SCHOTTENSTEIN EDITION

ששה סדרי משנה

THE MISHNAH ELUCIDATED

THE BOOK FAMILY EDITION OF SEDER NEZIKIN

ArtScroll® Series

זרעים
מועד
נשים
נזיקין
קדשים
טהרות

Rabbi Nosson Scherman / Rabbi Meir Zlotowitz
General Editors

A PROJECT OF THE

Mesorah Heritage Foundation

BOARD OF TRUSTEES

RABBI REUVEN FEINSTEIN
Rosh HaYeshivah, Yeshiva of Staten Island

JOEL L. FLEISHMAN Chairman
Director, Sam & Ronnie Heyman Center on Ethics,
Public Policy, and the Professions, Duke University

RABBI NOSSON SCHERMAN
General Editor, ArtScroll Series

HOWARD TZVI FRIEDMAN
Founding Partner, Lanx Management, LLC

JUDAH I. SEPTIMUS
Pres., Atlantic Land Title & Abstract, Ltd.

JOSEPH C. SHENKER
Senior Chair, Sullivan & Cromwell

JAMES S. TISCH
Chairman and CEO, Loews Corp.

RABBI GEDALIAH ZLOTOWITZ
President

RABBI DAVID FEINSTEIN ל"צז
Rosh HaYeshivah, Mesivtha Tifereth Jerusalem

RABBI MEIR ZLOTOWITZ ל"ז
Founder

AUDIT COMMITTEE

SAMUEL ASTROF
CFO/COO (Ret.) The Jewish
Federations of North America;
Partner (Ret.) Ernst & Young, LLP

JOEL L. FLEISHMAN
Director, Sam & Ronnie Heyman Center on Ethics,
Public Policy, and the Professions, Duke University

JUDAH I. SEPTIMUS
Pres., Atlantic Land Title & Abstract, Ltd.

JOSEPH C. SHENKER
Senior Chair, Sullivan & Cromwell

JAMES S. TISCH
Chairman and CEO, Loews Corp.

INTERNATIONAL BOARD OF GOVERNORS

JAY SCHOTTENSTEIN *(Columbus, OH)*
Chairman

STEVEN ADELSBERG
SIMCHA APPLEGRAD
MOSHE BEINHORN
RABBI RAPHAEL B. BUTLER
EDWARD MENDEL CZUKER *(Los Angeles)*
REUVEN D. DESSLER *(Cleveland)*
URI DREIFUS
YITZCHOK GANGER
MEIR R.Y. GRAFF *(Los Angeles)*
YITZCHOK MENACHEM HAAS
HASHI HERZKA
JACOB HERZOG *(Toronto)*
AMIR JAFFA *(Cleveland)*
ELAN JAFFA
JACK JAFFA
LLOYD F. KEILSON
MICHAEL KEST *(Los Angeles)*
ELLY KLEINMAN
ROBERT LOWINGER
EZRA MARCOS *(Tel Aviv)*
RABBI MEYER H. MAY *(Los Angeles)*
ASHER D. MILSTEIN

ANDREW J. NEFF
AARON J. ORLOFSKY *(Silver Spring)*
BARRY M. RAY *(Chicago)*
ZVI RYZMAN *(Los Angeles)*
JOSEPH A. SCHOTTENSTEIN
JONATHAN R. SCHOTTENSTEIN
JEFFREY A. SCHOTTENSTEIN
HERBERT E. SEIF *(Englewood, NJ)*
NATHAN B. SILBERMAN
ADAM M. SOKOL
A. JOSEPH STERN
JACQUES STERN *(Sao Paulo)*
ELLIOT TANNENBAUM
THOMAS J. TISCH
GARY TORGOW *(Detroit)*
STANLEY WASSERMAN *(New Rochelle)*
CHAIM WEALCATCH *(Baltimore)*
JOSEPH H. WEISS
MICHAEL WEISZ
STEVEN (CHANOCH) WEISZ
SHLOMO WERDIGER

שישה
סדרי משנה

ELUCIDATED

A PHRASE-BY-PHRASE
SIMPLIFIED TRANSLATION
WITH BASIC COMMENTARY

INCLUDES THE FULL HEBREW TEXT
OF THE COMMENTARY OF
RAV OVADIAH BERTINORO

SCHOTTENSTEIN EDITION

THE MISHNAH

THE BOOK FAMILY EDITION OF SEDER NEZIKIN

Published by

FIRST EDITION
Nine Impressions ... October 2015 — March 2022
Tenth Impression ... July 2023

Published and Distributed by
MESORAH PUBLICATIONS, Ltd.
313 Regina Avenue / Rahway, New Jersey 07065

Distributed in Europe by
LEHMANNS
Unit E, Viking Business Park
Rolling Mill Road
Jarrow, Tyne & Wear NE32 3DP
England

Distributed in Australia & New Zealand by
GOLDS WORLD OF JUDAICA
3-13 William Street
Balaclava, Melbourne 3183
Victoria Australia

Distributed in Israel by
SIFRIATI / A. GITLER — BOOKS
POB 2351
Bnei Brak 51122

Distributed in South Africa by
KOLLEL BOOKSHOP
Northfield Centre, 17 Northfield Avenue
Glenhazel 2192, Johannesburg, South Africa

ARTSCROLL® SERIES / THE SCHOTTENSTEIN EDITION
THE MISHNAH ELUCIDATED
SEDER NEZIKIN VOL. 1
BAVA KAMMA / BAVA METZIA

© Copyright 2015, by MESORAH PUBLICATIONS, Ltd.
313 Regina Avenue / Rahway, N.J. 07065 / (718) 921-9000 / FAX (718) 680-1875

ALL RIGHTS RESERVED. The Hebrew text of the Mishnah Elucidated has been edited,
corrected, and newly set; the English translation and commentary —
including introductory material, notes, and insights –
as well as the typographic layout and cover artwork, have been written, designed,
edited and/or revised as to content, form and style.
Additionally, new fonts have been designed for the texts and commentaries.
All of the above are fully protected under this international copyright.

No part of this volume may be reproduced
IN ANY FORM, including SCANNING, PHOTOCOPYING, OR FOR USE
WITH DIGITAL RETRIEVAL SYSTEMS, AS AN AUDIO OR VIDEO RECORDING
— EVEN FOR PERSONAL, STUDY GROUP, OR CLASSROOM USE —
without WRITTEN permission from the copyright holder,
except by a reviewer who wishes to quote brief passages
in connection with a review written for inclusion in magazines or newspapers.

NOTICE IS HEREBY GIVEN THAT THE PUBLICATION OF THIS WORK
INVOLVED EXTENSIVE RESEARCH AND COSTS,
AND THE RIGHTS OF THE COPYRIGHT HOLDER WILL BE STRICTLY ENFORCED

ITEM CODE: MEZ1H
ISBN 10: 1-4226-1659-2
ISBN 13: 978-1-4226-1659-8

Typography by CompuScribe at ArtScroll Studios, Ltd.
313 Regina Avenue / Rahway, N.J. 07065 / (718) 921-9000
Bound by Sefercraft, Quality Bookbinders, Ltd. Rahway, NJ

SEDER NEZIKIN VOL. I

מסכת בבא קמא
TRACTATE BAVA KAMMA

מסכת בבא מציעא
TRACTATE BAVA METZIA

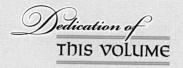
Dedication of
This Volume

This volume is dedicated in honor of our very dear friends and former neighbors,

Harry and Rachel Skydell

Not only is it a pleasure to know them, it is a privilege to be inspired by the wellspring of their chessed, love of learning, and support of Torah and chessed institutions. Their concern for others and understanding of their needs is perhaps best exemplified by the dozens of families that they brought into being through their phenomenal hachnasas orchim on Shabbos and Yom Tov.

The thriving Jewish communities of the Upper West Side and Monsey, as well as communities around the world, are immensely enriched by the warmth and generosity of Harry and Rachel.

May Hashem continue to bless them with good health, success, and nachas from their dear children, **Joseph and Eliana, Ephraim, Dena, Tamar, Shoshana, Yael, and Yehoshua** — for their blessing is a blessing for all who know and admire them.

Robin and Warren Shimoff

Lael and Jonathan,
Atara and David,
Alexander, Ariana

Dedication of
The Book Family Edition of Seder Nezikin

*T*his Seder is dedicated in loving memory to a remarkable Jewish Leader, and Educator, who changed the world.

Rabbi Meir Zlotowitz ז"ל
הרב מאיר יעקב בן הגאון הרב אהרן ז"ל
נפ׳ ל׳ סיון תשע"ז

*T*o Meir Zlotowitz ז"ל, *"Acheinu Bnei Yisrael"* meant exactly that:

"We are brothers." All of us stood together at Sinai, and received the Torah in all its beauty.
It belongs to all of us. If language was a barrier, he tore it down, and invited everyone in.

Our admiration for him is boundless.
Amy and I will forever be grateful to our friends Jeanie and Jay Schottenstein for introducing us to Meir and Rochel Zlotowitz in Jerusalem on Succoth, many years ago. While Rabbi Meir Zlotowitz ז"ל will always be remembered for his leadership and scholarship, we shall always remember his warm smile, charm, and amazing reservoir of energy. It is our honor and privilege to dedicate this Seder in his memory.

With the utmost respect and admiration,

Amy, Bob, and the Book Family

Dedication of
SCHOTTENSTEIN EDITION
THE MISHNAH ששה סדרי משנה
ELUCIDATED

The Mishnah Elucidated is lovingly dedicated in honor of
our parents and grandparents

Jerome ז"ל and Geraldine Schottenstein תחי׳
Leonard and Heddy Rabe שיחי׳

*T*hey were constant sources of strength
and role models of dignity,
integrity, loyalty to the past
and dedication to the future.

It is fitting that now,
as we dedicate The Mishnah Elucidated
we pay tribute to them,
for they symbolize to us
the values of our heritage,
their constant support day in day out,
and their encouragement
to go beyond our goals.

Jay and Jeanie Schottenstein

Joseph Aaron and Lindsay Brooke
Jacob Meir   Jonah Philip   Emma Blake
Jonathan Richard and Nicole Lauren
Winnie Simone   Teddi Isabella
Allegra Giselle   Elodie Yael
Jeffrey Adam and Ariella
Jerome Meir

PATRONS OF THE SEDARIM

The Mishnah is the basis of the Oral Law. In order to make this holy Torah legacy available to its heirs, these generous and visionary patrons have dedicated Sedarim/Orders of this edition of the Mishnah.

THE CZUKER EDITION OF SEDER ZERAIM

is lovingly dedicated by

Edward Mendel and Elissa Czuker and Family

(Los Angeles)

in loving memory of their beloved father

Jan Czuker ז״ל – ר׳ יוסף ב״ר מנחם מענדל ז״ל

נפ׳ פסח שני תש״ע

and יבל״ח in honor of their beloved mother

Mrs. Susanne Czuker שתחי׳

THE GRYFE EDITION OF SEDER MOED

is lovingly dedicated by

Daniel and Dena Gryfe

in honor of their parents

Josh and Nadja Graff   Moishe and Michele Gryfe

and as an inspiration to their children

Koby, Rikki, Alexander, Benjy and Mia

and their siblings

Elisha and Daniella   Zahava, Sabrina, Michal, and Tamara Graff,

Aviva and Gershon   Shoshana, Talia, and Esti Distenfeld,

Yehuda and Daniella   Yisroel, Aliza, Moshe, Ayelet, and Aryeh Graff

ESTHER KLAUS EDITION OF SEDER NASHIM

is lovingly dedicated by

Lester Klaus

Ari and Fradie (Rapp) Goldsmith

Benjy and Raizy Chesner   Menachem and Avigayil Rapp   Devorah, David and Esther
Shimmy, Bashi and Tzvi

Yankie and Sara Klaus   Bashie, Chedvah and Shimmy

Shmulie and Hindy Klaus   Dovie and Rachel Steier   Esther   Shana and Atara

Moshe Klaus

in loving memory of our quintessential wife and mother

אסתר בת צבי הירש ע״ה – ע״ה **Esther Klaus**

נפ׳ ט״ז ניסן תשע״ז

PATRONS OF THE SEDARIM

THE BOOK FAMILY EDITION OF SEDER NEZIKIN

is dedicated by

Amy, Bob, and the Book Family

in memory of

Rabbi Meir Zlotowitz ז"ל

הרב מאיר יעקב בן הגאון הרב אהרן ז"ל

נפ' ל' סיון תשע"ז

APPLEGRAD FAMILY EDITION OF SEDER KODASHIM

Dedicated by

Simcha and Shanie Applegrad

Yechiel   Mordechai Dovid   Yosef   Elisheva   Ayala   Chana

in loving memory of our grandparents,

Rav Avrohom Meyer and Chana Silverstein ז"ל

who were instrumental in laying the foundation for
the Torah community of Detroit and were patrons of its growth.

DIAMOND FAMILY EDITION OF SEDER TOHOROS

is lovingly dedicated by

Dr. David and Tzipi Diamond
Dr. Tzvi and Yocheved Diamond

Yitzchok   Yoni   Rachel   Tali   Rose

in loving memory of our beloved parents and grandparents,

Dr. Isaac and Rose Diamond ז"ל

ר' יצחק ב"ר ברוך בענדיט ז"ל

נפטר ד' חשון תשמ"ו

חי' רויזא בת אברהם משה ע"ה

נפטרה ה' ניסן תשס"ט

PATRONS OF THE MISHNAH

With generosity, vision, and devotion to the perpetuation of Torah study,
the following patrons have dedicated individual volumes of
The Mishnah Elucidated.

SEDER ZERAIM

◆§ BERACHOS, PEAH, DEMAI

Aron and Aliza Hirtz
Eliezer, Binyomin, Ariella, and Talia

in memory of our grandparents
Leslie and Lillian Hirtz ז"ל
אליעזר בן ישעיה ז"ל
לאה בת יוסף הלוי ע"ה

Yossi and Adina Hollander
Eitan Yaakov, Yonatan Meir, and Eliana Devora

In memory of our father
Max Hollander ז"ל
מאיר בן אברהם משה ז"ל

We all join in paying tribute to the memory of
our beloved grandparents
Rev. Yonason Neiman ז"ל
יונתן בן יעקב יהודה ז"ל
Yuspah Devora Dear ע"ה
יוספא דבורה בת בילא ע"ה

◆§ KILAYIM, SHEVIIS

Anonymous

◆§ TERUMOS, MAASROS

In honor of
Ira A. and Barbara K. Lipman and Family

◆§ MAASER SHENI, CHALLAH, ORLAH, BIKKURIM

The Jaffa Families

in memory of
Rabbi Meir Zlotowitz ז"ל
הרב מאיר יעקב בן הגאון הרב אהרן ז"ל

PATRONS OF THE MISHNAH

SEDER MOED

◆§ **SHABBOS, ERUVIN**

Amir and Edna Jaffa
Eby and Shani Schabes, Eli, Yaakov, and Rikki
in revered memory of our grandparents ז"ל
ר' חיים ישראל ב"ר מאיר זאב ז"ל
ורעיתו אלטע ויטא (ויקי) בת ר' אשר זעליג ע"ה – פריד
ר' נפתלי הירצקא ב"ר מנחם משה ז"ל
ורעיתו רבקה בת ר' יונה ע"ה – קליין
הרב אליהו ב"ר שמעון ז"ל – קמנצקי
ר' משה ליב ב"ר שניאור זלמן ז"ל
ורעיתו בלימא בת ר' אברהם משה ע"ה – יפה
and יבל"ח in honor of our grandmother עמו"ש
Mrs. Anita Kaminetsky שתחי'

◆§ **PESACHIM, SHEKALIM, YOMA, SUCCAH**

Barry and Harriet Ray and Family
dedicated to the memory of our dear parents
Emanuel M. and Zira G. (Siegel) Ray ז"ל
ר' מרדכי ב"ר ברוך ז"ל
צירל בת שמואל ע"ה

◆§ **BEITZAH, ROSH HASHANAH, TAANIS,**
MEGILLAH, MOED KATAN, CHAGIGAH

Norman and Cecily Davis
dedicated to the memory of our dear parents
Samuel and Sala Davis ז"ל
שלמה שמואל חיים בן דויד ז"ל
שינדל גיטל בת הרב צבי הירש הכהן ע"ה
Shaul and Yitta Cashdan ז"ל
שאול בן יוסף דוב הכהן ז"ל
חיה איטה בת חיים זעליג ע"ה

SEDER NASHIM

◆§ **YEVAMOS, KESUBOS**
dedicated to the memory of
Rabbi Menachem Gottesman זצ"ל
הרב אהרן מנחם בן הרב אשר זעליג זצ"ל

PATRONS OF THE MISHNAH

⊷§ NEDARIM, NAZIR
Andrew and Nancy Neff and Family
in honor of the ninetieth birthday of
our father, grandfather, and great-grandfather
Alan Martin Neff

⊷§ SOTAH, GITTIN, KIDDUSHIN
Joseph and Sheila Bistritzky and Family
dedicated in loving memory of
our dear parents and grandparents
Leibel Bistritzky ז״ל
ר׳ יהודה לייב בן ר׳ מרדכי ז״ל
Edah Bistritzky ע״ה
איטא בת ר׳ שלמה ע״ה

SEDER NEZIKIN

⊷§ BAVA KAMMA, BAVA METZIA
Robin and Warren Shimoff and Family
dedicated in honor of our very dear friends
Harry and Rachel Skydell

⊷§ BAVA BASRA, SANHEDRIN, MAKKOS, SHEVUOS
Adam and Suri Sokol and Family
dedicated to the prodigious, awe-inspiring memory of
Rabbi Meir Zlotowitz ז״ל
הרב מאיר יעקב בן הגאון הרב אהרן ז״ל

⊷§ EDUYOS, AVODAH ZARAH, AVOS, HORAYOS
Michael and Linda Elman
dedicated in loving memory of our dear parents
Julius Feigelman ז״ל
ר׳ יהודה ב״ר יחיאל מיכל ז״ל
Beatrice Feigelman ע״ה
בוניא בת ר׳ חיים אשר ע״ה
G. Leonard Rubin ז״ל
ר׳ גרשון ליפא ב״ר ליב עזריאל ז״ל
Bernice Rogoff Rubin ע״ה
באשא בת ר׳ בנימן ע״ה

PATRONS OF THE MISHNAH

SEDER KODASHIM

◆§ ZEVACHIM, MENACHOS
Shmuly and Batsheva Neuman and Family
dedicated in honor of our dear parents and grandparents
William and Gladys Neuman
Yanky and Perela Silber
Chaim and Suri Kassirer
Ruth Silber

and in memory of our dear grandparents
ז"ל Avrohom Neuman — אברהם בן זאב יהודה ז"ל
ע"ה Magda Neuman — מלכה בת אברהם יצחק ע"ה
ז"ל Nechemia Rabenstein — נחמיה בן שמואל חיים הכהן ז"ל
ע"ה Freida Rabenstein — שרה פייגא בת שלמה אלעזר ע"ה
ז"ל Kalman Silber — קלונימוס קלמן בן יהודה לייב ז"ל

◆§ CHULLIN, BECHOROS, ARACHIN
The Bak Families
dedicated in loving memory of our parents and grandparents
Bak — ר' שלום בן יהודה צבי ז"ל
Bak — ר' לייב בן ר' ניסן ז"ל
Zelmanovitz — הניא מלכה בת אברהם ישראל ע"ה
Scott — ר' ברוך בן חנוך ז"ל

and our uncles and aunts
Bak — ר' יצחק דוד בן יהודה צבי ז"ל
Bak — ר' גרשון בן יהודה צבי ז"ל
Zelmanowitz — מרים בת אברהם ישראל ע"ה
Zelmanowitz — חנה עקא בת אברהם ישראל ע"ה
Zelmanowitz — גיטל בת אברהם ישראל ע"ה

The Gastwirth Families
in memory of our beloved grandparents
Samuel and Beila Gastwirth ז"ל
ר' שמואל יעקב ב"ר צבי נחמן הלוי ז"ל
מרת בילה בת וואלף לייב הלוי ע"ה
Izzy and Ruthie Kalish ז"ל
ר' מרדכי יצחק ב"ר אהרן אבנר הלוי ז"ל
מרת רחל מרים בת מנחם צבי ע"ה

◆§ TEMURAH, KEREISOS, ME'ILAH, TAMID, MIDDOS, KINNIM
Sam and Laurie Friedland and family
dedicated in loving memory of our parents and grandparents
Friedland — ר' חיים מאיר בן שלמה זלמן ז"ל
Simon — ר' אליעזר בן משה יהודה ז"ל
Simon — שינא רחל בת דוד אליעזר ע"ה

PATRONS OF THE MISHNAH

SEDER TOHOROS

◆§ KEILIM (Vol. 1)
Woli and Chaja Stern
Jacques and Ariane Stern
לזכר ולעילוי נשמת
הורי ר׳ זאב
ר׳ צבי הלוי ב״ר חיים ומרים שטרן ז״ל
וזו׳ מרת דאכא ב״ר פרץ וברכה טאגר ע״ה
הורי חיה
ר׳ דוד אריה ב״ר יעקב ושינדל ברנר ז״ל
וזו׳ מרת איטלה (אירמה) ב״ר חיים ומדל שטרן ע״ה
אבי אריאן ר׳ ישכר טוביה ב״ר יוסף ופערל וייטמאן ז״ל

◆§ KEILIM (Vol. 2)
Woli and Chaja Stern
Jacques and Ariane Stern
לכבוד ולזכות
אם אריאן רחל (רוז׳ה) וויטמאן שתחי׳
ילדי ר׳ זאב וחיה
חיים אהרן ואריאלה ברכה סג״ל לנדא שיחיו
משה אפרים פישל ואילה (אנטי) קירשנבוים שיחיו
ילדי ר׳ יעקב ואריאן
יחזקאל וענת מינדל הרטמן שיחיו
מיכאל שלום ומרים אילנה פיינטוך שיחיו
צבי יונתן ומרים אביגיל שטרן שיחיו
יששכר טוביה ודבורה שטרן שיחיו
יחיאל משה ודאכא דינה מרזל שיחיו
ברוך משה ואיטלה טלי שטמברגר שיחיו

◆§ OHOLOS
The Gross, Strenger, Nadoff and Berger Families
in memory of our dear parents
Berish and Clara Berger ז״ל
יששכר בעריש בן יהושע ארי׳ ז״ל
שפרינצא בת אברהם ע״ה

◆§ NEGAIM, PARAH
Stephanie and George Saks
in memory of our dear friend
Rabbi Meir Zlotowitz ז״ל
הרב מאיר יעקב בן הגאון הרב אהרן ז״ל
and יבל״ח in honor of our dear friend
Rabbi Nosson Scherman שליט״א

PATRONS OF THE MISHNAH

☙ TOHOROS, MIKVAOS

As people who cherish the opportunity to join together for the greater good of Klal Yisrael, we took upon ourselves to share in this beautiful opportunity to dedicate this volume of Mishnah so that Jews across the world can benefit from its wisdom.

PLATINUM **David and Chanee Deutsch** לז"נ ברוך בן אשר זעליג הלוי ז"ל — Baruch Mappa
Benjamin (Binyamin) and Gabi Samuels   In honor of our son Baruch

GOLD **Dovid and Tikvah Azman**   In honor of our parents
Levi and Leeba Dessler   לז"נ ר' צבי יעקב בן ר' חיים ז"ל
Ari and Ariella Deutsch   לז"נ משה יהודה בן יהודה ז"ל
Aryeh and Malky Feller   לז"נ ישראל בן ישעיהו ז"ל   אהרן בן ישעיהו ז"ל
Moishe and Sue Heschel   לע"נ עלקא בת ר' זיסל ע"ה — Mrs. Elka Philipson
Chaim Sholom and Rivky Leibowitz   לע"נ דבורה בת משה ע"ה — Debbie Leibowitz
Avi (Ryan) and Tzivia Melohn   In honor of our parents and grandparents
Joseph (Yossi) and Malka Melohn   In honor of Alexander, Don, and Kate
Shalom and Reena Vegh   In honor of our parents
Michael and Katie Weisz   לז"נ ר' משה דוד זצ"ל בן ר' נוריאל נ"י

SILVER **Families of Alfred and Maurice Friedman**
Laibel Gerson   לז"נ עמנואל בן חיים יהודה ז"ל
Shari and Josh Goldberg   In honor of our children, Evelyn and Phillip
Shmuel Umlas   לע"נ אסתר בת אברהם ע"ה

☙ NIDDAH, MACHSHIRIN

Steven (Shlomo) and Rivky Weissman and Family
dedicated in loving memory of our dear father
ז"ל Marcel Weissman — הרב משה נתן בן יחזקאל ז"ל

☙ ZAVIM, TEVUL YOM, YADAYIM, UKTZIN

Aron and Rachel Solomon and Family
dedicated in memory of our dear father
ז"ל Cheskel Solomon — ר' יחזקאל ב"ר ישראל שלום ז"ל
In honor of our dear Grandmother and Parents
Razi Solomon
Vera Solomon
Pinchus and Judy Solomon
Also in memory of our dear Grandparents
Lipa and Mindel Goldberger ז"ל
ר' חנניה יו"ט ליפא ב"ר שלום ז"ל   מינדל בת ר' דוד ע"ה
ז"ל Yisroel Solomon — ר' ישראל שלום ב"ר שמואל ז"ל
Betzalel and Shaindel Solomon ז"ל
ר' בצלאל ב"ר דוב ז"ל   שיינדל בת ר' פינחס ע"ה
Yaakov Taivel and Rivkah Fixler ז"ל
ר' חיים אלטר יעקב טעבל ב"ר אליעזר ז"ל   רבקהביילא בת ר' צבי דוב ע"ה

Mishnah Associates

A fellowship of benefactors dedicated to
the dissemination of Mishnah Elucidated

❖

Moshe Finer and Steven Finer

❖

Phyllis and Chaim Shroot

In Memoriam — לזכר נשמת

Dedicated by the Mishnah Elucidated Associates
to those who forged eternal links

❖

ר' הירש בערל בן ר' אברהם לייב ז"ל   נעסע פייגעלה בת ר' יהודה ע"ה
חיה רבקה בת ר' הירש בערל ע"ה

❖

אלכסנדר בן חיים צדוק ז"ל   צייריל בת ארי' ע"ה
יוסף בן אברהם יהושע ז"ל   פסאה חייענה בת ארי' לייב ע"ה

Patrons of the Sedarim ❖ Digital Edition

SEDER ZERAIM

is dedicated by
Yisroel (Ira) and Rochi Zlotowitz
In memory of the unparalleled marbitz Torah, our beloved father,
Rabbi Meir Zlotowitz ז"ל
הרב מאיר יעקב בן הגאון הרב אהרן ז"ל

SEDER MOED

is dedicated by
Uri and Devorah Dreifus
May the limud haTorah from the Digital Edition of Mishnah Seder Moed
be a zechus for our children:
Avigail and Menasche, Eli, Chani, Shevy, Shira and Penina

SEDER NASHIM

is dedicated by
Ezra Birnbaum
In honor of my Rebbeim and chavrusas, without whom my life would not be the same
**Rabbi Chaim Tzvi Yair Senter   Rabbi Mordechai Kamenetzky   Rabbi Casreal Bloom
Rabbi Yossi Weberman   Rabbi Binyamin Prince   Rabbi Chili Birnbaum**
Acharon Acharon Chaviv **R' Meir Zlotowitz** ז"ל,
whose vision and dreams allow me on a daily basis to fulfill mine.

SEDER NEZIKIN

is dedicated by
**Menachem and Binah Braunstein
Daniella, Talia, Aryeh, and Binyamin**
In memory of our grandparents
Braunstein — הרב משה בן יששכר בעריש ז"ל   מרת יענטא בת הרב ישראל חיים ע"ה
Reichner — הרב משה אברהם בן הרב אשי ז"ל   מרת מרים בת מנחם מענדל ע"ה
Tajerstein — הרב יעקב ארי' בן הרב שבתי ז"ל
Weisner — הרב בנימין צבי בן הרב אליעזר ז"ל

SEDER KODASHIM

is dedicated by
Moshe and Esther Beinhorn
In memory of
Beinhorn — ר' יצחק אייזיק בן ר' יחיאל מיכל ז"ל   מרת טילא בת ר' יצחק ע"ה
Beinhorn — ר' יוסף דוד בן ר' יצחק אייזיק ז"ל   ר' אברהם זאב בן יחיאל מיכל ז"ל
Salamon — ר' יעקב בן ר' ישראל מרדכי ז"ל

SEDER TOHOROS

is dedicated by
The Yesh Foundation

Pillars of the Mishnah

We wish to acknowledge in this volume the friendship of the following:

Frank A. Compton

∞

Lee Farber

∞

Joel and Rachel Gedalius

∞

Mr. and Mrs. Michael Kagan

∞

Thomas Rumfelt

∞

Stuart and Nancy Schoenburg

∞

Richard Wineburgh

∞

The Written Word is Forever

We gratefully acknowledge the many Torah scholars who contributed to this volume.

General Editor:
Rabbi Chaim Malinowitz

Editorial Directors:
Rabbi Yosef Davis, Rabbi Yehezkel Danziger

Authors and Editors:
**Rabbi Doron Beckerman, Rabbi Binyomin Feldman,
Rabbi Zvi Goldberg, Rabbi Dovid Hollander,
Rabbi Yehudah Keilson, Rabbi Nechemya Klugman,
Rabbi Henoch Morris, Rabbi Doniel Rose,
Rabbi Mordechai Smilowitz, Rabbi Yisroel Weiss**

Scholars who reviewed and commented:
**Rabbi Eliyahu Meir Klugman, Rabbi Moshe Rosenblum,
Rabbi Yosaif Asher Weiss**

We also wish to thank our technical staff who worked so diligently to produce this volume.

Proofreaders:
Mrs. Judi Dick, Mrs. Mindy Stern, Mrs. Faygie Weinbaum

Typesetters:
**Mrs. Chumie Lipschitz
Mrs. Estie Dicker, Mrs. Esther Feierstein, Mrs. Toby Goldzweig**

Illustrator: **Yoav Elan**

Introduction

The Mishnah is the basis of the *Torah Shebe'al Peh*, the Oral Torah that was transmitted to Moses at Sinai. When conditions forced Rabbi Yehudah HaNasi and his compatriots to commit the Oral Torah to writing (completed in approximately 3950/190 CE), he composed the Mishnah in such a way that it could be understood only with the guidance of a teacher or with a broad knowledge of the subject matter. Therefore, the Mishnah cannot merely be read; it must be explained. One who has attained a basic knowledge of the entire Mishnah will find himself at home anywhere in the Talmud; he will have become familiar with the laws and concepts that were later discussed, broadened, and clarified by the Gemara and the countless commentaries. Traditionally, Mishnah has been studied not only by scholars, but also by students and laymen who had little knowledge of the Gemara. Obviously, therefore, Mishnah can be understood on many levels, from the most basic to the most scholarly. Additionally, because the Hebrew letters of the word משנה can be rearranged to spell נשמה, it is customarily studied as a source of merit for the departed, especially during the first year after their passing or on a *yahrzeit*.

⊷§ The Schottenstein Edition

To a significant degree, this 21-volume **SCHOTTENSTEIN EDITION OF THE MISHNAH ELUCIDATED** will do for students of the Mishnah what the universally acclaimed Schottenstein Edition of the Talmud does for students of the Talmud, in the sense that it is at once succinct and clear. The new, elucidated **Translation** is based on the universally accepted interpretation of Rabbeinu Ovadiah of Bertenoro, commonly referred to as *the Rav* or *the Bartenura*. The translation adds words and phrases to make the Mishnah text read smoothly and clearly, without reference to the notes. Thus, one who reads the translation will gain a clear understanding of the basic text of the Mishnah. This is ideal for someone who wants to study the Mishnah for a *yahrzeit* or to review his learning. The **Notes** section clarifies and explains the Mishnah further by drawing, where necessary, on the Gemara or other classic Mishnah commentaries. In the rare instances when the consensus of the major commentators differs from the *Rav*, the translation and notes follow the consensus.

In the planning stages of this edition, many versions of the format were circulated for comment among our scholars and editors, as well as among lay readers. No suggestion was ignored. The approach was refined and refined again, until we arrived at this final version that, we feel, accomplishes the goal we to seek to achieve, with Hashem's help.

Many years ago, we were privileged to publish the widely acclaimed 44-volume Mishnah Series with the now-classic YAD AVRAHAM commentary, dedicated by MR. AND MRS. LOUIS GLICK in memory of their son AVRAHAM YOSEF ע"ה. The anthologized YAD AVRAHAM is an encyclopedic, in-depth commentary that presents many explanations and explores nuances and complexities, raises questions, and cites a wide variety of works on the Mishnah and Talmud. Its thoroughness has won the praise of even masters of the Talmud throughout the world, so that those who study and benefit from this new SCHOTTENSTEIN EDITION OF THE MISHNAH ELUCIDATED may turn to the Yad Avraham commentary when they wish to delve into the nuances of the Mishnah more deeply and explore a wider range of comments. Thus, in effect, the two editions complement each other.

The idea of producing an elucidated Mishnah patterned after the Schottenstein Edition of the Talmud was first put forward by our friend **TUVIA ROTBERG**. It was **RABBI ASHER DICKER** who suggested what eventually became the initial model for the format of this new series. We are grateful for their foresight.

This new MISHNAH ELUCIDATED represents yet another monumental undertaking by **JAY AND JEANIE SCHOTTENSTEIN**. Their previous historic projects — the Schottenstein Editions of Talmud Bavli and Talmud Yerushalmi, the Schottenstein Editions of the Interlinear Chumash, Prayerbooks, Megillah, and Haggadah; and the Schottenstein Edition of *Sefer HaChinuch/Book of Mitzvos* — revolutionized the Torah study and Jewish lives of countless thousands, in homes, study halls, offices, commuter trains, and airplanes, wherever Jews have the desire and seek the opportunity to unite with their heritage. Thanks to Jay and Jeanie and their family, the Jewish world is a better place. Hundreds of thousands of Jews of all backgrounds have been touched by their vision and are now making Torah study and better prayer an integral part of their daily lives.

Now they have perceived a new need and, as always, they step forward to meet it. With their hallmark vision and generosity, they are enabling THE MISHNAH ELUCIDATED to bring the study of Mishnah within reach of all. This new series will add another jewel to the crown of their unprecedented service to the glory of Torah.

Gracious and generous, kind and caring, Jay and Jeanie open their hearts to countless people and causes. Quietly and considerately, they elevate the dignity and self-respect of those they help, they make their beneficiaries feel like their benefactors, and they imbue institutions with a stronger sense of mission. They not only give, they do.

In this dedication, Jay and Jeanie are joined by their children, **JOSEPH AND LINDSAY, JONATHAN**, and **JEFFREY**, so the next generation of this regal family

[xix] **INTRODUCTION**

of Torah dissemination carries on the family tradition of responsibility for Klal Yisrael, present and future. Already in Columbus and beyond, they are adding luster to the legacy of their unforgettable grandfather **JEROME** ז"ל. As the years go by, this legacy will be joined by **JACOB, JONAH,** and **EMMA,** as they take their places in the Schottenstein aristocracy of merit.

In the merit of their support of this and countless other Torah and *chessed* causes, may they all enjoy continued good health and success — and may the Jewish people continue to enjoy their leadership.

✥ Patrons of This Volume

This volume of Mishnah Elucidated is dedicated by **ROBIN AND WARREN SHIMOFF.** They are visionary people who discern a historic need and respond to it without being asked. Previously they dedicated a volume of the Talmud, a volume of Ramban, and both volumes of Midrash Rabbah on Shir HaShirim. Each time, they came forward of their own volition. It is a privilege for us to be associated with such generous people, whose desire to spread Torah study propels them to sponsor Torah projects for the benefit of Klal Yisrael.

ACKNOWLEDGMENTS

Over the years since the first ArtScroll book was published in 1976, we have been humbled to enjoy the guidance and encouragement of the great sages of the previous generation and our time. Their letters of approbation for various ArtScroll projects appear in volumes of those works. We are resolved בעזרת ה' to maintain the course set forth by them and their successors.

HAGAON HARAV DAVID FEINSTEIN שליט"א has been a guide, mentor, and friend since the first day of the ArtScroll Series, and we are honored that he regards our work as an important contribution to *harbatzas Torah*. Although complex halachic matters come to the Rosh Yeshivah from across the world, he always makes himself available to us whenever we consult him. He is also a founding Trustee of the Mesorah Heritage Foundation.

We are honored that this country's senior *roshei hayeshivah* have been so generous with their time and counsel. **HAGAON HARAV SHMUEL KAMENETSKY** שליט"א offers warm friendship and invaluable advice; **HAGAON HARAV AHARON SCHECHTER** שליט"א is unfailingly gracious and supportive; the Novominsker Rebbe, **HAGAON HARAV YAAKOV PERLOW** שליט"א, is a wise counselor, good friend, and staunch supporter of our efforts for *harbatzas Torah*. We are grateful beyond words to them all.

HAGAON HARAV DAVID COHEN שליט"א has been a dear friend for more than half a century; he places the treasury of his knowledge at our disposal whenever he is called upon, and has left his erudite mark on ArtScroll's projects from its inception. **HAGAON HARAV HILLEL DAVID** שליט"א is a warm and valued counselor and source of comment and advice. **HAGAON HARAV FEIVEL COHEN** שליט״א gladly interrupts his personal schedule whenever we call upon him.

A vast investment of time and resources will be required to make the twenty-one volumes of THE MISHNAH ELUCIDATED a reality. Only through the generous support of many people will it be possible not only to undertake and sustain such an important project, but to keep the price of the volumes within reach of the average family and student.

The Trustees of the MESORAH HERITAGE FOUNDATION saw the need to support the scholarship and production of this and other outstanding works of Torah literature. **HAGAON HARAV DAVID FEINSTEIN** שליט״א, as mentioned above, provides spiritual and halachic guidance. **PROF. JOEL L. FLEISHMAN** is the founding Trustee of the Foundation. It was he who recognized how much more could be accomplished with the aid of a Foundation. He conceived it and brought it into being. As chairman, he continues to guide us and lend his wisdom and prestige to our efforts. **SAM ASTROF** is nationally known in Jewish organizational life. His expertise and experience are invaluable. **HOWARD TZVI FRIEDMAN** is an old, dear friend and a fixture in the high echelons of public service. He unfailingly makes himself available. **JUDAH SEPTIMUS** is a *talmid chacham* and founding Trustee, who extends himself beyond belief in many ways, whenever he can be helpful. **JOSEPH SHENKER** is one of America's preeminent attorneys, a Torah scholar and good friend, who always makes time for our work. **JAMES S. TISCH**, one of the outstanding leaders of American industry and Jewish communal life, is a founding Trustee and a close friend. That such extraordinary people involve themselves closely with the work of the Foundation testifies to its importance. We are grateful to them and privileged to serve with them

We noted the Schottenstein family in the Introduction. **JAY SCHOTTENSTEIN** is chairman of the Board of Governors of Mesorah Heritage Foundation and has enlisted many others in support of its monumental projects. He and his wife **JEANIE**, and their children, **JOSEPH AND LINDSAY, JONATHAN,** and **JEFFREY**, have dedicated THE SCHOTTENSTEIN EDITION OF THE MISHNAH ELUCIDATED.

ELLY KLEINMAN is a dear friend who is renowned for his warmth, integrity, judgment, and generosity. In addition to individual Talmud volumes, he is the Patron of several historic and popular projects: the 5-volume KLEINMAN EDITION OF KITZUR SHULCHAN ARUCH, an elucidation of a halachic classic, including the rulings of *Mishnah Berurah* and Rabbi Moshe Feinstein; the INTERACTIVE MISHKAN DVD; the English full-color MISHKAN volume, and its Hebrew counterpart; 43 volumes of the three series of the KLEINMAN EDITION OF DAILY DOSE OF TORAH; and the monumental 17-volume KLEINMAN EDITION OF MIDRASH RABBAH.

RABBI ZVI AND BETTY RYZMAN, loyal and devoted friends, are patrons of several Talmud volumes and the inaugural dedicators of a tractate of TALMUD YERUSHALMI. Rabbi Ryzman is an exceptional *talmid chacham,* an internationally renowned *maggid shiur,* author of many *sefarim,* and the epitome of the Jew who combines Torah study with business success — and gives

[xxi] **INTRODUCTION**

priority to Torah. Most recently they have become the Patrons of this RYZMAN EDITION OF THE MISHNAH in Hebrew, which is already regarded as a classic, and which will be a major contribution to Torah study.

STANLEY AND ELLEN WASSERMAN are people of rare gentility, kindness, integrity, and dedication to worthy causes, both communal and private. They are patrons of several volumes of the SCHOTTENSTEIN EDITIONS OF THE TALMUD — BAVLI AND YERUSHALMI, of volumes of RAMBAN, and of the KLEINMAN EDITION OF MIDRASH RABBAH. Their two current projects are already of historic proportions: The WASSERMAN EDITION OF THE ARTSCROLL SIDDUR is becoming the Siddur of choice throughout the world. The WASSERMAN DIGITAL INITIATIVE harnesses the era of technology in the service of Torah and tefillah. In their community and far beyond, the Wassermans are admired and respected not only for what they do, but for what they are.

ASHER MILSTEIN has dedicated three major projects: the MILSTEIN EDITION OF SEDER NASHIM in Talmud Yerushalmi, the MILSTEIN EDITION OF THE FIVE MEGILLOS in Midrash Rabbah, and the MILSTEIN EDITION OF THE LATER PROPHETS. Not content with *sponsoring* Torah works, he has become a major disseminator of Torah in a unique way, by arranging for the distribution of huge numbers of ArtScroll/Mesorah volumes to synagogues, organizations, and individuals throughout the world. We are gratified that he has chosen us as a vehicle to accomplish this goal, and that his brother **ELISHA SHLOMO MILSTEIN** has dedicated the MILSTEIN EDITION OF SEDER TOHOROS in Talmud Yerushalmi, and the MILSTEIN EDITION OF SEFER BAMIDBAR in Midrash Rabbah.

We are honored to welcome **DANIEL AND DENA GRYFE** as the first dedicators of a Seder in The Mishnah Elucidated. The Gryfes have earned admiration in Toronto as people who support a wide variety of Torah and *chessed* efforts, in Israel, Canada, and America. Although they are generous supporters of many mainstream yeshivas and kollels, they are especially devoted to Kiruv institutions and to organizations that help the needy and the childless. It is our privilege that they have chosen to add our work to their long list of important causes.

We are proud that **IRA AND INGEBORG RENNERT**, widely respected, generous supporters of a host of worthy causes, are the first dedicators of a Seder in Talmud Yerushalmi. By having dedicated the RENNERT EDITION OF SEDER ZERAIM in both the Hebrew and English editions, they were instrumental in bringing this work to fruition, and in making available the major source of the agricultural laws of the Land of Israel.

JACOB M.M, AND PNINA (RAND) GRAFF of Los Angeles are in the top rank of those who make the classics of our heritage accessible to today's Jews.They have dedicated SEDER MOED in the HEBREW EDITION OF TALMUD BAVLI, SEDER MOED in the ENGLISH EDITION OF TALMUD YERUSHALMI, and the GRAFF-RAND STUDENT EDITION OF RAMBAN. Thanks to them, countless people are able to navigate the Sea of the Talmud and understand Chumash through the eyes of Ramban.

EDWARD MENDEL AND ELISSA CZUKER of Los Angeles are modest people who resist honors, but their commitment to Torah dissemination speaks for itself. They have dedicated the ELUCIDATION OF THE TORAH'S COMMANDMENTS IN SEFER HACHINUCH/THE BOOK OF MITZVOS, BEREISHIS-NOACH IN MIDRASH RABBAH, and TRACTATE ROSH HASHANAH IN THE ENGLISH TALMUD YERUSHALMI and the classic CZUKER EDITION MIKRAOS GEDOLOS on Chumash, and the forthcoming NEVIIM and KESUVIM. Their generosity will be rewarded in the generations that will enter the world of enhanced Torah learning thanks to them.

YAAKOV AND BEATRICE HERZOG of Toronto have dedicated SEDER KODASHIM in the HEBREW TALMUD YERUSHALMI and SEFER DEVARIM OF RAMBAN. Their devotion to learning is inspiring. Reb Yaakov is a *talmid chacham* whose love of learning is infectious. Thanks to the generosity of Mr. and Mrs. Herzog, his zeal for learning will be extended to others through the volumes they make possible.

We are deeply grateful to **RABBI HESHIE BILLET**, a distinguished rav, teacher, and good friend; **RABBI RAPHAEL B. BUTLER**, a constant friend and counselor, and the dynamic and imaginative founder of the Afikim Foundation; **RABBI YISRAEL H. EIDELMAN**, an effective, dedicated servant of Torah; **RABBI SHLOMO GERTZULIN**, whose competence and vision are invaluable assets to our people; **RABBI MOSHE M. GLUSTEIN**, an accomplished *marbitz Torah* and rosh yeshivah; **RABBI BURTON JAFFA**, the pioneer in giving hope to special children and their parents; **RABBI MICHOEL LEVI**, one of the community's most accomplished educators; **RABBI PINCHOS LIPSCHUTZ**, a leader in Torah journalism and a treasured friend; **RABBI SHIMSHON SHERER**, who inspires his congregation and honors us with his friendship; and **RABBI HOWARD ZACK**, a warm friend who is making an enormous impact for good in Columbus.

RABBI MEYER H. MAY of Los Angeles devotes his considerable acumen and prestige to the service of Torah. Thanks to him, many patrons have enlisted in support of the Foundation.

We are grateful also to many dear friends and loyal supporters. In alphabetical order, they are: **STEVE ADELSBERG**, a governor, and a dedicator in every edition of the Talmud; **ABRAHAM BIDERMAN**, Trustee Emeritus, who has many achievements for Torah and community; **REUVEN DESSLER**, a personal friend who adds luster to a distinguished family lineage; **YECHIEL BENZION FISHOFF**, the visionary, sensitive, and respected dedicator of several volumes; **ABRAHAM FRUCHTHANDLER**, who has placed support for Torah institutions on a new plateau; **LOUIS GLICK**, who sponsored the ArtScroll Mishnah Series with the Yad Avraham commentary; **HASHI HERZKA**, a pioneer dedicator and community activist; **MALCOLM HOENLEIN**, one of Jewry's truly great lay leaders, an eloquent and effective spokesman, who generously makes time to offer guidance and counsel; **SHIMMIE HORN**, patron of the HORN EDITION OF SEDER MOED of Talmud Bavli, a self-effacing person to whom support of Torah is a priority; **GEORGE KLEIN**, a major communal leader who has been in the forefront of Torah and community life for decades.

We are grateful to **MOTTY KLEIN**, dedicator of several Talmud volumes and of the OHEL SARAH WOMEN'S SIDDUR, a leader in his community and a force

INTRODUCTION

for Torah; **RABBI YEHUDAH LEVI**, whose service to Jewish children and worthy causes is extraordinary; **MOSHE MARX**, a respected and visionary supporter of Torah causes who prefers to remain in the background; **ANDREW NEFF**, dedicator of several volumes and a leader in his industry, who has made Mesorah his own cause; **DR. ALAN NOVETSKY**, the very first dedicator of an ArtScroll volume, who has continued his association and support over the years; **DAVID RETTER**, scion of a distinguished family and a leader in his own right; **GEOFFREY ROCHWARGER** of Bet Shemesh, Patron of SEDER NASHIM in the Hebrew Talmud Bavli.

We are grateful to **HESHE SEIF**, who displays constant interest in our work. He is Patron of the SEIF EDITION TRANSLITERATED PRAYERBOOKS, who has added our work to his long list of important causes; **FRED SCHULMAN**, whose generous spirit invigorates his surroundings; **AUBREY SHARFMAN** is more than a Dedicator. He lends his verve and talent to many worthy causes and makes every effort to recruit others to join our work; **A. JOSEPH STERN**, Inaugural ArtScroll Patron of the SEFARD ARTSCROLL MACHZORIM and of Talmud tractates, whose warmth and concern for Torah causes are legendary; **MENDY SILBER**, a dedicator and magnanimous supporter; **NATHAN SILBERMAN**, a leader in his profession, who makes his skills and judgment available in too many ways to mention; **ADAM SOKOL**, a generous dedicator; **WOLI STERN** (São Paulo), a man of unusual warmth and sincerity who, with his son and partner **JACQUES**, honors us with his friendship.

We are grateful to **ELLIOT TANNENBAUM**, a warm and gracious inaugural Patron of every Talmud edition, as well as several other volumes, including the very popular *"Ner Naftali"* Eretz Yisrael Siddur, whose example has motivated many others; **JOSEPH WEISS**, who has dedicated several volumes. He has made many astute comments as a contributing reader of Talmud Yerushalmi that were incorporated into the work, and he has influenced others to dedicate volumes; **STEVEN WEISZ**, a long-time personal friend and a true visionary whose infectious zeal for learning and service to good causes has brought many others under our banner; **SHLOMO WERDIGER**, an outstanding and selfless leader at the forefront of major causes, whose concern for the needs of Klal Yisrael is extraordinary, and who has been instrumental in our work since its inception; **YAAKOV WILLINGER**, an enthusiastic supporter; **MENDEL ZILBERBERG**, who carries on the family legacy of *askanus;* and להבחל"ח **HIRSCH WOLF** ז"ל, who was a valued friend and a fountain of encouragement from our very beginning, and an energetic, effective leader in many causes.

YERUCHAM LAX is more than an accountant. As a *talmid chacham* in his own right, he understands the importance of our work. His skill and expertise are indispensable in helping maintain our commitment to uncompromising accuracy.

Enough cannot be said about our dear friend and colleague **RABBI SHEAH BRANDER**, whose graphics genius set the standard of excellence in Torah publishing. He is a *talmid chacham* of note who added more than one dimension to the quality of every volume. Reb Sheah is involved in every aspect of the project, from scholarship to production. He has earned the respect, trust, and affection of the entire staff, to the point where it is inconceivable to envision the past and future success and quality of the work without him.

The graphics skill and innovative work of **ELI KROEN** distinguish many of our works.

We express our appreciation to our esteemed colleague **SHMUEL BLITZ**, who continues to coordinate the activities of our authors and editors in Israel with dedication and distinction. On this side of the ocean, **AVROHOM BIDERMAN** and **MENDY HERZBERG** do the same, as they shepherd works from manuscript to computer to print.

RABBI GEDALIAH ZLOTOWITZ is a key factor in our dissemination of Torah literature. He carries increasing responsibilities with aplomb and dedication. ArtScroll/Mesorah and the Foundation are grateful that he devotes his considerable talent to our work.

MRS. LEA BRAFMAN, the comptroller of Mesorah Publications Ltd. virtually since our founding, is indispensable to the efficient functioning of our work. Her loyalty and competence are unexcelled. She is very ably assisted by **MRS. LEYA RABINOWITZ** and **MRS. ROBERTA FUCHS**. **MRS. SARA LEA HOBERMAN** is the very loyal comptroller of Mesorah Heritage Foundation. Both organizations are fortunate to have such a highly skilled and loyal staff.

We conclude with gratitude to Hashem Yisbarach for His infinite blessings and for the privilege of being the vehicle to disseminate His word. May this work continue so that all who thirst for His word may find what they seek in the refreshing words of the Torah.

Rabbi Meir Zlotowitz / Rabbi Nosson Scherman

Cheshvan 5776/October 2015

מסכת בבא קמא
TRACTATE BAVA KAMMA

זרעים

מועד

נשים

נזיקין

קדשים

טהרות

General Introduction

This tractate is called *Bava Kamma,* which means "the first gate," because it is the first of a group of three tractates: *Bava Kamma* (the first gate), *Bava Metzia* (the middle gate), and *Bava Basra* (the last gate). According to the Amora Rav Yosef, they are not in fact separate tractates but three parts — each consisting of ten chapters — of one large tractate called *Nezikin* [literally: *damages*] (Gemara 102a; see *Ramban* to *Shevuos* 2a). *Bava Kamma* deals mainly with the laws of damages.

The Torah forbids a person to damage the body or property of another. He may not do damage with his own body or physical force, or neglect to prevent his property (such as an animal) from doing damage, or create a hazard (such as a fire or a pit) that can do damage. If he causes damage in any of these ways, the Torah commands him to pay the victim for his loss. The person responsible for the damage is called the מַזִּיק, *mazik,* and the one who suffered the damage is called the נִזָּק, *nizak.*

A damaging force that is mentioned in the Torah is called an אָב, *av* (literally, *father).* Any damaging force that is similar to the *av* but is not mentioned in the Torah is called a תּוֹלָדָה, *toladah* (literally, *descendant*).

I.

►§ The person himself

One is liable for damage he does with his body or physical force to another person's body or property (*Exodus* 21:18-19, 22-25; *Leviticus* 24:18-21). If one injures a *person,* he must pay the victim for as many as five things (where applicable): (a) נֶזֶק, *damage,* which is reckoned as the difference between the victim's theoretical value as a slave before the injury and afterward; (b) צַעַר, *pain* — the physical pain suffered by the victim; (c) רִפּוּי, *healing* — the victim's medical expenses; (d) שֶׁבֶת, *loss of work* — compensation for the money that the victim could have earned during his recovery; (e) בֹּשֶׁת, *embarrassment* — the embarrassment caused by the attack (see Mishnah 8:1).

Payment for the four things other than נֶזֶק, *damage,* applies only where one person injures another person. They do not apply where one's property injures a person or where a person injures an animal.

II.

►§ Animal

Damage done by an animal is divided into three categories:

(a) Shein (literally, *tooth*). The Torah speaks of an animal that does damage through eating (*Exodus* 22:4). Thus, eating is the *av* of this category. Its *tolados* include activities that are similar to eating insofar as they are normal activities from which the animal benefits. An example is where an animal scratches its back against a wall for its pleasure and thereby damages the wall.

The animal's owner must pay for *shein* damage only if the animal entered the field (or other property) of the victim and did the damage there. He is not liable for *shein* damage done in a public place (*Exodus* there; Mishnah 2:2).

(b) *Regel* (literally, *foot*). The *av* of this category is where an animal does damage with its foot in the course of normal walking (*Exodus* there). The *tolados* are where an animal does damage with other parts of its body (or with what it is carrying) as it moves in a normal way; for instance, its body brushes against an object and breaks it. As is the case with *shein*, the owner pays only for damage done in the property of the victim.

(c) *Keren* (literally, *horn*). The *av* is where an animal intentionally gores a person or other animal with its horns (*Exodus* 21:28-32, 35-36). Other types of intentional damage — such as pushing, biting, and kicking — are *tolados* of *keren* (*Rav* to Mishnah 1:4). Since intentional damage is unusual (for most animals), the category also includes any activity that is unusual. Thus, whenever an animal does damage in an unusual way, the rules of *keren* apply.

With respect to the category of *keren,* there are two types of animals: the תָּם, *tam* (literally, *simple, innocent*) and the מוּעָד, *muad* (literally, *warned*):

(i) A *tam* is an animal that is not expected to do damage in a particular way. Since such behavior is unusual for this animal, its owner is not required to prevent it from acting so. Therefore, if the animal happens to do damage in this manner, the owner need not pay the full amount of the victim's loss. He pays only half.[1] Furthermore, the half-damage payment is made only from "the body of the damaging animal" (Mishnah 1:4), which means that the animal's owner does not have to pay more than the animal is worth, and if the animal is not available (it died or is lost), he does not have to pay anything.

(ii) A *muad* is an animal that is expected to do damage in a certain way. When a *muad* does damage in that manner, the owner must pay in full, and his payment is not limited to the animal's "body."[2] A *tam* becomes a *muad* if it damages in an unusual way three times and, after each time, its owner is warned by the court to prevent it from doing so again. (For this reason, it is called *muad,* which means *warned.*) From that point on, the animal is a *muad* with regard to that type of behavior since the behavior is no longer unexpected. Its owner, therefore, must pay in full should it cause damage in that way a fourth time.

NOTES

1. By rights, the owner should not have to pay anything. The half payment is a fine that the Torah imposed on him (see Gemara 15a).

2. As far as *shein* and *regel* are concerned, every animal is a *muad,* since these are common and expected behaviors (Mishnah 1:4).

III.

✎§ Pit

A person may not create a hazard in a public place, where it could cause damage to people and animals that are passing by. If one does create such a hazard and it causes injury to a person or animal, he must pay for the damage. The *av* of this category is digging a pit and neglecting to cover it properly (*Exodus* 21:33-34). A pit is different from the other categories in that it does not move; rather, the injured party went to it. Any similar hazard is a *toladah*; for example, a stone that one leaves in a public street.

If one fails to cover his pit, and an animal falls in and is killed or injured, he must pay full damages for the animal. However, the Torah decrees that he is not liable to pay for damage to inanimate objects. Thus, if an animal that is carrying utensils fell into the pit and the utensils broke, he need not pay for the utensils. He must also pay if a person falls in and is *injured*, but he is not liable for damages if the person is *killed* (Mishnah 5:6).

IV.

✎§ Fire

One is also liable for damage done by a fire that he lit or owns and fails to prevent from spreading (*Exodus* 22:5). A fire tends to travel to what it destroys by means of the wind or other natural force. Among the *tolados* of this category, therefore, is where a person leaves a stone on a roof and the wind blows it off, causing it to fall on an object below and break it.

Chapter One

— רע״ב —

[א] אַרְבָּעָה אֲבוֹת נְזִיקִים: הַשּׁוֹר, וְהַבּוֹר, וְהַמַּבְעֶה, — פרק ראשון — ארבעה אבות.

(א) **ארבעה אבות נזיקין.** משום דאיכא לכל חד מינייהו תולדות, קרי להו אבות: **השור.** הוא הרגל, דהיינו מה שהבהמה מזקת ברגליה דרך הלוכה, כדכתיב (שמות כב,ד) ושלח את בעירה, ותניא (דף ג,ב) ושלח זה הרגל, וכן הוא אומר (ישעיה לב,כ) משלחי רגל השור והחמור. ותולדה דרגל היא, כשהזיקה בגופה דרך הלוכה, או בשערה דרך הלוכה שנדבקין כלים בשערה וגררתן ושברתן, או בשליף שעליה, והוא משאוי שבאמתחות ובמרצופין שעליה, או בזוג שבצוארה: **והבור.** הפותח בור ברשות הרבים, ונפל שמה שור או חמור, ומת — אם הבור עמוק עשרה טפחים, או הוזק — אם הוא פחות מעשרה טפחים, דכתיב (שמות כא,לג) כי יפתח איש בור וגו'. ותולדה דבור, כגון כיחו וניעו לאחר שנחו ברשות הרבים והזיקו: **והמבעה.** זה השן, שאכלה בהמתו בשדה חבירו, כדכתיב (שם כב,ד) וביער בשדה אחר. ונקרא

---

[1] When the property of a person, or a hazard that he created, damages the property of another, the person responsible for the damage (called the *mazik*) must pay the victim (called the *nizak*) for his loss. The Torah gives several examples of damage for which a *mazik* must pay. The specific object or force that does the damage in each of the Torah's examples is called a "primary damager." It is described as "primary" because it is mentioned in the Torah and it is the source for a broad category that includes many more cases. The Mishnah lists the "primary damagers:"

אַרְבָּעָה אֲבוֹת נְזִיקִים — There are **four primary damagers:**[1] הַשּׁוֹר — (1) **The ox,** which does damage with its feet as it walks: This is the category known as *regel* (foot), which includes any damage done by an animal in the course of walking or other movement.[2] וְהַבּוֹר — (2) **The pit,** into which people or animals fall: This is the category of *bor* (pit), which includes damage done by an obstacle that stays in place.[3] וְהַמַּבְעֶה — (3) **The tooth**[4] of an animal,

---

NOTES

[1]
1. Here, the word "damager" means the item that does the damage, such as an animal or a fire. In most other places, however, we shall use this word to denote the person who was responsible for preventing the damage (usually the owner of the item). Another word for the person is מַזִּיק, *mazik*, which means *one who causes damage*.

2. The Torah (*Exodus* 22:4) states that the owner of an animal (such as an ox) must pay for damage that it does as it walks (see Gemara 2b-3a). This example stands for a general category that is called *regel* (foot). Like the other categories, *regel* has a single *av* (primary case) and many *toladot* (derived cases). The *av* (primary case) is the example mentioned in the Torah, where an animal damages with its *feet* in the course of walking. The *toladot* (derived cases) are acts of damage that an animal does with other parts of its body (or with what

it is carrying) as it walks; for example, its body brushes up against a wall and knocks it over, its hair becomes entangled with a utensil and drags it until it breaks, or the load on its back or the bell hanging from its neck hits a utensil and breaks it (see *Rav* here and to Mishnah 2:1).

3. The Torah (verses 21:33-34 there) states that if a person digs a pit in a public place and an animal falls into it, he shall pay compensation to the owner of the animal. This is the *av* (primary case) of the category of *bor* (pit), which includes damage caused by any obstacle that, like a pit, does not move. An example of its *toladot* (derived cases) is someone who spits in a public area, and, after the spit lands on the ground, a person or animal is damaged by it (*Rav*).

4. Literally, *the uncovered thing*. This refers to a tooth, which is sometimes covered and sometimes uncovered [such as when the animal eats] (*Rav*).

[9] **MISHNAH BAVA KAMMA** / Chapter 1: *Arba'ah Avos*

— רע"ב —

הַשֵּׁן מִבְעָטָה, מִפְּנֵי שֶׁהוּא וְהַהֶבְעֵר. לֹא הֲרֵי הַשּׁוֹר כַּהֲרֵי הַמַּבְעֶה, פְּעָמִים מְכוּסֶּה פְּעָמִים

מְגוּלָה, מִלְּשׁוֹן נִבְטוּ מַלְפּוּנָיו (עובדיה ח,ו) דְּמִתַּרְגְּמִינָן אִגְלִיִין מִטְמְרוֹהִי. וְתוֹלַדְתָּה דָּשָׁן הִיא, כְּשֶׁנִּתְחַכְּכָה בְּכוֹתֶל לַהֲנָאָתָהּ, כְּדֶרֶךְ הַבְּהֵמוֹת שֶׁמִּתְחַכְּכוֹת, וְשָׁבְרָה אֶת הַכּוֹתֶל, אוֹ טָנְּפָה פֵּירוֹת כְּשֶׁנִּתְחַכְּכָה בָּהֶן לַהֲנָאָתָהּ: וְהַהֶבְעֵר. זוֹ הַדְּלֵקָה שֶׁיָּלְאָה וְהִזִּיקָה, כְּדִכְתִיב (שמות כב,ה) כִּי תֵצֵא אֵשׁ וְגוֹ' וְנֶאֱכַל גָּדִישׁ אוֹ הַקָּמָה אוֹ הַשָּׂדֶה. וְתוֹלַדְתּוֹ דְּאֵשׁ, אַבְנוֹ וְסַכִּינוֹ וּמַשָּׂאוֹ שֶׁהִנִּיחָן בְּרֹאשׁ גַּגּוֹ, וְנָפְלוּ בְּרוּחַ מְצוּיָה וְהִזִּיקוּ, דּוּמְיָא דְּאֵשׁ שֶׁהָרוּחַ מוֹלִיכָה. וְהָא דְּלֹא חָשִׁיב תַּנָּא דִּידָן קֶרֶן בְּכָלַל אֲבוֹת נְזִיקִין, מִשּׁוּם דְּלֹא מַיְירֵי אֶלָּא בִּנְזִיקִין שֶׁהֵם מוּעָדִים מִתְּחִלָּתָן, כְּלוֹמַר שֶׁמְּשַׁלְּמִין נֶזֶק שָׁלֵם מִתְּחִלָּתָן, אֲבָל בְּתַמָּן וְאַחַר כָּךְ מוּעָדִים לֹא קָא מַיְירֵי: לֹא הֲרֵי הַשּׁוֹר כַּהֲרֵי הַמַּבְעֶה. כְּלוֹמַר, אִי כָּתַב רַחֲמָנָא שׁוֹר לֹא נָפִיק מִבְעָטָה מִינֵּיהּ, דְּהָוָה אַמֵּינָא, רֶגֶל דְּהִזִּיקָה

---

which does damage when the animal eats: This is the category of *shein* (tooth), which includes damage that an animal does while doing something for its own pleasure, such as eating.[5] וְהַהֶבְעֵר — (4) **The fire,** which burns property: This is the category of *eish* (fire), which includes damage done by something that is left in one place but is blown elsewhere by the wind (or other force) and does damage as it travels.[6]

The Mishnah explains that the Torah had to mention these four categories, because if it had mentioned only some of them, we might not have known that a person is obligated to pay for the others:

לֹא הֲרֵי הַשּׁוֹר כַּהֲרֵי הַמַּבְעֶה — **The ox,** which damages through walking (*regel*)

NOTES

5. The Torah (verse 22:4) obligates a person to pay damages if his animal enters the property of another and eats something there. This is the *av* of the category of *shein* (tooth), which includes any damage that an animal does while doing an activity from which it benefits, similar to eating. Among its *tolados* is the case of an animal that scratches its back against a wall for its pleasure and thereby breaks the wall, or it rubs itself on fruits, making them dirty (*Rav*).

6. It is stated there (verse 22:5) that a person is responsible for damage done by a fire that he lit in his own property and was blown by the wind to the property of someone else. This is the *av* of the category of *eish* (fire), which includes any damage done by something that was moved by a wind or similar force. An example of its *tolados* is where a person leaves a stone on a roof and the wind blows it off, causing it to fall on an object and break it (*Rav*).

The Mishnah has listed two *avos* (primary damagers) that relate to an animal: *regel* (foot) and *shein* (tooth). However, there is a third one; namely, *keren* (horn). *Keren* refers to damage that the animal *intends* to do; for example, it attacks another animal with its horns (verses 21:35-36). The Mishnah leaves out *keren* because it deals only with damage that results from an animal's ordinary behavior (see end of the Mishnah). This includes *regel* and *shein*, which are normal activities, but excludes *keren*, which is not normal for most animals. For this reason, when an animal does damage through *keren*, the owner is not obligated to pay the entire amount of the victim's loss (he pays just half). Only after a particular animal has repeatedly damaged through *keren*, thus showing that *keren* is its normal behavior, must the owner pay in full (*Rav;* see Mishnah 4).

[The Mishnah does not speak of damage that a person does himself. The laws of this category, which is called *adam hamazik* (a person who damages), are found in several places in the tractate. See, for example, Mishnah 2:6.]

[The Gemara cites two explanations of the Mishnah. Following the commentary of *Rav,* we have explained שׁוֹר (ox) as referring to *regel,* and מַבְעֶה (tooth) as referring to *shein.* According to the Gemara's other explanation, שׁוֹר (ox) includes all the three types of damage that can be done by an animal (*regel, shein,* and *keren*). And the word מַבְעֶה does not mean *tooth;* rather, it means *person,* and it refers to *adam hamazik,* i.e., damage that a person does himself.]

וְלֹא הֲרֵי הַמַּבְעֶה כַּהֲרֵי הַשּׁוֹר. וְלֹא זֶה וָזֶה, שֶׁיֵּשׁ בָּהֶן רוּחַ חַיִּים, כַּהֲרֵי הָאֵשׁ, שֶׁאֵין בּוֹ רוּחַ חַיִּים,

— רע״ב —

מלוי חייביה רחמנא, שן דאין הזיקה מלוי לא חייביה רחמנא. ולוי כתב רחמנא שן

הוה אמינא, שן דיש הנאה להזיקה חייב, רגל דאין הנאה להזיקה אינו חייב. ולוי כתב רחמנא שן ורגל ולא כתב אש, הוה אמינא, שן ורגל שיש בהן רוח חיים, כלומר שבאים מכח בעלי חיים, חייב, אבל אש שאין בה רוח חיים לא לחייב. ואם נכתבו שלשתן ולא כתב רחמנא בור, הוה אמינא הני לחייבו. שדרכן לילך ולהזיק, אבל בור שאין דרכו לילך ולהזיק, לא לחייב עליו, משום הכי אילטריכו כולהו. ובגמרא (ה,ב) מסיק, דהי כתב בור וחד מהנך, אתו כולהו שאר לבד מקרן, בהלד השוה שבהן שדרכן להזיק. ולא הולרכו כולן, אלא מפני שהן חלוקים בהלכותיהן, יש בזה מה שאין בזה. שן ורגל פטורים ברשות הרבים, מה שאין כן בבור ואם. בור פטור ביה קרא אדם וכלים, דכתיב (שמות כא,לג) ונפל שמה שור או חמור, דדרשינן (דף כת,ב) שור ולא אדם, חמור ולא כלים, מה שאין כן בשאר אבות נזיקים. אם פטור בו את הטמון, שאם היו בגדים טמונים בגדיש, פטור המבעיר, דכתיב (שמות כב,ה) או הקמה, מה קמה בגלוי אף כל בגלוי. ובשאר אבות נזיקים לא פטר את הטמון:

---

is not like the tooth, which damages through eating (*shein*). The difference is that an animal often walks on another person's property but it does not often eat another person's property (it does so only when hungry).[7] Thus, if the Torah had said only that the owner must pay for damage done through walking (*regel*), which is common behavior, we might have thought that he need not pay for the damage done through eating (*shein*), which is relatively unusual.[8] So that we should not think this, the Torah added the example of eating (*shein*). וְלֹא הֲרֵי הַמַּבְעֶה כַּהֲרֵי הַשּׁוֹר — **And the tooth**, which damages through eating (*shein*) **is not like the ox**, which damages through walking (*regel*). The difference is that the owner of an animal benefits when it eats the property of others (since he does not have to feed it), but he does not benefit when it damages the property of others in the course of walking. Accordingly, if the Torah had said only that the owner must pay for the damage of eating, from which he benefits, we might have thought that he need not pay for the damage of walking, from which he gains nothing. To prevent this mistake, the Torah added the example of walking (*regel*). וְלֹא זֶה וָזֶה שֶׁיֵּשׁ בָּהֶן רוּחַ חַיִּים כַּהֲרֵי הָאֵשׁ שֶׁאֵין בּוֹ רוּחַ חַיִּים — **And [the ox] and [the tooth], in which there is life, are not like fire, in which there is no life.** The ox and the tooth represent damage done by a living animal, which must be watched carefully, because, having a mind of its own, it can decide at any time to go off and do what it wants. Animals, therefore, need more supervision than fire, which does not have a mind.[9] Thus, if the Torah had said only that a person must pay for damage done by his animal (through walking or eating), we might have thought that he need not pay for

---

NOTES

7. *Tiferes Yisrael.*

8. Since an animal often damages things when walking (*regel*), the owner must watch it very carefully to prevent it from doing so. However, he need not be all that careful to prevent it from eating the property of another (*shein*), because, provided that the animal has been fed,

it is unlikely to do that (*Tiferes Yisrael*).

9. *Tiferes Yisrael.* Leaving a fire alone is not as careless as leaving an animal alone because, unlike an animal, a fire cannot walk off whenever it chooses. It could be argued, then, that one is exempt from paying for damage done by fire.

[11] **MISHNAH BAVA KAMMA** / Chapter 1: *Arba'ah Avos*

— רע"ב —

הצד השוה שבהן וכו'. אף אני אביא כל שדרכו להזיק ושמירתו עליך, שאם הזיק נתחייב המזיק לשלם תשלומי הנזק שהזיק: במיטב הארץ. מעידית שבנכסיו, מן המשובח

וְלֹא זֶה וָזֶה, שֶׁדַּרְכָּן לֵילֵךְ וּלְהַזִּיק, כַּהֲרֵי הַבּוֹר, שֶׁאֵין דַּרְכּוֹ לֵילֵךְ וּלְהַזִּיק. הַצַּד הַשָּׁוֶה שֶׁבָּהֶן שֶׁדַּרְכָּן לְהַזִּיק, וּשְׁמִירָתָן עָלֶיךָ, וּכְשֶׁהִזִּיק, חָב הַמַּזִּיק לְשַׁלֵּם תַּשְׁלוּמֵי נֶזֶק בְּמֵיטַב הָאָרֶץ.

שבהם, אם בא ליתן לו קרקע בתשלומי נזקו, דכתיב (שם פסוק ד) מיטב שדהו ומיטב כרמו ישלם. אבל אם בא ליתן לו מטלטלין קיימא לן (דף ז,ב) כל מילי מיטב הוא, דאי לא מזדבן הכא מזדבן במתא אחריתי, ויהיב ליה כל מאי דבעי ואפילו סובין. והני מילי לנזקין, אבל לבטל חוב, אי אית ליה זוזי, מחייבינן ליה למיתן זוזי, ואי לית ליה זוזי, יהיב ליה מטלטלי מאי דבעי, ואי מגבי ליה ארעא יהיב ליה בבינונית. ושכיר, אפילו לית ליה למשכיר, לא מצי יהיב ליה באגרייהו אלא זוזי, ומחייבינן ליה לזבוני מנכסיה, עד דמשכח זוזי ויהיב ליה:

ולא **damage caused by fire. The Torah, therefore, added the example of fire.** וְלֹא זֶה וָזֶה שֶׁדַּרְכָּן לֵילֵךְ וּלְהַזִּיק כַּהֲרֵי הַבּוֹר שֶׁאֵין דַּרְכּוֹ לֵילֵךְ וּלְהַזִּיק — **And [an animal] and [fire], which tend to move and damage, are not like a pit, which does not tend to move and damage, but stays in one place. Since animals and fire move about, they must be watched more carefully than a pit, which does not move.**[10] **Thus, if the Torah had said only that a person must pay for damage done by his animal and his fire, we might have thought that he need not pay for damage caused by a pit. The Torah, therefore, also mentions a pit.**[11]

Despite the differences between these "primary damagers," a person must pay for all of them. The Mishnah explains what they have in common: הַצַּד הַשָּׁוֶה שֶׁבָּהֶן שֶׁדַּרְכָּן לְהַזִּיק — **Their common [characteristics] are that they tend to do damage** וּשְׁמִירָתָן עָלֶיךָ — **and the responsibility for watching them is on you** (that is, a person is responsible to prevent them from damaging, either because he owns them or he created them).[12] וּכְשֶׁהִזִּיק חָב הַמַּזִּיק לְשַׁלֵּם תַּשְׁלוּמֵי נֶזֶק בְּמֵיטַב הָאָרֶץ — **Accordingly, when [one of them] does damage, the damager** (i.e., the person responsible for guarding it)[13] **must pay damages with the best of the land** that he owns.[14]

——————————— NOTES ———————————

10. *Tiferes Yisrael*.

11. The Mishnah has not covered all the possibilities. For example, it has not explained why the Torah did not just mention *bor* on its own, or *bor* with one or two of the other three categories (*regel, shein, eish*). [In fact, the Gemara (5b) argues that it would have sufficed for the Torah to mention just *bor* and any one of the other three, and we could have derived the other categories from them.] The Torah nevertheless mentioned all the four categories, because each one has different laws [as will be explained in the coming chapters] (see *Rav*).

According to this, there was no need for the Mishnah to explain why some categories cannot be derived from others.

The Mishnah nevertheless included this discussion, because any serious analysis of the Torah is worth teaching so that יַגְדִּיל תּוֹרָה וְיַאְדִּיר, *the Torah will be made great and glorious* [Isaiah 42:21] (*Tos Yom Tov*).

12. We can therefore derive from the Torah's examples that in any case where a person is responsible for guarding something that tends to do damage, he must pay for the damage that it does (*Rav*).

13. In this sentence, "damager" (*mazik*) refers to the owner of the damaging item or someone that he asked to watch it (see note 1).

14. A person's land can be divided into three types: high quality, medium quality,

משניות בבא קמא / פרק א: ארבעה אבות

[ב] כָּל שֶׁחַבְתִּי בִּשְׁמִירָתוֹ, הִכְשַׁרְתִּי אֶת נִזְקוֹ. הִכְשַׁרְתִּי בְּמִקְצָת נִזְקוֹ, חַבְתִּי בְתַשְׁלוּמִין כְּהֶכְשֵׁר כָּל נִזְקוֹ. נְכָסִים שֶׁאֵין בָּהֶן מְעִילָה, נְכָסִים שֶׁל בְּנֵי בְרִית,

— רע"ב —

(ב) כל שחבתי בשמירתו וכו'. כל דבר שנתחייבתי לשמרו: הכשרתי את נזקו. אם לא שמרתי כראוי והזיק, אני הוא שהכשרתי וזמנתי אותו היזק, ואני חייב עליו, כגון המוסר שורו לחרש שוטה וקטן, חייב, שעליו היה מוטל שמירת שורו, והרי לא שמרו כראוי לו: הבשרתי במקצת נזקו וכו'. ואם תקנתיו וזמנתיו מקצת הנזק, אף על פי שלא זמנתי ותקנתי את כולו, נתחייבתי עליו כאילו זמנתיו כולו, כגון החופר בור תשעה ברשות הרבים ובא אחר והשלימו לעשרה, ונפל שמה שור או חמור ומת, האחרון חייב, אף על פי שלא תקן אלא מקצת הנזק, כאילו עשה כל הנזק, כיון דבתשעה ליכא מיתה: נבסים שאין בהם מעילה. ועל איזה נכסים אני חייב לשלם אם הזקתי, על נכסים שאין בהם מעילה, כגון נכסים שאינן הקדש. שאם הזקתי נכסים של הקדש איני חייב לשלם, דכתיב (שמות כא,לה) שור רעהו, ולא שור של הקדש. והוא הדין לכל שאר נזקים: נבסים שהם של בני ברית. שאם הזיק

---

[2] Some rules about when the obligation to pay damages applies: כָּל שֶׁחַבְתִּי בִּשְׁמִירָתוֹ — **Whatever I am required to guard** from doing damage, הִכְשַׁרְתִּי אֶת נִזְקוֹ — **I caused the damage that it does** if I failed to guard it properly; therefore, **I must pay**.[1] הִכְשַׁרְתִּי בְּמִקְצָת נִזְקוֹ — **In some cases, even if I caused** only **part of its damage,** חַבְתִּי בְתַשְׁלוּמִין כְּהֶכְשֵׁר כָּל נִזְקוֹ — **I am obligated to** make the **entire payment, as though I were the cause of all of its damage.**[2]

נְכָסִים שֶׁאֵין בָּהֶן מְעִילָה — The damager pays only for damage to **property that is not subject to** the laws of *me'ilah* (i.e., private property, which does not belong to the Temple),[3] נְכָסִים שֶׁל בְּנֵי בְרִית — and **property that**

NOTES

and low quality. [The definition of each type depends on the land owned by that person, and not on land in general.] One who is obligated to pay damages may pay with money, movable objects, or land. However, if he chooses to pay with land, he must give land of high quality, as stated in *Exodus* 22:4 (*Rav*). [People prefer a smaller amount of high-quality land to a larger amount of low-quality land.]

[2]

1. If a person is responsible to guard an animal (for example) from doing damage, and he fails to guard it properly, he must pay for any damage it does, because he made it possible for that damage to happen. Even if he had appointed someone else to watch the animal, but that person was not fit for the job (such as a minor), the first person must pay (*Rav*).

2. [This rule applies where one person created part of a dangerous object (or situation), but not enough of it to make it capable of causing damage, and then a second person completed it, making it into something that can cause damage. Even though the second person did not make all of it, he alone is responsible for whatever damage it causes, since he was the one who made it into a damaging force.] For example, if one person digs a pit that is nine *tefachim* deep, and a second person digs out another *tefach* (making it ten *tefachim* deep), and then an animal falls into the pit and dies, the second person must pay for the entire damage. This is because a pit is not considered deep enough to kill an animal unless it is at least ten *tefachim* deep (see Mishnah 5:5). Thus, although the second person dug only part of the pit, it is as if he dug all of it, since it would not have been deep enough to kill without the part that he added (*Rav*).

3. [The sin of using Temple property for one's own benefit is called *me'ilah*.] If a person caused damage to Temple

[13] MISHNAH BAVA KAMMA / Chapter 1: Arba'ah Avos

נִכְסִים הַמְיֻחָדִים, וּבְכָל מָקוֹם חוּץ מֵרְשׁוּת הַמְיֻחֶדֶת לַמַּזִּיק וּרְשׁוּת הַנִּזָּק וְהַמַּזִּיק.

— רע״ב —

נכסים של נכרי, פטור: **נכסים המיוחדים.** שיש להם בעלים מיוחדים, שאם הזיק נכסים של הפקר, פטור: **חוץ מרשות המיוחדת למזיק.** בכל מקום שהזיקו נכסיו את נכסי חבירו, חייב המזיק, חוץ מרשות המיוחדת למזיק, שאם נכנס שור ניזק ברשות המזיק, והזיקו שור המזיק, פטור, דאמר ליה תורך ברשותי מאי בעי. ודוקא כשהזיקו נכסיו, אבל המזיק עצמו שחבל בחברו, אף על פי שהוא עומד ברשותו, חייב, דאמר ליה הנחבל, נהי דאית לך רשותא לאפוקי, לאזוקי לית לך רשותא: **ורשות הניזק והמזיק.** ורשות המיוחדת לניזק ולמזיק, כגון חצר של שניהם, והזיק שורו של אחד מהם בחותה חצר, בשן ורגל, פטור. והוא שתהיה אותה חצר מיוחדת לשוורים גם כן, אבל אם היתה מיוחדת לפירות ולא לשוורים, והזיק בשן ורגל, חייב. ואם הזיק בקרן, בכל ענין חייב:

---

belongs to members of the covenant.[4]

נְכָסִים הַמְיֻחָדִים — He pays only if the item that did the damage was **property assigned** to him (i.e., he owned it) from the time of the damage until the court reached its verdict.[5]

וּבְכָל מָקוֹם — He pays for damage that happened **anywhere** חוּץ מֵרְשׁוּת הַמְיֻחֶדֶת לַמַּזִּיק — **except a place that belongs only to the damager** (*mazik*), וּרְשׁוּת הַנִּזָּק וְהַמַּזִּיק — **and a place that belongs to both the damager and the damaged party** (*nizak*).[6]

--- NOTES ---

property, he is not obligated to pay. This law is derived from the Torah [as explained in Mishnah 4:3] (*Rav*).

4. See Mishnah 4:3.

5. If he gave up ownership of the item, or if he donated it to the Temple, after it did the damage (but before the court obligated him to pay), he is exempt from payment (*Tiferes Yisrael*, from Gemara 13b).

6. The Mishnah is teaching two laws here:

(a) In regard to most categories of damage, it makes no difference where the damage happened. The *mazik* must pay regardless of whether the place of the damage was owned by the public, or by a private person, or it had no owner. The only exception is damage that occurred in the *mazik's* own property. For example, if one person's ox entered the field of another, and was attacked there by an animal belonging to the owner of the field, the *mazik* need not pay because he can say to the *nizak*: "What was your ox doing in my property!" That is, since you had no right to let your ox enter my property, I was not responsible to guard my ox so that it would not injure yours (*Rav*). [However, if the field owner himself did the damage, he *is* obligated to pay, because the *nizak* can say to him:

"You had the right to remove my animal from your property, but you had no right to damage it" (*Tos. Yom Tov*).]

(b) The categories of *regel* and *shein* are different from all the others. In their case, the Torah (*Exodus* 22:4) states: וּבִעֵר בִּשְׂדֵה אַחֵר, *and [the animal] damaged in the field of another,* which teaches that the *mazik* must pay for *shein* and *regel* only if the damage happened in the property of the *nizak*. If it happened in any other place, such as public property, or property belonging to a third person, or property belonging to both the *mazik* and the *nizak*, the *mazik* is exempt from having to pay, because it is not "the field of another" (*Rav, Tos. Yom Tov*).

It emerges that the Mishnah's two clauses refer to different types of damage. (a) When it says that one is liable for damage that happened "anywhere except a place that belongs only to the *mazik*," it refers to all categories of damage. (b) But when it adds "and [except] a place that belongs to both the *mazik* and the *nizak*," it refers specifically to the categories of *shein* and *regel*. Only in cases of *shein* or *regel* is the owner exempt from paying for damage that happened in a place owned by both him and the *nizak*. But in cases

משניות בבא קמא / פרק א: ארבעה אבות

וּכְשֶׁהִזִּיק, חָב הַמַּזִּיק לְשַׁלֵּם תַּשְׁלוּמֵי נֶזֶק בְּמֵיטַב הָאָרֶץ.

[ג] **שׁוּם** כֶּסֶף, וְשָׁוֶה כֶסֶף, בִּפְנֵי בֵית דִּין, וְעַל פִּי עֵדִים בְּנֵי חוֹרִין בְּנֵי בְרִית.

— רע״ב —

(ג) שׁוּם בְּסֶף. שׁוּם זֶה שֶׁל נְזָקִים, לֹא יְהֵא אֶלָּא בְּכֶסֶף, שֶׁיְּהוּ בֵּית דִּין שָׁמִין כַּמָּה שָׁוֶה הַנֵּזֶק, וְכָךְ יְשַׁלֵּם לוֹ. וְאִם הִזִּיקָה פָּרָתוֹ שֶׁל רְאוּבֵן טַלִּיתוֹ שֶׁל שִׁמְעוֹן, שֶׁדְּרָסָה עָלָיו בִּרְשׁוּת

הִזִּיק, וּשְׁבָרְתוֹ, וְאַחַר כָּךְ אֵירַע, שֶׁנִּשְׁבְּרָה רַגְלָהּ שֶׁל פָּרָה זוֹ שֶׁל רְאוּבֵן, בְּטַלִּיתוֹ שֶׁל שִׁמְעוֹן, בִּרְשׁוּת הָרַבִּים, דַּהֲוֵי נַמִי בּוֹר בִּרְשׁוּת הָרַבִּים, אֵין אוֹמְרִים, הוֹאִיל וְזֶה הִזִּיק וְזֶה הִזִּיק, יֵצֵא זֶה בְּהֶזֵּיקוֹ שֶׁל זֶה, אֶלָּא שָׁמִין שְׁנֵי הַנְּזָקִים בְּדָמִים, וּמִי שֶׁהִזִּיק לַחֲבֵירוֹ יוֹתֵר, יְשַׁלֵּם: שָׁוֶה בְסָף. וּכְסְבָּאִים לְשַׁלֵּם הַנִּיזָּק מִנִּכְסֵי הַיְּתוֹמִים, לֹא יִפָּרְעוּ אֶלָּא מִן הַקַּרְקָעוֹת, שֶׁהֵם שָׁוֶה כֶסֶף, וְלֹא מִמִּטַלְטְלִין שֶׁהֵם עַצְמָם כֶּסֶף, דְּכָל מִידֵי דִּמְטַלְטְלֵי חָשׁוּב כְּאִילּוּ הוּא כֶּסֶף, דְּאִי לֹא מִזְדַּבְּנָא הָכָא מִזְדַּבְּנָא בְמָתָא אַחֲרִיתִי: בִּפְנֵי בֵית דִּין. וְהַשּׁוּמָא וְהַתַּשְׁלוּמִין שֶׁל נְזָקִים, לֹא יִהְיוּ אֶלָּא בִּפְנֵי בֵית דִּין מוּמְחִין, וְלֹא בִּפְנֵי בֵית דִּין שֶׁל הֶדְיוֹטוֹת: וְעַל פִּי עֵדִים בְּנֵי חוֹרִין וּבְנֵי בְרִית. לְאַפּוֹקֵי עֲבָדִים וְעַכּוּ״ם, שֶׁאֵינָם כְּשֵׁרִים לְעֵדוּת שֶׁל נְזָקִין:

A rule about the payment itself:

חָב הַמַּזִּיק לְשַׁלֵּם תַּשְׁלוּמֵי נֶזֶק וּכְשֶׁהִזִּיק — When [something] does damage, בְּמֵיטַב הָאָרֶץ — the damager (i.e., the person responsible for guarding it) must pay damages with the best of the land that he owns.[7]

[3] Some more rules about payment for damage:

שׁוּם כֶּסֶף — The evaluation of damage must be in money.[1]

וְשָׁוֶה כֶסֶף — If a damager dies and leaves property to his heirs, the victim cannot collect money (or movable objects, which are equivalent to money), but only that which is merely **worth** money, i.e., land.[2]

בִּפְנֵי בֵית דִּין — These decisions (namely, the evaluation of damage and its collection from the damager or his family) must sometimes be made **by a court** of expert judges,[3] וְעַל פִּי עֵדִים בְּנֵי חוֹרִין בְּנֵי בְרִית — and they must be

---

NOTES

of other types of damage, he is liable for damage that happened in a place he owns together with the *nizak*, and he is exempt only if the place is entirely his.

7. This was stated in the previous Mishnah. It is repeated here to hint at a form of damage that was not mentioned there, i.e., *keren* [see note 6 there] (*Tos. Yom Tov*).

[3]

1. This teaches that if, for example, Reuven's cow stepped on Shimon's coat and damaged it, and later Reuven's cow broke its leg by slipping on Shimon's coat that was lying on the ground [where it is a hazard, like a pit], the court does not say that since both suffered a loss, neither one pays the other. Rather, it makes an exact monetary evaluation of each person's loss, and whoever owes the larger amount pays the difference (*Rav*).

2. Land is called "*worth* money" in contrast to movable property, which is called "money." Since movable property can be taken anywhere and is therefore easy to sell, it is almost as useful as money. Land, on the other hand, is merely "worth money," because it cannot be taken to buyers; rather, buyers must be brought to the land, which makes selling it more difficult (*Rav*).

As long as a *mazik* is alive, there is no difference between cash, movable property, and land; he must pay with whatever he has. After he dies, however, and leaves his estate to orphans, the *nizak* can take only the land in the estate, and not cash or movable objects (*Rav*).

3. That is, outstanding scholars who received *semichah*. [This refers to the *semichah* that was first granted by Moses to his students, who in turn granted it

MISHNAH BAVA KAMMA / Chapter 1: Arba'ah Avos

— רע״ב —

וְהַנָּשִׁים בִּכְלַל הַנֶּזֶק. וְהַנִּזָּק וְהַמַּזִּיק בַּתַּשְׁלוּמִין.

בֵּין שֶׁהַנִּזָּקִין הַמַּזִּיקִין, דִּין הָאִישׁ וְדִין הָאִשָּׁה שָׁוִין בִּנְזָקִין: וְהַנִּזָּק וְהַמַּזִּיק בַּתַּשְׁלוּמִין. פְּעָמִים שֶׁהַנִּזָּק שַׁיָּךְ עִם הַמַּזִּיק בַּתַּשְׁלוּמִין שֶׁל נִזָּק, כְּגוֹן אִם פָּחֲתָה הַנְּבֵלָה מִשְּׁעַת מִיתָה עַד שְׁעַת הָעֲמָדָה בַּדִּין, שְׁפַחַת נְבֵלָה דְּנִיזָּק הוּא, בֵּין בְּתָם בֵּין בְּמוּעָד, וְנִמְצָא שֶׁאֵין הַמַּזִּיק מְשַׁלֵּם לוֹ אֲפִלּוּ אוֹתוֹ חֲצִי נֶזֶק שֶׁזָּכְתָה לוֹ תּוֹרָה, אִם הוּא תָּם, אוֹ נֶזֶק שָׁלֵם אִם הוּא מוּעָד. הֲרֵי שֶׁהַנִּזָּק הוּא מַפְסִיד, וְשַׁיָּךְ בַּתַּשְׁלוּמִין הַלָּלוּ עִם הַמַּזִּיק:

based on the testimony of **witnesses** who are **free men** and **members of the covenant**.[4]

וְהַנָּשִׁים בִּכְלַל הַנֶּזֶק — **Women are included in the** laws of **damages**; that is, whether a woman causes damage or suffers damage, the law for her is the same as the law for a man.

וְהַנִּזָּק וְהַמַּזִּיק בַּתַּשְׁלוּמִין — **The victim and the damager** share **in the payment;** that is, there are cases in which the victim also "pays." For example, if an animal was killed and later its carcass decreased in value, the damager needs to pay only for the victim's loss at the time of the damage, and not for the loss that occurred later. Thus, the victim "pays" in the sense that he is not compensated for his entire loss.[5]

[4] Besides the four categories of damage listed in the first Mishnah, there is the category of *keren* (horn). *Keren* includes damage that an animal does intentionally; for example, it gores another animal with its horns.[1] Because intentional damage is unusual (for most animals), the category also includes any activity that is unusual. Thus, whenever an animal does damage in an unusual way, the rules of *keren* apply.

This Mishnah deals with the differences between a *tam* and a *muad*. (a) A *tam* is an animal that is not expected to do damage in a particular way. Since such behavior is unexpected for this animal, its owner does not have to guard it from damaging in such a manner. Therefore, if the animal happens to do damage in this way, the owner does not have to pay the full amount of the victim's loss (he pays only half).[2] (b) A *muad* (plural, *muadim*), on the other hand,

— NOTES —

to their students, and so on through the generations. It is not to be confused with modern-day *semichah*.]

In fact, the law allows for ordinary judges to decide most monetary cases, including claims of damage. Judges with *semichah* are required only where the damage is unusual or the payment is a "penalty," i.e., it is not the same as the actual loss [see Mishnah 7:1] (*Tiferes Yisrael*).

4. The testimony of free Jewish men is required.

5. For instance, an animal worth 100 *zuz* was killed and its carcass was worth 10 *zuz* at the time of death; thus, the *mazik* must pay 90 *zuz*. Before the case was decided in court, the carcass decreased in value from 10 *zuz* to 5 *zuz*. Even so, the *mazik* still has to pay only 90 *zuz*, and the *nizak* loses the 5 *zuz* of the carcass' depreciation (*Rav*).

[4]

1. The *av* (primary case) of the *keren* category is damage done by goring (*Exodus* 21:28,35; see Gemara 2b). Other types of intentional damage — such as pushing, biting, and kicking — are *toladôs* (derived cases) of *keren* (*Rav*; see Mishnah 1 with note 6).

2. Really, the *mazik* should not have to pay anything. The half payment is a fine that the Torah imposed on him (see Gemara 15a).

משניות בבא קמא / פרק א: ארבעה אבות

[ד] **חֲמִשָּׁה** תַּמִּין וַחֲמִשָּׁה מוּעָדִין, הַבְּהֵמָה אֵינָהּ מוּעֶדֶת לֹא לִגַּח, וְלֹא לִגּוֹף, וְלֹא לִשּׁוֹךְ, וְלֹא לִרְבֹּץ, וְלֹא לִבְעֹט. הַשֵּׁן מוּעֶדֶת לֶאֱכֹל אֶת הָרָאוּי לָהּ, הָרֶגֶל מוּעֶדֶת לִשְׁבֹּר בְּדֶרֶךְ הִלּוּכָהּ, וְשׁוֹר הַמּוּעָד,

— רע״ב —

(ד) חמשה תמין. שאינם רגילים להזיק, ואם הזיקו משלמין חצי נזק: **וחמשה מועדין.** שהם רגילין להזיק, ומשלמין נזק שלם: **בקרן:** לא ליגח. ולא ליגוף. דחיפת כל הגוף. וכולהו הוו תולדה דקרן ומשלמין חצי נזק. הרי חמשה תמין: **ושור המועד.** שלש פעמים ליגח, או לרבוץ, או לבטוט, או לשוך. הרי הן חמשה מועדים לשלם נזק שלם. ולגבי מועד חשיב להו חד:

---

is an animal that *is* expected to do damage in a certain way. Every animal is a *muad* with respect to damaging in the course of its normal activities, such as eating (*shein*) or walking (*regel*). Furthermore, a *tam* can become a *muad* if it damages in an unusual way three times and, after each time, its owner is warned by the court to guard it. From that point on, the animal is a *muad* with regard to that type of behavior since the behavior is no longer unexpected; its owner, therefore, must pay in full should it damage that way a fourth time.[3]

חֲמִשָּׁה תַּמִּין וַחֲמִשָּׁה מוּעָדִין — **There are** **five** **situations in which an animal is a** *tam* **and five** **situations in which it is a** *muad***.** הַבְּהֵמָה אֵינָהּ מוּעֶדֶת — **An animal is not a** *muad***, rather it is a** *tam***, the first three times that it damages in any of these unusual ways:** לֹא לִגַּח — **(1) It is not a** *muad* **to gore** with its horns, וְלֹא לִגּוֹף — **(2) nor to push** with its body, וְלֹא לִשּׁוֹךְ — **(3) nor to bite** something with intent to damage it, וְלֹא לִרְבֹּץ — **(4) nor to squat** on something with intent to break it, וְלֹא לִבְעֹט — **(5) nor to kick** something with intent to break it. Since these are unusual activities, the owner pays only half the amount of the damage.[4]

The Mishnah now lists the five situations in which every animal is always a *muad*, and thus full damages must be paid even the first time:

הַשֵּׁן מוּעֶדֶת לֶאֱכֹל אֶת הָרָאוּי לָהּ — **(1) In the case of damage through** *shein* (eating), an animal **is a** *muad* from the start, since it is normal for an animal **to eat food that is suitable for it;**[5] הָרֶגֶל מוּעֶדֶת לִשְׁבֹּר בְּדֶרֶךְ הִלּוּכָהּ — **(2) in the** case of damage through *regel* (walking), an animal **is a** *muad* from the start, since it is normal for an animal **to break things in the course of its walking;** וְשׁוֹר הַמּוּעָד — **(3) an ox** (or other animal) that became a *muad* by doing *keren*

--- NOTES ---

3. תָּם, *tam,* literally means *simple* or *innocent*. מוּעָד, *muad,* literally means *warned.* After each time that an animal damages in an unusual way, the court warns the owner to prevent it from doing so again.

4. These activities are considered unusual — and thus fall under the category of *keren* — only if they are done with intent to cause damage. But if, for example, an animal bites food because it wants to eat, which is normal, the damage belongs to the category of *shein*. And if an animal happens to squat on something as it bends its legs, or if it kicks something accidentally while it walks, the damage is *regel*. Regarding all actions that are defined as *shein* or *regel*, every animal is a *muad* (as the Mishnah will state), since these are common and expected behaviors.

5. However, if an animal eats an item that is clearly not food (such as clothing), it has done *keren* damage, for which it is a *tam* (Mishnah 2:2).

[17] MISHNAH BAVA KAMMA / Chapter 1: *Arba'ah Avos*

וְשׁוֹר הַמַּזִּיק בִּרְשׁוּת הַנִּזָּק, וְהָאָדָם. הַזְּאֵב, וְהָאֲרִי, וְהַדֹּב, וְהַנָּמֵר, וְהַבַּרְדְּלָס, וְהַנָּחָשׁ הֲרֵי אֵלּוּ מוּעָדִין. רַבִּי אֱלִיעֶזֶר אוֹמֵר, בִּזְמַן שֶׁהֵן בְּנֵי תַרְבּוּת, אֵינָן מוּעָדִין, וְהַנָּחָשׁ מוּעָד לְעוֹלָם.

— רע"ב —

ושור המזיק ברשות הניזק. אפילו קרן תמה הוי מועד לשלם נזק שלם. ומתניתין אתיא כמאן דאמר (דף טו,ב) משונה קרן בחצר הניזק, משלמת נזק שלם, ואפילו היא תמה. ואין כן הלכה: והאדם. הוי מועד מתחלתו נמי, ומשלם נזק שלם אם הזיק: [הזאב] והארי וכו'. מועדים מתחלתן. והא דלא תשיב להו בכלל חמשה מועדים דלעיל וליהוו אחד עשר מועדים, משום דהני לא שכיחי בישוב: ברדלס. חיה שקורין לה בערבי אלנב"ע: רבי אליעזר אומר: ואין הלכה כרבי אליעזר.

---

damage three times;[6] וְשׁוֹר הַמַּזִּיק בִּרְשׁוּת הַנִּזָּק — (4) an ox (or any animal) that does *keren* damage in an area owned by the damaged party is treated as though it were a *muad* even the first time it acts that way;[7] וְהָאָדָם — (5) and a person is a *muad* from the start.[8]

The Mishnah discusses certain species of animals that are aggressive by nature:

הַזְּאֵב וְהָאֲרִי וְהַדֹּב וְהַנָּמֵר וְהַבַּרְדְּלָס וְהַנָּחָשׁ הֲרֵי אֵלּוּ מוּעָדִין — The wolf, the lion, the bear, the leopard, the hyena, and the snake are *muadim* from the start even in respect to *keren* damage, because it is normal for these animals to deliberately attack.[9] רַבִּי אֱלִיעֶזֶר אוֹמֵר — However, R' Eliezer says: בִּזְמַן שֶׁהֵן בְּנֵי תַרְבּוּת אֵינָן מוּעָדִין — When they are domesticated, i.e., they were raised in someone's home, they are not *muadim* because they are presumably tame.[10] וְהַנָּחָשׁ מוּעָד לְעוֹלָם — But even R' Eliezer accepts that a snake is always a *muad* even if it was raised in a home, because he agrees that a snake can never be tamed.

--- NOTES ---

6. This clause refers to all the five activities listed above: goring, pushing, biting, squatting, and kicking (*Rav*). For example, if an animal deliberately pushes other animals three times and injures them, it is a *muad* with respect to pushing, because it has shown that this is its usual behavior. If it then pushes and damages a fourth time, the owner must pay in full.

7. The Mishnah taught above that an animal is a *tam* with respect to *keren* damage. However, if an animal entered the victim's property and did *keren* damage there, it has the law of a *muad* in that the owner must pay full compensation. This follows the opinion of R' Tarfon, but the Sages disagree, as taught in Mishnah 2:5 (*Rav*).

8. This is the category of *adam hamazik*, which is damage that a person does with his own body or force [for example, he strikes something with his hand or foot, or he shoots something with an arrow] (*Tiferes Yisrael*).

The Mishnah does not mention *eish* (fire) and *bor* (pit) among the five *muadim*, although they can be expected to do damage, because it deals only with living creatures (see *Tos. Yom Tov*).

9. These six animals were not added to the five cases of *muadim* listed above, which would have made a total of eleven, because these animals are not found where people live [and so are unlikely to be owned by a person or to damage property that belongs to a person] (*Rav*).

10. This is only the opinion of R' Eliezer. According to the Sages, however, these animals are always *muadim*, because even if they were raised among people, they cannot be assumed to be tame.

מַה בֵּין תָּם לְמוּעָד, אֶלָּא שֶׁהַתָּם מְשַׁלֵּם חֲצִי נֶזֶק מִגּוּפוֹ, וּמוּעָד מְשַׁלֵּם נֶזֶק שָׁלֵם מִן הָעֲלִיָּה.

— רע״ב —

מַה בֵּין תָּם לְמוּעָד. מְעִידִית שֶׁבִּנְכָסָיו. וַאֲפִלּוּ אֵין הַנּוֹגַחַת שָׁוֶה שִׁעוּר הַנֶּזֶק, דְּבַמּוּעָד כְּתִיב (שמות כא,לו) יְשַׁלֵּם שׁוֹר תַּחַת הַשּׁוֹר, וְלֹא כְּתִיב בֵּיהּ דְּמִגּוּף הַנּוֹגַחַת יִפְרַע:

The Mishnah teaches that there are two differences between a *tam* and a *muad* in regard to payment:

מַה בֵּין תָּם לְמוּעָד — **What** are the differences **between a** *tam* **and a** *muad*? אֶלָּא שֶׁהַתָּם מְשַׁלֵּם חֲצִי נֶזֶק מִגּוּפוֹ — **The differences are only that** when **a** *tam* damages, its owner **pays half damages,** and the payment is taken **from its body,** that is, the owner need give only the damaging animal as payment. If that animal's value is less than half the damage, he does not pay the difference.[11] And if it dies or becomes lost, he does not pay anything.[12] וּמוּעָד מְשַׁלֵּם נֶזֶק שָׁלֵם מִן הָעֲלִיָּה — **But** when **a** *muad* damages, its owner **pays full damages,** no matter how much the damaging animal is worth; and if he pays with land, he must pay **from the best** land he has.[13]

NOTES

11. For instance, if an ox worth 40 *zuz* gores another ox, causing 100 *zuz* in damage, the *mazik* need pay only 40 *zuz*. Even though the half-damage payment is 50 *zuz*, he is exempt from paying the 10 *zuz* that remain.

12. *Tiferes Yisrael*.

13. See Mishnah 1 note 14.

Chapter Two

משניות בבא קמא / פרק ב: כיצד הרגל

[א] **כֵּיצַד** הָרֶגֶל מוּעֶדֶת, לְשַׁבֵּר בְּדֶרֶךְ הִלּוּכָהּ. הַבְּהֵמָה מוּעֶדֶת לְהַלֵּךְ כְּדַרְכָּהּ וּלְשַׁבֵּר. הָיְתָה מְבַעֶטֶת, אוֹ שֶׁהָיוּ צְרוֹרוֹת מְנַתְּזִין מִתַּחַת רַגְלֶיהָ, וְשָׁבְרָה אֶת הַכֵּלִים, מְשַׁלֵּם חֲצִי נֶזֶק.

— רע״ב —

פרק שני — כיצד הרגל. (א) כיצד הרגל מועדת. כלומר, באיזה דבר הרגל מועדת. ומשני, לשבר בדרך הילוכה. בכך היא מועדת, שמשברת כלים דרך הלוכה: **הבהמה מועדת.** רישא

תנא אבות, רגל ממש, שדרסה ברגליה. וסיפא תנא תולדות, שבהמה מועדת להלך כדרכה ולשבר, בגופה, ובשערה, ובשליף שעליה, דרך הלוכה: **היתה מבעטת.** שינוי הוא זה, ותולדה דקרן, הלכך חצי נזק ותו לא: **או שהיו צרורות מנתזין.** אף על גב דלאו שינוי הוא, אלא אורחיה הוא, אף על פי כן חצי נזק ותו לא, דהלכתא גמירא לה. וברשות הניזק קאמר, דברשות הרבים פטור, דצרורות תולדה דרגל נינהו לפטרם ברשות הרבים:

---

[1] As explained in the last Mishnah of the previous chapter, the owner of an animal that did damage must pay full compensation only if the animal is a *muad* for that damage. It listed five situations in which an animal is a *muad*; these are: (a) damage by means of walking (*regel*), (b) damage by means of eating (*shein*), (c) *keren* damage[1] after three times, (d) *keren* damage in the property of the victim, (e) damage done by a person (*adam hamazik*). This chapter will elaborate upon each of these cases, beginning with *regel*:

כֵּיצַד הָרֶגֶל מוּעֶדֶת — **In what case is** an animal a *muad* with regard to *regel*? **לְשַׁבֵּר בְּדֶרֶךְ הִלּוּכָהּ** — An animal is a *muad* **to break** things with its feet (e.g., by stepping on them) **in the course of its walking;** **הַבְּהֵמָה מוּעֶדֶת לְהַלֵּךְ כְּדַרְכָּהּ וּלְשַׁבֵּר** — and **an animal is a *muad* to walk in its normal way and break** things with any other part of its body, or with an item that it is carrying.[2] In all these situations, therefore, the owner must pay full damages.

The Mishnah now presents two cases where an animal does damage with its feet and yet the owner pays only half of the victim's loss:

הָיְתָה מְבַעֶטֶת — **If it was kicking** with intent to damage, **אוֹ שֶׁהָיוּ צְרוֹרוֹת מְנַתְּזִין מִתַּחַת רַגְלֶיהָ** — **or if pebbles were flying out from under its feet** in the course of its normal walking, **וְשָׁבְרָה אֶת הַכֵּלִים** — **and,** in each of these circumstances, **it broke utensils,** **מְשַׁלֵּם חֲצִי נֶזֶק** — **[the owner] pays** only **half damages.** In the first of these two situations, he pays only half because the animal intended to damage, which makes it a case of *keren*.[3] And in the

---

NOTES

[1]
1. See Mishnah 1:4 note 4.
2. Although the Mishnah itself does not explain the difference between the first clause ("to break in the course of its walking") and the second clause ("to walk in its normal way and break"), the first clause is interpreted as referring to the *av* (primary case) of *regel*, which is damaging with the feet, while the second clause is interpreted as referring to the *tolados* (derived cases) of *regel*, which include damaging with other parts of the body or with things it is carrying; for example, its body brushes up against a wall and knocks it over (Rav; see Mishnah 1:1 note 2).

3. The first three times an animal does *keren* damage, the owner pays for half the damage, as taught in Mishnah 1:4. [Although the Mishnah is about *regel*, this particular case is one of *keren*.]

[21] MISHNAH BAVA KAMMA / Chapter 2: *Keitzad Haregel*

— רע"ב —

דָּרְסָה עַל הַכְּלִי וּשְׁבָרַתּוּ, וְנָפַל עַל כְּלִי וּשְׁבָרוֹ, עַל הָרִאשׁוֹן מְשַׁלֵּם נֶזֶק שָׁלֵם, וְעַל הָאַחֲרוֹן מְשַׁלֵּם חֲצִי נֶזֶק. הַתַּרְנְגוֹלִים מוּעָדִין לְהַלֵּךְ כְּדַרְכָּן וּלְשַׁבֵּר. הָיָה דְּלִיל קָשׁוּר בְּרַגְלָיו, אוֹ שֶׁהָיָה מְהַדֵּס וּמְשַׁבֵּר

ונפל על כלי אחר. ראשון נזקי רגל הן ומשלמת נזק שלם. והאחרון על ידי צרורות נשבר, הלכך חצי נזק: **דליל קשור ברגלו.** כל דבר הנקשר ברגל התרנגולת קרוי דליל. ואית דגרסי דלי: **מהדס.**

מרקד. ואית דמפרשי (עיין רמב"ם), חופר ברגליו באחר, כדרך התרנגולים: **משלם חצי נזק.** דדליל היינו צרורות, דבאתותו דליל אדיינהו לצרורות על הכלים. והדוס נמי כגון שהתיז, ואותן צרורות שברו הכלים:

---

second situation, he pays only half because the damage was inflicted not by the animal's body itself, but by the pebbles that flew out from under its feet.[4]

In the following case, an animal did damage both with its body and with something that it caused to move:

וְנָפַל עַל כְּלִי — דָּרְסָה עַל הַכְּלִי וּשְׁבָרַתּוּ — If it stepped on a vessel and broke it, וּשְׁבָרוֹ — and [a piece of the vessel] flew out, fell on another vessel and broke it, the law is as follows: עַל הָרִאשׁוֹן מְשַׁלֵּם נֶזֶק שָׁלֵם — For the first vessel, which the animal stepped on, [the owner] pays full damages, וְעַל הָאַחֲרוֹן מְשַׁלֵּם חֲצִי נֶזֶק — but for the last vessel, which was broken by a piece of the first one, [the owner] pays only half damages. Since the animal damaged the second vessel not with its body, but with something to which it gave force, only half damages need be paid.

The Mishnah applies these laws to birds:[5]

הַתַּרְנְגוֹלִים מוּעָדִין לְהַלֵּךְ כְּדַרְכָּן וּלְשַׁבֵּר — Chickens are *muadim* to walk in their normal way and break vessels, and therefore full payment must be made for the damage. הָיָה דְּלִיל קָשׁוּר בְּרַגְלָיו — However, if there was an object tied to [a chicken's] legs,[6] אוֹ שֶׁהָיָה מְהַדֵּס — or if it was hopping on its feet,

---
— NOTES —

4. Normally, there is no difference between damage done directly with the body of a person or animal (or something attached to the body) and damage done by something to which the body gave force, for example, a stone that a person threw. Either way, the *mazik* is fully liable. This principle is called כֹּחוֹ כְּגוּפוֹ, *his force is like his body*. In the laws of *regel*, however, there *is* a difference between an animal's body (or something attached to it) and its force. If damage was done by the animal's body (for example, it stepped on something) the owner pays in full, but if damage was done by something to which the animal gave force (such as pebbles that it accidentally kicked or that just flew out from under its feet), the owner need pay only half. This law, which is known as צְרוֹרוֹת, *pebbles*, was taught to Moses at Sinai and passed down through the generations from teacher to student (Gemara 17b).

Since damage through "pebbles" falls under the category of *regel*, payment is required only if the incident happened in the property of the victim, and not in public property (*Rav;* see Mishnah 1:2 note 6). This case is thus different from the previous one (kicking with intent to damage), which is *keren,* and where payment is required even if the damage occurred in a public place.

5. Even though the examples given in the Torah are of animals that damage, other verses teach that the same laws apply to birds as well (*Tos. Yom Tov*).

6. The word דְּלִיל refers to anything that is attached to the leg of a chicken. In some versions of the Mishnah's text, the word is דְּלִי, which means *bucket* (*Rav*).

משניות בבא קמא / פרק ב: כיצד הרגל

אֶת הַכֵּלִים, מְשַׁלֵּם חֲצִי נֶזֶק.

[ב] **כֵּיצַד** הַשֵּׁן מוּעֶדֶת, לֶאֱכֹל אֶת הָרָאוּי לָהּ. הַבְּהֵמָה מוּעֶדֶת לֶאֱכֹל פֵּרוֹת וִירָקוֹת. אָכְלָה כְּסוּת אוֹ כֵלִים, מְשַׁלֵּם חֲצִי נֶזֶק. בַּמֶּה דְבָרִים אֲמוּרִים, בִּרְשׁוּת הַנִּזָּק, אֲבָל בִּרְשׁוּת הָרַבִּים, פָּטוּר.

— רע״ב —

(ב) כיצד השן מועדת. באיזה דבר היא מועדת. ומשני, לאכול את הראוי לה: משלם חצי נזק. דמשונה הוא: במה דברים אמורים וכו׳. אאכלה פירות או ירקות קאי, דברשות הרבים פטור דבעינן ובער בשדה אחר (שמות כב,ד):

אבל אכלה כסות וכלים, אפילו ברשות הרבים, חייב חצי נזק, דעבדי אנשי דמנחי כסות וכלים ברשות הרבים לפי שעה, והוי קרן ברשות הרבים, וחייב:

וּמְשַׁבֵּר אֶת הַכֵּלִים — **and it broke vessels** because either the object or the chicken's feet caused pebbles to fly out and hit the vessels, מְשַׁלֵּם חֲצִי נֶזֶק — [the owner] pays for only half the damage, because it was the pebbles, and not the bird itself or anything attached to it, that broke the vessels.[7]

[2] The Mishnah explains the next category listed in Mishnah 1:4, which is *shein* (damage done by an animal in the course of eating):

כֵּיצַד הַשֵּׁן מוּעֶדֶת — **In what case is** an animal a *muad* with regard to *shein*? לֶאֱכֹל אֶת הָרָאוּי לָהּ — An animal is a *muad* to eat [food] that is suitable for it, הַבְּהֵמָה מוּעֶדֶת לֶאֱכֹל פֵּרוֹת וִירָקוֹת — and an animal is a *muad* to eat fruits and vegetables.[1] Thus, if someone's animal ate another person's fruit, vegetables, or any other suitable food, its owner must pay full damages. אָכְלָה כְּסוּת אוֹ כֵלִים — However, if it ate clothing or utensils, מְשַׁלֵּם חֲצִי נֶזֶק — he pays only half damages. Since an animal does not usually eat clothing or utensils, this is not a case of *shein*, but a case of unusual damage, which is *keren*; and when an animal does *keren* damage (the first three times), only half payment is required.

Having taught that the owner must pay in full for *shein* damage, the Mishnah limits this law:

בַּמֶּה דְבָרִים אֲמוּרִים — **In what case does it apply?** בִּרְשׁוּת הַנִּזָּק — It applies when the animal ate **in a place that belongs to the victim of the damage.** אֲבָל בִּרְשׁוּת הָרַבִּים פָּטוּר — But if it ate **in a public place, [its owner] is exempt**

NOTES

7. In the case of the object tied to the chicken's legs, the *mazik* pays half only if the object hit pebbles and it was the pebbles that did the damage. Since the damage was not done by the chicken's body, but rather by something to which the chicken gave "force" (i.e., the pebbles), half payment is enough. But if the object that was tied to the chicken did the damage, full payment would be required, because anything attached to or carried by an animal has the same law as its body (*Tiferes Yisrael*).

[2]

1. The second statement, "An animal is a *muad* to eat fruits and vegetables," does not seem to add anything to the previous one, "[An animal is a *muad*] to eat [food] that is suitable for it." The Gemara (17b) explains that the Mishnah makes two similar statements to allude to the fact that the laws of damages apply to both domestic animals (like sheep) and wild animals (like deer). Although the Torah always uses examples of domestic animals, the Mishnah teaches that the laws are the same for wild animals (*Tos. Yom Tov*).

[23] MISHNAH BAVA KAMMA / Chapter 2: *Keitzad Haregel*

— רע״ב —

משלם מה שנהנית. לאו תשלומין מעלייתא. אלא אם אכלה דבר שדמיו יקרים רואים אותו כאילו הן שעורים, ואינו משלם אלא דמי שעורים בזול, שהוא שליש פחות ממה שהם נמכרים בשוק.

אִם נֶהֱנֵית, מְשַׁלֵּם מַה שֶּׁנֶּהֱנֵית. כֵּיצַד מְשַׁלֵּם מַה שֶּׁנֶּהֱנֵית, אָכְלָה מִתּוֹךְ הָרְחָבָה, מְשַׁלֵּם מַה שֶּׁנֶּהֱנֵית, מִצִּדֵּי הָרְחָבָה, מְשַׁלֵּם מַה שֶּׁהִזִּיקָה. מִפֶּתַח הַחֲנוּת, מְשַׁלֵּם מַה שֶּׁנֶּהֱנֵית, מִתּוֹךְ הַחֲנוּת, מְשַׁלֵּם מַה שֶּׁהִזִּיקָה.

ואם אכלה דבר שדמיו פחותים מן השעורים, משלם דמי אותו דבר שאכלה, בזול. ואם אכלה דבר שהזיק לה, כגון שאכלה חטים, הואיל ולא נהנית פטור: מִצִּדֵּי הרחבה משלם מה שהזיקה. אם הלכה ועמדה בצדי הרחבה, במקום שאין דרך שוורים ללכת שם, לאו כרשות הרבים דמי, ומשלמת מה שהזיקה:

---

from payment.[2] אִם נֶהֱנֵית מְשַׁלֵּם מַה שֶּׁנֶּהֱנֵית — Nevertheless, even when it ate in a public place, **if it benefited** from the food, and the owner can therefore feed it less than usual, **he pays** the value of **what it benefited.** Since he saved the money he would have spent to buy that amount of animal food, he must pay for that benefit.[3]

The Mishnah elaborates:

כֵּיצַד מְשַׁלֵּם מַה שֶּׁנֶּהֱנֵית — **In what case** does he pay only **what it benefited?** אָכְלָה מִתּוֹךְ הָרְחָבָה מְשַׁלֵּם מַה שֶּׁנֶּהֱנֵית — **If it ate** food **in the middle of the street, he pays** only **what it benefited,** since that is a public place. מִצִּדֵּי הָרְחָבָה מְשַׁלֵּם מַה שֶּׁהִזִּיקָה — **But if it ate** food **from the sides of the street,** where animals do not usually walk, **he pays** in full for **what it damaged.** Since the owner of the food had a right to put it at the side of the street, where animals do not usually go, it is as if the animal entered the victim's property, in which case full payment is required.

A similar pair of rulings:

מִפֶּתַח הַחֲנוּת מְשַׁלֵּם מַה שֶּׁנֶּהֱנֵית — **If** an animal ate food **from the area in front of the entrance to a store,**[4] [the animal's owner] **pays** only **what it benefited,** because that is a public place. מִתּוֹךְ הַחֲנוּת מְשַׁלֵּם מַה שֶּׁהִזִּיקָה — **But if it**

NOTES

2. One does not have to pay for *regel* or *shein* damage unless the damage was done in the property of the victim (see Mishnah 1:2 note 6).

The Mishnah's case is where the animal ate suitable food, such as fruits and vegetables. If it ate clothing or utensils, which is *keren* damage, the owner would have to pay even if the incident occurred in a public place (*Rav*).

3. Although the owner does not have to pay for causing damage (מַזִּיק), he must pay for what he benefited (נֶהֱנֶה). It is a general rule that whenever someone benefits from the property of another and thereby causes the owner some loss, he must pay at least for the benefit. In our case, where the animal ate fruits or vegetables, the owner benefited in that he saved the money he would have spent on an equivalent amount of barley, which is a common animal food. He must therefore pay the victim the value of that amount of barley. He does not have to pay more even if the food it ate was more expensive than barley (*Rambam Commentary*). If it ate food that is harmful, he does not pay anything, since he had no benefit (*Rav*).

4. Storekeepers would display food on tables that they set up in the public area in front of their stores [where animals would walk] (*Tosafos* 21a ד״ה מפתח).

משניות בבא קמא / פרק ב: כיצד הרגל

[ג] **הַכֶּלֶב** וְהַגְּדִי שֶׁקָּפְצוּ מֵרֹאשׁ הַגַּג וְשִׁבְּרוּ אֶת הַכֵּלִים, מְשַׁלֵּם נֶזֶק שָׁלֵם, מִפְּנֵי שֶׁהֵן מוּעָדִין. הַכֶּלֶב שֶׁנָּטַל חֲרָרָה וְהָלַךְ לַגָּדִישׁ, אָכַל הַחֲרָרָה וְהִדְלִיק הַגָּדִישׁ, עַל הַחֲרָרָה מְשַׁלֵּם נֶזֶק שָׁלֵם, וְעַל הַגָּדִישׁ מְשַׁלֵּם חֲצִי נֶזֶק.

[ד] **אֵיזֶה** הוּא תָּם וְאֵיזֶה הוּא מוּעָד,

— רע״ב —

(ג) מפני שהן מועדין. לקפוץ. ובכרסות הניזק קאמר, דתולדה דרגל היא: חררה. עוגה שנאפית על גבי גחלים: על החררה משלם נזק שלם. דהוי שן בכרסות הניזק: ועל הגדיש משלם חצי נזק. דהוי כמו צרורות, דהלכתא גמירי לה שמשלם חצי נזק:

---

entered a store and ate food **from inside the store, he pays for what it damaged,** since the store is the victim's property.

[3] Having taught some general rules of *regel* and *shein*, the Mishnah deals with specific cases:[1]

הַכֶּלֶב וְהַגְּדִי שֶׁקָּפְצוּ מֵרֹאשׁ הַגַּג וְשִׁבְּרוּ אֶת הַכֵּלִים — **If a dog or young goat jumped from the top of a roof** onto someone's private property **and broke vessels when it landed,** מְשַׁלֵּם נֶזֶק שָׁלֵם — **[the animal's owner] pays full damages,** מִפְּנֵי שֶׁהֵן מוּעָדִין — **because [these animals] are** *muadim* in regard to jumping from roofs (i.e., it is normal behavior for them). Since it is not unusual for dogs and young goats to jump off roofs, this is a case of damage done in the course of an animal's usual movement (*regel*), for which the owner must pay in full.[2]

Another case:

הַכֶּלֶב שֶׁנָּטַל חֲרָרָה וְהָלַךְ לַגָּדִישׁ — **A dog** entered someone's property, **took a roll** that was baking there and which had hot coals sticking to it, **and went to a pile of grain** in that person's property carrying the roll and coals; אָכַל הַחֲרָרָה וְהִדְלִיק הַגָּדִישׁ — **then it ate the roll,** shaking the coals off onto the pile of grain,[3] **and thereby set the pile of grain on fire.** עַל הַחֲרָרָה מְשַׁלֵּם נֶזֶק שָׁלֵם — The law is that **for the roll, [the dog's owner] pays full damages,** because that is *shein* damage, וְעַל הַגָּדִישׁ מְשַׁלֵּם חֲצִי נֶזֶק — **but for the pile of grain, he pays** only **half damages.** Since the grain was damaged not by the dog's body but by the coals that were tossed onto the pile, this is like the case of "pebbles" (discussed in Mishnah 1), where only half payment is required.[4]

[4] This Mishnah deals with the third case listed in Mishnah 1:4, where an animal becomes a *muad*. An animal starts out as a *tam* in regard to *keren* damage (i.e., damage caused by unusual behavior), but becomes a *muad* after it has damaged in an unusual way three times.

אֵיזֶה הוּא תָּם וְאֵיזֶה הוּא מוּעָד — **Which** animal **is a** *tam* **and which** animal **is**

--- NOTES ---

[3]
1. Meiri.
2. Payment is required only if the damage occurred in the property of the *nizak*,

because this is *regel* damage, rather than *keren* (*Rav*).
3. *Tos. Yom Tov.*
4. See note 4 there.

[25] **MISHNAH BAVA KAMMA** / Chapter 2: *Keitzad Haregel*

— רע״ב —

(ד) משיחזור בו שלשה
ימים. שרוחה שוורים
ואינו נוגח, חוזר לתמותו:
שלשה פעמים. ואפילו
ביום אחד. ואין הלכה
כרבי [מאיר]. דלא הוי
מועד עד שיעידו בו
שלשה ימים: ממשמשים
בו. מושכים אותו ומשחקים בו, ואינו נוגח. ובהא הלכה [כרבי מאיר], שאין שור מועד חוזר לתמותו,
עד שיהו תינוקות משחקים בו:

מוּעָד כָּל שֶׁהֵעִידוּ בּוֹ שְׁלֹשָׁה יָמִים, וְתָם
מִשֶּׁיַּחֲזֹר בּוֹ שְׁלֹשָׁה יָמִים, דִּבְרֵי רַבִּי יְהוּדָה.
רַבִּי מֵאִיר אוֹמֵר, מוּעָד שֶׁהֵעִידוּ בּוֹ שְׁלֹשָׁה
פְעָמִים, וְתָם כָּל שֶׁיְּהוּ הַתִּינוֹקוֹת מְמַשְׁמְשִׁין
בּוֹ וְאֵינוֹ נוֹגֵחַ.

מוּעָד כָּל שֶׁהֵעִידוּ בּוֹ שְׁלֹשָׁה יָמִים — A *muad* is any animal about which they warned the owner that it did *keren* damage on **three days**.[1] **וְתָם מִשֶּׁיַּחֲזֹר בּוֹ שְׁלֹשָׁה יָמִים** — And a *muad* goes back to being **a *tam* if it changes** its behavior on **three days**; that is, it had the chance to do similar damage on three days but refrained.[2] **דִּבְרֵי רַבִּי יְהוּדָה** — These are **the words of R' Yehudah**. **רַבִּי מֵאִיר אוֹמֵר** — However, **R' Meir says**: **מוּעָד שֶׁהֵעִידוּ בּוֹ שְׁלֹשָׁה פְעָמִים** — A *muad* is an animal **about which they warned** the owner that it did *keren* damage **three times**, regardless of whether the incidents took place over three days or only one day.[3] **וְתָם כָּל שֶׁיְּהוּ הַתִּינוֹקוֹת מְמַשְׁמְשִׁין בּוֹ וְאֵינוֹ נוֹגֵחַ** — And a *muad* goes back to being **a *tam*** only if it becomes so tame that **children touch it** and pull it **and it does not gore** them.[4]

[5] This Mishnah deals with the fourth case of *muad* mentioned in Mishnah 1:4, where an animal does *keren* damage in an area owned by the victim of the damage. Even if the animal is actually a *tam*, its owner must pay full damages as though it were a *muad*. However, this law is not accepted by all; it is the subject of a disagreement:

--- NOTES ---

[4]

1. According to this Tanna, an animal that did *keren* damage three times on the same day does not become a *muad*. Rather, the three incidents must take place over a period of at least three days.

The three days do not have to be consecutive; for example, if it did *keren* damage on Sunday, Tuesday, and Thursday, it becomes a *muad*. However, the three days must not be separated by a day on which it had an opportunity to do *keren* damage but failed to act. For instance, if it gored an animal on Sunday and Tuesday, saw an animal on Wednesday but did not gore it, and then gored on Thursday, it remains a *tam* (*Piskei Riaz*).

2. For example, it saw animals on three days and did not gore them. A verse in the Torah teaches that in such a case it returns to being a *tam* (see *Tos. Yom Tov*).

3. R' Meir holds that if an animal can become a *muad* by goring three times on different days, it can certainly become a *muad* by goring three times on the same day, because the more frequently it attacks the more dangerous it is. According to R' Yehudah, however, a single day of goring is not enough for it to be *muad*, because it must show a pattern of aggressive behavior over a significant length of time, which the Torah says is three days (*Gemara* 24a; *Pnei Yehoshua* there).

4. *Rambam Commentary*.

R' Meir holds that holding back from attacking animals for three days [when it has the chance] is not enough reason for an animal to change back from a *muad* to a *tam*. The only way for it to become a *tam* again is by not goring children who touch and pull it (*Rav*, as explained by *Tosefos R' Akiva Eiger*).

— רע״ב —

כולן תולדות קרן הן: (ה) נגח נגף [וכו׳].

[ה] **שׁוֹר** הַמַּזִּיק בִּרְשׁוּת הַנִּזָּק כֵּיצַד, נָגַח, נָגַף, נָשַׁךְ, רָבַץ, בָּעַט, בִּרְשׁוּת הָרַבִּים, מְשַׁלֵּם חֲצִי נֶזֶק, בִּרְשׁוּת הַנִּזָּק, רַבִּי טַרְפוֹן אוֹמֵר, נֶזֶק שָׁלֵם. וַחֲכָמִים אוֹמְרִים: חֲצִי נֶזֶק. אָמַר לָהֶם רַבִּי טַרְפוֹן וּמָה בְּמָקוֹם שֶׁהֵקֵל עַל הַשֵּׁן וְעַל הָרֶגֶל, בִּרְשׁוּת הָרַבִּים, שֶׁהוּא פָטוּר, הֶחְמִיר עֲלֵיהֶם בִּרְשׁוּת הַנִּזָּק, לְשַׁלֵּם נֶזֶק שָׁלֵם, מָקוֹם שֶׁהֶחְמִיר עַל הַקֶּרֶן, בִּרְשׁוּת הָרַבִּים, לְשַׁלֵּם חֲצִי נֶזֶק, אֵינוֹ דִין שֶׁנַּחְמִיר עָלֶיהָ בִּרְשׁוּת הַנִּזָּק, לְשַׁלֵּם נֶזֶק שָׁלֵם.

שׁוֹר הַמַּזִּיק בִּרְשׁוּת הַנִּזָּק כֵּיצַד — **What is the case** of the ox (*tam*) that does *keren* damage in an area belonging to the victim of the damage? נָגַח נָגַף נָשַׁךְ רָבַץ בָּעַט בִּרְשׁוּת הָרַבִּים — **If it gored, pushed, bit, squatted, or kicked in a public place,** מְשַׁלֵּם חֲצִי נֶזֶק — **[its owner] pays half damages,** בִּרְשׁוּת הַנִּזָּק — **but if it did so in an area belonging to the victim,** רַבִּי טַרְפוֹן אוֹמֵר נֶזֶק שָׁלֵם — **R' Tarfon says** that he pays **full damages,** even though it is a *tam*; וַחֲכָמִים אוֹמְרִים חֲצִי נֶזֶק — while the Sages say that he pays only **half damages.**[1]

R' Tarfon bases his opinion on a logical argument (*kal vachomer*):[2]

אָמַר לָהֶם רַבִּי טַרְפוֹן וּמָה בְּמָקוֹם שֶׁהֵקֵל עַל — **R' Tarfon said to [the Sages]:** הַשֵּׁן וְעַל הָרֶגֶל בִּרְשׁוּת הָרַבִּים שֶׁהוּא פָטוּר — **Since [the Torah] is lenient regarding** *shein* **and** *regel* **that happened in a public place, ruling that [the owner] is exempt from paying,** הֶחְמִיר עֲלֵיהֶם בִּרְשׁוּת הַנִּזָּק לְשַׁלֵּם נֶזֶק שָׁלֵם — **and yet it is strict regarding [shein and regel]** that happened **in the victim's property, requiring the owner to pay full damages,** we see that stricter laws apply to damage done in the victim's property than to damage done in a public place. מָקוֹם שֶׁהֶחְמִיר עַל הַקֶּרֶן בִּרְשׁוּת הָרַבִּים לְשַׁלֵּם חֲצִי נֶזֶק — **If so, then since [the Torah] is stricter regarding** *keren* **in a public place,** in that it requires the owner **to pay half damages,** אֵינוֹ דִין שֶׁנַּחְמִיר עָלֶיהָ בִּרְשׁוּת הַנִּזָּק לְשַׁלֵּם נֶזֶק שָׁלֵם — **is it not logical that we should be stricter about [*keren*] in the victim's property** and require the owner **to pay full damages?** Since the victim's property is treated more strictly than a public place with respect to *shein* and *regel*, it should also be treated more strictly with respect to *keren*. Therefore, since the owner pays for half of *keren* damage done in a public place, he should pay in full for *keren* damage done in the victim's property.

The Sages respond:

NOTES

[5]

1. Mishnah 1:4, which states that full damages are required, follows R' Tarfon's opinion.

2. A *kal vachomer* compares two situations, one whose laws are generally lenient (*kal*) and one whose laws are generally strict (*chamur*). If the Torah applies a strict ruling to the lenient situation, logic tells us that the ruling certainly applies in the strict situation.

— רע"ב —

דיו לבא מן הדין להיות
כנדון. קרן ברשות הניזק
שאתה מביא מדין קרן
ברשות הרבים. דקאמרת,
קרן שהחמיר עליה ברשות
הרבים, אינו דין שנחמיר
עליה ברשות הניזק.
דיו להיות כנדון, כקרן
ברשות הרבים, ולא יהיה
חייב ברשות הניזק, אלא
חצי נזק, כמו שהוא חייב
ברשות הרבים: אני לא אדון קרן מקרן. כדאמרן לעיל, אלא קרן מרגל. מקום שהחמיר עליו בשן
ורגל, אינו דין שנחמיר בקרן:

אָמְרוּ לוֹ, דַּיּוֹ לַבָּא מִן הַדִּין לִהְיוֹת כַּנִּדּוֹן,
מַה בִּרְשׁוּת הָרַבִּים חֲצִי נֶזֶק, אַף בִּרְשׁוּת
הַנִּזָּק חֲצִי נֶזֶק. אָמַר לָהֶם, אֲנִי לֹא אָדוּן
קֶרֶן מִקֶּרֶן, אֲנִי אָדוּן קֶרֶן מֵרֶגֶל, וּמַה בְּמָקוֹם
שֶׁהֵקֵל עַל הַשֵּׁן וְעַל הָרֶגֶל בִּרְשׁוּת הָרַבִּים
הֶחְמִיר בַּקֶּרֶן, מָקוֹם שֶׁהֶחְמִיר עַל הַשֵּׁן וְעַל
הָרֶגֶל, בִּרְשׁוּת הַנִּזָּק, אֵינוֹ דִין שֶׁנַּחְמִיר בַּקֶּרֶן.

אָמְרוּ לוֹ — **They said to [R' Tarfon]**: דַּיּוֹ לַבָּא מִן הַדִּין לִהְיוֹת כַּנִּדּוֹן — **It is enough for the new law, which is taught by the** *kal vachomer,* **to be the same as the law from which it is derived**; it cannot be stricter than the law from which it is derived.[3] R' Tarfon's *kal vachomer* can teach that since the owner pays for half of *keren* damage done in a public place, he certainly pays for half of *keren* damage done in the victim's property; but it cannot teach that he must pay for *more* than half of *keren* damage done in the victim's property. מַה בִּרְשׁוּת הָרַבִּים חֲצִי נֶזֶק — **Rather, just as** the owner pays for **half** of *keren* **damage** done in **a public place,** אַף בִּרְשׁוּת הַנִּזָּק חֲצִי נֶזֶק — **so** does he pay for **half** of *keren* **damage** done **in the victim's property.**

In response, R' Tarfon presents a somewhat different *kal vachomer*:

אָמַר לָהֶם — **[R' Tarfon] said to them:** אֲנִי לֹא אָדוּן קֶרֶן מִקֶּרֶן — **I will not derive** the law of *keren* damage done in the victim's property **from** the law of *keren* damage done in a public place, as I did before; אֲנִי אָדוּן קֶרֶן מֵרֶגֶל — instead, **I will derive** the law of *keren* **from** the law of *regel* and *shein,* as follows: וּמַה בְּמָקוֹם שֶׁהֵקֵל עַל הַשֵּׁן וְעַל הָרֶגֶל בִּרְשׁוּת הָרַבִּים — **Since [the Torah] is lenient regarding** *shein* **and** *regel,* as we see from the fact that the owner pays nothing for *shein* or *regel* damage done **in a public place,** הֶחְמִיר בַּקֶּרֶן — and yet **it is strict about** *keren,* as we see from the fact that he pays something (half) for *keren* damage done in a public place, מָקוֹם שֶׁהֶחְמִיר עַל הַשֵּׁן וְעַל הָרֶגֶל בִּרְשׁוּת הַנִּזָּק — then in **a case where [the Torah] is strict regarding** *shein* **and** *regel* in that he must pay in full for such damage done in **the victim's property,** אֵינוֹ דִין שֶׁנַּחְמִיר בַּקֶּרֶן — **is it not logical that we should be** at least as **strict regarding** *keren* and require the owner to pay in full for *keren* damage done in the victim's property? Since in this case (i.e., where damage is done in the victim's property) he pays in full for *shein* and *regel* damage, whose laws are generally more lenient, he should certainly pay in full for *keren* damage, whose laws are generally stricter.

NOTES

3. A *kal vachomer* can tell us only that if a stringent ruling applies in a lenient situation, the *same* ruling applies in a strict situation. It cannot tell us that an even stricter ruling should apply in the strict situation.

משניות בבא קמא / פרק ב: כיצד הרגל

אָמְרוּ לוֹ, דַּיּוֹ לַבָּא מִן הַדִּין לִהְיוֹת כַּנִּדּוֹן. מַה בִּרְשׁוּת הָרַבִּים חֲצִי נֶזֶק, אַף בִּרְשׁוּת הַנִּזָּק חֲצִי נֶזֶק.

[ו] **אָדָם** מוּעָד לְעוֹלָם, בֵּין שׁוֹגֵג בֵּין מֵזִיד, בֵּין עֵר בֵּין יָשֵׁן. סִמֵּא אֶת עֵין חֲבֵרוֹ

— רע"ב —

דיו לבא מן הדין. דסוף סוף, אי לאו קרן ברשות הרבים, לא משכחת לה קל וחומר. ורבי טרפון, אף על גב דבטלמוד אית ליה דיו, מדאורייתא הוא, דכתיב (במדבר יב,יד) הלא תכלם שבעת ימים, קל וחומר לשכינה ארבעה עשר יום, אלא דיו מן הדין להיות כנדון, הלכך תסגר שבעת ימים ותו לא. מכל מקום הכא לית ליה דיו, דסתבירא ליה לרבי טרפון, דכי אמרינן דיו, היכא דלא מפריך קל וחומר, כגון התם, דשבעת ימים דשכינה לא כתיבי, אתא קל וחומר חייתי ארבייסר, אתא דיו אפיק שבעה, ואוקי שבעה, אשתכח דאהני קל וחומר להני שבעה דתוקימנא, ולא אפריך לגמרי. אבל הכא, חלי נזק כתיב בין ברשות הרבים בין בחצר הניזק, ואתא קל וחומר וחלי נזק אחריגא ונטשה נזק שלם, אי דרשת דיו ותוקמיה אחלי נזק כדמטיקרא, אפריך ליה קל וחומר, ולא אהני ולא מידי. ורבנן סברי, דאפילו היכא דמפריך קל וחומר, אמרינן דיו. והלכה כחכמים: (ו) **בין ער בין ישן.** אם היה ישן, ובא אחר וישן בצדו, והזיק שני לראשון, חייב. ואם הזיק ראשון לשני, פטור. ואם שכבו יחד, כל אחד מהם שהזיק את חברו חייב. לפי שעייהם מועדים זה לזה: **סימא את עין חברו.** אפילו בשוגג חייב בנזק. אבל לא בארבעה דברים, דלא מחייב בארבעה דברים אלא במזיד, או קרוב למזיד:

The Sages reject this *kal vachomer* as well:

אָמְרוּ לוֹ — **They said to him,** as above: דַּיּוֹ לַבָּא מִן הַדִּין לִהְיוֹת כַּנִּדּוֹן — **It is enough for** the new law, which is taught by the *kal vachomer,* to be the same **as the law from which it is derived;** it cannot be stricter than the law from which it is derived. Even R' Tarfon's second *kal vachomer* is based on the law of *keren* in a public place; thus, it can teach only that *keren* in the victim's property is the same as *keren* in a public place, but it cannot teach that it is stricter.[4] מַה בִּרְשׁוּת הָרַבִּים חֲצִי נֶזֶק — **Therefore, just as** the owner pays for half of *keren* damage done **in a public place,** אַף בִּרְשׁוּת הַנִּזָּק חֲצִי נֶזֶק — **so** does he pay for half of *keren* damage done **in the victim's property.**

[6] The Mishnah deals with the last *muad* listed in Mishnah 1:4, a person who does damage (*adam hamazik*):

אָדָם מוּעָד לְעוֹלָם — **A person is always a *muad*,** that is, he must always pay in full for any damage he does, בֵּין שׁוֹגֵג בֵּין מֵזִיד — **whether** he damages **by accident or on purpose,** בֵּין עֵר בֵּין יָשֵׁן — **whether** he damages when **awake or asleep.**[1] סִמֵּא אֶת עֵין חֲבֵרוֹ — For example, if **he blinded someone else's**

NOTES

4. R' Tarfon's second *kal vachomer* is based on the fact that *keren* is stricter than *shein* and *regel*. However, we know this only because *keren* damage done in a public place requires some payment, whereas *shein* or *regel* damage done in a public area requires no payment. Since the law of *keren* in a public place is needed for the *kal vachomer*, the law we derive from the *kal vachomer* cannot be stricter than it (*Rashi;* see *Tosafos* 25a ד"ה אני).

[6]

1. A person is responsible for what he does even in his sleep. For example, if someone goes to sleep next to some vessels and breaks them as he moves in his sleep, he must pay for the damage. Since he should have realized before he went to

וְשִׁבֵּר אֶת הַכֵּלִים, מְשַׁלֵּם נֶזֶק שָׁלֵם.

eye by accident, **וְשִׁבֵּר אֶת הַכֵּלִים** — **or if he broke vessels** by accident, **מְשַׁלֵּם נֶזֶק שָׁלֵם** — **he pays full damages.**[2]

NOTES

sleep that he might hit the vessels, he is liable for breaking them. However, if the vessels were placed next to him after he was already asleep, he is exempt from payment, because there was no way he could have known that the damage would occur. Even a person is not liable for damage that he could not possibly have avoided (*Tosafos* 4a ד"ה כיון דכייף).

2. We shall learn that when one person injures another, he makes five payments. He pays for the actual damage to the victim (i.e., the loss of his value were he to be sold as a slave), his pain, medical costs, lost wages, and shame (see Mishnah 8:1). Our Mishnah, however, mentions blinding an eye together with breaking a vessel, which implies that one who blinds an eye pays only for the actual damage, as is the law with breaking a vessel. This is because the Mishnah refers to one who blinded an eye by accident, and the rule in cases of accidental injury is that the *mazik* pays only for the actual damage, and not for any of the other four losses (*Rav, Tos. Yom Tov*).

Chapter Three

פרק ג: המניח

[א] הַמַּנִּיחַ אֶת הַכַּד בִּרְשׁוּת הָרַבִּים, וּבָא אַחֵר וְנִתְקַל בָּהּ וּשְׁבָרָהּ, פָּטוּר. וְאִם הֻזַּק בָּהּ, בַּעַל הֶחָבִית חַיָּב בְּנִזְקוֹ. נִשְׁבְּרָה כַדּוֹ בִּרְשׁוּת הָרַבִּים, וְהֻחְלַק אֶחָד בַּמַּיִם אוֹ שֶׁלָּקָה בַחֲרָסֶיהָ, חַיָּב.

— רע״ב —

פרק שלישי – המניח. (א) המניח את הכד וכו׳ ושברה פטור. לפי שאין דרך בני אדם להתבונן בדרכים: ואם הוזק בה בעל החבית חייב. ואפילו הפקירה, שכל המפקיר נזקיו שלא היה לו רשות מתחלה לעשותן, כאילו לא הפקירן: או שלקה בחרסיה חייב. דסבר נתקל פושע הוא, ולאו אונס הוא, ולכך חייב:

---

[1] This chapter deals with the second of the four categories of damage listed in Mishnah 1:1; namely, a pit in a public area (*bor*). This category includes any obstacle that, like a pit, does not move. The first Mishnah discusses a jug that was left in a public area, such as a street, where it caused damage or was damaged:

הַמַּנִּיחַ אֶת הַכַּד בִּרְשׁוּת הָרַבִּים — **If someone leaves a jug** on the ground **in a public place,** וּבָא אַחֵר וְנִתְקַל בָּהּ וּשְׁבָרָהּ — **and another person comes, stumbles over it, and breaks it,** פָּטוּר — **he is exempt** from paying for it. This is because people do not usually look down at the ground while they are walking; thus, the damager cannot be blamed for failing to notice something that was not expected to be there. וְאִם הֻזַּק בָּהּ — **And if he was injured by [the jug],** בַּעַל הֶחָבִית חַיָּב בְּנִזְקוֹ — **the owner of the jug**[1] **is obligated** to pay **for his injury,** because it was an obstacle in a public area, like a pit.[2]

A related case:

נִשְׁבְּרָה כַדּוֹ בִּרְשׁוּת הָרַבִּים — **If someone carrying a jug of water stumbled and fell, and his jug broke in a public place,** וְהֻחְלַק אֶחָד בַּמַּיִם — **and someone else slipped on the water,** אוֹ שֶׁלָּקָה בַחֲרָסֶיהָ — **or was injured by its shards** of pottery, חַיָּב — **[the owner of the jug] is obligated** to pay. Since the owner of the jug could have avoided stumbling and falling,[3] he is responsible for creating the hazard of the water and shards lying on the ground. He must therefore pay for whatever damage they cause.[4]

NOTES

[1]

1. Although the Mishnah previously used the word כַּד, *kad*, here it uses חָבִית, *chavis*, in order to teach that in certain regions these words have the same meaning. This is relevant to the laws of buying and selling, where the words used by the buyer and seller define the object being sold (see *Tos. Yom Tov*).

2. Even if he gave up ownership of the jug, he must pay for whatever damage it causes (*Rav*). This is derived from the laws of *bor*, a pit in a public area. The person who dug the pit is responsible for it as though he were its owner, although it does not actually belong to him (Gemara 29b).

3. According to this Tanna, a person who stumbles on the ground is considered negligent (*Rav*). [The person who slipped on the water, on the other hand, was not negligent, because his slipping was caused by an obstacle that he was not expected to see. Similarly, in the Mishnah's first case, where someone stumbled over a jug, his fall was caused by something unexpected.]

4. Since the jug carrier was negligent in that he stumbled, he is viewed as though he created the hazard with his own hands, similar to someone who dug a pit

— רע"ב —

בְּמִתְכַּוֵּין חַיָּב. אִם נִתְכַּוֵּין לִזְכּוֹת בַּחֲרָסֶיהָ וּבַמַּיִם אַחַר שֶׁנִּשְׁבְּרָה כַדּוֹ, חַיָּב בַּהֶזֵּקָן, דְּהָוֵי לֵיהּ בּוֹרוֹ שֶׁהִזִּיק. וְאִם לֹא נִתְכַּוֵּין לִזְכּוֹת בָּהֶן, הוֹאִיל וַעֲקָרָן אֻנְסָא הוּא, דִּסְבַר נִתְקַל לָאו פּוֹשֵׁעַ הוּא.

רַבִּי יְהוּדָה אוֹמֵר, בְּמִתְכַּוֵּין חַיָּב, בְּאֵינוֹ מִתְכַּוֵּין פָּטוּר.

[ב] **הַשּׁוֹפֵךְ** מַיִם בִּרְשׁוּת הָרַבִּים, וְהֻזַּק בָּהֶן אַחֵר, חַיָּב בְּנִזְקוֹ. הַמַּצְנִיעַ אֶת הַקּוֹץ וְאֶת הַזְּכוּכִית, וְהַגּוֹדֵר אֶת גְּדֵרוֹ בְּקוֹצִים,

הֲרֵי הַחֲרָסִים וְהַמַּיִם הֶפְקֵר לְאַחַר שֶׁנֶּאֶנַס, וּלְפִיכָךְ פָּטוּר. וַהֲלָכָה כְּרַבִּי יְהוּדָה דְּנִתְקַל לָאו פּוֹשֵׁעַ הוּא, וּמֵאַחַר דְּאָנוּס הוּא, וְלֹא נִתְכַּוֵּין לִזְכּוֹת בַּחֲרָסֶיהָ וּבַמַּיִם, הָוֵי כְּאִלּוּ לֹא הָיָה מֵעוֹלָם שֶׁלּוֹ, וּפָטוּר עַל נִזְקֵיהֶם: (ב) הַשּׁוֹפֵךְ מַיִם בִּרְשׁוּת הָרַבִּים. אַף עַל גַּב דְּבִרְשׁוּת קָעֲבִיד, כְּגוֹן בִּימוֹת הַגְּשָׁמִים שֶׁמֻּתָּר לִשְׁפּוֹךְ מַיִם בִּרְשׁוּת הָרַבִּים, אֲפִלּוּ הָכִי אִם הֻזַּק בָּהֶן אַחֵר, חַיָּב בְּנִזְקוֹ: הַמַּצְנִיעַ אֶת הַקּוֹץ וְכוּ'. וּכְגוֹן שֶׁהִגְלִיעַן

The next Tanna disagrees:

רַבִּי יְהוּדָה אוֹמֵר — R' Yehudah says: **בְּמִתְכַּוֵּין חַיָּב** — If he intends to keep the water and the shards, he is indeed obligated to pay (as stated above), **בְּאֵינוֹ מִתְכַּוֵּין פָּטוּר** — but if he does not intend to keep them he is exempt. According to R' Yehudah, this person is not viewed as having created the hazard, because he stumbled and fell through no fault of his own;[5] therefore, he is exempt from payment. However, if he intends to keep the water and shards, he is liable because they are his property.[6]

[2] The Mishnah continues to deal with the laws of an obstacle in a public area (*bor*):

הַשּׁוֹפֵךְ מַיִם בִּרְשׁוּת הָרַבִּים — If someone pours out water in a public place, at a time when he is permitted to do so,[1] **וְהֻזַּק בָּהֶן אַחֵר** — and someone else slipped on the water and was injured because of it, **חַיָּב בְּנִזְקוֹ** — he is obligated to compensate the victim for his injury. Even though he was permitted to pour out the water, he must pay for whatever damage it causes.[2] **הַמַּצְנִיעַ אֶת הַקּוֹץ וְאֶת הַזְּכוּכִית** — If someone hides a thorn or shard of glass in a public place,[3] **וְהַגּוֹדֵר אֶת גְּדֵרוֹ בְּקוֹצִים** — or if he builds a fence of thorns

---

NOTES

in public property. As such, he is liable even if he gave up ownership of the water and shards (*Rav;* see note 2).

5. Unlike the previous Tanna, R' Yehudah holds that stumbling is not negligence (*Rav*).

6. There are two situations in which a person can be liable for damage caused by an obstacle in a public area: (a) He created the obstacle, in which case he is always liable, even if he does not own it (for example, he dug a pit in a public street). (b) He did not create the obstacle but he owns it. If a person's property happens to be in a place where it could do damage, he must remove it, even if he did not put it there. And if he had time to remove it but failed to do so before damage occurs, he must pay for the damage (see Gemara 29a-29b).

[2]

1. For example, during the rainy season, when the ground is muddy, pouring water into a street is allowed [because it makes little difference to the condition of the street] (*Rav*).

2. He has to pay even though he does not want to keep the water. Since he created the hazard, he is responsible for it, despite the fact that it does not belong to him (*Tos. Yom Tov;* see note 2 on the previous Mishnah).

3. For example, he hid a thorn in a rickety wall that later fell into the street, and

[34] משניות בבא קמא / פרק ג: המניח

וְגָדֵר שֶׁנָּפַל לִרְשׁוּת הָרַבִּים, וְהִזִּיקוּ בָהֶן אֲחֵרִים, חַיָּב בְּנִזְקָן.

[ג] **הַמּוֹצִיא** אֶת תִּבְנוֹ וְאֶת קַשּׁוֹ לִרְשׁוּת הָרַבִּים לִזְבָלִים, וְהֻזַּק בָּהֶן אַחֵר, חַיָּב בְּנִזְקוֹ, וְכָל הַקּוֹדֵם בָּהֶן זָכָה.

— רע״ב —

ברשות הרבים. וכן הגודר גדרו בקוצים והפריחן לרשות הרבים, אבל המלמלס בתוך שלו והוזק בהן אחר, פטור, שאין דרך בני אדם להתחכך בכתלים: (ג) **לזבלים.** שירקבו התבן והקש, ונעשים זבל, לזבל שדות וכרמים: כל הקודם בהן זכה. דקנסינהו רבנן:

---

next to a public place,[4] וְגָדֵר שֶׁנָּפַל לִרְשׁוּת הָרַבִּים — or if his stone fence fell into a public place,[5] וְהִזִּיקוּ בָהֶן אֲחֵרִים — and other people were injured by any of [these items], חַיָּב בְּנִזְקָן — he is obligated to pay for their injuries.

[3] Another law about an obstacle in a public domain:

הַמּוֹצִיא אֶת תִּבְנוֹ וְאֶת קַשּׁוֹ לִרְשׁוּת הָרַבִּים לִזְבָלִים — If someone puts out his cut straw or his whole straw[1] into a public place to be converted into fertilizer,[2] וְהֻזַּק בָּהֶן אַחֵר — and another person was injured by them (for example, he slipped on the straw and fell), חַיָּב בְּנִזְקוֹ — [the owner] is obligated to pay for his injury. וְכָל הַקּוֹדֵם בָּהֶן זָכָה — And the first person to take [the straw] acquires it, because the Sages decreed that it no longer belongs to the original owner. In order to penalize someone who leaves his property in a public area when he is forbidden to do so, the Sages decreed that it does not belong to him and anyone may take it.

According to this Tanna, the owner is obligated to pay damages only if he was forbidden to place the straw in the public domain.[3] The next Tanna disagrees:

--- NOTES ---

the thorn caused damage there. Since he should have realized that the wall might collapse, he is liable for the damage (*Meiri*).

4. He owned land next to a public place and he made a wall of thorns between the two areas.

He is liable only if the thorns protrude into the public area [and thus people might walk into them]. However, if the thorns do *not* protrude into the public area and someone was injured by pressing himself against them, the owner of the fence is not liable. Because people generally do not press themselves against walls, he was not expected to think that such damage might occur (*Rav*).

5. If it was not his fault that the wall fell, he is not considered to have created the obstacle. Nevertheless, if he retained ownership of the stones and did not remove them as soon as he could, he must pay for whatever damage they cause (*Tos. Yom Tov*; see note 6 on the previous Mishnah).

[3]

1. "Whole straw" refers to complete stalks of grain while "cut straw" refers to stalks of grain that have been chopped up (*Rashi, Shabbos* 140a).

2. After straw rots, it can be used as fertilizer (*Rav*). People would leave their straw out in the street so that it would be crushed by people and animals passing over it [and thereby speed up the process of converting it into fertilizer] (*Gemara*).

3. However, if he was *permitted* to leave an object in a public area, he is not obligated to pay for damage it causes [and he certainly does not lose ownership of it] (see *Rav*). Thus, the previous Mishnah — which requires him to pay even where he has permission — does not follow the opinion of this Tanna; rather, it follows the

[35] **MISHNAH BAVA KAMMA** / Chapter 3: *Hamaniach* 3/4

רַבָּן שִׁמְעוֹן בֶּן גַּמְלִיאֵל אוֹמֵר, כָּל הַמְקַלְקְלִין בִּרְשׁוּת הָרַבִּים וְהִזִּיקוּ חַיָּבִין לְשַׁלֵּם, וְכָל הַקּוֹדֵם בָּהֶן זָכָה. הַהוֹפֵךְ אֶת הַגָּלָל בִּרְשׁוּת הָרַבִּים, וְהִזַּק בָּהֶן אַחֵר, חַיָּב בִּנְזָקוֹ.

[ד] **שְׁנֵי** קַדָּרִין שֶׁהָיוּ מְהַלְּכִין זֶה אַחַר זֶה, וְנִתְקַל הָרִאשׁוֹן וְנָפַל, וְנִתְקַל הַשֵּׁנִי בָּרִאשׁוֹן, הָרִאשׁוֹן חַיָּב בְּנִזְקֵי שֵׁנִי.

— רע״ב —

כל המקלקלים ברשות הרבים. ואפילו עושים ברשות, כגון בשעת הוצאת זבלים. אם הזיקו חייבים: היה הופך את הגלל. גרסינן בגמרא: (ד) הראשון חייב בנזקי שני. וכגון שהיה יכול לעמוד ולא עמד, דפושע הוא. אבל לא היה יכול לעמוד, פטור, דהא קיימא לן (לטיל משנה א) נתקל לאו פושע הוא:

כָּל — **Rabban Shimon ben Gamliel says:** רַבָּן שִׁמְעוֹן בֶּן גַּמְלִיאֵל אוֹמֵר הַמְקַלְקְלִין בִּרְשׁוּת הָרַבִּים — **All those who create hazards in a public place,** even if they had permission to do so,[4] וְהִזִּיקוּ — and thus **caused damage,** חַיָּבִין לְשַׁלֵּם — **are obligated to pay.** וְכָל הַקּוֹדֵם בָּהֶן זָכָה — **And** if he left them there until after the permitted period,[5] **the first** person **to take them acquires them.**

In the next case, someone became the owner of an obstacle that was already present in a public area:

הַהוֹפֵךְ אֶת הַגָּלָל בִּרְשׁוּת הָרַבִּים — **If someone turns over dung in a public area** with intent to acquire it, וְהִזַּק בָּהֶן אַחֵר — **and another** person **was injured by it,** חַיָּב בִּנְזָקוֹ — **he is obligated** to pay **for his injuries.** Once he acquired the dung it became his responsibility to remove it so that it will not cause harm, and if he did not do so he must pay damages.[6]

[4] In the next case, the very body of a person is an obstacle in a public area:

שְׁנֵי קַדָּרִין שֶׁהָיוּ מְהַלְּכִין זֶה אַחַר זֶה — **If two potters**[1] **were walking one behind the other** in a public place, וְנִתְקַל הָרִאשׁוֹן וְנָפַל — **and the first one stumbled and fell,** וְנִתְקַל הַשֵּׁנִי בָּרִאשׁוֹן — **and the second one stumbled over the first one** when the first one was still on the ground, הָרִאשׁוֹן חַיָּב בְּנִזְקֵי שֵׁנִי — **the first one is obligated** to pay **for the second one's injuries** if he

---

NOTES

opinion of Rabban Shimon ben Gamliel, which is cited next (*Shitah Mekubetzes*).

4. At the times of year when farmers would fertilizer their fields, it is permitted to put straw in a public area and leave it there for up to thirty days in order to convert it into fertilizer (Gemara).

[The previous Tanna, who refers to a case where putting out straw is forbidden, speaks of a person who put his straw in a public area at the wrong time of year, or one who left it there longer than thirty days.]

5. *Tosefos R' Akiva Eiger.*

6. Although he did not put the dung there in the first place, he is responsible for it. As we have learned, even someone who did not create an obstacle must pay for damage it causes if he owns it and did not remove it as soon as he could have (see Mishnah 1 note 6).

[4]

1. The Mishnah speaks of potters, who tend to carry large loads, because it is more common for someone to stumble and fall when he is carrying a heavy weight (*Meleches Shlomo*).

ג/ה

[ה] זֶה בָּא בְחָבִיתוֹ וְזֶה בָּא בְקוֹרָתוֹ, נִשְׁבְּרָה כַדּוֹ שֶׁל זֶה בְּקוֹרָתוֹ שֶׁל זֶה, פָּטוּר, שֶׁלָּזֶה רְשׁוּת לְהַלֵּךְ וְלָזֶה רְשׁוּת לְהַלֵּךְ. הָיָה בַעַל קוֹרָה רִאשׁוֹן וּבַעַל חָבִית אַחֲרוֹן, נִשְׁבְּרָה חָבִית בַּקּוֹרָה, פָּטוּר בַּעַל הַקּוֹרָה; וְאִם עָמַד בַּעַל הַקּוֹרָה, חַיָּב.

— רע״ב —

(ה) היה בעל קורה ראשון וכו׳ פטור. שזה מהלך כדרכו וזה מיהר לילכת:

---

could have picked himself up before the second one stumbled over him. Since he failed to remove the obstacle (i.e., his body lying on the ground) as soon as he could, he is liable for damage that it causes.[2]

[5] The Mishnah discusses various cases that involve two people walking in a public area, one carrying a beam and the other carrying a jug. In each case, the two items crash into each other with the result that the beam breaks the jug.

זֶה בָּא בְחָבִיתוֹ — If [one person] was coming from one direction **with a jug,** וְזֶה בָּא בְקוֹרָתוֹ — and [another person] was coming toward him from the opposite direction **with a beam,** and the items collide, נִשְׁבְּרָה כַדּוֹ שֶׁל זֶה בְּקוֹרָתוֹ שֶׁל זֶה — and **this one's jug was broken by that one's beam,** פָּטוּר — [the owner of the beam] **is not obligated** to pay for the jug, שֶׁלָּזֶה רְשׁוּת לְהַלֵּךְ וְלָזֶה רְשׁוּת לְהַלֵּךְ — **because they both have permission to walk** in the public domain; that is, since the owner of the beam was using the public domain in the usual way, he is not liable.[1]

Another case:

הָיָה בַעַל קוֹרָה רִאשׁוֹן — **If the owner of the beam was walking in front,** וּבַעַל חָבִית אַחֲרוֹן — **and the owner of the jug was walking behind** him at a faster pace, נִשְׁבְּרָה חָבִית בַּקּוֹרָה — and, as a result, **the jug was broken by the beam,** פָּטוּר בַּעַל הַקּוֹרָה — **the owner of the beam is not obligated** to pay for the jug, because the owner of the jug caused the accident.[2] וְאִם עָמַד בַּעַל הַקּוֹרָה — **But if the owner of the beam stopped** in order to rest for a while, which is unexpected in a place where people are walking, and the jug crashed into the beam and broke, חַיָּב — **[the owner of the beam] is obligated**

NOTES

2. He is not blamed for having created the obstacle because stumbling is an unavoidable accident and not an act of negligence (as taught by R' Yehudah in Mishnah 1). Nevertheless, because he "owns" the obstacle (his body), he should have removed it as soon as possible (*Rav;* see note 6 there).

[5]

1. The two people were walking toward each other when the damage occurred; therefore, it was the force of both that made the jug break. Since the owner of the beam did not provide the entire force that broke the jug, he need not pay for

it. However, he is exempt only if he was using the public place in the usual way. If, instead of walking, he was running, which is not usual behavior, he is liable (*Rashba*). [The next Mishnah will add that if *both* were running, the damager is exempt then, too, because both are equally to blame.]

2. When two people are walking one behind the other, it is always the responsibility of the person in the back to maintain a safe distance between them (*Tiferes Yisrael*). In this case, therefore, where the owner of the jug was walking behind the owner of the beam, it was his fault that the two items collided and his jug broke.

וְאִם אָמַר לְבַעַל הֶחָבִית עֲמֹד, פָּטוּר. הָיָה בַּעַל חָבִית רִאשׁוֹן וּבַעַל קוֹרָה אַחֲרוֹן, נִשְׁבְּרָה חָבִית בַּקּוֹרָה, חַיָּב, וְאִם עָמַד בַּעַל חָבִית, פָּטוּר. וְאִם אָמַר לְבַעַל קוֹרָה עֲמֹד, חַיָּב. וְכֵן זֶה בָּא בְנֵרוֹ, וְזֶה בְּפִשְׁתָּנוֹ.

[ו] שְׁנַיִם שֶׁהָיוּ מְהַלְּכִין בִּרְשׁוּת הָרַבִּים, אֶחָד רָץ וְאֶחָד מְהַלֵּךְ,

— רע״ב —

(ו) אחד רץ ואחד מהלך וכו׳. מתניתין חסורי מחסרא והכי קתני, אחד רץ ואחד מהלך בערבי שבתות וימים טובים, או שהיו שניהם רלים בשאר ימות השנה, שניהם פטורים. דבערבי שבתות וימים טובים, מי שרץ, רן ברשות, שהולך לדבר מלוה להכין לצרכי שבת ויום טוב, ומשום הכי פטור. ובשאר ימות השנה כשניהם.

to pay, because he caused the accident by doing something unexpected.[3] וְאִם אָמַר לְבַעַל הֶחָבִית עֲמֹד — **However, if he called out to the owner of the jug,** "**Stop!,**" פָּטוּר — **he is exempt** from payment, because the owner of the jug was warned and could have avoided the collision.

The Mishnah discusses the opposite of the previous situation:

וּבַעַל הָיָה בַּעַל חָבִית רִאשׁוֹן — **If the owner of the jug was walking in front,** וּבַעַל קוֹרָה אַחֲרוֹן — **and the owner of the beam was walking behind** him at a faster pace, נִשְׁבְּרָה חָבִית בַּקּוֹרָה — **and the jug was broken by the beam,** חַיָּב — **[the owner of the beam] is obligated** to pay, because the accident was his fault.[4] וְאִם עָמַד בַּעַל חָבִית — **But if the owner of the jug stopped** in order to rest for a while, and the beam crashed into the jug, פָּטוּר — **[the owner of the beam] is exempt** from payment, because it was the owner of the jug who caused the accident. וְאִם אָמַר לְבַעַל קוֹרָה עֲמֹד — **However, if he called out to the owner of the beam, "Stop!,"** חַיָּב — **[the owner of the beam] is obligated** to pay, because he was warned and could have avoided the collision.

The Mishnah adds another example:

וְכֵן זֶה בָּא בְנֵרוֹ וְזֶה בְּפִשְׁתָּנוֹ — **Similarly,** these laws apply **where one person comes with his lit candle and another comes with his bundle of flax, and the candle sets the flax on fire.**[5]

[6] Two more cases of collisions in a public area.

שְׁנַיִם שֶׁהָיוּ מְהַלְּכִין בִּרְשׁוּת הָרַבִּים — **If two people were moving in a public area,** אֶחָד רָץ וְאֶחָד מְהַלֵּךְ — **and it was Erev Shabbos or Erev Yom Tov,** when it is permitted to run in a public domain in order to prepare for Shabbos

---

NOTES

3. This law applies only where the owner of the beam stopped in order to rest. But if he stopped for just a moment in order to shift the weight of his burden, he is not liable, because this is normal behavior even in a public area [and the jug owner should have expected it] (*Tos. Yom Tov*).

4. In this case, where the owner of the beam was in back, he was responsible for the collision (see note 2).

5. The Mishnah adds this example because it could have been thought that since a flame can easily set flax on fire, the owner of the candle should have taken extra care to avoid a collision, and he is therefore liable in every situation. The Mishnah teaches that this is not so; rather, the owner of the candle has the same laws as the owner of the beam in the previous cases (*Tos. Yom Tov*).

אוֹ שֶׁהָיוּ שְׁנֵיהֶם רָצִים, וְהִזִּיקוּ זֶה אֶת זֶה, שְׁנֵיהֶם פְּטוּרִין.

[ז] **הַמְבַקֵּעַ** בִּרְשׁוּת הַיָּחִיד וְהִזִּיק בִּרְשׁוּת הָרַבִּים, בִּרְשׁוּת הָרַבִּים וְהִזִּיק בִּרְשׁוּת הַיָּחִיד, בִּרְשׁוּת הַיָּחִיד וְהִזִּיק בִּרְשׁוּת הַיָּחִיד אַחֵר, חַיָּב.

[ח] **שְׁנֵי** שְׁוָרִים תַּמִּים שֶׁחָבְלוּ זֶה אֶת זֶה,

— רע״ב —

רָצִים. הוֹאִיל וּשְׁנֵיהֶם מְשַׁנִּים, שְׁנֵיהֶם פְּטוּרִים: (ז) **הַמְבַקֵּעַ**. עֵצִים: וְהִזִּיק בִּרְשׁוּת הַיָּחִיד. שֶׁל אֲחֵרִים: בִּרְשׁוּת הַיָּחִיד. שֶׁלּוֹ: וְהִזִּיק בִּרְשׁוּת הַיָּחִיד. שֶׁל אֲחֵרִים, חַיָּב. וְאַף עַל גַּב דִּבְרְשׁוּתֵיהּ קָעָבֵיד, וְלֹא שְׁכִיחֵי רַבִּים שָׁם דְּנֵימָא הֲוָה לֵיהּ לְעַיּוּנֵי, אֲפִלּוּ הָכִי חַיָּב:

אוֹ שֶׁהָיוּ שְׁנֵיהֶם or Yom Tov,[1] and **one was running and one was walking**; רָצִים — or if it was a regular day and **both of them were running**, וְהִזִּיקוּ זֶה אֶת זֶה — and they accidentally **collided and injured one another**,[2] שְׁנֵיהֶם פְּטוּרִין — **both of them are exempt** from payment, because they are equally responsible. In the first case, the person running was allowed to do so; and in the second case, both were running. Thus, neither one was more responsible for the damage than the other.[3]

[7] הַמְבַקֵּעַ בִּרְשׁוּת הַיָּחִיד וְהִזִּיק בִּרְשׁוּת הָרַבִּים — **If someone was chopping** wood in his **private property**, causing chips of wood to fly through the air,[1] and he thereby **damaged** something **in a public place**, בִּרְשׁוּת הָרַבִּים וְהִזִּיק בִּרְשׁוּת הַיָּחִיד — or if he was chopping wood **in a public place** and thereby **damaged** something in another person's **private property**; בִּרְשׁוּת הַיָּחִיד וְהִזִּיק בִּרְשׁוּת הַיָּחִיד אַחֵר — or if he was chopping wood in his **private property** and thereby **damaged** something in another person's **private property**; חַיָּב — in each of these cases, **he is obligated** to pay damages.[2]

[8] The Mishnah discusses how damages are reckoned when two animals injure each other, or a person and an animal injure each other.

שְׁנֵי שְׁוָרִים תַּמִּים שֶׁחָבְלוּ זֶה אֶת זֶה — **If two oxen that are** *tamim* **injured** each

── NOTES ──

[6]

1. "Erev Shabbos" in this context refers to the period immediately before Shabbos, when people are in a rush to prepare for Shabbos (*Aruch HaShulchan, Choshen Mishpat* 378:18).
2. Each injury was caused by the forces of both the damager and the victim [for example, they were running toward each other when they collided] (*Nimukei Yosef*).
3. However, if one person was running and the other was walking, and it was not Erev Shabbos or Erev Yom Tov, and the runner injured the walker, the runner *would* have to pay damages. Since people do not usually run in a public area on an ordinary day, the runner was acting in an unexpected way, which makes him liable (Gemara 32a). This is so even in our Mishnah's case, where the injury was caused by the force of the victim as well (see Mishnah 5 note 1).

[7]

1. Or the blade of the axe flew off the handle (*Tos. Yom Tov*).
2. Although the damage was done not by the person's body but by the chips of wood, he is liable to pay, because he gave force to the wood, as though he threw it. This is an application of the rule כֹּחוֹ כְּגוּפוֹ, *His force is like his body* (*Tos. Yom Tov*; see Mishnah 2:1 note 4).

[39] **MISHNAH BAVA KAMMA** / Chapter 3: *Hamaniach*

— רע"ב —

מְשַׁלְּמִים בַּמּוֹתָר חֲצִי נֶזֶק. שְׁנֵיהֶם מוּעָדִים, מְשַׁלְּמִים בַּמּוֹתָר נֶזֶק שָׁלֵם. אֶחָד תָּם וְאֶחָד מוּעָד, מוּעָד בַּתָּם, מְשַׁלֵּם בַּמּוֹתָר נֶזֶק שָׁלֵם; תָּם בַּמּוּעָד, מְשַׁלֵּם בַּמּוֹתָר חֲצִי נֶזֶק. וְכֵן שְׁנֵי אֲנָשִׁים שֶׁחָבְלוּ זֶה בָזֶה, מְשַׁלְּמִים בַּמּוֹתָר נֶזֶק שָׁלֵם. אָדָם בְּמוּעָד וּמוּעָד בְּאָדָם, מְשַׁלֵּם בַּמּוֹתָר נֶזֶק שָׁלֵם. אָדָם בְּתָם, וְתָם בְּאָדָם, אָדָם בַּתָּם, מְשַׁלֵּם בַּמּוֹתָר נֶזֶק שָׁלֵם,

(ח) במותר חצי נזק. שמין מה הזיקו של זה יותר על נזקו של זה, ובאותו מותר משלם מי שהזיק יותר, את החצי: מועד בתם משלם במותר. כלומר, אם הוא הזיק את התם יותר ממה שהזיקו תם: אדם בתם משלם במותר נזק שלם. דאדם מועד לעולם:

מְשַׁלְּמִים בַּמּוֹתָר חֲצִי נֶזֶק — **half of the excess damages is paid.** That is, we reckon how much damage was done to each bull, and the owner of the bull that did more damage pays half of the difference (because only half is paid in the case of a *tam*).[1]
שְׁנֵיהֶם מוּעָדִים — **If** both are *muadim*, מְשַׁלְּמִים בַּמּוֹתָר נֶזֶק שָׁלֵם — **the entire excess damages are paid;** that is, the owner of the bull that did more damage pays the entire difference.
אֶחָד תָּם וְאֶחָד מוּעָד — **If** one is a *tam* and the other is a *muad*, מוּעָד בַּתָּם — then if the *muad* did more damage **to the** *tam* than the *tam* did to the *muad*, מְשַׁלֵּם בַּמּוֹתָר נֶזֶק שָׁלֵם — [the owner of the *muad*] **pays the entire excess damages,** תָּם בַּמּוּעָד — and if the *tam* did more damage **to the** *muad* than the *muad* did to the *tam*, מְשַׁלֵּם בַּמּוֹתָר חֲצִי נֶזֶק — [the owner of the *tam*] **pays half of the excess damages.**

The Mishnah applies these rules to people who injured each other:

וְכֵן שְׁנֵי אֲנָשִׁים שֶׁחָבְלוּ זֶה בָזֶה — **Similarly, if two people injured each other,** מְשַׁלְּמִים בַּמּוֹתָר נֶזֶק שָׁלֵם — whoever did more damage **pays the entire excess damages.**

In the next cases, a person fought with an animal that is a *muad* and they injured each other:

אָדָם בְּמוּעָד — **If** a person did more damage **to a** *muad* than it did to him, וּמוּעָד בְּאָדָם — or if a *muad* did more damage **to a person** than he did to it, מְשַׁלֵּם בַּמּוֹתָר נֶזֶק שָׁלֵם — whichever side did more damage **pays the entire excess damages.**

The Mishnah now deals with cases where a person fought with a *tam*:

אָדָם בְּתָם — **If** a person did more damage **to a** *tam* than it did to him, וְתָם בְּאָדָם — or the *tam* did more damage **to the person** than he did to it, אָדָם בַּתָּם מְשַׁלֵּם בַּמּוֹתָר נֶזֶק שָׁלֵם — then if the person did more damage **to the** *tam*,

---

NOTES

[8]
1. For example, if one ox did 100 *zuz* of damage and the other did 80 *zuz* of damage, in which case the difference is 20 *zuz*, the owner of the first ox pay half of that amount, i.e., 10 *zuz*.

תָּם בְּאָדָם, מְשַׁלֵּם בַּמּוֹתָר חֲצִי נֶזֶק. רַבִּי עֲקִיבָא אוֹמֵר, אַף תָּם שֶׁחָבַל בְּאָדָם מְשַׁלֵּם בַּמּוֹתָר נֶזֶק שָׁלֵם.

[ט] **שׁוֹר** שָׁוֶה מָנֶה שֶׁנָּגַח שׁוֹר שָׁוֶה מָאתַיִם, וְאֵין הַנְּבֵלָה יָפָה כְּלוּם, נוֹטֵל אֶת הַשּׁוֹר.

— רע"ב —

ותם באדם משלם במותר חצי נזק. דכתיב (שמות כא,לא) או בן יגח או בת יגח כמשפט הזה יעשה לו, כמשפט שור בשור כך משפט שור באדם, מה שור בשור תם משלם חצי נזק, ומועד משלם נזק שלם, אף שור באדם תם משלם חצי נזק,

ומועד משלם נזק שלם: רבי עקיבא אומר אף תם שחבל באדם משלם במותר נזק שלם. דדריש כמשפט הזה, לדינא דסליק האי קרא מיניה, דבשור מועד מיירי. והכי קאמר קרא, כמשפט שור מועד שמשלם נזק שלם, יעשה לו לכל שור שניגח את האדם ואפילו הוא שור תם. ואין הלכה כרבי עקיבא:

תָּם בְּאָדָם מְשַׁלֵּם בַּמּוֹתָר חֲצִי נֶזֶק — and if the *tam* did more damage to the person, [the owner of the *tam*] pays half of the excess damages.

The next Tanna disagrees in the case of a *tam* that injured a person:

רַבִּי עֲקִיבָא אוֹמֵר — R' Akiva says: **אַף תָּם שֶׁחָבַל בְּאָדָם** — Even if a *tam* does damage to a person, **מְשַׁלֵּם בַּמּוֹתָר נֶזֶק שָׁלֵם** — [its owner] pays the entire excess damages. R' Akiva holds that although the owner of a *tam* pays only half when it attacks property, he pays in full if it injures a person.[2]

[9] The Mishnah continues its discussion about what the owner of a *tam* must pay:

שׁוֹר שָׁוֶה מָנֶה שֶׁנָּגַח שׁוֹר שָׁוֶה מָאתַיִם — If a *tam* ox that is worth a *maneh* (100 zuz) gores and kills an ox that is worth 200 zuz, **וְאֵין הַנְּבֵלָה יָפָה כְּלוּם** — and the carcass is worth nothing, in which case the loss is 200 zuz, of which the damager pays half (100 zuz), **נוֹטֵל אֶת הַשּׁוֹר** — [the victim] takes the entire damaging ox because it happens to be worth the amount he is owed.[1]

The Torah states (*Exodus* 21:35) regarding the payment that must be made when a *tam* gores and kills another animal: וּמָכְרוּ אֶת הַשּׁוֹר הַחַי וְחָצוּ אֶת כַּסְפּוֹ, *they* [the damager and the victim] *shall sell the living ox* [i.e., the one that gored] *and divide its money in half.* The verse means that half the value of the living ox is kept by its owner (the damager) and half goes to the victim. The Mishnah gives an example of the type of case to which the verse refers:

NOTES

2. The opinions of R' Akiva and the first Tanna are based on Biblical sources (see *Rav*).

[9]

1. The Tanna of this Mishnah says that the victim "takes the ox" (i.e., he is entitled to seize the ox itself), because he holds that the damaging ox automatically becomes the property of the victim (*Tos. Yom Tov*).

If the damaging ox is worth more than the amount owed, the victim acquires a share in the ox that matches the amount he is owed. He thus becomes a joint owner of the ox together with the damager. They may sell the ox and divide the money according to each one's share.

שׁוֹר שָׁוֶה מָאתַיִם שֶׁנָּגַח שׁוֹר שָׁוֶה מָאתַיִם, וְאֵין הַנְּבֵלָה יָפָה כְּלוּם, אָמַר רַבִּי מֵאִיר, עַל זֶה נֶאֱמַר וּמָכְרוּ אֶת הַשּׁוֹר הַחַי וְחָצוּ אֶת כַּסְפּוֹ. אָמַר לוֹ רַבִּי יְהוּדָה, וְכֵן הֲלָכָה. קִיַּמְתָּ וּמָכְרוּ אֶת הַשּׁוֹר הַחַי וְחָצוּ אֶת כַּסְפּוֹ, וְלֹא קִיַּמְתָּ וְגַם אֶת הַמֵּת יֶחֱצוּן. וְאֵיזֶה, זֶה שׁוֹר שָׁוֶה מָאתַיִם שֶׁנָּגַח שׁוֹר שָׁוֶה מָאתַיִם, וְהַנְּבֵלָה יָפָה חֲמִשִּׁים זוּז,

— רע״ב —

(ט) וכן הלכה. ודאי כן הלכה דמנה נותן לו, דהיינו חצי נזק. אבל אין זה שור האמור בתורה, דקיימת ומכרו את השור החי וגו' (שמות כא, לה). ופלוגתא דרבי מאיר ורבי יהודה הוא בשבח נבלה, כגון שבשעת מיתה לא היתה שוה כלום, ונתייקרה אחר

כך, והיא שוה להאכילה לכלבים או למכרה לנכרי, רבי מאיר סבר, שבח נבלה דניזק הוי, ולא שקיל בה מזיק כלום, אלא נותן לו חצי נזק, והיינו דקאמר רבי מאיר על זה נאמר ומכרו את השור החי וחצו את כספו, כלומר, שצריך ליתן לו דמי חצי נזק מדמי שור החי, ואינו מנכה לו כלום בעבור השבח שהשביחה הנבלה. ורבי יהודה סבר דחצי שבח נבלה דמזיק הוי, וכשבא מזיק לשלם לניזק דמי חצי נזק, מנכה לו חצי שבח שהשביחה הנבלה משעת מיתה עד שעת העמדה בדין. והיינו דקאמר רבי יהודה לרבי מאיר, קיימת ומכרו את השור החי ולא קיימת את המת יחצון, שצריך לחלק השבח שהשביח המת, ושקיל ליה מזיק פלגא. והלכה כרבי יהודה:

שׁוֹר שָׁוֶה מָאתַיִם שֶׁנָּגַח שׁוֹר שָׁוֶה מָאתַיִם — If a *tam* ox that is worth 200 *zuz* gores and kills an ox that is also worth 200 *zuz*, וְאֵין הַנְּבֵלָה יָפָה כְּלוּם — and the carcass is worth nothing, אָמַר רַבִּי מֵאִיר — R' Meir said: עַל זֶה נֶאֱמַר — Regarding this case it is stated: "וּמָכְרוּ אֶת הַשּׁוֹר הַחַי וְחָצוּ אֶת כַּסְפּוֹ" — *they shall sell the living ox and divide its money in half.* Since the damager owes the victim 100 *zuz* (half the damage), and the living ox is worth 200 *zuz*, the victim is entitled to half the value of the living ox. In order to pay the victim, the damager may sell the living ox, and give half of the money to the victim.[2]

The next Tanna disagrees with this explanation of the verse:

וְכֵן הֲלָכָה — This is indeed the law (namely, that in this case the victim receives half the value of the living ox). However, this cannot be the situation to which the verse refers, קִיַּמְתָּ "וּמָכְרוּ אֶת הַשּׁוֹר הַחַי וְחָצוּ אֶת כַּסְפּוֹ" — because you have explained only the first half of the verse: *they shall sell the living ox and divide its money in half;* וְלֹא קִיַּמְתָּ "וְגַם אֶת הַמֵּת יֶחֱצוּן" — but you have not explained the second half: *and the dead one, too, they shall divide in half.* According to you, since the verse deals with a carcass that is not worth anything, how can it speak of dividing the "dead one"? וְאֵיזֶה — To what then, does the verse refer? זֶה שׁוֹר שָׁוֶה מָאתַיִם שֶׁנָּגַח שׁוֹר שָׁוֶה מָאתַיִם — It refers to an ox worth 200 *zuz* that gored and killed another ox worth 200 *zuz*, וְהַנְּבֵלָה יָפָה חֲמִשִּׁים זוּז — and the carcass is worth 50 *zuz*. In this case, the victim loses 150 *zuz* (200 — 50). Therefore, the damager, who pays half the loss, must give the

---

NOTES

2. The verse must refer to a case in which the two oxen were worth the same, because only then is the victim's payment, which is half the value of the ox that died, the same as half the value of the ox that gored. In this case, then, they sell the living ox and the victim takes half of the money.

שֶׁזֶּה נוֹטֵל חֲצִי הַחַי וַחֲצִי הַמֵּת, וְזֶה נוֹטֵל חֲצִי הַחַי וַחֲצִי הַמֵּת.

[י] **יֵשׁ** חַיָּב עַל מַעֲשֵׂה שׁוֹרוֹ וּפָטוּר עַל מַעֲשֵׂה עַצְמוֹ, פָּטוּר עַל מַעֲשֵׂה שׁוֹרוֹ וְחַיָּב עַל מַעֲשֵׂה עַצְמוֹ. שׁוֹרוֹ שֶׁבִּיֵּשׁ, פָּטוּר, וְהוּא שֶׁבִּיֵּשׁ,

— רע״ב —

(י) **שׁוֹרוֹ שֶׁבִּיֵּשׁ פָּטוּר.** דִּכְתִיב (ויקרא כז,יח) אִישׁ בַּעֲמִיתוֹ, וְלֹא שׁוֹר בַּעֲמִיתוֹ. אִי נַמִּי, אֵין הַמַּבְיִישׁ חַיָּב אֶלָּא כְּשֶׁמִּתְכַּוֵּן לְבַיֵּשׁ, וְשׁוֹר לָאו מִכַּוֵּן לְבַיֵּשׁ הוּא:

---

victim 75 *zuz*. The carcass belongs to the victim, but for the sake of arranging the payment, they may sell both the living ox and the carcass, and divide the money as follows: שֶׁזֶּה נוֹטֵל חֲצִי הַחַי וַחֲצִי הַמֵּת — **[The damager] takes half the** value of the **living** ox, which is 100 *zuz,* **and half the** value of the **carcass,** which is 25 *zuz*, making a total of 125 *zuz*. וְזֶה נוֹטֵל חֲצִי הַחַי וַחֲצִי הַמֵּת — Likewise, **[the victim] takes half the** value of the **living** ox (100 *zuz*) **and half the** value of the **carcass** (50 *zuz*), so that he too ends up with 125 *zuz*. The victim's 125 *zuz* is equivalent to half of his loss (75 *zuz*) together with the entire value of the carcass (50 *zuz*), which was his anyway. He has thus been paid for half of his loss.[3]

[10] The Mishnah contrasts a person's liability for damage done by his animal with a person's liability for damage done by himself:

יֵשׁ חַיָּב עַל מַעֲשֵׂה שׁוֹרוֹ — **There are** situations in which a person is **obligated** to pay **for the actions of his ox,** וּפָטוּר עַל מַעֲשֵׂה עַצְמוֹ — **but he is not obligated** to pay **for his own actions,** פָּטוּר עַל מַעֲשֵׂה שׁוֹרוֹ — **and there are** situations in which a person is **not obligated** to pay **for the actions of his ox,** וְחַיָּב עַל מַעֲשֵׂה עַצְמוֹ — **but he is obligated to pay for his own actions.**

The Mishnah gives two examples of a person being liable to pay for his own actions but not for the actions of his animal:

שׁוֹרוֹ שֶׁבִּיֵּשׁ — **If one's ox embarrassed** a person, פָּטוּר — **he is not obligated** to pay for the victim's embarrassment, וְהוּא שֶׁבִּיֵּשׁ — **but if it was he who**

--- NOTES ---

3. The same arrangement can be made wherever the two oxen are worth the same. The value of the carcass is irrelevant [the amount of 50 *zuz* is just an example] (*Rashi, Exodus* 21:35). The victim loses the difference between the value of his ox when it was alive (which he lost) and the value of the carcass (which he keeps). Since the ox that gored is a *tam*, the damager pays the victim only half of this difference. This half payment is the same as half the value of the ox that died minus half the value of its carcass. The payment can therefore be made in the following way: The damager sells the living ox (which is worth the same as the ox that died) and gives half the money to the victim. The victim sells the carcass and gives half the money to the damager. The victim thus ends up with the amount that is due him — half the value of his ox minus half the value of the carcass. According to R' Yehudah, this is the arrangement to which the verse refers when it says: *they shall sell the living ox and divide its money in half, and the dead one, too, they shall divide in half.*

R' Meir, however, explained the verse as referring to a case where the carcass was worth nothing. In his opinion, the words, *and the dead one, too, they shall divide in half,* are not meant literally. Rather, they are interpreted to mean: "in order to pay for the damage to the dead one, they shall divide *the living one* in half" (see Gemara 34a).

[43] **MISHNAH BAVA KAMMA** / Chapter 3: *Hamaniach*

חַיָּב. שׁוֹרוֹ שֶׁסִּמֵּא אֶת עֵין עַבְדּוֹ וְהִפִּיל אֶת שִׁנּוֹ, פָּטוּר, וְהוּא שֶׁסִּמֵּא אֶת עֵין עַבְדּוֹ וְהִפִּיל אֶת שִׁנּוֹ, חַיָּב.

שׁוֹרוֹ שֶׁחָבַל בְּאָבִיו וְאִמּוֹ, חַיָּב, וְהוּא שֶׁחָבַל בְּאָבִיו וְאִמּוֹ, פָּטוּר. שׁוֹרוֹ שֶׁהִדְלִיק אֶת הַגָּדִישׁ בְּשַׁבָּת, חַיָּב, וְהוּא שֶׁהִדְלִיק אֶת הַגָּדִישׁ בְּשַׁבָּת,

— רע״ב —

שורו שסימא את עין עבדו פטור. ואין העבד יוצא בן חורין על ידו: הוא שסימא את עין עבדו חייב. [שנאמר] (שמות כא,כו) לחפשי ישלחנו: שורו שחבל באביו ובאמו חייב. בתשלומי נזק: הוא שחבל באביו ובאמו פטור. מן התשלומין. שאין אדם מת ומשלם: שורו שהדליק את הגדיש בשבת חייב. חלי נזק. דמשונה הוא:

---

embarrassed someone, חַיָּב — he *is* obligated to pay for the embarrassment.[1]

שׁוֹרוֹ שֶׁסִּמֵּא אֶת עֵין עַבְדּוֹ — If one's ox blinded his Canaanite slave's eye, וְהִפִּיל אֶת שִׁנּוֹ — or knocked out his Canaanite slave's tooth, פָּטוּר — he is not obligated to free the slave. וְהוּא שֶׁסִּמֵּא אֶת עֵין עַבְדּוֹ — But if it was he who blinded his own Canaanite slave's eye וְהִפִּיל אֶת שִׁנּוֹ — or knocked out his tooth, חַיָּב — he *is* obligated to free the slave.[2]

The Mishnah now gives examples of the reverse, where a person must pay for the actions of his animal but not for his own actions:

שׁוֹרוֹ שֶׁחָבַל בְּאָבִיו וְאִמּוֹ — If one's ox wounded his father or his mother, חַיָּב — he is obligated to pay damages. וְהוּא שֶׁחָבַל בְּאָבִיו וְאִמּוֹ — But if it was he who wounded his father or mother, פָּטוּר — he is not obligated to pay damages, because wounding a parent is punishable by death, and a person cannot become subject to both the death penalty and a monetary obligation at the same time.[3]

שׁוֹרוֹ שֶׁהִדְלִיק אֶת הַגָּדִישׁ בְּשַׁבָּת — If one's ox set fire to another person's stack of grain on Shabbos, חַיָּב — he is obligated to pay damages, וְהוּא שֶׁהִדְלִיק אֶת הַגָּדִישׁ בְּשַׁבָּת — but if it was he who set fire to the stack of grain

---

NOTES

[10]

1. When one person injures another person, he is obligated to pay not only for the actual damage, but also for four other things, one of which is the shame that the victim suffered (see Mishnah 8:1). It is derived from the Torah that these extra payments are required only where the injury was done by a person, and not when it was done by an animal. If an animal wounds someone, its owner pays only for the actual damage (*Rav*).

2. The Torah states (*Exodus* 21:26) that if the master of a Canaanite slave blinds one of his eyes or knocks out one of his teeth, he must set the slave free. Although the Torah specifies an eye and a tooth, the same law applies to similar parts of the body (see *Kiddushin* 24a). The Torah teaches that he is obligated to free the slave only if he himself injured the slave, and not if his animal did so.

3. It is a general rule that if a person becomes subject to a severe punishment (such as the death penalty) and to a lighter punishment (such as a monetary obligation) at the same time, he receives only the severe punishment, and not the lighter one [קָם לֵיהּ בְּדְרַבָּה מִנֵּיהּ]. Wounding one's parent is punishable by death (*Exodus* 21:15). Accordingly, if a person wounds his parent, and thereby becomes subject to the death penalty, he is not obligated to pay damages (*Rav*).

ג/יא

פָּטוּר, מִפְּנֵי שֶׁהוּא מִתְחַיֵּב בְּנַפְשׁוֹ.

[יא] שׁוֹר שֶׁהָיָה רוֹדֵף אַחַר שׁוֹר אַחֵר וְהֻזַּק, זֶה אוֹמֵר, שׁוֹרְךָ הִזִּיק, וְזֶה אוֹמֵר, לֹא כִי, אֶלָּא בְסֶלַע לָקָה, הַמּוֹצִיא מֵחֲבֵרוֹ עָלָיו הָרְאָיָה. הָיוּ שְׁנַיִם רוֹדְפִים אַחַר אֶחָד, זֶה אוֹמֵר, שׁוֹרְךָ הִזִּיק,

— רע״ב —

(יא) בסלע לקה. מתחכך היה בסלע ולקה: **היו שנים רודפין אחר אחד.** שני שוורים של שני בני אדם רודפים אחר שור של אדם אחד:

מִפְּנֵי שֶׁהוּא פָּטוּר — he is not obligated to pay damages, on Shabbos, **מִתְחַיֵּב בְּנַפְשׁוֹ** — because he is liable to lose his life for violating Shabbos,[4] and, as stated above, one cannot become subject to the death penalty and a monetary obligation at the same time.

[11] The Mishnah deals with cases where it is unclear whether one must pay damages at all, or it is unclear how much he must pay. In situations of this type, the rule is הַמּוֹצִיא מֵחֲבֵרוֹ עָלָיו הָרְאָיָה, *The [burden of] proof rests on the one who wants to take [payment] from his fellow.* According to this rule, the person claiming to have suffered damage, who is the one seeking payment, cannot collect unless he proves that his claim is true:

שׁוֹר שֶׁהָיָה רוֹדֵף אַחַר שׁוֹר אַחֵר — One person's **ox was chasing another** person's **ox**, **וְהֻזַּק** — **and [the ox being chased] was** found **injured**, but it was not known what caused the injury. **זֶה אוֹמֵר שׁוֹרְךָ הִזִּיק** — [The owner of the injured ox] says, "Your ox did the damage!"; **וְזֶה אוֹמֵר לֹא כִי אֶלָּא בְסֶלַע לָקָה** — but [the owner of the chasing ox] says, "Not so! Rather, your ox became **injured** by pushing itself **against a boulder.**" **הַמּוֹצִיא מֵחֲבֵרוֹ עָלָיו הָרְאָיָה** — We apply the standard rule: The burden of **proof rests on the one who wants to take** payment **from his fellow.** Thus, the owner of the injured ox cannot collect payment from the owner of the chasing ox unless he proves that the damage was indeed done by the chasing ox.[1]

A related case:

הָיוּ שְׁנַיִם רוֹדְפִים אַחַר אֶחָד — **There were two oxen**, each owned by a different person, **chasing one** ox, which is owned by a third person, and the chased ox was injured by one of the first two oxen, but it is not known which one. The owners of the two chasing oxen disagree about which animal inflicted the injury. **זֶה אוֹמֵר שׁוֹרְךָ הִזִּיק** — **This one says, "Your ox did the damage,"**

NOTES

4. Starting or spreading a fire is one of the thirty-nine forms of labor (*melachah*) that are prohibited on Shabbos (*Shabbos* 7:2).

[11]

1. Even though it seems from the circumstances that the injury was inflicted by the chasing ox, that is not sufficient proof for the owner of the injured ox to be awarded damages. Rather, he must prove (usually, by having two witnesses testify in court) that the chasing ox was responsible. Moreover, even if the owner of the injured ox says he is sure that the injury was inflicted by the chasing ox, whereas the owner of the chasing ox does not really know what happened, the owner of the injured ox must still bring proof (*Tos. Yom Tov*).

MISHNAH BAVA KAMMA / Chapter 3: *Hamaniach*

וְזֶה אוֹמֵר, שׁוֹרְךָ הִזִּיק, שְׁנֵיהֶם פְּטוּרִין. אִם הָיוּ שְׁנֵיהֶן שֶׁל אִישׁ אֶחָד, שְׁנֵיהֶן חַיָּבִים. הָיָה אֶחָד גָּדוֹל וְאֶחָד קָטָן, הַנִּזָּק אוֹמֵר, גָּדוֹל הִזִּיק, וְהַמַּזִּיק אוֹמֵר, לֹא כִי, אֶלָּא קָטָן הִזִּיק; אֶחָד תָּם וְאֶחָד מוּעָד, הַנִּזָּק אוֹמֵר, מוּעָד הִזִּיק, וְהַמַּזִּיק אוֹמֵר, לֹא כִי, אֶלָּא תָּם הִזִּיק, הַמּוֹצִיא מֵחֲבֵרוֹ עָלָיו הָרְאָיָה.

שְׁנֵיהֶם וְזֶה אוֹמֵר שׁוֹרְךָ הִזִּיק — and this one says, "Your ox did the damage." **פְּטוּרִין** — Both of them are exempt from having to pay, unless proof is brought that the damage was done by a particular ox. **אִם הָיוּ שְׁנֵיהֶן שֶׁל אִישׁ אֶחָד** — However, if both [of the chasing oxen] belong to one person, **שְׁנֵיהֶן חַיָּבִים** —both of them are obligated; that is, the owner of the two chasing oxen is obligated to pay, since the animal that did the damage certainly belongs to him.[2]

The Mishnah presents two more cases in which both of the chasing oxen belong to the same person. In the first case, both of them are *tamim*:

הָיָה אֶחָד גָּדוֹל — There was one large ox, whose value would cover the half-damage payment, **וְאֶחָד קָטָן** — and one small ox, whose value was less than the half-damage payment.[3] **הַנִּזָּק אוֹמֵר גָּדוֹל הִזִּיק** — The victim says, "The large one did the damage," in which case he would be entitled to the entire half-damage payment; **וְהַמַּזִּיק אוֹמֵר לֹא כִי אֶלָּא קָטָן הִזִּיק** — but the damager says, "Not so! Rather, the small one did the damage," in which case he would not have to pay more than the value of the small ox. **אֶחָד תָּם וְאֶחָד מוּעָד** — A similar case is where one of the chasing oxen was a *tam* and one was a *muad*. **הַנִּזָּק אוֹמֵר מוּעָד הִזִּיק** — The victim says, "The *muad* did the damage," in which case he would be entitled to full damages, no matter how much the damaging ox is worth; **וְהַמַּזִּיק אוֹמֵר** — but the damager says, **לֹא כִי אֶלָּא תָּם הִזִּיק** — "Not so! Rather, the *tam* did the damage," in which case he would not have to pay more than the value of the damaging ox." **הַמּוֹצִיא מֵחֲבֵרוֹ עָלָיו הָרְאָיָה** — In both of these cases, we apply the rule:

--- NOTES ---

2. The Mishnah says "both [oxen] are obligated," and not the "[the owner] is obligated," for the following reason: We have learned that when the damaging ox is a *tam*, payment is made from "the body of the ox" (Mishnah 1:4). According to this rule, if the damaging ox is not worth anything or is unavailable, the victim is paid nothing. Thus, in our case, if the two chasing oxen are *tamim* and one of them went missing, the owner can claim that the damage was done by the missing ox, and he is therefore exempt from paying. The Mishnah hints to this law by saying "both [oxen] are obligated," that is, the obligation is based on the oxen, for the owner is not obligated to pay unless both oxen are available (*Rav*).

3. The rule cited in the previous note, "The owner of a *tam* pays from its body," also tells us that he need pay no more than the value of his animal.

ג/יא

— רע"ב —

הָיוּ הַנִּזּוֹקִין שְׁנַיִם, אֶחָד גָּדוֹל וְאֶחָד קָטָן, וְהַמַּזִּיקִים שְׁנַיִם, אֶחָד גָּדוֹל וְאֶחָד קָטָן, הַנִּזָּק אוֹמֵר, גָּדוֹל הִזִּיק אֶת הַגָּדוֹל, וְקָטָן אֶת הַקָּטָן, וּמַזִּיק אוֹמֵר, לֹא כִי, אֶלָּא קָטָן אֶת הַגָּדוֹל, וְגָדוֹל אֶת הַקָּטָן; אֶחָד תָּם וְאֶחָד מוּעָד, הַנִּזָּק אוֹמֵר, מוּעָד הִזִּיק אֶת הַגָּדוֹל, וְתָם אֶת הַקָּטָן, וְהַמַּזִּיק אוֹמֵר, לֹא כִי, אֶלָּא תָּם אֶת הַגָּדוֹל, וּמוּעָד אֶת הַקָּטָן.

קָטָן הִזִּיק אֶת הַגָּדוֹל. וְאַף עַל פִּי שֶׁחֲצִי נִזְקוֹ שֶׁל גָּדוֹל מְרוּבֶּה, לֹא תִּקַּח אֶלָּא קָטָן שֶׁלִּי, וַחֲצִי נִזְקוֹ שֶׁל קָטָן שֶׁלְּךָ, קַח מִן הַגָּדוֹל. וְכָל כָּךְ לָמָּה מַחְזִירִין עָלָיו הָרְאָיָה דִּתְנַן בְּמַתְנִיתִין, אִם לֹא הֵבִיא רְאָיָה, אֵין לוֹ כְלוּם וַאֲפִילּוּ דְּמֵי תָם, וַאֲפִילּוּ קָטָן שֶׁהוֹדָה לוֹ, אֵין לוֹ, שֶׁהֶטְעוֹתַן אֶת חֲבֵרוֹ חִטִּין וְהוֹדָה לוֹ בִּשְׂעוֹרִים, פָּטוּר אַף מִדְּמֵי שְׂעוֹרִים. וְכִי תָּפַס הִנִּיחַ שִׁיעוּר מַה שֶּׁהוֹדָה לוֹ הַמַּזִּיק, לֹא מַפְקִינַן מִינֵיהּ:

The burden of proof is on the one who wants to take payment from his fellow. Thus, the victim cannot collect payment unless he proves that it was the large ox (in the first case) or the *muad* ox (in the second case) that did the damage.[4]

In the following two cases, two oxen owned by one person injured two oxen owned by one person, but it is not known which ox inflicted which injury: הָיוּ הַנִּזּוֹקִין שְׁנַיִם — **There were two injured [oxen],** אֶחָד גָּדוֹל וְאֶחָד קָטָן — **one large and one small,** וְהַמַּזִּיקִים שְׁנַיִם — **and there were two attacking [oxen],** אֶחָד גָּדוֹל וְאֶחָד קָטָן — **one large and one small,** both of them *tamim*, and the small attacking ox is worth less than half the damage to the large injured ox. הַנִּזָּק אוֹמֵר — **The victim says,** גָּדוֹל הִזִּיק אֶת הַגָּדוֹל וְקָטָן אֶת הַקָּטָן — **"The large one injured the large one and the small one injured the small one";** וּמַזִּיק אוֹמֵר — **but the damager says,** לֹא כִי אֶלָּא קָטָן אֶת הַגָּדוֹל וְגָדוֹל אֶת הַקָּטָן — **"Not so! Rather, the small one injured the large one and the large one injured the small one,"** in which case he would not have to pay the entire half-damage payment for the large injured ox, but only as much as the small attacking ox is worth. אֶחָד תָּם וְאֶחָד מוּעָד — A similar case is where **one of** the damaging oxen was **a** *tam* **and one was a** *muad*, and the *tam* is worth less than half the damage to the large injured ox. הַנִּזָּק אוֹמֵר — **The victim says,** מוּעָד הִזִּיק אֶת הַגָּדוֹל וְתָם אֶת הַקָּטָן — **"The** *muad* **injured the large one and the** *tam* **injured the small one,"** in which case the damager would have to pay for the entire damage to the large ox"; וְהַמַּזִּיק אוֹמֵר — **but the damager says,** לֹא כִי אֶלָּא תָּם אֶת הַגָּדוֹל וּמוּעָד אֶת הַקָּטָן — **"Not so! Rather, the** *tam* **injured the large one and the** *muad* **injured the small one,"** in which case he would

---

— NOTES —

4. If the victim is unable to prove this, he is not entitled to any payment at all. He may not collect even the smaller amount, which the damager agrees that he owes. Since the victim said he was sure that the large ox (or the *muad*) did the damage, he has admitted, in effect, that it was *not* the other ox. He has thus denied the damager's statement that the small ox (or the *tam*) did the damage, and he has given up his claim even to the amount that the damager conceded (*Rav*).

הַמּוֹצִיא מֵחֲבֵרוֹ עָלָיו הָרְאָיָה.

not have to pay the entire half-damage payment for the large ox, but only as much as his *tam* ox is worth. הַמּוֹצִיא מֵחֲבֵרוֹ עָלָיו הָרְאָיָה — In both of these cases, we apply the rule: **The burden of proof rests on the one who wants to take** payment **from his fellow.** Thus, the victim cannot collect payment unless he proves that the injury to his large ox was inflicted by the large ox (in the first case) or by the *muad* ox (in the second case).

Chapter Four

משניות בבא קמא / פרק ד: שור שנגח

פרק רביעי – שור שנגח ארבעה וחמשה.
(א) שור שנגח ארבעה וחמשה. וכולם היו תפוסים מתחלה מגופו: ישלם.

[א] שׁוֹר שֶׁנָּגַח אַרְבָּעָה וַחֲמִשָּׁה שְׁוָרִים זֶה אַחַר זֶה, יְשַׁלֵּם לָאַחֲרוֹן שֶׁבָּהֶם. וְאִם יֵשׁ בּוֹ מוֹתָר, יַחֲזִיר לְשֶׁלְּפָנָיו.

— רע"ב —

חלי נזק לאחרון תחלה. בגמרא (לו,ב) מוקי למתניתין, כגון שתפסו לשור המזיק ניזק לגבות ממנו, ונעשה עליו שומר שכר. וכשילא מתחת ידו והזיק, הניזק הראשון חייב בנזקיו, לפיכך האחרון משתלם חלי נזקו משלם: **ואם יש בו מותר יחזיר לשלפניו.** הכי קאמר, אם יש בו מותר בנזקיו, יחזיר לשלפניו.

---

[1] This chapter continues to discuss the laws of an animal that attacks another animal. The first Mishnah cites a dispute about how damages are paid if a *tam* ox injured several animals, each of which is owned by a different person:

שׁוֹר שֶׁנָּגַח אַרְבָּעָה וַחֲמִשָּׁה שְׁוָרִים זֶה אַחַר זֶה — **If an ox gored four or five oxen**[1] **one after the other** while remaining a *tam*,[2] יְשַׁלֵּם לָאַחֲרוֹן שֶׁבָּהֶם — **[its owner] pays** the half-damage payment **to the last [victim],** and the others do not receive anything. This law applies in a specific situation; namely, where each victim seized the ox that gored in order to make sure that he would be paid. Once it is in his possession, he is responsible for any damage it does later.[3] After the ox gored the first time, the victim seized it; thus, when it gored the second time, it is the first victim (not the owner) who must pay. The second victim then seized the ox from the first victim; thus, when it gored the third time, the second victim must pay. The third victim then seized the ox, and so on. If the half-damage payment due each victim is the same — for instance, 100 *zuz* — the owner owes 100 *zuz* to the first victim, who owes 100 *zuz* to the second victim, who owes 100 to the third, etc. The last victim, however, does not owe anything, since the ox did not do any damage after he seized it. Thus, only the last victim gets to keep his payment (i.e., 100 *zuz* of the animal that he seized), while the others receive nothing. וְאִם יֵשׁ בּוֹ מוֹתָר — **However, if [the amount owed the second-to-last victim] is more** than the amount owed the last victim, יַחֲזִיר לְשֶׁלְּפָנָיו — **[the last victim] returns** the difference **to**

NOTES

[1]

1. The Mishnah's rulings apply regardless of how many oxen were gored. The phrase "four or five" is a figure of speech (*Tos. Yom Tov* to *Shabbos* 18:1).

2. Although the ox gored more than three times, it remained a *tam*, because the owner was not warned by the court after each goring (*Rav, Tos. Yom Tov*).

3. Each victim was afraid that the owner (or the previous victim) might hide the ox that gored and thereby prevent him from being paid (since payment is collected only from "the body of the ox"). Therefore, each one seized the ox so that he would be able to keep the part of its value that is due him and return the rest to the owner. Once he seized the ox, he became its legal guardian (שׁוֹמֵר), who is responsible to make sure that the ox does not do any damage in the future (*Rav*; see Mishnah 9). Thus, as far as the original owner is concerned, he is responsible only for the first goring. After making the half payment for that goring, he may keep everything that remains of his ox's value after the payment is deducted.

[If, however, the ox did each goring while still under the original owner's guardianship, he would be obligated to make *all* the half-damage payments (according to this Tanna). He would have to pay the first victim first, the second victim second, and so on, until the value of his ox is used up (see Gemara 36a-36b).]

MISHNAH BAVA KAMMA / Chapter 4: *Shor Shenagach*

— רע״ב —

וְאִם יֵשׁ בּוֹ מוֹתָר, יַחֲזִיר לְשֶׁלְּפָנָיו. וְהָאַחֲרוֹן אַחֲרוֹן נִשְׂכָּר, דִּבְרֵי רַבִּי מֵאִיר.

כגון שחלי נזקו של הראשון היה מנה, וחלי נזק האחרון היה חמשים, והשור שוה מאתים. מתחלה כשנגחה שור זה שורו של הניזק הראשון שחלי נזקו מנה, היה לניזק בשור זה ולבעלים מנה, וכשתפסו הניזק ונגח תחת ידו, אין לבעלים להפסיד מנה שהיה להם בו, שהרי לא היתה שמירתו עליהן אלא על הניזק שתפסו. וכשהזיק לשני והיה חלי נזקו חמשים, אבד הניזק הראשון מן המנה שלו חמשים ונותן לזה הניזק השני, והמותר עד המנה חוזר לו. והבעלים נוטלים המנה שלהם:

the one that came before him (i.e., the second-to-last victim). For example, every victim owes 100 *zuz* to the one that came after him, except for the second-to-last victim, who owes only 50 *zuz* to the last one. In this case, the last victim keeps for himself 50 *zuz* of the animal that he took, and he gives the remaining 50 *zuz* to the second-to-last victim.[4] Here, too, the last victim receives everything he is owed (50 *zuz*); however, the second-to-last victim receives less than what he is owed (50 *zuz* out of 100), and the others receive nothing. וְאִם יֵשׁ בּוֹ מוֹתָר — And if [the payment owed the third-to-last victim] is more than the total of the payments owed the last two victims together, יַחֲזִיר לְשֶׁלְּפָנָיו — [the last victim] returns part of the remainder to the second-to-last victim and part to the third-to-last victim.[5] For example, the payment due the third-to-last victim was 100 *zuz*, the payment due the second-to-last victim was 50 *zuz*, and the payment due the last victim was 20 *zuz*. In this case, where the last victim is entitled to only 20 *zuz*, he keeps just 20 *zuz* of the animal that he took. He gives 30 *zuz* (the difference between his payment and the previous victim's payment) to the previous victim, and he gives 50 *zuz* (the difference between the second-to-last victim's payment and the third-to-last victim's payment) to the third-to-last victim. Thus, the last victim keeps his full 20 *zuz*, the second-to-last victim gets 30 *zuz* (the 50 that he is owed minus the 20 that he owes), the third-to-last victim gets 50 *zuz* (the 100 that he is owed minus the 50 that he owes), and the other victims receive nothing. וְהָאַחֲרוֹן אַחֲרוֹן נִשְׂכָּר — In every case, regardless of how much each victim is owed, **the very last one benefits,**[6] since he is the only one who does not have to pay anyone else. דִּבְרֵי רַבִּי מֵאִיר — These are **the words of R' Meir.**

According to the previous Tanna, R' Meir, if a victim seizes the ox that gored to collect his payment from it, he becomes entirely responsible for the ox and must pay for any damage it does in the future. However, if he does not seize it, he is not liable to pay anything. The next Tanna (R' Shimon) disagrees. In his view, even if the victim does not seize the ox that gored, he automatically acquires a share of the animal that equals the amount he is owed. He thus

---

NOTES

4. The owner took his animal (or its monetary equivalent) back from the last victim, but since he owes 100 *zuz* to the first victim — which is ultimately owed to the last two victims — he left that amount with the last victim. Of that 100 *zuz*, the last victim keeps 50 and gives 50 to the victim that came before him.

5. Literally, *the one before the one that was before him.*

6. That is, the last victim always receives at least part of what he is owed. Any of the earlier victims, by contrast, might not receive anything (see *Tosafos* 36b ד״ה אם).

[52] משניות בבא קמא / פרק ד: שור שנגח ד/א

— רע"ב —

רבי שמעון אומר וכו'.
רבי שמעון סבר, שותפי
נינהו הבעלים והניזק
בשור המזיק, ושניהם
מתחייבים בנזקיו. כיצד,
שור שוה מאתים שנגח
וכו': ושלפניו. זה ניזק
ראשון. נוטל חמשים זוז,
והבעלים חמשים זוז,
דיש לניזק ראשון בו

רַבִּי שִׁמְעוֹן אוֹמֵר, שׁוֹר שָׁוֶה מָאתַיִם שֶׁנָּגַח שׁוֹר שָׁוֶה מָאתַיִם וְאֵין הַנְּבֵלָה יָפָה כְלוּם, זֶה נוֹטֵל מָנֶה, וְזֶה נוֹטֵל מָנֶה. חָזַר וְנָגַח שׁוֹר אַחֵר שָׁוֶה מָאתַיִם, הָאַחֲרוֹן נוֹטֵל מָנֶה. וְשֶׁלְּפָנָיו, זֶה נוֹטֵל חֲמִשִּׁים זוּז, וְזֶה נוֹטֵל חֲמִשִּׁים זוּז. חָזַר וְנָגַח שׁוֹר אַחֵר שָׁוֶה מָאתַיִם, הָאַחֲרוֹן נוֹטֵל מָנֶה,

החלי, הלכך משלם חלי תשלומי נזקו: חזר ונגח שור שוה מאתים. האחרון נוטל מנה, החלי מכל מי שהוא, דמגופו משתלם. ונמצא אותו שלפניו שהיה החלי שלו, משלם מחלקו חלי מנה חלי שלו שנוטל האחרון

becomes a part owner of the ox together with the original owner (and any other victims), and so he and the original owner share liability for damages.[7]

רַבִּי שִׁמְעוֹן אוֹמֵר — R' Shimon says: שׁוֹר שָׁוֶה מָאתַיִם שֶׁנָּגַח שׁוֹר שָׁוֶה מָאתַיִם — If a *tam* ox worth 200 *zuz* gored an ox worth 200 *zuz*, killing it, וְאֵין הַנְּבֵלָה יָפָה כְלוּם — and the carcass of the gored ox is worth nothing,[8] זֶה נוֹטֵל מָנֶה — [the victim] takes a *maneh* (100 *zuz*) of the ox that gored as his half-damage payment, וְזֶה נוֹטֵל מָנֶה — and [the owner] gets to keep the remaining 100 *zuz* of the ox. Thus, the victim and the owner each own half of the animal. חָזַר וְנָגַח שׁוֹר אַחֵר שָׁוֶה מָאתַיִם — If it then gored another ox worth 200 *zuz*, killing it, and the carcass is worth nothing, הָאַחֲרוֹן נוֹטֵל מָנֶה — the last one (i.e., the second victim) takes a *maneh* (100 *zuz*) as his half-damage payment. He collects half of his 100 *zuz* from the first victim and half from the owner (50 *zuz* from each), since each owns half of the animal. וְשֶׁלְּפָנָיו — Thus, the outcome regarding those who came before him — namely, the first victim and the owner — is as follows: זֶה נוֹטֵל חֲמִשִּׁים זוּז וְזֶה נוֹטֵל חֲמִשִּׁים זוּז — [The first victim] gets to keep 50 *zuz* of the animal, and [the owner] gets to keep 50 *zuz* of it.[9] At this point, the second victim owns half of the animal (100 *zuz*), the first victim owns a quarter (50 *zuz*), and the original owner owns a quarter (50 *zuz*). חָזַר וְנָגַח שׁוֹר אַחֵר שָׁוֶה מָאתַיִם — If [the ox] then gores another ox worth 200 *zuz*, killing it, and the carcass is worth nothing, הָאַחֲרוֹן נוֹטֵל מָנֶה — the last one (i.e., the third victim) takes a *maneh* (100 *zuz*) as his half-damage

---
NOTES

7. According to this opinion, it makes no difference whether the victim seizes the ox. When an animal (or any item) is owned by two people, sometimes one watches it and sometimes the other watches it, but both share responsibility for it at all times. Thus, even if the victim seizes the ox, he does not assume any more responsibility than he had before (*Tosafos* 36b ד"ה כגון; *Rav*, as explained by *Shach, Choshen Mishpat* 401:4).

8. [The Mishnah specifies that the dead animal is worth nothing in order to make the calculations simpler. If its carcass would have some value, the victim's loss would be the difference between the value of the living animal and the value of the carcass.]

9. The owner is left with 50 *zuz*, because he had 100 *zuz* (after the first goring) and then he paid 50 to the second victim. The same is true of the first victim. He also had 100 *zuz*, of which he paid 50 to the second victim.

[53] **MISHNAH BAVA KAMMA** / Chapter 4: *Shor Shenagach*

— רע״ב —

ושנים הראשונים. ניזק ראשון והבעלים שהיה להם לכל אחד רביע, משלמין כל אחד רביעית של נזקו: דינר זהב. שהם חמשה ועשרים דינרים של כסף: (ב) הועד לקטנים. לעגלים:

וְשֶׁלְּפָנָיו חֲמִשִּׁים זוּז, וּשְׁנַיִם הָרִאשׁוֹנִים דִּינַר זָהָב.

[ב] **שׁוֹר** שֶׁהוּא מוּעָד לְמִינוֹ וְאֵינוֹ מוּעָד לְשֶׁאֵינוֹ מִינוֹ, מוּעָד לְאָדָם וְאֵינוֹ מוּעָד לִבְהֵמָה, מוּעָד לִקְטַנִּים וְאֵינוֹ מוּעָד

---

payment. He collects this 100 *zuz* from its three owners (the original owner, the first victim, and the second victim) in proportion to the share of the animal that each one owns. Thus, he takes half of his payment (50 *zuz*) from the second victim, a quarter (25 *zuz*) from the first victim, and a quarter (25 *zuz*) from the original owner. וְשֶׁלְּפָנָיו חֲמִשִּׁים זוּז — It emerges that the second victim, **who came before him,** is left with **50** *zuz*, וּשְׁנַיִם הָרִאשׁוֹנִים דִּינַר זָהָב — **and** each of **the first two** (the owner and the first victim) is left with **a gold** *dinar* (25 *zuz*).[10]

[2] We have learned that once a *tam* animal gores (or otherwise attacks) three times, and its owner was warned each time, it becomes a *muad*. This Mishnah discusses the law where an animal gored certain types of animals three times but it refrained from goring other types of animals:

שׁוֹר שֶׁהוּא מוּעָד לְמִינוֹ וְאֵינוֹ מוּעָד לְשֶׁאֵינוֹ מִינוֹ — These are laws of **an ox that is a *muad* to** gore animals of **its own species but is not a *muad* to** gore animals that are **not of its own species,**[1] מוּעָד לְאָדָם וְאֵינוֹ מוּעָד לִבְהֵמָה — **or an ox that is a *muad* to** gore **people but is not a *muad* to** gore **animals,**[2] מוּעָד לִקְטַנִּים וְאֵינוֹ מוּעָד לִגְדוֹלִים — **or an ox that is a *muad* to** gore **young [animals]**

NOTES
---

10. The original owner once had full ownership of an ox worth 200 *zuz*. He then paid 100 *zuz* to the first victim, 50 to the second victim, and 25 to the third victim, which leaves him with 25 *zuz*. The first victim received 100 *zuz*, then paid 50 to the second victim and 25 to the third, which leaves him, too, with 25 *zuz*. As for the second victim, he received 100 *zuz*, and then paid 50 *zuz* to the third victim, which leaves him with 50 *zuz*.

In summary: (a) R' Meir holds that if a *tam* ox gores another ox, the victim does not automatically acquire part of the ox that gored. Therefore, if it gores again, it is the owner alone who pays the second victim. If there are several victims, the owner pays the first victim first, the second victim second, and so on, until the value of his ox is used up. However, if a victim seized the ox (to secure his payment), he alone, and not the owner, is liable to pay any future victims. If there are several victims and each one seized the ox from the one that came before him, the first victim pays the second, the second pays the third, etc. (b) According to R' Shimon, though, a victim automatically becomes a part owner of the ox that gored (regardless of whether he seized it). As such, he always pays part of all future damages. If there are several victims, the original owner and the first victim share in paying the second victim, all three of them share in paying the third victim, and so on.

[2]

1. The ox gored other oxen three times, but it did not gore any other types of animals though it had the chance to do so (*Rashi* to Gemara 37a ד״ה ואינו).

However, if the ox had no chance to gore any other species, we cannot say that it is still a *tam* in regard to them. Rather, since it is a *muad* for oxen, it is a *muad* for all other species as well (*Rashi* there).

2. It gored people three times but did not gore animals that it saw.

משניות בבא קמא / פרק ד: שור שנגח [54]

לִגְדוֹלִים, אֶת שֶׁהוּא מוּעָד לוֹ, מְשַׁלֵּם נֶזֶק שָׁלֵם, וְאֶת שֶׁאֵינוֹ מוּעָד לוֹ, מְשַׁלֵּם חֲצִי נֶזֶק. אָמְרוּ לִפְנֵי רַבִּי יְהוּדָה, הֲרֵי שֶׁהָיָה מוּעָד לְשַׁבָּתוֹת וְאֵינוֹ מוּעָד לְחוֹל, אָמַר לָהֶם, לְשַׁבָּתוֹת מְשַׁלֵּם נֶזֶק שָׁלֵם, לִימוֹת הַחוֹל מְשַׁלֵּם חֲצִי נֶזֶק. אֵימָתַי הוּא תָם, מִשֶּׁיַּחֲזֹר בּוֹ שְׁלֹשָׁה יְמֵי שַׁבָּתוֹת.

— רע"ב —

אמרו לפני רבי יהודה. שאלו תלמידיו ממנו. מועד לשבתות. מפני שהוא בטל ממלאכה ודעתו זחה עליו. אי נמי, לפי שרואה בני אדם במלבושים נאים של שבת, חשובים בעיניו נכרים ואינו מכירם:

ואינו מועד לחול. מה דינו: משיחזור בו שלשה ימי שבתות. לאחר שהועד לשבתות, העבירו

אֶת שֶׁהוּא מוּעָד לוֹ מְשַׁלֵּם נֶזֶק but is not a *muad* to gore grown [animals]:[3] שָׁלֵם — If it later gored those animals (or people) toward which it is a *muad*, [its owner] pays full damages, וְאֶת שֶׁאֵינוֹ מוּעָד לוֹ מְשַׁלֵּם חֲצִי נֶזֶק — but if it gored those toward which it is not a *muad*, he pays only half damages. Although the animal is a *muad* in regard to the types of animals that it attacked, it remains a *tam* in regard to the types that it refrained from attacking; therefore, if it does attack an animal of the second type, the owner pays only half.

A question about a similar case:

אָמְרוּ לִפְנֵי רַבִּי יְהוּדָה — They (i.e., the students) said before R' Yehudah: הֲרֵי שֶׁהָיָה מוּעָד לְשַׁבָּתוֹת וְאֵינוֹ מוּעָד לְחוֹל — What is the law where [the ox] is a *muad* to gore on Shabbos but is not a *muad* to gore on weekdays?[4] אָמַר לָהֶם — [R' Yehudah] said to them: לְשַׁבָּתוֹת מְשַׁלֵּם נֶזֶק שָׁלֵם — For goring on Shabbos [its owner] pays full damages, because it is a *muad* on Shabbos, לִימוֹת הַחוֹל מְשַׁלֵּם חֲצִי נֶזֶק — but for goring on the weekdays he pays half damages, because it is a *tam* on weekdays.

R' Yehudah adds:

אֵימָתַי הוּא תָם — And when is [this animal] a *tam*? That is, how can it go back to being a *tam*, even on Shabbos? מִשֶּׁיַּחֲזֹר בּוֹ שְׁלֹשָׁה יְמֵי שַׁבָּתוֹת — When it refrains from goring on three consecutive Shabbos days.[5]

— NOTES —

3. For example, it gored three calves but did not gore mature oxen even though it had the opportunity to do so (see *Rav*).

The same applies to people: The ox gored three children but refrained from goring adults that it saw (*Tos. Yom Tov*).

4. That is, it gored on three consecutive Shabbos days, but did not gore animals that it saw on weekdays. If we say that its goring is linked specifically to Shabbos, the owner would have to pay in full for damage it does on Shabbos, but only half for what it does on weekdays. However, if we say that all days are considered the same, and thus its goring is not linked to Shabbos, the ox is not a *muad* at all, because it refrained from goring during the days that came between each Shabbos and the next (see Mishnah 2:4 note 1). According to the second approach, the owner would have to pay only half even for damage it does on Shabbos (*Tos. Yom Tov*).

The reason to link an animal's goring specifically to Shabbos is that since an animal does not work on Shabbos, it feels more arrogant on that day [a feeling that might make it more aggressive]. A different explanation is that since people wear special clothing on Shabbos, the animal will not recognize even people that it sees often [which might provoke it into attacking] (*Rav*).

5. That is, after the animal became a

MISHNAH BAVA KAMMA / Chapter 4: Shor Shenagach

[ג] **שׁוֹר** שֶׁל יִשְׂרָאֵל שֶׁנָּגַח שׁוֹר שֶׁל הֶקְדֵּשׁ, וְשֶׁל הֶקְדֵּשׁ שֶׁנָּגַח לְשׁוֹר שֶׁל יִשְׂרָאֵל, פָּטוּר, שֶׁנֶּאֱמַר, שׁוֹר רֵעֵהוּ וְלֹא שׁוֹר שֶׁל הֶקְדֵּשׁ. שׁוֹר שֶׁל יִשְׂרָאֵל שֶׁנָּגַח לְשׁוֹר שֶׁל עוֹבֵד כּוֹכָבִים, פָּטוּר, וְשֶׁל עוֹבֵד כּוֹכָבִים שֶׁנָּגַח לְשׁוֹר שֶׁל יִשְׂרָאֵל,

— רע״ב —

לפניו שוורים בשלש שבתות, ולא נגח, חזר לתמותו. ואם חזר ונגח, אינו משלם אלא חצי נזק: (ג) שור של ישראל שנגח שור של עובד כוכבים. דכתיב (חבקוק ג,ו) עמד וימודד ארץ ראה ויתר גוים, ראה שבע מצות שנצטוו בני נח, כיון שלא קיימו אותן, עמד והתיר ממונן לישראל. ואומר (דברים לג,ב) הופיע מהר פארן, גלה ממונן של עובד כוכבים והתירן, מהר פארן, משעה שסבב והחזיר את התורה על העובדי כוכבים ולא קבלוה:

[3] שׁוֹר שֶׁל יִשְׂרָאֵל שֶׁנָּגַח שׁוֹר שֶׁל הֶקְדֵּשׁ — If the ox of a Jew gored an ox of *hekdesh*, i.e., an ox that belongs to the Temple treasury, or one that was sanctified as an offering, וְשֶׁל הֶקְדֵּשׁ שֶׁנָּגַח לְשׁוֹר שֶׁל יִשְׂרָאֵל — or if [an ox] of *hekdesh* gored the ox of a Jew, פָּטוּר — [the owner of the ox that gored] is not obligated to pay for the damage,[1] שֶׁנֶּאֱמַר "שׁוֹר רֵעֵהוּ" — as it is stated: *If the ox of a man strikes* **the ox of his fellow** ... *he [the owner] shall surely pay* (Exodus 21:35-36). By stating *the ox of his fellow*, the verse implies that it refers only to an ox belonging to an ordinary Jew, וְלֹא שׁוֹר שֶׁל הֶקְדֵּשׁ — and **not to an ox of** *hekdesh*. It is derived from here that damages are not paid where an ox of *hekdesh* is involved, whether it was the animal that gored or the victim of the goring.[2]

A similar law:

שׁוֹר שֶׁל יִשְׂרָאֵל שֶׁנָּגַח לְשׁוֹר שֶׁל עוֹבֵד כּוֹכָבִים — If the ox of a Jew gored the ox of an idolater, whether the ox that gored was a *tam* or a *muad*, פָּטוּר — he is not obligated to pay for the damage.[3] וְשֶׁל עוֹבֵד כּוֹכָבִים שֶׁנָּגַח לְשׁוֹר שֶׁל יִשְׂרָאֵל — But if [the ox] of an idolater gored the ox of a Jew,

---- NOTES ----

muad to gore on Shabbos, they led animals (or people) in front of it on three consecutive Shabbos days and it did not attack them. It thus goes back to being a *tam*. If it then gores again even on a Shabbos, its owner pays only half damages (*Rav*). [This is consistent with R' Yehudah's opinion in Mishnah 2:4; see *Yam Shel Shlomo* 3 and *Tos. Yom Tov*.]

[3]

1. In the Mishnah's first case, the owner does not have to pay the Temple treasury for the damage that his animal did; in the second case, the Temple treasury does not have to pay for the damage that *its* animal did.

These exemptions apply whether the ox that gored was a *tam* or a *muad* (*Tos.*

Yom Tov, Tiferes Yisrael).

2. By describing the *nizak* as a "fellow" of the *mazik*, the Torah implies that they must be similar to each other in order for one to have to pay damages to the other. The verse thus excludes the Temple treasury, which is not similar to an ordinary individual (*Tos. Yom Tov*).

Although the Mishnah speaks only of goring [the category of *keren*], the same applies to other types of damage [the categories of *bor, shein,* and *regel*] (*Rav* to Mishnah 1:2).

3. In the time of the Mishnah, idolaters did not obligate a person to pay for damage caused by his animals. We deal with them according to their own laws (*Rambam, Hilchos Nizkei Mamon* 8:5, with *Maggid Mishneh*).

בֵּין תָּם בֵּין מוּעָד, מְשַׁלֵּם נֶזֶק שָׁלֵם. [ד] **שׁוֹר** שֶׁל פִּקֵּחַ שֶׁנָּגַח שׁוֹר שֶׁל חֵרֵשׁ, שׁוֹטֶה, וְקָטָן, חַיָּב. וְשֶׁל חֵרֵשׁ, שׁוֹטֶה, וְקָטָן שֶׁנָּגַח שׁוֹר שֶׁל פִּקֵּחַ, פָּטוּר. שׁוֹר שֶׁל חֵרֵשׁ, שׁוֹטֶה, וְקָטָן שֶׁנָּגַח, בֵּית דִּין מַעֲמִידִין לָהֶן אַפּוֹטְרוֹפּוֹס, וּמְעִידִין לָהֶן בִּפְנֵי אַפּוֹטְרוֹפּוֹס.

— רע"ב —

(ד) ושל חרש שוטה וקטן שנגח שור של פקח פטור. שאין מעמידין אפוטרופוס לתם לגבות מגופו, דמטלטלי הוא, ואמרינן בפרק קמא [דף יב:] שוה כסף, מלמד שאין בית דין נזקקים אלא לנכסים שיש להן אחריות, ואוקימנא ביתמי: מעמידין להן אפוטרופוס וכו'. אם הוחזקו נגחנים, מעמידין להם אפוטרופוס, ולא לשלם חצי נזק, אלא לשוייה מועד, דכי הדר נגח משלם מן העליה, ויגבו הניזק מקרקע של יתומים:

בֵּין תָּם בֵּין מוּעָד — *whether* the ox that gored was *a* tam *or a* muad, מְשַׁלֵּם נֶזֶק שָׁלֵם — *he pays full damages.*[4]

[4] שׁוֹר שֶׁל פִּקֵּחַ — *If the ox of a competent person* (i.e., a normal adult) שֶׁנָּגַח שׁוֹר שֶׁל חֵרֵשׁ שׁוֹטֶה וְקָטָן — *gored the ox of a deaf-mute, an insane person, or a minor,*[1] חַיָּב — *[the damager] is obligated* to pay for the damage.[2] וְשֶׁל חֵרֵשׁ שׁוֹטֶה וְקָטָן — *But if [the ox] of a deaf-mute, an insane person, or a minor* שֶׁנָּגַח שׁוֹר שֶׁל פִּקֵּחַ — *gored the ox of a competent person,* פָּטוּר — *[the damager] is not obligated* to pay for the damage, for since he is not mentally competent, he cannot be held responsible for guarding his animal. שׁוֹר שֶׁל חֵרֵשׁ שׁוֹטֶה וְקָטָן שֶׁנָּגַח — *However, if the ox of a deaf-mute, an insane person, or a minor gored* repeatedly, thereby showing that it is wild and aggressive, בֵּית דִּין מַעֲמִידִין לָהֶן אַפּוֹטְרוֹפּוֹס — *the court appoints a guardian* to watch over the ox *for them,*[3] וּמְעִידִין לָהֶן בִּפְנֵי אַפּוֹטְרוֹפּוֹס — *and witnesses testify about them before [the court] in the presence of the guardian.* That is, if witnesses testify that the ox gored three times after the guardian took charge, the ox becomes a *muad*. Then, if the ox gores a fourth time, the court can collect full damages from

— NOTES —

4. Idolaters were not careful in those times to prevent their animals from doing damage. They were therefore penalized so that they would have responsibility for their animals (*Rambam* there).

The Mishnah's rulings apply only to uncivilized nations. We may not discriminate against nations that have codes of law and civility (*Meiri*).

[4]

1. A חֵרֵשׁ (deaf-mute) is someone who can neither hear nor speak (*Terumos* 1:2). A minor is a boy under thirteen years of age or a girl under twelve. The Torah considers a deaf-mute, a minor, and a person who is insane to be legally incompetent and thus not responsible for their actions (see Mishnah 8:4).

2. Since the owner of the ox that gored is a normal, competent adult, he is responsible to watch his ox and prevent it from damaging (*Meiri*).

3. The word אַפּוֹטְרוֹפּוֹס (*guardian, administrator*) is usually used for a person who is appointed to protect the affairs of young orphans or other people who are legally incompetent. The guardian discussed here, though, is appointed not to protect the owner, but to secure his ox and prevent it from doing damage (see *Yam Shel Shlomo* 13).

[57] **MISHNAH BAVA KAMMA** / Chapter 4: *Shor Shenagach*

נִתְפַּקֵּחַ הַחֵרֵשׁ, נִשְׁתַּפָּה הַשּׁוֹטֶה, וְהִגְדִּיל הַקָּטָן, חָזַר לְתַמּוּתוֹ, דִּבְרֵי רַבִּי מֵאִיר. רַבִּי יוֹסֵי אוֹמֵר, הֲרֵי הוּא בְחֶזְקָתוֹ. שׁוֹר הָאִצְטָדִין אֵינוֹ חַיָּב מִיתָה, שֶׁנֶּאֱמַר, כִּי יִגַּח וְלֹא שֶׁיַּגִּיחוּהוּ.

— רע״ב —

חוזר לתמותו. דקסבר מועד שילא מרשות בעליו, ונכנס לרשות בעלים אחרים, חוזר לתמותו. דרשות משונה, משנה את דין הִתרְאָתוֹ: שׁוֹר הָאִצְטָדִין. שמיוחד לנגיחות, ומלמדין אותו לכך:

---

the property of the owner (the deaf-mute, insane person, or minor).[4] נִתְפַּקֵּחַ הַחֵרֵשׁ — If the ox became a *muad* after the guardian was appointed and then **the deaf-mute became able to hear and speak,** נִשְׁתַּפָּה הַשּׁוֹטֶה — or **the insane person became sane,** וְהִגְדִּיל הַקָּטָן — or **the minor became an adult,** so that the responsibility for the ox goes from the guardian back to the owner (since the owner is now mentally competent), חָזַר לְתַמּוּתוֹ — **[the ox] returns to its *tam* status,** and its owner pays only half damages if it gores again. דִּבְרֵי רַבִּי מֵאִיר — These are **the words of R' Meir.**[5]

A dissenting view:

רַבִּי יוֹסֵי אוֹמֵר — **R' Yose says:** הֲרֵי הוּא בְחֶזְקָתוֹ — **[The ox] remains in its present *muad* state** even after its owner becomes competent, and so he must pay full damages if it gores again.[6]

The Torah states (*Exodus* 21:28) that an ox that killed a person is put to death.[7] The Mishnah teaches an exception to this law:

שׁוֹר הָאִצְטָדִין אֵינוֹ חַיָּב מִיתָה — **An ox of the stadium,** i.e., an ox that is trained to fight for the purpose of entertaining spectators in a stadium,[8] **is not liable to** be put to **death** if it killed a person, שֶׁנֶּאֱמַר "כִּי יִגַּח" — **because it is stated:** *If an ox gores* a man or a woman and [the victim] dies, the ox shall surely be stoned (*Exodus* there). By stating "if an ox gores," the verse implies that the sentence of death is applied only if the ox gored on its own, וְלֹא שֶׁיַּגִּיחוּהוּ — **and not if others cause it to gore,** for example, by training it.[9]

NOTES

4. The law is that an animal does not became a *muad* unless its owner was warned in court three times, once after each goring (see *Exodus* 21:29). But in this case, warning the owner is meaningless, since he is legally incompetent. Therefore, even if the ox gored more than three times, it does not become a *muad*, but remains a *tam*. Even after the guardian takes over, the animal remains a *tam* until it gores another three times and the guardian is warned in court after each time. Only then does it become a *muad*, and if it gores a fourth time, full damages must be paid from the property of the owner (*Tosafos*).

5. According to R' Meir, when the ox moved from the jurisdiction of the guardian to that of the newly competent owner, it goes back to being a *tam* (*Rav*). This is because the owner can claim that if he himself had been warned about the ox he would have guarded it more effectively and prevented it from goring three times. He therefore cannot be held responsible for its having become a *muad* (*Tos. Yom Tov*).

6. R' Yose holds that the ox did not really move to a new jurisdiction when its owner became competent, because the guardian simply stood in place of the owner. The ox therefore remains a *muad*, and does not go back to being a *tam* (*Rambam, Hilchos Nizkei Mamon* 6:6).

7. See the next Mishnah.

8. *Tiferes Yisrael*.

9. [The Mishnah speaks of a trained ox

משניות בבא קמא / פרק ד: שור שנגח

[ה] **שׁוֹר** שֶׁנָּגַח אֶת הָאָדָם וָמֵת, מוּעָד, מְשַׁלֵּם כֹּפֶר, וְתָם, פָּטוּר מִן הַכֹּפֶר. וְזֶה וָזֶה חַיָּבִים מִיתָה. וְכֵן בַּבֵּן וְכֵן בַּבַּת. נָגַח עֶבֶד אוֹ אָמָה, נוֹתֵן שְׁלֹשִׁים סְלָעִים, בֵּין שֶׁהוּא יָפֶה מֵאָה מָנֶה, וּבֵין שֶׁאֵינוֹ יָפֶה אֶלָּא דִּינָר אֶחָד.

— רע"ב —

(ה) מועד משלם כופר. ואף על גב דבקמא דנגח קטלינן ליה, אשכחינן מועד, כגון שהרג שלשה עכו"ם. אי נמי, שהרג שלשה ישראלים טרפה, דלטרפה לא קטלינן ליה, דגברא קטילא קטיל. אי נמי, דקטיל וערק לאגמא לאחר שהעידו בו: **וכן בבן וכן בבת.** תינוק ותינוקת. חייב עליהן סקילה וכופר כגדולים:

[5] The Torah states (verses 29-30 there) that if an animal kills a person, its owner is liable to death at the hands of Heaven, but he can save himself from death by paying a *kofer* (ransom)[1] to the heirs of the victim. The Mishnah teaches when this law applies:

שׁוֹר שֶׁנָּגַח אֶת הָאָדָם וָמֵת — **If an ox gored a person and he died,** מוּעָד מְשַׁלֵּם כֹּפֶר — **the law is that if the ox was a *muad*,** i.e., it had already gored and killed three people, **[its owner] pays the *kofer*;** וְתָם פָּטוּר מִן הַכֹּפֶר — **but if the ox was a *tam*,** i.e., it had not killed three people before this killing, **[its owner] is exempt from paying the *kofer*.**[2] וְזֶה וָזֶה חַיָּבִים מִיתָה — **However, both this one and that one** (the *tam* and the *muad*) **are liable to be put to death** by stoning for having killed a person.[3] וְכֵן בַּבֵּן וְכֵן בַּבַּת — **The same laws apply even where** the victim is just **a boy or a girl,** and not an adult (that is, the ox is stoned, and if the ox is a *muad*, its owner pays the *kofer*).[4]

The Torah also states (verse 32 there) that if the victim is a Canaanite slave, the owner of the animal pays thirty *shekels*. The Mishnah elaborates upon this law:

נָגַח עֶבֶד אוֹ אָמָה — **If [an ox] gored a male** Canaanite **slave or a female** Canaanite **slave** and killed him or her, the ox is put to death, נוֹתֵן שְׁלֹשִׁים סְלָעִים — **and [its owner] must give thirty *sela'im*** (shekels) to the owner of the slave,[5] בֵּין שֶׁהוּא יָפֶה מֵאָה מָנֶה וּבֵין שֶׁאֵינוֹ יָפֶה אֶלָּא דִּינָר אֶחָד — **whether [the**

— NOTES —

that killed a person. There is a difference of opinion whether the exemption also applies to *damage* caused by such an ox; see *Meiri* and *Meleches Shlomo*.]

[5]

1. The *kofer* amount is equal to the victim's value just before his death had he been sold then as a slave. This payment is made to the victim's heirs (*Tos. Yom Tov, Tiferes Yisrael*).

2. This difference between a *tam* and a *muad* is implied by verses in the Torah (see *Tiferes Yisrael*).

3. Although an animal is put to death for killing a person just once, it can become

a *muad* (i.e., one that has killed three times) if it ran away after each killing (*Rav*).

4. This law appears in the Torah: *Whether it gores a boy or it gores a girl*, etc. (verse 31 there). It could have been thought that the ox is not put to death nor does the owner pay *kofer* if it killed a minor, who is not yet obligated in mitzvos. The Torah therefore teaches otherwise (*Tos. Yom Tov*).

5. [The Mishnah refers to the *shekels* of the Torah as *sela'im*.]

Here, too, the owner pays the fine only if the ox is a *muad*, but the ox is put to death even if it is a *tam* (*Meiri*).

[6] שׁוֹר שֶׁהָיָה מִתְחַכֵּךְ בַּכֹּתֶל וְנָפַל עַל הָאָדָם, נִתְכַּוֵּן לַהֲרוֹג אֶת הַבְּהֵמָה וְהָרַג אֶת הָאָדָם, לְעוֹבֵד כּוֹכָבִים וְהָרַג בֶּן יִשְׂרָאֵל, לִנְפָלִים וְהָרַג בֶּן קַיָּמָא פָּטוּר.

[7] שׁוֹר הָאִשָּׁה, שׁוֹר הַיְתוֹמִים, שׁוֹר

— רע״ב —

(ו) שׁוֹר שהיה מתחכך בכותל וכו׳. פטור מן המיתה. ואם היה מועד, כגון שהיה מועד להתחכך בכתלים ולהפילם על בני אדם, ונתחכך בכותל להנאתו, והפילו על האדם ומת, השור פטור מן המיתה, והבעלים משלמים את הכופר. השור פטור מן המיתה, דכתיב (שמות כא,כט) השור יסקל וגם בעליו יומת, כמיתת הבעלים כך מיתת השור, מה בעלים אין חייבין אם הרגו את הנפש עד שיהרגו בכוונה, כך השור אינו חייב עד שיהרוג בכוונה. והבעלים משלמים את הכופר, דכתיב (שם פסוק ל) אם כופר, שהיה יכול לכתוב כופר יושת עליו, מאי אם כופר, לרבות ההורג שלא בכוונה לחיוב כופר: (ז) וְשׁוֹר הַיְתוֹמִים. שאין להם אפוטרופוס:

---

slave] is worth one hundred *maneh* (2,500 *sela'im*), **or whether [the slave] is worth only a single *dinar*** (a quarter of a *sela*).[6]

[6] The Mishnah states the law that applies to an ox that killed a person unintentionally:

שׁוֹר שֶׁהָיָה מִתְחַכֵּךְ בַּכֹּתֶל וְנָפַל עַל הָאָדָם — **If an ox was rubbing itself against a wall and [the wall] fell on a person** and killed him,[1] נִתְכַּוֵּן לַהֲרוֹג אֶת הַבְּהֵמָה וְהָרַג אֶת הָאָדָם — **or if it intended to kill an animal but** instead **killed a person** who was nearby,[2] לְעוֹבֵד כּוֹכָבִים וְהָרַג בֶּן יִשְׂרָאֵל — **or if it intended to kill an idolater but** instead **killed a Jew,** לִנְפָלִים וְהָרַג בֶּן קַיָּמָא — **or if it intended to kill infants that will not live**[3] **but** instead **killed one that will live,** פָּטוּר — in all these cases **[the ox] is not liable** to be put to death, because it did not intend to kill the actual victim.[4]

[7] The Mishnah lists various cases in which an animal is put to death for killing a person:

שׁוֹר הָאִשָּׁה — **An ox of a woman,** שׁוֹר הַיְתוֹמִים — **an ox of** minor **orphans,** שׁוֹר

--- NOTES ---

6. The Torah fixed thirty *sela'im* as the *kofer* where the victim is a Canaanite slave, regardless of the slave's actual value (see *Rambam, Hilchos Nizkei Mamon* 11:1).

[6]

1. The ox rubbed against the wall for its own pleasure (to scratch itself), but did not intend to kill the person (*Tos. Yom Tov, Tiferes Yisrael*).

2. In this case (and those that follow), the ox *did* intend to kill, but it failed to kill its intended target and killed another animal or person instead.

3. This refers to infants who were born prematurely and are not expected to survive.

4. In the Mishnah's first case (where the ox rubbed against the wall and it collapsed on a person), the ox is not put to death because it did not intend to kill anyone. In the next three cases, although the ox intended to kill and in fact killed, since it would not have been condemned to death for killing its *intended* victim, it is not put to death for accidentally killing its *actual* victim.

In all of the cases, if the animal is a *muad*, although it is not put to death, the owner must pay the *kofer* to the victim's heirs (*Rav*).

[60] משניות בבא קמא / פרק ד: שור שנגח

הָאַפּוֹטְרוֹפּוֹס, שׁוֹר הַמִּדְבָּר, שׁוֹר הַהֶקְדֵּשׁ, שׁוֹר הַגֵּר שֶׁמֵּת וְאֵין לוֹ יוֹרְשִׁים, הֲרֵי אֵלּוּ חַיָּבִים מִיתָה. רַבִּי יְהוּדָה אוֹמֵר, שׁוֹר הַמִּדְבָּר, שׁוֹר הַהֶקְדֵּשׁ, שׁוֹר הַגֵּר שֶׁמֵּת, פְּטוּרִים מִן הַמִּיתָה, לְפִי שֶׁאֵין לָהֶם בְּעָלִים.

— רע"ב —

ושור האפוטרופוס. השור של יתומים הוא, אלא שעל האפוטרופוס לשמרו: הרי אלו חייבין. דשבעה שור כתובים בפרשה בנוגח אדם. חד לגופיה, ושאה, לשאה שוורים הללו:

רבי יהודה אומר שור הקדש שור הגר שמת ואין לו יורשים פטורים מן המיתה. אפילו נגח ואחר כך הקדיש, נגח ואחר כך מת הגר, היה פוטר רבי יהודה. ואין הלכה כרבי יהודה:

הָאַפּוֹטְרוֹפּוֹס — an ox of minor orphans that is in the charge of a guardian,[1] שׁוֹר הַמִּדְבָּר — an ox of the wild (i.e., an ox that does not belong to anyone),[2] שׁוֹר הַהֶקְדֵּשׁ — an ox of *hekdesh* (i.e., it belongs to the Temple treasury or was designated as an offering), שׁוֹר הַגֵּר שֶׁמֵּת וְאֵין לוֹ יוֹרְשִׁים — and an ox of a convert to Judaism who died and has no heirs, and thus is not owned by anyone, הֲרֵי אֵלּוּ חַיָּבִים מִיתָה — all of these are liable to be put to death if they kill a person.[3]

The next Tanna disagrees with the inclusion of the last three cases:

רַבִּי יְהוּדָה אוֹמֵר — R' Yehudah says: שׁוֹר הַמִּדְבָּר שׁוֹר הַהֶקְדֵּשׁ שׁוֹר הַגֵּר שֶׁמֵּת פְּטוּרִים מִן הַמִּיתָה — An ox of the wild, an ox of *hekdesh*, and an ox of a convert who died without heirs are not liable to be put to death for killing a person, לְפִי שֶׁאֵין לָהֶם בְּעָלִים — because they have no owners.[4]

NOTES
---

[7]

1. See Mishnah 4.
2. *Lechem Shamayim.*
3. The Torah mentions the word "ox" seven times in reference to an ox's death penalty (*Exodus* 21:28-32). The six extra times teach that the ox is put to death in each of these six cases (*Rav*).

We might have assumed that the ox should be spared in these cases, and so the Torah had to teach otherwise: (a) *An ox of a woman*: Since the Torah (verse 28 there) refers to the ox's owner in the masculine form [בַּעַל הַשּׁוֹר], it could have been thought that only an ox owned by a man is executed (*Rashi* ד"ה שור האשה). (b) *An ox of orphans*: Since minors, due to their lack of maturity, are not responsible to guard their animals (see Mishnah 4), it could have been thought that they should not be made to lose their ox. (c) *An ox in the charge of the orphans' guardian*: Since an ox watched by a guardian is less likely to kill again, *and it is the property of orphans,* it could have been thought

that the Torah would rule leniently here and spare the ox from execution. (d) *An ox of the wild*: Since the Torah refers numerous times to *the owner of the ox,* it could have been thought that only an ox that has an owner is put to death. (e) *An ox of hekdesh*: It could have been thought that a consecrated ox is not executed so that the Temple will not suffer a loss. (f) *An ox of the convert who dies without heirs*: This is another case of an ownerless ox [like an "ox of the wild"] (*Tos. Yom Tov;* see there for an explanation of why the Mishnah includes two cases of an ownerless ox).

4. R' Yehudah derives from the verse, *and its owner had been warned* (*Exodus* 21:29), that an ox that killed is not put to death unless it has an owner (*Tosefta* 4:6).

Even if the ox had an owner and was unconsecrated when it killed, but became ownerless or consecrated before its case was judged, it is not put to death, because its status at the time of the judgment is what counts (*Rav*).

[ח] שׁוֹר שֶׁהוּא יוֹצֵא לְהִסָּקֵל וְהִקְדִּישׁוֹ בְּעָלָיו, אֵינוֹ מֻקְדָּשׁ. שְׁחָטוֹ, בְּשָׂרוֹ אָסוּר. וְאִם עַד שֶׁלֹּא נִגְמַר דִּינוֹ הִקְדִּישׁוֹ בְּעָלָיו, מֻקְדָּשׁ. וְאִם שְׁחָטוֹ, בְּשָׂרוֹ מֻתָּר.

— רע״ב —

(ח) ואם שחטו אסור. באכילה. דכתיב (שמות כא,כח) סקול יסקל השור ולא יאכל את בשרו, ממשמע שנאמר סקול יסקל השור, איני יודע שהיא נבלה, ונבילה אסורה באכילה, ומה תלמוד לומר ולא יאכל את בשרו, אלא לומר לך, שאם קדם ושחטו לאחר שנגמר דינו, אסור: הקדישו בעליו מוקדש. ונפקא מינה, דאי מתהני מיניה מעל:

---

[8] This Mishnah presents laws that apply to an ox that has been condemned to death:

שׁוֹר שֶׁהוּא יוֹצֵא לְהִסָּקֵל — If an ox was being taken out of the courthouse to be stoned,[1] וְהִקְדִּישׁוֹ בְּעָלָיו — and its owner consecrated it for the Temple, אֵינוֹ מֻקְדָּשׁ — it is not consecrated, because it is no longer his to consecrate;[2] שְׁחָטוֹ בְּשָׂרוֹ אָסוּר — and if [its owner] slaughtered it before it was stoned by the court, its meat is forbidden, because once an animal has been sentenced to death, the Torah forbids having benefit from it.[3] וְאִם עַד שֶׁלֹּא נִגְמַר דִּינוֹ הִקְדִּישׁוֹ בְּעָלָיו — However, if [its owner] consecrated [the ox] before its judgment was decided, מֻקְדָּשׁ — it is consecrated; וְאִם שְׁחָטוֹ — and if he slaughtered it before its judgment was decided,[4] בְּשָׂרוֹ מֻתָּר — its meat is permitted to be eaten, because the prohibition against benefit does not take effect until it has been sentenced to death.[5]

[9] The Mishnah discusses the laws that apply where one person is responsible for watching the animal of another:

NOTES

[8]

1. The same laws apply as soon as it is sentenced to death, even before it is taken out of the courthouse (*Tos. Yom Tov*).

2. See the next note.

3. This law is derived from *Exodus* 21:28 (see *Rav*).
  This is also the reason that the owner cannot consecrate it after the judgment has been passed. In order to consecrate an item to the Temple, one must own it (*Gemara* 68b). Once the court sentences an ox to death, however, it no longer belongs to anyone, because the Torah prohibits benefiting from it in any way. Since even the owner may not benefit from it, his rights of ownership are worth nothing, and he is thus unable to consecrate it (*Rashi* to *Gemara* 45a ד״ה אינו מוקדש; *Nimukei Yosef*).

4. For the same reason, the owner can consecrate it before it is sentenced to death. Since it is still permitted with regard to benefit, it still belongs to him, and he can therefore consecrate it. It is true that nothing may be done with the consecrated animal, because it must be put to death [according to the first Tanna of the previous Mishnah, who holds that even a consecrated animal is put to death]. Nevertheless, since the consecration took effect, anyone who benefits from it violates the prohibition of *me'ilah* [having forbidden benefit from Temple property] (*Rav*).

5. Actually, it is forbidden to slaughter an animal that killed a person, because one thereby avoids the obligation to bring it to court and have it judged (see *Chullin* 140a). The Mishnah refers to a sinner, who violated this prohibition (*Yam Shel Shlomo* 18).

[ט] מְסָרוֹ לְשׁוֹמֵר חִנָּם, וּלְשׁוֹאֵל, לְנוֹשֵׂא שָׂכָר, וּלְשׂוֹכֵר, נִכְנְסוּ תַּחַת הַבְּעָלִים, מוּעָד מְשַׁלֵּם נֶזֶק שָׁלֵם, וְתָם מְשַׁלֵּם חֲצִי נֶזֶק. קְשָׁרוֹ בְעָלָיו בְּמוֹסֵרָה, וְנָעַל בְּפָנָיו כָּרָאוּי, וְיָצָא וְהִזִּיק, אֶחָד תָּם וְאֶחָד מוּעָד, חַיָּב, דִּבְרֵי רַבִּי מֵאִיר.

— רע״ב —

(ט) ונעל בפניו כראוי. בדלת שיכולה לעמוד ברוח מצויה. והיינו שמירה פחותה:

מְסָרוֹ לְשׁוֹמֵר חִנָּם וּלְשׁוֹאֵל לְנוֹשֵׂא שָׂכָר וּלְשׂוֹכֵר — If [the owner of an animal] handed it over to an unpaid watchman, a borrower, a paid watchman, or a renter,[1] and it did damage, **נִכְנְסוּ תַּחַת הַבְּעָלִים** — they take the place of the owner, i.e., they are responsible for the damage as if they were the owner: **מוּעָד מְשַׁלֵּם נֶזֶק שָׁלֵם וְתָם מְשַׁלֵּם חֲצִי נֶזֶק** — If the animal is a *muad* [the watchman] pays full damages, and if it is a *tam* he pays half damages.

If the owner of an animal takes measures to prevent it from doing damage, but it nevertheless damages, he is not obligated to pay. The Mishnah cites a three-way dispute about the level of supervision necessary to free the owner from paying. The first opinion:

קְשָׁרוֹ בְעָלָיו בְּמוֹסֵרָה — If its owner tied it up with a leash that will restrain it only in normal conditions, **וְנָעַל בְּפָנָיו כָּרָאוּי** — or he locked the gate **before it properly**, that is, he locked it in a pen with a gate that will remain standing in a normal wind, but not in an unusually strong wind,[2] **וְיָצָא וְהִזִּיק** — and the animal tore the leash, or an unusually strong wind knocked down the gate, and it **got out and did damage**, **אֶחָד תָּם וְאֶחָד מוּעָד חַיָּב** — whether it is a *tam* or a *muad*, [the owner] is **obligated** to pay (half damages for a *tam*, full damages for a *muad*). **דִּבְרֵי רַבִּי מֵאִיר** — These are the words of R' Meir. According to R' Meir, the owner must guard the animal in a superior manner in order to be freed from paying damages.[3] Therefore, an owner who secures his animal in ways that are effective only in normal circumstances is liable if the animal gets out and does damage.

— NOTES —

[9]
1. These are the four cases listed in the Torah (*Exodus* 22:6-14) where one person is responsible to guard the property of another: (a) the שׁוֹמֵר חִנָּם, *unpaid watchman*, who agrees to guard someone's property without being paid; (b) the שׁוֹמֵר שָׂכָר, *paid watchman*, who is paid to guard someone's property; (c) the שׂוֹכֵר, *renter*, who pays for the right to use the property of another; and (d) the שׁוֹאֵל, *borrower*, who is allowed to use it for free. Each of these people is obligated to prevent the item from being damaged (see *Bava Metzia*, Chapters 3, 7, and 8), and also to prevent it from doing damage.

An unpaid watchman is obligated to pay only if he was negligent. The others, however, must always pay unless they provided the same level of supervision that the owner himself is required to provide [which is defined below] (*Tos. Yom Tov*).

2. Both the leash and the gate are considered "lesser" (i.e., ordinary) forms of guarding the animal [שְׁמִירָה פְּחוּתָה] (*Rav*). [The superior manner of guarding (שְׁמִירָה מְעֻלָּה) would be to tie the animal with an iron chain, which does not break no matter how hard the animal pulls and struggles, or to lock it behind a door that can withstand even unusually strong winds (*Meiri*).]

3. See note 2.

[63] **MISHNAH BAVA KAMMA** / Chapter 4: *Shor Shenagach* 4/9

— רע"ב —

רַבִּי יְהוּדָה אוֹמֵר, תָּם חַיָּב וּמוּעָד פָּטוּר, שֶׁנֶּאֱמַר, וְלֹא יִשְׁמְרֶנּוּ בְּעָלָיו, וְשָׁמוּר הוּא זֶה. רַבִּי אֱלִיעֶזֶר אוֹמֵר, אֵין לוֹ שְׁמִירָה אֶלָּא סַכִּין.

ומועד פטור. מלד העדאה שבו. אבל לד תמות במקומה עומדת, ומשלם חלי נזק כתם. דכתיב ולא ישמרנו גבי מועד, הא שמרו כל דהו פטור מלד העדאה: רבי אליעזר אומר. אין לו שמירה למועד, אלא סכין, עד שישחטנו. ושלש מחלוקות בדבר. לרבי מאיר, בשמירה פחותה חייב ובמעולה פטור. ולרבי יהודה, בשמירה פחותה נמי פטור מלד העדאה שבו, אבל חייב על לד תמות שבו, עד שישמרנו שמירה מעולה. ולרבי אליעזר במעולה נמי חייב. והלכה כרבי יהודה. ומיהו, לכתחלה מלוה לשחוט שור המועד, כדי לסלק היזיקו:

The second opinion:

רַבִּי יְהוּדָה אוֹמֵר — **R' Yehudah says:** תָּם חַיָּב — **If the animal is a** *tam,* **[the owner] is** indeed **obligated** to pay half damages (as R' Meir ruled), וּמוּעָד פָּטוּר — **but if it is a** *muad,* **he is not obligated** to pay full damages, but pays only half.[4] שֶׁנֶּאֱמַר "וְלֹא יִשְׁמְרֶנּוּ בְּעָלָיו" — **This is because it is stated** regarding the payment of full damages in the case of a *muad:* **And its owner did not guard it** (*Exodus* 21:36), which implies that he must pay full damages only if he did not guard it at all, וְשָׁמוּר הוּא זֶה — **but** in our case [the animal] **was guarded** in a manner that would be effective in normal circumstances, and so he does not have to pay full damages.

The third opinion:

רַבִּי אֱלִיעֶזֶר אוֹמֵר — **R' Eliezer says:** אֵין לוֹ שְׁמִירָה אֶלָּא סַכִּין — **[A** *muad*] **cannot be watched except with the knife;** that is, the only method of properly guarding a *muad* is to slaughter it, thereby completely preventing it from ever damaging again. Therefore, if the owner did not slaughter it and it did further damage, he must pay in full, no matter how well he guarded it.[5]

NOTES

4. R' Yehudah exempts the owner only from paying the *second* half of the full damages. He must still pay the half that he would have had to pay had the ox been a *tam* (*Rav*).

5. The Mishnah has presented three views regarding a *muad* that did damage: (a) According to R' Meir, the owner must pay full damages unless he had guarded it in a superior way. (b) According to R' Yehudah, methods that work in normal circumstances are enough to exempt him from paying for half of the damage, but superior methods are needed to exempt him from the other half. (c) R' Eliezer holds that he must always pay in full, no matter how well he guarded it (*Rav*). [All agree, however, that for damage done by a *tam,* he must pay half unless he guarded it in a superior manner.]

[The Mishnah deals only with the category of *keren.* Regarding the categories of *shein* and *regel,* everyone agrees that an ordinary level of guarding is enough. See Mishnah 6:1 and note 1 there.]

Chapter Five

פרק ה: שור שנגח

[א] שׁוֹר שֶׁנָּגַח אֶת הַפָּרָה וְנִמְצָא עֻבָּרָהּ בְּצִדָּהּ, וְאֵין יָדוּעַ אִם עַד שֶׁלֹּא נְגָחָהּ יָלְדָה, אִם מִשֶּׁנְּגָחָהּ יָלְדָה, מְשַׁלֵּם חֲצִי נֶזֶק לַפָּרָה וּרְבִיעַ נֶזֶק לַוָּלָד. וְכֵן פָּרָה שֶׁנָּגְחָה אֶת הַשּׁוֹר וְנִמְצָא וְלָדָהּ בְּצִדָּהּ,

— רע"ב —

פרק חמישי — שור
שנגח את הפרה. (א)
שור שנגח את הפרה.
מעוברת: ונמצא עוברה
בצדה. מת: ואין ידוע
אם עד שלא נגח ילדה.
ולא מת מחמת הנגיחה:
אם משנגחה. ומחמת

הנגיחה הפילתו: **ורביע נזק.** דתם חייב חצי נזק, והאי ולד מוטל בספק הוא, וחולקין. ומתניתין סומכוס היא דאמר ממון המוטל בספק חולקין. אבל חכמים אומרים, זה כלל גדול בדין המוציא מחבירו עליו הראיה. והלכה כחכמים. ואפילו ניזק אומר ברי, ומזיק אומר שמא, המוציא מחבירו עליו הראיה: **וכן פרה שנגחה את השור וכו'.** משלם חצי נזק מן הפרה, אם נמלאת הפרה, כדין תם שמשלם חצי נזק מגופו. ואם לא נמלאת הפרה, משלם רביע נזק מן הולד. שאם היה ידוע שקודם שילדה נגחה, היה

---

[1] This chapter continues with the laws of an animal that does damage. The first Mishnah discusses a case where it is uncertain how much the animal's owner is obligated to pay:

שׁוֹר שֶׁנָּגַח אֶת הַפָּרָה — A *tam* ox gored and killed a cow that was known to be pregnant some time before the attack, וְנִמְצָא עֻבָּרָהּ בְּצִדָּהּ — and [the cow's] fetus was then found dead at its mother's side, וְאֵין יָדוּעַ אִם עַד שֶׁלֹּא נְגָחָהּ יָלְדָה — but it is not known whether [the cow] had given birth before [the ox] gored it, in which case the fetus was not killed by the ox and the ox's owner would not have to pay for it, אִם מִשֶּׁנְּגָחָהּ יָלְדָה — or whether [the cow] gave birth after [the ox] gored it, in which case the fetus was presumably killed by the ox and the ox's owner *would* have to pay for it.[1] מְשַׁלֵּם חֲצִי נֶזֶק לַפָּרָה וּרְבִיעַ נֶזֶק לַוָּלָד — The law is that [the ox's owner] pays half damages for the loss of the cow and one-quarter damages for the loss of the fetus. Since it is unknown whether he is obligated to pay for the fetus, he pays only half the usual half-damage payment, which comes to a quarter.[2]

The opposite situation, where the cow gored the ox:

וְכֵן פָּרָה שֶׁנָּגְחָה אֶת הַשּׁוֹר — And the law is similar where a *tam* cow that was previously known to be pregnant gored an ox וְנִמְצָא וְלָדָהּ בְּצִדָּהּ — and

---

— NOTES —

[1]

1. Witnesses saw the ox gore the cow from a distance [so the ox's owner must definitely pay for the damage to the cow]. They later approached the cow and found a dead fetus next to it, but they do not know whether the fetus died before or after the goring (*Meiri*).

2. Since the ox is a *tam,* the owner is liable to pay for only half the damage (Mishnah 1:4). With respect to the damage to the cow itself, for which he is certainly liable, he makes the usual half-damage payment. But with respect to the fetus, for which his liability is uncertain, he divides the amount in question with the victim. Thus, he pays only one-quarter of the fetus' value (*Rav*).

This requirement to pay one-quarter follows the opinion of Sumchos, who rules that when a doubt arises as to who owns something, it is divided evenly between the two sides. The Sages, however, rule that since the owner of the fetus is trying to collect payment from the owner of the ox, it is up to him to prove his claim (namely, that it died because of the attack) [הַמּוֹצִיא מֵחֲבֵרוֹ עָלָיו הָרְאָיָה]; if he cannot do so, he receives nothing (*Rav*; see Mishnah 3:11).

— רע"ב —

מוסיף כל חצי נזק מן הולד, שמעוברת שנגחה, היא ועוברה נגחו. ואם לאחר שילדה נגחה, לא היה משלם מן הולד כלום, שהרי הולד לא נגח, ואין התם משלם אלא מגופו. עכשיו שהוא בספק, חולקים, ומן החצי נזק שיש לו לשלם, משלם

וְאֵין יָדוּעַ אִם עַד שֶׁלֹּא נָגְחָה יָלְדָה, אִם מִשֶּׁנָּגְחָה יָלְדָה, מְשַׁלֵּם חֲצִי נֶזֶק מִן הַפָּרָה וּרְבִיעַ נֶזֶק מִן הַוָּלָד.

[ב] **הַקַּדָּר** שֶׁהִכְנִיס קְדֵרוֹתָיו לֶחָצֵר בַּעַל הַבַּיִת שֶׁלֹּא בִרְשׁוּת, וְשִׁבְּרָתַן בְּהֶמְתּוֹ שֶׁל בַּעַל הַבַּיִת, פָּטוּר.

וְאֵין יָדוּעַ אִם עַד שֶׁלֹּא נָגְחָה — its newborn[3] calf was then found at its side, יָלְדָה — but it is not known whether [the cow] had given birth before it gored the ox, in which case the calf was not part of the goring animal, and so the owner would have to pay only from the "body of the cow," and not from "the body of the calf," אִם מִשֶּׁנָּגְחָה יָלְדָה — or whether [the cow] gave birth after it gored the ox, in which case the calf was still part of the cow at the time of the attack, and thus the owner would have to pay from "the body of the calf" as well.[4] מְשַׁלֵּם חֲצִי נֶזֶק מִן הַפָּרָה וּרְבִיעַ נֶזֶק מִן הַוָּלָד — [The cow's owner] pays half damages from the body of the cow and one-quarter damages from the body of the newborn calf.[5] In this situation, too, since it is uncertain whether the calf was part of the goring animal, its owner need pay only half of the usual half-damage payment from it (i.e., one quarter).[6]

[2] The Mishnah discusses damage that results from someone bringing his possessions into the property of another:

הַקַּדָּר שֶׁהִכְנִיס קְדֵרוֹתָיו לֶחָצֵר בַּעַל הַבַּיִת שֶׁלֹּא בִרְשׁוּת — If a potter brought his pots into a homeowner's courtyard without permission, וְשִׁבְּרָתַן בְּהֶמְתּוֹ שֶׁל בַּעַל הַבַּיִת — and an animal belonging to the homeowner broke them, פָּטוּר — [the homeowner] is not obligated to pay for the pots, because the potter did not have permission to bring them there.[1]

NOTES

3. Tos. Yom Tov.

4. We have learned that when a *tam* does damage, the victim takes the *tam* itself as payment [up to the value of half the damage] (Mishnah 1:4). In our case, if the cow was still pregnant with this calf when it gored the ox, and thus the calf was part of the animal that gored, the victim may also take the calf. But if the calf was born before the attack, the victim may take only the cow.

5. If the cow is available, the victim can collect his entire half-damage payment from it. But if the cow is not available (for example, it ran away), and so the victim has to collect his payment from the body of the calf, he can take only half of that payment, i.e., a quarter of the damage (*Rav*).

Another practical application of the Mishnah's law is that even if the cow *is* available, but it is worth less than the payment he is owed, the victim collects only *half* the difference from the calf (*Tos. Yom Tov*).

6. This ruling, too, follows the opinion of Sumchos (see note 2). According to the Sages, the victim (i.e., the owner of the ox) cannot collect anything from the body of the calf unless he proves that the cow gave birth after the goring and the fetus was therefore part of the goring animal (*Rif*).

[2]

1. See Mishnah 1:2 note 6 (a).

משניות בבא קמא / פרק ה: שור שנגח

וְאִם הֻזְּקָה בָהֶן, בַּעַל הַקְּדֵרוֹת חַיָּב. וְאִם הִכְנִיס בִּרְשׁוּת, בַּעַל חָצֵר חַיָּב. הִכְנִיס פֵּרוֹתָיו לַחֲצַר בַּעַל הַבַּיִת שֶׁלֹּא בִרְשׁוּת, וַאֲכָלָתַן בְּהֶמְתּוֹ שֶׁל בַּעַל הַבַּיִת, פָּטוּר. וְאִם הֻזְּקָה בָהֶן, בַּעַל הַפֵּרוֹת חַיָּב. וְאִם הִכְנִיס בִּרְשׁוּת, בַּעַל הֶחָצֵר חַיָּב.

— רע״ב —

רביע נזק מן הולד: (ב) ואם הוזקה בהם בעל הפירות חייב. והני מילי שהוחלקה ונכשלה בהן. אבל אם אכלה מהן עד שמתה, בטל הפירות

וְאִם הֻזְּקָה בָהֶן — **And if [the homeowner's animal] was damaged by [the pots]**, for example, it tripped over them and was injured, בַּעַל הַקְּדֵרוֹת חַיָּב — **the owner of the pots is obligated** to pay for the damage to the animal, since he created a hazard (*bor*) in his neighbor's property without permission.[2] וְאִם הִכְנִיס בִּרְשׁוּת — **But if [the potter] brought** his pots **into** the courtyard **with permission**, and they were broken there, בַּעַל חָצֵר חַיָּב — **the owner of the courtyard** (i.e., the homeowner) **is obligated** to pay for the pots, because by allowing them to be brought into his courtyard, he presumably agreed to protect them, even if he did not say so explicitly.[3]

A similar case:

הִכְנִיס פֵּרוֹתָיו לַחֲצַר בַּעַל הַבַּיִת שֶׁלֹּא בִרְשׁוּת — **If someone brought his produce into a homeowner's courtyard without permission,** וַאֲכָלָתַן בְּהֶמְתּוֹ שֶׁל בַּעַל הַבַּיִת — **and an animal belonging to the homeowner ate it,** פָּטוּר — **[the homeowner] is not obligated** to pay for it, because the owner of the produce did not have permission to bring it there. וְאִם הֻזְּקָה בָהֶן — **And if [the homeowner's animal] was damaged by [the produce],** for example, it slipped on the produce and was injured, בַּעַל הַפֵּרוֹת חַיָּב — **the owner of the produce is obligated** to pay for the damage to the animal, since he created a hazard in his neighbor's property without permission.[4] וְאִם הִכְנִיס בִּרְשׁוּת — **But if [the owner of the produce] brought** the produce **into** the courtyard **with the** homeowner's **permission**, and the homeowner's animal ate it, בַּעַל הֶחָצֵר חַיָּב — **the owner of the courtyard** (i.e., the homeowner) **is obligated** to pay for the produce, because by allowing it to be brought into the courtyard, he presumably agreed to protect it.[5]

NOTES

2. *Meiri*, first explanation.

3. The Tanna of this Mishnah holds that when the homeowner allowed the potter to bring the pots into his courtyard, he automatically accepted to become their watchman (*shomer*). As a watchman, he is required to protect the pots from damage. And if they are damaged (as a result of his negligence) in any way — even if the wind tips them over and breaks them — he must pay the owner (*Tos. Yom Tov*). [The next Mishnah cites a Tanna who disagrees.]

In this case, if the homeowner's animal was damaged by the pots, the potter does not have to pay. Since he had permission to bring his pots into the courtyard, he is not responsible for damage that they might cause there (*Tos. Yom Tov*).

4. The owner of the produce must pay only if the animal tripped or slipped on the produce and was thereby injured. If, however, the animal became sick from *eating* the produce, the owner of the produce is exempt, because he cannot be held liable for damage that the animal brought upon itself willingly (*Rav, Tos. Yom Tov*).

5. The Mishnah adds the case of the produce to teach that a homeowner who

MISHNAH BAVA KAMMA / Chapter 5: *Shor Shenagach*

— רע"ב —

[ג] **הַכְנִיס** שׁוֹרוֹ לַחֲצַר בַּעַל הַבַּיִת שֶׁלֹּא בִרְשׁוּת, וּנְגָחוֹ שׁוֹרוֹ שֶׁל בַּעַל הַבַּיִת, אוֹ שֶׁנְּשָׁכוֹ כַּלְבּוֹ שֶׁל בַּעַל הַבַּיִת, פָּטוּר. נָגַח הוּא שׁוֹרוֹ שֶׁל בַּעַל הַבַּיִת, חַיָּב. נָפַל לְבוֹרוֹ וְהִבְאִישׁ מֵימָיו, חַיָּב. הָיָה אָבִיו אוֹ בְנוֹ לְתוֹכוֹ, מְשַׁלֵּם אֶת הַכֹּפֶר. וְאִם הִכְנִיס בִּרְשׁוּת, בַּעַל הֶחָצֵר חַיָּב.

פטור, דהוה לה שלא תאכל:
(ג) היה אביו או בנו. של בעל הבית בתוכו. והוא הדין לשאר אנשים, אלא אורחא דמלתא נקט: משלם את הכופר. וכגון שהיה מועד להפיל עצמו על בני אדם בבורות, והאידנא חזי ירקא בבור, והפיל עצמו לבור לאכול ירקא, והרג את האדם. שהשור פטור ממיתה, הואיל והרג שלא בכונה. והבעלים משלמין את הכופר, דאתרבי כופר אפילו שהרג שלא בכונה,

---

[3] This Mishnah deals with a third case of damage that results from someone bringing his possessions into another's property:

הַכְנִיס שׁוֹרוֹ לַחֲצַר בַּעַל הַבַּיִת שֶׁלֹּא בִרְשׁוּת — **If someone brought his ox into a homeowner's courtyard without permission,** וּנְגָחוֹ שׁוֹרוֹ שֶׁל בַּעַל הַבַּיִת — **and the homeowner's ox gored it** אוֹ שֶׁנְּשָׁכוֹ כַּלְבּוֹ שֶׁל בַּעַל הַבַּיִת — **or the homeowner's dog bit it,** פָּטוּר — **[the homeowner] is not obligated** to pay for the damage, because the victim did not have permission to bring his ox there. נָגַח הוּא שׁוֹרוֹ שֶׁל בַּעַל הַבַּיִת — **And if [the ox that was brought in] gored the homeowner's ox,** חַיָּב — **[the person who brought the ox in] is obligated** to pay for the damage. נָפַל לְבוֹרוֹ וְהִבְאִישׁ מֵימָיו — **Likewise, if [the ox that was brought in] fell into [the homeowner's] water-pit and made its waters dirty** and unfit for drinking, חַיָּב — **[the owner of the ox] is obligated** to pay for the ruined water. הָיָה אָבִיו אוֹ בְנוֹ לְתוֹכוֹ — **And if [the homeowner's] father or son was in [the pit]**[1] and was killed by the falling ox, מְשַׁלֵּם אֶת הַכֹּפֶר — **[the owner of the ox] pays** *kofer* (the "ransom" that must be paid by someone whose animal killed a person).[2]

וְאִם הִכְנִיס בִּרְשׁוּת — **However, if he brought** his ox **into the courtyard with permission,** and it was injured there, בַּעַל הֶחָצֵר חַיָּב — **the owner of the courtyard is obligated** to pay for the damage, because by allowing the ox to be brought into the courtyard, the homeowner presumably agreed to protect it, even if he did not say so explicitly.[3]

NOTES
---

gives permission for someone to put items in his property accepts responsibility not only for pottery, which is fragile and easily damaged, but even for produce, which is not as easily damaged [and thus is less likely to require protection] (*Tos. Yom Tov*).

[3]

1. The same law applies when any other person was in the pit. The Mishnah chose to speak of his father or son only because that is the usual case [i.e., it is common for a homeowner's relatives to be on his property] (*Rav*).

2. See Mishnah 4:5. [This part of the Mishnah must refer to an ox that is a *muad*, because the owner of a *tam* is exempt from paying *kofer* (see *Rav*).]

3. In this case, the *homeowner* would be obligated to pay *kofer* if the ox was a *muad* and it killed a person (*Tiferes Yisrael*).

רַבִּי אוֹמֵר, בְּכֻלָּן אֵינוֹ חַיָּב עַד שֶׁיְּקַבֵּל עָלָיו לִשְׁמֹר.

[ד] **שׁוֹר** שֶׁהָיָה מִתְכַּוֵּן לַחֲבֵרוֹ וְהִכָּה אֶת הָאִשָּׁה, וְיָצְאוּ יְלָדֶיהָ, פָּטוּר מִדְּמֵי וְלָדוֹת. וְאָדָם שֶׁהָיָה מִתְכַּוֵּן לַחֲבֵרוֹ וְהִכָּה אֶת הָאִשָּׁה, וְיָצְאוּ יְלָדֶיהָ, מְשַׁלֵּם דְּמֵי וְלָדוֹת.

— רע"ב —

רבי אומר וכו'. והלכה כרבי. הלכך אם הכניס שורו ברשות בעל הבית, סתם, ולא קבל עליו לשמור, בעל הבית פטור, דהא לא קבל עליה נטירותא. והמכניס נמי פטור, לפי שהכניס ברשות: **(ד) שור שהיה מתכוין** לחבירו וכו'. איידי דבעי למיתני סיפא, אדם שהיה מתכוין לחבירו, תנא רישא נמי, שור שהיה מתכוין לחבירו. דאפילו היה מתכוין לאשה, פטור השור מדמי ולדות, שאין חייב בדמי ולדות אלא אדם בלבד:

כדאמרינן לעיל (ו,ו):

The next Tanna disagrees with the last point:

רַבִּי אוֹמֵר — **Rebbi** (i.e., R' Yehudah HaNasi) **says:** בְּכֻלָּן אֵינוֹ חַיָּב עַד שֶׁיְּקַבֵּל עָלָיו לִשְׁמֹר — **In all of these [cases]** cited in this Mishnah and the previous Mishnah, where one brought things (pots, produce, or an ox) into another's property, even if the homeowner gave him permission, **[the homeowner] is not obligated** to pay for damages that occur in his property to them, **unless** he explicitly **accepts upon himself to protect** them.[4]

[4] The Torah (*Exodus* 21:22) states that if someone accidentally struck a pregnant woman and caused her to miscarry, he must pay for the loss of the fetus. The Mishnah contrasts the law where a *person* struck a pregnant woman with the law where an *animal* struck a pregnant woman:

שׁוֹר שֶׁהָיָה מִתְכַּוֵּן לַחֲבֵרוֹ וְהִכָּה אֶת הָאִשָּׁה וְיָצְאוּ יְלָדֶיהָ — **If an ox intended to gore another ox and it struck a** pregnant **woman instead and caused her to miscarry,** פָּטוּר מִדְּמֵי וְלָדוֹת — **[the owner of the ox] is not obligated to pay the value of the fetus.** וְאָדָם שֶׁהָיָה מִתְכַּוֵּן לַחֲבֵרוֹ — **But if a** *person* **intended to** strike **another** person וְהִכָּה אֶת הָאִשָּׁה וְיָצְאוּ יְלָדֶיהָ — **and he struck a** pregnant **woman instead and caused her to miscarry,** מְשַׁלֵּם דְּמֵי וְלָדוֹת — **he must pay the value of the fetus.**[1]

NOTES

4. This Mishnah and the last one stated that one who allows another person to bring items into his property automatically commits himself to protect them. According to Rebbi, however, he makes no such commitment (unless he clearly says so). Thus, if the items are damaged, the homeowner is exempt from paying. However, even according to Rebbi the owner of the items is exempt from paying for any damage that his items cause on the property, since, after all, he had permission to place them there (*Rav*).

[4]

1. The Torah (*Exodus* 21:22) states that a *man* who caused a woman to miscarry must pay, which implies that if an *animal* did so its owner is not obligated to pay (*Rav* to Mishnah 8:2; *Tosefos R' Akiva Eiger,* from Gemara 42a).

Actually, it makes no difference whether the ox intended to gore another ox or the woman; in either case, the ox's owner does not have to pay for the fetus. The Mishnah mentions that it intended to gore another ox only because in its next case, where a *man* struck a pregnant woman, he is required to pay even if he intended to hit another man and struck the woman by accident (see *Rav*).

— רע"ב —

אִם כֵּן מִשֶּׁהָאִשָּׁה יוֹלֶדֶת מַשְׁבַּחַת. אִם כֵּן דְּכָךְ שַׁיְימִין כִּדְקָאָמְרַתְּ, אִשְׁתְּכַח דְּלֹא יָהֵיב לֵיהּ מִידֵּי, שֶׁהֲרֵי מִשֶּׁהָאִשָּׁה יוֹלֶדֶת מַשְׁבַּחַת, שֶׁדָּמֶיהָ פְּחוּתִין לִימָּכֵר קוֹדֶם שֶׁתֵּלֵד, שֶׁמְּסוּכֶּנֶת הִיא לָמוּת בְּצַעַר הַלֵּידָה: הָיְתָה שִׁפְחָה וְנִשְׁתַּחְרְרָה. כְּלוֹמַר, הָיְתָה מְשׁוּחְרֶרֶת נְשׂוּאָה לְגֵר אוֹ לְעֶבֶד מְשׁוּחְרָר, אוֹ גִּיוֹרֶת נְשׂוּאָה לְאֶחָד מֵהֶן, וּמֵת הַבַּעַל, פָּטוּר. דְּהַמַּחֲזִיק בְּנִכְסֵי הַגֵּר שֶׁמֵּת וְאֵין לוֹ יוֹרְשִׁים, זָכָה, וְזֶה קוֹדֵם לִזְכּוֹת בָּמָּה שֶׁבְּיָדוֹ. וְהוּא הַדִּין נַמִּי, לְיִשְׂרְאֵלִית הַנְּשׂוּאָה לְגֵר, וּמֵת הַגֵּר, דְּפָטוּר, דְּהָא דְּמֵי וְלָדוֹת לַבַּעַל. אֶלָּא מִשּׁוּם דִּסְתָם מְשׁוּחְרֶרֶת וְגִיּוֹרֶת נְשׂוּאוֹת לְגֵר וְלִמְשׁוּחְרָר, לְהָכִי נָקַט שִׁפְחָה וְגִיוֹרֶת:

כֵּיצַד מְשַׁלֵּם דְּמֵי וְלָדוֹת, שָׁמִין אֶת הָאִשָּׁה כַּמָּה הִיא יָפָה עַד שֶׁלֹּא יָלְדָה, וְכַמָּה הִיא יָפָה מִשֶּׁיָּלְדָה. אָמַר רַבָּן שִׁמְעוֹן בֶּן גַּמְלִיאֵל, אִם כֵּן מִשֶּׁהָאִשָּׁה יוֹלֶדֶת מַשְׁבַּחַת, אֶלָּא שָׁמִין אֶת הַוְּלָדוֹת כַּמָּה הֵן יָפִין. וְנוֹתֵן לַבַּעַל, וְאִם אֵין לָהּ בַּעַל, נוֹתֵן לְיוֹרְשָׁיו. הָיְתָה שִׁפְחָה וְנִשְׁתַּחְרְרָה,

---

The Mishnah explains how the value of the fetus is calculated:

כֵּיצַד מְשַׁלֵּם דְּמֵי וְלָדוֹת — **How does one pay the value of the fetus? שָׁמִין אֶת הָאִשָּׁה כַּמָּה הִיא יָפָה עַד שֶׁלֹּא יָלְדָה** — **They** (i.e., the court) **estimate how much the woman was worth before giving birth** had she been sold then as a slave, **וְכַמָּה הִיא יָפָה מִשֶּׁיָּלְדָה** — **and how much she would have been worth after giving birth** (if she would have given birth normally).[2] The difference is considered the value of the fetus, which the damager must pay.[3]

The next Tanna disagrees:

אָמַר רַבָּן שִׁמְעוֹן בֶּן גַּמְלִיאֵל — **Rabban Shimon ben Gamliel said: אִם כֵּן מִשֶּׁהָאִשָּׁה יוֹלֶדֶת מַשְׁבַּחַת** — **If so,** that we reckon the value of the woman before and after the pregnancy, the damager will pay nothing, because **a woman increases** in value after she gives birth! A pregnant woman is worth less as a slave than one who is not pregnant, because the danger presented by the approaching childbirth reduces her value. **אֶלָּא שָׁמִין אֶת הַוְּלָדוֹת כַּמָּה הֵן יָפִין** — **Rather, we estimate how much the fetus was worth** just before the attack and the damager pays that amount.[4]

The Mishnah discusses to whom the payment is made:

וְנוֹתֵן לַבַּעַל — **[The damager] gives** the value of the fetus **to the** woman's **husband,** i.e., the baby's father.[5] **וְאִם אֵין לָהּ בַּעַל** — **And if she has no husband,** i.e., the father died, **נוֹתֵן לְיוֹרְשָׁיו** — **he gives** it to [the husband's] **heirs. הָיְתָה שִׁפְחָה וְנִשְׁתַּחְרְרָה** — **If she was a** Canaanite slave-woman who had been freed and had married a freed Canaanite slave,

---

NOTES

2. *Tos. Yom Tov.*

3. [This payment covers only damages related to pregnancy. If she suffered additional injuries to her body, we assess those damages separately, in the manner stated in Mishnah 8:1.]

4. The Gemara (49a) explains that Rabban Shimon ben Gamliel disagrees only in the case of a woman who was pregnant for the first time, when it is unknown whether she can survive childbirth. Once she has given birth, however, the risk is greatly reduced, and Rabban Shimon ben Gamliel agrees that she is in fact considered more valuable on account of her pregnancy (*Tos. Yom Tov*).

5. This law is derived from the Torah (see *Tos. Yom Tov*).

[ה]

אוֹ גִיּוֹרֶת, פָּטוּר.

[ה] הַחוֹפֵר בּוֹר בִּרְשׁוּת הַיָּחִיד וּפְתָחוֹ לִרְשׁוּת הָרַבִּים, אוֹ בִּרְשׁוּת הָרַבִּים וּפְתָחוֹ לִרְשׁוּת הַיָּחִיד, בִּרְשׁוּת הַיָּחִיד וּפְתָחוֹ לִרְשׁוּת הַיָּחִיד אַחֵר, חַיָּב.

— רע"ב —

(ה) בִּרְשׁוּת הַיָּחִיד וּפְתָחוֹ לִרְשׁוּת הַיָּחִיד אַחֶרֶת. אַף עַל גַּב דְּאֵין כָּאן צַד רְשׁוּת הָרַבִּים, חַיָּב. וּבִלְבַד אִם הִפְקִיר רְשׁוּתוֹ, אוֹתָהּ שֶׁפִּי הַבּוֹר לְתוֹכָהּ:

אוֹ גִיּוֹרֶת — or if she was **a convert** to Judaism who married a male convert, and, in each of these cases, her husband died without leaving any heirs, פָּטוּר — **[the damager] is not obligated** to pay the value of the fetus to anyone.[6]

[5] From here until the end of the chapter, the Mishnah discusses the category of damage called *bor* (a pit), which includes obstacles that a person makes in a public space:[1]

הַחוֹפֵר בּוֹר בִּרְשׁוּת הַיָּחִיד וּפְתָחוֹ לִרְשׁוּת הָרַבִּים — **If someone digs a pit in** his **private domain and opens it to the public domain**, for example, he digs a pit in the public domain at an angle so that the floor of the pit is in his own property,[2] אוֹ בִּרְשׁוּת הָרַבִּים וּפְתָחוֹ לִרְשׁוּת הַיָּחִיד — **or** he digs a pit **in the public domain and opens it to** his **private domain**, for example, he digs in his own property at an angle so that the floor of the pit is under the public domain,[3] בִּרְשׁוּת הַיָּחִיד וּפְתָחוֹ לִרְשׁוּת הַיָּחִיד אַחֵר — **or** he digs a pit **in** his **private domain and opens it to another private domain** that he owns,[4] חַיָּב — in all of these cases, **he is obligated** to pay for damages caused by the pit.[5]

--- NOTES ---

6. [The Mishnah refers to a convert or freed slave who did not have children after he converted or was freed; thus, he has no legal relatives who can inherit him.] The law is that when he dies, his property becomes ownerless (*hefker*), and the first person to seize it acquires it. In the Mishnah's case, therefore, the damager may keep the payment, for since he still has it in his possession, he has already "seized" it (*Rav*).

Although the Mishnah says that the woman herself was a convert or a freed Canaanite slavewoman, the same law applies to any woman, even one who is Jewish by birth, because it is the *husband's* status that affects to whom the payment is made. The Mishnah mentions a convert and a freed slavewoman only because it was common for people of similar backgrounds to marry each other (*Rav*).

[5]

1. See Mishnah 1:1.
2. *Meiri*. Since the pit opens into the public domain, an animal walking in the public domain could fall into it.

3. The Mishnah refers to a case where the digger gave up his ownership of the area around the opening of the pit, thus making it part of the public domain, where people and animals may walk. If he had kept that area as part of his private property and not declared it ownerless, he would not be obligated to pay for damage caused by the pit, because he could say to the victim, "What were you doing on my property?" (*Rav*, *Tos. Yom Tov*; see Mishnah 1:2 note 6).

4. In this case, too, he gave up his ownership of the area around the pit's opening, thereby making it part of the public domain (*Rav*).

[The Mishnah could have said that the floor of the pit and its opening were in the same private domain. However, in keeping with the style of the preceding cases, it describes the pit's opening and floor as being in two different domains (*Tos. Yom Tov*).]

5. In summary, it makes no difference

[73] MISHNAH BAVA KAMMA / Chapter 5: *Shor Shenagach* 5/5

הַחוֹפֵר בּוֹר בִּרְשׁוּת הָרַבִּים, וְנָפַל לְתוֹכוֹ שׁוֹר אוֹ חֲמוֹר וָמֵת, חַיָּב. אֶחָד הַחוֹפֵר בּוֹר, שִׁיחַ, וּמְעָרָה, חֲרִיצִין, וּנְעִיצִין, חַיָּב. אִם כֵּן לָמָּה נֶאֱמַר בּוֹר, מַה בּוֹר שֶׁיֵּשׁ בּוֹ כְּדֵי לְהָמִית, עֲשָׂרָה טְפָחִים, אַף כֹּל שֶׁיֵּשׁ בּוֹ כְּדֵי לְהָמִית, עֲשָׂרָה טְפָחִים. הָיוּ פְּחוּתִין מֵעֲשָׂרָה טְפָחִים, וְנָפַל לְתוֹכוֹ שׁוֹר אוֹ חֲמוֹר וָמֵת, פָּטוּר, וְאִם הוּזַּק בּוֹ, חַיָּב.

— רע״ב —

אחד החופר בור. הוא עשוי עגול: שיח. ארוך וקצר: מערה. מרובעת ומכוסה בקירוי, אלא שיש לה פה: חריצין. רחבים ומרובעים כמערה, אלא שאינן מקורין: נעיצין. קצרין מלמטה ורחבים מלמעלה: מה בור שיש בו כדי להמית עשרה טפחים. דסתם בור הוא גבוה עשרה טפחים:

In the preceding cases the damager owned either the pit or its opening. The Mishnah now cites a case where the damager owns neither:

וְנָפַל הַחוֹפֵר בּוֹר בִּרְשׁוּת הָרַבִּים — If someone digs a pit in the public domain לְתוֹכוֹ שׁוֹר אוֹ חֲמוֹר וָמֵת — and an ox or a donkey (or any other animal)[6] fell into it and died, חַיָּב — he is obligated to pay for it. Even though the entire pit (the floor and its opening) is in the public domain and no part of it belongs to the one who dug it, he is responsible for the damage that it causes.[7]

The Mishnah lists various types of pits for which one is liable if he digs (or uncovers) them:

אֶחָד הַחוֹפֵר בּוֹר שִׁיחַ וּמְעָרָה חֲרִיצִין וּנְעִיצִין — Whether one digs a typical round pit, a ditch (a long and narrow pit), a vault (a square pit covered with a roof in which there is an opening), square pits (square pits that are uncovered), or wedge-like pits (pits that are wide on top and narrow at the bottom), חַיָּב — he is obligated to pay for the damage that they cause. אִם כֵּן לָמָּה נֶאֱמַר בּוֹר — If so, why is only a standard pit mentioned in the Torah (*Exodus* 21:33-34)? This is to teach the following: מַה בּוֹר שֶׁיֵּשׁ בּוֹ כְּדֵי לְהָמִית עֲשָׂרָה טְפָחִים — Just as a standard pit is able to cause death, because a standard pit is ten *tefachim* deep, which is deep enough to kill an animal that falls into it, אַף כֹּל שֶׁיֵּשׁ בּוֹ כְּדֵי לְהָמִית עֲשָׂרָה טְפָחִים — so too, any other type of pit must be able to cause death, that is, it must be at least ten *tefachim* deep. הָיוּ פְּחוּתִין מֵעֲשָׂרָה טְפָחִים — If any of [these pits] were less than ten *tefachim* deep, וְנָפַל לְתוֹכוֹ שׁוֹר אוֹ חֲמוֹר וָמֵת — and an ox or a donkey fell into it and died, פָּטוּר — [the digger] is not obligated to pay, because it is completely unexpected that such a shallow pit would cause an animal's death and so the digger cannot be blamed. וְאִם הוּזַּק בּוֹ — However, if [an animal] was merely injured by falling into it (a pit less than ten *tefachim* deep), חַיָּב — [the digger] is obligated to pay, because even shallow pits can cause injury.[8]

---- NOTES ----

where one digs a pit; as long as its opening is accessible to the public, the digger is liable for any damage it causes (see *Tos. Yom Tov*).

6. The Mishnah speaks of an ox or donkey because these are the animals mentioned in the verse (*Exodus* 21:33) about a pit that causes damage (*Shitah Mekubetzes*, citing *Rabbeinu Yehonasan*; see Mishnah 7).

7. The Gemara (49b) derives this law from a verse (see *Tos. Yom Tov*).

8. *Tos. Yom Tov.*

[ו] **בּוֹר** שֶׁל שְׁנֵי שֻׁתָּפִין, עָבַר עָלָיו הָרִאשׁוֹן וְלֹא כִסָּהוּ, וְהַשֵּׁנִי וְלֹא כִסָּהוּ, הַשֵּׁנִי חַיָּב. כִּסָּהוּ הָרִאשׁוֹן, וּבָא הַשֵּׁנִי וּמְצָאוֹ מְגֻלֶּה וְלֹא כִסָּהוּ, הַשֵּׁנִי חַיָּב.

— רע״ב —

(ו) השני חייב. והוא שמסר לו ראשון לשני כשהלך, כסוי הבור לכסותו, ולא כסהו השני:

[6] The Torah states that not only digging a pit, but merely uncovering a pit makes one obligated for any damage it causes (*Exodus* 21:33). The Mishnah discusses these laws regarding a pit that is owned by two people. Normally, both owners would be obligated to pay for any damage caused by their pit, but in the following cases only one is obligated:

בּוֹר שֶׁל שְׁנֵי שֻׁתָּפִין — If there is **a pit that belongs to two partners,**[1] עָבַר עָלָיו הָרִאשׁוֹן וְלֹא כִסָּהוּ — **and the first one passed by it,** uncovered it (to draw water, for example), **and did not cover it** again, וְהַשֵּׁנִי וְלֹא כִסָּהוּ — **and,** before he left, **the second one** passed by and the first one gave the cover to the second, **but [the second one], too, did not cover it,** הַשֵּׁנִי חַיָּב — only **the second one is obligated** to pay for any damage caused later by the pit. The second one must pay because he should have covered the pit. The first partner, though, does not have to pay because he fulfilled his responsibility by giving the cover to the second one.[2]

Another case regarding a pit that belongs to two people:

כִּסָּהוּ הָרִאשׁוֹן — **If the first one covered it** properly, וּבָא הַשֵּׁנִי וּמְצָאוֹ מְגֻלֶּה — **and the second one came** some time afterward **and found it uncovered,** because, for example, the cover had become wormy and broke,[3] וְלֹא כִסָּהוּ — **and [the second one] did not cover it,** הַשֵּׁנִי חַיָּב — **the second one is obligated** to pay for any damage later caused by the pit, since he should have covered it but did not do so. The first partner, however, does not have to pay, because he covered it properly; although it later become wormy, that was an unlikely accident, which he was not expected to foresee.[4]

— NOTES —

[6]
1. For example, two people owned a courtyard in which there was a pit. They gave up their ownership of the courtyard but kept the pit (*Tos. Yom Tov;* see previous Mishnah, note 3).

2. By giving the cover to the second partner, it is as though the first partner asked him to watch the pit. Therefore, if any accident happens, it is entirely the second one's fault (*Tos. Yom Tov*).

However, if *both* partners passed by their uncovered pit and left it uncovered, they are equally liable for the damage (*Meleches Shlomo,* citing *Rashi* to 51b ד״ה וראשון).

3. *Rashi.* [The case cannot be that a person uncovered it, because that person would become entirely responsible for the pit, as the Gemara (49b) derives from *Exodus* 21:33.]

4. Once he covered the pit properly, he is not required to constantly go back and check whether the cover is still strong and has not become wormy (*Rabbeinu Yehonasan*).

If, however, the first partner did find out that the cover was weak (and he had enough time to make a new one, or hire someone to make a new one and cover the pit with it), both are obligated to pay for damage caused by the pit, since both knew that it was not covered properly and failed to fix it (*Tos. Yom Tov*).

— רע"ב —

כִּסָּהוּ כָּרָאוּי, וְנָפַל לְתוֹכוֹ שׁוֹר אוֹ חֲמוֹר וָמֵת, פָּטוּר. לֹא כִסָּהוּ כָּרָאוּי, וְנָפַל לְתוֹכוֹ שׁוֹר אוֹ חֲמוֹר וָמֵת, חַיָּב. נָפַל לְפָנָיו מִקּוֹל הַכְּרִיָּה, חַיָּב. לְאַחֲרָיו מִקּוֹל הַכְּרִיָּה, פָּטוּר. נָפַל לְתוֹכוֹ שׁוֹר וְכֵלָיו וְנִשְׁתַּבְּרוּ, חֲמוֹר וְכֵלָיו וְנִתְקָרְעוּ,

כסהו כראוי ונפל לתוכו. כגון שהתליע הכסוי: נפל לפניו מקול הברייה חייב. שהיה חופר בבור, ושמע השור קול פטיש ונבעת, ונפל בבור ומת, חייב. ואף על גב דכיון דמשום גרמא דקול הכרייה נפל, הוה לן למימר דאסתלק חיובא דבור מיניה, ורמיא אפסיעותא דקול הכריה והוה גרמא בעלמא ופטור, אפילו הכי חייב, הואיל ובתוך הבור נמצא הנזק: לאחריו מקול הברייה פטור. אם נבעל השור מקול הכרייה על שפת הבור, ונפל לאחריו חוץ לבור ומת, פטור. שהרי לא נמלא הנזק בבור, וקול הכרייה גרמא בעלמא הוא ופטור: ונשתברו, ונתקרעו. בכלי שור שייך שבירה, ובכלי חמור שייך קריעה, כטול והמחרישה. בכלי חמור שייך קריעה, חבילת בגדים ומרדעת שעל גביו:

The Mishnah now teaches some general laws of a pit (which apply regardless of how many people own it):

כִּסָּהוּ כָּרָאוּי וְנָפַל לְתוֹכוֹ שׁוֹר אוֹ חֲמוֹר וָמֵת — If [the owner of a pit] **covered it properly, and** nevertheless **an ox or a donkey fell into it and died,** because, for example, the cover had become wormy in the meantime, **פָּטוּר** — **he is not obligated** to pay damages, since he covered it properly and was not expected to foresee that it would become wormy.[5] **לֹא כִסָּהוּ כָּרָאוּי וְנָפַל לְתוֹכוֹ שׁוֹר אוֹ חֲמוֹר וָמֵת** — But if **he did not cover [the pit] properly and an ox or a donkey fell into it and died,** **חַיָּב** — he **is obligated** to pay.[6]

The Mishnah considers the law where an animal fell into a pit not because it stepped into the pit's airspace, but because a worker was digging inside a pit and the noise of the digging startled the animal, causing it to fall:

נָפַל לְפָנָיו מִקּוֹל הַכְּרִיָּה — If it was near a pit and **fell forward** into the pit because it was startled **by the noise of the digging,** **חַיָּב** — **[the owner of the pit] is obligated** to pay for the damage. Even though it was the noise (rather than the pit) that caused the animal to fall, the owner of the pit is liable because the damage occurred in his pit. **לְאַחֲרָיו מִקּוֹל הַכְּרִיָּה** — But if the animal fell **backward** onto the ground outside the pit because it was startled **by the noise of the digging,** **פָּטוּר** — **[the owner of the pit] is not obligated** to pay, because in this case the damage happened outside the pit.[7]

The Mishnah discusses what type of damage the owner of a pit is obligated to pay for:

נָפַל לְתוֹכוֹ שׁוֹר וְכֵלָיו וְנִשְׁתַּבְּרוּ — If **an ox fell into it** together **with its gear** (such as its yoke and plow) and the ox was injured **and [the yoke or plow] broke,** **חֲמוֹר וְכֵלָיו וְנִתְקָרְעוּ** — or **a donkey** fell into it together **with its gear** (such as the blanket under its saddle, or a bundle of clothes it was carrying), and the

---

NOTES

5. See previous note.

6. This ruling is obvious. The Gemara (52b) suggests that it is included only to round out this section of the Mishnah. Since the Tanna began the section with "he covered it properly, etc.," he ends it with "he did not cover it properly, etc."

7. In either case, the worker who made the noise does not have to pay, because he caused the damage only indirectly (*Rav*).

חַיָּב עַל הַבְּהֵמָה, וּפָטוּר עַל הַכֵּלִים. נָפַל לְתוֹכוֹ שׁוֹר חֵרֵשׁ, שׁוֹטֶה, וְקָטָן, חַיָּב. בֶּן אוֹ בַת, עֶבֶד אוֹ אָמָה, פָּטוּר.

— רע״ב —

ופטור על הכלים. דכתיב (שמות כא,לג) ונפל שמה שור או חמור, שור ולא אדם, חמור ולא כלים: שור חרש שוטה וקטן חייב. שור שהוא חרש ושהוא שוטה ושהוא קטן, חייב עליו אם נפל לבור. אבל שור שהוא פקח, אינו חייב עליו, דאיבעי ליה לעיוני ומיזל.

---

donkey was injured and [the items] were torn, חַיָּב עַל הַבְּהֵמָה — [the owner of the pit] is obligated to pay for the damage to the animal, וּפָטוּר עַל הַכֵּלִים — but he is not obligated to pay for the damage to the gear. This is because the Torah states (Exodus 21:33-34): *If a man uncovers a pit or digs a pit ... and an ox or a donkey falls there, the owner of the pit shall pay.* By mentioning only animals, the verse implies that he must pay only for damage to animals, and not for damage to their gear (or other objects they are carrying).

The Mishnah defines the type of animal for whose injury or death the owner of a pit must pay:

נָפַל לְתוֹכוֹ שׁוֹר חֵרֵשׁ שׁוֹטֶה וְקָטָן — If an ox that is deaf, foolish, or young (i.e., it has not yet been trained to pull a plow)[8] fell into [a pit] and was injured or it died, חַיָּב — [the owner of the pit] is obligated to pay, because such animals do not take care to avoid pits.[9] But he need not pay for damage done to a normal animal. Since a normal animal looks where it is going and tries to keep away from pits, its falling into a pit is an unexpected occurrence for which the owner of the pit is not responsible.[10]

The verse quoted above, which mentions only animals (*and an ox or a donkey falls there*), excludes not just objects but also people. The Torah thus teaches that even if a person falls into a pit and dies, the owner of the pit is exempt from payment. The Mishnah elaborates upon this law:

בֶּן אוֹ בַת — Even if a young boy or girl עֶבֶד אוֹ אָמָה — or a male Canaanite slave or female Canaanite slave fell into a pit and died, פָּטוּר — [the owner of the pit] is not obligated to pay, because the verse implies that he must pay only for the death of animals, and not for the death of any people, regardless of their age or status.[11]

NOTES

8. *Meiri.* Before an ox has been trained to pull a plow, it runs about wildly and does not avoid obstacles.

9. The same law applies to an animal walking at night, or a blind one even during the day (*Tiferes Yisrael*).

10. This ruling applies only where the pit is open, in which case a normal ox would see the pit and walk around it. If, however, it is covered (but the cover is not strong enough to prevent an ox from falling in), an ox cannot be expected to see the danger. Therefore, if an ox stepped on the cover and fell into the pit, the owner of the pit must pay damages (*Rosh*).

[Only animals are expected to avoid obstacles when they are walking. People are less likely to avoid obstacles, because they are often busy with their thoughts and do not pay attention to where they are going (see Mishnah 3:1). Accordingly, if any person, even one who is mature and sane, falls into a pit and is injured, the owner of the pit cannot claim that this was an unexpected accident (*Meiri* to 27b).]

11. Although this law applies to all people,

— רע"ב —

(ז) אחד שור ואחד כל
בהמה לנפילת הבור.
דכתיב (שמות כא,לד) כסף
ישיב לבעליו, לכל מידי דאית
ליה בעלים: ולהפרשת הר
סיני. דכתיב (שם יט,יג) אם בהמה אם איש לא יחיה, וחיה בכלל בהמה. אם, לרבות את העופות:
לתשלומי כפל. כדכתיב (שם כב,ח) על כל דבר פשע, כל מידי דבר פשיעה הוא: להשבת אבידה.
לכל אבדת אחיך (דברים כב,ג):

[ז] **אֶחָד** שוֹר וְאֶחָד כָּל בְּהֵמָה לִנְפִילַת הַבּוֹר, וּלְהַפְרָשַׁת הַר סִינַי, וּלְתַשְׁלוּמֵי כֶפֶל, וְלַהֲשָׁבַת אֲבֵידָה,

---

[7] Although the verse that speaks of damage caused by a pit mentions only an *ox* and a *donkey* (see previous Mishnah), this Mishnah teaches that the verse's laws apply to other animals as well. The Mishnah then goes on to teach that the same is true of other verses in the Torah that mention only certain animals.

אֶחָד שׁוֹר וְאֶחָד כָּל בְּהֵמָה — **The same** law that applies to **an ox** applies **also** to any **domestic animal**[1] in regard to the following laws: לִנְפִילַת הַבּוֹר — (1) paying damages for **its falling into a pit,** וּלְהַפְרָשַׁת הַר סִינַי — (2) **separation** from **Mount Sinai** at the Giving of the Torah,[2] וּלְתַשְׁלוּמֵי כֶפֶל — (3) **the double payment** that a thief must make for stealing an animal,[3] וְלַהֲשָׁבַת אֲבֵידָה —

NOTES
---

the Mishnah mentions only children and Canaanite slaves. It mentions children in order to teach that although children cannot be expected to avoid obstacles, and thus the blame for their death lies with the owner of the pit, the Torah exempts him from payment (*Tos. Yom Tov*). And it mentions Canaanite slaves in order to teach that although they are owned by others, the law exempting the owner from payment for the death of people applies to Canaanite slaves as well, since they, too, are people (see *Tiferes Yisrael* and *Tosefos R' Akiva Eiger*).

The owner of a pit is exempt only where the victim died. If the victim was merely injured, the owner must pay. This is because the verse that mentions an ox and a donkey — from which it is derived that no payment is required for people and objects — speaks of an ox or a donkey that *died* (*Exodus* 21:33-34). Thus, when this verse excludes people, it refers only to people who died and not to those who were injured. As far as objects are concerned, the owner of the pit is exempt even if they just broke, because the breaking of an object is equivalent to its "death" (*Tos. Yom Tov* ד"ה ופטור).

[7]
1. The term בְּהֵמָה refers to domestic animals, such as cows, sheep, and goats. The Mishnah states below that wild animals and birds are also included.

2. When the *Shechinah* (Divine Presence) rested upon Mount Sinai, animals and people were not allowed to go on the mountain or even to touch its edge, as it is stated: *Beware of ascending the mountain or touching its edge; whoever touches the mountain ... whether animal* (בְּהֵמָה) *or person, he shall not live* (*Exodus* 19:12-13). Although the Torah uses the word בְּהֵמָה (domestic animal), the prohibition applied to all types of animals.

3. The Torah commands a thief to pay the owner "double" — that is, the item he stole (or its value) plus an additional fine of the same amount. The source for this double payment is the verse (22:3 there): *If the theft shall be found in his possession, whether it is a live ox or a donkey or a seh* [a word that refers to sheep and goats], *he shall pay double*. This law, too, pertains to all animals, despite the fact that the verse mentions only certain species.

[In fact, the double payment must be made even by one who steals an inanimate object, as stated in Mishnah 7:1. The double-payment obligation is nevertheless listed here, because this is

משניות בבא קמא / פרק ה: שור שנגח

לִפְרִיקָה, לַחֲסִימָה, לְכִלְאַיִם, וּלְשַׁבָּת.

— רע"ב —

לפריקה. עזוב תעזוב עמו (שמות כג,ה). אף על גב דכתיב (שם) חמור שונאך, כל בהמה בכלל, דילפינן חמור חמור משבת (גמרא נד,ב), שנאמר בו (דברים ה,יד) שורך וחמורך וכל בהמתך: לחסימה. לא תחסום שור בדישו (שם כה,ד), ילפינן שור שור משבת (גמרא נד,ב): לכלאים. הרבעתה, אף על גב דכתיב (ויקרא יט,יט) בהמתך לא תרביע כלאים, הוי נמי חיה ועוף בכלל, דילפינן בהמה בהמה משבת (גמרא נד,ב). וכן לענין כלאים דהנהגה דלא תחרוש בשור ובחמור יחדיו (דברים כב,י), ילפינן שור שור משבת (גמרא נד,ב), דהוא הדין לכל שני מינים של בהמה חיה ועוף. ומיהו לענין פסק ההלכה, מן התורה אינו חייב אלא כשחורש ומנהיג בשני מינים, שאחד טמא ואחד טהור, דומיא דשור וחמור. אלא שאסרו חכמים כל שני מינים, בין שניהם טמאים, בין שניהם טהורים: ולשבת. דכתיב (דברים ה,יד) שורך וחמורך וכל בהמתך, והיה בכלל בהמה. וכל, רבויא הוא לרבות עופות:

---

(4) **returning a lost [animal]**,[4] לִפְרִיקָה — (5) **unloading** a burden from an animal,[5] לַחֲסִימָה — (6) the prohibition of **muzzling** an animal when it is threshing grain,[6] לְכִלְאַיִם — (7) the prohibition of **kilayim**, i.e., mating or plowing with two different species of animals together,[7] וּלְשַׁבָּת — and (8) the prohibition of having one's animals work on **Shabbos**.[8] In every one of these eight cases, the same rules that apply to an ox (or the other animals mentioned in the various verses) apply to *all* domestic animals.[9]

NOTES

another example of a verse that specifies certain animals and yet its law does not apply to them alone (*Raavad*).]

4. It is a mitzvah to return a lost object to its owner, as the Torah states: *You shall not see the ox of your brother or his seh* [sheep or goat] *going astray, and hide yourself from them; you shall surely return them to your brother* (*Deuteronomy* 22:1). The Mishnah teaches that the mitzvah applies to all types of animals.

[Here, too, even inanimate objects are included, as verse 3 there states: *So shall you do for any lost article of your brother* (*Rav*; see previous note).]

5. One must help to unload a burden from an animal that is struggling beneath it, as the Torah states: *If you see the donkey of your enemy ... sitting under its load, would you refrain from helping him [unload it]? You must surely help with him* (*Exodus* 23:5). The obligation applies to all animals, not just donkeys (*Rav*).

[There is a parallel mitzvah to help someone *load* an animal whose burden has fallen off. Regarding this mitzvah as well, although the Torah mentions only an ox and a donkey (*Deuteronomy* 22:4),

all animals are included (*Tiferes Yisrael*).]

6. The Torah (*Deuteronomy* 25:4) commands: *You shall not muzzle an ox when it is threshing* (or performing other kinds of agricultural labor). This prohibition applies to all animals, not just oxen.

7. There are two prohibitions that concern the "mixing" of two types of animals. The Torah forbids mating different species of animals together, as it states: *You shall not mate your animal* (בְּהֶמְתְּךָ) *with another species* (*Leviticus* 19:19). It also forbids making different species work together: *You shall not plow with an ox and a donkey together* (*Deuteronomy* 22:10). All types of animals are included in both prohibitions.

8. It is written (*Deuteronomy* 5:14): *But the seventh day is Shabbos to Hashem, your God. You shall not do any work — you, your son, your daughter, your male slave, your female slave, your ox, your donkey, and your every animal* (בְּהֶמָה). This prohibition applies to all living creatures, even wild animals and birds (*Rav*), as the Mishnah teaches below.

9. The Gemara (54b) derives from verses referring to these laws that they apply to all creatures (see *Rav*).

[79] MISHNAH BAVA KAMMA / Chapter 5: *Shor Shenagach*

וְכֵן חַיָּה וָעוֹף כַּיּוֹצֵא בָהֶן. אִם כֵּן, לָמָּה נֶאֱמַר שׁוֹר אוֹ חֲמוֹר, אֶלָּא שֶׁדִּבֶּר הַכָּתוּב בַּהֹוֶה.

— רע״ב —
שֶׁדִּבֶּר הַכָּתוּב בַּהֹוֶה.
בְּדָבָר הָרָגִיל לִהְיוֹת:

וְכֵן חַיָּה וָעוֹף כַּיּוֹצֵא בָהֶן — **Furthermore, any wild beast or bird is the same as [domestic animals]** in these matters.

The Mishnah explains why the Torah mentions only certain animals:

אִם כֵּן לָמָּה נֶאֱמַר שׁוֹר אוֹ חֲמוֹר — **If so**, that the law about damage done by a pit applies to all other animals and birds, **why is it stated "an *ox* or *donkey*"?** אֶלָּא שֶׁדִּבֶּר הַכָּתוּב בַּהֹוֶה — It **is only because the verse speaks about the usual** case. That is, the Torah mentions the ox and the donkey because it was common for these animals to walk freely in the streets, where they might fall into a pit.[10] Similarly, to illustrate each of the laws listed above, the Torah chose the most common examples.

NOTES

10. Since oxen were used for threshing grain (and other field work) and donkeys were used to carry burdens, these animals were frequently on the streets (*Shoshanim LeDavid*).

Chapter Six

משניות בבא קמא / פרק ו: הכונס

[א] הַכּוֹנֵס צֹאן לַדִּיר וְנָעַל בְּפָנֶיהָ כָּרָאוּי, וְיָצְאָה וְהִזִּיקָה, פָּטוּר. לֹא נָעַל בְּפָנֶיהָ כָּרָאוּי, וְיָצְאָה וְהִזִּיקָה, חַיָּב. נִפְרְצָה בַלַּיְלָה, אוֹ שֶׁפְּרָצוּהָ לִסְטִים, וְיָצְאָה וְהִזִּיקָה פָּטוּר.

— רע״ב —

פרק ששי – הכונס.
(א) הכונס. פטור. דהא נטרה, ומאי הוי ליה למעבד:

---

[1] After discussing damage caused by a pit (*bor*), the tractate returns to the subject of damage done by an animal, either through eating (*shein*) or through walking (*regel*).

As a rule, if the owner of an animal secured it but it nevertheless escaped and did damage, he does not have to pay. This Mishnah defines how well a person must secure his animal in order to be exempt from payment:

הַכּוֹנֵס צֹאן לַדִּיר וְנָעַל בְּפָנֶיהָ כָּרָאוּי — If someone brought his **sheep into a pen and locked** the gate **before it properly** (i.e., the gate can withstand a normal wind), but an unusually strong wind blew it open, **וְיָצְאָה וְהִזִּיקָה** — **and [the sheep] got out and damaged** another person's property, **פָּטוּר** — **he is not obligated** to pay for the damage, because he fulfilled his duty by locking it up in a way that would secure it in normal circumstances.[1] **לֹא נָעַל בְּפָנֶיהָ כָּרָאוּי** — But if **he did not lock** the gate **before it properly** (i.e., the gate cannot withstand even a normal wind), **וְיָצְאָה וְהִזִּיקָה** — **and it got out and did damage**, **חַיָּב** — **he is obligated** to pay, because he locked it up in a way that would not work even in normal circumstances.

Having ruled about a sheep that escaped through the gate of its pen, the Mishnah now rules about one that escaped through a hole in the wall:

נִפְרְצָה בַלַּיְלָה אוֹ שֶׁפְּרָצוּהָ לִסְטִים — If the owner of the sheep locked the pen properly but **[its wall] was breached** in an unexpected manner[2] **at night, or robbers breached it** at night, **וְיָצְאָה וְהִזִּיקָה** — **and it got out** through the gap in the wall **and damaged** another person's property, **פָּטוּר** — **he is not obligated** to pay for the damage, because the wall broke through no fault of his own.[3]

NOTES

[1]
1. Although the owner of an animal must prevent it from doing damage, it is enough for him to use methods that are effective in normal circumstances. He does not have to secure it in a "superior" way, which prevents the animal from doing damage even in circumstances that are unusual. Even R' Meir, who requires "superior" security (Mishnah 4:9), applies that standard only in the case of preventing a *muad* from doing *keren* damage. He agrees that normal supervision is enough with respect to *regel* and *shein* (see Gemara 55b).

2. The wall was sturdy but the sheep somehow made a hole in it or it collapsed by itself [because of some unforeseeable circumstance] (*Tiferes Yisrael*).

3. The owner is exempt from payment only if the wall was breached at night (as implied by the Mishnah). Since a hole in a wall is unlikely to be seen at night, the owner presumably did not know about it. Therefore, he cannot be blamed for failing to run after his escaped animal and prevent it from doing damage. But if the wall was breached in the daytime, when people would have seen and told the owner, he is obligated to recover the animal, and if he fails to do so, he is responsible for what it does (*Tos. Yom Tov*). In the Mishnah's previous case, where

[83] **MISHNAH BAVA KAMMA** / Chapter 6: *Hakoneis* 6/2

— רע״ב —

הוֹצִיאוּהָ לִסְטִים, לִסְטִים חַיָּבִים.

[ב] הִנִּיחָהּ בַּחַמָּה, אוֹ שֶׁמְּסָרָהּ לְחֵרֵשׁ, שׁוֹטֶה, וְקָטָן, וְיָצְאָה וְהִזִּיקָה,

הוציאוה לסטים. אף על גב דלא הוליאוה ממש, אלא שעמדו בפניה עד שילאה, הוי כאילו הוליאוה בידים, וחייבים:
(ב) הניחה בחמה. מלערה לה שמשא, ולא סגי לה בנעילה כראוי, שהיא בדלת שיכולה לעמוד ברוח מלויה בלבד:

In the previous case, neither the owner nor the robbers have to pay for the damage done by the sheep. The owner is exempt because he secured the sheep properly, and the robbers are exempt because they do not own the sheep and they caused the damage only indirectly.[4] The Mishnah now presents a case in which the robbers *are* obligated to pay:

הוֹצִיאוּהָ לִסְטִים — If the **robbers took it out** of the pen and it damaged someone's property, לִסְטִים חַיָּבִים — the **robbers are obligated** to pay for the damage. By taking it out, they performed an act of acquisition (*kinyan*) with the animal, which makes it theirs in certain ways, including giving them the responsibility to prevent it from doing damage.[5]

[2] The Mishnah continues with the laws of preventing an animal from doing damage:

הִנִּיחָהּ בַּחַמָּה — If he locked up his sheep in its pen properly[1] but **left it in the** hot **sun,** אוֹ שֶׁמְּסָרָהּ לְחֵרֵשׁ שׁוֹטֶה וְקָטָן — or **if he handed it over to a deaf-mute, an insane person, or a minor** (that is, he had one of these people watch the sheep for him), וְיָצְאָה וְהִזִּיקָה — **and it escaped and did damage,**

--- NOTES ---

the gate was blown open, there is no difference between day and night. People who see an open gate do not realize that anything is wrong and would not say anything to the owner. Even in the daytime, then, he might not have known that the gate was open, and so we cannot hold him liable for failing to retrieve the animal (*Tiferes Yisrael*).

4. Only the owner of an animal is liable for damage that he indirectly caused it to do (for example, he failed to secure it properly and it got out and did damage). Anyone else is not liable unless he made the animal do damage directly. In our case, the robbers are neither the owners, nor did they cause the animal to do damage directly; thus, they are not required to pay.

5. When one buys something, he does not acquire it until he performs a *kinyan* (act of acquisition) with it. Similarly, if one takes something from another person without permission, he has not committed "theft," which makes him responsible for the stolen object, until he performs a *kinyan*. There are several types of *kinyanim* (acts of acquisition) that can be performed with an animal. One is the simple act of pulling the animal, which is called *meshichah* (pulling). In the Mishnah's case, therefore, after the robbers took the sheep out of the pen (thus performing *meshichah*), they are responsible to prevent it from doing damage, and if it does do damage, they must pay (*Tos. Yom Tov*).

[It is not necessary for the robbers to actually pull the animal or otherwise make it walk. Even if they just surrounded it in such a way that it could go in only one direction (*Rav*), they are considered to have performed a *kinyan*. The Sages decreed that this is a *kinyan* in order to punish the robbers (*Tos. Yom Tov*, explaining *Rav*).]

[2]

1. He locked the pen with a gate that can withstand a normal wind.

[84] מִשְׁנָיוֹת בָּבָא קַמָּא / פֶּרֶק ו: הַכּוֹנֵס

— רע״ב —

חַיָּב. מְסָרָהּ לְרוֹעֶה, נִכְנַס רוֹעֶה תַחְתָּיו. נָפְלָה לְגִנָּה וְנֶהֱנֵית, מְשַׁלֶּמֶת מַה שֶׁנֶּהֱנֵית.

נכנס הרועה תחתיו. ולא אמרינן בכהאי גוונא שומר שמסר לשומר חייב, שדרך הרועה הגדול למסור לרועה הקטן שתחתיו, ולפיכך הרועה שתחתיו חייב: נפלה לגינה. וכגון שהוחלקה ונפלה באונס. אבל דחו חותה חברותיה והפילוה, משלם מה שהזיקה, דהיינו פשע בה, דהוי ליה לעבורינהו חדא חדא: מה שנהנית. לפי הנאתה ולא לפי הזיקה:

חַיָּב — [the owner] is obligated to pay for the damage, because he acted negligently by leaving the sheep out in the sun[2] or entrusting it to an unreliable person. **מְסָרָהּ לְרוֹעֶה** — But if **he handed it over to** a normal, adult **shepherd**, **נִכְנַס רוֹעֶה תַחְתָּיו** — **the shepherd takes the place of [the owner]**, which means that the shepherd must pay for any damage, and not the owner.[3]

The Mishnah discusses the law where an animal damaged growing produce: **נָפְלָה לְגִנָּה וְנֶהֱנֵית** — If it accidentally **fell into a garden**[4] where crops were growing, damaged the crops, **and benefited** from the damage it caused,[5] **מְשַׁלֶּמֶת מַה שֶׁנֶּהֱנֵית** — **he must pay what it benefited** from the crops, but he does not have to pay for the damage, because the animal's fall into the garden was an unforeseeable accident, for which he is not responsible.[6]

NOTES

2. Although the gate would not fall as a result of a normal wind, it might not be able to withstand the desperate attempts of an overheated sheep to break out. Therefore, using such a gate is negligent if the animal will be exposed to the sun (Rav).

3. Only the shepherd is obligated to pay damages. The owner is not liable because he took care of the animal properly by entrusting it to a reliable person.

   The Gemara (56b) objects that these laws have already been taught in Mishnah 4:9. Therefore, the Gemara explains that the Mishnah refers to a special case, where the owner entrusted his sheep to a shepherd, and then that shepherd gave it to his assistant to watch. The general rule is that if the owner of an object entrusts it to a *shomer* (the term for someone who watches the property of another), and the *shomer* hands it over to another *shomer*, the first *shomer* remains responsible for the object, because the owner did not give him permission to entrust it to anyone else. In our case, then, the first shepherd should remain responsible for the sheep even after he gave it to his assistant. The Mishnah teaches that this is not so; rather, the first shepherd ceases to be responsible, and the assistant takes his place. Since it is standard practice for a shepherd to entrust his sheep to his assistants, the owner of the sheep presumably expected this to happen, and it is as though he gave permission. The responsibility for the sheep was thus transferred to the assistant, and it is he who must pay for any damage (Rav). [When the Mishnah says, מְסָרָהּ לְרוֹעֶה, נִכְנַס רוֹעֶה תַחְתָּיו, he handed it over to a shepherd, the shepherd takes his place, it means that if the first shepherd handed it over to a second shepherd (i.e., his assistant), the second shepherd takes the place of the first one (see Gemara 56b).]

4. For example, the sheep was walking on its owner's roof that is next to the garden, or in a public area that is above the garden, and it accidentally slipped (Rashi).

5. For example, the crops cushioned the sheep's fall and thereby saved it from injury, or the sheep ate the crops (*Tiferes Yisrael*, from Gemara 58a).

6. Although the owner does not have to pay for causing damage (מַזִּיק), he must pay for what he benefited (נֶהֱנֶה). It is a general rule that whenever someone benefits from the property of another and thereby causes the owner some loss, he must pay at least for the benefit.

— רע״ב —

שָׁמִין בֵּית סְאָה בְּאוֹתָהּ שָׂדֶה. אֵין שָׁמִין אֶת הָעֲרוּגָה לְבַדָּהּ, מִפְּנֵי שֶׁמַּפְסִיד מַזִּיק, שֶׁשָּׁמִין אוֹתָהּ בְּכָל שָׁוֶה, וְרַחֲמָנָא אָמַר (שמות כב,ד) וּבִעֵר בִּשְׂדֵה אַחֵר, וְדָרְשִׁינַן

יָרְדָה כְּדַרְכָּהּ וְהִזִּיקָה, מְשַׁלֶּמֶת מַה שֶּׁהִזִּיקָה. כֵּיצַד מְשַׁלֶּמֶת מַה שֶּׁהִזִּיקָה, שָׁמִין בֵּית סְאָה בְּאוֹתָהּ שָׂדֶה כַּמָּה הָיְתָה יָפָה וְכַמָּה הִיא יָפָה. רַבִּי שִׁמְעוֹן אוֹמֵר, אָכְלָה פֵּרוֹת גְּמוּרִים,

(נח,ב) מְלַמֵּד שֶׁשָּׁמִין אוֹתָהּ עַל גַּב שָׂדֶה אַחֶרֶת. אֶלָּא שָׁמִין בֵּית סְאָה בְּאוֹתָהּ שָׂדֶה, כַּמָּה הָיְתָה שָׁוֶה קוֹדֶם שֶׁנֶּאֶכְלָה מִמֶּנָּה הָעֲרוּגָה הַזֹּאת, וְכַמָּה הִיא שָׁוֶה עַכְשָׁיו, וְהִשְׁתָּא לֹא מְשַׁלֵּם כֻּלָּהּ דָּמֶיהָ, דְּמֵי שְׁלוּקָה בֵּית סְאָה כְּשֶׁהִיא בִּתְבוּאָתָהּ, אֵינוֹ מוֹזִיל בָּהּ בִּשְׁבִיל הֶפְסֵד עֲרוּגָה אַחַת, כִּי אִם דָּבָר מוּעָט: רַבִּי שִׁמְעוֹן אוֹמֵר אָכְלָה פֵּירוֹת גְּמוּרִים. שֶׁכְּבָר בְּטֵלוּ כָּל צָרְכָּן, מְשַׁלֶּמֶת כָּל הַהֶזֵּק. וְהֵיכָא שַׁיְּימִינַן לְגַב שָׂדֶה, הֵיכָא דְּעַדַיִן לֹא נִגְמְרוּ. וַהֲלָכָה כְּרַבִּי שִׁמְעוֹן:

יָרְדָה כְּדַרְכָּהּ וְהִזִּיקָה — However, if the sheep did not fall, rather **it went down** to the neighboring garden **in its usual manner and it did damage** there, **מְשַׁלֶּמֶת מַה שֶּׁהִזִּיקָה** — **he pays** the full value of **what it damaged**, because in this case he was negligent in letting the sheep enter the garden.

The Mishnah explains how we assess damage done to a crop that was attached to the ground:

כֵּיצַד מְשַׁלֶּמֶת מַה שֶּׁהִזִּיקָה — **How** much **does he pay for what it damaged?** **שָׁמִין בֵּית סְאָה בְּאוֹתָהּ שָׂדֶה כַּמָּה הָיְתָה יָפָה** — **We assess how much a** *beis se'ah* of land (a relatively large area)[7] **in that field was worth** before the animal damaged the produce of a small part of it, **וְכַמָּה הִיא יָפָה** — **and how much** [that *beis se'ah*] **is worth** after the damage. The owner of the animal pays the difference.[8]

According to the previous Tanna, the owner does not pay the cost of the damaged produce, but only the reduction in the value of the land. The next Tanna basically agrees with this rule, but he makes the following exception:

רַבִּי שִׁמְעוֹן אוֹמֵר — **R' Shimon says:** **אָכְלָה פֵּרוֹת גְּמוּרִים** — **If it ate ripe**

— NOTES —

How to calculate the benefit that the sheep received depends on how the crops were damaged. If they were eaten, the sheep's owner must pay what it would have cost him to feed his animal with cheap animal food (see Mishnah 2:2 note 3). If they were crushed by the sheep's fall, the owner is liable for the amount he would have paid to cushion his animal's fall and prevent it from being injured (*Meiri* 57b).

7. A *beis se'ah* is an area of 2,500 square *amos*. When in the shape of a square, it measures 50 x 50 *amos*.

8. We do not assess the value of the eaten produce itself (that is, how much money such produce costs in the market); instead, we assess how much the *land* went down in value because some of its produce was eaten. This is much less than the value of the produce on its own. Furthermore, although the animal ate the produce of only a small area of land, we do not reckon how much the value of that small area was reduced. It is derived from the Torah that we look at a *beis se'ah* in which that small area was located, and we reckon how much the entire *beis se'ah* went down in value. This makes the payment even lower, because someone buying an entire *beis se'ah* does not care all that much if the produce of a small area within it was eaten (*Rav*).

מְשַׁלֶּמֶת פֵּרוֹת גְּמוּרִים, אִם סְאָה סְאָה, אִם סָאתַיִם סָאתָיִם.

[ג] הַמַּגְדִּישׁ בְּתוֹךְ שָׂדֶה שֶׁל חֲבֵירוֹ שֶׁלֹּא בִרְשׁוּת, וַאֲכָלָתַן בְּהֶמְתּוֹ שֶׁל בַּעַל הַשָּׂדֶה פָּטוּר. וְאִם הֻזְּקָה בָּהֶן, בַּעַל הַגָּדִישׁ חַיָּב. וְאִם הִגְדִּישׁ בִּרְשׁוּת, בַּעַל הַשָּׂדֶה חַיָּב.

— רע״ב —

(ג) וְאִם הִגְדִּישׁ בִּרְשׁוּת בַּעַל הַשָּׂדֶה חַיָּב. בַּגְּמָרָא (נט,ג) מוּקֵי לָהּ בְּבִקְטָה, שֶׁרְגִילִין כּוּלָּן לַעֲשׂוֹת בְּגוֹרֶן אֶחָד זֶה גָּדִישׁוֹ וְזֶה גָּדִישׁוֹ, וּמַמְּנִין שׁוֹמֵר. וְכֵיוָן שֶׁאָמַר הַשּׁוֹמֵר טַיֵּיל וְגָדוֹשׁ, הָוֵי כְּאִילּוּ אָמַר טַיֵּיל וְאֶנְטוֹר לָךְ.

אֲבָל בִּשְׁאָר בְּנֵי אָדָם, אֲפִילּוּ הִגְדִּישׁ בִּרְשׁוּת, אֵין בַּעַל הַשָּׂדֶה חַיָּב עַד דִּמְקַבֵּל עֲלֵיהּ נְטִירוּתָא:

מְשַׁלֶּמֶת פֵּרוֹת גְּמוּרִים — produce, which is ready to be harvested and sold, he pays the value of the **ripe produce;** **אִם סְאָה סְאָה** — for example, if the animal ate a *se'ah* of produce, he pays the price of a *se'ah* of produce; **אִם סָאתַיִם סָאתָיִם** — and if it ate two *se'ahs* of produce, he pays the price of two *se'ahs* of produce. This Tanna holds that damage done to *ripe* produce (which no longer needs the ground) is assessed according to the value of the produce itself. Only damage to *unripe* produce (which still needs to be attached to the ground) is assessed according to the value of the land.

[3] The Mishnah continues to discuss damage that an animal does by eating (*shein*):

הַמַּגְדִּישׁ בְּתוֹךְ שָׂדֶה שֶׁל חֲבֵירוֹ שֶׁלֹּא בִרְשׁוּת — If someone made **stacks** of his grain in his neighbor's field without permission, **וַאֲכָלָתַן בְּהֶמְתּוֹ שֶׁל בַּעַל הַשָּׂדֶה** — and an animal belonging to the owner of the field ate from them, **פָּטוּר** — [the owner of the field] is not obligated to pay for the eaten grain because the owner of the grain had no right to put it there. **וְאִם הֻזְּקָה בָּהֶן** — And if [the landowner's animal] was damaged by [the stacks], for example, it slipped on them and was injured, **בַּעַל הַגָּדִישׁ חַיָּב** — the owner of the stack **is obligated** to pay for the damage to the animal, since he created a hazard (*bor*) in his neighbor's field without permission.[1] **וְאִם הִגְדִּישׁ בִּרְשׁוּת** — But if someone made stacks of his grain in his neighbor's field with permission, and an animal belonging to the owner of the field ate from them, **בַּעַל הַשָּׂדֶה חַיָּב** — the owner of the field is obligated to pay for the eaten grain, because, by allowing the grain to be stored in his field, he presumably agreed to protect the grain from damage, even though he did not say so explicitly.[2]

NOTES

[3]
1. These laws were already taught in Mishnah 5:2. They are repeated here in order to teach that one may not place his produce even in an open field unless he has the landowner's permission (*Tiferes Yisrael*).

2. The Tanna of our Mishnah seems to hold that whenever a landowner allows things to be stored on his property, it is assumed that he accepts the responsibility to protect them from harm. In Mishnah 5:3, however, Rebbi ruled that the owner of a courtyard does *not* automatically become responsible to protect an ox (or other item) that he allows on his property. To bring our Mishnah in line with Rebbi's ruling, the Gemara (59b) explains our Mishnah as referring to a special case, namely, where the farmers

[ד] **הַשּׁוֹלֵחַ** אֶת הַבְּעֵרָה בְּיַד חֵרֵשׁ, שׁוֹטֶה, וְקָטָן, פָּטוּר בְּדִינֵי אָדָם, וְחַיָּב בְּדִינֵי שָׁמַיִם. שָׁלַח בְּיַד פִּקֵּחַ, הַפִּקֵּחַ חַיָּב.

[4] Having completed its discussion of damage caused by animals, the Mishnah turns to the laws of damage caused by fire:

הַשּׁוֹלֵחַ אֶת הַבְּעֵרָה בְּיַד חֵרֵשׁ שׁוֹטֶה וְקָטָן — **If someone sent** a **source of fire** (e.g., a hot coal)[1] **in the hands of a deaf-mute, an insane person, or a minor,** who fanned it into a fire and burned another person's property with it, **פָּטוּר בְּדִינֵי אָדָם** — the one who sent the source of the fire is **not obligated** to pay **under the laws of man,** since he did not make the fire,[2] **וְחַיָּב בְּדִינֵי שָׁמַיִם** — **but he is obligated** to pay **under the laws of Heaven,** because he was an indirect cause of the damage.[3] **שָׁלַח בְּיַד פִּקֵּחַ** — If **he sent** it **in the hands of a competent person,** who burned another person's property with it, **הַפִּקֵּחַ חַיָּב** — the **competent person is obligated** to pay for the damage (even under the laws of man), and the one who sent it is completely exempt (even under the laws of Heaven).[4]

―――――― NOTES ――――――

of the area would stack their grain in one person's field each year, and they would appoint him to guard it. Even if the owner of that field only said, "Bring your grain into my field," without adding, "and I will guard it," Rebbi would agree that he presumably agrees to guard it (*Rav, Meiri*).

[4]

1. *Tiferes Yisrael,* from Gemara 22b.

2. Although one must guard his fire to prevent it from doing damage (just as he must guard his animal to prevent it from doing damage), the first person in the Mishnah's case is not liable because he did not have a fire; he had only a hot coal, which is not considered a damaging force, like a fire. It was the deaf mute, the insane person, or the minor who made the coal into a damaging force.

However, if the first person handed over a fire or even just a flame (e.g., a burning candle) to a deaf-mute, he is certainly liable for any damage that it causes, since it was his fire and he failed to guard it properly. This is like handing over one's animal to a deaf-mute, where the law is that the owner must pay, as taught in Mishnah 2 (*Tiferes Yisrael;* see Gemara 22b with *Rashi*).

3. "Obligated under the laws of Heaven"

means that the person has a religious duty to pay, and if he fails to do so, he is a thief (*Meiri* 56b); however, the court cannot force him to pay. Of course, the deaf-mute, insane person, or minor is not obligated at all, since he is not responsible for his actions (*Meiri* 59b).

4. The first person is completely exempt because he entrusted it to a person of sound mind, who can be relied upon to prevent it from causing damage. This is true not only where he gave him a hot coal but even where he gave him a flame, such as a burning candle (*Meiri*).

Furthermore, the first person is exempt even if he *told* the second one to do the damage, This is despite the fact that the second person would then be serving as his agent, and the rule is that the actions of an agent are viewed as though they were done by the one who sent him [שְׁלוּחוֹ שֶׁל אָדָם כְּמוֹתוֹ, *The agent of a person is like himself*]. Since the first person told him to commit a sin (damaging the property of another), he can say, "I did not expect him to listen to my instructions rather than the instructions of God." Therefore, if the agent goes ahead and does the damage, it is his decision and only he is responsible [אֵין שָׁלִיחַ לִדְבַר עֲבֵרָה, *There is no agent for a matter of sin*] (*Tos. Yom Tov*).

[88] משניות בבא קמא / פרק ו: הכונס

אֶחָד הֵבִיא אֶת הָאוּר וְאֶחָד הֵבִיא אֶת הָעֵצִים, הַמֵּבִיא אֶת הָעֵצִים חַיָּב. אֶחָד הֵבִיא אֶת הָעֵצִים, וְאֶחָד הֵבִיא אֶת הָאוּר, הַמֵּבִיא אֶת הָאוּר חַיָּב. בָּא אַחֵר וְלִבָּה, הַמְלַבֶּה חַיָּב, לִבְּתָה הָרוּחַ, כּוּלָּן פְּטוּרִין. הַשּׁוֹלֵחַ אֶת הַבְּעֵרָה וְאָכְלָה עֵצִים, אוֹ אֲבָנִים, אוֹ עָפָר, חַיָּב שֶׁנֶּאֱמַר,

— רע״ב —

(ד) בא אחר וליבה. נפח באש והעלה שלהבת, כמו בלבת אש (שמות ג,ב). ואית ספרים דגרסי נבה, מגזרת ניב שפתים (ישעיה נז,יט), כאחדס מדבר מנענע בשפתיו ורוח יוצא: או עפר. שלחכה נירו ונתקלקל:

The Mishnah determines who is liable when a number of people contributed to making a fire:

וְאֶחָד הֵבִיא אֶת הָעֵצִים — אֶחָד הֵבִיא אֶת הָאוּר — If one person brought a flame, — and one person brought wood and put it on the flame, thus creating a fire that could spread and do damage, הַמֵּבִיא אֶת הָעֵצִים חַיָּב — the one who brought the wood is obligated to pay for any damage done by the fire, because he was the one who made it capable of doing damage. The one who brought the flame, however, is exempt from payment, since his flame on its own would not have done any harm.[5] אֶחָד הֵבִיא אֶת הָעֵצִים — In the opposite case, where one person brought wood, וְאֶחָד הֵבִיא אֶת הָאוּר — and one person brought a flame and set the wood alight, הַמֵּבִיא אֶת הָאוּר חַיָּב — the one who brought the flame is certainly obligated to pay for any damage done by the fire (since he alone created it), while the one who brought the wood is exempt.[6] בָּא אַחֵר וְלִבָּה — However, in either of the previous cases, if the flame did not set the wood alight, and then another person then came and blew it into a fire that could do damage,[7] הַמְלַבֶּה חַיָּב — the one who blew it is obligated to pay, and the others are exempt. לִבְּתָה הָרוּחַ כּוּלָּן פְּטוּרִין — If the damaging fire was created only because an unusually strong wind blew it, all three of them are exempt.[8]

Other laws about damage caused by fire:

הַשּׁוֹלֵחַ אֶת הַבְּעֵרָה — If someone sent a fire, that is, he lit a fire within his own premises and it spread to someone else's property, וְאָכְלָה עֵצִים אוֹ אֲבָנִים אוֹ עָפָר — where it consumed wood, blackened stones, or scorched the earth,[9] חַיָּב — he is obligated to pay damages, שֶׁנֶּאֱמַר — because it is stated

---
NOTES

5. Tos. Yom Tov.
6. [Here, it is even more apparent that the first person is exempt and the second one is liable, because the first one merely brought wood, rather than a flame, while the second person brought a flame and set the wood alight.]
7. Tiferes Yisrael.
8. Since they were not required to expect such a wind, they are not obligated to pay for any resulting damage (Tos. Yom Tov).
  In all the preceding cases, the last person is liable only if the fire he created was capable of spreading in a usual wind (Tiferes Yisrael).
9. The fire scorched the surface of a plowed field and damaged it (Rav). Since the earth is now dry and hard, the owner has to plow it again (Rashi to Exodus 22:5).

— רע״ב —

או דרך הרבים. **שש** כִּי תֵצֵא אֵשׁ וּמָצְאָה קוֹצִים וְנֶאֱכַל גָּדִישׁ אוֹ
עשרה אמה, כדגלי המדבר: הַקָּמָה אוֹ הַשָּׂדֶה, שַׁלֵּם יְשַׁלֵּם הַמַּבְעִר אֶת
הַבְּעֵרָה. עָבְרָה גָּדֵר שֶׁהוּא גָבוֹהַּ אַרְבַּע אַמּוֹת, אוֹ דֶרֶךְ הָרַבִּים,
אוֹ נָהָר, פָּטוּר. הַמַּדְלִיק בְּתוֹךְ שֶׁלּוֹ, עַד כַּמָּה תַעֲבוֹר הַדְּלֵקָה, רַבִּי
אֶלְעָזָר בֶּן עֲזַרְיָה אוֹמֵר, רוֹאִין אוֹתוֹ כְּאִלּוּ הוּא בְּאֶמְצַע בֵּית כּוֹר.

"כִּי תֵצֵא אֵשׁ וּמָצְאָה קֹצִים וְנֶאֱכַל גָּדִישׁ אוֹ הַקָּמָה אוֹ הַשָּׂדֶה" (*Exodus* 22:5):
שַׁלֵּם יְשַׁלֵּם הַמַּבְעִר אֶת הַבְּעֵרָה" — *If a fire shall go forth and find thorns, and a stack of grain or the standing grain or the field is consumed, the one who lit the blaze shall surely pay.* By adding the word *field*, the verse teaches that one must pay even for stones that were blackened or earth that was scorched.[10]

The Mishnah discusses the laws regarding barriers that block fire:

עָבְרָה גָּדֵר שֶׁהוּא גָבוֹהַּ אַרְבַּע אַמּוֹת — **If someone lit a pile of wood in his own premises and [the fire] passed** over a stone wall[11] that is **four** *amos* **higher** than the pile of wood,[12] אוֹ דֶרֶךְ הָרַבִּים — **or it crossed a public road** that is at least sixteen *amos* wide,[13] אוֹ נָהָר — **or it crossed a river** that is at least eight *amos* wide,[14] פָּטוּר — the one who created the fire is **not obligated** to pay for any damage caused by the fire, because these barriers are usually enough to prevent a fire from spreading.[15]

According to the previous Tanna, a road (or any similar strip of land) is an effective barrier if it is sixteen *amos* wide. The Mishnah teaches that this is only one of several opinions:

הַמַּדְלִיק בְּתוֹךְ שֶׁלּוֹ — **If someone lights** a fire **within his own** property, עַד כַּמָּה תַעֲבוֹר הַדְּלֵקָה — **how far will the fire go?** That is, how far must he distance his fire from neighboring property to prevent it from spreading into that property? רַבִּי אֶלְעָזָר בֶּן עֲזַרְיָה אוֹמֵר — **R' Elazar ben Azaryah says:** רוֹאִין אוֹתוֹ כְּאִלּוּ הוּא בְּאֶמְצַע בֵּית כּוֹר — **We view him as though he were in the center of a *beis***

NOTES

10. *Tos. Yom Tov,* from Gemara 60a.
The verse teaches that the person is liable even though it is unusual for fire to damage stones or earth (*Tosafos* 10a ד״ה וליחכה).

11. The word used here for wall (גָּדֵר) usually refers to a barrier of stone (see *Rav* to *Bava Metzia* 2:3).

12. *Tos. Yom Tov.*

13. This measurement is based on the Jewish camp in the Wilderness (*Rav*), whose public roads needed to be 16 *amos* wide to accommodate the wagons that carried the beams of the Mishkan (*Shabbos* 98a). [It is not necessary for the 16-*amah* strip to actually be used as a road. Any strip of that width suffices to exempt the one who lit the fire (see the end of this Mishnah).]

14. Even though the strip of land must be 16 *amos* wide, the river need only be 8 *amos* wide, due to the water in it (*Rambam, Hilchos Nizkei Mamon* 14:2).

15. He is exempt even if he did nothing to prevent the fire from spreading, but simply relied on the barrier to stop it (*Meiri*). Since it is unusual for a fire to cross such barriers, the resulting damage is an unavoidable accident for which he cannot be blamed.

רַבִּי אֱלִיעֶזֶר אוֹמֵר, שֵׁשׁ עֶשְׂרֵה אַמּוֹת כְּדֶרֶךְ רְשׁוּת הָרַבִּים. רַבִּי עֲקִיבָא אוֹמֵר חֲמִשִּׁים אַמָּה. רַבִּי שִׁמְעוֹן אוֹמֵר, שַׁלֵּם יְשַׁלֵּם הַמַּבְעִיר אֶת הַבְּעֵרָה, הַכֹּל לְפִי הַדְּלֵקָה.

[ה] **הַמַּדְלִיק** אֶת הַגָּדִישׁ, וְהָיוּ בּוֹ כֵלִים וְדָלְקוּ, רַבִּי יְהוּדָה אוֹמֵר, יְשַׁלֵּם מַה שֶּׁבְּתוֹכוֹ, וַחֲכָמִים אוֹמְרִים, אֵינוֹ מְשַׁלֵּם אֶלָּא גָדִישׁ שֶׁל חִטִּין אוֹ שֶׁל שְׂעוֹרִים.

— רע״ב —

רבי שמעון אומר הכל לפי הדליקה. לפי גובה הדליקה, וגודל שיעורה. שכשהאש גדולה קופצת למרחוק. והלכה כרבי שמעון: (ה) המדליק את הגדיש. שהדליק בתוך שלו, והלכה ואכלה בתוך של חבירו: רבי יהודה אומר ישלם כל מה שבתוכו. לדרבי יהודה מחייב על נזקי טמון באש, דלית ליה דרשא דאו הקמה

(שמות כב,ה), מה קמה גלויה אף כל גלוי: וחכמים אומרים אינו משלם אלא גדיש וכו׳. דלית להו דרשא דאו הקמה, ופטרי על נזקי טמון באש. אלא שמשערין מקום הכלים כאילו הוא גדיז, ומפלם גדיש כשעור גופן של כלים. ומדקאמרי סיפא, ומודים חכמים לרבי יהודה במדליק את הבירה שהוא משלם כל מה שבתוכה, מוכח בגמרא (סא,ב), שנחלקו רבי יהודה וחכמים גם במדליק בתוך של חברו, שרבי

---

kor. That is, if half a *beis kor* (which has a width of 137 *amos*)[16] separates the fire from the surrounding properties, he is not obligated to pay for any damage the fire does there. שֵׁשׁ עֶשְׂרֵה — **R' Eliezer says:** רַבִּי אֱלִיעֶזֶר אוֹמֵר — **The required distance is sixteen *amos,*** like the minimum width of **a public road** (as the Mishnah stated above). רַבִּי עֲקִיבָא אוֹמֵר — **R' Akiva says:** חֲמִשִּׁים אַמָּה — **The required distance is fifty *amos.*** רַבִּי שִׁמְעוֹן אוֹמֵר — **R' Shimon says:** ״שַׁלֵּם יְשַׁלֵּם הַמַּבְעִיר אֶת הַבְּעֵרָה״ — **The Torah states** (*Exodus* 22:5): **the one who ignited the fire shall pay.** הַכֹּל לְפִי הַדְּלֵקָה — By stating *the fire,* the verse implies that **it all depends on the fire.** Thus, the required distance must be determined on a case-by-case basis, depending on the fire's size.

[5] The Mishnah continues to discuss damage caused by fire: הַמַּדְלִיק אֶת הַגָּדִישׁ וְהָיוּ בּוֹ כֵּלִים וְדָלְקוּ — **If someone lit** a fire on his own premises and it spread to another person's property where it burned down **a stack of grain in which utensils were** hidden, **and they were burned** too, רַבִּי יְהוּדָה אוֹמֵר — **R' Yehudah says:** יְשַׁלֵּם מַה שֶּׁבְּתוֹכוֹ — **He pays** not only for the stack of grain but even **for what was** hidden **inside it.**[1] וַחֲכָמִים אוֹמְרִים — **But the Sages say:** אֵינוֹ מְשַׁלֵּם אֶלָּא גָדִישׁ שֶׁל חִטִּין אוֹ שֶׁל שְׂעוֹרִים — **He pays only for a stack of wheat or** a stack **of barley** and not for the hidden utensils, because (according to the Sages) the Torah does not hold one liable for burning things that are hidden.[2]

— NOTES —

16. A *beis kor* (the area in which a *kor* of seed is sown) measures 75,000 square *amos.* When in the shape of a square, each side is about 274 *amos* long (*Rambam, Hilchos Arachin* 4:4). Thus, the center of a square *beis kor* is about 137 *amos* from the border.

[5]

1. R' Yehudah holds that he is liable even for things that are unlikely to be hidden in a haystack, such as a purse (*Rashi* 61b ד״ה בתרתי).

2. In describing damage done by a fire,

הָיָה גְּדִי כָפוּת לוֹ וְעֶבֶד סָמוּךְ לוֹ, וְנִשְׂרַף עִמּוֹ, חַיָּב. עֶבֶד כָּפוּת לוֹ וּגְדִי סָמוּךְ לוֹ, וְנִשְׂרַף עִמּוֹ, פָּטוּר.

— רע"ב —

יהודה סבר, כשהדליק בשל חברו, משלם כל מה שבתוכו, ואפילו ארנקי. ורבנן סברי, כלים שדרכן להטמין בגדים, כגון מוריגין וכלי בקר, הוא דמשלם, כלים שאין דרכן להטמין בגדים, לא משלם. והלכה כחכמים: **היה גדי כפות לו חייב.** דבעלי חיים נמי אתרבו מלו הקמה. ומשום דקם ליה בדרבה מיניה, ליכא למפטריה. דאינו חייב מיתה על העבד, הואיל ואינו כפות היה לו לברוח, ופטור עליו ממיתה, ומן התשלומין. אבל [אם] היה עבד כפות לו, פטור אפילו על הגדי ועל הגדיש, דחייב מיתה על העבד, וקם ליה בדרבה מיניה. ובגדי, לא שני לן בין כפות לאינו כפות. ואיידי דנקט בעבד נקט בגדי:

The Mishnah discusses two other cases where items were burned together with a stack of grain:

הָיָה גְּדִי כָפוּת לוֹ — If a kid goat was tied to [a stack of grain], וְעֶבֶד סָמוּךְ לוֹ — and a slave was near [the stack] but he was not tied to it, וְנִשְׂרַף עִמּוֹ — and the goat or slave was burned with [the stack], חַיָּב — [the damager] is obligated to pay for the goat (and obviously, the stack). But he is not liable for killing the slave because the slave could have run away.[3] However, if the slave was tied to [the stack] עֶבֶד כָּפוּת לוֹ and the kid goat was near it וּגְדִי סָמוּךְ לוֹ — and [the slave] was burned with it, וְנִשְׂרַף עִמּוֹ — [the damager] is not obligated to pay anything at all, because murdering a slave is

---

NOTES

the Torah (*Exodus* 22:5) states: *If a fire shall go forth and find thorns, and a stack of grain or the standing grain or the field is consumed.* By adding the example of *standing grain*, the Torah teaches that the damager need pay only for objects that, like standing grain, are exposed, and not for objects that are hidden. However, he must pay as though the space taken up by the utensils was filled with grain. If the grain is wheat, he pays the value of that volume of wheat, and if it is barley he adds the value of that volume of barley (*Rav*).

Since the exemption from paying for hidden things is a special Biblical decree (rather than being based on human logic), it applies in all cases. Therefore, the person who lit the fire is exempt even if the hidden items would be expected to be in the place where they were burned; for example, his fire burned a haystack in which farmer's tools were hidden (*Rashi* 61b בתרתי ד"ה). Furthermore, he is exempt even if he *knew* that the items were there (*Chazon Ish*).

[The Mishnah refers here to a person who lit a fire in his own premises and it traveled outside. The law of a fire lit in the victim's property is stated below.]

3. If someone deliberately kills a Canaanite slave, he is liable to the death penalty. In this case, however, the damager is neither put to death nor even required to pay the owner for the loss of his slave. Since the slave was not tied to the stack and could have run away, he is considered to have brought his own death upon himself (*Rav*). The same law applies where the victim is a free man. The Mishnah speaks of a slave because a slave is likely to be found in a grain field (*Tiferes Yisrael*).

Although the Mishnah states that the goat was tied, the damager would be obligated to pay for the goat even if it was not tied, but was merely near the stack. We do not say that the goat should have escaped, because a goat does not have the sense to run away from fire until it is too late. Nevertheless, the Mishnah describes the goat as "tied" in order to parallel the next case, where one [the goat] is loose and the other [the slave] is tied (*Rav*).

ו/ה

וּמוֹדִים חֲכָמִים לְרַבִּי יְהוּדָה בְּמַדְלִיק אֶת הַבִּירָה, שֶׁהוּא מְשַׁלֵּם כָּל מַה שֶּׁבְּתוֹכָהּ, שֶׁכֵּן דֶּרֶךְ בְּנֵי אָדָם לְהַנִּיחַ בַּבָּתִּים.

— רע"ב —

במדליק את הבירה. דמדליק בתוך של חבירו הוא, והוי כמאבד בידים. **ואפילו הכי, טעמא** משום דדרך בני אדם להניח כלים בבתים. אבל בגדים דאין דרך בני אדם להניח, אלא כגון מורינין וכלי בקר, אף על גב דאדליק לתוך של חבירו, אינו משלם אליבא דחכמים אלא דברים שדרכן להטמין בגדיש:

punishable by death,[4] and a person cannot become subject to both the death penalty and a monetary obligation at the same time.[5]

The Sages stated above that one is not liable for burning that which is hidden. The Mishnah cites an exception to the Sages' ruling:

וּמוֹדִים חֲכָמִים לְרַבִּי יְהוּדָה בְּמַדְלִיק אֶת הַבִּירָה — **But the Sages agree with R' Yehudah where someone lit** a fire on another person's property and it burned down **a large house** there, שֶׁהוּא מְשַׁלֵּם כָּל מַה שֶּׁבְּתוֹכָהּ — **that he must pay for everything inside [the house],** including hidden objects, שֶׁכֵּן דֶּרֶךְ בְּנֵי אָדָם לְהַנִּיחַ בַּבָּתִּים — **because it is the way of people to place** all sorts of things **in their houses.** Since the fire was started on the victim's property and it is common for anything to be hidden in a house, the Sages agree that the damager must pay even for the hidden items.[6]

---— NOTES ---—

4. In this situation, where the slave was tied to the stack, the one who lit the fire is liable for killing him, since he could not have run away.

5. See Mishnah 3:10.

6. When someone starts a fire in his neighbor's property without permission and it causes damage there, he is viewed as someone who did damage with his own hands (*Rav*). As such, the damage does not belong to the category of *eish* (fire), but to the category of *adam hamazik* (a person who damages). Therefore, since the Biblical decree exempting a person from payment for hidden things was stated only in connection with *eish*, it does not apply here.

Even in this situation, however, the Sages hold one liable for burning a hidden object only if an object of that type is sometimes found in the place where it was burned (for example, a farmer's tools in a haystack). Since he should have considered the possibility that the object is present, he is responsible for burning it. But if the hidden item was not expected to be there (for example, a wallet in a haystack), its burning is an unforeseeable accident, for which he is not liable. To teach this point, the Sages added, "because it is the way of people to place [all sorts of things] in [their] houses." A person who burned down a house must pay for its hidden things only because he should have expected that anything may be hidden inside a house (*Rav*).

To summarize: The Sages and R' Yehudah disagree on two points: (a) According to the Sages, the Torah decrees that one who lights a fire *on his own premises* is not liable for burning that which is hidden. But according to R' Yehudah, there is no such Biblical decree and so he is liable. This dispute applies both to objects that were expected to be in the place where they were burned (e.g., a farmer's tools in a haystack) and objects that were not expected to be there (e.g., a wallet in a haystack). (b) If the damager lit the fire *on the victim's premises,* even the Sages rule that the Biblical decree does not apply (because this is not a case of *eish*), but they reason that a person cannot be held responsible for burning something that was not expected to be where it was burned. R' Yehudah disagrees even with this. As stated in note 1, R' Yehudah holds that one must pay for burning *anything,* even a hidden item that was not expected to be present (*Rav*).

[93] **MISHNAH BAVA KAMMA** / Chapter 6: *Hakoneis*

— רע״ב —

[ו] גֵּץ שֶׁיָּצָא מִתַּחַת הַפַּטִּישׁ וְהִזִּיק, חַיָּב. גָּמָל שֶׁהָיָה טָעוּן פִּשְׁתָּן וְעָבַר בִּרְשׁוּת הָרַבִּים, וְנִכְנַס פִּשְׁתָּנוֹ לְתוֹךְ הַחֲנוּת, וְדָלְקוּ בְּנֵרוֹ שֶׁל חֶנְוָנִי, וְהִדְלִיק אֶת הַבִּירָה, בַּעַל הַגָּמָל חַיָּב. הִנִּיחַ חֶנְוָנִי נֵרוֹ מִבַּחוּץ, הַחֶנְוָנִי חַיָּב. רַבִּי יְהוּדָה אוֹמֵר, בְּנֵר חֲנֻכָּה פָּטוּר.

(ו) גץ. ניצוץ של אש: רבי יהודה אומר בנר חנוכה פטור. כיון דבמצוה קא עסיק. ואין הלכה כרבי יהודה:

[6] This Mishnah rules on more cases of fire damage:

גֵּץ שֶׁיָּצָא מִתַּחַת הַפַּטִּישׁ וְהִזִּיק — **If a spark flew out from under the hammer** of a blacksmith **and damaged** someone else's property, חַיָּב — **he is obligated** to pay for the damage.[1]

Another case:

גָּמָל שֶׁהָיָה טָעוּן פִּשְׁתָּן וְעָבַר בִּרְשׁוּת הָרַבִּים — **If a camel passing through a public street was loaded with** a large bundle of **flax,** וְנִכְנַס פִּשְׁתָּנוֹ לְתוֹךְ הַחֲנוּת וְדָלְקוּ בְּנֵרוֹ שֶׁל חֶנְוָנִי — **and its flax extended into a shop and was set on fire by the shopkeeper's lamp,** וְהִדְלִיק אֶת הַבִּירָה — **and then it** (i.e., the camel with its bundle of burning flax) **set fire to a large house,** בַּעַל גָּמָל חַיָּב — **the owner of the camel is obligated** to pay for the damage to the house, because it was negligent of him to load his animal with a bundle of flax wide enough to extend into shops.[2] הִנִּיחַ חֶנְוָנִי נֵרוֹ מִבַּחוּץ — **However, if the shopkeeper had put his lamp outside** in the street, and the camel's load of flax caught fire as it passed the lamp and then it set fire to a house, הַחֶנְוָנִי חַיָּב — **the *shopkeeper* is obligated** to pay for the flax and the house, because he was negligent in placing his lamp where it could cause damage.[3]

The next Tanna holds that there is an exception to the last ruling:

רַבִּי יְהוּדָה אוֹמֵר — **R' Yehudah says:** בְּנֵר חֲנֻכָּה פָּטוּר — **If the shopkeeper's lamp was a Chanukah light, he is not obligated** to pay damages. Since it is a Rabbinic mitzvah to place the Chanukah light outside, where it can be seen by people,[4] the shopkeeper is not responsible if it causes damage.[5]

NOTES

[6]
1. As the blacksmith was banging with his hammer on the hot piece of metal he was shaping, a spark happened to fly outside and cause damage (for example, it flew into the street and burned a bundle of flax that someone was carrying there). He is liable to pay because he should have been working so far inside his premises that sparks could not have flown outside (*Meiri*).
2. *Tos. Yom Tov.*
3. It was common for animals loaded with materials like flax to walk down the street. Thus, the camel carrying the fire to the house is like a normal wind blowing a fire to someone's field, in which case the person who lit the fire must pay for any damage it does there.

[If the owner of the camel could have prevented it from burning the house, he too is responsible for the damage, and he and the shopkeeper each pay half (*Meleches Shlomo*).]

4. In this way, the miracle of Chanukah is brought to the attention of the people passing by (*Rashi* 22a).

5. Because the shopkeeper had permission to place his lamp in the street, and it was even a mitzvah for him to do so, he cannot be held liable for damage it causes.

The first Tanna disagrees with R' Yehudah, because in his view the shopkeeper should have watched over his lamp to make sure that it does no harm (*Tos. Yom Tov*).

Chapter Seven

משניות בבא קמא / פרק ז: מרבה

[א] מְרֻבָּה מִדַּת תַּשְׁלוּמֵי כֶפֶל מִמִּדַּת תַּשְׁלוּמֵי אַרְבָּעָה וַחֲמִשָּׁה, שֶׁמִּדַּת תַּשְׁלוּמֵי כֶפֶל נוֹהֶגֶת בֵּין בְּדָבָר שֶׁיֵּשׁ בּוֹ רוּחַ חַיִּים וּבֵין בְּדָבָר שֶׁאֵין בּוֹ רוּחַ חַיִּים, וּמִדַּת תַּשְׁלוּמֵי אַרְבָּעָה וַחֲמִשָּׁה אֵינָהּ נוֹהֶגֶת אֶלָּא בְּשׁוֹר וָשֶׂה בִּלְבָד, שֶׁנֶּאֱמַר, כִּי יִגְנֹב אִישׁ שׁוֹר אוֹ שֶׂה וּטְבָחוֹ אוֹ מְכָרוֹ וְגוֹ'.

— רע"ב —

פרק שביעי – מרובה. (א) מרובה. בדבר שיש בו רוח חיים ובדבר שאין בו רוח חיים. דכתיב (שמות כב, ח) על שה על שלמה על כל אבדה וגו' ישלם שנים:

---

[1] The rest of the tractate (except for Chapter 8) deals with the laws of theft.

There are two types of thieves: The גַּנָּב, *ganav*, who steals secretly, and the גַּזְלָן, *gazlan*, who robs openly by force or by threatening force. A *ganav* is subject to special laws. He not only has to return the stolen item but must also pay the owner a fine equivalent to its value (*Exodus* 22:3). Thus, he pays double: the object itself plus its value in money. The extra payment is called כֶּפֶל (literally, *double*).[1] Another fine that must be paid by a *ganav* is the תַּשְׁלוּמֵי אַרְבָּעָה וַחֲמִשָּׁה, *the fourfold or fivefold payments*. If he steals a sheep or a goat and slaughters or sells it, he pays four times its value. If he steals an ox and slaughters or sells it, he pays five times its value (*Exodus* 21:37).[2] This Mishnah points out a difference between the double payment and the fourfold and fivefold payments:

מְרֻבָּה מִדַּת תַּשְׁלוּמֵי כֶפֶל מִמִּדַּת תַּשְׁלוּמֵי אַרְבָּעָה וַחֲמִשָּׁה — **The rule of the double payment applies to more items than the rule of the fourfold and fivefold payments does,** שֶׁמִּדַּת תַּשְׁלוּמֵי כֶפֶל נוֹהֶגֶת בֵּין בְּדָבָר שֶׁיֵּשׁ בּוֹ רוּחַ חַיִּים וּבֵין בְּדָבָר שֶׁאֵין בּוֹ רוּחַ חַיִּים — **for the rule of the double payment applies to the theft of both living things and non-living things,**[3] וּמִדַּת תַּשְׁלוּמֵי אַרְבָּעָה וַחֲמִשָּׁה אֵינָהּ נוֹהֶגֶת אֶלָּא בְּשׁוֹר וָשֶׂה בִּלְבָד — **while the rule of the fourfold and fivefold payments applies only to the theft of an ox or a sheep,**[4] שֶׁנֶּאֱמַר — **as it is stated** regarding the fourfold and fivefold payments (*Exodus* 21:37): כִּי יִגְנֹב אִישׁ שׁוֹר אוֹ שֶׂה וּטְבָחוֹ אוֹ מְכָרוֹ וְגוֹ' — **If a man shall steal an ox or a sheep, and he slaughters it or sells it,** *etc.* [he shall pay five cattle in place of the ox, and four sheep in place of the sheep].[5]

--- NOTES ---

[1]
1. For example, if he stole one *zuz*, he pays two *zuz*. If he stole a coat that is worth a *zuz*, he returns the coat and pays a *zuz*. If the coat is not available, he pays two *zuz*.
2. The fourfold and fivefold payments include the double payment. Thus, in effect, he pays the double payment plus another double payment (in the case of a stolen sheep or goat that he slaughtered or sold) or the double payment plus a triple payment (in the case of a stolen ox).

3. By stating: *for an ox, for a donkey, for a sheep, for a garment, for any lost item ... he shall pay double to his fellow* (*Exodus* 22:8), the Torah includes all types of items, whether living or not (*Rav*).

4. The word שֶׂה refers to both sheep and goats (see *Rashi* to *Exodus* 12:5). We have translated it as *sheep* because there is no exact English translation.

5. In several places where the Torah mentions an "ox," all animals are included (as listed in Mishnah 5:7). However, the

[97] MISHNAH BAVA KAMMA / Chapter 7: *Merubah* — 7/2

אֵין הַגּוֹנֵב אַחַר הַגַּנָּב מְשַׁלֵּם תַּשְׁלוּמֵי כֶפֶל, וְלֹא הַטּוֹבֵחַ וְלֹא הַמּוֹכֵר אַחַר הַגַּנָּב מְשַׁלֵּם תַּשְׁלוּמֵי אַרְבָּעָה וַחֲמִשָּׁה.

[ב] **גָּנַב** עַל פִּי שְׁנַיִם, וְטָבַח וּמָכַר עַל פִּיהֶם, אוֹ עַל פִּי שְׁנַיִם אֲחֵרִים, מְשַׁלֵּם תַּשְׁלוּמֵי אַרְבָּעָה וַחֲמִשָּׁה. גָּנַב וּמָכַר בְּשַׁבָּת,

— רע״ב —

אין הגונב אחר הגנב וכו׳. דכתיב (שם ו) וגונב מבית האיש, ולא מבית הגנב: (ב) גנב על פי שנים. כלומר שנים מעידין אותו שגנב: גנב ומכר בשבת. אבל טבח שהוא ענוש סקילה, קם ליה בדרבה מיניה:

A law that applies to all of these fines: אֵין הַגּוֹנֵב אַחַר הַגַּנָּב מְשַׁלֵּם תַּשְׁלוּמֵי כֶפֶל — **One who steals** a stolen item **from a thief does not make the double payment** (either to the original owner or to the thief), וְלֹא הַטּוֹבֵחַ וְלֹא הַמּוֹכֵר אַחַר הַגַּנָּב מְשַׁלֵּם תַּשְׁלוּמֵי אַרְבָּעָה וַחֲמִשָּׁה — **nor does one who slaughters or sells** an ox or a sheep that he stole **from a thief make the fourfold or fivefold payment.**[6]

[2] The Mishnah lists various cases in which a thief makes the fourfold or fivefold payment:

גָּנַב עַל פִּי שְׁנַיִם — **If someone stole** an ox or a sheep **according to two witnesses,** וְטָבַח וּמָכַר עַל פִּיהֶם אוֹ עַל פִּי שְׁנַיִם אֲחֵרִים — **and he slaughtered or sold** the animal **according to them** (the same witnesses) **or according to two others,** מְשַׁלֵּם תַּשְׁלוּמֵי אַרְבָּעָה וַחֲמִשָּׁה — **he makes the fourfold or fivefold payment.** Although the witnesses who saw the sale or slaughter of the animal did not see the theft, their testimony is valid.[1] גָּנַב וּמָכַר בְּשַׁבָּת — **If someone stole** an ox or a sheep **and then sold it on Shabbos,**[2]

NOTES

law of the fourfold and fivefold payments applies only to the animals named in the verse: oxen and sheep (see *Tos. Yom Tov*).

6. The Torah (*Exodus* 22:6) specifies: *it is stolen from the house of the man,* i.e., the owner, which teaches that the penalties must be paid only if the item was stolen from the owner, and not from another thief (*Rabbeinu Yehonasan*).

[2]

1. The Torah states (*Deuteronomy* 19:15): *According to two witnesses ... shall "a matter" be established,* which implies that testimony is valid only when it is a complete matter, and not a partial matter [דָּבָר וְלֹא חֲצִי דָבָר] (Gemara 70b). In our Mishnah's case, however, although the second group of witnesses did not testify about the theft, rather they testified only that someone slaughtered or sold an ox or a sheep, their testimony is a "complete matter," because they testified about everything they could have seen at that time (*Tos. Yom Tov*). [The testimony about the *theft* is certainly a "complete matter" since the theft alone is enough to find the thief guilty and require him to repay the victim.]

2. The Mishnah will state that in this case and all the following ones, the thief is obligated to make the fourfold or fivefold payment.

We have learned that if a person becomes subject to a severe punishment and a lighter punishment (such as the death penalty and a monetary obligation) at the same time, he receives only the severe punishment and is exempt from the lighter one [קָם לֵיהּ בְּדְרַבָּה מִנֵּיהּ] (*Mishnah* 3:10). That rule, however, does not apply here. Since selling things on Shabbos does not carry a severe punishment (it is prohibited only by Rabbinic decree), it

גָּנַב וּמָכַר לַעֲבוֹדָה זָרָה, גָּנַב וְטָבַח בְּיוֹם הַכִּפּוּרִים, גָּנַב מִשֶּׁל אָבִיו, וְטָבַח וּמָכַר, וְאַחַר כָּךְ מֵת אָבִיו, גָּנַב וְטָבַח, וְאַחַר כָּךְ הִקְדִּישׁ, מְשַׁלֵּם תַּשְׁלוּמֵי אַרְבָּעָה וַחֲמִשָּׁה.

— רע"ב —

וטבח ביום הכפורים. שאין זדונו אלא כרת, וכגון דלא אתרו ביה ולא לקי, דקיימא לן כל חייבי מלקיות שוגגים, חייבים בתשלומין (עח, א). אבל

חייבי מיתות בית דין, אפילו שוגגים, פטורים מן התשלומין: וטבח ומכר ואחר כך מת אביו. תנא סיפא דפטור, דשלו הוא טובח ושלו הוא מוכר, שהרי ירש את אביו: אבל מת אביו ואחר כך טבח,

---

גָּנַב וּמָכַר לַעֲבוֹדָה זָרָה — or he stole an ox or a sheep and sold it for purposes of idolatry,[3] גָּנַב וְטָבַח בְּיוֹם הַכִּפּוּרִים — or he stole an ox or a sheep and then slaughtered it on Yom Kippur,[4] גָּנַב מִשֶּׁל אָבִיו וְטָבַח וּמָכַר וְאַחַר כָּךְ מֵת אָבִיו — or he stole an ox or a sheep from his father and slaughtered or sold it, and afterward his father died,[5] גָּנַב וְטָבַח וְאַחַר כָּךְ הִקְדִּישׁ — or he stole an ox or a sheep and slaughtered it, and afterward he consecrated it (i.e., he donated it to the Temple treasury),[6] מְשַׁלֵּם תַּשְׁלוּמֵי אַרְבָּעָה וַחֲמִשָּׁה — in all these cases, he makes the fourfold or fivefold payment.

— NOTES —

does not exempt him from the monetary obligation.

The Mishnah says only that the thief *sold* the animal. If he *slaughtered* it on Shabbos, which is punishable by death, he would indeed be exempt from payment (Mishnah 4).

3. Selling an animal to someone who will sacrifice it to an idol is Biblically forbidden (because he thereby enables someone to sin), but it does not carry a severe punishment. Hence, there is no reason to exempt the thief from the fourfold or fivefold payment.

However, if the thief himself slaughtered the animal as a sacrifice to an idol, he is subject to the death penalty and thus exempt from payment (Mishnah 4).

4. A person who slaughters an animal on Yom Kippur is punished with *kares* (a Divinely imposed punishment that takes the form of premature death). According to the Tanna of our Mishnah, the rule that "a severe punishment overrides a lighter one" applies only where the severe punishment is of a type imposed by a human court (such as execution or *malkus*), and not where it is of a type imposed by Heaven (such as *kares*). Therefore, although this thief became subject to *kares*, he must make the fourfold or fivefold payment.

[Even though the Mishnah says that he *slaughtered* the animal on Yom Kippur,

the same ruling certainly applies if he *sold* it, since that is merely a Rabbinic transgression. See note 2.]

5. He became obligated to make the payments when his father was still alive. After his father dies, he must pay his father's heirs. However, because he is one of the heirs, he keeps his portion of the payment, and he pays the other heirs only their portions (Gemara 71b).

If he slaughtered or sold the animal *after* his father's death, he would not have to pay the fine at all (Mishnah 4).

6. When an animal is consecrated, it becomes the property of the Temple treasury and no longer belongs to its previous owner. Thus, if the thief would have consecrated it first and then slaughtered it, he would be exempt from the fourfold or fivefold payment, since the animal was not the owner's property at the time of the slaughter (Mishnah 4). In the Mishnah's case, however, where he slaughtered the animal before he consecrated it, the animal still belonged to the owner at the time of the slaughter, so he must make the fourfold or fivefold payment. [For explanation of how a thief can consecrate a stolen article, see Mishnah 4 note 5.]

[The Mishnah says only that he *slaughtered* the animal, and not that he *sold* it, because after selling it, he can no longer consecrate it.]

[99] MISHNAH BAVA KAMMA / Chapter 7: *Merubah*

גָּנַב וְטָבַח לִרְפוּאָה אוֹ לִכְלָבִים, הַשּׁוֹחֵט וְנִמְצָא טְרֵפָה, הַשּׁוֹחֵט חֻלִּין בַּעֲזָרָה, מְשַׁלֵּם תַּשְׁלוּמֵי אַרְבָּעָה וַחֲמִשָּׁה. רַבִּי שִׁמְעוֹן פּוֹטֵר בִּשְׁנֵי אֵלּוּ.

— רע"ב —

בשני אלו. בטרפה ובחולין בעזרה. דקסבר רבי שמעון שחיטה שאינה ראויה לאו שמה שחיטה. אבל לרפואה ולכלבים, שחיטה ראויה היא, דאי בעי, מלי אכיל מינה:

גָּנַב וְטָבַח לִרְפוּאָה — **If someone stole** an ox or a sheep **and slaughtered** it to use the meat **for healing purposes** (i.e., medicine), and not for food, אוֹ לִכְלָבִים — **or** he slaughtered it for the purpose of feeding it **to dogs**; הַשּׁוֹחֵט וְנִמְצָא טְרֵפָה — **or** he slaughtered it **and it is found to be a** *tereifah*, which may not be eaten;[7] הַשּׁוֹחֵט חֻלִּין בַּעֲזָרָה — **or if he slaughtered a non-consecrated [animal] in the Temple Courtyard** and thus made it forbidden;[8] מְשַׁלֵּם תַּשְׁלוּמֵי אַרְבָּעָה וַחֲמִשָּׁה — in all these cases, **he makes the fourfold or fivefold payment.** Although the *shechitah* (slaughtering) did not make the animal fit to be eaten, or the thief did not intend for the animal to be eaten, it is still an act of *shechitah*.

The next Tanna disagrees in the last two cases, where the thief slaughtered a *tereifah*, or he slaughtered a non-consecrated animal in the Temple Courtyard: רַבִּי שִׁמְעוֹן פּוֹטֵר בִּשְׁנֵי אֵלּוּ — **R' Shimon exempts** him from the fourfold or fivefold payment **in these two** cases, because (according to R' Shimon) an act of slaughtering that does not permit the animal to be eaten is not called *shechitah*. As such, it cannot make the thief liable to the fourfold or fivefold payment.[9]

[3] *Zomemin* witnesses: There are two main ways in which the testimony of one group of witnesses can be contradicted by the testimony of a second group: (a) One group of witnesses testifies that they saw an event in a certain time and place, and then a second group of witnesses testifies that they were in that place at that time and saw that the event did not occur. In this case, the testimonies of both groups are treated equally. (b) The second group of witnesses testify that the first witnesses were in a different place at that time, and therefore could not have seen the event. Thus, the second witnesses do not claim to know anything about the event; they are testifying only about the first witnesses themselves. The Torah decrees that in this situation we are to

---

NOTES

7. A *tereifah* is an animal with certain fatal wounds or defects. Even if it is slaughtered properly, it may not be eaten (see *Exodus* 22:30).

8. He stole an ordinary (non-sacred) animal and then slaughtered it in the Temple Courtyard. The Torah prohibits eating or having any other type of benefit from such an animal.

9. R' Shimon derives from a Biblical source that wherever the Torah mentions *shechitah*, it refers only to an act that makes the animal permitted for consumption (*Chullin* 85a).

R' Shimon agrees, however, that in the previous two cases (where the thief slaughtered the animal to be used as medicine or dog food), the thief must indeed make the fourfold or fivefold payment. Even though he intended to use the meat for other purposes, the fact is that it may be eaten by people, and thus he has performed an act of *shechitah* (*Rav*).

[ג] גָּנַב עַל פִּי שְׁנַיִם, וְטָבַח וּמָכַר עַל פִּיהֶם, וְנִמְצְאוּ זוֹמְמִין, מְשַׁלְּמִין הַכֹּל. גָּנַב עַל פִּי שְׁנַיִם וְטָבַח וּמָכַר עַל פִּי שְׁנַיִם אֲחֵרִים, אֵלּוּ וָאֵלּוּ נִמְצְאוּ זוֹמְמִין, הָרִאשׁוֹנִים מְשַׁלְּמִין תַּשְׁלוּמֵי כֶפֶל, וְהָאַחֲרוֹנִים מְשַׁלְּמִין תַּשְׁלוּמֵי שְׁלֹשָׁה.

— רע"ב —

(ג) הָאַחֲרוֹנִים מְשַׁלְּמִים שְׁלֹשָׁה. לְשׁוֹר. וְכגון שהוזמו אחרונים תחלה, דאי ע"י גניבה הוזמו תחלה, בטלה לה עדות טביחה, דלמא בטלים מכרוהו לו, וכי מתזמי אמאי משלמי:

---

believe only the second witnesses and assume that the first witnesses were lying. These lying witnesses are called *zomemin* (plotters) because they plotted against the person whom they falsely accused.[1] The Torah also decrees that *zomemin* receive the same punishment that the person they accused would have received. Since they tried to have him punished in that manner, the same punishment is imposed on them (*Deuteronomy* 19:19).

The Mishnah applies these rules to various situations where witnesses testify that someone stole an ox or a sheep and then slaughtered or sold it:

גָּנַב עַל פִּי שְׁנַיִם — **If someone stole** an ox or a sheep **according to two** witnesses, וְטָבַח וּמָכַר עַל פִּיהֶם — **and he** also **slaughtered or sold it according to them,** וְנִמְצְאוּ זוֹמְמִין — **and [these witnesses] were found to be** *zomemin,* מְשַׁלְּמִין הַכֹּל — **they pay everything;** that is, they pay the entire fourfold or fivefold payment to the person they accused of stealing, since that is the punishment he would have received according to their testimony.

גָּנַב עַל פִּי שְׁנַיִם — **If someone stole** an ox **according to two** witnesses, וְטָבַח וּמָכַר עַל פִּי שְׁנַיִם אֲחֵרִים — **and he slaughtered or sold it according to two others,** אֵלּוּ וָאֵלּוּ נִמְצְאוּ זוֹמְמִין — and both **these and those were found to be** *zomemin,* הָרִאשׁוֹנִים מְשַׁלְּמִין תַּשְׁלוּמֵי כֶפֶל — the law is that **the first ones,** who testified about the theft, **make the double payment,** וְהָאַחֲרוֹנִים מְשַׁלְּמִין תַּשְׁלוּמֵי שְׁלֹשָׁה — **and the later ones,** who testified about the slaughter or sale, **make a triple payment.** The first witnesses pay twice the value of the ox, because they accused someone of stealing, which would have obligated him to pay double. The second witnesses pay three times the value of the ox, because they accused him of slaughtering or selling it, which would have obligated him to pay an additional three times its value (the second part of the fivefold payment).[2]

NOTES

[3]
1. For example, one pair of witnesses say that they saw someone eat *cheilev* (certain fats and other forbidden parts of an animal) at a certain time and in a certain place, and then another pair of witnesses says, "You were with us (in a different place) at that time." The first pair of witnesses receives the punishment for eating *cheilev,* which is *malkus.*
2. The Mishnah refers to an ox (*Rav*), in which case the thief pays fivefold. If the animal were a sheep, for which a thief pays only fourfold, the first witnesses would have to pay twice its value and the second witnesses would also have to pay twice its value.

The Mishnah's ruling applies only where the second pair of witnesses was found to be *zomemin* before the first pair. In the reverse case, where the first pair was found to be *zomemin* before the

[101] MISHNAH BAVA KAMMA / Chapter 7: Merubah

נִמְצְאוּ אַחֲרוֹנִים זוֹמְמִין, הוּא מְשַׁלֵּם תַּשְׁלוּמֵי כֶפֶל, וְהֵן מְשַׁלְּמִין תַּשְׁלוּמֵי שְׁלֹשָׁה. אֶחָד מִן הָאַחֲרוֹנִים זוֹמֵם, בָּטְלָה עֵדוּת שְׁנִיָּה. אֶחָד מִן הָרִאשׁוֹנִים זוֹמֵם, בָּטְלָה כָּל הָעֵדוּת, שֶׁאִם אֵין גְּנֵיבָה, אֵין טְבִיחָה וְאֵין מְכִירָה.

— רע״ב —

בטלה עדות שניה. והוא משלם כפל משום עדות ראשונים. והן פטורין, דאין עדים משלמין ממון עד שיזומו שניהם: בטלה כל העדות. והוא פטור והם פטורים. ואפילו חזרו והוזמו אחרונים אחר כך, אין משלמין, שהרי בטלה עדותן כבר והוכחשו, כיון דלא גנב לא טבח, [ומהיכי] לא מחייבו, אלא אטמונו הייתם שהוזהרה גופה של עדות. וכל שכן אם הוזמו שנים הראשונים תחלה, שעדות שניה בטלה אלא שבזמן שלא הוזמו אלא אחד אחד, בטלו שניהם. אבל כשהוזמו שניהם, לא בטלה עדות ראשונה, אלא משלמין כפל:

נִמְצְאוּ אַחֲרוֹנִים זוֹמְמִין — If only **the later [witnesses]**, who testified about the slaughter or sale, **were found to be** *zomemin*, but the first ones, who testified about the theft, were not found to be *zomemin*, הוּא מְשַׁלֵּם תַּשְׁלוּמֵי כֶפֶל — [the thief] **makes the double payment,** וְהֵן מְשַׁלְּמִין תַּשְׁלוּמֵי שְׁלֹשָׁה — and **[the later witnesses] make a triple payment.** Since the testimony about the theft is valid, the thief must make the double payment. But he does not make the additional triple payment, because the testimony about the slaughter or sale was rejected; rather, it is the *zomemin* who must make the triple payment. אֶחָד מִן הָאַחֲרוֹנִים זוֹמֵם — **Even if only one of the later ones,** who testified about the slaughter or sale, was found to be a *zoeim*,[3] בָּטְלָה עֵדוּת שְׁנִיָּה — **the second testimony is rejected,** because only a single witness remains of the second pair. As a result, the thief no longer has to make the additional triple payment; and *both* of the later witnesses, including the one found to be a *zoeim*, are also exempt.[4] אֶחָד מִן הָרִאשׁוֹנִים זוֹמֵם — **Even if only one of the first ones,** who testified about the theft, was found to be a *zoeim*, בָּטְלָה כָּל הָעֵדוּת — **all the testimony** (both the testimony about the theft and the testimony about the slaughter or sale) **is invalid,** שֶׁאִם אֵין גְּנֵיבָה אֵין טְבִיחָה וְאֵין מְכִירָה — **because "if there is no theft, there is no slaughter or sale."** That is, since we do not know that he

— NOTES —

slaughter or sale, "You were with us (in a different place) at that time." They do not say this about his fellow witness.

4. The thief must make the double payment, because the testimony to the theft is still valid. He is exempt from the additional triple payment, because the court has only one valid witness attesting to the slaughter or sale. [These are monetary matters, for which at least two witness are required.] As far as the witnesses are concerned, even the one who was found to be a *zoeim* is exempt from payment, because the rule is that a *zoeim* witness is not punished unless his fellow witness is also a *zoeim* (*Rav*).

second pair, the second pair would not have to pay anything. Once the court discovers that the first witnesses were *zomemin* and rejects their testimony, it has no evidence that the accused person stole the animal at all (he might have bought it from the previous owner). At that point, the testimony of the second pair, that he slaughtered or sold the animal, becomes irrelevant because it no longer obligates him to pay anything. Therefore, even if the second witnesses are later found to be *zomemin*, they do not receive the punishment of *zomemin* (*Rav*).

3. Two witnesses say regarding *one* of the witnesses who testified about the

[102] **משניות בבא קמא / פרק ז: מרובה**

[ד] **גָּנַב** עַל פִּי שְׁנַיִם, וְטָבַח וּמָכַר עַל פִּי עֵד אֶחָד אוֹ עַל פִּי עַצְמוֹ, מְשַׁלֵּם תַּשְׁלוּמֵי כֶפֶל, וְאֵינוֹ מְשַׁלֵּם תַּשְׁלוּמֵי אַרְבָּעָה וַחֲמִשָּׁה. גָּנַב וְטָבַח בְּשַׁבָּת, גָּנַב וְטָבַח לַעֲבוֹדָה זָרָה,

— רע״ב —

(ד) עַל פִּי עֵד אֶחָד. אַף עַל גַּב דִּמְלְתָא דִּפְשִׁיטָא הִיא, דְּאֵין מְשַׁלֵּם אַרְבָּעָה וַחֲמִשָּׁה עַל פִּי עֵד אֶחָד, הָא קָא מַשְׁמַע לָן דְּעַל פִּי עַצְמוֹ דּוּמְיָא דְּעַל

פִּי עֵד אֶחָד, מָה עַד אֶחָד אִי אָתֵי עֵד אֶחָד בָּתַר הָכִי מִצְטָרֵף בַּהֲדֵיהּ, וּמְחַיֵּיב, אִי אָתוּ עֵדִים בָּתַר הוֹדָאָתוֹ, מְחַיְּיבֵי לֵיהּ, דְּמוֹדֶה בִּקְנָס וְאַחַר כָּךְ בָּאוּ עֵדִים חַיָּיב. וְהָנֵי מִילֵי בְּאוֹמֵר לֹא גָּנַבְתִּי וּבָאוּ עֵדִים שֶׁגָּנַב, וְחָזַר וְאָמַר טָבַחְתִּי וּמָכַרְתִּי, וּבָאוּ עֵדִים אַחַר כָּךְ שֶׁטָּבַח וּמָכַר, חַיָּיב, שֶׁהֲרֵי כְּשֶׁאָמַר טָבַחְתִּי וּמָכַרְתִּי, אֵינוֹ מְחַיֵּיב עַצְמוֹ בִּכְלוּם, שֶׁיּוֹדֵעַ הוּא שֶׁמּוֹדֶה בִּקְנָס פָּטוּר, וְאֵין כָּאן הוֹדָאָה שֶׁל כְּלוּם. אֲבָל בְּאוֹמֵר גָּנַבְתִּי וּבָאוּ עֵדִים שֶׁגָּנַב, פָּטוּר. דְּחַיֵּיב עַצְמוֹ לְשַׁלֵּם קֶרֶן מֵחֲמַת הוֹדָאָתוֹ, הִלְכַּךְ הוֹדָאָה גְּמוּרָה הִיא וּפָטוּר מִכֶּפֶל, אַף עַל פִּי שֶׁאַחַר כָּךְ בָּאוּ עֵדִים:

---

stole the animal (because only one of the two witnesses to the theft remains), the fact that he slaughtered or sold the animal does not obligate him to pay anything. In this case, therefore, the accused person and both pairs of witnesses are exempt from all payments.[5]

[4] Mishnah 2 listed several cases where the thief is obligated to make the fourfold or fivefold payment. Our Mishnah cites related cases in which he is *not* obligated to pay.

גָּנַב עַל פִּי שְׁנַיִם — If someone stole an ox or a sheep **according to two** witnesses, וְטָבַח וּמָכַר עַל פִּי עֵד אֶחָד אוֹ עַל פִּי עַצְמוֹ — **and he slaughtered or sold** the animal **according to** only **one witness or according to himself** (i.e., he admitted that he slaughtered or sold it), מְשַׁלֵּם תַּשְׁלוּמֵי כֶפֶל — he makes **the double payment**, because two witnesses testified that he stole the animal, וְאֵינוֹ מְשַׁלֵּם תַּשְׁלוּמֵי אַרְבָּעָה וַחֲמִשָּׁה — **but he does not make the fourfold or fivefold payment**, because the testimony of a single witness or his own admission is not enough to obligate him to pay.[1]

גָּנַב וְטָבַח בְּשַׁבָּת — If someone stole an ox or a sheep **and** then **slaughtered** it **on Shabbos**;[2] גָּנַב וְטָבַח לַעֲבוֹדָה זָרָה — **or he stole** an ox or a sheep **and**

--- NOTES ---

5. The accused thief is exempt because only one valid witness testified to the theft. The witnesses who testified about the theft are exempt because only one of them is a *zomeim*. And the witnesses who testified about the slaughter or sale are exempt because they are not *zomemin*. Moreover, even if the later witnesses *were* found to be *zomemin*, they would be exempt, because once the testimony to the theft has been rejected, their testimony about the slaughter or sale is irrelevant [as explained in note 2] (*Tos. Yom Tov*).

[4]

1. Although someone who admits that he owes money is usually obligated to pay, that rule applies only to regular monetary obligations (debts, damages, and the like), and not to fines, such as the fourfold and fivefold payments. One who admits that he owes a fine does not have to pay it.

2. Here, we apply the rule that a person who became subject to the death penalty (or other severe punishment) and a lighter punishment at the same time receives only the severe punishment. Slaughtering an animal is one of the 39 *melachos* (activities) that are forbidden on Shabbos and which are punishable by death. Therefore, if a thief slaughters a stolen animal on Shabbos, he becomes

[103] **MISHNAH BAVA KAMMA** / Chapter 7: *Merubah* 7/4

גָּנַב מִשֶּׁל אָבִיו וּמֵת אָבִיו וְאַחַר כָּךְ טָבַח וּמָכַר, גָּנַב וְהִקְדִּישׁ וְאַחַר כָּךְ טָבַח וּמָכַר, מְשַׁלֵּם תַּשְׁלוּמֵי כֶפֶל, וְאֵינוֹ מְשַׁלֵּם תַּשְׁלוּמֵי אַרְבָּעָה וַחֲמִשָּׁה.

— רע״ב —

וּמֵת אָבִיו. וְהוּא יוֹרְשׁוֹ, וְלֹא הֲוָיָא טְבִיחָה כּוּלָּהּ בְּאִיסוּרָא: גָּנַב וְהִקְדִּישׁ. כִּי קָא טָבַח, דְּהֶקְדֵּשׁ קָא טָבַח, וְלֹא דִּבְעָלִים:

---

slaughtered it for idolatry;[3] גָּנַב מִשֶּׁל אָבִיו וּמֵת אָבִיו וְאַחַר כָּךְ טָבַח וּמָכַר — or he stole an ox or a sheep from his father, then his father died, and afterward he slaughtered or sold it;[4] גָּנַב וְהִקְדִּישׁ וְאַחַר כָּךְ טָבַח וּמָכַר — or he stole an ox or a sheep and consecrated it,[5] and afterward he slaughtered or sold it;[6] מְשַׁלֵּם תַּשְׁלוּמֵי כֶפֶל — in all these cases, he makes the double payment, וְאֵינוֹ מְשַׁלֵּם תַּשְׁלוּמֵי אַרְבָּעָה וַחֲמִשָּׁה — but he does not make the fourfold or fivefold payment.

Having spoken about a thief who stole an animal and then consecrated it, the Mishnah deals with a thief who stole an animal that had already been consecrated (that is, he stole an offering from someone). The Sages rule in another tractate that one who steals an offering is exempt from the fourfold and fivefold payments.[7] Our Mishnah cites a different view:

———————— NOTES ————————

liable only to the death penalty, and not to the fourfold or fivefold payment (*Rav* to Mishnah 2).

He is exempt even if he does not actually receive the death penalty (for example, he did *melachah* on Shabbos without knowing that it is forbidden), because doing a sin that *can* be punished with a severe penalty is enough to exempt him from a monetary obligation incurred at the same time (*Rav* to Mishnah 2).

3. Idol worship carries the death penalty. Accordingly, if a thief slaughters the stolen animal as a sacrifice to an idol, which makes him liable to the death penalty, he is exempt from the fourfold or fivefold payment (see previous note).

4. The thief and his brothers inherited the stolen animal upon their father's death. Thus, when he slaughtered the animal, the act of slaughter was not entirely prohibited, since he then owned part of the animal (*Rav*). A Biblical source teaches that the fourfold or fivefold payment is imposed only when the slaughter or sale of the animal is entirely prohibited, and not in a case such as this, where part of the animal belongs to the thief. He is thus exempt from paying *anything*, even the shares of his brothers (*Tos. Yom Tov* to Mishnah 5).

5. That is, he designated the animal as an offering. [Although "consecration" can also mean giving an item to the Temple treasury, that is not its meaning here, because consecration of that type is considered a sale (see *Tosafos* 79a ד״ה גנב).]

It is normally impossible for a thief to consecrate stolen property, since it is not his. The Mishnah, though, refers to a situation where he consecrated the animal after the original owner had despaired of getting it back, in which case the consecration does take effect (see *Tos. Yom Tov*).

6. When he slaughtered the animal, it was already consecrated. It is derived from the Torah that if a thief slaughtered or sold an animal that he consecrated, he is exempt from the fourfold or fivefold payment (see *Rashi* 68b ד״ה ואינו).

7. The ruling of the Sages is found in *Bava Metzia* 4:9. The Torah states: וְגֻנַּב מִבֵּית הָאִישׁ, *and it was stolen from the house of the man* (Exodus 22:6), which teaches that one who steals an offering or other consecrated property (*hekdesh*) is exempt from the double payment, because he did not steal from the "house of the man (i.e., an ordinary Jew)," but rather from "the house of *hekdesh*." And if he slaughters or sells it, he is exempt from the fourfold or fivefold payment

— רע"ב —

רבי שמעון אומר שחייב באחריותו וכו'. רבי שמעון לאו אמילתיה דתנא קמא קאי, ולא פליג עליה בגנב והקדיש ואחר

רַבִּי שִׁמְעוֹן אוֹמֵר, קָדָשִׁים שֶׁחַיָּב בְּאַחֲרָיוּתָם מְשַׁלֵּם תַּשְׁלוּמֵי אַרְבָּעָה וַחֲמִשָּׁה, שֶׁאֵין חַיָּב בְּאַחֲרָיוּתָם, פָּטוּר.

כך טבח ומכר. אלא שמעינהו רבי שמעון לרבנן בדוכתא אחריתי, דאמרי, הגונב מבית בעלים פטור, דכתיב (שמות כב,ו) וגונב מבית האיש ולא מבית הקדש. ועלה קאי רבי שמעון ואמר, קדשים שחייב באחריותן חייב, דקרינן ביה וגונב מבית האיש, דכיון דהבעל חייב באחריותם, כי קא קא טבח, דמריה קא טבח. ובקדשים שחייב באחריותן, נמי לא מחייב רבי שמעון תשלומי ארבעה וחמשה, אלא כשסחטן תמימים בפנים לשם בעלים, אלא שנשפך הדם. או שסחטן בעלי מומין בחוץ. ואף על פי שלא נפלו, סבר כל העומד לפדות כפדוי דמי, והויא שחיטה ראויה. אבל אם שחטן תמימים בחוץ, הויא שחיטה שאינה ראויה, ושמעינן ליה לרבי שמעון דאמר, שחיטה שאינה ראויה לאו שמה שחיטה, וחייב עליה תשלומי ארבעה וחמשה. ואין הלכה כרבי שמעון:

רַבִּי שִׁמְעוֹן אוֹמֵר — R' Shimon says: קָדָשִׁים שֶׁחַיָּב בְּאַחֲרָיוּתָם — If he stole and slaughtered **a consecrated [animal] for which [the owner] is responsible** (that is, the owner would have to replace it with another animal if it is lost),[8] מְשַׁלֵּם תַּשְׁלוּמֵי אַרְבָּעָה וַחֲמִשָּׁה — he makes the **fourfold or fivefold payment** to the owner. Because the owner is responsible for the animal, it is still his "property" and the thief must therefore pay for it.[9] שֶׁאֵין חַיָּב בְּאַחֲרָיוּתָם — However, if he stole and slaughtered a consecrated animal **for which [the owner] is not responsible** (that is, the owner would not have to replace it if it is lost),[10] פָּטוּר — **he is exempt** from payment. Since this animal did not

---

NOTES

(see *Rav*). [However, he must return the animal itself or, if it is unavailable, pay its value. He is exempt only from the fines.]

8. If someone says, "I accept upon myself to bring an offering," and designates an animal as his offering, and the animal then becomes unavailable (for example, it dies or is stolen), he must designate and bring another in its place. Since he said, "I accept upon *myself*, etc." he accepted a general obligation upon himself, which is not limited to any particular animal. Thus, if the designated animal is lost, he must replace it (see *Megillah* 1:6). Similarly, if someone is obligated by the Torah to bring an offering (for example, he committed a sin for which he must bring a *chatas*), and he designated an animal for that purpose and then lost it, he must designate another one.

9. Since the animal still belongs to the original owner to some degree, one who steals it is considered to be stealing "from the house of the man," in which case he must make the fourfold or fivefold payment (*Rav*). [If he did not slaughter or sell it, he is liable to the double payment.]

The Mishnah must be referring to an act of *shechitah* (slaughter) that makes the offering permitted to be eaten, because R' Shimon holds that the thief would not be liable to the fine otherwise (see Mishnah 2). One possibility is that it was slaughtered in the Temple Courtyard, like any other offering. Another possibility is that it developed a blemish that disqualified it from being offered, in which case it may be slaughtered outside the Courtyard. However, if it did not become blemished and he slaughtered it outside the Courtyard, the *shechitah* would not count according to R' Shimon, because such an animal may not be eaten (*Rav*).

R' Shimon agrees that in the Mishnah's previous case, where the thief stole an ordinary animal and then consecrated it himself (before he slaughtered or sold it), he is exempt from the fourfold or fivefold payment (see note 6). R' Shimon requires the thief to pay only if he stole an animal that had already been consecrated (*Rav*).

10. He set aside an animal and said "This is an offering." If the animal then

[105] **MISHNAH BAVA KAMMA** / Chapter 7: *Merubah*

— רע"ב —

(ה) מכרו חוץ מאחד ממאה שבו. גנב
שמכר כל השור חוץ
מדבר מועט שבו, מן
הדברים הניתרים עמו
בשחיטה, פטור, דכתיב
(שמות כא,לז) וטבחו
או מכרו, עד שימכור כל הדברים הניתרים בטביחה. לאפוקי שאם השאיר גידיה או קרניה,
דלא הוי שיור, ולא מפטר בהכי: **הנוחר.** קורטו מנחיריו עד לבו: **והמעקר.** עוקר סימנים,
פטור. ואפילו לרבנן דאמרי, שחיטה שאינה ראויה שמה שחיטה, דהא לאו שחיטה היא כלל:

[ה] **מְכָרוֹ** חוּץ מֵאֶחָד מִמֵּאָה שֶׁבּוֹ, אוֹ
שֶׁהָיְתָה לוֹ בּוֹ שׁוּתָּפוּת, הַשּׁוֹחֵט
וְנִתְנַבְּלָה בְיָדוֹ, הַנּוֹחֵר וְהַמְעַקֵּר, מְשַׁלֵּם תַּשְׁלוּמֵי
כֶפֶל, וְאֵינוֹ מְשַׁלֵּם תַּשְׁלוּמֵי אַרְבָּעָה וַחֲמִשָּׁה.

belong to its original owner at all when it was stolen, the thief does not have to pay.[11]

[5] The Mishnah lists more cases where the thief is exempt from the fourfold or fivefold payment:

מְכָרוֹ חוּץ מֵאֶחָד מִמֵּאָה שֶׁבּוֹ — **If he sold [the animal] except for one-hundredth of it,** that is, he sold 99 percent of the animal and kept 1 percent for himself;[1] אוֹ שֶׁהָיְתָה לוֹ בּוֹ שׁוּתָּפוּת — **or if he had part ownership of it** before he stole it;[2] הַשּׁוֹחֵט וְנִתְנַבְּלָה בְיָדוֹ — **or if he slaughtered it but it became a *neveilah* in his hand,** that is, he slaughtered the animal incorrectly,[3] thereby making it a *neveilah*, which may not be eaten; הַנּוֹחֵר וְהַמְעַקֵּר — **or if he slit the pipes lengthwise or tore the pipes out,** which are invalid forms of slaughtering (*shechitah*);[4] מְשַׁלֵּם תַּשְׁלוּמֵי כֶפֶל וְאֵינוֹ מְשַׁלֵּם תַּשְׁלוּמֵי אַרְבָּעָה וַחֲמִשָּׁה — **in all**

NOTES

becomes unavailable, he does not have to replace it, because he designated only that animal as an offering, and did not accept a general obligation upon himself to bring any animal (see *Megillah* 1:6).

11. Here, R' Shimon agrees with the Sages (see note 7).

[5]

1. It is derived from the Torah that a thief does not become obligated to make the fourfold or fivefold payment unless he sells all the parts of the animal that become permitted to be eaten through *shechitah*. Thus, if he keeps any edible part of the animal for himself, he is exempt from these payments, as the Mishnah will state. However, if he keeps an inedible part (such as its wool or a horn), he does have to pay (*Rav*).

2. Since part of the animal belongs to him, he is exempt from the fourfold or fivefold payment. As taught earlier (Mishnah 4 note 4), these payments are required only if the thief's slaughter or sale of the animal was completely prohibited,

and not in a case such as this, where part of the animal was always his (*Tos. Yom Tov*).

3. For example, he used a knife that is flawed, or he paused in the middle of the *shechitah*, which makes the *shechitah* invalid (*Rashi* to *Chullin* 17a). [*Neveilah* is the term for an animal that died without proper *shechitah*.]

4. Proper *shechitah* requires sliding a sharp knife across the trachea (windpipe) and esophagus (food pipe) until most of each pipe is cut. Cutting through the pipes lengthwise or ripping them out is not a valid *shechitah*.

The Sages in Mishnah 2 ruled that the thief must make the fourfold or fivefold payment even if his *shechitah* does not permit the meat to be eaten. However, that is true only where the *shechitah* was done properly and the animal is prohibited for some other reason (for example, it was a *tereifah*). If the *shechitah* itself was invalid, the Sages agree that the thief does not need to pay (*Rav*).

גָּנַב בִּרְשׁוּת הַבְּעָלִים וְטָבַח וּמָכַר חוּץ מֵרְשׁוּתָם, אוֹ שֶׁגָּנַב חוּץ מֵרְשׁוּתָם, וְטָבַח וּמָכַר בִּרְשׁוּתָם, אוֹ שֶׁגָּנַב וְטָבַח וּמָכַר חוּץ מֵרְשׁוּתָם, מְשַׁלֵּם תַּשְׁלוּמֵי אַרְבָּעָה וַחֲמִשָּׁה. אֲבָל גָּנַב וְטָבַח וּמָכַר בִּרְשׁוּתָם, פָּטוּר.

these cases **he makes the double payment** for the theft, **but does not make the fourfold or fivefold payment** for slaughtering or selling the animal.

Kinyan: When one buys something, he does not acquire it until he performs a *kinyan* (act of acquisition) with it. Similarly, if one takes something from another person without permission, he has not committed "theft," which makes him subject to the obligations of a thief, until he performs a *kinyan*. Therefore, if one stole an ox or a sheep and then slaughtered or sold it before he performed a *kinyan,* he is not obligated to make the fourfold or fivefold payment.[5] There are several types of *kinyanim* (acts of acquisition) that can be performed with an animal. One is the simple act of pulling the animal, which is called *meshichah* (pulling). However, in order to be effective, *meshichah* must be done outside the property of the owner. The Mishnah teaches how these rules relate to the fourfold and fivefold payments:

גָּנַב בִּרְשׁוּת הַבְּעָלִים וְטָבַח וּמָכַר חוּץ מֵרְשׁוּתָם — **If he stole** the animal when it was **inside the owner's property and slaughtered or sold** it **outside [the owner's] property**,[6] אוֹ שֶׁגָּנַב חוּץ מֵרְשׁוּתָם וְטָבַח וּמָכַר בִּרְשׁוּתָם — **or if he stole** the animal when it was **outside [the owner's] property and slaughtered or sold** it **inside [the owner's] property**, אוֹ שֶׁגָּנַב וְטָבַח וּמָכַר חוּץ מֵרְשׁוּתָם — **or if he stole** the animal **and slaughtered or sold** it **outside [the owner's] property**,[7] מְשַׁלֵּם תַּשְׁלוּמֵי אַרְבָּעָה וַחֲמִשָּׁה — **he makes the fourfold or fivefold payment.** Since in all these cases he must have pulled the animal at least a short distance when it was already outside the owner's property, he performed a valid act of *meshichah* (pulling), which makes him subject to the obligations of a thief, including the fourfold and fivefold payments. אֲבָל גָּנַב וְטָבַח וּמָכַר בִּרְשׁוּתָם — **But if he stole** the animal **and slaughtered or sold** it **in [the owner's] property**, in which case it remained inside the owner's premises all the time, פָּטוּר — **he is exempt.** Since the animal did not leave the owner's property, he did not perform a valid act of *meshichah*.[8]

NOTES

5. This Mishnah deals with the fourfold and fivefold payments. The principal and the double payment (*keifel*) are discussed in the next Mishnah.

6. He found the animal on the owner's property, pulled it outside, and then sold or slaughtered it. He became subject to the laws of a thief when it left the owner's property [since that was when the *kinyan* of *meshichah* took effect] (*Rashi*).

7. In these last two cases, the "theft" occurred as soon as he pulled the animal, since it was already outside the owner's domain (*Rashi*).

8. Thus, he is not held liable for stealing the animal. However, he must compensate the owner for any damage he did to it (*Piskei Rid*).

[6] **הָיָה** מוֹשְׁכוֹ וְיוֹצֵא, וּמֵת בִּרְשׁוּת הַבְּעָלִים, פָּטוּר. הִגְבִּיהוֹ אוֹ שֶׁהוֹצִיאוֹ מֵרְשׁוּת הַבְּעָלִים וָמֵת חַיָּב. נְתָנוֹ לִבְכוֹרוֹת בְּנוֹ, אוֹ לְבַעַל חוֹבוֹ, לְשׁוֹמֵר חִנָּם, וּלְשׁוֹאֵל,

— רע״ב —

(ו) היה מושכו ויוצא. פטור מכפל: הגביהו. אפילו ברשות בעלים, שהרי הגבהה קונה בכל מקום: נתנו. גנב לכהן, בחמש סלעים של פדיון בנו:

---

[6] The previous Mishnah taught that a thief who did not perform *meshichah* (or any other *kinyan*) with the stolen object is exempt from the fourfold and fivefold payments. This Mishnah teaches that he is also exempt from the principal and *keifel* payments.[1]

הָיָה מוֹשְׁכוֹ וְיוֹצֵא וּמֵת בִּרְשׁוּת הַבְּעָלִים — If a thief found an animal[2] in the owner's land, and, as **he was pulling it out, it died**[3] while still **in the owner's property,** פָּטוּר — **he is exempt** from all payments (including the principal and *keifel*), because this act of pulling is not a valid *meshichah*, since it took place entirely inside the owner's property. הִגְבִּיהוֹ — **If, however, he lifted it,** which is a valid act of acquisition (*hagbahah*) regardless of where it is done,[4] אוֹ שֶׁהוֹצִיאוֹ מֵרְשׁוּת הַבְּעָלִים — **or if he took** (pulled) **it out of the owner's property,** thereby performing *meshichah* outside the owner's domain, וָמֵת — **and** then **it died,** חַיָּב — **he is obligated** to make the principal and *keifel* payments.

In the following cases, someone entered the premises of another person and took an animal without permission, but before he "acquired" it (by pulling it out of the owner's domain or by lifting it) he gave it to someone else:

נְתָנוֹ לִבְכוֹרוֹת בְּנוֹ — **If,** while the animal was still in the owner's property, **he gave it** to a Kohen **for the redemption of his firstborn son,**[5] אוֹ לְבַעַל חוֹבוֹ — **or to** his **lender** as payment for a debt, לְשׁוֹמֵר חִנָּם — **or to an unpaid** *shomer* (watchman) to watch the animal for him, וּלְשׁוֹאֵל — **or to a**

NOTES

[6]

1. As stated in the introduction to Mishnah 1, a thief who cannot return the stolen item must pay the owner its value (the principal). If the thief is a *ganav* (who steals secretly), he also pays a fine equivalent to the item's value (*keifel*). Like the fourfold and fivefold payments, these two obligations apply only if what he did can be legally defined as "theft" (*Tos. Yom Tov*). [Of course, regardless of whether he committed "theft" or not, if he can return the stolen item itself, he must do so.]

2. This Mishnah's rulings apply to *all* animals (not just sheep or oxen), since it is discussing the principal and *keifel* payments, and not the fourfold and fivefold payments.

3. [The animal died a natural death. If its death was caused by the thief, he would have to pay for killing it.]

4. "Lifting" (הַגְבָּהָה) is another way to acquire an animal or object. This *kinyan* works in all places, even the domain of the owner (*Rav*).

5. The Torah obligates a father to redeem his firstborn son, which he does by giving a Kohen five silver *sela'im* (*Numbers* 18:16). In the Mishnah's case, the thief asked a Kohen (who did not know that the animal was stolen) to take the animal in place of the five *sela'im* (*Rav*). The Kohen then pulled the animal out of the owner's domain, having been told to do so by the thief (*Meiri*).

לְנוֹשֵׂא שָׂכָר, וּלְשׂוֹכֵר, וְהָיָה מוֹשְׁכוֹ, וּמֵת בִּרְשׁוּת הַבְּעָלִים, פָּטוּר. הִגְבִּיהוֹ אוֹ שֶׁהוֹצִיאוֹ מֵרְשׁוּת הַבְּעָלִים, וָמֵת, חַיָּב.

[ז] **אֵין** מְגַדְּלִין בְּהֵמָה דַקָּה בְּאֶרֶץ יִשְׂרָאֵל,

— רע״ב —

היה מושכו. הכהן או בעל חוב או השומר: ומת ברשות בעלים: פטור. הגנב מכלוס: (ז) אין מגדלין בהמה דקה בארץ ישראל. משום ישוב ארץ ישראל,

---

borrower to use it, **לְנוֹשֵׂא שָׂכָר** — or **to a paid** *shomer* **to watch it for him,** **וּלְשׂוֹכֵר** — **or to a renter** **to use it,** **וְהָיָה מוֹשְׁכוֹ וּמֵת בִּרְשׁוּת הַבְּעָלִים** — **and, as he** (the person who received the animal) **was pulling it, it died** while still **in the owner's domain,** **פָּטוּר** — [the thief] **is exempt** from all payments, because neither he nor the person to whom he gave the animal performed a *kinyan* with it. **הִגְבִּיהוֹ** — However, if **he** (the person who received the animal) **lifted it,** which is a valid *kinyan* even inside the owner's domain, **אוֹ שֶׁהוֹצִיאוֹ מֵרְשׁוּת הַבְּעָלִים** — **or if he took it out of the owner's domain,** in which case he performed the *kinyan* of *meshichah*, **וָמֵת** — **and** then **it died,** **חַיָּב** — [the thief] **is obligated** to pay the principal and the *keifel* payments. In all these cases, the thief asked the recipient to do the *kinyan* for him. The recipient thus acted as the thief's agent, and the rule is that an act done by an agent is viewed as though it were done by the person who asked him to do it.[6] Accordingly, the thief "acquired" the animal (through his agent's act of pulling or lifting it), which makes him subject to the obligations of a thief, including the principal and *keifel* payments.

[7] After teaching the Torah's laws about damage involving animals, the chapter finishes with several *Rabbinic* decrees that concern animals:[1] **אֵין מְגַדְּלִין בְּהֵמָה דַקָּה בְּאֶרֶץ יִשְׂרָאֵל** — **We may not raise small domestic animals** (sheep and goats) **in Eretz Yisrael,** because they might damage the crops;[2]

NOTES

6. This is the rule of שְׁלוּחוֹ שֶׁל אָדָם כְּמוֹתוֹ, *The agent of a person is like himself.*

Normally, this rule does not apply where the agent was asked to commit a sin, as in our case, where he was asked to steal something [אֵין שָׁלִיחַ לִדְבַר עֲבֵרָה, *There is no agent for a matter of sin*]. However, the reason for this exception is that the one who asked the agent can say that he did not expect him to disobey the word of God (see Mishnah 6:4 note 4), and this reason is relevant only where the agent *knew* that he would be committing a sin. Therefore, in the Mishnah's cases, if the agent did not know that he was being asked to sin (because he thought that the animal belonged to the thief), we go back to the regular rule, which states that the actions of an agent are viewed as though they were done

by the one who sent him (*Tos. Yom Tov*).

[7]

1. *Meleches Shlomo.*

2. The Sages wished to strengthen Jewish settlement of Eretz Yisrael. For this reason, they prohibited raising small animals (goats and sheep) there, because these animals tend to destroy vegetation that farmers have planted (*Rav*).

However, raising *large* animals (such as oxen or horses) is permissible, even though they also damage crops. This is because large animals are needed for work (carrying burdens, pulling plows), and the Sages avoided making laws that would be too difficult for the people to keep. Small animals, on the other hand, were mainly used for food, and could be brought in from other countries (*Meiri*).

[109] **MISHNAH BAVA KAMMA** / Chapter 7: *Merubah* 7/7

— רע"ב —

שֶׁמַּפְסִידִין אֶת הַזְּרָעִים: **אֲבָל מְגַדְּלִין בְּסוּרְיָא.** אַרְלוּת שֶׁכִּבֵּשׁ דָּוִד. דְּלָאו שְׁמֵיהּ כִּבּוּשׁ, וְלֹא חָיְישִׁינַן בָּהּ לִישּׁוּב, וְאִם יַפְסִידוּ שָׂדוֹת אֲחֵרִים יְשַׁלְּמִינְהוּ: **אֵין מְגַדְּלִין תַּרְנְגוֹלִים בִּירוּשָׁלַיִם מִפְּנֵי הַקֳּדָשִׁים.** שֶׁאוֹכְלִין שָׁם.

אֲבָל מְגַדְּלִין בְּסוּרְיָא וּבַמִּדְבָּרוֹת שֶׁבְּאֶרֶץ יִשְׂרָאֵל. אֵין מְגַדְּלִין תַּרְנְגוֹלִים בִּירוּשָׁלַיִם מִפְּנֵי הַקֳּדָשִׁים, וְלֹא כֹהֲנִים בְּאֶרֶץ יִשְׂרָאֵל מִפְּנֵי הַטְּהָרוֹת. אֵין מְגַדְּלִין חֲזִירִים בְּכָל מָקוֹם. לֹא יְגַדֵּל אָדָם אֶת הַכֶּלֶב אֶלָּא אִם כֵּן הָיָה קָשׁוּר בְּשַׁלְשֶׁלֶת.

וְדֶרֶךְ תַּרְנְגוֹלִים לְנַקֵּר בָּאַשְׁפָּה, וְשֶׁמָּא יוֹצִיאוּ עַכָּ"ס [כַּטְּהוֹרָה] מִן הַשֶּׁרֶץ, וְיַטְמְאוּ אֶת הַקֳּדָשִׁים: **וְלֹא** יְגַדְּלוּ כֹּהֲנִים תַּרְנְגוֹלִים בְּכָל אֶרֶץ יִשְׂרָאֵל: **מִפְּנֵי הַטְּהָרוֹת.** שֶׁהַכֹּהֲנִים אוֹכְלִים תְּרוּמָה, וּצְרִיכִים לְשָׁמְרָהּ בִּטְהָרָה: **חֲזִירִים.** מְפָרֵשׁ טַעְמָא בַּגְּמָרָא (פב,ב), כְּשֶׁצָּרוּ מַלְכֵי חַשְׁמוֹנַאי זֶה עַל זֶה, הָיוּ רְגִילִים בְּכָל יוֹם, שֶׁהָיוּ אֵלּוּ שַׁבְּחוּץ מַעֲלִים לָהֶם תְּמִידִים לְאֵלּוּ שֶׁבִּפְנִים. יוֹם אֶחָד הֶעֱלוּ לָהֶם חֲזִיר, כֵּיוָן שֶׁהִגִּיעַ לַחֲצִי חוֹמָה, נָעַץ צִפָּרְנָיו בַּחוֹמָה, וְנִזְדַּעְזְעָה אֶרֶץ יִשְׂרָאֵל אַרְבַּע מֵאוֹת פַּרְסָה עַל אַרְבַּע מֵאוֹת פַּרְסָה. בְּאוֹתָהּ שָׁעָה אָמְרוּ אָרוּר הַמְגַדֵּל חֲזִירִים: **אֶת הַכֶּלֶב.** מִפְּנֵי שֶׁנּוֹשֵׁךְ וּמְנַבֵּחַ, וּמַפֵּלֶת אִשָּׁה מִירָאָתוֹ:

אֲבָל מְגַדְּלִין בְּסוּרְיָא — but we may raise them **in Surya**, which is not part of Eretz Yisrael,[3] וּבַמִּדְבָּרוֹת שֶׁבְּאֶרֶץ יִשְׂרָאֵל — and **in the wilderness areas of Eretz Yisrael**, where there are no crops to be damaged. אֵין מְגַדְּלִין תַּרְנְגוֹלִים בִּירוּשָׁלַיִם מִפְּנֵי הַקֳּדָשִׁים — **We may not raise chickens in Jerusalem because of the offerings** that are eaten there, which the chickens might cause to become *tamei*.[4] וְלֹא כֹהֲנִים בְּאֶרֶץ יִשְׂרָאֵל מִפְּנֵי הַטְּהָרוֹת — **And Kohanim** may **not** raise chickens anywhere **in Eretz Yisrael because of the** *tahor* **food** (i.e., terumah) that they receive, which they must prevent from becoming *tamei*.[5] לֹא אֵין מְגַדְּלִין חֲזִירִים בְּכָל מָקוֹם — **We may not raise pigs in any place.**[6] יְגַדֵּל אָדָם אֶת הַכֶּלֶב אֶלָּא אִם כֵּן הָיָה קָשׁוּר בְּשַׁלְשֶׁלֶת — **A person may not raise**

NOTES

3. This is Aram Tzova (north of Eretz Yisrael), which King David conquered. The Tanna of our Mishnah holds that this region did not gain the status of Eretz Yisrael proper (see *Gittin* 8b).

4. The meat of some offerings (*shelamim*, *pesach*, etc.) did not have to be eaten in the Temple, but could be eaten anywhere in Jerusalem, provided that it was *tahor*. The Sages were concerned that chickens, which pick at piles of garbage, might pull out a piece of a dead *sheretz* (one of certain types of creeping creatures that transmit *tumah* when dead) and bring it into contact with sacred meat, making it *tamei*. To prevent this, they prohibited raising chickens in Jerusalem (*Rav*).

5. *Terumah* is the first portion that must be separated from produce grown in Eretz Yisrael. It is given to a Kohen and may be eaten only by Kohanim and the members of their households. *Terumah* is sacred and must be kept *tahor*. The Sages, therefore, forbade Kohanim to raise chickens wherever they live, because these birds might contaminate their *terumah* [as described in the previous note] (*Rav*).

6. This decree resulted from an incident that took place when Hyrkanos and Aristobolus — sons of King Alexander Yannai — were fighting each other for the crown. One held Jerusalem while the other besieged the city. Every day, those inside the city would lower money in a basket over the city wall, and the besiegers would take the money and place lambs in the basket for the two daily *tamid* offerings. One day, the besiegers wanted to disrupt the sacrificial service, so they placed a pig in the basket instead of the usual lambs. When the pig reached halfway up the wall, it stuck its hoofs into the wall, and the entire Eretz Yisrael shook. At that time, the Sages declared, "Cursed be the man who shall raise pigs" (*Rav*).

[110] משניות בבא קמא / פרק ז: מרבה

אֵין פּוֹרְסִין נְשָׁבִים לַיוֹנִים, אֶלָּא אִם כֵּן הָיָה רָחוֹק מִן הַיִּשׁוּב שְׁלֹשִׁים רִיס.

— רע"ב —

נְשָׁבִים. פַּחִים. **שֶׁלֹּא יִלְכְּדוּ בָּהֶם יוֹנֵי בְּנֵי הַיִּשׁוּב: שְׁלֹשִׁים רִיס.** אַרְבָּעָה מִילִין:

---

a dog unless it is tied up with a chain, because an untied dog might frighten a pregnant woman and cause her to miscarry.[7] אֵין פּוֹרְסִין נְשָׁבִים לַיוֹנִים אֶלָּא אִם כֵּן הָיָה רָחוֹק מִן הַיִּשׁוּב שְׁלֹשִׁים רִיס — **We may not spread traps for** wild **doves unless [the trap] is** at least **thirty** *ris* **away from the** nearest **settled area,** because a trap that is closer to a settled area might capture doves that belong to the people who live there.[8]

NOTES

7. The prohibition applies to fierce dogs, which bite and bark at people they do not know. Raising tame dogs is permitted, even if they are not chained up (*Tos. Yom Tov*).

8. Doves tend not to travel more than thirty *ris* from where they usually reside.

Thirty *ris* is four *milin* (*Rav*), and four *milin* is 8,000 *amos*. [Thus, based on the various opinions regarding the length of an *amah*, 30 *ris* is between 2.4 and 2.9 miles (3.8 and 4.6 kilometers).]

Chapter Eight

משניות בבא קמא / פרק ח: החובל

[א] הַחוֹבֵל בַּחֲבֵרוֹ, חַיָּב עָלָיו מִשּׁוּם חֲמִשָּׁה דְבָרִים, בְּנֶזֶק, בְּצַעַר, בְּרִפּוּי, בְּשֶׁבֶת, וּבְבֹשֶׁת. בְּנֶזֶק כֵּיצַד. סִמֵּא אֶת עֵינוֹ, קָטַע אֶת יָדוֹ, שִׁבֵּר אֶת רַגְלוֹ, רוֹאִין אוֹתוֹ כְּאִלּוּ הוּא עֶבֶד נִמְכָּר בַּשּׁוּק, וְשָׁמִין כַּמָּה הָיָה יָפֶה וְכַמָּה הוּא יָפֶה. צַעַר, כְּוָאוֹ בְשַׁפּוּד אוֹ בְמַסְמֵר, וַאֲפִלּוּ עַל צִפָּרְנוֹ, מָקוֹם שֶׁאֵינוֹ עוֹשֶׂה חַבּוּרָה,

— רע"ב —

פרק שמיני – החובל. (א) החובל. וכמה הוא יפה. שאלו היה צריך היה מוכר עצמו בעבד עברי, וזה שהזיקו הפסידו ממון זה:

---

[1] This chapter deals with the laws of physical injuries inflicted by one person on another. The first Mishnah lists and explains the different payments that the attacker must make to the victim:

הַחוֹבֵל בַּחֲבֵרוֹ חַיָּב עָלָיו מִשּׁוּם חֲמִשָּׁה דְבָרִים — **Someone who wounds another person is obligated to pay him for five things,** i.e., five aspects of the injury: בְּנֶזֶק — (1) **for the damage** itself (i.e., the victim's loss of value), בְּצַעַר — (2) **for the pain** that he suffered, בְּרִפּוּי — (3) **for the expenses of healing,** בְּשֶׁבֶת — (4) **for loss of employment,** וּבְבֹשֶׁת — (5) **and for embarrassment.**[1]

The Mishnah elaborates on each of these five categories, starting with "damage":

בְּנֶזֶק כֵּיצַד — **How is** the payment for **"damage" calculated?** סִמֵּא אֶת עֵינוֹ קָטַע אֶת יָדוֹ שִׁבֵּר אֶת רַגְלוֹ — **If, for example, he blinded [the victim's] eye, cut off his hand, or broke his leg,** רוֹאִין אוֹתוֹ כְּאִלּוּ הוּא עֶבֶד נִמְכָּר בַּשּׁוּק — **we view [the victim] as though he were a servant being sold in the market,** וְשָׁמִין כַּמָּה הָיָה יָפֶה וְכַמָּה הוּא יָפֶה — **and we estimate how much he was worth** when he still had the eye, hand, or leg, **and how much he is worth** without it. The attacker must pay the difference.[2]

The second payment, "pain":

צַעַר — **How is** the payment for **"pain" calculated?** כְּוָאוֹ בְשַׁפּוּד אוֹ בְמַסְמֵר — **If, for example, he burned [the victim] with a** hot iron **spit or with a hot nail,** וַאֲפִלּוּ עַל צִפָּרְנוֹ מָקוֹם שֶׁאֵינוֹ עוֹשֶׂה חַבּוּרָה — **even if he burned him on his fingernail,** which is **a place where [a burn] does not make a wound** that would

--- NOTES ---

[1]

1. Each of these five types of payments is derived from a verse (see *Rav* ד"ה והמתבייש).

The Mishnah means that the attacker can be obligated to pay for up to five categories of damage. If he inflicted all five, he must pay for all five. If he inflicted fewer than five (for example, he burned the victim lightly, causing pain but none of the other types of damage), he pays only for what he inflicted (*Meiri*).

2. A Jew in need of money can sell himself as a servant (*eved ivri*). Now that the victim's value has been reduced because of the injury, he cannot sell himself for as much as he could before. Since the attacker made him "lose" that amount of money, he must compensate him for it (*Rav*).

MISHNAH BAVA KAMMA / Chapter 8: *HaChoveil*

— רע״ב —

אוֹמְדִין כַּמָּה אָדָם כַּיּוֹצֵא בָזֶה רוֹצֶה לִטוֹל לִהְיוֹת מִצְטַעֵר כָּךְ. רִפּוּי, הִכָּהוּ, חַיָּב לְרַפֹּאתוֹ. עָלוּ בוֹ צְמָחִים, אִם מֵחֲמַת הַמַּכָּה, חַיָּב; שֶׁלֹּא מֵחֲמַת הַמַּכָּה, פָּטוּר. חָיְתָה וְנִסְתְּרָה, חָיְתָה וְנִסְתְּרָה, חַיָּב לְרַפֹּאתוֹ. חָיְתָה כָּל צָרְכָּהּ, אֵינוֹ חַיָּב לְרַפֹּאתוֹ.

כיוצא בזה. לפי מה שהוא מעונג, רב לערכו וכלאחבו. צמחין. אבעטבועות לבנות:

אוֹמְדִין כַּמָּה אָדָם כַּיּוֹצֵא בָזֶה רוֹצֶה לִטוֹל לִהְיוֹת reduce his market value,[3] מִצְטַעֵר כָּךְ — **we estimate how much** money **a man like this [victim], with his particular sensitivity and tolerance of pain, would want to take to suffer such pain,** and the attacker must pay him that amount.[4]

The third category, "healing":

רִפּוּי — **What is "healing"?** הִכָּהוּ חַיָּב לְרַפֹּאתוֹ — **If one** person **struck [another], he is obligated to heal him,** that is, he must pay the expenses of healing the injury, such as doctors' bills and medicines.

Some laws about the obligation to pay for healing:

עָלוּ בוֹ צְמָחִים — **If blisters developed on [his skin],** near the wound, אִם מֵחֲמַת הַמַּכָּה חַיָּב — the law is that **if** they developed **as a result of the wound, [the attacker] is obligated** to pay for healing them as well,[5] שֶׁלֹּא מֵחֲמַת הַמַּכָּה פָּטוּר — **but** if they did **not** develop **as a result of the wound, he is not obligated** to pay for healing them.[6] חָיְתָה וְנִסְתְּרָה חָיְתָה וְנִסְתְּרָה — **If [the wound] healed and returned** and then again **it healed and returned** (i.e., it kept returning because it never fully healed), חַיָּב לְרַפֹּאתוֹ — **[the attacker] is obligated to heal him,** that is, he must pay for the medical expenses again and again until it is healed completely. חָיְתָה כָּל צָרְכָּהּ — **If,** however, **[the wound] healed completely** and then returned, אֵינוֹ חַיָּב לְרַפֹּאתוֹ — **[the attacker] is not obligated to heal him.**[7]

— NOTES —

3. In this case the attacker pays for "pain" but not for "damage" (*Meiri*).

4. The Mishnah seems to mean that the court makes the following assessment: If the victim was offered money in order to suffer the level of pain that was inflicted upon him, how much money would he demand? However, the Gemara (85a) argues that this cannot be the Mishnah's meaning, because a person would not agree to suffer great pain even if he were paid all the money in the world. Therefore, the Gemara explains that we assess the payment for pain as follows: How much would the victim *give* in order to *avoid* the pain? For example, if his hand had to be cut off in any event, how much would he pay to have the operation done in such a way that he would not feel pain? The amount he would pay is the amount the attacker must give him (*Tos. Yom Tov*).

5. Even if the blisters appeared later, if they were caused by the wound, the attacker must pay to heal them (*Tiferes Yisrael*).

6. That is, if the blisters resulted from the victim's negligence (for example, he did not follow the doctor's orders), the attacker does not have to pay to heal them, even though they would not have developed had there been no wound in the first place (*Rav* ד״ה והמתבייש; *Tos. Yom Tov*).

When the Mishnah mentions "blisters," it is merely giving an example. The same laws apply to any infection or sickness that results from the injury (see *Rav* there).

7. The victim cannot claim that the

שֶׁבֶת, רוֹאִין אוֹתוֹ כְּאִלּוּ הוּא שׁוֹמֵר קִשּׁוּאִין, שֶׁכְּבָר נָתַן לוֹ דְּמֵי יָדוֹ וּדְמֵי רַגְלוֹ. בֹּשֶׁת, הַכֹּל לְפִי הַמְבַיֵּשׁ וְהַמִּתְבַּיֵּשׁ.

— רע״ב —

שבת. כל ימי החולי רואין אותו כאילו הוא שומר קשואין, ונותן שכירותו של כל יום, שהרי אין ראוי למלאכה אחרת אפילו בלא

חולי, שהרי נקטע ידו ורגלו, והוא כבר נתן לו דמיהן: הכל לפי המבייש. אדם קל שבייש בשתו מרובה: והמתבייש. לפי חשיבותו בשתו [מרובה]. וכולהו חמשה דברים מקרא נפקי. נזק, דכתיב (שמות כא,כד) עין תחת עין, ואין לומר עין ממש דכתיב (במדבר לה,לא) ולא תקחו כופר לנפש רוצח, לנפש רוצח אי אתה לוקח כופר, אבל אתה לוקח כופר לראשי אברים, שאם סימא את עין חבירו נותן לו דמי עינו, והיינו עין תחת עין. צער, נפקא לן מפצע תחת פצע (שמות כא,כה), דקרא יתירא הוא לחייב על הצער ואפילו במקום נזק. דלמא תימא הרי קנה ידו ויש עליו לחתכה, אלא אומרים, היה עליו לחתכה בסם, וזה חתכה בברזל ולטרן, לפיכך משלם את הצער. רפוי ושבת, רק שבתו יתן ורפא ירפא (שם יט). ודוקא כשהחולי בא מחמת מכה, אבל אם פשע החולה בעצמו, ועבר על דברי הרופא, שוב אין המזיק חייב בשבת ורפוי, שצריכין מחמת פשיעותא. בשת, דכתיב (דברים כה,יב) וקצותה את כפה, ממון. ודין תורה שאין יכולים לדון בשום דין שבטבולם, אלא דיינים הסמוכים בארץ ישראל, דכתיב (שמות כב,ח) עד האלהים יבא דבר שניהם, ואין נקראים אלהים אלא דיינים הסמוכים בארץ ישראל. אלא שבהלואות, ומקח וממכר, והקנאות, והודאות, וכפירות, דנין בהם בחולה לארץ, כאילו הם שלוחים של בית דין של ארץ ישראל, ושליחותייהו קעבדינן. וזה בלבד בדבר המצוי ויש בו חסרון כיס, [וכן] בהמה

The fourth payment, "loss of employment":

שֶׁבֶת — How is **"loss of employment"** calculated? If the victim cannot do the type of work that he did before (for example, he lost a hand and he cannot work without it), רוֹאִין אוֹתוֹ כְּאִלּוּ הוּא שׁוֹמֵר קִשּׁוּאִין — we view him as though he were a watchman of a field of **cucumbers,** because that is all he is fit to do now. The attacker must pay him the wages of a cucumber watchman for every day that his illness (which was caused by the injury) keeps him bedridden and prevents him from doing even such simple work. However, the attacker does not have to pay him the wages he was earning before he was wounded, שֶׁכְּבָר נָתַן לוֹ דְּמֵי יָדוֹ וּדְמֵי רַגְלוֹ — **because he has already given him the value of his hand or the value of his foot** when he paid for "damage," and that amount included whatever he would have earned had he not been injured.[8]

The fifth payment, "embarrassment":

בֹּשֶׁת — How is **"embarrassment"** calculated? הַכֹּל לְפִי הַמְבַיֵּשׁ וְהַמִּתְבַּיֵּשׁ — It

---

NOTES

---

wound returned because of the original injury. Rather, since the wound healed completely, we assume that it returned as a result of some other factor, for which the attacker is not responsible (*Tiferes Yisrael; Meiri*).

8. The Mishnah's case is where the victim was injured in such a way that he will never be able to return to his previous profession, and for the rest of his life he will have to do simple, low-paying jobs, such as watching a patch of cucumbers. Furthermore, the injury caused him to be sick for some time, during which he

could not work at all. The permanent reduction of salary (from that of his previous profession to that of a watchman) is included in the payment for "damage," since "damage" is the change in value between a servant who could do his old profession and one who can only be a watchman. Thus, after paying "damage," all that remains is for the attacker to compensate him for his inability to do *any* work (even watching a small field) when he was sick and bedridden. This is the payment for "loss of employment" (*Rav*).

[115] MISHNAH BAVA KAMMA / Chapter 8: HaChoveil

הַמְבַיֵּשׁ אֶת הֶעָרֹם, הַמְבַיֵּשׁ אֶת הַסּוּמָא, וְהַמְבַיֵּשׁ אֶת הַיָּשֵׁן, חַיָּב. וְיָשֵׁן שֶׁבִּיֵּשׁ, פָּטוּר. נָפַל מִן הַגָּג, וְהִזִּיק וּבִיֵּשׁ, חַיָּב עַל הַנֶּזֶק וּפָטוּר עַל הַבֹּשֶׁת, שֶׁנֶּאֱמַר, וְשָׁלְחָה יָדָהּ וְהֶחֱזִיקָה בִּמְבֻשָׁיו,

— רע"ב —

שהזיקה בשן ורגל שהם מועדים, או שהזיק אדם בבהמה. אבל בהמה שהזיקה אדם, או אדם באדם, אין דנין אותו בחוץ לארץ כלל. אלא מנדין את החובל או את המזיק, עד שיפעלנו עם בעל דינו לארץ ישראל, או שיתן פשרה קרוב למה שנראה בעיני הדיין, אבל דבר קצוב אין פוסקים עליו. וכן הדין בכל הקנסות הכתובות בתורה ובכולה תלמודא, אין גובין אותן דייני חוצה לארץ, אלא שמנדין מי שנתחייב בהן כמו שבארנו:

all depends on the status of **the one who caused the embarrassment, and** the status of **the one who was embarrassed.** The lower the status of the attacker, the greater the disgrace he causes, and the higher the status of the victim, the greater the disgrace he suffers. We estimate how much a person of the victim's status would pay to avoid being embarrassed by someone of the attacker's status, and the attacker must pay that amount.[9]

Some laws about the payment for embarrassment:

הַמְבַיֵּשׁ אֶת הֶעָרֹם — If someone embarrasses a naked person (for example, he spits on him or slaps him);[10] הַמְבַיֵּשׁ אֶת הַסּוּמָא — or if he embarrasses a blind person, who senses that he is being disgraced even though he cannot see it;[11] וְהַמְבַיֵּשׁ אֶת הַיָּשֵׁן — or if he embarrasses a sleeping person, who, upon waking, realizes that he had been disgraced in his sleep;[12] חַיָּב — in each of these cases, he is obligated to pay for the disgrace that he caused, because people suffer disgrace even if they are unclothed, blind, or asleep at the time.[13] וְיָשֵׁן שֶׁבִּיֵּשׁ פָּטוּר — But if a sleeping person embarrassed someone (for example, he kicked another person in his sleep, or he fell off his bed on top of him) he is not obligated to pay, because one must pay for embarrassing someone only if he attacked him intentionally, as derived from the verse quoted below.

נָפַל מִן הַגָּג וְהִזִּיק וּבִיֵּשׁ — If someone fell from a roof by accident, and injured and embarrassed another person by falling on him, חַיָּב עַל הַנֶּזֶק — he is obligated to pay for the damage, because a person must pay "damage," even if the attack was unintentional,[14] וּפָטוּר עַל הַבֹּשֶׁת — but he is not obligated to pay for the embarrassment, because payment for embarrassment is required only in the case of an intentional attack, שֶׁנֶּאֱמַר "וְשָׁלְחָה יָדָהּ וְהֶחֱזִיקָה בִּמְבֻשָׁיו" — as it is stated regarding the payment for embarrassment (Deuteronomy 25:11): *If men fight one another... and the wife of one of them approaches to rescue her husband from the hand of the one who is hitting him*

NOTES

9. See *Rambam, Hilchos Naarah Besulah* 2:5.

10. *Tos. Yom Tov,* citing *Tosafos.* Although he is naked, he is shamed by these acts (though not as much as a clothed person would be).

11. *Tiferes Yisrael.*

12. *Tos. Yom Tov.*

13. However, the attacker is not obligated to pay as much as one who embarrasses a clothed, seeing, or awake person (*Tos. Yom Tov, Tiferes Yisrael*).

14. Mishnah 2:6.

ח/ב

משניות בבא קמא / פרק ח: החובל

אֵינוֹ חַיָּב עַל הַבֹּשֶׁת עַד שֶׁיְהֵא מִתְכַּוֵּן.

[ב] זֶה חֹמֶר בָּאָדָם מִבְּשׁוֹר, שֶׁהָאָדָם מְשַׁלֵּם נֶזֶק, צַעַר, רִפּוּי, שֶׁבֶת, וּבֹשֶׁת, וּמְשַׁלֵּם דְּמֵי וְלָדוֹת, וְשׁוֹר אֵינוֹ מְשַׁלֵּם אֶלָּא נֶזֶק וּפָטוּר מִדְּמֵי וְלָדוֹת.

— רע״ב —

(ב) ושור אינו משלם אלא נזק. דכתיב (ויקרא כד,יט) איש בעמיתו, ולא שור בעמיתו: ופטור מדמי ולדות. דכתיב (שמות כא,כב) כי ינצו אנשים, אנשים ולא שוורים:

---

and [to do so] she stretches out her hand and grasps his embarrassing place (i.e., his private parts, to embarrass him and thus stop him from hitting her husband). The words, and she stretches out her hand, imply that she attacks him intentionally;[15] — אֵינוֹ חַיָּב עַל הַבֹּשֶׁת עַד שֶׁיְהֵא מִתְכַּוֵּן — therefore, one is not obligated to pay for embarrassing someone unless he intended to harm him.[16]

[2] The Mishnah contrasts the law of a *person* who injures a person with the law of an *animal* that injures a person.

זֶה חֹמֶר בָּאָדָם מִבְּשׁוֹר — **This is a stringency that** applies to **a person rather than to an ox;** that is to say, a person who injures another person is treated more stringently in the following respects than the owner of an ox (or any other animal) that injures a person: שֶׁהָאָדָם מְשַׁלֵּם נֶזֶק צַעַר רִפּוּי שֶׁבֶת וּבֹשֶׁת — **A person** who injures another person **pays for damage, pain, healing, loss of employment, and embarrassment** (as taught in the previous Mishnah), וּמְשַׁלֵּם דְּמֵי וְלָדוֹת — **and** if he injures a pregnant woman, causing her to miscarry, he **pays the value of the fetus.**[1] וְשׁוֹר אֵינוֹ מְשַׁלֵּם אֶלָּא נֶזֶק — **But the** owner of **an ox** that injures a person **pays only** for **damage,**[2] וּפָטוּר מִדְּמֵי וְלָדוֹת — **and** if it causes a pregnant woman to miscarry, **he is exempt** from paying **the value of the fetus.**[3]

[3] The first part of this Mishnah is based on the following laws: (a) A person who hits his parent and causes bleeding or bruising is liable to the death penalty.[1] (b) A person who hits anyone on Shabbos and causes bleeding or bruising is liable to the death penalty, but not if he does so on Yom Kippur.[2]

NOTES

15. Tos. Yom Tov.

16. However, if he *did* intend to harm the victim, he must pay for embarrassment, even if he intended only to injure him, and not to embarrass him (*Tos. Yom Tov*).

[2]

1. See Mishnah 5:4.

2. The Torah states: *And if a man inflicts a blemish* (wound) *on his fellow, as he did, so shall be done to him* [i.e., he shall make the five payments] (*Leviticus* 24:19). By stating "man," the verse implies that

only a *person* who injures another person must make all five payments, but if an *ox* injures a person, its owner need not pay all of them (*Rav*).

3. See Mishnah 5:4 note 1.

[3]

1. *Sanhedrin* 11:1.

2. Wounding a living creature is a *melachah* (work that is forbidden on Shabbos and other holy days). One who performs *melachah* on Shabbos is liable to the death penalty, but one who does so on Yom Kippur is liable to *kares*.

[117] MISHNAH BAVA KAMMA / Chapter 8: HaChoveil

— רע״ב —

(ג) והחובל בחבירו ביום הכפורים חייב. אף על גב דבכל התורה כולה, העובר עבירה שחייב עליה מלקות ותשלומין, לוקה ואינו משלם, הכא משלם ואינו לוקה, דפטירוט רבתה תורה חובל בחבירו לתשלומין ולא למלקות.

[ג] **הַמַּכֶּה** אֶת אָבִיו וְאֶת אִמּוֹ, וְלֹא עָשָׂה בָּהֶם חַבּוּרָה, וְחוֹבֵל בַּחֲבֵרוֹ בְּיוֹם הַכִּפּוּרִים, חַיָּב בְּכֻלָּן. הַחוֹבֵל בְּעֶבֶד עִבְרִי, חַיָּב בְּכֻלָּן חוּץ מִן הַשֶּׁבֶת בִּזְמַן שֶׁהוּא שֶׁלּוֹ. הַחוֹבֵל בְּעֶבֶד כְּנַעֲנִי שֶׁל אֲחֵרִים, חַיָּב בְּכֻלָּן. רַבִּי יְהוּדָה אוֹמֵר, אֵין לַעֲבָדִים בֹּשֶׁת.

מדכתיב (דברים כה,יא) יד ביד, דהיינו ממון. מכדי כתיב (ויקרא כד,יט) כאשר עשה כן יעשה לו, יד ביד למה לי, אלא להביא חובל בחבירו ביום הכפורים, שמשלם ואינו לוקה: רבי יהודה אומר אין לעבדים בושת. דכתיב (דברים כה,יא) כי ינצו אנשים יחדיו איש ואחיו, במי שיש לו אחוה, יצא עבד שאין לו אחוה. ואין הלכה כרבי יהודה:

הַמַּכֶּה אֶת אָבִיו וְאֶת אִמּוֹ וְלֹא עָשָׂה בָּהֶם חַבּוּרָה — If someone hits his father or his mother, but does not inflict a wound upon them, that is, he does not draw blood or even make a bruise, **וְחוֹבֵל בַּחֲבֵרוֹ בְּיוֹם הַכִּפּוּרִים** — or if someone wounds another on Yom Kippur, **חַיָּב בְּכֻלָּן** — he is obligated to pay all of them, i.e., all the five payments (damage, pain, healing, loss of employment, and embarrassment). Although the rule is that someone who becomes subject to the death penalty and a monetary obligation at the same time is exempt from the monetary obligation,[3] that rule does not apply in these cases. In the first case, the attacker is not subject to the death penalty because he did not cause bleeding or bruising, and in the second case, he is not subject to the death penalty because he made the wound on Yom Kippur (as opposed to Shabbos). Thus, there is no reason to exempt him from his monetary obligations.[4]

Another law about the five payments:

הַחוֹבֵל בְּעֶבֶד עִבְרִי חַיָּב בְּכֻלָּן — One who wounds a Hebrew servant is obligated to make all [the payments], **חוּץ מִן הַשֶּׁבֶת בִּזְמַן שֶׁהוּא שֶׁלּוֹ** — except for loss of employment when [the servant] is his, since it is his own loss that his servant is unable to work.[5] **הַחוֹבֵל בְּעֶבֶד כְּנַעֲנִי שֶׁל אֲחֵרִים חַיָּב בְּכֻלָּן** — One who wounds a Canaanite slave who belongs to others is obligated to make all [the payments], because wounding a Canaanite slave is like wounding a free man.[6]

The next Tanna disagrees on one point:

רַבִּי יְהוּדָה אוֹמֵר — R' Yehudah says: **אֵין לַעֲבָדִים בֹּשֶׁת** — Canaanite slaves have no payment for embarrassment. One who injures a Canaanite slave

— NOTES —

3. See Mishnah 3:10.

4. Although *melachah* on Yom Kippur is punishable by *kares*, according to this Tanna that punishment does not exempt a person from monetary payments (*Meiri*).

5. If he wounds someone else's Hebrew servant, he pays the loss of employment to the servant's master, and the other four payments to the servant himself.

6. All the payments are made to his master (*Meiri*), with the exception of "healing," which is made to a doctor to heal the slave (see *Tosafos*).

[ד] חֵרֵשׁ, שׁוֹטֶה וְקָטָן פְּגִיעָתָן רָעָה, הַחוֹבֵל בָּהֶן חַיָּב, וְהֵם שֶׁחָבְלוּ בַאֲחֵרִים, פְּטוּרִין. הָעֶבֶד וְהָאִשָּׁה פְּגִיעָתָן רָעָה, הַחוֹבֵל בָּהֶן חַיָּב, וְהֵם שֶׁחָבְלוּ בַאֲחֵרִים פְּטוּרִין, אֲבָל מְשַׁלְּמִין לְאַחַר זְמָן, נִתְגָּרְשָׁה הָאִשָּׁה, נִשְׁתַּחְרֵר הָעֶבֶד, חַיָּבִין לְשַׁלֵּם.

— רע"ב —

(ד) עבד ואשה שחבלו באחרים פטורים. שאין להם מה לשלם: נתגרשה האשה ונשתחרר העבד. וקנו נכסים, חייבין לשלם. שהרי מתחלה הן חייבין, אלא שאין להם מה לשלם, שנכסי מלוג של אשה, משועבדים לבעל לפירות ולירושה:

is not obligated to pay for embarrassment but only for the other four losses (damage, pain, healing, and loss of employment).[7]

חֵרֵשׁ שׁוֹטֶה וְקָטָן פְּגִיעָתָן רָעָה [4] — **Fighting with a deaf-mute, an insane person, and a minor**[1] **is always harmful** to a person because, either way, he loses: הַחוֹבֵל בָּהֶן חַיָּב — **If someone wounds them, he is obligated** to make **the five payments,** וְהֵם שֶׁחָבְלוּ בַאֲחֵרִים פְּטוּרִין — **but if they wound others, they are exempt** from making any payment, because they are not responsible for their actions.[2]

הָעֶבֶד וְהָאִשָּׁה פְּגִיעָתָן רָעָה — Similarly, **fighting with a** Canaanite **slave or a** married **woman is** always **harmful:** הַחוֹבֵל בָּהֶן חַיָּב — **If someone wounds them, he is obligated** to make the five payments, וְהֵם שֶׁחָבְלוּ בַאֲחֵרִים פְּטוּרִין — **but if they wound others, they are exempt** from making any payment, because they have no money of their own with which to pay.[3] אֲבָל מְשַׁלְּמִין — **However, they must pay afterward,** נִתְגָּרְשָׁה הָאִשָּׁה נִשְׁתַּחְרֵר לְאַחַר זְמָן הָעֶבֶד חַיָּבִין לְשַׁלֵּם — that is, if **the woman is** later **divorced** (or widowed) or **the**

NOTES

7. The verse that speaks of the payment for embarrassment states: *If men fight one another, a man against his brother* etc. (Deuteronomy 25:11). The word "brother" implies that the verse refers to someone who can achieve "brotherhood" with Jews. Since Canaanite slaves and slavewomen cannot marry ordinary Jews (see *Kiddushin* 3:12), R' Yehudah rules that one who embarrasses a Canaanite slave is exempt from this payment (*Rav; Tos. Yom Tov,* citing *Rashi*).

The first Tanna, however, holds that a Canaanite slave *is* considered a "brother" because he is obligated in most mitzvos (*Tos. Yom Tov*).

[4]

1. See Mishnah 4:4 note 1.
2. Even after the minor becomes an adult, or the deaf-mute or insane person is cured, he remains exempt from liability for the damage he caused, since he was not responsible for his actions at the time of the attack (*Tos. Yom Tov*).

However, someone who wounds these mentally incompetent people is liable for all the five categories or some of them, depending on the victim. A deaf-mute receives all five payments, even loss of employment, because he is capable of working. An insane person is paid for damage, pain, and healing, but not for loss of employment, because he is incapable of working, and not for embarrassment, because he does not experience shame. A minor, too, suffers no loss of employment, but, depending on his age and maturity, he can feel shame (*Meiri*).

3. Anything acquired by a Canaanite slave automatically becomes the property of his master. A wife does keep her own property but her husband has the right to use it, and she cannot deprive him of that right by selling it or by using it to pay a monetary obligation (*Rav*).

[119] **MISHNAH BAVA KAMMA** / Chapter 8: *HaChoveil* 8/5-6

— רע״ב —

(ה) מפני שהוא נדון בנפשו. שאף על פי שהוא מקלקל, מתקן הוא אצל ילדו, שסככה חמתו ונח רוגזו בכך: (ו) התוקע לחבירו. שמחבר אצבעותיו בפס ידו, ומכה אותו באגרוף: נותן לו סלע. דמי בשתו. ואין הלכה כרבי יהודה שאומר מנה:

[ה] **הַמַּכֶּה** אָבִיו וְאִמּוֹ וְעָשָׂה בָּהֶן חַבּוּרָה, וְהַחוֹבֵל בַּחֲבֵרוֹ בְּשַׁבָּת פָּטוּר מִכֻּלָּן, מִפְּנֵי שֶׁהוּא נִדּוֹן בְּנַפְשׁוֹ. וְהַחוֹבֵל בְּעֶבֶד כְּנַעֲנִי שֶׁלּוֹ, פָּטוּר מִכֻּלָּן.

[ו] **הַתּוֹקֵעַ** לַחֲבֵרוֹ, נוֹתֵן לוֹ סֶלַע. רַבִּי יְהוּדָה אוֹמֵר מִשּׁוּם רַבִּי יוֹסֵי

---

slave is freed and then they have property of their own, **they are obligated to pay** for the damage they did while married or enslaved.[4]

[5] Like Mishnah 3, this Mishnah is based on the rule that one who becomes liable to the death penalty and a monetary payment at the same time is exempt from the payment. The earlier Mishnah cited two cases where this rule does not apply and now this Mishnah cites two similar cases where it does apply:

הַמַּכֶּה אָבִיו וְאִמּוֹ וְעָשָׂה בָּהֶן חַבּוּרָה — **If someone strikes his father or his mother and inflicts a wound upon them** (that is, he draws blood or makes a bruise), וְהַחוֹבֵל בַּחֲבֵרוֹ בְּשַׁבָּת — **or if someone wounds another on Shabbos,** פָּטוּר מִכֻּלָּן — **he is exempt from** making any of [the five payments], מִפְּנֵי שֶׁהוּא נִדּוֹן בְּנַפְשׁוֹ — **because he is punished with** losing **his life** instead.[1]

Another case in which an attacker is exempt:

וְהַחוֹבֵל בְּעֶבֶד כְּנַעֲנִי שֶׁלּוֹ פָּטוּר מִכֻּלָּן — **And someone who wounds his** own **Canaanite slave is** also **exempt from** making any [of the payments], because the slave belongs to him.[2]

[6] The Mishnah lists certain cases where the Sages established a standard payment for embarrassing someone:[1]

הַתּוֹקֵעַ לַחֲבֵרוֹ נוֹתֵן לוֹ סֶלַע — **Someone who punches another must give him a** *sela* (4 *zuz*) for the embarrassment he caused. רַבִּי יְהוּדָה אוֹמֵר מִשּׁוּם רַבִּי יוֹסֵי

--- NOTES ---

4. A Canaanite slave and a married woman are obligated to pay for the damage they cause (unlike a deaf-mute, insane person, and minor); they are exempt only because they have no property available. Therefore, as soon as they gain property, they must pay (*Rav, Tos. Yom Tov*).

At the time of the injury, the court assesses the five payments and gives the victim a written record of them, so that he will be able to collect from the Canaanite slave or the woman when he or she has the means to pay (*Rosh*).

[5]
1. See Mishnah 3.
2. Although it is wrong for a master to even treat his Canaanite slave harshly, let alone wound him (see *Rambam, Hilchos Avadim* 9:8), he is exempt from payment.

[6]
1. The other payments incurred in these cases (damage, pain, healing, and loss of employment) are assessed according to the methods described in Mishnah 1 (see *Tos. Yom Tov*).

משניות בבא קמא / פרק ח: החובל

הַגְּלִילִי, מָנֶה. סְטָרוֹ, נוֹתֵן לוֹ מָאתַיִם זוּז. לְאַחַר יָדוֹ, נוֹתֵן לוֹ אַרְבַּע מֵאוֹת זוּז. צָרַם בְּאָזְנוֹ, תָּלַשׁ בִּשְׂעָרוֹ, רָקַק וְהִגִּיעַ בּוֹ רֻקּוֹ, הֶעֱבִיר טַלִּיתוֹ מִמֶּנּוּ, פָּרַע רֹאשׁ הָאִשָּׁה בַּשּׁוּק, נוֹתֵן אַרְבַּע מֵאוֹת זוּז. זֶה הַכְּלָל, הַכֹּל לְפִי כְבוֹדוֹ. אָמַר רַבִּי עֲקִיבָא, אֲפִלּוּ עֲנִיִּים שֶׁבְּיִשְׂרָאֵל רוֹאִין אוֹתָם כְּאִלּוּ הֵם בְּנֵי חוֹרִין שֶׁיָּרְדוּ מִנִּכְסֵיהֶם, שֶׁהֵם בְּנֵי אַבְרָהָם, יִצְחָק, וְיַעֲקֹב.

— רע"ב —

סטרו. שֶׁהִכָּהוּ בְּפַס יָדוֹ עַל לֶחְיוֹ, וַאֲכִילָא בְּשֵׁת טְפֵי: צרם. מָשַׁךְ. לְשׁוֹן מַחַר, פָּגַם: הכל לפי כבודו. כָּל אֵלּוּ הַדָּמִים שֶׁהֻזְכְּרוּ בַּמִּשְׁנָה, אֵינָם אֶלָּא לִמְכֻבָּד בְּיוֹתֵר. אֲבָל לְאָדָם בָּזוּי פּוֹחֲתִין לוֹ: אמר רבי עקיבא וכו'. רַבִּי עֲקִיבָא פָּלִיג אַתַּנָּא קַמָּא, וּסְבַר דְּאֵין מְכֻבָּד בֵּין בָּזוּי, כֻּלָּן שָׁוִין לְדִינֵי קְנָסוֹת הַלָּלוּ. וְאֵין הֲלָכָה כְרַבִּי עֲקִיבָא:

הַגְּלִילִי — R' Yehudah says in the name of R' Yose HaGlili: מָנֶה — He must give him a *maneh* (100 *zuz*).

סְטָרוֹ נוֹתֵן לוֹ מָאתַיִם זוּז — If he slapped him on his cheek, which is more embarrassing than being punched, he must give him 200 *zuz*; לְאַחַר יָדוֹ נוֹתֵן לוֹ אַרְבַּע מֵאוֹת זוּז — if he slapped him on his cheek with the back of his hand, which is even more embarrassing, he must give him 400 *zuz*.

צָרַם בְּאָזְנוֹ — If he pulled his ear,[2] תָּלַשׁ בִּשְׂעָרוֹ — or pulled out his hair, רָקַק וְהִגִּיעַ בּוֹ רֻקּוֹ — or spat at him and his spit landed on him, הֶעֱבִיר טַלִּיתוֹ מִמֶּנּוּ — or removed his cloak from him, פָּרַע רֹאשׁ הָאִשָּׁה בַּשּׁוּק — or uncovered the head of a woman in the street, נוֹתֵן אַרְבַּע מֵאוֹת זוּז — he must give him (or her) 400 *zuz*.

The Mishnah adds that these amounts are maximums:

זֶה הַכְּלָל — However, **this is the rule:** הַכֹּל לְפִי כְבוֹדוֹ — **Everything depends on his level of honor**; the more honorable the victim, the greater his embarrassment. The amounts listed above are required only if the victim was an important person. People of lesser status suffer less embarrassment and therefore receive smaller amounts.[3]

The next Tanna disagrees:

אָמַר רַבִּי עֲקִיבָא — **R' Akiva said:** אֲפִלּוּ עֲנִיִּים שֶׁבְּיִשְׂרָאֵל רוֹאִין אוֹתָם כְּאִלּוּ הֵם בְּנֵי חוֹרִין שֶׁיָּרְדוּ מִנִּכְסֵיהֶם — **Even the poorest Jews are considered like noblemen who have lost their wealth,** שֶׁהֵם בְּנֵי אַבְרָהָם יִצְחָק וְיַעֲקֹב — **because they are all the children of Abraham, Isaac, and Jacob.** Therefore, the amounts listed above are paid to any victim, regardless of his or her apparent importance.[4]

--- NOTES ---

2. *Rav*, first explanation.
3. *Rav*; see Mishnah 1.
4. According to R' Akiva, poor people are treated like "wealthy people who lost their money," who are still highly sensitive to shame. Since there are wealthy people who are less sensitive to shame, and there are poor people who are more sensitive, it is difficult to assess each person individually. Everyone is therefore treated equally (*Tos. Yom Tov*).

[121] **MISHNAH BAVA KAMMA** / Chapter 8: *HaChoveil*

— רע״ב —

ונתן לו זמן. והני מילי לכסת דלא חסריה ממונא, יהבינן זמן. אבל לנזקין דחסריה ממונא, לא יהבינן זמן: שימר. המתין לה, עד שראהו אותה עומדת על פתח חצרה. ובו כאיסר שמן. שמן קנוי כאיסר: לזו אני נותן ארבע מאות זוז. שעל כאיסר שמן, זלזלה בעצמה לגלות ראשה, ומראה היא, שאינה מקפדת על הבושת:

וּמַעֲשֶׂה בְּאֶחָד שֶׁפָּרַע רֹאשׁ הָאִשָּׁה בַּשּׁוּק. בָּאת לִפְנֵי רַבִּי עֲקִיבָא, וְחִיְּבוֹ לִתֵּן לָהּ אַרְבַּע מֵאוֹת זוּז. אָמַר לוֹ, רַבִּי, תֶּן לִי זְמַן, וְנָתַן לוֹ זְמַן. שְׁמָרָהּ עוֹמֶדֶת עַל פֶּתַח חֲצֵרָהּ, וְשָׁבַר אֶת הַכַּד בְּפָנֶיהָ וּבוֹ כְּאִסָּר שֶׁמֶן. גִּלְּתָה אֶת רֹאשָׁהּ וְהָיְתָה מְטַפַּחַת וּמַנַּחַת יָדָהּ עַל רֹאשָׁהּ. הֶעֱמִיד עָלֶיהָ עֵדִים וּבָא לִפְנֵי רַבִּי עֲקִיבָא. אָמַר לוֹ, רַבִּי, לָזוֹ אֲנִי נוֹתֵן אַרְבַּע מֵאוֹת זוּז? אָמַר לוֹ, לֹא אָמַרְתָּ כְּלוּם. הַחוֹבֵל בְּעַצְמוֹ, אַף עַל פִּי שֶׁאֵינוֹ רַשַּׁאי, פָּטוּר,

The Mishnah relates an incident where R' Akiva applied his ruling in practice: וּמַעֲשֶׂה בְּאֶחָד שֶׁפָּרַע רֹאשׁ הָאִשָּׁה בַּשּׁוּק — **It once happened that someone uncovered the head of a woman in the street.** בָּאת לִפְנֵי רַבִּי עֲקִיבָא — **She came before R' Akiva** to judge her case, וְחִיְּבוֹ לִתֵּן לָהּ אַרְבַּע מֵאוֹת זוּז — **and he obligated [her assailant] to give her 400** *zuz* **for her embarrassment,** following his view that everyone is paid equally.[5] אָמַר לוֹ רַבִּי תֶּן לִי זְמַן — **He said to [R' Akiva]: "My teacher, give me time** to come up with the money." וְנָתַן לוֹ זְמַן — **So [R' Akiva] gave him time.** שְׁמָרָהּ עוֹמֶדֶת עַל פֶּתַח חֲצֵרָהּ — **[The assailant] waited for her until he saw her standing at the entrance of her courtyard,** where she could be seen publicly, וְשָׁבַר אֶת הַכַּד בְּפָנֶיהָ וּבוֹ כְּאִסָּר שֶׁמֶן — **and then he broke a jug in front of her containing an** *issar's* **worth of oil.**[6] גִּלְּתָה אֶת רֹאשָׁהּ — **[The woman] uncovered her head,** וְהָיְתָה מְטַפַּחַת — and began scooping up some of the spilled oil and וּמַנַּחַת יָדָהּ עַל רֹאשָׁהּ — **and began scooping up** some of the spilled oil and **putting her hand on her head** to apply the oil to her hair. הֶעֱמִיד עָלֶיהָ עֵדִים — **He set up witnesses** to see what she was doing and testify **against her,** וּבָא לִפְנֵי רַבִּי עֲקִיבָא — **and he came** with them **before R' Akiva.** אָמַר לוֹ — **He said to [R' Akiva]:** רַבִּי לָזוֹ אֲנִי נוֹתֵן אַרְבַּע מֵאוֹת זוּז — **"My teacher! To this [woman],** who disgraced herself and uncovered her own head for such a small amount of oil, **I must give 400** *zuz***?!"** She herself has demonstrated that she is not embarrassed to uncover her head in public! אָמַר לוֹ — **[R' Akiva] said to him:** לֹא אָמַרְתָּ כְּלוּם — **"You have said nothing** (i.e., your argument is flawed), הַחוֹבֵל בְּעַצְמוֹ אַף עַל פִּי שֶׁאֵינוֹ רַשַּׁאי פָּטוּר — **because we find that someone who wounds himself, even though he is not permitted** to do so,[7] is

— NOTES —

5. Although she was poor, R' Akiva obligated her assailant to pay her the full amount stated above (400 *zuz*), which the first Tanna would award only to a very honorable person (*Raavad*).

6. That is, the jug contained a small amount of oil, which could be purchased with as little as an *issar* [a coin of little value] (see *Rav*).

7. A *nazir* is called a sinner (see *Numbers* 6:11), because he denied himself the pleasure of drinking wine. Certainly, then, it is a sin for someone to injure himself (*Tos. Yom Tov*).

אֲחֵרִים שֶׁחָבְלוּ בוֹ, חַיָּבִין. וְהַקּוֹצֵץ נְטִיעוֹתָיו, אַף עַל פִּי שֶׁאֵינוֹ רַשַּׁאי, פָּטוּר, אֲחֵרִים שֶׁקִּצְצוּ אֶת נְטִיעוֹתָיו, חַיָּבִים.

[ז] **אַף** עַל פִּי שֶׁהוּא נוֹתֵן לוֹ, אֵין נִמְחָל לוֹ עַד שֶׁיְּבַקֵּשׁ מִמֶּנּוּ, שֶׁנֶּאֱמַר, וְעַתָּה הָשֵׁב אֵשֶׁת וְגוֹ׳. וּמִנַּיִן שֶׁלֹּא יְהֵא הַמּוֹחֵל אַכְזָרִי, שֶׁנֶּאֱמַר, וַיִּתְפַּלֵּל אַבְרָהָם אֶל הָאֱלֹהִים וַיִּרְפָּא

אֲחֵרִים שֶׁחָבְלוּ בוֹ חַיָּבִין — exempt from liability (as there is no one to pay), וְהַקּוֹצֵץ נְטִיעוֹתָיו אַף עַל פִּי שֶׁאֵינוֹ רַשַּׁאי yet **others who wound him are liable.** פָּטוּר — **Also, someone who cuts down his own saplings, even though he is not permitted** to do so,[8] **is exempt** from liability, אֲחֵרִים שֶׁקִּצְצוּ אֶת נְטִיעוֹתָיו חַיָּבִים — yet **others who cut down his saplings are liable."** Even though he does not seem to care about his own body or trees — since he injured himself or cut them down himself — *others* who do the same thing to him are obligated to pay. Therefore, the fact that this woman disgraced herself is not a reason to exempt someone else who embarrassed her.

[7] The Mishnah teaches what an attacker must do in order to be forgiven by God for the sin of hurting a person:

אַף עַל פִּי שֶׁהוּא נוֹתֵן לוֹ — **Even though he gives [his victim]** the five payments, אֵין נִמְחָל לוֹ עַד שֶׁיְּבַקֵּשׁ מִמֶּנּוּ — **he is not forgiven** by God **until he asks** for forgiveness **from [the victim]**,[1] שֶׁנֶּאֱמַר ״וְעַתָּה הָשֵׁב אֵשֶׁת וְגוֹ׳״ — **as it is stated:** *God came to Avimelech in a dream by night and said to him, "Behold you are going to die because of the woman [Sarah] you have taken, and she is a married woman ... **But now, return the man's wife** etc.,* for he [Abraham] is a prophet, and he will pray for you and you will live..." (Genesis 20:3, 7).[2] The verse implies that it was not enough for Avimelech to merely return Sarah to Abraham. He also had to ask Abraham's forgiveness until Abraham would forgive him so wholeheartedly that he would even pray on Avimelech's behalf.[3] וּמִנַּיִן שֶׁלֹּא יְהֵא הַמּוֹחֵל אַכְזָרִי — **And from where** do we know **that [the victim] should not be cruel** and refuse to forgive? שֶׁנֶּאֱמַר ״וַיִּתְפַּלֵּל אַבְרָהָם אֶל הָאֱלֹהִים וַיִּרְפָּא

— NOTES —

8. One who needlessly destroys a fruit tree violates the prohibition (*Deuteronomy* 20:19): *You shall not destroy its trees* [בַּל תַּשְׁחִית] (*Rashi*).

[7]

1. The five payments discussed in this chapter are only monetary compensations for the damage done to the victim. The grief and anguish that he suffered, however, cannot be relieved with money. The attacker must therefore appease the victim and ask his forgiveness (see Gemara 92a).

In fact, this is true of all sins against another person. God does not forgive the sinner until the person he has wronged forgives him (*Meiri*; see *Yoma* 8:9).

2. When Abraham and Sarah traveled to Gerar (a Philistine city), Avimelech the king of Gerar sent messengers to take Sarah and bring her to him. However, God prevented him from touching her and struck his household with a plague. God also appeared to Avimelech in a dream and warned him that he would die if he did not return Sarah to Abraham (*Genesis* Chapter 20).

3. *Meiri*.

[123] **MISHNAH BAVA KAMMA** / Chapter 8: *HaChoveil*

אֱלֹהִים אֶת אֲבִימֶלֶךְ וְגוֹ'. הָאוֹמֵר, סַמֵּא אֶת עֵינִי, קְטַע אֶת יָדִי, שַׁבֵּר אֶת רַגְלִי, חַיָּב. עַל מְנָת לִפְטֹר, חַיָּב.
קָרַע אֶת כְּסוּתִי, שָׁבַר אֶת כַּדִּי, חַיָּב.

– רע"ב –

(ז) עַל מְנַת לִפְטוֹר חַיָּב. אִם שְׁאָלוֹ חוֹבֵל לַנֶּחְבָּל, עַל מְנַת לִפְטוֹר אוֹתִי אַתָּה אוֹמֵר סַמֵּא אֶת עֵינִי, וְהֱשִׁיבוֹ הַנֶּחְבָּל הֵן, אַף עַל פִּי כֵן חַיָּב, שֶׁיֵּשׁ הֵן שֶׁהוּא כְלָאו, וּבִלְשׁוֹן תֵּימָה אָמַר לוֹ הֵן, שֶׁאֵין דֶּרֶךְ בְּנֵי אָדָם לִמְחֹל עַל צַעַר גּוּפוֹ. אֲבָל הָאוֹמֵר לַחֲבֵירוֹ שְׁבֹר אֶת כַּדִּי, וְשָׁאֲלוֹ הַמַּזִּיק, עַל מְנָת לִפְטוֹר אוֹתִי אַתָּה אוֹמֵר וְנִיזּוֹק לָאו, זֶה הֲלֹא הוּא כֹהֵן, וּכְאִלּוּ אָמַר לוֹ, וְכִי לֹא אָמַרְתִּי לְךָ עַל מְנַת לִפְטוֹר, וּלְפִיכָךְ פָּטוּר, שֶׁכֵּן דֶּרֶךְ בְּנֵי אָדָם לִמְחֹל עַל נִזְקֵי מָמוֹן:

אֱלֹהִים אֶת אֲבִימֶלֶךְ וְגוֹ׳ — **For it is stated:** *Abraham prayed to God and God healed Avimelech, etc.* (verse 17 there). Abraham indeed forgave Avimelech and prayed on his behalf. So too, anyone who suffers at the hands of others should forgive them when they ask for forgiveness.[4]

The Mishnah moves to a new subject, namely, where one person asks another to injure him:

הָאוֹמֵר סַמֵּא אֶת עֵינִי קְטַע אֶת יָדִי שַׁבֵּר אֶת רַגְלִי — **If one** person **said** to another, **"Blind my eye,"** or **"Cut off my hand,"** or **"Break my leg,"** and the other person did so, חַיָּב — **[the attacker] is obligated** to pay for the injury (even though the victim asked him to injure him), because the victim was not serious.[5]

עַל מְנָת לִפְטֹר — Moreover, even if the attacker replied, "When you asked me to injure you, did you mean **to exempt** me from liability?" and the victim said "Yes," חַיָּב — **[the attacker] is obligated** to pay, because a person is unlikely to want to suffer pain, and thus did not seriously mean to exempt the attacker. Although the victim said "Yes," he was presumably expressing astonishment (as in "Do you really think I am exempting you from payment?").[6]

The law is different when one person asks another to damage his *possessions*:

קָרַע אֶת כְּסוּתִי שָׁבַר אֶת כַּדִּי — **If** one person said to another, **"Tear my garment,"** or **"Break my jug,"** and the other person did so, חַיָּב — **[the damager] is obligated** to pay for the damage, because the owner was not serious.[7]

─────────── NOTES ───────────

4. Since Abraham set the example of forgiving Avimelech, his descendants are expected to follow in his ways (see *Meiri*).

A victim who does not forgive his attacker is "cruel," because he thereby shows that he does not care about the Heavenly punishment the attacker will otherwise suffer (*Meiri*).

5. It is common knowledge that no one really wants to be injured (*Rambam, Hilchos Choveil U'Mazik* 5:11). Thus, if someone asked to be injured, he surely did not mean it, but was speaking only out of distress or anger (*Rashba* to 93a), or he was joking (*Tiferes Yisrael*).

6. This ruling applies only where the attacker asked whether he would be exempt and the victim agreed. But if the victim said explicitly, "Injure me and you will not be liable," the attacker *would* be exempt, since the victim clearly exempted him (*Rashi* to 93a ד"ה הכני).

7. The Mishnah refers only to a case where the owner had asked the other person to watch the property. When that person committed himself to be a watchman (*shomer*), he accepted liability for damage that might occur in the future. In this situation, if the owner later said, "Break it," he did not mean to exempt him from payment; rather, he meant, "You may break it but you will have to pay for it."

עַל מְנָת לִפְטֹר, פָּטוּר. עָשָׂה כֵן לְאִישׁ פְּלוֹנִי עַל מְנָת לִפְטֹר, חַיָּב, בֵּין בְּגוּפוֹ בֵּין בְּמָמוֹנוֹ.

עַל מְנָת לִפְטֹר — But if the damager replied, "When you asked me to damage your property, did you mean **to exempt** me from liability?" then even if the owner said "No," **פָּטוּר** — [the damager] **is not obligated** to pay, because it is not unusual for a person to forgo payment for damage to his possessions. Since he already said, "Tear my garment," we interpret "No" as an expression of astonishment (as in, "Do you really think that I will hold you liable?").

A related case:

עָשָׂה כֵן לְאִישׁ פְּלוֹנִי עַל מְנָת לִפְטֹר — If one person said to another, **"Do this damage to So-and-so** or to his possessions," even if he adds, "And I intend **to exempt** you from liability (that is, I will pay for the damage),"[8] **חַיָּב בֵּין בְּגוּפוֹ בֵּין בְּמָמוֹנוֹ** — [the damager] **is obligated** to pay **whether** he damaged [the victim's] **body or his possessions.** One person cannot exempt a second person from payments that he incurs for damaging a third person. The damager must therefore pay.[9]

NOTES

If, however, the damager never agreed to watch the item and the owner told him to break it, the damager would indeed be exempt (*Tos. Yom Tov*).

8. See *Tos. Yom Tov*.

9. In fact, only the one who did the damage is liable, while the one who sent him is exempt. Although the actions of an agent are usually viewed as though they were done by the one who sent him, that rule does not apply where the agent was asked to do a sin, such as injuring a person or damaging his property [אֵין שָׁלִיחַ לִדְבַר עֲבֵרָה] (*Tos. Yom Tov*; see Mishnah 6:4 note 4).

Nevertheless, the one who sent him is a wicked man, because he misled his fellow and encouraged him to sin (*Rambam, Hilchos Chovel U'Mazik* 5:13).

Chapter Nine

משניות בבא קמא / פרק ט: הגזול עצים

[א] הַגּוֹזֵל עֵצִים וַעֲשָׂאָן כֵּלִים, צֶמֶר וַעֲשָׂאָן בְּגָדִים, מְשַׁלֵּם כִּשְׁעַת הַגְּזֵלָה. גָּזַל פָּרָה מְעֻבֶּרֶת וְיָלְדָה, רָחֵל טְעוּנָה וּגְזָזָהּ, מְשַׁלֵּם דְּמֵי פָרָה הָעוֹמֶדֶת לֵילֵד,

— רע״ב —

פרק תשיעי – הגזול עצים. (א) הגוזל. משלם בשעת הגזילה. דמי עצים ולמר. ואין חייב להחזיר לו כלים, דקני בשינוי:

---

[1] The Torah states: וְהֵשִׁיב אֶת הַגְּזֵלָה אֲשֶׁר גָּזָל, *He shall return the stolen property that he stole* (Leviticus 5:23). Here, the Torah commands a thief to return the stolen article to the owner. However, by adding the words *that he stole,* the verse teaches that he must return the stolen article only if it is still the one "that he stole." If it has changed since then, the thief acquires it and pays its monetary value to the owner. The first four Mishnahs of this chapter define how much the article must change in order for the thief to acquire it.[1]

הַגּוֹזֵל עֵצִים וַעֲשָׂאָן כֵּלִים — If someone steals **pieces of wood and makes them into utensils,** צֶמֶר וַעֲשָׂאָן בְּגָדִים — or if he steals **wool and makes it into garments,** he does not have to return the utensils or the garments; מְשַׁלֵּם כִּשְׁעַת הַגְּזֵלָה — rather, **he pays according to** what the wood or wool was worth **at the time of the robbery.** Since the item that he stole changed into something else, he acquires it and he pays the owner what it was worth when he stole it.[2]

גָּזַל פָּרָה מְעֻבֶּרֶת וְיָלְדָה — **If someone stole a pregnant cow and it gave birth,** רָחֵל טְעוּנָה וּגְזָזָהּ — or if he stole **a ewe laden** with wool **and he sheared it,** he does not have to return the calf or the wool; מְשַׁלֵּם דְּמֵי פָרָה הָעוֹמֶדֶת לֵילֵד —

NOTES

[1]
1. The acquisition discussed here should not be confused with the acquisition discussed in Mishnahs 7:5-6. There, the subject was the *kinyan* through which one who stole something becomes subject to the obligations of a thief (for example, he must make the *keifel* payment, and if he stole an ox or a sheep and then slaughtered or sold it, he must make the fourfold or fivefold payment). At that point, though, the stolen item does not belong to the thief, and if it is still available he must return it. Here, however, the discussion is about a change in the item that makes it the thief's property. He is then allowed to keep it and pay the owner money instead.

The laws presented in the following Mishnahs apply to both the גַּנָּב and the גַּזְלָן. See the introduction to Mishnah 8:1.

2. These changes cannot be reversed. He stole a raw piece of wood and planed it to make it into a utensil, or he stole raw wool and made it into felt. [Felt is a fabric created by pressing fibers of wool together. Although the Mishnah says "garments," it refers to felt, which is used in making garments.] In these cases, the wood and wool can never go back to what they were at the time of the theft. In addition, their names have changed: the wood is now called a "utensil," and the wool is now called "felt." The combination of these two changes makes the stolen item into something new, which the thief need not return because it is not the item "that he stole" (*Tos. Yom Tov*).

If the change *is* reversible, the thief does not acquire the item, even if its name changed. For example, he stole planks of wood that were already planed and nailed them together to make a utensil, or he stole threads of wool and wove them into cloth. Since he can take the utensil apart, or unravel the cloth, he must do so and return the planed wood or the woolen threads to the owner (see *Tos. Yom Tov*). On the other hand, there are cases in which the physical change is so great that the thief acquires the item even if its name remains the same (see the next Mishnah).

[127] MISHNAH BAVA KAMMA / Chapter 9: *Hagozeil Eitzim* 9/1

— רע״ב —

דְּמֵי רָחֵל הָעוֹמֶדֶת לִיגָּזֵז. גָּזַל פָּרָה וְנִתְעַבְּרָה אֶצְלוֹ וְיָלְדָה, רָחֵל וְנִטְעֲנָה אֶצְלוֹ וּגְזָזָהּ, מְשַׁלֵּם כְּשָׁעַת הַגְּזֵלָה. זֶה הַכְּלָל, כָּל הַגַּזְלָנִים מְשַׁלְּמִין כְּשָׁעַת הַגְּזֵלָה.

דמי רחל העומדת ליגזז. והטעודף ששוה יותר הולד והגיזה, שלו הוא, דקנינהו בשינוי: זה הכלל. לאתויי גנב טלה ונעשה איל, עגל ונעשה שור, וטבחו או מכרו, שהוא פטור מתשלומי ארבעה וחמשה. שכיון שנעשה שינוי בידו, קנאו, ושלו הוא טובח הוא ושלו הוא מוכר:

---

rather, **he pays the value of a cow that is ready to give birth** דְּמֵי רָחֵל הָעוֹמֶדֶת לִיגָּזֵז — **or the value of a ewe that is ready to be shorn.** That is, he returns the cow or the ewe as it is, and he pays the difference between what it is worth now and what it was worth when it was stolen (i.e., when the cow was pregnant, and the ewe still had its wool). Since the animal remained basically the same and did not change significantly, he does not acquire it and he must return it. However, he need not return the newborn calf or the wool because it changed completely, going from fetus to calf, or from part of a ewe to detached wool.[3]

גָּזַל פָּרָה וְנִתְעַבְּרָה אֶצְלוֹ וְיָלְדָה — If someone stole **a cow and it became pregnant while** it was **with him** and then **it gave birth,** רָחֵל וְנִטְעֲנָה אֶצְלוֹ וּגְזָזָהּ — or if he stole **a ewe and it became laden** with wool **while** it was **with him and** then **he sheared it,** מְשַׁלֵּם כְּשָׁעַת הַגְּזֵלָה — **he pays according to** what it was worth at **the time of the robbery.** That is, he returns the cow or ewe itself, since it did not change,[4] but he keeps the calf or the wool, which did not even exist until after the robbery.

The Mishnah states the general rule for a stolen article that changed in value after the theft:

זֶה הַכְּלָל — **This is the rule:** כָּל הַגַּזְלָנִים מְשַׁלְּמִין כְּשָׁעַת הַגְּזֵלָה — **All robbers pay according to** what the stolen property was worth at **the time of the robbery.**[5]

NOTES
---

3. For example, if a cow is worth 100 *zuz*, a pregnant cow 130 *zuz*, and a calf 50 *zuz*, the robber would return the cow itself, pay 30 *zuz*, and keep the 50-*zuz* calf. The extra 20 *zuz*, which is the amount the fetus increased in value when it was born, belong to the thief, since he acquired the calf through its change: it was previously a fetus and then became a newborn animal (*Rav;* see *Tos. Yom Tov*).

4. Although the cow became pregnant while in his possession, this is not considered a physical change in the cow (just as a pregnant cow that gives birth is not considered to have changed, as mentioned in note 3). He must therefore return the cow (*Tos. Yom Tov*).

5. The Mishnah mentions this rule again in order to teach that a thief can acquire the stolen item even through a small change [as long as the change is irreversible and its name also changes] (*Tosefos Rid*). For example, if he stole a lamb that then grew into a ram (at the age of 13 months) or a calf that then grew into an ox (at the age of two years), he thereby acquires it. If he slaughters or sells the grown animal, he is exempt from the fourfold for fivefold payment, because it was his when he slaughtered or sold it (*Rav*).

He need pay the owner only the amount the animal was worth when it was stolen, and if a double (*keifel*) payment is required, he pays twice that amount (*Tos. Yom Tov*).

[ב] **גָּזַל** בְּהֵמָה וְהִזְקִינָה, עֲבָדִים וְהִזְקִינוּ, מְשַׁלֵּם כִּשְׁעַת הַגְּזֵלָה. רַבִּי מֵאִיר אוֹמֵר, בַּעֲבָדִים אוֹמֵר לוֹ, הֲרֵי שֶׁלְּךָ לְפָנֶיךָ. גָּזַל מַטְבֵּעַ וְנִסְדַּק, פֵּרוֹת וְהִרְקִיבוּ, יַיִן וְהֶחֱמִיץ, מְשַׁלֵּם כִּשְׁעַת הַגְּזֵלָה.

- רע"ב -

(ב) בעבדים אומר לו הרי שלך לפניך. דקרקע דמו. וברשותא דמרייהו קיימי. **והלכה כרבי מאיר: מטבע ונסדק.** שינוי הניכר הוא: **פירות והרקיבו.** בשהרקיבו מקצתן, [ואומר] לו הרי שלך לפניך. אבל הרקיבו כולם, משלם כשעת הגזילה: **מטבע ונפסל.** שאינו עובר באותה מדינה, אבל עובר הוא במדינה אחרת:

---

[2] In the cases of this Mishnah, the stolen item undergoes a change that *decreases* its value:

גָּזַל בְּהֵמָה וְהִזְקִינָה — **If someone stole an animal and it became old,** עֲבָדִים וְהִזְקִינוּ — **or if he stole Canaanite slaves and they became old,** מְשַׁלֵּם כִּשְׁעַת הַגְּזֵלָה — **he pays according to** their value at **the time of the robbery.** Since the stolen animal or slaves changed physically by growing old and weak, the robber acquires them. He pays what they were worth at the time of the robbery, when they were young and strong.[1]

The next Tanna disagrees regarding slaves:

רַבִּי מֵאִיר אוֹמֵר — **R' Meir says:** בַּעֲבָדִים אוֹמֵר לוֹ הֲרֵי שֶׁלְּךָ לְפָנֶיךָ — **In the case of slaves, [the robber] can say to** [the original owner], **"Behold, what is yours is** here **before you;** take him back as he is." According to R' Meir, it is not legally possible to steal a slave and acquire him; rather, he remains the property of his owner.[2] Thus, even after the slave grows old, the thief returns him and need not pay for the loss of value.

Other cases in which stolen property went down in value:

גָּזַל מַטְבֵּעַ וְנִסְדַּק — **If someone stole a coin and it cracked,** פֵּרוֹת וְהִרְקִיבוּ — **or fruits and they rotted,** יַיִן וְהֶחֱמִיץ — **or wine and it soured,** מְשַׁלֵּם כִּשְׁעַת הַגְּזֵלָה — **he pays according to** what it was worth **at the time of the robbery.** The article has changed enough for it to become the thief's property; he therefore keeps it and pays the owner its original value.[3]

In the following cases, the stolen item undergoes a change that is not obvious:

NOTES

[2]

1. It is a significant change for slaves (or animals) to grow old, since they can no longer work or have children (*Tosefos Rid*). [This is such a great change that the thief acquires the slave, even though there was no change in name: before he was called a slave and now he is also called a slave (*Chazon Ish* 17:21).]

2. R' Meir derives this law from verses in the Torah (see *Rav*).

3. All of these changes are easy to recognize. The crack in the coin and the rotten fruit are clearly visible, and the souring of wine can easily be detected through its change in smell and taste (*Tos. Yom Tov*).

The Mishnah's case of rotting fruit is where all the fruit rotted (*Rav*). If just some rotted, this is not considered a change, because it is common for fruits to spoil (*Tos. Yom Tov*).

[129] MISHNAH BAVA KAMMA / Chapter 9: *Hagozeil Eitzim*

— רע"ב —

מַטְבֵּעַ וְנִפְסַל, תְּרוּמָה וְנִטְמֵאת, חָמֵץ וְעָבַר עָלָיו הַפֶּסַח, בְּהֵמָה וְנֶעֶבְדָה בָה עֲבֵרָה, אוֹ שֶׁנִּפְסְלָה מֵעַל גַּבֵּי הַמִּזְבֵּחַ, אוֹ שֶׁהָיְתָה יוֹצְאָה לִסָּקֵל, אוֹמֵר לוֹ, הֲרֵי שֶׁלְּךָ לְפָנֶיךָ.

[ג] נָתַן לְאֻמָּנִין לְתַקֵּן וְקִלְקְלוּ, חַיָּבִין לְשַׁלֵּם.

וְנֶעֶבְדָה בָּה עֲבֵירָה. שֶׁנִּרְבְּעָה אוֹ נֶעֶבְדָה לַעֲבוֹדָה זָרָה], שֶׁהִיא פְסוּלָה לְקָרְבָּן: שֶׁנִּפְסְלָה לַמִּזְבֵּחַ. כְּמוּם שֶׁאֵינוֹ נִכָּר, כְּגוֹן בְּדוּקִין שֶׁבָּעַיִן: (ג) נָתַן לְאֻמָּנִין לְתַקֵּן. נָתַן לָהֶם עֵצִים לַעֲשׂוֹת כְּלִי. וּלְאַחַר שֶׁנַּעֲשָׂה הַכְּלִי קִלְקְלוּהוּ, חַיָּבִים לְשַׁלֵּם דְּמֵי הַכְּלִי, וְלֹא דְמֵי עֵצִים בִּלְבַד:

מַטְבֵּעַ וְנִפְסַל — **If he stole a coin and it became disqualified**, that is, the local people stopped accepting it as money;[4] תְּרוּמָה וְנִטְמֵאת — **or he stole *terumah* and it became *tamei*,** which makes it forbidden to be eaten;[5] חָמֵץ וְעָבַר עָלָיו הַפֶּסַח — **or he stole *chametz* and it was** with him **during Pesach,** thus becoming permanently forbidden;[6] בְּהֵמָה וְנֶעֶבְדָה בָה עֲבֵרָה — **or he stole an animal and a sin was performed with it,** such that it may no longer be used for an offering;[7] אוֹ שֶׁנִּפְסְלָה מֵעַל גַּבֵּי הַמִּזְבֵּחַ — **or it became disqualified from** being offered **on the** Temple **Altar** because it developed a blemish (however, the blemish cannot be seen easily);[8] אוֹ שֶׁהָיְתָה יוֹצְאָה לִסָּקֵל — **or it was being taken out to be stoned** because it killed a person and the court condemned it to death;[9] אוֹמֵר לוֹ הֲרֵי שֶׁלְּךָ לְפָנֶיךָ — **[the robber] can say to [the original owner], "Behold, what is yours is here before you; take it back as it is."** In all these cases, where the change is not obvious, the item is not considered to have changed to the extent that it becomes the robber's property. The robber can therefore return the article in its current state and he is not obligated to pay for its loss of value.

[3] The Mishnah discusses the laws of a craftsman who damaged an item that he was hired to make or repair:

נָתַן לְאֻמָּנִין לְתַקֵּן וְקִלְקְלוּ — **If someone gave** wood **to craftsmen to improve** and make into a utensil, and they made it into a utensil **but then they ruined** it, חַיָּבִין לְשַׁלֵּם — **they are obligated to pay** the value of the utensil, rather

--- NOTES ---

4. After the thief stole the coin, it stopped being used in the place where the owner lived, but it was still used in other places (*Rav*). The coin is not considered to have changed, because the owner can take it somewhere else and spend it there (*Tos. Yom Tov*).

5. The Torah forbids everyone (even a Kohen) to eat *terumah* that is *tamei*. Nevertheless, since the change cannot be seen, it is not considered a change that makes the food the property of the thief (*Tos. Yom Tov*).

6. *Chametz* that was in the possession of a Jew during Pesach is Rabbinically forbidden even after Pesach is over (*Pesachim* 2:2). Here, too, the robber does not acquire it since the change cannot be seen (*Tos. Yom Tov*).

7. For example, it was worshiped as an idol, which makes it unfit to be an Altar offering (*Rav*).

8. For example, a cataract formed in its eye (*Rav*).

9. An animal that killed a person is put to death (as discussed earlier, Mishnahs 4:5-8). Once it has been condemned, no one may have any benefit from it.

[130] משניות בבא קמא / פרק ט: הגוזל עצים

נָתַן לְחָרָשׁ שִׁדָּה תֵּבָה וּמִגְדָּל לְתַקֵּן וְקִלְקֵל, חַיָּב לְשַׁלֵּם. וְהַבַּנַּאי שֶׁקִּבֵּל עָלָיו לִסְתּוֹר אֶת הַכֹּתֶל וְשִׁבֵּר אֶת הָאֲבָנִים אוֹ שֶׁהִזִּיק, חַיָּב לְשַׁלֵּם.

– רע"ב –

נתן לחרש. השתא אשמועינן, שאם נתן כלי עשוי לאומן כדי לתקנו, וקלקלו, חייב לשלם דמי הכלי. ותנא סיפא לגלויי רישא, דלא תימא רישא מיירי בכלי עשוי: שידה. עגלה של עץ העשויה למרכב נשים:

---

than the value of the wood they were given, because it was the utensil that they damaged.[1]

In the next cases, a craftsman was hired to repair a broken object:

נָתַן לְחָרָשׁ שִׁדָּה תֵּבָה וּמִגְדָּל לְתַקֵּן — If one gave a carpenter a carriage,[2] a box, or a closet to fix, וְקִלְקֵל — and he ruined it, חַיָּב לְשַׁלֵּם — he is obligated to pay the value of the object that he was given, since that is what he damaged.[3]

Another situation in which a worker is hired to do a job:

וְהַבַּנַּאי שֶׁקִּבֵּל עָלָיו לִסְתּוֹר אֶת הַכֹּתֶל — If a builder accepts to take down a wall, וְשִׁבֵּר אֶת הָאֲבָנִים אוֹ שֶׁהִזִּיק — and he broke the stones or caused damage with them (for example, they fell on people passing by), חַיָּב לְשַׁלֵּם — he is obligated to pay for the damage to the stones or the damage caused by the stones. When he agreed to take down the wall, it was understood that he would keep the stones intact, so that they can be used in the future. He must therefore pay for damaging them. He is also liable for the damage done *by* the stones, because by agreeing to do the job, he accepted responsibility to prevent any resulting damage.[4]

NOTES

[3]

1. It could have been thought that when a craftsman improves something, the value of the improvement belongs to him (until he is paid). If so, the craftsman in the Mishnah's case would own the difference in value between the wood and the finished utensil. Thus, when he broke the utensil, it would be his loss and he would not have to pay the owner for it (he pays only for the wood itself). The Mishnah teaches that this is not true. Any improvement made by a craftsman immediately becomes the property of the owner, and he must therefore pay the owner for the damage to the finished utensil (*Meiri*).

Mishnah 1 taught that if a thief stole wood and made it into a utensil, he does not have to return the utensil (because it is not what he stole); rather, he may keep the utensil and pay only for the wood. That law, though, applies only to a thief, who took the wood for himself, and not to a craftsman, who works for the owner and never intended to steal. A craftsman does not acquire what he was given even after it changes completely (*Tos. Yom Tov*).

2. The wooden section of a carriage where women would sit while riding (*Rav*).

3. This ruling seems unnecessary because the Mishnah already taught that a craftsman must pay for breaking a utensil that he was working on. The Tanna adds it in order to imply that there is a difference between the Mishnah's two cases. While the second case is where a craftsman *repairs* a broken utensil (as the Mishnah itself states), the first case is where he *makes* a new one (*Rav*). From there we learn that even where a craftsman makes a new utensil, he does not acquire the value of the improvements that he made, and so he must pay for breaking it (see note 1).

4. Since the builder is responsible to prevent damage, it is only he, and not the owner of the wall, who must pay for the damage done by the falling stones (see *Meiri*).

הָיָה סוֹתֵר מִצַּד זֶה וְנָפַל מִצַּד אַחֵר, פָּטוּר. וְאִם מֵחֲמַת הַמַּכָּה, חַיָּב.

[ד] **הַנּוֹתֵן** צֶמֶר לְצַבָּע, וְהִקְדִּיחַתּוּ יוֹרָה, נוֹתֵן לוֹ דְּמֵי צַמְרוֹ. צְבָעוֹ כָאוּר,

הָיָה סוֹתֵר מִצַּד זֶה — **If he was taking down** a wall **from one side** (for example, he was hired to remove one half of a long wall) וְנָפַל מִצַּד אַחֵר — **and it fell from the other side** (i.e., the other side of the wall collapsed), because the second side was being supported by the first side and it lost that support, פָּטוּר — **he is not obligated** to pay, because he was not expected to realize that the second side was supported by the first side and could not stand on its own.[5] וְאִם מֵחֲמַת הַמַּכָּה — **But if** the second side fell directly **because of a blow** to the first side (that is, he hit the first side so hard that the impact caused the second side to fall), חַיָּב — **he is obligated** to pay, because he should have been careful not to make the second side move.[6]

[4] The Mishnah deals with more cases in which a craftsman did not do his job properly:

הַנּוֹתֵן צֶמֶר לְצַבָּע — **If someone gives wool to a dyer** so that the dyer will color it, וְהִקְדִּיחַתּוּ יוֹרָה — **and the cauldron** (large pot) used for dyeing **burns it** and it becomes ruined, נוֹתֵן לוֹ דְּמֵי צַמְרוֹ — **[the dyer] pays him the value of his wool.**[1]

Having stated the law of a dyer who destroyed the wool, the Mishnah presents the law of one who improved the wool but not as much as he should have:

צְבָעוֹ כָאוּר — **If he dyed it poorly** (that is, he used dye of low quality),[2] he cannot demand his fee, since he did not do his job properly. Nevertheless, because he increased the value of the wool, he has the right to be paid as

---
NOTES

5. The collapse of the wall was not his fault but an accident beyond his control [אָנוּס] (*Rabbeinu Yehonasan*).

6. Although he did not directly hit the second side of the wall, he is liable for the damage done by the force of his blow, just like a person who shoots an arrow that does damage far away (*Meiri*).

[4]

1. Wool would be dyed by heating it with dye in a large pot. In this case, the dyer overheated the pot, ruining the wool. He must therefore compensate the owner for the wool. He has no right to be paid even for his expenses (let alone his regular fee) since he did not improve the wool at all (*Rav;* see note 3).

He pays the owner the value of the plain wool (as it was when he received it) only if it was burned before the dye took hold. If it was dyed first and then it was burned, he must pay the value of the *dyed* wool because that is what he damaged (*Tos. Yom Tov*).

2. He used the residue of the dye, which increases the wool's value to some degree, but the improvement is far less than it would have been had he used good dye (*Rabbeinu Yehonasan*).

- רע"ב -

ואם השבח. שהשביח הצמר, יתר על היציאה של לבע. נותן לו ללבע את היציאה, ולא שכר שלם, ומקבל צמרו. ודמי צמרו לא אמרינן דנייתיב ליה, דנקי' אינהו שבחא דלמר, דהא בלבע שהתנה עמו לבע, וליכא שינויא דנקני':

אִם הַשֶּׁבַח יוֹתֵר עַל הַיְצִיאָה, נוֹתֵן לוֹ אֶת הַיְצִיאָה. וְאִם הַיְצִיאָה יְתֵירָה עַל הַשֶּׁבַח, נוֹתֵן לוֹ אֶת הַשֶּׁבַח. לִצְבֹּעַ לוֹ אָדֹם, וּצְבָעוֹ שָׁחֹר, שָׁחֹר וּצְבָעוֹ אָדֹם, רַבִּי מֵאִיר אוֹמֵר, נוֹתֵן לוֹ דְּמֵי צַמְרוֹ. רַבִּי יְהוּדָה אוֹמֵר, אִם הַשֶּׁבַח יָתֵר עַל הַיְצִיאָה,

לצבוע לו אדום וכו'. קנייה בשינוי. לרבי מאיר, לא יהיב אלא [דמי] צמרו, או זה יתן שכרו, משלם, ויקח הצמר: רבי יהודה אומר וכו'. דקניס ליה להאי דצבע להיות ידו על התחתונה, ולא נתהני משבחא,

אִם הַשֶּׁבַח יוֹתֵר עַל הַיְצִיאָה — If the improvement he made to the wool is greater than his expenses, נוֹתֵן לוֹ אֶת הַיְצִיאָה — [the owner] pays him his expenses; וְאִם הַיְצִיאָה יְתֵירָה עַל הַשֶּׁבַח — and if his expenses were greater than the improvement to the wool, נוֹתֵן לוֹ אֶת הַשֶּׁבַח — [the owner] pays him for the improvement.[3]

In the next case, the dyer used the wrong color:

לִצְבֹּעַ לוֹ אָדֹם וּצְבָעוֹ שָׁחֹר — If the owner asked him to dye the wool red for him, but he dyed it black, שָׁחֹר וּצְבָעוֹ אָדֹם — or if he asked him to dye it black, and he dyed it red, רַבִּי מֵאִיר אוֹמֵר — R' Meir says: נוֹתֵן לוֹ דְּמֵי צַמְרוֹ — He pays [the owner] the value of his raw wool. Since the dyer acted against the owner's wishes, he is considered a thief. Therefore, like a thief, he acquired the "stolen property" (i.e., the wool) when it underwent a change by being dyed. He thus keeps the dyed wool and he pays the owner the amount that the wool was worth at the time of the "theft."[4]

The next Tanna disagrees. In his view, the craftsman does not acquire the dyed wool (as R' Meir said); rather, he must return it the owner, and he is paid as follows:

רַבִּי יְהוּדָה אוֹמֵר — R' Yehudah says: אִם הַשֶּׁבַח יָתֵר עַל הַיְצִיאָה — If the

---
NOTES

3. Although he does not receive his fee, he is paid something for increasing the value of the wool. He is like a person who entered someone else's land without permission and made improvements to it. He is entitled to his expenses or the value of his improvement, whichever is less, as taught in *Bava Metzia* 101a (see *Sma, Choshen Mishpat* 306:9, and *Shach* there #5).

4. *Rabbeinu Yehonasan.*

This case is different from the previous one, where the dyer used a dye of poor quality. There, he is not considered a thief, because he used the color that the owner wanted; he just used an inferior dye. He thus returns the dyed wool and collects either his expenses or the value of the improvement. But in this case, where he dyed it the *wrong* color, he utterly disobeyed the owner's instructions. Therefore, like a thief, he keeps the changed article (i.e., the dyed wool) and pays the owner its original worth.

Nevertheless, even in this case, since the dyer did not intend to steal, he is not treated completely like a thief. In contrast to a thief, who fully acquires the stolen object when it changes, a dyer who uses the wrong color does not fully acquire the wool. If the owner wants, he may indeed let the dyer keep the wool, but if he wants he can take it back (against the dyer's wishes) as long as he pays the dyer his regular fee (*Rav, Tos. Yom Tov*).

[133] MISHNAH BAVA KAMMA / Chapter 9: *Hagozeil Eitzim* 9/5

נוֹתֵן לוֹ אֶת הַיְצִיאָה, וְאִם הַיְצִיאָה יְתֵרָה עַל הַשֶּׁבַח, נוֹתֵן לוֹ אֶת הַשֶּׁבַח.

[ה] הַגּוֹזֵל אֶת חֲבֵירוֹ שָׁוֶה פְּרוּטָה וְנִשְׁבַּע לוֹ, יוֹלִיכֶנּוּ אַחֲרָיו אֲפִלּוּ לְמָדַי.

– רע״ב –

ואגרא נמי לא נשקול, אלא
יציאה. ואם יציאה יתירה
על השבח, יתן לו השבח
שהשבית. ואם ירצה לתת
את שכרו, משלם. שבח
יותר על השכר, יתן
שכרו. והלכה כרבי יהודה:

(ה) נשבע לו. על שקר, והודה: יוליכנו אחריו אפילו למדי. דאין לו כפרה עד שיחזיר לנגזל עצמו.
דגבי נשבע על שקר כתיב (ויקרא ה,כד) לאשר הוא לו יתננו:

---

improvement he made to the wool **is greater than** his **expenses,** נוֹתֵן לוֹ אֶת הַיְצִיאָה — [the owner] **pays him** his **expenses;** וְאִם הַיְצִיאָה יְתֵרָה עַל הַשֶּׁבַח — **and if** his **expenses** were **greater than the improvement** to the wool, נוֹתֵן לוֹ אֶת הַשֶּׁבַח — [the owner] **pays him for the improvement.**[5]

[5] The Torah (*Leviticus* 5:21-26, *Numbers* 5:6-7) states that if someone has money or property that belongs to someone else (for example, he stole or borrowed money and has not returned it), and he swore falsely that he is not liable to pay the owner,[1] and then he admitted that he was lying, he must pay the owner the principal amount that he owes plus a fifth,[2] and he must also bring an *asham* offering. From here until the end of the chapter, the Tanna discusses these laws:

הַגּוֹזֵל אֶת חֲבֵירוֹ שָׁוֶה פְּרוּטָה — **If one steals**[3] **from another something that is worth** at least **a** *perutah*,[4] וְנִשְׁבַּע לוֹ — **and swore** falsely **to him** denying the theft, but later confesses,[5] יוֹלִיכֶנּוּ אַחֲרָיו אֲפִלּוּ לְמָדַי — **he must bring**

--- NOTES ---

5. If the dyer were to be treated as a thief (as R' Meir holds), he would benefit from disobeying the owner's instructions, because he gets to keep the dyed wool for himself and pays only the value of the plain wool (or he is paid his regular fee, as stated in the previous note). R' Yehudah argues that this is unfair. He therefore rules that the dyer may not keep the dyed wool, but must return it to the owner (without receiving his regular fee). Nevertheless, since he did improve the wool, he is entitled to either his expenses or the improvement, whichever is less (*Rav*).

[5]

1. For example, he said, "I hereby make a *shevuah* (oath) that I did not steal it from you," or "that I already returned it to you."

2. The "fifth" is actually a quarter of the amount owed. The Torah refers to it as a "fifth" because it is a fifth of the entire sum after the extra is added. For example, if someone stole 80 *zuz*, he must return the 80 *zuz* and pay an extra 20 *zuz*, for a total of 100 *zuz*. Thus, the extra payment (20) is a quarter of the principal (80), but a fifth of the total (100).

3. Although the Mishnah mentions "stealing," the same laws apply wherever one person owes money or property to another. For example, he borrowed money and did not pay it back, he hired workers and did not pay them, he was given an object to safeguard and did not return it, etc. (see Mishnah 7).

4. Although the Torah forbids making a false oath about any amount, the special laws discussed here apply only where the amount is at least a *perutah* (the smallest coin).

5. The obligations of the fifth and the *asham*, as well as the laws presented in this Mishnah, apply only where the thief confesses (see Mishnah 7 note 8).

משניות בבא קמא / פרק ט: הגוזל עצים

לֹא יִתֵּן לֹא לִבְנוֹ וְלֹא לִשְׁלוּחוֹ, אֲבָל נוֹתֵן לִשְׁלִיחַ בֵּית דִּין. וְאִם מֵת, יַחֲזִיר לְיוֹרְשָׁיו.

רע״ב — לא יתן לא לבנו. של נגזל. דלא הוי השבה עד דמטי לידיה: לשליח בית דין. תקנה הוא: ואם מת. הנגזל.

דעבוד רבנן מפני תקנת השבים, שלא נתייאשו לזה להוליך מנה בהולאת הדרך: **ואם מת.** הנגזל.

[the stolen item] to him even to Media (a distant country); that is, he must bring the stolen property, or its value, to the owner even if the owner is very far away.[6] לֹא יִתֵּן לֹא לִבְנוֹ וְלֹא לִשְׁלוּחוֹ — He may not give it to [the owner's] son or to [the owner's] agent and ask him to deliver it; rather, he must return it to the owner himself.[7]

The Sages, however, provided a way for the thief to fulfill his obligation without traveling to the victim:

אֲבָל נוֹתֵן לִשְׁלִיחַ בֵּית דִּין — But he may give [the stolen item] to an agent of the court, who then holds it on behalf of the owner. The Sages decreed that this is enough because they wanted to make it easier for a thief to repent.[8]

The Mishnah continues:

וְאִם מֵת יַחֲזִיר לְיוֹרְשָׁיו — If [the owner] dies before he was paid, [the thief] must return the stolen property to his heirs.[9]

NOTES

6. The Torah (*Leviticus* 5:24) states: *to the one to whom it belongs shall he give it*. Even if the owner is in a distant land, the thief does not gain atonement unless he goes to the owner and gives the money or stolen property to him (*Rav*). And he cannot bring his *asham* offering until the owner has been paid (Mishnah 12).

Normally, if the victim of a theft travels out of town, the thief is not required to go after him; he only needs to let the owner know that he is ready to pay him back. The obligation to travel any distance applies only in the Torah's specific case, where the thief swore falsely and then confessed (*Tos. Yom Tov*, citing *Tur, Choshen Mishpat* 367).

7. In fact, any thief who must return stolen property cannot just give it to the owner's son or agent; he must deliver it to the owner himself. The thief discussed here, who swore and confessed, is different only in that he must pursue the owner even to a distant land, whereas an ordinary thief does not have to do so, as stated in the previous note (*Sma, Choshen Mishpat* 367:5).

8. As soon as the thief gives the property to an agent of the local court, he has fulfilled his duty, and he may then bring his *asham* offering. The agent of the court safeguards it until the owner collects it (*Rashi*, as understood by *Tosafos*).

The Sages were concerned that a thief might be discouraged from repenting if he has to pursue the owner to a distant land. To make his repentance easier, they allowed him to bring it to the local court instead (*Rav*). [When the Mishnah said that the thief must follow the owner even to Media, it was teaching the Biblical law, which was in force before the Rabbis decreed that giving the item to the court or its agent suffices (*Shitah Mekubetzes*, citing *Rosh*).]

9. The heirs take the place of the owner in all respects. The thief pays the extra fifth to them, and he must follow them even to a distant land [unless he gives it to the court] (*Tos. Yom Tov*).

- רע"ב -

(ו) חוץ מפחות משווה פרוטה וכו'. ולא חיישינן שמא יתייקר וישוב על שוה פרוטה, ואפילו הגזל בעין, אינו צריך להוליכו אחריו:

[ו] נָתַן לוֹ אֶת הַקֶּרֶן וְלֹא נָתַן לוֹ אֶת הַחֹמֶשׁ, מָחַל לוֹ עַל הַקֶּרֶן וְלֹא מָחַל לוֹ עַל הַחֹמֶשׁ, מָחַל לוֹ עַל זֶה וְעַל זֶה, חוּץ מִפָּחוֹת מִשָּׁוֶה פְרוּטָה בַּקֶּרֶן, אֵינוֹ צָרִיךְ לֵילֵךְ אַחֲרָיו. נָתַן לוֹ אֶת הַחֹמֶשׁ וְלֹא נָתַן לוֹ אֶת הַקֶּרֶן, מָחַל לוֹ עַל הַחֹמֶשׁ וְלֹא מָחַל לוֹ עַל הַקֶּרֶן, מָחַל לוֹ עַל זֶה וְעַל זֶה חוּץ מִשָּׁוֶה פְרוּטָה בַּקֶּרֶן, צָרִיךְ לֵילֵךְ אַחֲרָיו.

---

[6] This Mishnah elaborates upon the main law of the previous Mishnah, namely, that one who swore falsely that he does not owe money and then confesses must travel any distance to pay the owner:

נָתַן לוֹ אֶת הַקֶּרֶן וְלֹא נָתַן לוֹ אֶת הַחֹמֶשׁ — If, after swearing falsely and confessing, **he paid [the owner] the principal but did not pay him the fifth,** מָחַל לוֹ עַל הַקֶּרֶן וְלֹא מָחַל לוֹ עַל הַחֹמֶשׁ — or **[the owner] forgave him the principal but did not forgive him the fifth,** מָחַל לוֹ עַל זֶה וְעַל זֶה חוּץ מִפָּחוֹת מִשָּׁוֶה פְרוּטָה בַּקֶּרֶן — or **he forgave him this and that** (the principal and the fifth) **except for less than a** *perutah's* **worth of the principal,** אֵינוֹ צָרִיךְ לֵילֵךְ אַחֲרָיו — **he need not pursue him** to pay him what remains. In all of these cases, the thief only has to pay the fifth (or less than a *perutah's* worth of the principal). Therefore, he is not obligated to pursue the owner to a distant land, because that obligation applies only where he must pay him the principal (or at least a *perutah's* worth of it), and not where he has to pay him only the fifth.[1]

The reverse cases:

נָתַן לוֹ אֶת הַחֹמֶשׁ וְלֹא נָתַן לוֹ אֶת הַקֶּרֶן — However, if **he paid him the fifth but did not pay him the principal,** מָחַל לוֹ עַל הַחֹמֶשׁ וְלֹא מָחַל לוֹ עַל הַקֶּרֶן — or **[the owner] forgave him the fifth but did not forgive him the principal,** מָחַל לוֹ עַל זֶה וְעַל זֶה חוּץ מִשָּׁוֶה פְרוּטָה בַּקֶּרֶן — or **he forgave him this and that** (the principal and the fifth) **except for a** *perutah's* **worth of the principal,** צָרִיךְ לֵילֵךְ אַחֲרָיו — **he must pursue him.** Since in all these cases, he still owes the principal (or a *perutah's* worth of it), he must pursue the owner to give it to him, no matter how far he needs to travel.[2]

[7] The Tanna continues with the laws of a thief who swore falsely and then confessed, who is obligated to pay the principal and a fifth and to bring an *asham* offering:

NOTES

[6]

1. He does not have to deliver the fifth (or less than a *perutah's* worth of the principal) to the owner, unless the owner is in town (see note 6 to the previous Mishnah).

2. This is the Biblical law. According to Rabbinic law, it is enough to give the money to an agent of the court, as stated in the previous Mishnah.

[ז] נָתַן לוֹ אֶת הַקֶּרֶן וְנִשְׁבַּע לוֹ עַל הַחֹמֶשׁ, הֲרֵי זֶה מְשַׁלֵּם חֹמֶשׁ עַל חֹמֶשׁ עַד שֶׁיִּתְמַעֵט הַקֶּרֶן פָּחוֹת מִשָּׁוֶה פְּרוּטָה. וְכֵן בְּפִקָּדוֹן, שֶׁנֶּאֱמַר, בְּפִקָּדוֹן אוֹ בִתְשׂוּמֶת יָד אוֹ בְגָזֵל אוֹ עָשַׁק אֶת עֲמִיתוֹ אוֹ מָצָא אֲבֵדָה וְכִחֶשׁ בָּהּ וְנִשְׁבַּע עַל שָׁקֶר, הֲרֵי זֶה מְשַׁלֵּם קֶרֶן וְחֹמֶשׁ וְאָשָׁם.

– רע"ב –

(ז) **ונשבע לו על החומש.** שבועה שניה שנתנו לו, והודה שלא נתנו: **הרי זה משלם חומש על חומש.** חומשו של חומש. דחומש ראשון נעשה קרן: **עד שיתמעט וכו'.** שאם חזר ונתן לו חומש ראשון, ונשבע על השני, והודה, משלם חומשו וחומשו של חומש שני, וכן לעולם. שנאמר (ויקרא ה,כד) וחמישיתיו יוסף עליו, התורה רבתה חמשיות הרבה לקרן אחד: **תשומת יד.** הלואה: **עשק את עמיתו.** שכר שכיר: **משלם קרן.** דאין חומש ואשם אלא אם כן הודה. דכתיב בגזל הגר בפרשת נשא (במדבר ה,ז), והתודה:

נָתַן לוֹ אֶת הַקֶּרֶן וְנִשְׁבַּע לוֹ עַל הַחֹמֶשׁ — If **he paid [the owner] the principal** but not the fifth, **and** when asked for payment, he **swore** falsely **to him about the fifth,** claiming that he had already paid it, and later he confessed to this new sin as well, **הֲרֵי זֶה מְשַׁלֵּם חֹמֶשׁ עַל חֹמֶשׁ — he must pay a fifth for the fifth** that he denied. That is, in addition to paying the fifth for his first false oath, he must pay a fifth of that fifth because of the second false oath.[1] Then, if he pays only the first fifth, and swears falsely that he paid the second fifth and confessed, he must add a fifth of the second fifth because of the third false oath. **עַד שֶׁיִּתְמַעֵט הַקֶּרֶן פָּחוֹת מִשָּׁוֶה פְּרוּטָה** — This can continue **until the principal** amount about which he swears falsely (i.e., the latest fifth) **is reduced to less than the value of a *perutah*.**[2]

Until now, the Tanna discussed these laws in the context of a thief. Here, the Tanna adds:

וְכֵן בְּפִקָּדוֹן — And the same laws apply **to a deposit.** That is, if something was deposited with a person (for example, he was given money or property to safeguard) and he did not return it, and he falsely swore to deny his obligation,[3] and then he confessed, he is subject to the same laws as a thief who swore falsely and confessed. **שֶׁנֶּאֱמַר** — This is **as it is stated** (*Leviticus* 5:21-22): **"בְּפִקָּדוֹן אוֹ בִתְשׂוּמֶת יָד אוֹ בְגָזֵל אוֹ עָשַׁק אֶת עֲמִיתוֹ אוֹ מָצָא אֲבֵדָה וְכִחֶשׁ בָּהּ וְנִשְׁבַּע עַל שָׁקֶר"** — *If a person will sin ... by lying to his fellow* ***regarding a deposit, or a loan, or a robbery; or by cheating his fellow;***[4] ***or he found a lost item and denied it — and he swore falsely,*** etc. **הֲרֵי זֶה מְשַׁלֵּם קֶרֶן וְחֹמֶשׁ וְאָשָׁם — This**

NOTES

[7]

1. When he swore falsely about the first fifth, that fifth became the *principal* of his new oath (*Rav*). Therefore, his new sin requires an additional fifth.

For example, if he originally swore falsely about 80 *zuz* and then he confessed, he became obligated to pay an extra 20 *zuz* (see Mishnah 5 note 2). If he later swore falsely that he paid the 20 *zuz* and then he confessed, he becomes obligated to pay another 5 *zuz*.

2. Once it is less than a *perutah*, he is not obligated to pay an additional fifth (or bring an *asham*), as taught in Mishnah 5.

3. For example, he claimed that the item was never deposited with him or that he had already returned it.

4. He did not pay his worker (*Rav*).

הֵיכָן פִּקְדוֹנִי, אָמַר לוֹ, אָבַד. מַשְׁבִּיעֲךָ אֲנִי, וְאָמַר, אָמֵן, וְהָעֵדִים מְעִידִים אוֹתוֹ שֶׁאֲכָלוֹ, מְשַׁלֵּם קֶרֶן. הוֹדָה מֵעַצְמוֹ, מְשַׁלֵּם קֶרֶן וָחֹמֶשׁ וְאָשָׁם.

[ח] הֵיכָן פִּקְדוֹנִי, אָמַר לוֹ, נִגְנַב. מַשְׁבִּיעֲךָ אֲנִי, וְאָמַר, אָמֵן,

one (i.e., the sinner mentioned in the verse) **pays the principal, and the fifth,** and brings **an** *asham* **offering,** as the passage continues (verses 24-25): *He shall repay its principal and add its fifth to it ... And he shall bring his asham offering to Hashem.*[5]

The obligation to pay the fifth and bring an *asham* does not apply unless a certain condition is met:

הֵיכָן פִּקְדוֹנִי — If one person said to another, **"Where is my deposit** that I gave you to safeguard?," אָמַר לוֹ אָבַד — and **he replied, "It was lost,"** in which case he would not be obligated to return it or pay its value,"[6] מַשְׁבִּיעֲךָ אֲנִי — and the owner then said to him, "I hereby **make you swear** that it is indeed lost," וְאָמַר אָמֵן — **and he answered, "Amen"** (which is the same as making the oath himself),[7] וְהָעֵדִים מְעִידִים אוֹתוֹ שֶׁאֲכָלוֹ — **and afterward witnesses testified against him that he consumed it** or kept it for himself, מְשַׁלֵּם קֶרֶן — **he pays** only **the principal.** הוֹדָה מֵעַצְמוֹ — **But if he confessed on his own,** מְשַׁלֵּם קֶרֶן וָחֹמֶשׁ וְאָשָׁם — **he pays the principal and the fifth** and brings the ***asham*** **offering.** It is only where the thief confessed that the obligations of the fifth and the *asham* apply.[8]

[8] In the last case of the previous Mishnah, the *shomer* (i.e., person who is given money or property to safeguard) claimed that the deposit was *lost*. In the following case, he claims that it was *stolen*:

הֵיכָן פִּקְדוֹנִי — If one person said to another, **"Where is my deposit** that I gave you to safeguard?," אָמַר לוֹ נִגְנַב — and **he replied, "It was stolen,"** in which case he would not be obligated to return it or pay its value, מַשְׁבִּיעֲךָ אֲנִי — and the owner then said to him, "I hereby **make you swear** that it was indeed stolen," וְאָמַר אָמֵן — **and he answered, "Amen"** (which is the same

---
NOTES

5. He is also obligated to bring the principal to the owner no matter how far he must travel (see Mishnah 5 note 6).
6. The Mishnah refers to an unpaid *shomer* (watchman), who is exempt from paying for a deposit that was lost, unless he was negligent (see Mishnah 4:9 note 1).
7. Answering "Amen" is an acceptance of the oath, which is equal to the oath itself (*Meiri*).
8. This law is derived from the Torah (see *Rav*). The reason why confession is necessary is that the purpose of the fifth and the *asham* is to provide the thief with atonement (God's forgiveness), and there can be no atonement except for one who repents and confesses his sin (*Rambam Hil. Gezeilah* 7:8). If he fails to confess, then even if witnesses testify against him, he is exempt from the fifth and the *asham*. He is also exempt from the special obligation to travel any distance to pay the owner.

[Although the Mishnah's words, "he confessed *on his own*," imply that he confessed before witnesses testified against him, the same laws apply even where he confessed after witnesses testified (see *Tosefos R' Akiva Eiger*).]

משניות בבא קמא / פרק ט: הגוזל עצים

וְהָעֵדִים מְעִידִין אוֹתוֹ שֶׁגְּנָבוֹ, מְשַׁלֵּם תַּשְׁלוּמֵי כֶפֶל. הוֹדָה מֵעַצְמוֹ, מְשַׁלֵּם קֶרֶן וְחֹמֶשׁ וְאָשָׁם.

[ט] הַגּוֹזֵל אֶת אָבִיו וְנִשְׁבַּע לוֹ וָמֵת, הֲרֵי זֶה מְשַׁלֵּם קֶרֶן וְחֹמֶשׁ לְבָנָיו אוֹ לְאֶחָיו.

- רע"ב -

(ח) תשלומי כפל. ואם הודה מעצמו אינו משלם כפל, דכתיב (שמות כב,ח) אשר ירשיעון אלהים, פרט למרשיע את עצמו:
(ט) הרי זה משלם קרן וחומש לבניו או לאחיו. אם אין לו בנים. ואף על גב דנפלה ירושה קמיה דהיאך, בעי למיעבד תשובה, ואין מטכב אללו אפילו כנגד חלקו. דכתיב (ויקרא ה,כג) והשיב את הגזלה, אין לו תקנה עד שיוציא גזילו מתחת ידו. ובלבד שתהא הגזילה בעין, דלא קנייה בשינוי:

---

as making the oath himself), וְהָעֵדִים מְעִידִין אוֹתוֹ שֶׁגְּנָבוֹ — and afterward witnesses testified against him that he stole it himself (that is, he still had it at the time of the oath or he had consumed it), מְשַׁלֵּם תַּשְׁלוּמֵי כֶפֶל — he makes the **double payment** (*keifel*) that a regular thief must make.[1] But he does not pay the extra fifth or bring an *asham* offering, because he did not confess, and those two obligations apply only where the thief confessed on his own (as taught in the previous Mishnah). הוֹדָה מֵעַצְמוֹ — However, if **he did confess on his own,** מְשַׁלֵּם קֶרֶן וְחֹמֶשׁ וְאָשָׁם — he pays the **principal and the fifth and** brings the *asham* **offering.** But he is exempt from the double payment, because that is a "fine," and the rule is that a person's confession does not obligate him to pay a fine.[2]

[9] Another law that concerns a thief who falsely swore that he does not have to pay and then confessed:

הַגּוֹזֵל אֶת אָבִיו וְנִשְׁבַּע לוֹ — **If someone robbed his father and swore** falsely **to him,** claiming that he is not liable, וָמֵת — **and then [the father] died** and the son confessed, הֲרֵי זֶה מְשַׁלֵּם קֶרֶן וְחֹמֶשׁ לְבָנָיו אוֹ לְאֶחָיו — **he pays the principal and the fifth to [his father's] sons or [the father's] brothers.** That is, he must pay the *entire* principal and the *entire* fifth —including the share that he inherits — to the other heirs of his father, such as his father's other sons (the robber's brothers) or the father's brothers.[1] Although the thief also inherits his father, he may not keep anything for himself, but must pay everything to the other heirs.[2]

NOTES

[8]

1. An unpaid *shomer* who does not return the item entrusted to him is exempt from payment if he swears that it was lost or stolen. However, if he swears that it was stolen and witnesses testify that it was *not* stolen (for example, they say that he still has it), the Torah teaches that he is treated like a thief in that he must pay the value of the article plus a fine that equals the value of the article (*Bava Metzia* 3:1). This is the *keifel* fine that a thief must pay (see the beginning of Chapter 7).

2. Normally, when a person says that he owes money, he becomes obligated to pay it. But if he says that he owes a fine, he is exempt. This rule is derived from the Torah (see *Rav*).

In fact, the "fifth" is also a fine. He must nevertheless pay it in order to gain atonement (*Tiferes Yisrael*).

[9]

1. If someone dies without sons, he is inherited by his brothers.
2. The thief discussed here (who swore falsely and then confessed) does not gain

[139] **MISHNAH BAVA KAMMA** / Chapter 9: *Hagozeil Eitzim* 9/10

– רע״ב –

אֵין לוֹ. נכסים כל כך שיכול לוותר על חלקו: אוֹ שֶׁאֵינוֹ רוֹצֶה. להפסיד חלקוֹ: לוֹוֶה. מאחרים, ומחזיר את הגזל לאחיו, לקיים מצות השבה: וּבַעֲלֵי הַחוֹב. שלוה זה הגזלן מהם: בָּאִים

וְאִם אֵינוֹ רוֹצָה, אוֹ שֶׁאֵין לוֹ, לֹוֶה וּבַעֲלֵי חוֹב בָּאִים וְנִפְרָעִים.

[י] הָאוֹמֵר לִבְנוֹ, קוֹנָם אִי אַתָּה נֶהֱנֶה מִשֶּׁלִי, אִם מֵת, יִירָשֶׁנּוּ.

וְנִפְרָעִים. מן הגזילה הזאת, החלק שיש לגזלן בה. ואם אין יורש לחבי אלא הוא, נותן הוא עצמו הגזילה לבעל חובו בפרעון החוב, וצריך להודיעו ולומר לו זה גזל אבא. או נותן על דרך זה, לכתובת אשתו או לקופת הצדקה. ובכולן צריך שיודיע שזה גזל אבוו:

The Tanna provides a way for him to avoid losing his share of the stolen item, while still fulfilling his obligation to return everything he stole:

וְאִם אֵינוֹ רוֹצֶה — **But if he does not want to** give up his share of the stolen item, אוֹ שֶׁאֵין לוֹ — **or he does not have** enough money to afford giving it up, לֹוֶה — **he may borrow** money from someone, וּבַעֲלֵי חוֹב בָּאִים וְנִפְרָעִים — **and then his lender can come and collect** the debt from the portion of the stolen property that he inherited and gave away. That is, the thief borrows an amount that equals his share of the stolen item, then he gives the entire item to the other heirs, and then the lender collects his debt from the other heirs. In this way, the robber fulfills his obligation to return the entire item, and yet he also benefits from his share by borrowing that amount and not paying it back.[3]

[10] In continuation of the previous Mishnah, the Tanna discusses another case of an heir who may not keep his inheritance:

הָאוֹמֵר לִבְנוֹ קוֹנָם אִי אַתָּה נֶהֱנֶה מִשֶּׁלִי — **If someone says to his son, "Konam if you benefit from what is mine,"** that is, he made a vow (*neder*) forbidding his son to have benefit from his property,[1] אִם מֵת יִירָשֶׁנּוּ — **when he dies,**

--- NOTES ---

atonement unless he returns *all* of the stolen item (and the fifth), including the share that he inherited. This is in contrast to a regular thief, who may keep his own share and return just the shares of the other heirs (*Tiferes Yisrael;* see *Tos. Yom Tov*).

This requirement to return everything applies only where the stolen item itself must be returned. If the thief pays its monetary value instead (for example, because the item changed and he thereby acquired it), he need not make the *entire* payment to the other heirs, but may keep the share of the principal (and the fifth) that he inherited (*Rav*).

3. For example, if the robber has two brothers, and he inherited a third of the stolen item, he borrows an amount equal to a third of its value. The borrower then seizes that amount from the heirs.

Generally, if a borrower gives (or sells) movable property to someone before paying off his debt, the lender *cannot* take it from the recipient. (He can take only land, not movable property.) This thief, however, did not actually give his share of the stolen item to his brothers; he merely surrendered his rights to it so that he could gain atonement. Since the brothers did not receive it as a gift, the lender is entitled to take it from them (see *Tos. Yom Tov*).

[10]

1. A *neder* is a statement through which a person forbids himself or anyone else to use an item or to benefit from it. For example, he says, "This loaf of bread is prohibited to me," or "My chair is prohibited to you." (One can prohibit anyone's property to himself, but only his own property to others.) One way to

משניות בבא קמא / פרק ט: הגזול עצים

בְּחַיָּיו וּבְמוֹתוֹ, אִם מֵת, לֹא יִירָשֶׁנּוּ, וְיַחֲזִיר לְבָנָיו אוֹ לְאֶחָיו. וְאִם אֵין לוֹ, לֹוֶה וּבַעֲלֵי חוֹב בָּאִים וְנִפְרָעִים.

— רע״ב —

(י) ואם אין לו. מה יאכל. לוה ואוכל, ובעלי חוב באים ונפרעים מן הירושה את חלקו. ולא תשיבא הנאה מה שפורע חובו באותם מעות, דהא תנן בנדרים (דף לג,ח) המודר הנאה מחבירו פורע לו חובו:

[the son] **inherits him**; that is, the son is allowed to have benefit from his father's estate. Since the father said, "what is *mine*," he intended to prohibit his property only as long as it belonged to him, and not after his death, when it is no longer his.[2] בְּחַיָּיו וּבְמוֹתוֹ — However, if he declares his property forbidden to his son **during his lifetime and after his death,** for example, he said, "Konam if you benefit from what is mine during my lifetime and after my death," אִם מֵת לֹא יִירָשֶׁנּוּ — **when he dies, [the son] does not inherit him** (that is, he may not benefit even from his own share of his father's estate), because the father said that the prohibition lasts even after his death.[3] וְיַחֲזִיר לְבָנָיו אוֹ לְאֶחָיו — And so **he must return** his share of the estate **to [his father's] sons or [his father's] brothers,** i.e., the other heirs of his father.[4]

The Tanna provides a way for the son to keep his share:

וְאִם אֵין לוֹ — **But if he does not have** enough money to buy food, לֹוֶה — **he may borrow** money, וּבַעֲלֵי חוֹב בָּאִים וְנִפְרָעִים — **and** then his **lender can come and collect** the debt from his share of the estate. This is permitted because the son thereby benefits from his share only indirectly.[5]

NOTES
---

express a *neder* is by linking its subject to a general category of objects that are prohibited, for example, "This loaf of bread is like a *korban* (sacred offering) to me." The person who made the *neder* thereby forbids himself to have benefit from the bread. The word *konam* used in our Mishnah means the same as *korban* (Nedarim 1:2). Thus, the father's expression in our Mishnah, "Konam if you benefit from what is mine," means, "My property is forbidden to you like a *korban* if you benefit from it" (see *Tos. Yom Tov*).

2. *Meiri*.

3. Although a person cannot make a *neder* forbidding other people to have benefit from something he does not own (see note 1), the father is able to prohibit his estate even after his death, when it is no longer his. Since he started the prohibition in his lifetime, when it did belong to him, the prohibition remains in force even after it leaves his hands (*Nedarim* 47a).

4. The son may not give the property as a gift in the usual manner, because he would thereby benefit from it. (The recipient's gratitude is a form of benefit that the giver enjoys.) Instead, he may tell the other heirs, "My father prohibited this property to me and I do not know what to do with it; you may take it and use it as you wish." This is not considered a gift, but a surrendering of his rights, which is permitted (*Tos. Yom Tov*).

5. In this way, the son does not receive a positive gain from the estate; rather, the estate is used to pay off his debt and save him from a loss. This is an indirect form of benefit, which is permitted according to the laws of *nedarim* (*Rav* to *Nedarim* 4:2). Since only indirect benefit is allowed, the son may not keep his inheritance and have the lender take it from him directly. Rather, he must give it to his brothers and have the lender take it from them (*Ran, Nedarim* 47a).

[Here, *Rav* explains the phrase וְאִם אֵין לוֹ, *But if he does not have,* to mean that the son does not have anything *to eat,* while in the previous Mishnah *Rav* explained the same phrase as meaning

MISHNAH BAVA KAMMA / Chapter 9: *Hagozeil Eitzim*

- רע"ב -

(יא) שנאמר ואם אין לאיש גואל. ואין לך אדם בישראל שאין לו גואלים למעלה עד יעקב אבינו. אלא זה הגר שמת, ואין לו יורשין: ומת. הגזלן:

[יא] **הַגּוֹזֵל** אֶת הַגֵּר וְנִשְׁבַּע לוֹ, וָמֵת, הֲרֵי זֶה מְשַׁלֵּם קֶרֶן וְחֹמֶשׁ לַכֹּהֲנִים וְאָשָׁם לַמִּזְבֵּחַ, שֶׁנֶּאֱמַר, וְאִם אֵין לָאִישׁ גֹּאֵל לְהָשִׁיב הָאָשָׁם אֵלָיו, הָאָשָׁם הַמּוּשָׁב לַה׳ לַכֹּהֵן, מִלְּבַד אֵיל הַכִּפֻּרִים אֲשֶׁר יְכַפֶּר בּוֹ עָלָיו:

---

[11] The Tanna returns once more to the topic of one who swore falsely to deny a monetary obligation. Mishnah 9 taught that if the victim dies, the robber pays the principal and fifth to his heirs. Our Mishnah discusses how the sinner can gain atonement if the deceased victim has no heirs:

הַגּוֹזֵל אֶת הַגֵּר וְנִשְׁבַּע לוֹ — **If someone robs a convert and swears** falsely **to him,** claiming that he is not liable, וָמֵת — **and [the convert] dies** without leaving heirs,[1] הֲרֵי זֶה מְשַׁלֵּם קֶרֶן וְחֹמֶשׁ לַכֹּהֲנִים — **[the thief] pays the principal and the fifth to the Kohanim,** וְאָשָׁם לַמִּזְבֵּחַ — **and brings an *asham* offering to be burned on the Altar.** שֶׁנֶּאֱמַר — **This is as it is stated** (Numbers 5:8): וְאִם אֵין לָאִישׁ גֹּאֵל לְהָשִׁיב הָאָשָׁם אֵלָיו — "*But if the man has no relative to whom the guilt payment can be returned* [i.e., he does not have an heir to whom the principal and fifth can be paid],[2] הָאָשָׁם הַמּוּשָׁב לַה׳ לַכֹּהֵן — *the guilt payment that is returned is for Hashem, for the Kohen,* מִלְּבַד אֵיל הַכִּפֻּרִים אֲשֶׁר יְכַפֶּר בּוֹ עָלָיו" — *aside from the ram of atonement* [the *asham*] *with which he* [the Kohen] *shall provide him atonement.*[3]

NOTES

that the son faces financial difficulty. (Also, the previous Mishnah said that the same law applies even if the son simply *does not want* to give away his share.) The reason for this difference is that in the previous Mishnah's case — where a son stole from his father who then died — the son is not prohibited to have benefit from the stolen property. He is just required to give away his share in order to fulfill the mitzvah of returning what he stole. To fulfill this mitzvah, he is allowed to give away his share and then have it collected by his borrower. In our Mishnah, however, where the son is *prohibited* to have benefit from his father's property, the Sages forbade him to use this scheme unless he has nothing to eat (*Tos. Yom Tov*).]

[11]

1. Only a convert can die without heirs. Every born Jew has relatives who inherit him, no matter how distant, since all born Jews are descended from Jacob. However, when a non-Jew converts to Judaism, it is as if he were reborn (כְּקָטָן שֶׁנּוֹלַד דָּמֵי), which means that his biological relatives are no longer viewed as being related to him (see *Yevamos* 97b). Thus, unless he marries a Jewish woman and has children after he converts, he does not have any heirs (*Rav, Rambam Commentary*). [When he dies, his property is *hefker* (i.e., it does not have an owner) and can be taken by anyone.]

2. This must refer to a convert. See previous note.

3. When the convert died and his property became ownerless (see note 1), the thief acquired the stolen item since he already had it in his possession. This verse teaches that he must nevertheless give it (or its value) and the fifth to the Kohanim in order to gain atonement for his false oath (*Rav*).

הָיָה מַעֲלֶה אֶת הַכֶּסֶף וְאֶת הָאָשָׁם, וָמֵת, הַכֶּסֶף יִנָּתֵן לְבָנָיו, וְהָאָשָׁם יִרְעֶה עַד שֶׁיִּסְתָּאֵב, וְיִמָּכֵר, וְיִפְּלוּ דָמָיו לִנְדָבָה.

[יב] נָתַן אֶת הַכֶּסֶף לְאַנְשֵׁי מִשְׁמָר וָמֵת, אֵין הַיּוֹרְשִׁים יְכוֹלִין לְהוֹצִיא מִיָּדָם,

- רע"ב -

הכסף ינתן לבניו. של גזלן. שכבר זכה בהן ממיתת הגר. אלא דהשבה בעי למעבד, כי היכי דתיהוי ליה כפרה אצבועתיה, והשתא תו ליכא כפרה, כיון דמית ליה: והאשם ירעה. כדין אשם שמתו בעליו,

דקיימא לן (קי,3) כל שבחטאת מתה באשם רועה. עד שיסתאב: ויפלו דמיו לנדבה. לקיץ המזבח לקנות מהם עולות: (יב) לאנשי משמר ומת. קודם שיביא קרבן. אין יורשי הגזלן יכולים להוציא מיד הכהנים, מאחר שזכו בהן כבר:

The Mishnah continues:

הָיָה מַעֲלֶה אֶת הַכֶּסֶף וְאֶת הָאָשָׁם — If [the thief] was bringing up the money and *asham* to Jerusalem, to give the money to the Kohanim and to offer the *asham,* וָמֵת — and he died along the way, הַכֶּסֶף יִנָּתֵן לְבָנָיו — the money shall be given to his sons who inherit him, and not to the Kohanim,[4] וְהָאָשָׁם יִרְעֶה עַד שֶׁיִּסְתָּאֵב — and the *asham* offering grazes until it develops a blemish, וְיִמָּכֵר וְיִפְּלוּ דָמָיו לִנְדָבָה — and it is then sold, and the money from the sale goes toward the purchase of voluntary communal offerings.[5]

[12] The previous Mishnah taught that if the thief died before he paid the Kohanim, the payments are kept by his heirs and the *asham* can no longer be offered. Moreover, even if the thief died after he paid the Kohanim, the *asham* is not offered. The Mishnah addresses the question of whether the Kohanim have to return the money:

נָתַן אֶת הַכֶּסֶף לְאַנְשֵׁי מִשְׁמָר וָמֵת — If he gave the money to the men of the *mishmar* (the group of Kohanim serving that week in the Temple)[1] and then died before his *asham* was offered, אֵין הַיּוֹרְשִׁים יְכוֹלִין לְהוֹצִיא מִיָּדָם — his heirs cannot take the money back from them, even though the thief is no

---

NOTES

4. The reason he must give it to the Kohanim is only so that he will receive atonement. Thus, after the thief died and can no longer receive atonement, nothing will be gained by having the payment taken from his estate. The stolen property and the fifth may therefore be kept by his heirs (*Rav*).

5. The purpose of any *asham* is to atone for its owner. Therefore, if the owner of an *asham* dies, it is not offered, since he can no longer receive atonement. The animal is left to graze until it develops a blemish, at which point it is sold. The money from the sale is sacred and must be used to buy communal *olah* offerings. These *olah* offerings are burned on the Altar when no other offerings are being burned there, so that the Altar will never be idle and unused (*Rav*).

[12]

1. The Kohanim were divided into twenty-four family groups, each of which served in the Temple for one week at a time (see *Taanis* 4:2). Each group was known as a *mishmar*. When the thief comes to make the payment, he may not give it to any Kohen of his choosing; rather, he must give it to the Kohanim of that week's *mishmar*, who share it among themselves (*Tiferes Yisrael*; see *Rashi* 109b ד"ה בשהוא אומר for the Biblical source).

[143] MISHNAH BAVA KAMMA / Chapter 9: *Hagozeil Eitzim*

שֶׁנֶּאֱמַר, אִישׁ אֲשֶׁר יִתֵּן לַכֹּהֵן לוֹ יִהְיֶה.
נָתַן הַכֶּסֶף לִיהוֹיָרִיב וְאָשָׁם לִידַעְיָה, יָצָא.
אָשָׁם לִיהוֹיָרִיב וְכֶסֶף לִידַעְיָה, אִם קַיָּם
הָאָשָׁם, יַקְרִיבוּהוּ בְּנֵי יְדַעְיָה, וְאִם לָאו,

- רע"ב -

ליהויריב. היא משמרה ראשונה של עשרים וארבעה משמרות כהונה שבמקדש. ושל ידעיה אחריה: נתן. הגזלן את הכסף ליהויריב במשמרתו, ואחר כך נתן האשם לידעיה במשמרתו, יצא. כדמפרש ואזיל, שהמביא גזלו עד שלא הביא קרבן אשמו, יצא. וזה המשמר זכה בשלו, וזה בשלו. אבל נתן אשם ליהויריב, שהביא אשמו תחלה, ואחר כך הביא גזלו ונתן למשמר שלאחריו, אם האשם קיים, שלא הקריבוהו בני יהויריב, יקריבוהו בני ידעיה, ויהא גזלו ואשמו לידעיה. ואם אין אשמו קיים, לא יצא באשם שנתן ליהויריב, כיון שלא נתן גזלו. ויחזור ויביא אשם אחר:

---

longer able to gain atonement with his *asham*. שֶׁנֶּאֱמַר — **This is because it is stated** (*Numbers* 5:10): "אִישׁ אֲשֶׁר יִתֵּן לַכֹּהֵן לוֹ יִהְיֶה" — **what a man gives to the Kohen shall be his,** which teaches that once the Kohanim are paid, the money is completely theirs and need not be returned.[2]

The Mishnah discusses cases where the thief gave the money to one *mishmar* and his *asham* was offered by another *mishmar*.

נָתַן הַכֶּסֶף לִיהוֹיָרִיב וְאָשָׁם לִידַעְיָה — **If he gave the money to Yehoyariv** (the first *mishmar*) during its week **and gave the** *asham* **to Yedayah** (the second *mishmar*) during *its* week,[3] יָצָא — **he has fulfilled** his obligation, because the payment was made before the *asham* was offered, which is the correct order.[4] If however, he did the reverse: אָשָׁם לִיהוֹיָרִיב וְכֶסֶף לִידַעְיָה — **that** is, he gave the *asham* **to Yehoyariv** (the first *mishmar*) **and the money to Yedayah** (the second *mishmar*), the law is as follows: אִם קַיָּם הָאָשָׁם — **If the** *asham* **still exists** (that is, the first *mishmar*, Yehoyariv, did not offer it), יַקְרִיבוּהוּ בְּנֵי יְדַעְיָה — **the members of Yedayah** (the second *mishmar*) **offer it** instead,[5] וְאִם לָאו — **but if the** *asham* **does not exist** anymore (because the

---

NOTES

2. It could have been thought that the thief's heirs have the following claim: "Our father paid the Kohanim only to gain atonement. Therefore, now that he cannot have atonement in any event (because he died before bringing his *asham*), the payment was based on a mistake, and the Kohanim must return what they received." The Torah teaches that this is not a valid claim, because the payment itself — even without the *asham* — gives some degree of atonement. The Kohanim may thus keep the money regardless of whether the *asham* is offered (*Tos. Yom Tov*).

3. The first of the twenty-four *mishmaros* was the family of Yehoyariv, and the second was the family of Yedayah (*I Chronicles* 24:7). The robber made the payment to the *mishmar* of Yehoyariv during their week, but he did not bring the *asham* until the next week, when it was the turn of Yedayah to serve (*Rav*).

4. As the Mishnah explains below, the robber gains atonement only if the *asham* is offered after he makes the payment.

5. Because the *asham* was given to Yehoyariv (the first *mishmar*), they should be allowed to keep it until after the payment is made and their next time to serve in the Temple arrives. The Sages decreed, however, that since Yehoyariv acted improperly by accepting the *asham* before the thief made his payment, we take the offering out of their hands and give it to the next *mishmar*, Yedayah (*Rav, Rashi*).

יַחֲזֹר וְיָבִיא אָשָׁם אַחֵר, שֶׁהַמֵּבִיא גְּזֵלוֹ עַד שֶׁלֹּא הֵבִיא אֲשָׁמוֹ יָצָא, הֵבִיא אֲשָׁמוֹ עַד שֶׁלֹּא הֵבִיא גְּזֵלוֹ לֹא יָצָא. נָתַן אֶת הַקֶּרֶן, וְלֹא נָתַן אֶת הַחֹמֶשׁ, אֵין הַחֹמֶשׁ מְעַכֵּב.

- רע״ב -

נתן הקרן. לכהנים. אין החומש מעכב. מלהקריב את האשם. אם לא נתן עדיין, ולבסוף נתן:

יַחֲזֹר וְיָבִיא אָשָׁם אַחֵר — [the first *mishmar*, Yehoyariv, had already offered it), [the thief] **must go back and bring another** *asham,* because the *asham* provides atonement only if it is offered after the payment is made.

The Mishnah states the rule on which these laws are based:

שֶׁהַמֵּבִיא גְּזֵלוֹ עַד שֶׁלֹּא הֵבִיא אֲשָׁמוֹ יָצָא — This is **because one who brought the payment for his theft before he brought his** *asham* **has fulfilled his obligation,** הֵבִיא אֲשָׁמוֹ עַד שֶׁלֹּא הֵבִיא גְּזֵלוֹ לֹא יָצָא — but **one who brought his** *asham* **before he brought** the payment for **his theft has not fulfilled** his obligation. The thief does not receive atonement unless he pays first and brings the *asham* later.

The Mishnah states which part of the payment must be made before the *asham* is offered:

נָתַן אֶת הַקֶּרֶן וְלֹא נָתַן אֶת הַחֹמֶשׁ — **If he gave** the Kohanim **the principal** that he stole **but did not give** them **the fifth,** אֵין הַחֹמֶשׁ מְעַכֵּב — **the fifth does not hold back** his atonement. As long as the *asham* is offered after the *principal* is paid, it atones for him, even though the fifth has not yet been paid.[6]

NOTES

6. He must, however, pay the fifth later (*Tos. Yom Tov, Tiferes Yisrael*).

Chapter Ten

משניות בבא קמא / פרק י: הגזול

[א] הַגּוֹזֵל וּמַאֲכִיל אֶת בָּנָיו וְהִנִּיחַ לִפְנֵיהֶם, פְּטוּרִין מִלְּשַׁלֵּם. וְאִם הָיָה דָבָר שֶׁיֵּשׁ בּוֹ אַחֲרָיוּת, חַיָּבִין לְשַׁלֵּם.

— רע"ב —

פרק עשירי – הגזול ומאכיל. (א) הגזול ומאכיל. והניח לפניהם. או שהניח לפניהם הגזילה קיימת: פטורים מלשלם.

אם אכלוה אחר מיתת אביהם ולא איתא בעינה, פטורים מלשלם. דהא אינהו לא גזול מידי, ומטלטלי לא משתעבדי לבעל חוב. ואם לא אכלוה והיא בעינה, חייבים להחזיר: אם היה דבר שיש בו אחריות. כלומר, ואם הניח להם אביהם דבר שיש בו אחריות, שהם קרקעות, חייבים לשלם אף על פי שאכלוה כבר. הכי מתרצה מתניתין בגמרא (קיא, ב). ולעניין פסק הלכה, הגזול ומאכיל את בניו. בין שאכלו לפני יאוש, בין שאכלו לאחר יאוש, חייבים לשלם ממונו שהניח להם אביהם, בין מנכסים שיש להם אחריות, בין מנכסים שאין להם אחריות. דהאידנא מטלטלי משתעבדי לבעל חוב. ואם לא הניח הגזלן כלום. אם אכלו הבנים הגזילה לפני יאוש, חייבים לשלם משלהם. ואם לאחר יאוש אכלו, אין חייבים לשלם משלהם, אלא אם כן הניח להם אביהם:

---

[1] This chapter continues to deal with the laws of theft. The first Mishnah teaches when a thief's children are obligated to pay for items that their father stole:

הַגּוֹזֵל וּמַאֲכִיל אֶת בָּנָיו — **If someone steals** something **and feeds** it **to his children** and then he dies, וְהִנִּיחַ לִפְנֵיהֶם — **or if he** dies and **leaves** the stolen item **to them** as an inheritance and then they eat it, פְּטוּרִין מִלְּשַׁלֵּם — **they are not obligated to pay** the owner, because although they ate the item, it was their father who stole it, and they are not required to pay for what he did.[1] וְאִם הָיָה דָבָר שֶׁיֵּשׁ בּוֹ אַחֲרָיוּת — **However, if there was real estate**[2] (i.e., land or houses) in their inheritance, חַיָּבִין לְשַׁלֵּם — **they are obligated to pay** with the real estate, because it is mortgaged to pay for their father's obligations.

--- NOTES ---

[1]

1. The Mishnah refers to a case where the thief left only movable goods (מִטַּלְטְלִין) to his children. The law is that orphans are not obligated to pay their father's debts (which include payments for items he stole) with movable items that they inherited from him [and they are certainly not obligated to pay with their own possessions] (Rav). [The Mishnah below states the law where they inherited real estate from their father.]

The children are exempt from payment only if the owner had already given up hope of getting the stolen property back (יֵאוּשׁ) before they ate it. If he had *not* yet given up hope, the children themselves are considered to have stolen it when they ate it, in which case they would have to pay the owner even with their own money (Rav; see note 2 on the next Mishnah).

As stated in the Mishnah, the children *ate* the item (before or after the thief died). If they did not eat it and it is still intact, they must return it to its owner (Rav).

2. Literally, *possessions that have responsibility*. Real estate is referred to in this way because a person's real estate is "responsible" for (i.e., guarantees) his financial obligations. For example, if a borrower has no money to repay his loan, the lender can take that amount from the land the borrower owned at the time of the loan, even if the borrower has already sold the land to someone else [but the lender cannot take *movable property* that the borrower had sold] (Rav to Kiddushin 1:5). In our case, too, since the thief owes money to the owner of the stolen item, the owner can collect his payment from the thief's land even after he has died and it has been passed on to his sons.

[147] MISHNAH BAVA KAMMA / Chapter 10: *Hagozeil* 10/2

אֵין פּוֹרְטִין לֹא מִתֵּבַת הַמּוֹכְסִין וְלֹא מִכִּיס שֶׁל גַּבָּאִין, וְאֵין נוֹטְלִין מֵהֶם צְדָקָה. אֲבָל נוֹטֵל הוּא מִתּוֹךְ בֵּיתוֹ אוֹ מִן הַשּׁוּק.

[ב] **נָטְלוּ** מוֹכְסִין אֶת חֲמוֹרוֹ וְנָתְנוּ לוֹ חֲמוֹר

— רע״ב —

אין פורטין. אין מחליפים סלעים בפרוטות: **מתיבת המוכסין.** ליטול פרוטות מתיבתן שנותנים בה מעות המכס: ולא **מכיס של [גבאים].** גבאי המלך שגובה כסף גולגולת וארנונה. לפי שהן של גזל. ודוקא במוכס עכו״ם, או מוכס ישראל שאין לו קצבה, שלוקח כמו שהוא רוצה. אבל מוכס ישראל שהעמידו אפילו מלך עכו״ם, ולוקח דבר קצוב בחוק המלכות, אינו בחזקת גזלן, ופורטין מתיבתו. ולא עוד, אלא שאסור להבריח מן המכס שלו, דדינא דמלכותא דינא: **מתוך ביתו.** של מוכס שהוא בחזקת גזלן: **או מן השוק.** אם יש לו מעות בביתו או בשוק שאינם בתיבת המכס. ואם חייב אדם פרוטות למוכס, מן המכס, בתלי דינר, ואין לו פרוטות, נותן לו דינר כסף, ומקבל ממנו פרוטות בשוה חציו, ואף על פי שנותן לו מתיבת המכס, מפני שהוא כמציל מידו:

The Mishnah cites other laws about using property that was stolen by another:

אֵין פּוֹרְטִין לֹא מִתֵּבַת הַמּוֹכְסִין — **We may not take change**[3] from coins in the **customs-collector's box,** וְלֹא מִכִּיס שֶׁל גַּבָּאִין — **or** from coins in the **tax-collector's purse,** וְאֵין נוֹטְלִין מֵהֶם צְדָקָה — **nor may we take charity from them.** Those who collected taxes and customs fees were suspected of stealing;[4] therefore, the box or purse that they use for collecting might contain stolen money, which may not be used even for a mitzvah, such as giving charity.[5]

אֲבָל נוֹטֵל הוּא מִתּוֹךְ בֵּיתוֹ אוֹ מִן הַשּׁוּק — **However, one may take from** coins the collector has **in his house or from** coins he carries in **the street,** because only the coins in his official tax-collecting box or purse are presumed to have been stolen, but not his personal coins.

[2] The Mishnah cites cases where it is *permitted* to benefit from stolen goods: נָטְלוּ מוֹכְסִין אֶת חֲמוֹרוֹ וְנָתְנוּ לוֹ חֲמוֹר אַחֵר — **If customs-collectors**

NOTES

3. That is, to exchange larger coins for smaller ones (see *Rav*).

4. In earlier times, it was common for kings to obtain their income by selling the right to collect taxes. A person would pay the king a large sum of money in exchange for the right to collect taxes and keep the payments for himself (*Rashi* 113a). The Mishnah refers to a collector who is permitted to collect any amount of tax. He is likely to charge unfairly, increasing the obligations of some and decreasing the obligations of others, as he chooses. Since this is unjust, the money that he collects is considered stolen (*Tos. Yom Tov* to *Nedarim* 3:4).

However, a tax collector who is authorized by the king to collect a limited amount from each person or for each type of merchandise is not a thief, because any king or government (whether Jewish or not) has the right to impose laws on its people, including the obligation to pay taxes. The laws of the land are binding according to halachah (דִּינָא דְמַלְכוּתָא דִּינָא); thus, a Jew has a religious duty to pay taxes and is forbidden to avoid paying them. It is certainly permitted in such a case to take change from a tax- or customs-collector (*Rav*).

5. See *Tos. Yom Tov*.

[In addition, taking stolen money for charity is prohibited because it encourages thieves to steal, since they mistakenly believe that giving the money to charity justifies their sin and exempts them from having to pay the owner (*Meiri*).]

משניות בבא קמא / פרק י: הגוזל

אַחֵר, גְּזָלוּ לִסְטִים אֶת כְּסוּתוֹ וְנָתְנוּ לוֹ כְּסוּת אַחֶרֶת, הֲרֵי אֵלּוּ שֶׁלּוֹ, מִפְּנֵי שֶׁהַבְּעָלִים מִתְיָאֲשִׁין מֵהֶן. הַמַּצִּיל מִן הַנָּהָר, אוֹ מִן הַגַּיִס, אוֹ מִן הַלִּסְטִים, אִם נִתְיָאֲשׁוּ הַבְּעָלִים, הֲרֵי אֵלּוּ שֶׁלּוֹ.

— רע״ב —

(ב) הֲרֵי אֵלּוּ שֶׁלּוֹ. דְּמִסְתָּמָא נִתְיָאֲשׁוּ הַבְּעָלִים מִיָּד, וְקִנְּנָהוּ הֵיאַךְ בְּיֵאוּשׁ וְשִׁנּוּי רְשׁוּת: אִם נִתְיָאֲשׁוּ הַבְּעָלִים. דְּשַׁמְעִינְהוּ דְּאָמְרֵי וַוי לְחֶסְרוֹן כִּיס. אֲבָל סְתָמָא לֹא. וְרֵישָׁא דְּנָטְלוּ לִסְטִים אֶת כְּסוּתוֹ דְּמַשְׁמַע דְּמִסְתָּמָא מִתְיָאֲשׁוּ, מַיְירֵי בְּלִסְטִים יִשְׂרָאֵל, דְּכֵיוָן דְּדַיְינֵי יִשְׂרָאֵל אָמְרֵי הַבָּא עֵדִים הַבָּא רְאָיָה, מִכִּי נַטְלוּ לוֹ לִסְטִים מְיָאֵשׁ. וְסֵיפָא בְּלִסְטִים עַכּוּ״ם, שֶׁדַּיָּינֵי עַכּוּ״ם דָּנִין בְּגַאֲוָה וּבִזְרוֹעַ וּבְאֻמְדָּן דַּעַת, בְּלֹא עֵדִים וְלֹא רְאָיָה, וְהַנִּגְזָל מֵהֶם לֹא מְיָאֵשׁ. וּמִשּׁוּם הָכִי אִי שַׁמְעִינְהוּ דְּאַיְּאוּשׁ אִין, אֲבָל סְתָמָא לֹא:

---

confiscated [someone's] donkey and gave him a different donkey that they had confiscated from someone else,[1] גְּזָלוּ לִסְטִים אֶת כְּסוּתוֹ וְנָתְנוּ לוֹ כְּסוּת אַחֶרֶת — **or if bandits stole [someone's] clothing and gave him other clothing** that they had stolen from someone else, הֲרֵי אֵלּוּ שֶׁלּוֹ — **they are his to keep,** מִפְּנֵי שֶׁהַבְּעָלִים מִתְיָאֲשִׁין מֵהֶן — **because** it may be assumed that **the owners gave up hope of** getting **them** back.[2]

A similar situation:

הַמַּצִּיל מִן הַנָּהָר אוֹ מִן הַגַּיִס אוֹ מִן הַלִּסְטִים — In a case where **one rescues** another's belongings **from** a flooding **river, from an army, or from bandits,** אִם נִתְיָאֲשׁוּ הַבְּעָלִים הֲרֵי אֵלּוּ שֶׁלּוֹ — **if** it is known that **the owner gave up hope** of getting them back before the rescuer took them, **they are [the rescuer's] to keep.**[3]

NOTES

[2]
1. After seizing his donkey, the customs-collectors took pity on him and gave him one worth less money than his, which was clearly the property of another of their victims (*Meiri*).
2. Stolen property is legally acquired by a third party when two conditions are met: (a) The original owner gives up hope of getting the item back (יֵאוּשׁ). (b) After he gives up hope, the object goes from the hands of the thief to the hands of a third person (שִׁנּוּי רְשׁוּת). Both of these conditions were met in our case, because it may be assumed that a person whose property was taken by a tax collector or bandit despairs of recovering it, and it was then transferred from the tax collector or bandit to a third person. Therefore, the third person may keep it (*Rav, Tos. Yom Tov*).
3. He may keep them in the case of an army or bandits for the reason stated in the previous note. In the case of a flooding river, where the object is lost (not stolen), he may keep it simply because the owner gave up hope of getting it back (see *Bava Metzia* 22b). [Unlike stolen goods, *lost* items belong to the finder provided that he found them after the owner gave up hope, even though they never entered the hands of a third person (see *Bava Metzia* 2:1).]

Here, the Mishnah refers to situations where the owner had a fair chance of retrieving his items. Thus, it says that the rescuer may keep them "if" he knows that the owner has despaired of getting them back (for example, the owner was heard to say "Woe for the loss that I suffered"). The first part of the Mishnah, however, deals with situations where the owner had very little chance of recovering the stolen items. It therefore said that the one who received them may keep them "because" it may be assumed that owner has given up hope (see *Rav*).

וְכֵן נְחִיל שֶׁל דְּבוֹרִים, אִם נִתְיָאֲשׁוּ הַבְּעָלִים, הֲרֵי אֵלּוּ שֶׁלּוֹ. אָמַר רַבִּי יוֹחָנָן בֶּן בְּרוֹקָה, נֶאֱמֶנֶת אִשָּׁה אוֹ קָטָן לוֹמַר, מִכָּאן יָצָא נְחִיל זֶה. וּמְהַלֵּךְ בְּתוֹךְ שָׂדֶה חֲבֵרוֹ לְהַצִּיל אֶת נְחִילוֹ. וְאִם הִזִּיק מְשַׁלֵּם מַה שֶּׁהִזִּיק. אֲבָל לֹא יָקֹץ אֶת שׂוֹכוֹ עַל מְנָת לִתֵּן אֶת הַדָּמִים.

A third case: וְכֵן נְחִיל שֶׁל דְּבוֹרִים — **Similarly, should someone find a swarm of bees** that had flown from another person's beehive and settled in this person's property,[4] אִם נִתְיָאֲשׁוּ הַבְּעָלִים הֲרֵי אֵלּוּ שֶׁלּוֹ — **if it is known that the owner** of the bees **gave up hope** of getting them back before they settled in his property, **they are his** to keep.[5]

The Mishnah teaches another law regarding the ownership of bees: אָמַר רַבִּי יוֹחָנָן בֶּן בְּרוֹקָה — **R' Yochanan ben Berokah said:** נֶאֱמֶנֶת אִשָּׁה אוֹ קָטָן לוֹמַר מִכָּאן יָצָא נְחִיל זֶה — **If** we do not know to whom a swarm of bees belongs, **a woman or a minor is believed to say, "This swarm** of bees **came out from here,"** and thereby identify its owner. Although the testimony of a woman or minor is usually invalid, it is accepted in this case.[6]

If someone's bees fly to another's field, he may do the following to bring them back:

וּמְהַלֵּךְ בְּתוֹךְ שָׂדֶה חֲבֵרוֹ לְהַצִּיל אֶת נְחִילוֹ — **And one may walk into another's field to save** (i.e., retrieve) **his swarm** of bees that had settled there; וְאִם הִזִּיק מְשַׁלֵּם מַה שֶּׁהִזִּיק — **but if he** thereby **damaged** the field (for example, he stepped on crops that were growing there), **he must pay for what he damaged.**[7] אֲבָל לֹא יָקֹץ אֶת שׂוֹכוֹ — **However,** if the bees came to rest on a branch of a tree in the field, **he may not cut off the branch of [the other's]** tree to take back the entire swarm at once,[8] עַל מְנָת לִתֵּן אֶת הַדָּמִים — **even with**

NOTES

4. *Tiferes Yisrael.*

5. The Mishnah implies that if the owner had *not* given up hope, the bees are still his, and the finder must return them. According to Biblical law, bees are always considered ownerless (because they tend to fly away), but the Rabbis enacted that a person is deemed to own bees that nest in his property. Thus, it is Rabbinic law that prohibits the finder to keep them unless the owner had given up hope (*Tos. Yom Tov*).

6. Since the ownership of bees is only a Rabbinic enactment (see previous note), the Sages had the authority to accept testimony that would normally be invalid.

Even so, they allowed such testimony only in particular circumstances (see *Tos. Yom Tov*).

7. The owner of the bees is allowed to enter the other's field even if he knows for certain that he will cause damage, because he does so only to recover his bees, and he plans to pay for the damage (*Meiri*).

8. The bees' owner does not want to take the bees one by one because he fears that the others will fly away in the meantime. He prefers instead to cut the entire branch off the tree and thereby retrieve all the bees at once (*Rav*).

רַבִּי יִשְׁמָעֵאל בְּנוֹ שֶׁל רַבִּי יוֹחָנָן בֶּן בְּרוֹקָה אוֹמֵר, אַף קוֹצֵץ וְנוֹתֵן אֶת הַדָּמִים.

[ג] הַמַּכִּיר כֵּלָיו וּסְפָרָיו בְּיַד אַחֵר, וְיָצָא לוֹ שֵׁם גְּנֵבָה בָּעִיר, יִשָּׁבַע לוֹ הַלּוֹקֵחַ כַּמָּה נָתַן, וְיִטּוֹל. וְאִם לָאו, לֹא כָּל הֵימֶנּוּ,

— רע"ב —

רבי ישמעאל כו'. ואין הלכה כרבי ישמעאל: (ג) המכיר כליו וספריו וכו'. מתניתין באדם שאינו עשוי למכור כליו, דכיון דיצא לו שם גניבה בעיר, ואיכא סהדי שאלו הכלים והספרים שלו היו, לא חיישינן דלמא זבנינהו: ישבע לוקח כמה נתן ויטול. ויחזיר לו כליו. ולפני יאוש קמיירי:

---

the intention of paying for the branch, because the branch of a tree cannot be replaced (unlike the crops).[9]

A dissenting opinion:

רַבִּי יִשְׁמָעֵאל בְּנוֹ שֶׁל רַבִּי יוֹחָנָן בֶּן בְּרוֹקָה אוֹמֵר — R' Yishmael the son of R' Yochanan ben Berokah says: אַף קוֹצֵץ וְנוֹתֵן אֶת הַדָּמִים — He may even cut the branch off to recover the bees and then pay for the branch.[10]

[3] The Mishnah deals with a case where someone is accused of having bought stolen property:

הַמַּכִּיר כֵּלָיו וּסְפָרָיו בְּיַד אַחֵר — If someone recognizes his utensils or books in the possession of another person, וְיָצָא לוֹ שֵׁם גְּנֵבָה בָּעִיר — and a report of theft had spread in the town about him (i.e., it was widely rumored that he had been the victim of a theft), but the one who has the items in his possession says that he bought them from someone else, יִשָּׁבַע לוֹ הַלּוֹקֵחַ כַּמָּה נָתַן וְיִטּוֹל — the buyer must return them to the claimant and swear to him how much he paid, and he takes that amount from the claimant.[1] וְאִם לָאו — But if there was no report of theft, לֹא כָּל הֵימֶנּוּ — [the claimant] is not believed[2]

NOTES

9. *Meiri*.

10. When Joshua divided up Eretz Yisrael, he obligated the new owners to observe certain laws (Gemara 114b). According to R' Yishmael the son of R' Yochanan ben Berokah, these laws included that the owner of bees may cut off the branch of another person's tree in order to retrieve his bees, provided that he pays for the damage (*Tos. Yom Tov*).

[3]

1. The Mishnah's ruling applies only where it is known that these items once belonged to the claimant. In addition, it is known that he does not usually sell his things. Furthermore, he says that he had not yet given up hope of getting them back (see the previous Mishnah). Only where all these conditions are met *and* a widespread rumor supports his claim that they were stolen may he take the items back (*Rav*).

He must nevertheless pay the buyer for the items (even though they are his), because of a Rabbinic law known as תַּקָּנַת הַשּׁוּק, literally, *the enactment of the marketplace*. People might be reluctant to buy goods for fear that if they are found to be stolen, they will have to return them to the real owner and lose their money. Therefore, to encourage the buying and selling of goods in the marketplace, the Rabbis decreed that if anything is found to be stolen and must be returned, the owner must pay the buyer (see *Tos. Yom Tov*). [Should the owner want to recover the money he paid the buyer, he would have to take up his case with the thief (see Gemara 115a).]

2. Literally, *it is not all from him* (see *Rav* to *Gittin* 8:8).

[151] **MISHNAH BAVA KAMMA** / Chapter 10: *Hagozeil*   10/4

— רע"ב —

(ד) אין לו אלא שכרו.
שכר כלי ושכר פעולה:

שֶׁאֲנִי אוֹמֵר מְכָרָן לְאַחֵר וּלְקָחָן זֶה הֵימֶנּוּ.

[ד] זֶה בָּא בְּחָבִיתוֹ שֶׁל יַיִן, וְזֶה בָּא בְּכַדּוֹ שֶׁל דְּבַשׁ, נִסְדְּקָה חָבִית שֶׁל דְּבַשׁ, וְשָׁפַךְ זֶה אֶת יֵינוֹ וְהִצִּיל אֶת הַדְּבַשׁ לְתוֹכוֹ, אֵין לוֹ אֶלָּא שְׂכָרוֹ. וְאִם אָמַר,

---

to say that the objects were stolen, and the buyer does not have to give them to him,[3] שֶׁאֲנִי אוֹמֵר מְכָרָן לְאַחֵר וּלְקָחָן זֶה הֵימֶנּוּ — **for I say,** i.e., it is possible to argue, that they were not stolen from him; rather, **he sold them to another, and this** person [the one who has them in his possession] **bought them from him** [the one to whom they were sold].[4]

[4] The Mishnah discusses the law where one person suffered a loss as he was saving the property of another:

זֶה בָּא בְּחָבִיתוֹ שֶׁל יַיִן וְזֶה בָּא בְּכַדּוֹ שֶׁל דְּבַשׁ — Two people were walking, **this one** carrying[1] **his barrel of wine, and this one carrying his jug of honey,** נִסְדְּקָה חָבִית שֶׁל דְּבַשׁ — **and the barrel**[2] **of honey cracked** and the honey began to leak out. וְשָׁפַךְ זֶה אֶת יֵינוֹ וְהִצִּיל אֶת הַדְּבַשׁ לְתוֹכוֹ — **The one** who was carrying wine **poured out his wine** from its barrel, **and saved the honey in it** (i.e., he poured the honey into the empty wine barrel).[3] He now demands that the owner of the honey pay him for the wine that he lost. אֵין לוֹ אֶלָּא שְׂכָרוֹ — The law is that [the owner of the wine] **receives only his fee,** i.e., the fee for his labor and for the use of his barrel,[4] but he is not paid for his lost wine.[5] וְאִם אָמַר — **But if,** before he poured out the wine, **he said** to the

---

NOTES

3. *Tiferes Yisrael.*

4. If there is no widespread rumor that the claimant was robbed, it is possible that he was in need of money and sold these items [even though he does not usually do so; see note 1], and now that he has money, he regrets the sale and invented the story of theft in order to retrieve his property (*Meiri*). The buyer, therefore, is under no obligation to return the goods.

[4]

1. Literally, *was coming with*.

2. [The Tanna uses the words barrel (חָבִית) and jug (כַּד) interchangeably; see Mishnah 3:1 note 1.]

3. He did this because the other person's honey was worth more than his wine (*Tiferes Yisrael*), but the same ruling would apply where they were worth the same (see note 7).

4. Saving the honey is a fulfillment of the mitzvah to return a lost object (הֲשָׁבַת אֲבֵדָה). Although one may not usually accept payment for this mitzvah, this case is different, because saving the honey requires him to lose his wine, and there is no obligation to save the property of another at the expense of one's own. Thus, by pouring out his wine for the sake of saving the honey, this person went beyond the requirements of the mitzvah, and, as such, he is entitled to payment [for his labor and the use of his barrel] (*Tos. Yom Tov*).

5. Since he did not make an agreement with the owner of the honey to be paid for his wine, he is not entitled to compensation (*Tos. Yom Tov,* citing *Rosh* to *Bava Metzia* 31b).

The Mishnah refers to a case in which the barrel of honey was wrapped with something that prevented the honey from flowing out all at once, allowing it to drip

משניות בבא קמא / פרק י: הגזול

אַצִיל אֶת שֶׁלְּךָ, וְאַתָּה נוֹתֵן לִי דְּמֵי שֶׁלִּי, חַיָּב לִתֶּן לוֹ. שָׁטַף נָהָר חֲמוֹרוֹ וַחֲמוֹר חֲבֵרוֹ, שֶׁלּוֹ יָפֶה מָנֶה, וְשֶׁל חֲבֵרוֹ מָאתַיִם, הִנִּיחַ זֶה אֶת שֶׁלּוֹ וְהִצִּיל אֶת שֶׁל חֲבֵרוֹ, אֵין לוֹ אֶלָּא שְׂכָרוֹ. וְאִם אָמַר לוֹ, אֲנִי אַצִּיל אֶת שֶׁלְּךָ, וְאַתָּה נוֹתֵן לִי אֶת שֶׁלִּי, חַיָּב לִתֶּן לוֹ.

— רע״ב —

שטף נהר חמורו. צריכא למיתני תרי בבי דמתניתין. דאי תנא רישא, הוה אמינא, התם הוא דכי פריש יהיב ליה דמי כולה, משום דבידים קא פסיד, ששפך את יינו בידים בשבילו, אבל סיפא דממילא, אימא אין לו אלא שכרו. ואי אשמועינן סיפא, הכא הוא דבסתמא אין לו אלא שכרו משום דממילא, אבל התם דבידים, אימא אפילו בסתמא יהיב ליה דמי כולה. צריכא.

---

owner of the honey, אַצִיל אֶת שֶׁלְּךָ וְאַתָּה נוֹתֵן לִי דְּמֵי שֶׁלִּי — "I will save your [honey], but you must **give me the value of my [wine]**," and the owner of the honey agreed,[6] חַיָּב לִתֶּן לוֹ — [the owner of the honey] **is obligated to give him** the value of the wine.

A similar case:

שָׁטַף נָהָר חֲמוֹרוֹ וַחֲמוֹר חֲבֵרוֹ — **A river overflowed and swept away [some-**one's] **donkey and the donkey of another** person. שֶׁלּוֹ יָפֶה מָנֶה וְשֶׁל חֲבֵרוֹ מָאתַיִם — **His** donkey **was worth a** *maneh* (100 *zuz*) **and the other's was worth 200** *zuz*,[7] הִנִּיחַ זֶה אֶת שֶׁלּוֹ וְהִצִּיל אֶת שֶׁל חֲבֵרוֹ — **so he left his [donkey]** to drown, **and saved the other person's [donkey].** He then demands that the owner of the more expensive donkey pay him the value of his lost donkey. אֵין לוֹ אֶלָּא שְׂכָרוֹ — The law is that **he receives only his fee,** i.e., the amount it would have cost to hire a person to rescue the donkey from the river, but he is not paid for the loss of his donkey. וְאִם אָמַר לוֹ — **But if,** before he abandoned his donkey, **he said to [the owner of the other donkey],** אֲנִי אַצִּיל אֶת שֶׁלְּךָ וְאַתָּה נוֹתֵן לִי אֶת שֶׁלִּי — "**I will save your [donkey], but you must give me the value of my [donkey],"** and the other agreed, חַיָּב לִתֶּן לוֹ — [the owner of the saved donkey] **is obligated to give him** the value of his lost donkey.

[5] The Mishnah deals with a case where someone stole land and it was then taken from *him*. His obligation to return the stolen land is discussed:

NOTES

only a little at a time. Since the honey drips out slowly, there is a possibility it can be saved; therefore, it is not considered ownerless (*hefker*). But if the barrel is not wrapped and it cracked in a way that allows all the honey to flow out immediately, the owner loses his ownership of it (since he is unable to save it from going to waste), and it would belong to the owner of the wine when he saves it (*Tos. Yom Tov*).

6. *Tos. Yom Tov.*

If the owner of the honey is not present, the rescuer can make this condition in front of a court (*Tos. Yom Tov* ד״ה ואם).

7. The law would be the same where both donkeys were of equal value. The Mishnah mentions that they were worth different amounts only because a person is unlikely to sacrifice his own property in order to save the property of another unless the property being saved is worth more (*Tos. Yom Tov*).

— רע״ב —

[ה] **הַגּוֹזֵל** שָׂדֶה מֵחֲבֵרוֹ, וּנְטָלוּהָ מַסִּיקִין, אִם מַכַּת מְדִינָה הִיא, אוֹמֵר לוֹ, הֲרֵי שֶׁלְּךָ לְפָנֶיךָ, וְאִם מֵחֲמַת הַגַּזְלָן, חַיָּב לְהַעֲמִיד לוֹ שָׂדֶה אַחֵר. שְׁטָפָהּ נָהָר, אוֹמֵר לוֹ, הֲרֵי שֶׁלְּךָ לְפָנֶיךָ.

(ה) נטלוה מסיקין. אנסים גזלוה מן הגזלן. תרגום גנב, סקאה (דברים כח, מב), שהארבה גזלן הוא, שאוכל בשדות אחרים: אם מכת מדינה היא. שאנסו קרקע של אחרים עם זו:

הַגּוֹזֵל שָׂדֶה מֵחֲבֵרוֹ — **If someone steals a field from another,**[1] וּנְטָלוּהָ מַסִּיקִין — **and then marauders take it from him** [the thief], the law is as follows: אִם מַכַּת מְדִינָה הִיא — **If it is a state-wide "plague,"** that is, they were also taking the fields of others, אוֹמֵר לוֹ הֲרֵי שֶׁלְּךָ לְפָנֶיךָ — **[the thief] can say to [the owner]: "Behold, what is yours is before you,"** and he does not have to pay for the loss of the field. The owner cannot blame the thief for losing the stolen field to the marauders, since they would have taken it regardless of who had it.[2] וְאִם מֵחֲמַת הַגַּזְלָן — **But if** the field was taken by the marauders **because of the thief,** that is, they took it only because it was in the thief's possession, חַיָּב לְהַעֲמִיד לוֹ שָׂדֶה אַחֵר — **[the thief] is obligated to provide [the owner] with another field** of the same value, or pay him the field's value.[3]

A similar situation:

שְׁטָפָהּ נָהָר — If someone steals a field from another, and **a river flooded it** and ruined it, אוֹמֵר לוֹ הֲרֵי שֶׁלְּךָ לְפָנֶיךָ — **[the thief] can say to [the owner of the field]: "Behold, what is yours is before you,"** and he does not have to pay for the field, since he had nothing to do with its destruction.

―――――― NOTES ――――――

[5]

1. That is, he moved the boundary marker between his field and the other's field so that his field now included part of the other's (*Tosefos Rid*), or he forced the owner out of the field and occupied it himself.

2. *Meiri.*

We have learned that once a thief performs a *kinyan* with the property he stole, he becomes responsible for it (see Mishnah 7:5). Should it suffer any loss or damage, even due to an accident he could not have prevented, he must pay the owner what it was worth when it was stolen. This law, however, is limited to movable objects. Land, by contrast, can never be said to be in the possession of a thief; rather, it remains in the possession of the one from whom it was taken (קַרְקַע אֵינָה נִגְזֶלֶת, *land cannot be stolen*). Thus, if the land is damaged or stolen after the thief took it, the owner has to bear the loss, and the thief is not obligated to compensate him. In the Mishnah's case, then, where marauders seized the land from the thief, he does not have to pay the owner (*Meiri*). [If the owner wants his land back, he must take his case up with the marauders.]

As stated, this law applies only to land. If someone stole *movable* property, he indeed becomes responsible for anything that happens to it (*Meiri*). He must pay the owner even for loss, damage, or theft that he could not have prevented (see Mishnah 9:2).

3. *Aruch HaShulchan, Choshen Mishpat* 371:3.

Although "land cannot be stolen," and thus the thief is not responsible for what happens to it (see the previous note), the Rabbis punished him and obligated him to pay for the field, since the marauders would not have seized it had he not taken it in the first place (*Tiferes Yisrael; Rashba,* citing *Yerushalmi*).

משניות בבא קמא / פרק י׃ הגוזל [154]

[ו] **הַגּוֹזֵל** אֶת חֲבֵרוֹ, אוֹ שֶׁלָּוָה הֵימֶנּוּ, אוֹ שֶׁהִפְקִיד לוֹ, בַּיִּשּׁוּב, לֹא יַחֲזִיר לוֹ בַּמִּדְבָּר. עַל מְנָת לָצֵאת בַּמִּדְבָּר, יַחֲזִיר לוֹ בַּמִּדְבָּר.

[ז] **הָאוֹמֵר** לַחֲבֵרוֹ, גְּזַלְתִּיךָ, הִלְוִיתַנִי, הִפְקַדְתָּ אֶצְלִי, וְאֵינִי יוֹדֵעַ אִם הֶחֱזַרְתִּי לְךָ אִם לֹא הֶחֱזַרְתִּי לְךָ, חַיָּב לְשַׁלֵּם.

— רע״ב —

(ו) על מנת לצאת במדבר. לא שיאמר לו בפירוש, על מנת שתהא במדבר ותפרעני, דהא מלתא דפשיטא היא. אלא כגון שאמר לו חבירו, הוי האי פקדון גבך, דלמחר למדבר נפיקנא, ואמר ליה אידך, ואנא נמי למדבר בעינא למיפק, והשתא אי בעי לאהדוריה במדבר, מהדר להו: (ז) האומר

לחבירו גזלתיך וכו׳. וכגון שתבירו טוענו בריא גזלתני, והוא אומר אמת גזלתיך, אבל איני יודע אם החזרתי לך, חייב לשלם. אבל אם חבירו טוענו שמא גזלתני או הלויתיך, והוא אומר אמת גזלתיך או הלויתני, ואיני יודע אם החזרתי לך, פטור מדיני אדם. ואם בא לצאת ידי שמים, ישלם לו:

[6] הַגּוֹזֵל אֶת חֲבֵרוֹ אוֹ שֶׁלָּוָה הֵימֶנּוּ אוֹ שֶׁהִפְקִיד לוֹ — **If someone steals** something **from another, or borrows** money **from him, or had an item deposited with him** for safekeeping, and he wishes to return it, the law is as follows: בַּיִּשּׁוּב — **If** he stole, borrowed, or received it for safekeeping **in an inhabited area,** לֹא יַחֲזִיר לוֹ בַּמִּדְבָּר — **he may not return it to** [the owner] **in a wilderness,** where people do not live, since it will be unsafe there.[1] עַל מְנָת לָצֵאת בַּמִּדְבָּר — However, if he (specifically, the borrower or watchman) accepted it **on condition that he may go out to the wilderness** to return it, יַחֲזִיר לוֹ בַּמִּדְבָּר — **he may return it to** [the owner] **in the wilderness.**[2]

[7] הָאוֹמֵר לַחֲבֵרוֹ — **If one** person **says to another,** גְּזַלְתִּיךָ הִלְוִיתַנִי הִפְקַדְתָּ אֶצְלִי — **"I stole** something **from you,"** or **"You lent me** money," or **"You deposited** an item **with me** for safekeeping," וְאֵינִי יוֹדֵעַ אִם הֶחֱזַרְתִּי לְךָ אִם לֹא הֶחֱזַרְתִּי לְךָ — and he continues, **"but I do not know whether I returned it to you or I did not return it to you,"** חַיָּב לְשַׁלֵּם — **he is obligated to pay,**

— NOTES —

[6]
1. If the owner does not want to take back his item or money in an uninhabited area (because it is difficult to protect things there) the robber, borrower, or watchman cannot require him to accept it there (*Tos. Yom Tov*). The owner can say, "Since the item came into your possession in a populated area, you are responsible for it until you return it to me in a populated area" (*Rambam, Hilchos She'eilah U'Fikadon* 7:11).

If he *did* return the item in an uninhabited area (against the owner's will), he remains responsible for it, and if harm befalls it, he is obligated to pay (*Meiri*).
2. That is, the borrower or watchman told the owner that he is taking the object only if he can return it in an uninhabited area, and the owner accepted this condition. The borrower or watchman can then fulfill his duty by returning it in such a place.

The Gemara (118a) argues that this ruling is obvious. It therefore explains the Mishnah as referring to a case where the owner gave him the money or item and told him that he was leaving for the wilderness, and the borrower or watchman replied that he too was going to the wilderness. Even though he did not explicitly say that he might return it there, he implies as much. Therefore, since the owner did not object, he may return it even in the wilderness (*Rav*).

[155] **MISHNAH BAVA KAMMA** / Chapter 10: *Hagozeil* 10/8

— רע״ב —

אֲבָל אִם אָמַר לוֹ, אֵינִי יוֹדֵעַ אִם גְּזַלְתִּיךָ, אִם הִלְוִיתַנִי, אִם הִפְקַדְתָּ אֶצְלִי, פָּטוּר מִלְּשַׁלֵּם.

[ח] **הַגּוֹנֵב** טָלֶה מִן הָעֵדֶר וְהֶחֱזִירוֹ, וּמֵת אוֹ נִגְנַב, חַיָּב בְּאַחֲרָיוּתוֹ. לֹא יָדְעוּ הַבְּעָלִים לֹא בִּגְנֵבָתוֹ וְלֹא בַּחֲזִירָתוֹ,

איני יודע אם גזלתיך וכו׳ פטור מלשלם. ומיהו ישבע שאינו יודע שחייב לו, דלא עדיף שמא מברי. דהא אי נמי הוה טעין ליה אין לך בידי כלום, הוה משבעינן ליה שבועת היסת: (ח) חייב באחריותו. דמכי גנבה

קם ליה ברשותיה, והשבה דעבד לאו השבה היא: ואם לא ידעו בו וכו׳. מתניתין הכי מתרצא. חייב באחריותו בין מנו בין לא מנו, אימתי, בזמן שלא ידעו בו הבעלים בגניבתו ובחזרתו. אבל ידעו הבעלים בגנבתו, ומנו את הצאן והיא שלימה, פטור מלשלם. והכי פירושה, מת או נגנב הטלה לאחר שהחזירו הגנב

---

because he certainly took the item or money, whereas it is only possible that he returned it.[1] **אֲבָל אִם אָמַר לוֹ** — **But if he said to him,** **אֵינִי יוֹדֵעַ אִם גְּזַלְתִּיךָ אִם הִלְוִיתַנִי אִם הִפְקַדְתָּ אֶצְלִי** — **"I do not know whether I stole from you,"** or **"I do not know whether you lent me** money," or **"I do not know whether you deposited** an item **with me** for safekeeping," **פָּטוּר מִלְּשַׁלֵּם** — he **is not obligated to pay,** since in this case he might not have taken the item or money in the first place.[2]

[8] A thief is responsible for the item he stole until he returns it. Thus, if it is damaged (for example) before he returns it, he must pay the owner, but if it is damaged afterward, the owner suffers the loss. The Mishnah defines when a thief is considered to have "returned" an animal that he stole from a flock: **הַגּוֹנֵב טָלֶה מִן הָעֵדֶר וְהֶחֱזִירוֹ** — **If someone steals a lamb from a flock** of sheep, **וּמֵת אוֹ נִגְנַב** — **and he** then **returns it** to the flock, without telling the owner, **and** later **it died or was stolen,** **חַיָּב בְּאַחֲרָיוּתוֹ** — **[the thief] is responsible for it.** **לֹא יָדְעוּ הַבְּעָלִים לֹא בִּגְנֵבָתוֹ וְלֹא בַּחֲזִירָתוֹ** — This ruling applies where **the owner**

--- NOTES ---

[7]

1. *Rif, Tiferes Yisrael.*
The Mishnah's ruling applies where the claimant (victim of the theft, lender, owner of safeguarded item) is *sure* that he is owed the money or the item. Only then must the defendant pay. If the claimant himself is not sure (or he makes no claim at all), the defendant is exempt. Nevertheless, he should pay in order to fulfill a moral obligation [לָצֵאת יְדֵי שָׁמַיִם] (*Rav, Tos. Yom Tov*).

2. *Tiferes Yisrael.*
In this case, even if the claimant is sure that the defendant took the money, whereas the defendant is unsure, the defendant is exempt [though here, too, he has a moral duty to pay (*Tos. Yom Tov*)]. This is an application of the rule: הַמּוֹצִיא

מֵחֲבֵרוֹ עָלָיו הָרְאָיָה, *The burden of proof is on the one who wants to collect property from his fellow* (see Mishnah 3:11). Since the claimant must prove his case but cannot, he has no right to collect payment.

[Although the defendant is under no obligation to pay, the claimant can force him to take an oath in court (known as שְׁבוּעַת הֶסֵּת) that he in fact does not know whether he owes the money (*Rav*).]

This case is different from the previous one, where both agree that the defendant took the item or money, and the only doubt is whether he returned it. Since the defendant was definitely obligated at some point, and it is not known whether he ever fulfilled that obligation, he must pay even though the claimant has no proof (see *Rif*).

משניות בבא קמא / פרק י: הגזול

וּמָנוּ אֶת הַצֹּאן, וּשְׁלֵמָה הִיא, פָּטוּר.

[ט] **אֵין** לוֹקְחִין מִן הָרוֹעִים צֶמֶר, וְחָלָב, וּגְדָיִים, וְלֹא מִשּׁוֹמְרֵי פֵרוֹת עֵצִים וּפֵרוֹת;

— רע"ב —

חייב באחריותו, בין שמנו הבעלים הצאן והיא שלימה, בין שלא מנו הצאן. אימתי, בזמן שלא ידעו הבעלים בגניבת הטלה. שכל זמן שהיה רגילה לצאת חוץ, צריך ליזהר בה ביותר, וזו הואיל ולא ידעו הבעלים בגניבתה, ושמירתה למודה לצאת, ולא נזהרו בה, חייב הגנב לשלם, שבגרמתו נאבדה הטלה. אבל אם ידעו הבעלים בגניבת הטלה, ואחר כך מנו הצאן ונמצאת שלימה, שהוחזר הטלה הגנוב, אם כן כבר ידעו שיש לטלה אחת שלמודה לצאת חוץ, והיה להם להזהר בה, ואם לא נזהרו אינהו דאפסוד, ופטור הגנב מלשלם: (ט) אין לוקחין מן הרועים. דאיכא למימר, שמא גנבו מלאנו של בעל הבית המסור להם:

---

was not aware of its theft or its return. Since the owner did not know that the animal was stolen, it is not enough for the thief to simply put it back in the flock. Rather, he remains responsible for the sheep until he tells the owner that it was stolen and has been returned.[1] וּמָנוּ אֶת הַצֹּאן וּשְׁלֵמָה הִיא — However, if the owner was aware of the theft, **and after the thief returns it, [the owner] counts the sheep and** finds that **[the flock] is complete,** פָּטוּר — **[the thief] is not obligated** for any harm that befalls it later. In this case, where the owner *knew* that it had been stolen, the thief only has to put the animal back in the flock and does not need to tell the owner anything. As soon as the owner becomes aware of its return (by counting his flock and finding that it contains the same number as before the theft), the thief ceases to be responsible.

[9] The Mishnah lists items that one is forbidden to buy from others because they might be stolen:

אֵין לוֹקְחִים מִן הָרוֹעִים צֶמֶר וְחָלָב וּגְדָיִים — **We may not buy wool, milk, or kids** (young goats or sheep) **from shepherds** who are hired to care for other people's flocks, because shepherds are suspected of stealing these items from the flocks of their employers; וְלֹא מִשּׁוֹמְרֵי פֵרוֹת עֵצִים וּפֵרוֹת — **nor may** we buy **wood or fruit from watchmen** who are hired to guard fruit orchards, because they are suspected of stealing these things from the orchard.[1]

NOTES
---

[8]

1. A stolen animal requires extra protection after it is returned, because, having once been separated from the flock, it is more likely than the others to wander off on its own. The thief therefore remains responsible for the animal until he tells the owner that it was stolen and returned, so that the owner can guard it properly. Thus, if the thief did not tell the owner anything, even if the owner counts the sheep and finds that none are missing, the thief must pay for any subsequent damage to the lamb, since the owner was not aware of the theft and did not know that it required extra supervision (*Rav*).

This ruling obviously applies only where an *animal* was stolen. If an inanimate object was stolen and returned without the owner's knowledge (for example, a thief stole money and slipped it back into the owner's wallet), the thief has fulfilled his obligation to return the object and is not responsible for any future mishap (*Rambam, Hilchos Geneivah* 4:11).

[9]

1. It is great sin to buy stolen goods from a thief, because one thereby encourages him to steal more things. If no one would buy from him, he would stop stealing (*Rambam, Hilchos Geneivah* 5:1).

[157] MISHNAH BAVA KAMMA / Chapter 10: Hagozeil

— רע״ב —

אֲבָל לוֹקְחִין מִן הַנָּשִׁים כְּלֵי צֶמֶר בִּיהוּדָה, וּכְלֵי פִשְׁתָּן בַּגָּלִיל, וַעֲגָלִים בַּשָּׁרוֹן. וְכֻלָּן שֶׁאָמְרוּ לְהַטְמִין, אָסוּר. וְלוֹקְחִין בֵּיצִים וְתַרְנְגוֹלִים מִכָּל מָקוֹם.

[י] מוֹכִין שֶׁהַכּוֹבֵס מוֹצִיא הֲרֵי אֵלּוּ שֶׁלּוֹ, וְשֶׁהַסּוֹרֵק מוֹצִיא הֲרֵי אֵלּוּ שֶׁל

צֶמֶר ביהודה ופשתן בגליל. מלאכת הנשים היא. והן עלמן עושות ומוכרות, ולדעת בעליהן הוא: ועגלים הרועים בשרון. שם מקום שמגדלין בו עגלים. וטלהן הן: (י) מוכין שהכובס מוציא. מלבן הלמר מוליא מן הלמר דבר מועט על ידי שטיפה: הרי אלו שלו. שאין הבעל [בית] מקפיד, ואם הקפיד לא הוי קפידא: ושהסורק מוציא. הסורק את הלמר והמנפנו, מה שמוליא, הוי דבר חשוב, ורגילים להקפיד:

אֲבָל לוֹקְחִין מִן הַנָּשִׁים כְּלֵי צֶמֶר בִּיהוּדָה וּכְלֵי פִשְׁתָּן בַּגָּלִיל וַעֲגָלִים בַּשָּׁרוֹן — **But we may buy** the following articles even **from** married **women: woolen garments in Judea, linen garments in the Galilee, and calves in the Sharon.** It was common for the women of Judea to make and sell woolen garments, for the women of the Galilee to make and sell linen garments, and for women of the Sharon to raise and sell calves.[2] Since this was the standard practice in those places, it may be assumed that the women have the permission of their husbands, so there is no question of theft. וְכֻלָּן שֶׁאָמְרוּ לְהַטְמִין אָסוּר — **But if any of [these women] told** the buyer **to hide** what he bought, and not reveal it to others, **it is prohibited** to buy even these items from them, because it is clear that they stole their merchandise and are afraid of being caught. וְלוֹקְחִין בֵּיצִים וְתַרְנְגוֹלִים מִכָּל מָקוֹם — **And we may buy eggs and chickens anywhere,** from any person,[3] because they are common and inexpensive, and thus unlikely to have been stolen.[4]

[10] Often, after a worker or craftsman has finished his work, some pieces of material are left over. The Mishnah deals with the question of which pieces may be kept by the craftsman and which must be returned to the owner: מוֹכִין שֶׁהַכּוֹבֵס מוֹצִיא הֲרֵי אֵלּוּ שֶׁלּוֹ — **The shreds of wool that a launderer removes** when he rinses wool[1] **belong to him,** because very little wool is removed in this process and the owner does not care for it to be returned.[2] וְשֶׁהַסּוֹרֵק מוֹצִיא הֲרֵי אֵלּוּ שֶׁל בַּעַל הַבַּיִת — **But the shreds that a comber**

NOTES

2. Calves were very cheap in the Sharon (the coastal area of Eretz Yisrael between Jaffa and Mount Carmel). The women living there would buy their own calves to raise and sell (*Rav, Rashi*).

3. *Tos. Yom Tov.*

4. A person would not risk getting caught stealing these items for the small profit they would bring (see *Meiri*).

Even in this case, though, if the seller told the buyer to hide his purchase, buying them is forbidden (*Tos. Yom Tov*).

[10]

1. When a launderer rinses wool, a small amount comes off (*Rav*).

2. Even if a certain owner *does* want the shreds of wool to be returned to him, the launderer may keep them. Since the vast majority of owners do not care about these leftover shreds, the attitude of this owner is not taken seriously [בָּטְלָה דַעְתּוֹ אֵצֶל כָּל אָדָם] (see *Rav*).

[158] **משניות בבא קמא / פרק י: הגזול**

בַּעַל הַבַּיִת. הַכּוֹבֵס נוֹטֵל שְׁלֹשָׁה חוּטִין, וְהֵן שֶׁלּוֹ. יָתֵר מִכֵּן, הֲרֵי אֵלּוּ שֶׁל בַּעַל הַבַּיִת. אִם הָיָה הַשָּׁחוֹר עַל גַּבֵּי הַלָּבָן, נוֹטֵל אֶת הַכֹּל וְהֵן שֶׁלּוֹ. הַחַיָּט שֶׁשִּׁיֵּר מִן הַחוּט כְּדֵי לִתְפֹּר בּוֹ, וּמַטְלִית שֶׁהִיא שָׁלֹשׁ עַל שָׁלֹשׁ,

— רע"ב —

הכובס נוטל שלשה חוטים. דרך בגדי צמר להניח בסוף אריגתן שלשה חוטי ממין אחר, והכובס נוטלן, ומשוה הבגד ומיפהו. ואם חוטין שחורין הם ארוגים בבגד לבן, רשאי הכובס ליטול

הכל, לפי שהשחור בלבן מגנה אותו ביותר: **החייט ששייר מן החוט כדי לתפור בו**. שהוא כמלא אורך המחט: **ומטלית שהיא שלש על שלש**. גרסינן. חייט שהשוה את תפירתו, וקילע ממנה מטלית קטנה שלש אצבעות על שלש אצבעות, חייב להחזיר לבעל הבגד:

---

removes[3] belong to the owner, because this process removes a significant amount of wool, which the owner would presumably want to keep.

הַכּוֹבֵס נוֹטֵל שְׁלֹשָׁה חוּטִין וְהֵן שֶׁלּוֹ — After washing a woolen garment **the launderer takes out three threads** at the edge of the garment[4] **and they belong to him**, because such a small number of threads have little use and the owner is not interested in them. יָתֵר מִכֵּן הֲרֵי אֵלּוּ שֶׁל בַּעַל הַבַּיִת — But if he took out **more than that, they belong to the owner,** because more than three threads are useful and the owner would want to keep them.[5] אִם הָיָה הַשָּׁחוֹר עַל גַּבֵּי הַלָּבָן נוֹטֵל אֶת הַכֹּל וְהֵן שֶׁלּוֹ — However, **if it was black on white,** that is, if black threads were woven onto the edge of a white garment, **[the launderer] may take off all of them, and they belong to him.** Since black ruins the appearance of a white garment, the launderer may take all the black threads (even if there are more than three).[6]

The law regarding a tailor:

הַחַיָּט שֶׁשִּׁיֵּר מִן הַחוּט כְּדֵי לִתְפֹּר בּוֹ — If **a tailor** was given material and thread for use in sewing a garment,[7] and he **left over enough thread with which to sew,**[8] וּמַטְלִית שֶׁהִיא שָׁלֹשׁ עַל שָׁלֹשׁ — or if he evened out the garment by cutting off **a piece of cloth that is** at least **three fingerbreadths**[9] **by three**

NOTES

3. After the raw wool is washed, it is combed and beaten with a stick [to untangle it and prepare it for spinning] (*Rav, Tos. Yom Tov*).

4. It was the standard practice of weavers to weave an extra three threads of another type of material at the edges of a woolen garment so that the edges of the garment itself do not unravel in the laundering process. [After washing the garment] the launderer pulls out these three threads and straightens out the edges of the garment so that it looks neat (*Rav*).

5. That is, if more than three threads were added by the weaver, and the launderer removed them, the owner would want them all back, since this is a significant number of threads, which he would find useful (*Tos. Yom Tov*).

6. If the weaver added black threads to a white garment, he clearly intended for all of them to be removed [and the owner does not want them since they are of a different color] (*Rashba*).

7. *Meiri.*

8. This is twice the length of the needle (*Tos. Yom Tov,* from Gemara).

9. The opinions regarding the measure of a fingerbreadth range between .8 and .95 inches (2-2.4 cm.).

[159] **MISHNAH BAVA KAMMA** / Chapter 10: *Hagozeil* 10/10

— רע"ב —

הֲרֵי אֵלּוּ שֶׁל בַּעַל הַבַּיִת. מַה שֶּׁהֶחָרָשׁ מוֹצִיא בְּמַעֲצָד הֲרֵי אֵלּוּ שֶׁלּוֹ. וּבַכַּשִּׁיל, שֶׁל בַּעַל הַבַּיִת. וְאִם הָיָה עוֹשֶׂה אֵצֶל בַּעַל הַבַּיִת, אַף הַנְּסֹרֶת שֶׁל בַּעַל הַבַּיִת.

מעצד. כלי שמחליק בו הנגר את פני הלוח. וספחין שהוא מוציא דקין הן: כשיל. קרדוס. ומפיל שפחין גסין: אצל בעל הבית.

כשכיר יוס: אף הנסרות. דק דק היולא מתחת המקדח שהם דקים מחד. של בעל הבית:

הֲרֵי אֵלּוּ שֶׁל בַּעַל הַבַּיִת — they **belong to the owner**, because thread and material are useful in these amounts. Smaller amounts, however, may be kept by the tailor because the owner does not care about them.

The law regarding a carpenter:

מַה שֶּׁהֶחָרָשׁ מוֹצִיא בְּמַעֲצָד הֲרֵי אֵלּוּ שֶׁלּוֹ — **[The shavings] that a carpenter removes** when he scrapes wood **with a plane**[10] **belong to him,** because they are so thin that the owner does not care about them; *וּבַכַּשִּׁיל שֶׁל בַּעַל הַבַּיִת* — but the chips that he removes when he chops wood **with an ax belong to the owner,** because they are large pieces that the owner would want returned to him. *וְאִם הָיָה עוֹשֶׂה אֵצֶל בַּעַל הַבַּיִת אַף הַנְּסֹרֶת שֶׁל בַּעַל הַבַּיִת* — **However, if he was working on the owner's property,** all the wood, **even the sawdust** that falls when he drills a hole, **belongs to the owner.** Since the wood is already in the owner's property, he would not want it to be taken from him.[11]

NOTES

10. A scraping tool that is used to smooth planks of wood (*Rav*).

11. Because the shavings and sawdust are already in the owner's yard and do not need to be carried there, he wishes to keep them for himself (*Sma; Shulchan Aruch, Choshen Mishpat* 358:14).

All the rulings of this Mishnah regarding which leftover materials may be kept by the craftsman and which ones must be returned to the owner apply only in a place where there is no accepted custom. If there is an established custom, the custom should be followed (see *Rambam, Hilchos Geneivah* 6:8).

מסכת בבא מציעא
TRACTATE BAVA METZIA

זרעים

מועד

נשים

נזיקין

קדשים

טהרות

General Introduction

Bava Metzia (literally, *the middle gate*) is the second tractate of Seder *Nezikin* (literally, *damages*). The group of tractates known as the *"Bavas"* (*Bava Kamma, Bava Metzia,* and *Bava Basra*) are, according to the Amora Rav Yosef, not really three separate tractates, but three parts — each consisting of ten chapters — of a single large tractate called *Nezikin* (*Bava Kamma* 102a; see *Ramban* to *Shevuos* 2a).

Bava Metzia deals with aspects of civil law other than damages, such as the rules for returning lost items [הֲשָׁבַת אֲבֵדָה]; the obligations and responsibilities of *shomrim* [שׁוֹמְרִים], people entrusted with the safekeeping of other peoples' property; the prohibition of *ona'ah* [אוֹנָאָה], unfair pricing; the prohibition against taking interest on a loan [רִבִּית]; the hiring of artisans, workers, and animals; loans of objects for use; sharecropping agreements; rental of apartments; and various related topics. These topics will each be explained in the chapters that deal with them. The rest of this Introduction will focus on some of the general rules of monetary law and lawsuits.

◆§ מֻחְזָק, *possession*

One of the most basic principles of Torah civil law is the legal principle of מֻחְזָק, *possession*. The general rule in monetary cases is that הַמּוֹצִיא מֵחֲבֵרוֹ עָלָיו הָרְאָיָה, *the burden of proof is on the one who wants to take property from his fellow.* This means that when a person claims that money or property being held by someone else really belongs to him, the person holding the property (the *muchzak*) does *not* have to prove that he has a right to keep it; rather, the person trying to take it from him must prove *his* right to take it. The Gemara (*Bava Kamma* 46b) holds this principle to be so logically self-evident that no Scriptural basis for it is necessary.

Nevertheless, there are Tannaim who maintain that in cases where something happened that might affect the ownership of property, but it is impossible for either of the parties to know what really happened, the property in question is divided between them, even though it is presently in the possession of one of them. Several Mishnahs in this tractate and in tractate *Bava Kamma* follow this view (see, for example, *Bava Kamma* 5:1 and *Bava Metzia* 8:2, 4).[1]

◆§ קִנְיָן, *kinyan*

Another basic principle of Torah civil law is that a change of ownership must

---
NOTES

1. Nevertheless, the majority of Sages disagree with this view and hold that the person in possession is always assumed to have the right to keep it until it is proven otherwise. The halachah follows their view (*Bava Kamma* 46a; see *Choshen Mishpat* 399:2,3).

happen through a legally recognized act known as a *kinyan*. This act is performed by the person acquiring the property, with the consent of the person transferring it to him. Different types of property are subject to different kinds of *kinyanim* (see *Kiddushin* 1:4,5).

Until the proper *kinyan* has been made, the property remains under the ownership of the one who had it until now, even if the buyer has paid for it. And once a buyer has made the proper *kinyan,* ownership of it goes over to him, even if he has not yet paid for it.[2] This is true not just for sales but for gifts as well. In the case of ownerless property (*hefker*), until the proper *kinyan* is made the property remains ownerless, even if someone is holding it. Therefore, if another person comes along and makes a proper *kinyan* on it, *he* becomes the owner.

≈§ Rules of Evidence and Oaths

As is true in most other areas of Torah law, monetary obligations can be established only on the basis of the testimony of two valid witnesses. One witness cannot prove a claim. Nevertheless, the testimony of a single witness is enough to force the person being sued to swear that he does not owe the money (*Shevuos* 40a). If he does not swear, he must pay the claim (*Shevuos* 41a; *Rambam, Hilchos To'ein VeNitan* 1:4).

There are also other situations where a person must swear to avoid having to pay. Someone who admits to *part* of a claim but denies the other part of it [מוֹדֶה בְּמִקְצָת] must swear about the part he denies in order to avoid paying for it (see Mishnah 4:7). Also, a *shomer* who claims that the item he was keeping for someone was lost in a way that would exempt him from paying for it must swear that this is what happened, and that he did not take the item to use for himself (see Mishnah 3:1).

NOTES

2. The money then becomes a debt owed by the buyer to the seller.

Chapter One

משניות בבא מציעא / פרק א: שנים אוחזין

[א] שְׁנַיִם אוֹחֲזִין בְּטַלִּית, זֶה אוֹמֵר, אֲנִי מְצָאתִיהָ, וְזֶה אוֹמֵר, אֲנִי מְצָאתִיהָ, זֶה אוֹמֵר, כֻּלָּהּ שֶׁלִּי, וְזֶה אוֹמֵר, כֻּלָּהּ שֶׁלִּי, זֶה יִשָּׁבַע שֶׁאֵין לוֹ בָּהּ פָּחוֹת מֵחֶצְיָהּ,

— רע"ב —

פרק ראשון – שנים אוחזין. (א) שנים אוחזין בטלית. בגמרא (ב, א) מוקי למתניתין, כגון שאחד מהם תופס בחוטין שבשפת הבגד מצד זה, והאחד תופס בחוטין שבשפת הבגד מצד זה. אבל אם הם אדוקים בבגד עצמו, זה נוטל עד מקום שידו מגעת, וזה נוטל עד מקום שידו מגעת, והשאר חולקים בשוה, ובשבועה: זה אומר בולה שלי. אני קניתיה, ולי מכרה המוכר ולא לך. והמוכר מכר לאחד מהם, ולקח המעות משניהם, מאחד מדעתו ומאחד בעל כרחו, ואינו יודע מהי מדעתו ומהי בעל כרחיה. דאילו ידע והיה אומר לזה מכרתי, היה כאן עד אחד, והיה שכנגדו חייב שבועה דאורייתא להכחיש העד. עכשיו שאינו יודע, שניהם נשבעים שבועה זו האמורה במתניתין. ובדין הוא שיהיו חולקים בלא שבועה, אלא שתקנו חכמים שלא יטול שום אחד מהם אלא בשבועה, כדי שלא יהא כל אחד הולך ותוקף בטליתו של חבירו ואומר שלי היא. ואיצטריך תנא לאשמועינן בזה שלא אמרי אנחנו מצאתיה דהיינו במליאה, וזה אומר כולה שלי דהיינו מקח וממכר. אי תנא מליאה, הוה אמינא, מליאה הוא דרמו רבנן שבועה עליה, משום דמורה התירא לאחוז בה כי שלא כדין דאמר, חברי לאו מידי חסר בה, אחיל ואתפוס ואפלוג בהדיה. אבל מקח וממכר, דאי לא הוה להו מהדר אבתרה למזבנה, וזה שבא לחלוק עמו ולינה חלי דמיה, שלא כדין כי מחסרו, וליכא למימר דמורי התירא, אימא לא רמו רבנן שבועה עליה. ואי אשמועינן במקח וממכר, הוה אמינא, מקח וממכר הוא דרמו רבנן שבועה עליה, משום דמורי [התירא] ואמר, חברי דמי קא יהיב ואנא דמי קא יהיבנא, השתא דליכחד לדידי אשקליה אנא, וחברי לטרח וליזיל וליזבן אחריתי. אבל מליאה דליכא למימר הכי, אימא לא, צריכא:

---

[1] This chapter deals with disputes that have to do with finding lost objects. The following Mishnah discusses a case where two people come to court holding a lost object they found, and each one claims that he acquired it first:[1]

שְׁנַיִם אוֹחֲזִין בְּטַלִּית — Two people come to court holding onto the edges of a cloak they found in the street. זֶה אוֹמֵר "אֲנִי מְצָאתִיהָ" — This one says, "I found it and picked it up first, and it is mine," וְזֶה אוֹמֵר "אֲנִי מְצָאתִיהָ" — and the other one says, "I found it and picked it up first, and it is mine."[2] Or, two people come to court holding onto a cloak they bought in a store, זֶה אוֹמֵר "כֻּלָּהּ שֶׁלִּי" — and this one says, "It is all mine because the owner sold it to me," וְזֶה אוֹמֵר "כֻּלָּהּ שֶׁלִּי" — and the other one says, "It is all mine because the owner did not sell it to you but to me."[3] The law in both of these cases is: זֶה יִשָּׁבַע שֶׁאֵין לוֹ בָּהּ פָּחוֹת מֵחֶצְיָהּ — This one must swear that he owns not

---

NOTES

[1]

1. The Mishnah speaks of the type of lost item that may be kept by the person who finds it (*Meiri*). The rules for which lost items must be returned and which may be kept by the finder are taught in the next chapter.

2. Each person says that he reached the cloak first and picked it up, while the other person grabbed onto it afterward. Lifting an item is a type of *kinyan* [formal act of acquisition], and thus whoever picked up the cloak first becomes its owner (*Meiri*).

3. These two people were shopping in a store and were both interested in buying the same cloak. Both people gave money for the cloak, but the owner agreed to accept the money from only one of them. He does not remember now which person he agreed to sell it to [due to the confusion of both people wanting the cloak and paying for it] (see *Rav*).

[7] MISHNAH BAVA METZIA / Chapter 1: *Shenayim Ochazin*

— רע״ב —

וְזֶה יִשָּׁבַע שֶׁאֵין לוֹ בָהּ פָּחוֹת מֵחֶצְיָהּ,
וְיַחֲלֹקוּ. זֶה אוֹמֵר, כֻּלָּהּ שֶׁלִּי, וְזֶה אוֹמֵר,
חֶצְיָהּ שֶׁלִּי, הָאוֹמֵר כֻּלָּהּ שֶׁלִּי יִשָּׁבַע
שֶׁאֵין לוֹ בָהּ פָּחוֹת מִשְּׁלֹשָׁה חֲלָקִים,

ישבע שאין לו בה פחות
מחציה. ואינו נשבע
שכולה שלו כדקא טעין
מעיקרא, דהא לא יהבי ליה
כולה. ואי משתבע שחליה
שלו כדקא יהבי ליה, הוה
מרע ליה לדבוריה קמא
דאמר כולה שלי. הלכך ישבע שאין לו בה פחות מחליה, דמשמע הכי, כולה שלי כדקא אמינא
מעיקרא, ולדבריכם שאין אתם מאמינים לי בכולה, שבועה שיש לי בה, ואין לי בה פחות מחליה:

וְזֶה יִשָּׁבַע שֶׁאֵין לוֹ בָהּ פָּחוֹת מֵחֶצְיָהּ — and the other **one must swear that he owns not less than half of it**,[4] וְיַחֲלֹקוּ — **and they** then **divide** the cloak equally.[5] Since both people are holding the cloak, they are both in equal possession of it. And since we do not know who the real owner is, the law is that the cloak must be given to whoever has it in his possession. Since they both have possession of it, each one receives half the cloak.[6] However, the Rabbis required that before taking anything, each must swear that he owns at least that part of the cloak that he will get.[7]

The Mishnah considers a variation of the previous case:

זֶה אוֹמֵר "כֻּלָּהּ שֶׁלִּי" — **If two people are holding onto a cloak they found in the street, and this one says, "[The cloak] is all mine** because I picked it up first," וְזֶה אוֹמֵר "חֶצְיָהּ שֶׁלִּי" — **and the other one says, "Half [the cloak] is mine** because we both lifted it at the same time and thus we are both partners in it," — הָאוֹמֵר "כֻּלָּהּ שֶׁלִּי" יִשָּׁבַע שֶׁאֵין לוֹ בָהּ פָּחוֹת מִשְּׁלֹשָׁה חֲלָקִים — the law is that **the one who says, "[The cloak] is all mine," must swear that he owns**

— NOTES —

4. He does not swear to his claim that the whole cloak is his, since in the end he will receive only half the cloak. But he cannot say that he owns half the cloak, since he claims that he owns the whole thing. Thus, he swears that he owns no less than half (*Rav*, from Gemara 5b).

5. If it is possible to physically divide the cloak (without the cut halves losing their value) they do so. If not, they sell it and divide the money (*Tos. Yom Tov*).

[In the case of the bought cloak, each person receives half the cloak plus half of the extra money given to the seller (see *Rashi* 2b ד״ה אבל).]

6. [This follows the most basic rule of monetary law: We assume that a person owns whatever is in his possession until it is proven otherwise (הַמּוֹצִיא מֵחֲבֵרוֹ עָלָיו הָרְאָיָה, *the one who wishes to take money from someone else must bring proof*). Since both people are holding the edges of the cloak and are in equal possession of it, and neither one can prove that he owns the other half as well, each one is assumed to own half of it.]

However, if only one person is holding the cloak but the other one claims he found it first, the one holding it gets the entire cloak (*Rashi*). Similarly, if they are both holding the cloak somewhere in the middle (rather than at its edges), we view each person as being in possession of the cloak up to the point he is holding, and they divide only what still remains between them (*Rav*).

7. This is because the Rabbis were afraid that people might simply grab onto another person's item (even while the owner himself is holding onto it) and claim falsely that it is theirs. They therefore decreed that one must take an oath before being given a portion of such a disputed item (*Rav*, from Gemara). [If, however, one of them refuses to swear, the other one swears that the whole cloak is his, and receives the whole cloak (see *Choshen Mishpat* 138:1).]

א/ב

משניות בבא מציעא / פרק א: שנים אוחזין [8]

וְהָאוֹמֵר חֶצְיָהּ שֶׁלִּי יִשָּׁבַע שֶׁאֵין לוֹ בָהּ פָּחוֹת מֵרְבִיעַ, זֶה נוֹטֵל שְׁלֹשָׁה חֲלָקִים, וְזֶה נוֹטֵל רְבִיעַ.

[ב] **הָיוּ** שְׁנַיִם רוֹכְבִין עַל גַּבֵּי בְהֵמָה, אוֹ שֶׁהָיָה אֶחָד רוֹכֵב וְאֶחָד מַנְהִיג,

— רע"ב —

(ב) **היו שנים רוכבים על גבי בהמה.** הא קמשמע לן דרוכב קני, ואף על פי שאינו מנהיג שלא זה הבהמה ממקומה: **או שהיה אחד רוכב ואחד מנהיג.** בזמן שרוכב מנענע ברגליו כי היכי דתיזיל הבהמה מחמתיה, הוא דשויס רוכב ומנהיג. ואם לא היה אלא רוכב בלבד, מנהיג קנה, רוכב לא קנה. ואם הודו או באו עדים, אפילו לאחר שנפסק הדין עליהם שיחלוקו בשבועה, חולקים שלא בשבועה:

וְהָאוֹמֵר not less than three parts [that is, three-quarters] of the cloak, **"חֶצְיָהּ שֶׁלִּי" יִשָּׁבַע שֶׁאֵין לוֹ בָהּ פָּחוֹת מֵרְבִיעַ** — and the one who says, "Half [the cloak] is mine," must swear that he owns not less than one-fourth of the cloak. **זֶה נוֹטֵל שְׁלֹשָׁה חֲלָקִים** — This one (the person who claims the whole cloak is his) then **takes three parts** [three-quarters] of the cloak, **וְזֶה נוֹטֵל רְבִיעַ** — and the other one (the person who says half is his) **takes one-fourth** of it. Since the person claiming half the cloak agrees that the other half belongs to the one claiming the whole, that half certainly goes to him. The only dispute is about the second half. Since they are both holding onto the cloak and are in equal possession of it, they divide the part of the cloak that is in dispute.[8] Therefore, they divide the second half equally.[9] But before they do so, they must swear that they own at least the amount they are getting, as in the previous case.[10]

[2] The Mishnah now discusses a case where two people are arguing about an animal that they found:

הָיוּ שְׁנַיִם רוֹכְבִין עַל גַּבֵּי בְהֵמָה — **Two** people were **riding on an animal** that they found,[1] **אוֹ שֶׁהָיָה אֶחָד רוֹכֵב וְאֶחָד מַנְהִיג** — **or one was riding** the

---

NOTES

8. [Since they are both holding onto the cloak by its edges, they are considered to be in equal possession of whatever part of the cloak is in dispute (see *Rashi* ד"ה וזה).]

9. Thus, the one claiming the whole gets the first half, which is surely his, plus half of the second half that is being disputed. His total share is thus three-quarters of the entire cloak. The one claiming half, however, receives only half of the disputed second half. Thus, he receives a quarter of the entire cloak.

10. Although their dispute is only about half the cloak, the person claiming the whole cloak must swear about the three-fourths he is getting, not just about

his part of the disputed half (i.e., one-fourth). If he would merely swear that he owns one-fourth of the cloak, he could be referring to the part that is surely his and not the disputed part. Therefore, he must swear that three-fourths are his, which surely includes his part of the disputed half (*Tos. Yom Tov*, from *Nimukei Yosef*).

[2]

1. The act of "riding" an animal, i.e., sitting on it and holding the reins, even without causing it to move, is considered a *kinyan* with respect to ownerless items (*Rav*; *Rambam*, *Hil. Gezeilah* 17:7; *Rashi* and *Rif*, cited by *Tos. Yom Tov*; see there for other opinions).

זֶה אוֹמֵר, כֻּלָּהּ שֶׁלִּי, וְזֶה אוֹמֵר, כֻּלָּהּ שֶׁלִּי, זֶה יִשָּׁבַע שֶׁאֵין לוֹ בָּהּ פָּחוֹת מֵחֶצְיָהּ, וְזֶה יִשָּׁבַע שֶׁאֵין לוֹ בָּהּ פָּחוֹת מֵחֶצְיָהּ, וְיַחֲלֹקוּ. בִּזְמַן שֶׁהֵם מוֹדִים, אוֹ שֶׁיֵּשׁ לָהֶן עֵדִים, חוֹלְקִים בְּלֹא שְׁבוּעָה.

animal **and the other one was leading it.**[2] זֶה אוֹמֵר "כֻּלָּהּ שֶׁלִּי" — **This one says, "It is all mine** because I was riding the animal before you started to ride or lead it," וְזֶה אוֹמֵר "כֻּלָּהּ שֶׁלִּי" — **and the** other **one says, "It is all mine** because *I* was riding (or leading) the animal before you."[3] זֶה יִשָּׁבַע שֶׁאֵין לוֹ בָּהּ פָּחוֹת מֵחֶצְיָהּ — **The law is that this one swears that he owns not less than half of [the animal],** וְזֶה יִשָּׁבַע שֶׁאֵין לוֹ בָּהּ פָּחוֹת מֵחֶצְיָהּ — **and the** other **one swears that he owns not less than half of it,** וְיַחֲלֹקוּ — **and they** then **divide** the animal. This is because riding or leading an animal is considered to be like holding onto it.[4] Thus, just as two people holding onto an item each swear and take half (as we learned in the previous Mishnah), the same is true where they are both riding an animal, or one is riding and the other is leading.

The Mishnah cites cases in which something is divided *without* an oath:

בִּזְמַן שֶׁהֵם מוֹדִים — **Whenever they** both **agree** that they acquired an item at the same time and are therefore equal partners in it,[5] אוֹ שֶׁיֵּשׁ לָהֶן עֵדִים — **or they have witnesses** who testify that they acquired it at the same time, חוֹלְקִים בְּלֹא שְׁבוּעָה — the law is that **they divide** the item **without** taking **an oath.**[6] This is because an oath is required only to attempt to verify each person's claim. However, in these cases, there is no need for verification, since it is clear (through admission or witnesses) that each one owns half.

[3] The Mishnah discusses another case where it is unclear who acquired a found item. Here the question is not who picked it up first, but if the person who picked it up meant to acquire it for himself or for someone else:

NOTES

2. "Leading" an animal, i.e., causing it to move, is considered a *kinyan* (called *meshichah*).

3. Thus, each of these people claims that he did one of these actions first and thereby acquired the entire animal for himself (*Meiri*).

[*Rav* explains that in the case where one person is riding the animal and the other one is leading it, the rider must cause the animal to move by spurring it with his feet. In this way his *kinyan* is equal to the *kinyan* of the one leading it, and they therefore both have equal possession of the animal. However, if the rider just sits on the animal without moving it, it is considered that the one leading has sole possession of the animal, and he gets the whole thing. See, however, *Tos. Yom Tov.*]

4. *Meiri*.

5. Even if at the beginning each one claimed that he had acquired it first, but then later both of them admitted that they really acquired it at the same time.

6. Even if the court has already ruled that they must take an oath before collecting half, if they now agree that they acquired it at the same time, or witnesses come and say that this is what happened, they each take half without having to swear (*Rav* ד"ה או, *Rambam Commentary*).

משניות בבא מציעא / פרק א: שנים אוחזין

[ג] הָיָה רוֹכֵב עַל גַּבֵּי בְהֵמָה וְרָאָה אֶת הַמְּצִיאָה, וְאָמַר לַחֲבֵרוֹ, תְּנֶה לִי, נְטָלָהּ וְאָמַר, אֲנִי זָכִיתִי בָהּ, זָכָה בָהּ. אִם מִשֶּׁנְּתָנָהּ לוֹ אָמַר, אֲנִי זָכִיתִי בָהּ תְּחִלָּה, לֹא אָמַר כְּלוּם.

[ד] רָאָה אֶת הַמְּצִיאָה וְנָפַל עָלֶיהָ, וּבָא אַחֵר וְהֶחֱזִיק בָּהּ,

— רע״ב —

(ג) אמר לחבירו תנה לי וכו'. אבל אמר זכה לי בה, קנה הרוכב, ואין המגביה יכול לומר אני זכיתי בה: לא אמר כלום. שקנאה זה משמשכה מיד חבדו, וכל זמן שהיתה ביד המגביה, הפקר היתה:

רָאָה אֶת — **Someone was riding on an animal,** הָיָה רוֹכֵב עַל גַּבֵּי בְהֵמָה — הַמְּצִיאָה — **and he saw a lost item**[1] **on the ground.** וְאָמַר לַחֲבֵרוֹ "תְּנֵה לִי" — **He then said to his friend** who was standing next to the item, **"Give it to me."**[2] נְטָלָהּ וְאָמַר "אֲנִי זָכִיתִי בָהּ" — **[The friend] took [the item]** off the ground in order to give it to the rider, **and then said, "I have acquired it** for myself," meaning that he has now decided *not* to give it to the rider, but to take it for himself instead. זָכָה בָהּ — **The law in this case is that [the friend] has indeed acquired it.** Although he originally picked it up for the rider, he did not intend to acquire it for him. Rather, his intention was to then hand it to the rider, so that the rider could lift it and acquire it for himself.[3] Thus, the rider did not acquire the lost item, and when the friend then decided to take it for himself, he acquired it.

In the following case, however, the law is different:

אִם מִשֶּׁנְּתָנָהּ לוֹ אָמַר "אֲנִי זָכִיתִי בָהּ תְּחִלָּה" — **But if after [the friend] had given it to [the rider]** he said, **"I acquired it** for myself **first,"** that is, he claims that when he picked it up he meant to acquire it for himself and not for the rider, לֹא אָמַר כְּלוּם — **he has not said anything;** that is, his claim is not believed, because if it were true, he would not have given it to the rider. Rather, we assume that he picked it up only with the intention of giving it to the rider, as the rider had requested. Thus, the rider acquired it when it was handed to him.

[4] The Mishnah teaches which acts are effective for acquiring lost items that one may keep:

רָאָה אֶת הַמְּצִיאָה וְנָפַל עָלֶיהָ — **If someone saw a lost item**[1] **and fell on it** in order to acquire it, וּבָא אַחֵר וְהֶחֱזִיק בָּהּ — **and another** person came and

---

NOTES

[3]

1. Literally, *a found item*. [As in the previous Mishnahs, the Mishnah refers to a lost item that can be kept by the finder.]
2. Since he was on the horse and could not reach the item, he asked his friend to get it for him (see *Tos. Yom Tov*).
3. This is because the rider said, "*Give* it to me," as opposed to, "*Acquire* it for me," by which he meant, *hand* it to me (not acquire it for me). We therefore assume that the friend followed the rider's instructions

and picked up the item only to hand it to the rider and not to acquire it for him (Gemara 10a, as explained by *Tos. Yom Tov*; but see *Tur, Choshen Mishpat* 269).

[If the friend had picked it up to acquire it for *himself*, it would surely be his. The point of the Mishnah is that even though he originally picked it up to give it to the rider, he may still change his mind and keep it for himself.]

[4]

1. Or, any ownerless item (see *Meiri*).

[11] **MISHNAH BAVA METZIA** / Chapter 1: *Shenayim Ochazin* 1/4

— רע"ב —

זֶה שֶׁהֶחֱזִיק בָּהּ זָכָה בָּהּ. רָאָה אוֹתָן רָצִין אַחַר מְצִיאָה אַחַר צְבִי שָׁבוּר, אַחַר גּוֹזָלוֹת שֶׁלֹּא פָרְחוּ, וְאָמַר, זָכְתָה לִי שָׂדִי, זָכְתָה לוֹ.

(ד) **זה שהחזיק בה** זכה בה. ודוקא שהיתה המציאה ברשות הרבים, שאין ארבע אמות של אדם קונות לו ברשות הרבים, לפיכך המחזיק בה זכה. אבל בסמטא שהיא שביל של יחיד, או בצדי רשות הרבים שאין רבים דוחקים שם, ארבע אמות של אדם קונות לו כל מליאה שבאה בארבע אמות, ואין אחר רשאי לתפסו. ותקינו ליה רבנן כי היכי דלא ליתו לאינצויי: **אחר צבי שבור.** שאינו יכול לרוץ, ומשתמר בתוך השדה אם לא יטלוהו אחרים, והוא כמליאה: **זכתה לו.** שדהו. והוא שעומד בצד שדהו, וכגון שיכול לרוץ אחריהן ומגיען קודם שילאו משדהו:

זֶה שֶׁהֶחֱזִיק בָּהּ זָכָה בָּהּ — the one who took hold of [the item] and lifted it, took hold of it acquired it. Falling on an item is not considered a *kinyan*. Therefore, the first person never acquired it. Thus, when the second person lifted it, he acquired it.[2]

The Mishnah teaches that a person can sometimes acquire a lost item merely by the fact that it entered his property:

רָאָה אוֹתָן רָצִין אַחַר מְצִיאָה — If someone saw [people] running to take a lost item that was in his field,[3] **אַחַר צְבִי שָׁבוּר אַחַר גּוֹזָלוֹת שֶׁלֹּא פָרְחוּ** — or he saw them running after an ownerless **lame deer** that had wandered into his field, or after ownerless **young pigeons that cannot** yet **fly, וְאָמַר "זָכְתָה לִי שָׂדִי" and he said, "My field has acquired them for me," זָכְתָה לוֹ** — then [his field] **acquired** these items **for him** and the people running after them cannot take them. Since the lame deer and young pigeons cannot quickly escape from his field and are easy for him to catch before they leave it, they are considered to be held in the field.[4] A person's property can acquire for him any item that is held securely in it.[5]

---------- NOTES ----------

2. Lifting is a valid *kinyan* (act of acquisition), as we learned in Mishnah 1.

[There are certain semipublic areas (known as *simta*) in which a person can acquire property simply by standing within four *amos* of the item he wishes to acquire. [This is a Rabbinic enactment known as "the *kinyan* of four *amos*."] If the lost item was in such a place, then the person who fell on it acquires it as soon as he comes within four *amos* of it, and it therefore belongs to him. The Mishnah, however, discusses a case where the item was not in such an area, but in a regular public place such as a street. Therefore, he did not acquire it with the *kinyan* of four *amos* (*Rav*; but see *Tiferes Yisrael*).]

3. The Mishnah speaks here of an object that is not alive and cannot move out of the field on its own (*Rashi*; see *Rav* ד"ה אחר).

4. The Mishnah speaks of a case where he is standing next to the field and is able to run after the lame deer or young birds and prevent them from leaving the field (*Rav*, from Gemara).

5. This is known as a *kinyan chatzeir* (acquisition by courtyard). The Gemara learns from a verse that just as a person can acquire something by taking it in his hands, so too he can acquire something by holding it in his property (see Gemara 10b).

[If the field was protected by a fence, even a healthy deer would be considered "held" in it, since it could not escape. Our Mishnah, however, is talking about an unfenced field. In such a case, the deer is considered "held" only because it is lame and the owner of the field is standing nearby, so that he can prevent it from leaving the field (*Tos. Yom Tov*).]

משניות בבא מציעא / פרק א: שנים אוחזין

הָיָה צְבִי רָץ כְּדַרְכּוֹ אוֹ שֶׁהָיוּ גּוֹזָלוֹת מַפְרִיחִין,
וְאָמַר, זָכְתָה לִי שָׂדִי, לֹא אָמַר כְּלוּם.
[ה] **מְצִיאַת** בְּנוֹ וּבִתּוֹ הַקְּטַנִּים, מְצִיאַת
עַבְדּוֹ וְשִׁפְחָתוֹ הַכְּנַעֲנִים,
מְצִיאַת אִשְׁתּוֹ, הֲרֵי אֵלּוּ שֶׁלּוֹ.

— רע״ב —

(ה) הקטנים. כל סמוך על שלחן אביו אפילו הוא גדול, קרי ליה קטן, ומליאתו לאביו משום איבה. והבת בין קטנה בין נערה מליאתה לאביה, דהתורה זכתה כל שבח נעוריה לאביה:

עבדו ושפחתו הכנעניים. שהרי גופן קנוי לו, כדכתיב (ויקרא כה, מו) והתנחלתם אותם: מציאת אשתו. רבנן תקינו ליה משום איבה:

In the following case, however, a person does not acquire the items in his field:

הָיָה צְבִי רָץ כְּדַרְכּוֹ אוֹ שֶׁהָיוּ גּוֹזָלוֹת מַפְרִיחִין — However, **if a deer was running** through his field **in its usual manner** (i.e., it was not lame), **or young pigeons were flying** in his field,[6] and other people were running to acquire them, וְאָמַר, "זָכְתָה לִי שָׂדִי" — **and he said, "My field has acquired** them **for me,"** לֹא אָמַר כְּלוּם — **he has said nothing,** and the field does *not* acquire these items for him. This is because he cannot stop the deer and birds from leaving his field, and something that is not secure within a person's property cannot be acquired by him through his property.[7] Rather, whichever person chasing them reaches them first and performs a valid *kinyan* on them acquires them.

[5] The Mishnah discusses who keeps the lost or ownerless items that are found by the members of a person's household:

מְצִיאַת בְּנוֹ וּבִתּוֹ הַקְּטַנִּים — **The [things] found by someone's young son or daughter,** or any child being supported by his father,[1] מְצִיאַת עַבְדּוֹ וְשִׁפְחָתוֹ הַכְּנַעֲנִים — **and the [things] found by someone's Canaanite slave or slavewoman,** מְצִיאַת אִשְׁתּוֹ — **and the [things] found by a person's wife,** הֲרֵי אֵלּוּ שֶׁלּוֹ — **these belong to him.** What a daughter under the age of 12½ finds belongs to her father under Biblical law.[2] Similarly, what a Canaanite slave finds belongs to his master under Biblical law.[3] In the case of a wife, and a child

--- NOTES ---

6. The Mishnah earlier discussed very young pigeons that could not yet fly. Here the Mishnah refers to young pigeons that were slightly older and could fly.

7. The deer does not actually have to be running or the birds flying to prevent his field from acquiring them. As long as the deer and birds are *able* to run or fly, his field cannot acquire them.

[5]

1. In the context of this Mishnah, the term קָטָן (which usually means an underage child, one who is not yet an adult) refers to any child who is being supported by his father, regardless of the age. On the other hand, even a very young boy is considered an adult in regard to this law if he supports himself. In the case of a daughter, even if she supports herself she is considered a "young child" until the age of 12½ (*Rav*, as explained by *Tos. Yom Tov*; but see note 2 to *Kesubos* 4:4).

2. From the time a girl develops signs of maturity (usually at the age of 12) until six months after that she is known as a *naarah*. We learn from a verse that when a girl is a *naarah* (and certainly when she is under 12 and not yet a *naarah*) all that she acquires (even her earnings) belongs to her father (*Rav, Rambam Commentary;* see, however, *Tos. Yom Tov*).

3. A Canaanite slave is considered the

מְצִיאַת בְּנוֹ וּבִתּוֹ הַגְּדוֹלִים, מְצִיאַת עַבְדּוֹ וְשִׁפְחָתוֹ הָעִבְרִים, מְצִיאַת אִשְׁתּוֹ שֶׁגֵּרְשָׁהּ, אַף עַל פִּי שֶׁלֹּא נָתַן כְּתֻבָּתָהּ, הֲרֵי אֵלּוּ שֶׁלָּהֶן.

being supported by his father, the Rabbis instituted that what they find belongs to the husband and father in order to prevent bad feelings between them.[4] מְצִיאַת בְּנוֹ וּבִתּוֹ הַגְּדוֹלִים — However, the [things] found by someone's adult son or daughter who support themselves, or a son of any age who supports himself,[5] מְצִיאַת עַבְדּוֹ וְשִׁפְחָתוֹ הָעִבְרִים — and the [things] found by someone's Hebrew servant or maidservant,[6] מְצִיאַת אִשְׁתּוֹ שֶׁגֵּרְשָׁהּ אַף עַל פִּי שֶׁלֹּא נָתַן כְּתֻבָּתָהּ — and the [things] found by a person's wife whom he has divorced, even though he has not yet given her *kesubah* (the money due to a wife when she is divorced) to her, הֲרֵי אֵלּוּ שֶׁלָּהֶן — these belong to them, not him. This is because even under Biblical law a father has no rights to his daughter once she reaches the age of 12½,[7] nor are Hebrew servants considered his property. And once a wife has been divorced or a child has become self-supporting, there is no further concern for resentment, so the Rabbis did not award the finds of these people to the father or husband.[8]

[6] The rest of the chapter deals with a person who finds lost documents. The Mishnah will discuss a number of different types of documents, and teach whether they should be returned to any of the parties mentioned in them. The first case discussed is lost loan documents:[1]

NOTES
---

property of his master. Therefore, anything he acquires is also the property of his master.

4. Since the father is supporting this child, he might feel resentful if he does not receive in return the valuables that his child finds. This might cause him to stop supporting the child. The Rabbis therefore instituted that he should receive the things that his child finds (*Rav*; see also *Tos. Yom Tov*). Similarly, since a husband provides food for his wife, he might be resentful if he does not have rights to the items she finds, and this could lead to marital conflict. The Rabbis therefore decreed that he should receive these things (*Rav*).

5. See note 1.

6. A "Hebrew servant" is a Jew who was sold as a servant for a fixed amount of time (see *Kiddushin* 1:2). Although he has an obligation to work for his master, he is not considered his master's property.

7. See note 4.

8. The Mishnah refers to a case where the woman received a *get* in a way that makes it unclear whether the divorce took effect. In such a case, the husband is not obligated to pay the *kesubah,* but if he chooses not to pay it, he must continue supporting her. The Mishnah teaches that although normally a husband who must support his wife receives her finds to prevent bad feelings between them (note 4), here that is not a consideration, since there are in any case bad feelings between them (*Tiferes Yisrael,* from Gemara).

[6]

1. When a person borrows money, a document is written saying that the borrower owes this amount of money to the lender. This document is signed by witnesses and kept by the lender. When the loan is repaid, the document is returned to the borrower. When such a document is lost and then found, we do not know whether the lender lost it before it was paid, or whether the borrower lost it after getting it back from the lender.

משניות בבא מציעא / פרק א: שנים אוחזין

[ו] מָצָא שִׁטְרֵי חוֹב, אִם יֵשׁ בָּהֶן אַחֲרָיוּת נְכָסִים, לֹא יַחֲזִיר, שֶׁבֵּית דִּין נִפְרָעִין מֵהֶן. אֵין בָּהֶן אַחֲרָיוּת נְכָסִים, יַחֲזִיר, שֶׁאֵין בֵּית דִּין נִפְרָעִין מֵהֶן, דִּבְרֵי רַבִּי מֵאִיר.

— רע״ב —

(ו) אחריות נכסים. שיעבוד קרקעות שינגבה מהם: לא יחזיר. דחיישינן לפרעון ולקנוניא, שמא שטר פרוע הוא ומן הלוה נפל, והאי דקא מודה לא פרעתי, עלה על דעתו היא ביניהם, לטרוף את הלקוחות שלקחו ממנו קרקע שלא באחריות, ויחלקו ביניהם:

מָצָא שִׁטְרֵי חוֹב — If a person found loan documents, and both the lender and the borrower agree that the loans have not yet been paid,[2] **אִם יֵשׁ בָּהֶן** **אַחֲרָיוּת נְכָסִים לֹא יַחֲזִיר** — if [the documents] contain a lien on the property (land) of the borrower,[3] [the finder] should not return them to the lender. **שֶׁבֵּית דִּין נִפְרָעִין מֵהֶן** — This is because the court can collect the amount written in the document **from [the properties]** of the borrower that were later sold to someone else. We must therefore suspect that the borrower might be lying when he says that he still owes the money, so that the lender will be able to collect those properties from the buyers, and then divide them with him.[4] **אֵין בָּהֶן אַחֲרָיוּת נְכָסִים יַחֲזִיר** — However, if [the documents] do *not* contain a lien on the property of the borrower, and the borrower admits that he still owes the money, then [the finder] should return them to the lender. **שֶׁאֵין בֵּית דִּין** **נִפְרָעִין מֵהֶן** — This is because the court cannot collect such a debt from [the properties] that were sold by the borrower. Since there is no concern that the buyers will lose anything and the borrower admits that he did not pay, the document should be returned to the lender so that he can collect from the borrower's unsold property.[5] **דִּבְרֵי רַבִּי מֵאִיר** — These are the words of R' Meir.

NOTES

2. If the borrower claims that he *did* pay the loan, it is obvious that the document cannot be returned to the lender, since he could then use it to collect again. Similarly, it cannot be returned to the borrower, since he might still owe the money. The Mishnah must therefore be discussing a case where the borrower admits that he has not yet paid off the loan (see Gemara 12b).

3. A lien on the borrower's property allows the lender to collect that property (if the borrower has no money to pay the debt) even if the property is later sold to someone else (see *Gittin* 5:2). However, this is only if the loan is recorded in a document (*Bava Basra* 10:8).

4. That is, we suspect that the borrower may really have paid the debt and gotten the document back from the lender and then lost it. When he realized that it was lost and had been found, he entered into a scheme with the lender to defraud the buyers by saying that he still owes the money, so that the lender should be able to collect illegally from the buyers. In exchange, the lender will give him back a portion of the illegally collected property (*Rav*, from Gemara).

The reason we suspect a fraud is that a lender is generally careful to guard his documents, since he needs them to collect his debts. Thus, when a loan document is lost, it is more likely that the borrower lost it after paying off the loan and getting back the document (see *Tos. Yom Tov*; see also *Tiferes Yisrael*).

[The Mishnah discusses a case where the borrower did not have any property of his own, and therefore the court can collect from the buyers. However, if he did have property, the document should be returned to the lender, since in this case the lender cannot collect from the buyers (*Tiferes Yisrael*).]

5. Because a lender may collect from whatever property a borrower has in

[15] MISHNAH BAVA METZIA / Chapter 1: *Shenayim Ochazin*

— רע"ב —

בֵּין כָּךְ וּבֵין כָּךְ לֹא יַחֲזִיר. דְּשֶׁטָּר שֶׁאֵין בּוֹ אַחֲרָיוּת מְמַשְׁעַבְּדֵי נַמִי גָּבֵי, דְּאַחֲרָיוּת טָעוּת סוֹפֵר הוּא, וְחַיְישִׁינַן לִפְרָעוֹן וּלְקְנוּנְיָא. וְהִלְכְתָא כְּחַכָמִים. וְדַוְקָא בִּשְׁטָר שֶׁאֵין נִזְכָּר בּוֹ אַחֲרָיוּת אָמְרוּ חֲכָמִים דְּטָעוּת סוֹפֵר הוּא, וְגָבֵי מְמַשְׁעַבְּדֵי כְּאִילוּ הָיָה הָאַחֲרָיוּת כָּתוּב בּוֹ. אֲבָל אִם פֵּירֵשׁ בַּשְּׁטָר שֶׁאֵינוֹ רוֹצֶה לְקַבֵּל עָלָיו אַחֲרָיוּת, מוֹדִים חֲכָמִים דְּיַחֲזִיר, דְּהַשְׁתָּא לֵיכָּא לְמֵיחַשׁ לִקְנוּנְיָא: (ז) דְּיַיתִיקִי. נוּחַת שְׁכִיב מְרַע. דָּא תְּהֵא לְמֵיקָם וְלִהְיוֹת. וְשׁוֹבְרִים. שֶׁטָעוּשָה מַלְוֶה לְלֹוֶה שֶׁנִפְרַע מִמֶּנּוּ שְׁטָר חוֹבוֹ:

וַחֲכָמִים אוֹמְרִים, בֵּין כָּךְ וּבֵין כָּךְ לֹא יַחֲזִיר, מִפְּנֵי שֶׁבֵּית דִּין נִפְרָעִין מֵהֶן.

[ז] **מָצָא** גִּטֵּי נָשִׁים, וְשִׁחְרוּרֵי עֲבָדִים, דְּיַתִיקִי, מַתָּנָה, וְשׁוֹבָרִים, הֲרֵי זֶה לֹא יַחֲזִיר, שֶׁאֲנִי אוֹמֵר, כְּתוּבִים הָיוּ,

---

The Sages disagree:

וַחֲכָמִים אוֹמְרִים — **But the Sages say:** בֵּין כָּךְ וּבֵין כָּךְ לֹא יַחֲזִיר — **In either case,** that is, whether the documents contain a lien or whether they do not, [the finder] should *not* return them to the lender, מִפְּנֵי שֶׁבֵּית דִּין נִפְרָעִין מֵהֶן — **because the court can collect** the debt **from [the properties]** sold by the borrower even if the document does not mention a lien.[6]

[7] The Mishnah discusses various other types of lost documents that should not be returned:

מָצָא גִּטֵּי נָשִׁים — **If someone found divorce documents,** וְשִׁחְרוּרֵי עֲבָדִים — **or freedom documents of** Canaanite **slaves,**[1] דְּיַתִיקִי — **or sickbed wills** dictated by a person close to death,[2] מַתָּנָה — **or gift** documents given by healthy people,[3] וְשׁוֹבָרִים — **or receipts** that state that a borrower has repaid a loan, הֲרֵי זֶה לֹא יַחֲזִיר — **he should not return them** to the people named in the documents,[4] שֶׁאֲנִי אוֹמֵר — **because I say** (i.e., we suspect) כְּתוּבִים הָיוּ

NOTES

his possession even without a lien. [The document can thus serve as proof to the lender's claim if the borrower later decides to deny it.]

6. According to the Sages, every loan recorded in a document is assumed to include a lien on the borrower's property even if the lien is not mentioned in the document. This is because a lender would not lend money unless he has a lien on the borrower's property. It is therefore assumed that both the lender and the borrower agreed to a lien, but the scribe forgot to write it [אַחֲרָיוּת טָעוּת סוֹפֵר] (see *Tos. Yom Tov*). [See *Bava Basra* 10:8 for why this is only true for a loan recorded in a document.]

[7]

1. These are documents given by a master to his slave to free him from slavery.

2. A person who is near death can give his property to another person with just a verbal declaration. The gift takes effect when he dies but until then he can change his mind. The Mishnah refers to a document written to serve as proof of the gift, by those who heard his declaration (see *Tiferes Yisrael*).

3. This refers to documents used to transfer a gift of land (which cannot simply be handed over).

4. That is, he should not hand the *get* (divorce document) to the wife, or give the freedom document to the slave, or the will or gift document to the people named as recipients, or give the receipt to the borrower.

וְנִמְלַךְ עֲלֵיהֶם שֶׁלֹּא לִתְּנָם.

[ח] **מָצָא** אִגְּרוֹת שׁוּם, וְאִגְּרוֹת מָזוֹן,

— רע״ב —

(ח) אגרות שום. ששמו בית דין נכסי לוה למלוה, בחובו: ואגרות מזון. שקבל עליו לזון את בת אשתו. פירוש אחר, שימכרו מקרקע הבעל למזון האשה והבנות:

וְנִמְלַךְ עֲלֵיהֶם שֶׁלֹּא לִתְּנָם — that although [these documents] were originally written to be given to the people named in them, [the writer] changed his mind and decided **not to give them**, and he then lost them. Thus, if the finder gives the documents to the people named in them, he would enable those people to misuse them and claim what is not theirs.[5] Therefore, he should not return the documents to these people.[6]

Since we do not know who lost these documents, the finder should not return them to anyone.

[8] The Mishnah lists certain types of lost documents that *should* be returned:

מָצָא אִגְּרוֹת שׁוּם — **If someone found letters of appraisal,** that is, documents that state that a borrower's land was appraised by the court and then foreclosed and given to the lender as payment for a loan;[1] **וְאִגְּרוֹת מָזוֹן** — or he found **letters of support,** that is, documents that state that the court has

— NOTES —

5. A woman is divorced only when she receives the *get* from her husband. If she simply finds it, or someone else gives it to her, she is not divorced (unless that person was the husband's agent). The same is true of a freedom document; the slave is freed by it only if he receives it from his master. If he finds it, or someone (who is not the master's agent) gives it to him, he is not freed by it. Similarly, gift documents are not effective in transferring the property unless they are given by the giver to the beneficiary of the gift. Since we do not know whether the husband or owner ever gave the document that was found, we cannot assume that the wife was divorced, or that the slave was freed or that the land was transferred.

In the case of the will of someone close to death, it is his verbal declaration that transfers the property; the document is merely a record of what he said. Nevertheless, since he can cancel the gift at any point before he dies, we suspect that he may have done so (and then lost the document), so that the will never took effect (see note 2). In the case of the receipt the concern is that the lender wrote the receipt to have ready to give to the borrower when he paid him, but

the borrower did not end up paying. The receipt can therefore not be returned to the borrower.

[The Mishnah speaks of a case where the writer of the document claims that he lost it and that he no longer wants to make the transaction, or the writer is unavailable and we do not know whether he changed his mind. However, if the writer says that he still wants to go through with the transaction, the document *is* given to the one who was supposed to get it (see *Tos. Yom Tov*).]

6. He should also not return them to the writer of the documents, since it is also possible that the writer *did* hand over the documents, and the recipients lost them.

[8]

1. The borrower was not able to repay the loan, so the court foreclosed on his property and gave it to the lender. Before doing so, they must appraise the land to make sure that it is valued at its fair market price. The appraisal is recorded in a document that states that the land has been given to the lender in payment of a debt (see *Rav*). The purpose of this document is to show that the lender now owns the land, so that the borrower cannot claim that it is still his (*Tos. Yom Tov*).

[17] **MISHNAH BAVA METZIA** / Chapter 1: *Shenayim Ochazin*

— רע״ב —

ומיאונין. שכותבים שְׁטָרֵי חֲלִיצָה וּמֵאוּנִין, וְשִׁטְרֵי בֵרוּרִין, וְכָל בשטר בפנינו מיאנה מַעֲשֵׂה בֵית דִּין, הֲרֵי זֶה יַחֲזִיר. פלונית בפלוני בעלה. ובקטנה שהשיאוה אמה ואחיה, שאינה צריכה גט: שטרי בירורין. זה בורר לו אחד וזה בורר לו אחד שידועו להם:

---

sold land from a man's estate in order to support his wife and daughters;[2] שְׁטָרֵי חֲלִיצָה — or he found **documents** that state that a woman has received *chalitzah*;[3] וּמֵאוּנִין — or he found documents that record a marriage being dissolved through the act of *mi'un*;[4] וְשִׁטְרֵי בֵרוּרִין — or he found documents concerning the **selection** of judges for a monetary case;[5] וְכָל מַעֲשֵׂה בֵית דִּין — or he found documents that record any other **act of the court**;[6] הֲרֵי זֶה יַחֲזִיר — the law in all these cases is that **[the finder] should return** the documents to the people who are supposed to have received them. This is because these documents are all issued by a court, and a court writes them only when the events recorded in the documents actually take place. Thus, it is clear that these documents were actually given to the people who were supposed to receive them and were then lost by those people. We therefore return the documents to them.[7]

— NOTES —

2. One of the obligations a man has to his wife is that if he dies, she and their young daughters receive support from his estate (see *Kesubos* 4:11-12). If the heirs refuse to pay, the court authorizes the wife to sell some of the property of the estate to pay for this support. The court writes a document to show that she has the right to sell the property (*Rav*, second explanation; *Rambam Commentary*).

3. If a man dies without children, there is a mitzvah for his brother to marry the widow (*yibum*). If he does not wish to marry her, he must perform the procedure of *chalitzah* (*removal of the shoe*) with her, to permit her to marry someone else (*Deuteronomy* 25:5-9). Once this procedure is performed, the court writes a document for the woman as proof that *chalitzah* was done.

4. Under Biblical law, a girl under the age of 12 may be married off by her father. If the father dies, the Rabbis authorized her mother and brothers to marry her off (so that she will not be taken advantage of by others). Since this marriage is only Rabbinically valid, the Rabbis said that if at any point the girl wishes to leave the marriage, she does not need a *get*. She must merely state this wish in front of the court, and she is no longer married. This procedure is known as *mi'un* (literally, *refusal*). The court then gives her a document stating that *mi'un* has taken place, and she is free to marry another man (*Tiferes Yisrael, Rashi*).

5. Monetary cases are judged by a court of three (*Sanhedrin* 1:1). This does not need to be done before a regular court. If the litigants agree, they may each select one judge and have those two judges choose a third judge (*Rav;* see *Sanhedrin* 4:1). The court then writes a document stating whom the litigants chose, to prevent them from later changing their minds (*Rashi* 20a ד״ה זה).

6. This refers to various types of court orders involving the collection of debts. For example, the court issued a lender a warrant to seize the borrower's land for his loan (*Meiri,* from Gemara 16b; see there and *Tos. Yom Tov* for an additional example).

7. The documents listed in the previous Mishnah, however, may have been written some time *before* the actual event. It is therefore possible that the writer then changed his mind, and then lost them without ever using them (*Tos. Yom Tov* ד״ה אגרות שום, citing *Rashi*).

משניות בבא מציעא / פרק א: שנים אוחזין

מָצָא בַחֲפִיסָה אוֹ בִדְלֻסְקְמָא תַּכְרִיךְ שֶׁל שְׁטָרוֹת אוֹ אֲגֻדָּה שֶׁל שְׁטָרוֹת, הֲרֵי זֶה יַחֲזִיר.

— רע״ב —

מצא. שטרות: בחפיסה: חמת של עור קטנה: **ודלוסקמא:** כלי עור שהזקנים מניחים בה כלי תשמישם שלא יטרחו לחפש אחריהם: **ותכריך של שטרות:** שלשה שטרות או יותר כרוכין זה בזה: **ואגודה.** מושכבים זה על זה, ארכו של זה על ארכו של זה: **הרי זה יחזיר.** דדבר שיש בו סימן הוא. שהכלי סימן כשיאמרו הבעלים בכלי פלוני מונחת אותם, וכן תכריך ואגודה סימן הוא:

The Mishnah now teaches about cases where even the documents listed in the previous Mishnahs (such as divorce and loan documents) should be returned:

מָצָא בַחֲפִיסָה אוֹ בִדְלֻסְקְמָא — **If someone found** documents **in a small leather bag**[8] **or in a large leather box**,[9] תַּכְרִיךְ שֶׁל שְׁטָרוֹת — **or he found a roll of documents**, i.e., several documents wrapped around one another,[10] אוֹ אֲגֻדָּה שֶׁל שְׁטָרוֹת — **or he found a bundle of documents**, i.e., a stack of several documents rolled together,[11] הֲרֵי זֶה יַחֲזִיר — **he should return** them to the person who correctly identifies what type of container they were in, or the way in which they were rolled.[12] For example, if loan documents were found and the lender gives the correct description, the documents are returned to him. If the borrower gives the correct description, they are returned to him.[13]

When identifying a "bundle" of documents, it is not enough to just say how they are rolled. The person must also know the number of documents in the roll, as the Mishnah will now explain:

NOTES

8. The Mishnah refers to a specific type of leather container normally used to store wine (*Rashi* 20b ד״ה חמת). The person found this type of container in the street, and there were documents in it.

9. This refers to a box usually used by elderly people to hold their regular utensils, so that they can easily find them (*Rav*).

10. The innermost document is rolled up like a scroll, and the next one is rolled up around it. A third document is then rolled up around the second one (*Rav*, as explained by *Tos. Yom Tov*).

11. The documents are placed down one on top of the other and then rolled together into a single roll (see *Rav*). [Each coil of the roll is thus made up of all the documents.]

12. It is unusual for people to store documents in wine flasks or containers used by elderly people for their utensils. Thus, these features are considered a *siman* (identifying mark) and it can be assumed that the one who knows them is the correct owner (*Tos. Yom Tov*, in explanation of *Rav*). Similarly, multiple documents are not usually rolled together in the ways described in the Mishnah (*Rashi* ibid.). Thus, the way in which the documents are rolled is also considered a *siman*, and the one who can identify it can be assumed to be the one who lost it. This is the law for all lost items, as we will learn in the next chapter.

13. Normally, we cannot return a lost document to either party because we do not know if the debt was paid or not (see Mishnah 6 note 1). However, where one of the parties can identify the unusual way in which the document was rolled or stored, we can safely assume that he was the one who lost it.

Similarly, if a woman can correctly identify the unusual way in which her *get* was rolled or stored, this proves that she *did* in fact receive the document and is divorced. Thus, the concern that the husband wrote it and then decided not to give it (see Mishnah 7) does not apply (see *Meiri*).

[19] **MISHNAH BAVA METZIA** / Chapter 1: *Shenayim Ochazin*

— רע״ב —

וְכַמָּה אֲגֻדָּה שֶׁל שְׁטָרוֹת, שְׁלֹשָׁה קְשׁוּרִין זֶה בָּזֶה. רַבָּן שִׁמְעוֹן בֶּן גַּמְלִיאֵל אוֹמֵר, אֶחָד הַלֹּוֶה מִשְּׁלֹשָׁה, יַחֲזִיר לַלֹּוֶה; שְׁלֹשָׁה הַלֹּוִין מֵאֶחָד, יַחֲזִיר לַמַּלְוֶה. מָצָא שְׁטָר בֵּין שְׁטָרוֹתָיו,

אחד הלוה משלשה. אם שלשה שטרות של לוה אחד הן, שלוה משלשה בני אדם, יחזירם המוצא ללוה, דודאי מידו נפלו, שאם מיד נפלו, מי קבלם למקום אחד.

ודוקא שהשטרות מקויימים בבית דין, אבל [אם] אינם מקויימים, חיישינן דלמא לקיומינהו הוליכום שלשה המלוים אצל סופר הדיינים, ונפלו מיד הסופר. ואין לחוש שמא לאחר שקיימו אותם נפלו מיד הסופר, דלא משהי אינש קיומיה בידא דספרא. ואם שלשה לויים הם, שלוו מאדם אחד, יחזירם המוצא למלוה, שהדבר ידוע שממנו נפלו. ואם היו שלשתן כתיבת סופר אחד, חיישינן שמא מיד הסופר נפלו, ולא לוו מעולם, ולפיכך לא יחזיר: מצא שטר בין שטרותיו ואינו יודע מה טיבו. אלמא, אם הלוה הפקידו אצלו או המלוה, או שמא מקלטו פרוע ומסרוהו לו להיות שליש ביניהם:

וְכַמָּה אֲגֻדָּה שֶׁל שְׁטָרוֹת — **How many** documents must there be in **the bundle of documents?** שְׁלֹשָׁה קְשׁוּרִין זֶה בָּזֶה — **Three** documents or more **bound to one another** by being rolled together. The owner must know how many documents were in the bundle in addition to knowing that they were rolled as a "bundle."[14]

In certain cases a bundle (or roll) of documents can be identified by the nature of the documents themselves:

רַבָּן שִׁמְעוֹן בֶּן גַּמְלִיאֵל אוֹמֵר — **Rabban Shimon ben Gamliel says:** אֶחָד הַלֹּוֶה מִשְּׁלֹשָׁה יַחֲזִיר לַלֹּוֶה — **If** someone found three loan documents, and all three loans were from **one** person **who borrowed from three** different people, **he should return** the documents **to the borrower.** Three lenders would not have had their documents rolled together. Thus, these documents must have fallen from the borrower, who repaid the loans and received the documents back from the lenders. He then rolled them together and lost them. The same logic can also be applied to the opposite case: שְׁלֹשָׁה הַלֹּוִין מֵאֶחָד יַחֲזִיר לַמַּלְוֶה — If the three documents are about **three** people **who borrowed from one** lender, [the finder] should return them **to the lender.** Had the borrowers lost them, they would not have been rolled together. Rather, all three documents must have been in the possession of the single lender who rolled all his unpaid documents together.

The Mishnah discusses cases where one finds documents in his possession, but does not remember why he has them:

מָצָא שְׁטָר בֵּין שְׁטָרוֹתָיו — **If someone found a document** regarding another

---- NOTES ----

14. Because only both of these identifications together are considered a *siman* (see *Rashi* 20b ד״ה שטרי; but see *Tos. Yom Tov*).

When a person finds a lost item and wishes to return it, he makes an announcement about his find, so that the one who lost it will come to him and identify it (see introduction to Chapter 2). Since a person who finds documents must announce that he found "documents" (in the plural), it is obvious that there are at least two of them. Thus, knowing the number of documents is a proof only where there are at least three documents, and the owner provides the correct number (*Tos. Yom Tov*). [The same is true for a "roll" of documents (see *Rav* ד״ה ותבריך).]

משניות בבא מציעא / פרק א: שנים אוחזין

וְאֵינוֹ יוֹדֵעַ מַה טִיבוֹ, יְהֵא מֻנָּח עַד שֶׁיָּבוֹא אֵלִיָּהוּ. אִם יֵשׁ עִמָּהֶן סִמְפּוֹנוֹת, יַעֲשֶׂה מַה שֶּׁבַּסִּמְפּוֹנוֹת.

— רע״ב —

יהא מונח. בידו, ולא יחזיר לא לזה ולא לזה: אם יש עמהן סמפון. המולא בין שטרותיו שובר שנכתב על אחד

משטרותיו: יעשה מה שבסמפון. והשטר בחזקת פרוע. ואף על פי שהיה ראוי לשובר זה להיות מונח ביד הלוה ולא ביד המלוה, אמרינן האמינו הלוה למלוה, ואמר, למחר תנהו לי, ושכח. והוא שמצא המלוה השטר הזה שנכתב עליו השובר, בין השטרות קרועים, אף על פי שלא נקרע:

---

person's loan **among his** own **documents,** וְאֵינוֹ יוֹדֵעַ מַה טִיבוֹ — **and he does not know its status;** that is, he does not remember if the loan was not paid and the lender gave it to him to hold, or if it *was* paid and the borrower received the document and then deposited it with him, or if only part of the loan was paid and the borrower and lender both agreed that he should hold the document until the loan was fully paid.[15] יְהֵא מֻנָּח עַד שֶׁיָּבוֹא אֵלִיָּהוּ — **The law is that [the document] should be set aside until** the Prophet **Eliyahu comes** and tells us what happened.[16] The finder should not return it to either the lender or the borrower because he does not know to whom it really belongs.

Another case where one finds unknown documents in his possession:

אִם יֵשׁ עִמָּהֶן סִמְפּוֹנוֹת — **If** one finds that **there are receipts among [his documents],** that is, he had loan documents regarding money that he lent, and among them was a receipt that stated that one of the debts was paid, and he does not remember if indeed the debt was paid or not, יַעֲשֶׂה מַה שֶּׁבַּסִּמְפּוֹנוֹת — **he should do whatever is** written **in the receipts** and he should consider those loans for which there are receipts as paid.[17]

NOTES

15. When a borrower repays part of a loan, he does not want the lender to keep the original loan document because he could then present it in court and collect the *entire* debt from him. On the other hand, the lender does not want to return the document to the borrower, because the borrower could then claim that he paid the *entire* debt. It was therefore customary in such a case to deposit the document with a third person, who would ensure that the debt was fully paid before giving the document back to the borrower (*Rav*).

16. Eliyahu HaNavi will come right before the Final Redemption to announce the coming of the Messiah. At that time he will clarify all unresolved halachic questions.

17. Although if the loan had been paid the receipt should have been in the possession of the borrower, not the lender, it is possible that when the borrower came to repay the loan, the receipt was not ready and he trusted the lender to give it to him the next day. In the end the borrower forgot to get the receipt, which is why it is still in the lender's possession (*Rav*).

[The Mishnah discusses a case where the lender found the original loan document together with documents that were torn because they were paid. We therefore assume that this document was also paid, as the receipt states. But if the document was not with torn documents, we assume it was *not* paid even though there was a receipt (*Rav*, from Gemara).]

Chapter Two

The second chapter of *Bava Metzia* deals with the mitzvah of returning a lost object to its owner. The Torah states (*Deuteronomy* 22:1-3): *You shall not see your brother's ox or his sheep getting lost and turn away from them; you must return them to your brother. If your brother is not close to you, and you do not know him, you shall gather it into your house, and it shall be with you until your brother comes looking for it, and you shall return it to him. So shall you do for his donkey, so shall you do for his garment, and so shall you do for any lost object of your brother, which will be lost from him and you will find it; you may not turn away.*

In order to be able to return a lost item to its owner, the finder must make a public announcement (הַכְרָזָה) about what he found, so that the owner will know that it was found and where he can claim it.

Before returning a lost object to someone, we must be sure that it is really his. The person claiming the object must therefore be able to identify it by describing some unusual mark or feature on it, which only the owner is likely to know. Such an identifying mark is known as a סִימָן, *siman*. A standard item that has no unusual mark on it does not need to be returned, since it is not possible for the owner to identify it.

Once the owner of a lost object gives up hope of getting it back, it becomes ownerless (*hefker*) and it is permissible for anyone who finds the object to keep it. [Giving up hope is known as יֵאוּשׁ, *ye'ush*.][1]

NOTES

1. It is for this reason that the finder may keep an object that has no *siman* on it. Since the owner will not be able to identify it, he gives up hope of getting it back, which makes it permissible for anyone to take it (*Rav* and *Rashi* to Mishnah 1).

משניות בבא מציעא / פרק ב: אלו מציאות

[א] **אֵלוּ** מְצִיאוֹת שֶׁלּוֹ, וְאֵלּוּ חַיָּב לְהַכְרִיז. אֵלוּ מְצִיאוֹת שֶׁלּוֹ. מָצָא פֵּרוֹת מְפֻזָּרִין, מָעוֹת מְפֻזָּרוֹת, כְּרִיכוֹת בִּרְשׁוּת הָרַבִּים, וְעִגּוּלֵי דְבֵלָה, כִּכָּרוֹת שֶׁל נַחְתּוֹם, מַחֲרוֹזוֹת שֶׁל דָּגִים, וַחֲתִיכוֹת שֶׁל בָּשָׂר, וְגִזֵּי צֶמֶר הַבָּאוֹת מִמְּדִינָתָן, וַאֲנִיצֵי פִשְׁתָּן,

— רע״ב —

פרק שני—אלומציאות. (א) אלו מציאות. מצא פירות מפוזרים. סתמן נתייאשו הבעלים, והפקר הם: מעות מפוזרות. הואיל ואין להם סימן ניכר [כבד] מיאושי מיאשי והפקר כן. והיינו טעמא דכלהו: ברשות הרבים. שהכל דשין עליהם, ואפילו היה בהן סימן, נפסד: של נחתום. אין בהם סימן, שכולם שוים, אבל של בעל הבית יש להם סימן: הבאות ממדינתן. לאפוקי הבאות מבית האומן, כדקתני סיפא: עמרים קטנים: ברשות

---

[1] If someone finds a lost object, there are times when he must announce what he found and try to return it to its owner, and there are times when he may keep it for himself (see the introduction to this chapter). The first Mishnah lists items that a finder may keep and does not have to announce:

וְאֵלוּ — אֵלוּ מְצִיאוֹת שֶׁלּוֹ — Which found objects are [the finder's] to keep, חַיָּב לְהַכְרִיז — and which found objects **must he announce** and try to return to their owner? אֵלוּ מְצִיאוֹת שֶׁלּוֹ — These are the found objects that [a finder] may keep: מָצָא פֵּרוֹת מְפֻזָּרִין — If he found **scattered produce**, מָעוֹת מְפֻזָּרוֹת — or **scattered coins** (which have no *siman*),[1] כְּרִיכוֹת בִּרְשׁוּת הָרַבִּים — or he found **small bundles** of grain-stalks **in a public place** (where they get kicked or stepped on by the people passing by, and lose any *siman* they may have), וְעִגּוּלֵי דְבֵלָה — or **round cakes of pressed figs**,[2] כִּכָּרוֹת שֶׁל נַחְתּוֹם — or **loaves** of bread **from a baker**,[3] מַחֲרוֹזוֹת שֶׁל דָּגִים — or **strings of fish**, וַחֲתִיכוֹת שֶׁל בָּשָׂר — or **slices of meat**,[4] וְגִזֵּי צֶמֶר הַבָּאוֹת מִמְּדִינָתָן — or **fleeces** of raw **wool that come from the province** without having been processed,[5] וַאֲנִיצֵי פִשְׁתָּן — or ordinary **bundles of flax** fibers,[6]

NOTES

[1]
1. [Fruits and vegetables have no *siman* of their own. Nevertheless, if they are stacked or bundled together, the way in which are they stacked, or the place where they were left, can serve as a *siman*.] Once they are scattered, they have no *siman* and the owner gives up hope of getting them back (*Rav*). The same is true for coins.
2. In Mishnaic times it was common for people to dry figs and press them into round "cakes" [which made them convenient to store or carry on a trip] (*Tiferes Yisrael*). Since everyone did this the same way, they generally had no *siman*.
3. Breads made in a bakery all look the same and have no *siman*. Homemade loaves, however, are different from one another and are thus identifiable, as we will learn in the next Mishnah (*Rav, Rashi*).
4. Fishermen would tie a standard number of fish onto one string. Slices of meat were also of a standard shape and weight (*Meleches Shlomo*, from Gemara 23b).
5. [That is, from the countryside in that district, where the sheep are raised and their wool is sheared.] All the raw wool in that area looks the same and has no *siman*. Once the wool is given to a craftsman to process, however, he makes a sign in each batch to identify whose wool it is (*Tiferes Yisrael*).
6. That is, flax that has been broken apart and combed into fibers but has not yet been spun into linen thread (*Tiferes Yisrael*).

— רע"ב —

ולשונות של ארגמן.
נמר לבוע ארגמן ומשוך
כמין לשון: מצא עיגול.
של דבלה:

וּלְשׁוֹנוֹת שֶׁל אַרְגָּמָן, הֲרֵי אֵלּוּ שֶׁלּוֹ; דִּבְרֵי רַבִּי מֵאִיר. רַבִּי יְהוּדָה אוֹמֵר, כָּל שֶׁיֵּשׁ בּוֹ שִׁנּוּי חַיָּב לְהַכְרִיז. כֵּיצַד, מָצָא עִגּוּל וּבְתוֹכוֹ חֶרֶס, כִּכָּר וּבְתוֹכוֹ מָעוֹת.

הֲרֵי אֵלּוּ שֶׁלּוֹ — **all of these are his** to keep, because they have no *siman,* and their owner gives up hope of getting them back;[8] וּלְשׁוֹנוֹת שֶׁל אַרְגָּמָן — or "**tongues**" **of purple wool**,[7] דִּבְרֵי רַבִּי מֵאִיר — these are **the words of R' Meir.**

According to R' Meir, even if there is something irregular about these objects that might serve as a *siman,* if the irregularity could have occurred on its own (as in the following cases), so that the owner may not have known about it, it is not considered a *siman,* and the finder may keep the objects. The next Tanna disagrees:

רַבִּי יְהוּדָה אוֹמֵר — **R' Yehudah says:** כָּל שֶׁיֵּשׁ בּוֹ שִׁנּוּי חַיָּב לְהַכְרִיז —**Anything that has some irregularity in it,** [the finder] **must announce** in public and return it to its owner, even if the irregularity may have occurred on its own and not through the owner. כֵּיצַד — **For example,** מָצָא עִגּוּל וּבְתוֹכוֹ חֶרֶס — if **he found a round cake** of pressed figs **with a** piece of **pottery in it,** כִּכָּר וּבְתוֹכוֹ מָעוֹת — or **a loaf** of bread **from a baker with coins in it,** he must announce his find and try to return it to the owner. Although it is quite possible that the broken piece of pottery got stuck in the cake of pressed figs without the owner's knowledge, and that the coins fell into the dough accidentally,[9] R' Yehudah considers these things a *siman,* since the owner *might* be aware of them and use them to identify the lost cake or loaf. Therefore, the finder must announce these items and try to return them to the owner.[10]

---------- NOTES ----------

7. Wool that had been combed and dyed purple was rolled into long wads called "tongues" (because of their tongue-like shape). These were common in those days [and could not be identified one from the other] (*Rav, Rashi*).

8. Since all of these items have no *siman,* even if they are found the owner cannot identify them, and he gives up hope of ever getting them back. They therefore become ownerless (*hefker*) and the finder may keep them (*Rav, Rashi*). [In the case of the small bundles found in a public place, even if they still do have a *siman,* the finder may keep them. Since the owner knows that they will get stepped on and kicked around, he does not expect the *siman* to remain in place and he therefore gives up hope of getting them back (see *Tos. R' Akiva Eiger*).]

A finder may keep something only if the owner gave up hope of getting it back *before* he found it. In all of these cases it can be assumed that the owner already knew that he lost the item and gave up hope before the finder picked it up, either because they are valuable and the owner is always checking on them, or because they are bulky and heavy, so that he soon notices when they are missing (*Tos. Yom Tov,* from Gemara 21b-22b).

9. It would be very unusual for a person to put a broken piece of pottery into his cake of figs, or to put coins into his bread. It is more likely that these fell in without the owner's knowledge (*Tiferes Yisrael*).

10. R' Meir, however, is of the opinion that we assume that the owner was unaware of these things. Since there is no other identifying mark, he gives up hope of getting the items back, and the finder may keep them (*Tiferes Yisrael*).

[24] משניות בבא מציעא / פרק ב: אלו מציאות

רַבִּי שִׁמְעוֹן בֶּן אֶלְעָזָר אוֹמֵר, כָּל כְּלִי אַנְפּוֹרְיָא אֵין חַיָּב לְהַכְרִיז.

[ב] **וְאֵלּוּ** חַיָּב לְהַכְרִיז, מָצָא פֵּרוֹת בִּכְלִי, אוֹ כְלִי כְּמוֹת שֶׁהוּא, מָעוֹת בְּכִיס, אוֹ כִיס כְּמוֹת שֶׁהוּא, צִבּוּרֵי פֵרוֹת, צִבּוּרֵי מָעוֹת, שְׁלֹשָׁה מַטְבְּעוֹת זֶה עַל גַּב זֶה,

— רע"ב —

אנפוריא. כלים חדשים שלא שבעתן העין, ואין לבעלים בהם טביעות עין. שפעמים שמחזירים אבדה בטביעות עינא, כגון לצורבא מרבנן דלא משני בדבוריה. ואלו הכלים שידוע שאין לבעליהן בהן טביעות עין, אינו חייב להכריז.

והלכה כרבי שמעון בן אלעזר. ואימתי בזמן שמצאן אחד אחד, אבל מצאן שנים שנים חייב להכריז, דמינכרא הוי סימן. והמוצא מליאה בסרטיא ופלטיא גדולה, בעיר שרובה עכו"ם, אפילו דבר שיש בו סימן אינו חייב להכריז, ובעיר שרובה ישראל, חייב להכריז: (ב) בכלי. וכלי יש בו סימן: כמות שהוא. ריקן: צבורי פירות. סימנא, מנין או מקום: שלשה מטבעות זה על גב זה. או יותר. והמכריז, מכריז מטבעות מצאתי, וזה בא ואומר כך וכך היו מונחים זה על זה:

The rule is that if a Torah scholar says that he recognizes a lost item as his, we return it to him even if he cannot provide any specific *siman*. This is because a Torah scholar can be trusted not to lie about recognizing an item.[11] Thus, in a place where Torah scholars live, a person who finds something must announce his find even if it has no obvious *siman*. The next Tanna will explain that even in such a place, it is not necessary to try and return every found object:

כָּל כְּלִי אַנְפּוֹרְיָא — R' Shimon ben Elazar says: רַבִּי שִׁמְעוֹן בֶּן אֶלְעָזָר אוֹמֵר — **Any new and unused vessels**, which the eye of the owner has not grown accustomed to, and which he can therefore not recognize,[12] אֵין חַיָּב לְהַכְרִיז — **[the finder] is not obligated to announce** finding them; rather, they are his to keep, even in a place where there are Torah scholars.

[2] This Mishnah lists items that a finder must announce and return to the owner because they have a *siman*.

וְאֵלּוּ חַיָּב לְהַכְרִיז — **These are the found objects that [a finder] is obligated to announce and return**: מָצָא פֵּרוֹת בִּכְלִי אוֹ כְלִי כְּמוֹת שֶׁהוּא — **If he found a utensil with produce in it, or a utensil as is**, i.e., empty;[1] מָעוֹת בְּכִיס אוֹ כִיס כְּמוֹת שֶׁהוּא — or he found **a purse with money in it, or a purse as is**, i.e., empty;[2] צִבּוּרֵי פֵרוֹת — or **piles of produce**, in which case the location of the pile of fruits or their number is considered a *siman*;[3] צִבּוּרֵי מָעוֹת, שְׁלֹשָׁה מַטְבְּעוֹת זֶה עַל גַּב זֶה — or **piles of money**, for example, **three** or more **coins** piled **one upon the**

NOTES

11. *Rav,* from Gemara 23b.

12. The term אַנְפּוֹרְיָא is a contraction of the Hebrew words אֵין פֹּה רְאִיָּה (*ein poh re'iyah*), which means, "there is no visual [recognition] here" (*Rashi* there).

[2]

1. A utensil (in this case, a container of some kind) usually has a *siman* (*Rav*). [If the utensil can be identified, the produce in it is assumed to belong to the owner of the utensil (Gemara 25a).]

2. A purse also usually has a *siman*, and any money in it is assumed to belong to the owner of the purse.

3. Since the produce is piled up and not scattered, it was certainly placed there intentionally, and its location or quantity therefore serves as its *siman* (*Rav*).

בְּרִיכוֹת בִּרְשׁוּת הַיָּחִיד, וְכִכָּרוֹת שֶׁל בַּעַל הַבַּיִת, וְגִזֵּי צֶמֶר הַלְּקוּחוֹת מִבֵּית הָאֻמָּן, כַּדֵּי יַיִן, וְכַדֵּי שֶׁמֶן, הֲרֵי אֵלּוּ חַיָּב לְהַכְרִיז.

[ג] **מָצָא** אַחַר הַגַּפָּה אוֹ אַחַר הַגָּדֵר גּוֹזָלוֹת מְקֻשָּׁרִין, אוֹ בִּשְׁבִילִין שֶׁבַּשָּׂדוֹת, הֲרֵי זֶה לֹא יִגַּע בָּהֶן.

— רע"ב —

(ג) אחר הגפה. סתימת כותל של עץ או של קנים: גדר. של אבנים: גוזלות מקושרין. בכנפיהן. דכולי עלמא הכי מקטרי להו, וקשר כזה לא הוי סימן: לא יגע בהן. דאמרינן, הני, אינש אצנעינהו, ואי שקיל להו לית להו למרייהו סימנא בגוויה, הלכך לשכינהו, עד דאתי מריייהו ושקיל להו:

---

other, in which case the location of the coins or their number is considered a *siman*;[4] בְּרִיכוֹת בִּרְשׁוּת הַיָּחִיד — or **small bundles** of grain-stalks (which have a *siman*) **in a private area,** where they are *not* kicked by people passing by and do not lose their *siman*;[5] וְכִכָּרוֹת שֶׁל בַּעַל הַבַּיִת — or **homemade loaves** of bread;[6] וְגִזֵּי צֶמֶר הַלְּקוּחוֹת מִבֵּית הָאֻמָּן — or **fleeces of** processed **wool taken from a craftsman's shop,** where each customer's fleece is tied with a unique knot that serves as its *siman*;[7] כַּדֵּי יַיִן וְכַדֵּי שֶׁמֶן — or **jugs of wine or jugs of oil,** which, though manufactured in standard sizes, are sealed shut by their owners and marked for identification;[8] הֲרֵי אֵלּוּ חַיָּב לְהַכְרִיז — all **these** are items that [a finder] **is obligated to announce** and return, because they have a *siman*, and their owner does not give up hope of getting them back.

[3] מָצָא אַחַר הַגַּפָּה אוֹ אַחַר הַגָּדֵר גּוֹזָלוֹת מְקֻשָּׁרִין — **If someone found young pigeons tied** together by their wings[1] standing **behind** a wooden **fence or a stone wall,** אוֹ בִּשְׁבִילִין שֶׁבַּשָּׂדוֹת — **or in the paths through the fields** (where not many people go), הֲרֵי זֶה לֹא יִגַּע בָּהֶן — **he should not touch them,** because it is possible that the owner put them there for safekeeping and will soon return for them.[2] Since they have no *siman*, if he takes them the owner

---

NOTES

4. Here too, a pile of coins is assumed to have been placed there by their owner, and their location or number serves as their *siman* (*Rav*; *Tos. Yom Tov*).

[If there were only two coins, even if one was lying on top of the other, they are assumed to have fallen and are treated like the scattered coins of the previous Mishnah (*Tos. Yom Tov*).]

5. For example, they were found in a planted field, which few people walk through (*Tos. Yom Tov*), so that their *siman* is not likely to be lost.

6. Literally, *loaves of a homeowner*. Homemade loaves are made differently by each person and are thus identifiable.

7. When a craftsman is given wool to process (i.e., to clean or dye), he ties a special knot around each person's fleece in order to be able to identify it. The owner of the wool thus has a *siman* with which to claim it as his own (*Meiri*).

8. The clay seal that closes the top of the jug was made with a mark in it to identify its owner (*Tos. Yom Tov*).

[3]

1. It was common to tie young pigeons together by their wings to prevent them from flying away. Thus, the fact that they were tied this way is not a *siman* (*Rav*).

2. It is not certain that the owner left them here intentionally, because these are not completely protected places. Nevertheless, it is possible that he did so, since they are somewhat protected (*Tos. Yom Tov*).

[26] **משניות בבא מציעא / פרק ב: אלו מציאות**

— רע״ב —

מָצָא כְלִי בָאַשְׁפָּה, אִם מְכֻסֶּה, לֹא יִגַּע בּוֹ, אִם מְגֻלֶּה, נוֹטֵל וּמַכְרִיז. מָצָא בְגַל וּבְכוֹתֶל יָשָׁן, הֲרֵי אֵלּוּ שֶׁלּוֹ. מָצָא בְכוֹתֶל חָדָשׁ,

מבוסה לא יגע בו. דאין זה אבידה שיהא מוזהר עליה בלא תוכל להתעלם (דברים כב,ג), דמשתמר הוא:

מצא בגל ובכותל ישן הרי אלו שלו. מפני שיכול לומר לבעל הגל ולבעל הכותל, של אמוריים שהורישו אבותינו היה. ובלבד שיהיה בו חלודה רבה, שניכר שמזמן הרבה היה טמון שם:

—————————— NOTES ——————————

will surely not be able to get them back. Therefore, it is better to leave them where they are.[3]

In the preceding case, we discussed something that was found in a place that is partially protected but not well protected. The Mishnah now discusses what to do when we find something in a place that is well protected:[4]

מָצָא כְלִי בָאַשְׁפָּה — **If he found a utensil** (which typically has a *siman*) **in a garbage heap,**[5] the law is as follows: אִם מְכֻסֶּה לֹא יִגַּע בּוֹ — **If [the utensil] is covered** in the garbage heap, and thus well protected,[6] **he should not touch it** even if it has a *siman*, because its owner probably left it there for protection and will return to get it.[7] אִם מְגֻלֶּה נוֹטֵל וּמַכְרִיז — **If, however, it is uncovered** and thus not protected, **he must take** it **and announce** what he found, because it surely was not placed there for protection but must have been lost.[8]

The Mishnah lists cases of lost items that one may keep even if they have a *siman*, and even if they were found in a well-protected place:[9]

מָצָא בְגַל וּבְכֹתֶל יָשָׁן — **If one found** items buried **in a pile** of stones from an old wall that collapsed, **or in the hole of an old wall** that is still standing, and the items show signs of age (for example, they are very rusty or corroded),[10] הֲרֵי אֵלּוּ שֶׁלּוֹ — **they are his to keep** even if they have a *siman*. He does not have to return them to the current owner of the wall.[11] מָצָא בְכֹתֶל חָדָשׁ — **If,**

—————————— NOTES ——————————

3. *Rav*. However, if they do have a *siman*, he should take them and announce his find, since it is possible that the owner lost them and does not know where to find them (*Tos. Yom Tov*).

4. *Tos. Yom Tov*.

5. The Mishnah speaks of a garbage heap that is left in place and not removed. Thus, it is a good place to hide something for a while.

[A utensil (*kli*) is anything that has been formed into an object used by people, such as a dish, cup, fork, chair, lamp, etc. It stands in contrast to an unformed object, such as a lump of clay, piece of wood, chunk of metal, or stone.]

6. Since it is hidden from sight.

7. There is no obligation to take an item and return it unless it is "lost." Since this utensil appears to have been left there intentionally and it is completely covered and protected, it is not "lost" and there is no obligation to return it (*Rav*).

Although it does have a *siman* and it *could* be taken and announced, this would just make it more difficult for the owner to get it back, since he would then have to track down the finder and give a *siman* to prove it was his. Therefore, it is better to leave it where it is (see *Rambam, Hil. Gezeilah VaAveidah* 15:1).

8. No one deliberately leaves his possessions in an open, unprotected place. We must therefore assume that the owner lost this item on the garbage heap (*Ritva*).

9. *Ritva*.

10. *Rav*, from Gemara 25b-26a.

11. The Mishnah refers to a wall in the Land of Israel, which has been standing since the time of the original conquest of

[27] MISHNAH BAVA METZIA / Chapter 2: *Eilu Metzios*

— רע״ב —

מֶחֱצָיוֹ וְלַחוּץ שֶׁלּוֹ, מֶחֱצָיוֹ וְלִפְנִים שֶׁל בַּעַל הַבָּיִת. אִם הָיָה מַשְׂכִּירוֹ לַאֲחֵרִים,

מחציו ולחוץ. בְּאֹתֶל מחורי כותל הסמוכים לרשות הרבים. אִם מָלְאָה מְחֻלֵּי טוּבְיוֹ שֶׁל כּוֹתֶל ולחוץ, שֶׁלּוֹ, דְּאַמְרִינָן אֶחָד מִבְּנֵי רְשׁוּת הָרַבִּים נְתָנוּ שָׁם, וְשָׁכַח, וְתוֹלֶדָה שֶׁטְּעָלָיו מוֹכַחַת שֶׁמִּזְּמַן הַרְבֵּה הָיָה שָׁם וּבְוַדַּאי נִתְיָאֲשׁוּ הַבְּעָלִים. וְדִין זֶה דַּוְקָא בִּלְשׁוֹן זָהָב וַחֲתִיכַת כֶּסֶף וְכַיּוֹצֵא בָזֶה. אֲבָל אִם הָיָה כְלִי וּבְתוֹכוֹ מָעוֹת, אִם פִּי הַכְּלִי לַחוּץ, הֲרֵי הוּא שֶׁלּוֹ, וְאִם פִּי הַכְּלִי לִפְנִים, הֲרֵי הוּא שֶׁל בַּעַל הַבָּיִת:

however, **he found** them **in** a hole in **a new wall**[12] that stands next to a street, the rule is as follows: מֶחֱצָיוֹ וְלַחוּץ שֶׁלּוֹ — **If they were found in the outer half of the wall,**[13] on the side closer to the street, then **they are his** to keep, because we may assume that someone traveling in the street put them in the hole, forgot where he put them, and then gave up hope of getting them back.[14]   מֶחֱצָיוֹ וְלִפְנִים שֶׁל בַּעַל הַבַּיִת — **If they were found in the inner half of the wall, they belong to the owner of the house,** because we assume that he (or the ancestor from whom he inherited the house) is the one who left them there.[15]

The Mishnah ends with a case where the finder may keep an item even if it was found inside a house:

אִם הָיָה מַשְׂכִּירוֹ לַאֲחֵרִים — **If [the owner] would** regularly **rent [this property]**

— NOTES —

the Land. Since the wall, or its remaining pile of stones, is ancient, and the found item itself shows signs of great age, the finder can claim that the item never belonged to the family that now owns the property, but was left there by the original Amorites, who lived there before the land was conquered. He is therefore allowed to keep it (*Rav*). [The same is true outside the Land of Israel, if the wall is old enough to have been there before the land was bought by Jews (*Tos. Yom Tov*).]

[The present owner of the property cannot claim that his property acquired the item for him (*kinyan chatzeir*; see Mishnah 1:4), because a person's property does not acquire for him things he may never discover on his own (*Tos. Yom Tov; Tosafos* 26a ד"ה דשתיך).]

12. That is, a wall known to have been built by a Jew after the conquest of the Land of Israel. This wall is now owned by the builder's descendants (*Tos. Yom Tov*).

13. Literally, *from the middle [of the wall] and outward.*

14. Here too, the Mishnah speaks of a case where the item shows signs of having been there for a very long time. Therefore, even if it had a *siman*, we may assume that the person who left it there has given up hope by now of ever finding it (*Rav*).

15. The Mishnah refers to a case where the owner of the house claims that the items are his, or that it is possible that they belonged to one of his ancestors from whom he inherited the house (*Tos. Yom Tov*). Although the items show signs of great age, which indicates that the original owner gave up hope of finding them, they do not become ownerless. Giving up hope (*ye'ush*) makes an item ownerless only when it is no longer in the owner's possession [or the possession of his heirs]. It does not affect an item that is still physically in his possession (*Ramban, Ran*).

The Mishnah speaks of things that could have been placed in the wall from either side. We therefore look at which side they are closer to in deciding whether they were put there by the owner of the property or by a passerby in the street. However, if the find was something like a bag of coins, which is usually held by its opening and pushed into a hole bottom first, the side that the opening faces tells us where it came from, regardless of whether it is closer to the street or the inside of the property (*Rav*).

אֲפִילוּ בְּתוֹךְ הַבַּיִת הֲרֵי אֵלּוּ שֶׁלּוֹ.

[ד] מָצָא בַּחֲנוּת הֲרֵי אֵלּוּ שֶׁלּוֹ, בֵּין הַתֵּבָה וְלַחֶנְוָנִי שֶׁל חֶנְוָנִי. לִפְנֵי שֻׁלְחָנִי הֲרֵי אֵלּוּ שֶׁלּוֹ, בֵּין הַכִּסֵּא וְלַשֻּׁלְחָנִי הֲרֵי

— רע"ב —

אפילו בתוך הבית הרי אלו שלו. דלא ידע דמאן נינהו, ובעליו נואשו: (ד) מצא בחנות הרי אלו שלו. בדבר שאין בו סימן מיירי, דהווה דנפל מיניה מייאש, שהכל ככנסים

לשם: **בין תיבה.** שהחנווני יושב לפניו, ותמיד נוטל ממנה ונותן לפניו לפני ומוכר, ומעות שנותנין לו נותן בתוכה, ולא נפל שום דבר אלא מיד חנווני: **לפני שולחני הרי אלו שלו.** דאמרינן מן הבאים להחליף מעות נפלו, שהרי השלחן מפסיק בין שולחני למעות שנמצאו, ואם מן השולחני הם, היה להם להמלא בינו ולכסא שהשלחן מונח עליו:

---

to others, and the last renter was not a Jew, **אֲפִילוּ בְּתוֹךְ הַבַּיִת הֲרֵי אֵלּוּ שֶׁלּוֹ** — even if items were found **inside the house** itself, **they are [the finder's] to keep**, because he may assume that they were left there by the last renter, who was not a Jew.[16]

[4] This Mishnah discusses the law regarding items that a person finds in a store, at a moneychanger's booth, or in merchandise that he bought:

מָצָא בַחֲנוּת הֲרֵי אֵלּוּ שֶׁלּוֹ — If **someone found** money or any other item that has no *siman* **in a store, it is his** to keep, because a store is open to the public and anyone who lost something there certainly gave up hope of getting it back, since it has no *siman*.[1] **בֵּין הַתֵּבָה וְלַחֶנְוָנִי שֶׁל חֶנְוָנִי** — If he found it **between the case and the storekeeper,** where it must have fallen from the storekeeper, it belongs to **the storekeeper.**[2] **לִפְנֵי שֻׁלְחָנִי הֲרֵי אֵלּוּ שֶׁלּוֹ** — Similarly, if someone found coins **in front of a moneychanger,**[3] that is, in front of the table at which he sits, **they are [the finder's]** to keep, because it can be assumed that they fell from someone who came to exchange money. Since coins have no *siman,* the person who dropped them gave up hope of getting them back.[4] **בֵּין הַכִּסֵּא וְלַשֻּׁלְחָנִי הֲרֵי**

NOTES

16. Each renter usually checks the house before he leaves to make sure that he did not forget anything. The finder may therefore assume that the item was lost by the last person there (see *Shekalim* 7:2), who, in this case, was not a Jew (*Tos. Yom Tov*).

[4]

1. He cannot hope to get it back from the store, because many people enter a store and can pick up the lost item; therefore, he can only hope to get it back if one of the customers will announce finding it and he will identify it. But since it has no *siman*, he cannot identify it, and he thus gives up hope of getting it back (*Rav*). This makes it permissible for the finder to keep it. [See Mishnah 3 note 11.]

2. The stores of those days were arranged differently than our stores. The storekeeper kept his merchandise in a large case or chest, from which he would take out the items requested by the customers. The storekeeper sat *in front* of the case, between it and the customers. After being paid, he would put the money in the case. Thus, whatever items were found between him and the case must have fallen from him (see *Rav, Rashi*). [These are not "lost" because they are still in the storekeeper's possession (see Mishnah 3 note 15).]

3. Someone who exchanges coins of different denominations for a small fee. The moneychanger sat on one side of a table and his customers stood across it and placed the coins they wished to exchange on the table (*Rashi* 26b).

4. Since the area in front of the table is

[29] **MISHNAH BAVA METZIA** / Chapter 2: *Eilu Metzios* — 2/4

— רע״ב —

הלוקח פירות מחבירו
וכו׳. וכגון שחבירו זה
תגר, שלקח תבואה זו
או פירות הללו מאנשים
הרבה, ולא ידיע דמאן
נינהו, וכיון דלית

אֵלּוּ לַשֻּׁלְחָנִי. הַלּוֹקֵחַ פֵּרוֹת מֵחֲבֵרוֹ, אוֹ
שֶׁשָּׁלַח לוֹ חֲבֵרוֹ פֵּרוֹת, וּמָצָא בָהֶן מָעוֹת,
הֲרֵי אֵלּוּ שֶׁלּוֹ. אִם הָיוּ צְרוּרִין, נוֹטֵל
וּמַכְרִיז.

בהו סימן נתיאשו הבעלים. אבל אם זה שמכר את הפירות לקטן הוא עצמו מן הקרקע שלו,
שודאי המעות הללו שלו הן, חייב להחזיר: **ואם היו צרורים**. הקשר או מנין שלהם הוי סימן:

אֵלּוּ לַשֻּׁלְחָנִי — **If,** however, he found coins **between the stool** (upon which the moneychanger's table was placed) **and the moneychanger,** that is, he found the coins behind the table at which the moneychanger sits, **they belong to the moneychanger,** because they must have fallen from him and not from a customer.

הַלּוֹקֵחַ פֵּרוֹת מֵחֲבֵרוֹ — **If someone buys produce from his friend,** and the friend is a merchant who buys produce from different farms and then sells it, **אוֹ שֶׁשָּׁלַח לוֹ חֲבֵרוֹ פֵּרוֹת** — **or his friend sent him produce** as a gift, **וּמָצָא בָהֶן מָעוֹת** — **and he found coins in [the produce],**[5] **הֲרֵי אֵלּוּ שֶׁלּוֹ** — **they belong to him** (the buyer or receiver) because there is no way of knowing from which farmer the merchant got this bundle of produce. Since the coins have no *siman,* the owner of the coins certainly gave up hope of getting them back, and the finder may keep them. **אִם הָיוּ צְרוּרִין** — However, **if [the coins] were tied in a bundle,** in which case they have a *siman* and can be identified by their owner,[6] **נוֹטֵל וּמַכְרִיז** — **[the finder] must take** them **and announce** his find, and return them to their owner.[7]

[5] The verse regarding the mitzvah of returning a lost object states (*Deuteronomy* 22:1-3): *You shall not see your brother's ox or his sheep wandering and turn away from them; you must return them to your brother... So shall you do for his donkey, so shall you do for his garment, and so shall you do for any lost object of your brother, which will be lost from him and you will find it; you may not turn away.*

Since the verse says that *any* lost article must be returned to its owner, why does it list his "garment" specifically? The Mishnah explains what this teaches:[1]

NOTES
---

open to the public, anyone can pick up the coins. The person who lost them therefore does not expect to get them back, since they have no *siman* (*Rav*).

5. The bundle of fruits or vegetables had some coins in it.

6. For example, by their number or by the type of knot used to tie the bundle (*Rav*).

7. In this case the owner does not give up hope of getting them back, because he hopes the finder will announce what he has found and he will then go and get them.

[5]

1. The same question can be asked about the other items mentioned in the verse. Our Mishnah focuses on the "garment" because it is from this example that we learn about returning an item based on a *siman* and about not having to return an item if the owner has given up hope of getting it back. The Gemara (27a) explains what we learn from the other items mentioned in the verse.

משניות בבא מציעא / פרק ב: אלו מציאות [30]

[ה] אַף הַשִּׂמְלָה הָיְתָה בִּכְלַל כָּל אֵלֶּה. לָמָּה יָצָאת, לְהַקִּישׁ אֵלֶיהָ, לוֹמַר לְךָ, מַה שִּׂמְלָה מְיֻחֶדֶת, שֶׁיֵּשׁ בָּהּ סִימָנִים וְיֵשׁ לָהּ תּוֹבְעִים, אַף כָּל דָּבָר שֶׁיֵּשׁ בּוֹ סִימָנִים וְיֵשׁ לוֹ תּוֹבְעִים חַיָּב לְהַכְרִיז.

[ו] וְעַד מָתַי חַיָּב לְהַכְרִיז, עַד כְּדֵי שֶׁיֵּדְעוּ בּוֹ שְׁכֵנָיו, דִּבְרֵי רַבִּי מֵאִיר.

— רע״ב —

(ה) בכלל כל אלה. בכלל כל אבדת אחיך (דברים כב,ג): ולמה יצאת. וכן תעשה לשמלתו (שם): מה שמלה מיוחדת. סתם שמלה יש בה סימן, וכל שמלה יש לה בעלים תובעים אותה, שנתעסק בידי אדם ולא באת מן ההפקר: אף כל שיש לו תובעים. למטוטי מידי דמייאש. וייאוש הוא

דסמטעיניה דאמר וי ליה לחסרון כיס. (ו) שכניו. שכני מקום שנמצאת בו האבידה, שמא שלהן היא:

אַף הַשִּׂמְלָה הָיְתָה בִּכְלַל כָּל אֵלֶּה — The "garment," too, was included in the rule of all of these "lost objects of your brother," which the Torah commands us to return. לָמָּה יָצָאת — Why then was it singled out in the verse? לְהַקִּישׁ אֵלֶיהָ — To compare all lost articles to [garments], לוֹמַר לְךָ מַה שִּׂמְלָה מְיֻחֶדֶת — to tell you that just as a garment is unique שֶׁיֵּשׁ בָּהּ סִימָנִים וְיֵשׁ לָהּ תּוֹבְעִים — in that it has *simanim* (identifying marks) and it has owners who will claim it as their own,[2] which is why a person who finds it is required to announce his find and return it to its owner if he can identify its *siman*, אַף כָּל דָּבָר שֶׁיֵּשׁ בּוֹ סִימָנִים וְיֵשׁ לוֹ תּוֹבְעִים חַיָּב לְהַכְרִיז — so, too, with any lost article that has *simanim* and has owners who can claim it as their own, [the person] who finds it is required to announce his find and return it to its owner if he can identify its *siman*.[3]

[6] The Mishnah discusses how long a person must announce finding a lost item:

וְעַד מָתַי חַיָּב לְהַכְרִיז — Until when must a person who found a lost item announce that he found it?[1] עַד כְּדֵי שֶׁיֵּדְעוּ בּוֹ שְׁכֵנָיו — Until the neighbors who live in the area where the item was found know about it.[2] דִּבְרֵי רַבִּי מֵאִיר —

--- NOTES ---

2. A typical garment has some unusual mark on it by which it can be identified. Moreover, since it is man-made, it generally has an owner who will be looking to claim it (*Rav*).

3. We learn from the example of "garment" that even if the lost object has a *siman*, if it no longer has an owner who is looking to get it back, there is no obligation to announce the find. Thus, if we know that the owner gave up hope of getting it back [for example, we heard him say, "Woe for the loss I suffered"], there is no need to announce it (*Rav*). The item is now considered ownerless, and whoever finds it can keep it. Similarly, in cases where it can be assumed that the owner gave up hope of getting it back, the item is considered ownerless and may be kept by whoever finds it.

[6]

1. If someone announced that he found a lost item but no one came to claim it, how long must he continue to announce it? (*Meiri*).

2. [Although it is possible that the item was lost by someone who was passing through this area and does not live here, the Torah required a person to announce his find only to the people who live in the area where it was found] because of the possibility that it belongs to one of them

[31] **MISHNAH BAVA METZIA** / Chapter 2: *Eilu Metzios*

רַבִּי יְהוּדָה אוֹמֵר, שָׁלשׁ רְגָלִים, וְאַחַר הָרֶגֶל הָאַחֲרוֹן שִׁבְעָה יָמִים, כְּדֵי שֶׁיֵּלֵךְ לְבֵיתוֹ שְׁלֹשָׁה, וְיַחֲזֹר שְׁלֹשָׁה, וְיַכְרִיז יוֹם אֶחָד.

[ז] **אָמַר** אֶת הָאֲבֵדָה, וְלֹא אָמַר סִימָנֶיהָ,

— רע"ב —

כדי שילך כל אחד לביתו בשלשה ימים. משישמע ההכרזה, וידע אם אבד לו כלום, ואם יראה שאבד, יחזור שלשה, ויכריז יום אחד אני אבדתי ואלו סימניה. והלכה כרבי יהודה. ומשחרב בית המקדש התקינו שיהיו מכריזין בבתי כנסיות ובבתי מדרשות. ומשרבו האנסין דאמרי אבידתא למלכא, התקינו שיהא מודיע לשכניו ולמיודעיו, ודיו:

These are **the words of R' Meir.** רַבִּי יְהוּדָה אוֹמֵר — **R' Yehudah says:** שָׁלשׁ רְגָלִים — He must announce it in Jerusalem during each of the **three festivals** of the year (Pesach, Shavuos, and Succos), when most Jews are in Jerusalem,[3] וְאַחַר הָרֶגֶל הָאַחֲרוֹן שִׁבְעָה יָמִים — **and** he must then wait in Jerusalem **after the final festival**[4] another **seven days,** כְּדֵי שֶׁיֵּלֵךְ לְבֵיתוֹ שְׁלֹשָׁה וְיַחֲזֹר שְׁלֹשָׁה וְיַכְרִיז יוֹם אֶחָד — to give someone who heard the last announcement **enough** time **to travel home for three** days, check his belongings for missing items, **travel back** to Jerusalem **for three** days, **and announce** what he lost with its *siman* **for one day,** so that he can get it back from the one who found it.[5]

[7] Someone who finds a lost item must make sure he is returning it to its true owner. The Mishnah explains how he goes about doing this: אָמַר אֶת הָאֲבֵדָה וְלֹא אָמַר סִימָנֶיהָ — **If he** (the person who claims he lost it) **said** what **the lost object** was, **but he did not say** what **its** *simanim* are,

---

NOTES

(*Rav*, *Rashi*). Therefore, once all the residents in that area have heard the announcement, there is no need to continue announcing it.

3. According to R' Yehudah, the Torah requires someone who finds a lost item to announce it to all of Israel. This is done by making an announcement in Jerusalem during the festivals of Pesach, Shavuos, and Succos, when all Jews are obligated to go to the Temple to celebrate these festivals (see *Deuteronomy* 16:16). Although people sometimes miss going for one or two festivals, everyone is likely to come at least once a year. Therefore, the announcement must be made three festivals in a row (*Meiri*).

There was a special place in Jerusalem designated for announcing lost items (*Gemara* 28b).

4. That is, after the third festival in which he announces finding the item (*Tiferes Yisrael*). [The announcement made clear that this was the third and last festival during which this item would be announced (*Gemara* 28a).]

5. He does not have to wait in Jerusalem an extra seven days after the first two festivals because the person who discovers that he lost something knows that he can wait until the next festival to reclaim his item (*Gemara* 28a-28b).

Although there were parts of Eretz Yisrael that were more than three days journey from Jerusalem, the Sages did not burden the finder to wait longer than seven days after the festival (*Tos. Yom Tov,* from *Gemara* 28a).

Today, when there is no Temple, a finder need only announce a lost item in the synagogue of the community or among his friends and neighbors (see *Rav*).

משניות בבא מציעא / פרק ב: אלו מציאות

לֹא יִתֵּן לוֹ. וְהָרַמַּאי אַף עַל פִּי שֶׁאָמַר סִימָנֶיהָ לֹא יִתֵּן לוֹ, שֶׁנֶּאֱמַר, עַד דְּרשׁ אָחִיךָ אֹתוֹ, עַד שֶׁתִּדְרשׁ אֶת אָחִיךָ אִם רַמַּאי הוּא אִם אֵינוֹ רַמַּאי.

כָּל דָּבָר שֶׁעוֹשֶׂה וְאוֹכֵל יַעֲשֶׂה וְיֹאכַל,

— רע״ב —

(ז) כל דבר שעושה ואוכל. אם האבדה דבר שיכולים להאכילו את שכר מעשיו, כגון שור וחמור: יעשה ויאכל. ולא ימכור אותו המוצא, שכל אדם נוח לו בבהמתו שהכירה בו כבר [ולימדה] לרצונו.

ואינו חייב להטפל בה לעולם, אלא תרנגולת ובהמה גסה, מטפל בה שנים עשר חדש. עגלים וסייחים של רעיה, כלומר שאין מגדלים אותם לפטם, וכן גדיים וטלאים, מטפל בהם שלשה חדשים. ועגלים של פטם, מטפל בהם שלשים יום. אווזין ותרנגולים זכרים, הקטנים, מטפל בהן שלשים יום, והגדולים שאוכלים

לֹא יִתֵּן לוֹ — [the finder] should not give it to him;[1] **וְהָרַמַּאי** — and if the claimant is known to be **a dishonest person**, **אַף עַל פִּי שֶׁאָמַר סִימָנֶיהָ** — even if he said what its *simanim* are, **לֹא יִתֵּן לוֹ** — [the finder] should not give it to him, because we suspect he may have had knowledge of his neighbor's item and is now using that information dishonestly.[2] **שֶׁנֶּאֱמַר "עַד דְּרשׁ אָחִיךָ אֹתוֹ"** — As the verse states (*Deuteronomy* 22:2): *and it shall be with you until your brother comes looking for it, and you shall return it to him.*[3] This is expounded to mean: **עַד שֶׁתִּדְרשׁ אֶת אָחִיךָ אִם רַמַּאי הוּא אִם אֵינוֹ רַמַּאי** — Do not return the item **until you look into the** nature of **your brother,** to see **whether he is a dishonest person or not.**[4] If he is an honest person and provides its *simanim*, return it to him; but if he is a dishonest person, even if he provides its *simanim*, do not return it to him.[5]

Someone who finds a lost item is obligated to take care of it until the owner comes for it. However, he does not have to lose money by taking care of it; rather, the owner must reimburse him for any expenses. The Mishnah explains what should be done to prevent the expenses from consuming the value of the found object:

כָּל דָּבָר שֶׁעוֹשֶׂה וְאוֹכֵל — Any found **item that works and eats,** for example, an ox or a donkey, whose work is worth the cost of its care, **יַעֲשֶׂה וְיֹאכַל** —

NOTES

[7]

1. When a finder announces that he found something, he must specify what type of item it is. For example, if he found a shirt, he must announce that he found a shirt, and he may not simply say, "I found a lost item." Obviously, if someone comes to him and says, "I lost a shirt," the finder does not give it back to him since the person was merely repeating what the finder announced. What the Mishnah means is that even if the person provided a general description of the shirt (for example, he specified its color), but he could not provide a more specific *siman* (for example, its size), the finder should not give it to him (*Tos. R' Akiva Eiger*, from Gemara 28b).

2. See *Rashi* 28b ד״ה חיישינן לרמאי.

3. See the introduction to this chapter.

4. The Torah could have said *and it shall be with you,* without adding *until your brother comes looking for it.* Obviously, you cannot give it to him until he comes for it! The verse is therefore expounded to mean that it is *you* (the finder) who must look into your brother (who is claiming the lost item) before giving it back to him (Gemara 27b; *Rashi* ד״ה דרשהו).

5. Such a person can get back his item only if he has witnesses who say that it is his (*Tiferes Yisrael*).

[33] MISHNAH BAVA METZIA / Chapter 2: *Eilu Metzios*

וְדָבָר שֶׁאֵין עוֹשֶׂה וְאוֹכֵל, יִמָּכֵר, שֶׁנֶּאֱמַר, וַהֲשֵׁבֹתוֹ לוֹ, רְאֵה הֵיאַךְ תְּשִׁיבֶנּוּ לוֹ. מַה יְּהֵא בַדָּמִים, רַבִּי טַרְפוֹן אוֹמֵר, יִשְׁתַּמֵּשׁ בָּהֶן, לְפִיכָךְ אִם אָבְדוּ חַיָּב בְּאַחֲרָיוּתָן.

— רע״ב —

הרבה, מטפל בהן שלשה ימים. מכאן ואילך, לוקח אותם הוא לעצמו בשומא כפי שוויין, או מוכרן לאחרים, ומניח הדמים אצלו: לפיכך אם אבדו חייב באחריותן. כיון

דשרו ליה רבנן לאשתמושי בהו, אף על גב דלא אשתמש בהו, כמאן דאשתמש דמי, וחייב באחריותן. והלכה כרבי טרפון בדמי אבדה של אבדה, כגון שמלא מעות בכיס או שלש מטבעות זו על גב זו, לא ישתמש בהם כלל:

---

should work to earn its keep, **and eat** from what it produces.[6] **וְדָבָר שֶׁאֵינוֹ עוֹשֶׂה וְאוֹכֵל** — However, a found **item that does not work but eats,** for example a rooster or a calf, which cannot earn their keep,[7] **יִמָּכֵר** — **should be sold,** and the money received in payment should be returned to the owner when he comes to claim the item. **שֶׁנֶּאֱמַר ״וַהֲשֵׁבֹתוֹ לוֹ״** — **As the verse states** (*Deuteronomy* 22:2): **and you shall return it to him,** which means, **רְאֵה הֵיאַךְ תְּשִׁיבֶנּוּ לוֹ** — **see how you can** best **return it to him,** without causing him a loss.[8]

The Mishnah discusses what the finder may do with the money he receives from selling the lost item, until the owner comes to claim it:

רַבִּי טַרְפוֹן אוֹמֵר **מַה יְּהֵא בַדָּמִים** — **What may be done with the money? יִשְׁתַּמֵּשׁ בָּהֶן** — **R' Tarfon says: [The finder] may use it** for his own needs and then give his own money to the owner when he comes to claim what he lost;[9] **לְפִיכָךְ אִם אָבְדוּ חַיָּב בְּאַחֲרָיוּתָן** — **therefore, if [the money] was lost** before he could return it, even if it was lost accidentally, **[the finder] is responsible for it** and he must pay the owner from his own money.[10]

— NOTES —

6. If someone found an ox or a donkey, he should hire them out and use the money to pay for their food. [Similarly, if he found chickens that lay eggs, he should sell the eggs to pay for their food.] He should not sell the items he found and return the money to the owner, because the owner would rather get back the animal he trained than have to buy a new one (*Rav*).

He does not have to maintain these arrangements indefinitely. After a certain amount of time, depending on what the item is, he may sell it and hold the money for the owner. See *Rav*.

7. In which case the finder would have to spend money to feed them, and they would not produce anything in return.

8. [If the expense of feeding the animal will cost as much as the animal is worth, the finder is not giving anything back to the owner when he comes to claim it, since the owner will have to reimburse the finder for his expenses.] Indeed, even if the expenses add up to more than half of the animal's worth, the finder should sell the animal instead of feeding it, because returning an item that is worth less than half its value is not considered "returning it" (*Rashi* 28b).

9. In exchange for the trouble of caring for the item and then selling it (when caring for it became too expensive), the Rabbis gave the finder permission to use the money for his own needs until the owner comes for it (*Tos. Yom Tov*).

10. Normally, someone who is caring for a lost object is not responsible for any accidents that happen to it while it is in his care (as will be explained in the next note). In our case, however, since the Rabbis granted him the right to *use* the

רַבִּי עֲקִיבָא אוֹמֵר, לֹא יִשְׁתַּמֵּשׁ בָּהֶן, לְפִיכָךְ אִם אָבְדוּ אֵין חַיָּב בְּאַחֲרָיוּתָן.

[ח] מָצָא סְפָרִים, קוֹרֵא בָּהֶן אַחַת לִשְׁלֹשִׁים יוֹם, וְאִם אֵינוֹ יוֹדֵעַ לִקְרוֹת גּוֹלְלָן. אֲבָל לֹא יִלְמַד בָּהֶן בַּתְּחִלָּה, וְלֹא יִקְרָא אַחֵר עִמּוֹ.

רַבִּי עֲקִיבָא אוֹמֵר לֹא יִשְׁתַּמֵּשׁ בָּהֶן — R' Akiva says: He may not use the money for his own needs; לְפִיכָךְ אִם אָבְדוּ אֵינוֹ חַיָּב בְּאַחֲרָיוּתָן — therefore, if it was lost accidentally, he is not responsible for it.[11]

[8] As part of his obligation to return the lost item to its owner, the finder must make sure that it does not become damaged while in his possession. The Mishnah gives some examples of what a finder must do to protect the item from damage that comes from long-term storage:

מָצָא סְפָרִים קוֹרֵא בָּהֶן אַחַת לִשְׁלֹשִׁים יוֹם — If he found books (i.e., scrolls), he should read through them once every thirty days to air them out;[1] וְאִם אֵינוֹ יוֹדֵעַ לִקְרוֹת גּוֹלְלָן — and if he does not know how to read, he should roll them from end to end once every thirty days. אֲבָל לֹא יִלְמַד בָּהֶן בַּתְּחִלָּה — However, he may not study in them any text that he is learning for the first time, since he will then keep the scroll open longer than necessary, which might lead to its damage.[2] וְלֹא יִקְרָא אַחֵר עִמּוֹ — Even if he is just reading through it, another person may not read from it together with him, because each person might pull the scroll in his direction and cause it to tear.[3]

— NOTES —

money he received from selling the item, he is treated as a "borrower" [שׁוֹאֵל] in regard to that money. A borrower must pay even for losses that could not have been prevented [אֳנָסִים; see introduction to Chapter 3] (Rav; Tos. Yom Tov, from Gemara).

11. According to R' Akiva, the Rabbis did not give the finder the right to use the money he received from selling the item he found. Therefore, the finder is no more responsible for the money than he was for the lost item itself. The law for someone who is caring for an item that he found is that he is treated either as a paid shomer [שׁוֹמֵר שָׂכָר], who is responsible for loss and theft but not for accidents, or as an unpaid shomer [שׁוֹמֵר חִנָּם], who is responsible only for negligence. This is the subject of a dispute in the Gemara (29a-29b). But according to both of these opinions, he is not responsible for accidents.

[8]

1. In the times of the Mishnah, books were written on scrolls [like our Sifrei Torah and Megillos] (Rav). If they were left unopened for a long time, they would begin to decay. To prevent this, someone who finds a scroll must open it and roll it out from end to end to expose every part of it to the air (Rav). The Rabbis permitted him to do this by reading through it once every thirty days, even though this might cause some wear and tear (Meiri).

2. Rav. [This is true for Books of Scripture (Tanach). However, with books of Gemara, the more a person knows of a text, the more deeply he goes into it the next time he reads it. Therefore, even if he has studied this volume before, he may not read through a book of Gemara that he found (Tos. Yom Tov, Nimukei Yosef).]

3. This is so only if they are reading the

[35] **MISHNAH BAVA METZIA** / Chapter 2: *Eilu Metzios*

— רע"ב —

מָצָא כְסוּת, מְנַעֲרָהּ אַחַת לִשְׁלֹשִׁים יוֹם,
וְשׁוֹטְחָהּ לְצָרְכָּהּ, אֲבָל לֹא לִכְבוֹדוֹ. כְּלֵי כֶסֶף
וּכְלֵי נְחֹשֶׁת, מִשְׁתַּמֵּשׁ בָּהֶן לְצָרְכָּן, אֲבָל לֹא
לְשָׁחֳקָן. כְּלֵי זָהָב וּכְלֵי זְכוּכִית, לֹא יִגַּע בָּהֶן
עַד שֶׁיָּבֹא אֵלִיָּהוּ. מָצָא שַׂק אוֹ קֻפָּה, וְכָל דָּבָר
שֶׁאֵין דַּרְכּוֹ לִטֹּל, הֲרֵי זֶה לֹא יִטֹּל.

שׁוֹטְחָהּ לְצָרְכָּהּ. לְשַׁלּוֹט בָּהּ אֲוִיר שֶׁלֹּא תֹאכְלֶנָּה עָשׁ: לְצָרְכָּן. שֶׁמִּתְעַפְּשִׁים בַּקַּרְקַע שֶׁצָּרִיךְ לִתְּנָן בַּקַּרְקַע דְּזוּ הִיא שְׁמִירָתָן. וּלְפִיכָךְ מִשְׁתַּמֵּשׁ בָּהֶם לִפְרָקִים: אֲבָל לֹא לִשְׁחָקָן. וְלֹא יִשְׁתַּמֵּשׁ בָּהֶן זְמַן אָרוֹךְ עַד שֶׁיִּשְׁחֲקוּ: לֹא יִגַּע בָּהֶן.

זָהָב אֵינוֹ מִתְעַפֵּשׁ בָּאָרֶץ, וְכֵן זְכוּכִית. וְעוֹד שֶׁהוּא נֹחַ לְהִשָּׁבֵר: שֶׁאֵין דַּרְכּוֹ לִיטֹּל. דָּבָר שֶׁגְּנַאי הוּא לוֹ. וְהַתּוֹרָה אָמְרָה וְהִתְעַלַּמְתָּ מֵהֶם (דברים כב,ג), פְּעָמִים שֶׁאַתָּה מִתְעַלֵּם, כְּגוֹן זָקֵן וְאֵינוֹ לְפִי כְבוֹדוֹ:

לִשְׁלֹשִׁים יוֹם אַחַת מְנַעֲרָהּ כְּסוּת מָצָא — **If he found a garment, he must shake it out once every thirty days,** לְצָרְכָּהּ וְשׁוֹטְחָהּ — **and spread it out** over a bed or table **for its benefit,** i.e., to let the air get to all parts of the garment and prevent it from decaying and becoming moth-eaten;[4] לִכְבוֹדוֹ לֹא אֲבָל — but he may **not** do so **for his own honor,** i.e., to decorate his home.

נְחֹשֶׁת וּכְלֵי כֶסֶף כְּלֵי — **If he found silver utensils or copper utensils,** which need to be stored in the ground to protect them from being stolen,[5] and which may therefore become corroded if they are left there too long, בָּהֶן מִשְׁתַּמֵּשׁ לְצָרְכָּן — **he may use them** occasionally **for their needs,** as often as necessary to keep them from being ruined,[6] לְשָׁחֳקָן לֹא אֲבָל — **but not** to the extent that he **wears them down.** זְכוּכִית וּכְלֵי זָהָב כְּלֵי — However, if he found **gold utensils or glass utensils,** which do not corrode in the ground, and which are (in the case of glass) breakable, אֵלִיָּהוּ שֶׁיָּבֹא עַד בָּהֶן יִגַּע לֹא — **he should not touch them** once they are stored in the ground, **until the Prophet Eliyahu comes** and reveals the identity of their owner.[7]

The Mishnah now teaches that there are cases where a person does not have to pick up a lost object and try to return it:

לִטֹּל דַּרְכּוֹ שֶׁאֵין דָּבָר וְכָל קֻפָּה אוֹ שַׂק מָצָא — **If he found a sack,** a large **container, or any** other **object that it is not his practice to pick up,** because it is beneath his dignity to be seen carrying such an item,[8] יִטֹּל לֹא זֶה הֲרֵי — **he does not have to pick** it **up** and return it to its owner.[9]

NOTES
---

same passage. If they are reading different passages, this is not a concern [because they can unroll the scroll enough for both to read comfortably] (Gemara 29b, as explained by *Rashi*).

4. *Rav; Rashi* 29b.

5. The Gemara (42a) states that valuables can be protected properly only by being buried in the ground (*Rav; Rashi*).

6. These types of utensils need to be used to prevent them from becoming corroded (*Meiri*; cf. *Tosafos* 30a ד"ה לצורכן).

7. That is, if the owner does not come forward and identify them, he should leave them buried in the ground until Eliyahu HaNavi comes and identifies the owner (see above, 1:8 note 16).

8. That is, he would not pick it up and carry it through the street even if it was his own, because it is embarrassing for him to be seen carrying it.

9. This is learned from the verses that state (*Deuteronomy* 22:1,3): *You shall not see the ox of your brother or his sheep*

[ט] **אֵיזוֹ** הִיא אֲבֵדָה, מָצָא חֲמוֹר אוֹ פָּרָה רוֹעִין בַּדֶּרֶךְ אֵין זוֹ אֲבֵדָה, חֲמוֹר וְכֵלָיו הֲפוּכִין, פָּרָה רָצָה בֵּין הַכְּרָמִים, הֲרֵי זוֹ אֲבֵדָה. הֶחֱזִירָהּ וּבָרְחָה, הֶחֱזִירָהּ וּבָרְחָה, אֲפִלּוּ אַרְבָּעָה וַחֲמִשָּׁה פְעָמִים, חַיָּב לְהַחֲזִירָהּ, שֶׁנֶּאֱמַר, הָשֵׁב תְּשִׁיבֵם.

— רע"ב —

(ט) איזו היא אבדה. שנכר בה שאין הבעלים יודעים שהיא שם: אין זו אבדה. ואינו חייב להחזיר, שמדעת הניחוה שם: רצה בין הכרמים. שמתקלקלים רגליה: השב תשיבם. התורה רבתה השבות הרבה:

---

[9] If someone finds an animal roaming around, he does not necessarily have to take it and return it, since it may not be lost. The owner may have left it out to graze, knowing that it will come back on its own or that he will know where to find it. The Mishnah teaches what signs show that an animal is indeed lost:

מָצָא אֵיזוֹ הִיא אֲבֵדָה — **What is** considered **lost** in the case of an animal? חֲמוֹר אוֹ פָּרָה רוֹעִין בַּדֶּרֶךְ אֵין זוֹ אֲבֵדָה — **If he found a donkey or a cow grazing by** the side of **the road, this is not** considered **a lost** [animal] and he does not have to take it and return it, because the owner probably left it there to graze. חֲמוֹר וְכֵלָיו הֲפוּכִין פָּרָה רָצָה בֵּין הַכְּרָמִים — If, however, he found **a donkey with its gear out of place,**[1] or **a cow running through the vineyards,** where its feet will get bruised by the vines,[2] הֲרֵי זוֹ אֲבֵדָה — **this is** a sign that it is **a lost** [animal], and the finder must return it to the owner, since it is clear that the owner does not know where it is.

How many times must one return an animal?

הֶחֱזִירָהּ וּבָרְחָה הֶחֱזִירָהּ וּבָרְחָה — **If someone returned [a lost animal]** to its owner **and it ran away** again, **and he returned it** to the owner a second time, **and it ran away** again, אֲפִלּוּ אַרְבָּעָה וַחֲמִשָּׁה פְעָמִים חַיָּב לְהַחֲזִירָהּ — **even if** this happened **four or five times, he is obligated to return it** again, שֶׁנֶּאֱמַר "הָשֵׁב תְּשִׁיבֵם" — **because the verse states:** *You must surely return them to your brother* (Deuteronomy 22:1). This teaches that there is no limit to the number of times a finder must return a lost object to its owner.[3]

— NOTES —

getting lost and turn away from them; you must return them to your brother ... and so shall you do for any lost object of your brother ... you may not turn away. Since the last verse says clearly that a person who sees a lost item may not ignore it ("you may not turn away"), it seems unnecessary for the first verse to have said this as well ("You shall not see ... and turn away from them"). The Gemara therefore explains that when the first verse says "and turn away from them," it means to imply that there are times when you *may* turn away. For example, if the finder is a Torah scholar or an elderly man, for whom it is embarrassing to be seen carrying such an item in the street — and he would not do it for himself — he need not pick it up and carry it to return to someone else (*Rav*).

[9]

1. For example, if its saddle had slipped down and was hanging from its belly instead of resting on its back (*Meiri*).

2. *Rav*.

3. The word הָשֵׁב, *return*, is absolute; it does not imply any limits. Thus, it teaches that the finder must return the found item as many times as necessary, even

— רע"ב —

הָיָה בָּטֵל מִסֶּלַע לֹא יֹאמַר לוֹ, תֵּן לִי
סֶלַע, אֶלָּא נוֹתֵן לוֹ שְׂכָרוֹ כְּפוֹעֵל בָּטֵל.
אִם יֵשׁ שָׁם בֵּית דִּין, מַתְנֶה בִּפְנֵי בֵּית דִּין.

לא יאמר לו תן לי
סלע. שזה אומר לו,
אם עשית מלאכתך היית
מרבה טורח, עכשיו לפי
מה שטרחת כפועל
בטל. כמה אדם רוצה ליטול ולפחות משכרו לבטל ממלאכה זו כדבר שהוא עוסק בה, ולעשות
במלאכה קלה כזו: אם יש שם בית דין. אם אינו רוצה לבטל ממלאכתו שׁשְּׂכָרָהּ מרובה, מה יעשה.
אם יש שם שלשה בני אדם, מתנה בפניהם ואומר, ראו שאני משתכר כך וכך, ואי אפשי לבטל ליטול
שכר מועט, אם תאמרו שאטול שכרי משלם, אטפל בהשבת אבדה זו:

We learned in Mishnah 7 that the owner must pay the finder for any expenses he had in caring for the item. Likewise, the owner must compensate the finder for any loss of income he suffers while returning the item.[4] The Mishnah explains how much the owner must pay the finder for his lost income:

הָיָה בָּטֵל מִסֶּלַע — **If [the finder] stopped** doing his job, **from** which he could have earned **a sela,** in order to return an object to its owner, לֹא יֹאמַר לוֹ תֵּן לִי סֶלַע — **[the finder] may not say to [the owner]: "Give me** the entire *sela* that I lost." אֶלָּא נוֹתֵן לוֹ שְׂכָרוֹ כְּפוֹעֵל בָּטֵל — **Rather, [the owner] may give him his wage like a worker who stopped** doing a difficult job in order to perform an easier job, such as returning a lost item.[5]

The above is true if the finder, like most people, is willing to be paid less and perform an easier job. The Mishnah now discusses the law in a case where the finder would rather work hard and earn more:

אִם יֵשׁ שָׁם בֵּית דִּין — **If there is a court** of three available,[6] and the finder claims that instead of returning the item and earning less, he would rather work hard at his own job and earn more, מַתְנֶה בִּפְנֵי בֵּית דִּין — **he may declare before the court** that he is willing to return the item to the owner only if the owner compensates him for his entire loss. If he then returns the item to the owner, he may demand the full amount from the owner.

NOTES

as many as one hundred times (*Tos. Yom Tov*, from *Rambam Commentary*, from Gemara 31a; see, however, *Rav*). ["Four or five times" is just the Mishnah's way of saying "over and over again" (*Tos. Yom Tov*).]

The Mishnah teaches that although the animal may have run away because of its owner's negligence, this does not exempt the finder from his obligation to return it (*Tiferes Yisrael*).

4. For example, he found a lost animal and he had to stop working to go and catch the animal and return it to the owner, or bring it back to his own barn where he could keep it safely until the owner came for it.

5. For example, the finder was hired to do a difficult job (such as lifting heavy loads) for which he is being paid a *sela* (four *dinars*). Most people would be willing to take an easier job (such as returning an animal to its owner) for two *dinars* rather than have to work so hard for four *dinars*. In this case, the finder may not demand the four *dinars* that he loses by neglecting his difficult job and returning the item; rather, he may demand only two *dinars* for the "work" of returning the lost item (*Rav*).

6. That is, three people [who can serve as a temporary court for his declaration]. They need not be regular judges (see *Rav; Aruch HaShulchan* 265:4).

אִם אֵין שָׁם בֵּית דִּין, בִּפְנֵי מִי יַתְנֶה, שֶׁלּוֹ קוֹדֵם.

[י] מְצָאָהּ בְּרֶפֶת, אֵינוֹ חַיָּב בָּהּ; בִּרְשׁוּת הָרַבִּים, חַיָּב בָּהּ. וְאִם הָיְתָה בֵּית הַקְּבָרוֹת, לֹא יִטַּמֵּא לָהּ. אִם אָמַר לוֹ אָבִיו, הִטַּמֵּא,

— רע״ב —

שלו קודם. ומניח את האבדה: (י) מצאה ברפת. אף על פי שאינה משתמרת בה כגון שאינה נעולה: ואם היתה בבית הקברות. והוא כהן:

לא יטמא לה. שהשבת אבדה עשה, השב תשיבם לאחיך (דברים כב,א), ובטומאת כהן עשה דקדושים יהיו (ויקרא כא,ו) ולא תעשה דלנפש לא יטמא בעמיו (שם א), ואין עשה דוחה את לא תעשה ועשה:

אִם אֵין שָׁם בֵּית דִּין בִּפְנֵי מִי יַתְנֶה — **If**, on the other hand, **there is no court** of three available, **before whom should he make this declaration?** שֶׁלּוֹ קוֹדֵם — In such a case, since there is no way for him to collect full compensation, **his** own financial concerns **come before** those of **others,** and he need not take off from his job to return the item.[7]

[10] The Mishnah continues its discussion of when an animal is considered lost:

מְצָאָהּ בְּרֶפֶת אֵינוֹ חַיָּב בָּהּ — **If he found [the animal] in an** unlocked **barn, he is not obligated to** take **it** and return it to its owner, even though it is not properly guarded, because he can assume that the owner knows it is there and will come back for it himself.[1] בִּרְשׁוּת הָרַבִּים חַיָּב בָּהּ — **If,** however, he found it wandering **on the public roads, he is obligated to** take **it** and return it to its owner.[2]

The Mishnah lists other factors that affect whether or not a person is obligated to return a lost item to its owner:

וְאִם הָיְתָה בֵּית הַקְּבָרוֹת — **If [the animal],** or any other item, **was in a cemetery**,[3] לֹא יִטַּמֵּא לָהּ — **[a Kohen],** who is forbidden to become *tamei* from a human corpse or a grave,[4] **may not** enter the cemetery and **become *tamei* to take it** to return to the owner.[5] אִם אָמַר לוֹ אָבִיו הִטַּמֵּא — **If [the Kohen's] father told him, "Become *tamei* and**

— NOTES —

7. A person does not have to lose money to save the money of another person (see Mishnah 11). Hence, he need not spend time returning a lost item if he will not be compensated for his loss.

[10]

1. *Rav; Aruch HaShulchan* 261:3. If the barn is locked, the animal is obviously not considered lost and there is no reason for the Mishnah to say that he should leave it where it is. The Mishnah speaks of a case where the barn is not fully guarded [for example, the barn door is unlocked (*Rashi* 32a, *Rav*)], so that the animal can get out, but there is nothing pushing the animal to leave the barn [for example, there is still enough food there for it (*Ritva*)]. The Mishnah teaches that in

such a case the animal is not considered lost (Gemara 32a; see *Tos. Yom Tov*).

2. The last Mishnah taught that an animal running in the vineyards is considered lost. This Mishnah adds that if it is roaming aimlessly in a public area and it appears lost, one is also obligated to return it (see *Tos. Yom Tov*).

3. In which case it is considered lost.

4. See *Leviticus* 21:1.

5. A positive commandment usually overrides a negative commandment [עֲשֵׂה דּוֹחֶה לֹא תַעֲשֶׂה]. It might therefore be thought that the positive commandment to return a lost item overrides the negative commandment that prohibits a Kohen to become *tamei*. The Mishnah therefore teaches that a Kohen is exempt in this

[39] **MISHNAH BAVA METZIA** / Chapter 2: *Eilu Metzios*

— רע"ב —

או שאמר לו אל
תחזיר. והאבידה במקום
שמלוה להחזיר, הרי זה לא
ישמע לו, דכתיב (שם יט,ג)
איש אמו ואביו תיראו
ואת שבתותי תשמרו, שאם אביך אומר לך חלל את השבת אל תשמע לו. וכן בשאר כל המצות:

אוֹ שֶׁאָמַר לוֹ, אַל תַּחֲזִיר, לֹא יִשְׁמַע לוֹ. פָּרַק וְטָעַן, פָּרַק וְטָעַן, אֲפִילוּ אַרְבָּעָה וַחֲמִשָּׁה פְעָמִים, חַיָּב, שֶׁנֶּאֱמַר, עָזֹב תַּעֲזֹב.

return the item," i.e., go into the cemetery and get the lost item so that you can return it to its owner,[6] **אוֹ שֶׁאָמַר לוֹ אַל תַּחֲזִיר** — or if, in the case of an item that was found anywhere, [the finder's father] told him, "Do not return the item," **לֹא יִשְׁמַע לוֹ** — he should not listen to [his father], because a son may not violate a law of the Torah to listen to his father.[7]

The Mishnah now mentions two other obligations similar to returning a lost item, which a person must also fulfill "even four or five times."[8] These are the obligation to help unload an animal that has collapsed under its load, and the obligation to help an owner reload an animal whose load has come off:[9]

פָּרַק וְטָעַן פָּרַק וְטָעַן — If someone saw an animal sitting under its load, and he **unloaded** its burden and stood the animal up, **and** then he **loaded** it back onto the animal, but it sat down again under its load, and **he unloaded** its burden a second time, stood the animal up **and** then again **loaded** it back onto the animal, **אֲפִילוּ אַרְבָּעָה וַחֲמִשָּׁה פְעָמִים חַיָּב** — **even** if this happened **four or five times, he is obligated** to unload it and load it again, **שֶׁנֶּאֱמַר "עָזֹב תַּעֲזֹב"** — because the verse states: *you must surely help* (to unload the animal), which teaches that one is obligated to do so over and over again, as many times as necessary.[10]

— NOTES —

case, because the prohibition for him to become *tamei* is based on both a positive commandment (see *Leviticus* 21:6) and a negative commandment (see v. 1 there). A positive commandment cannot override a negative commandment that has a positive commandment with it (*Rav*).

6. Thus, he now has two positive commands pushing him to become *tamei* — the mitzvah to return a lost item and the mitzvah to obey his father's command.

7. The Torah states (*Leviticus* 19:3): *Every man — your mother and your father you shall fear, and My Shabbos you shall observe; I am Hashem.* The phrase, *I am Hashem,* teaches that God's honor, for example, observing His Shabbos or any of His other mitzvos (such as those mentioned in our Mishnah), takes precedence over the honor of one's parents (*Rav; Tos. Yom Tov*). [Thus, the mitzvah to obey a father's command cannot override a prohibition.]

8. *Meiri,* introduction to this chapter.

9. The Torah states that when someone sees a person's animal collapsed under its load, he is obligated to assist the owner in unloading the burden from the animal. This is referred to as פְּרִיקָה, *unloading* (see *Exodus* 23:5). Similarly, if he sees that bundles of goods have fallen off an animal, he is obligated to help the owner reload the fallen items. This is referred to as טְעִינָה, *loading* (see *Deuteronomy* 22:4).

10. The verse states: *If you see the donkey of your enemy sitting under its load, would you refrain from helping him? You must surely help, with him* (*Exodus* 23:5). The command to help implies no limits; you must do it as many times as necessary (*Tos. Yom Tov; Rambam Commentary* to Mishnah 9).

Similarly, the verse in *Deuteronomy* 22:4 states: *You shall not see the donkey of your brother or his ox falling on the*

הָלַךְ וְיָשַׁב לוֹ, וְאָמַר, הוֹאִיל וְעָלֶיךָ מִצְוָה, אִם רְצוֹנְךָ לִפְרֹק פְּרֹק, פָּטוּר, שֶׁנֶּאֱמַר, עִמּוֹ. אִם הָיָה זָקֵן אוֹ חוֹלֶה, חַיָּב. מִצְוָה מִן הַתּוֹרָה לִפְרֹק, אֲבָל לֹא לִטְעֹן. רַבִּי שִׁמְעוֹן אוֹמֵר, אַף לִטְעֹן.

Having mentioned the obligations of helping someone unload and reload his animal, the Mishnah teaches several additional details about these obligations: הָלַךְ וְיָשַׁב לוֹ וְאָמַר — If [the owner] of the animal that was collapsed under its load **walked away** from the animal, **sat himself down, and said** to a passerby: הוֹאִיל וְעָלֶיךָ מִצְוָה אִם רְצוֹנְךָ לִפְרֹק פְּרֹק — "**Since there is a mitzvah upon you** to unload my animal, **if you want to unload it, unload** it on your own, while I sit here and watch," פָּטוּר — [the passerby] **is exempt** from unloading the animal, שֶׁנֶּאֱמַר "עִמּוֹ" — **because that verse states:** *You must surely help with him,* which implies that you are only obligated to help along with him (the owner). If he refuses to do anything, you are not obligated to do it on your own. אִם הָיָה זָקֵן אוֹ חוֹלֶה חַיָּב — **If,** however, [the owner] **was an elderly or a sickly man,** who is unable to help, [the passerby] **is obligated** to unload or load the animal on his own.[11]

The Mishnah cites a dispute about the extent of the obligations to unload and load:

מִצְוָה מִן הַתּוֹרָה לִפְרֹק — **It is a Biblical commandment** to help **unload** an animal that has collapsed under its burden, without being paid for doing so, אֲבָל לֹא לִטְעֹן — **but it is not** a Biblical commandment **to help load** an animal whose load has come off without being paid for doing so.[12] רַבִּי שִׁמְעוֹן אוֹמֵר אַף לִטְעֹן — **R' Shimon says:** It is a Biblical commandment **even to** help **load** an animal without being paid.[13]

── NOTES ──

road and turn away from them; you must surely stand [them] up with him. The words *stand [them] up* [הָקֵם תָּקִים] refer to the animal's load, that is, you must "stand the load up" again on the animal by reloading it (see Gemara 32a). This command also does not imply any limit. Thus, it teaches that one must assist the owner in loading his animal as many times as needed (*Tos. Yom Tov*).

11. This exception is learned from a verse (see Gemara 31a).

12. There are two separate verses that teach the obligations to help unload and load an animal (see note 10). Seemingly, it would have been enough for the Torah to write just the obligation to help load and we would have concluded on our own

that there is also an obligation to help unload. This is because loading benefits only the owner of the animal, whereas unloading not only helps the owner but also relieves the suffering of the animal that is collapsed under the load. Why then did the Torah add a separate verse to teach the obligation to help unload? It means to teach that unloading carries with it a greater obligation, namely, that he cannot demand to be paid for it (*Tos. Yom Tov,* from Gemara 32a).

13. R' Shimon argues that the Torah *needed* to add the second verse to teach the mitzvah of loading. This is because the words of this verse could actually be explained to refer to the mitzvah of *un*loading. [The words *stand them up*

[41] MISHNAH BAVA METZIA / Chapter 2: *Eilu Metzios*

רַבִּי יוֹסֵי הַגְּלִילִי אוֹמֵר, אִם הָיָה עָלָיו יָתֵר עַל מַשָּׂאוֹ, אֵין זָקוּק לוֹ, שֶׁנֶּאֱמַר, תַּחַת מַשָּׂאוֹ, מַשּׂוּי שֶׁיָּכוֹל לַעֲמוֹד בּוֹ.

[יא] **אֲבֵדָתוֹ** וַאֲבֵדַת אָבִיו, אֲבֵדָתוֹ קוֹדֶמֶת, אֲבֵדָתוֹ וַאֲבֵדַת רַבּוֹ, שֶׁלּוֹ קוֹדֶמֶת. אֲבֵדַת אָבִיו וַאֲבֵדַת רַבּוֹ, שֶׁל רַבּוֹ קוֹדֶמֶת, שֶׁאָבִיו הֱבִיאוֹ לָעוֹלָם הַזֶּה, וְרַבּוֹ שֶׁלִּמְּדוֹ חָכְמָה מְבִיאוֹ לְחַיֵּי הָעוֹלָם הַבָּא.

— רע״ב —

רבי יוסי הגלילי אומר
וכו׳. ואין הלכה כרבי יוסי:
(יא) אבדתו קודמת.
דאמר קרא (דברים טו,ד)
אפס כי לא יהיה בך אביון,
הזהר שלא תהיה אתה
אביון: של רבו קודמת.
והוא שיהיה רבו מובהק,
שלמד רוב חכמתו ממנו,
וכן כל היכא דרבו דאמרינן
במתניתין שקודמים לאביו,
אינו אלא ברבו מובהק:

A final ruling regarding the mitzvah of unloading:

אִם הָיָה עָלָיו יָתֵר עַל מַשָּׂאוֹ — רַבִּי יוֹסֵי הַגְּלִילִי אוֹמֵר — R' Yose HaGlili says: אֵין זָקוּק לוֹ — If [the animal] was loaded with more than it could bear, and it collapsed under its load, [the passerby] is not obliged to unload it, שֶׁנֶּאֱמַר "תַּחַת מַשָּׂאוֹ" — as the verse states (*Exodus* 23:5): *If you see the donkey ... sitting under its load,* which implies that the obligation to help unload applies only to a load than can be called *its* load,[14] מַשּׂוּי שֶׁיָּכוֹל לַעֲמוֹד בּוֹ — that is, **a load that it is** normally **able to stand with.**

[11] This Mishnah deals with someone who finds lost items belonging to different people, and the finder is able to return only one of them:

אֲבֵדָתוֹ וַאֲבֵדַת אָבִיו אֲבֵדָתוֹ קוֹדֶמֶת — If someone finds **his own lost item and his father's lost item** and he is able to take only one of them, saving **his own lost item takes precedence** over saving his father's. אֲבֵדָתוֹ וַאֲבֵדַת רַבּוֹ שֶׁלּוֹ קוֹדֶמֶת — Likewise, if he finds **his own lost item and his teacher's lost item** and he is able to take only one of them, saving **his own lost item takes precedence** over saving his teacher's. Where it is not possible to do both, a person's own needs come before those of others.[1] אֲבֵדַת אָבִיו וַאֲבֵדַת רַבּוֹ שֶׁל רַבּוֹ קוֹדֶמֶת — If he finds **his father's lost item and his teacher's lost item** and he is able to take only one of them, saving **his teacher's lost item takes precedence** over saving his father's, שֶׁאָבִיו הֱבִיאוֹ לָעוֹלָם הַזֶּה — because **his father brought him** only **into this world,** וְרַבּוֹ שֶׁלִּמְּדוֹ חָכְמָה מְבִיאוֹ לְחַיֵּי הָעוֹלָם הַבָּא — **whereas his teacher, who taught him wisdom** (that is, Torah), **brings**

NOTES

(הָקֵם תָּקִים) quoted in note 10 could be referring to the animals, not the loads.] It is only because there is already another verse for the mitzvah of unloading that we explain the second verse to be referring to the mitzvah of loading. Therefore, the second verse is not extra and cannot be used to teach a greater obligation for unloading than for loading (*Tos. Yom Tov*; see Gemara for further explanation).

14. *Tiferes Yisrael.*

[11]

1. The Torah states (*Deuteronomy* 15:4): *Only, that there shall not be any poor man among you.* This teaches that one must take steps to avoid becoming poor himself (*Rav*). We learn from this that one should save his own money before saving someone else's money, even that of his father or teacher.

וְאִם אָבִיו חָכָם, שֶׁל אָבִיו קוֹדֶמֶת. הָיָה אָבִיו וְרַבּוֹ נוֹשְׂאִין מַשָּׂאוּי, מֵנִיחַ אֶת שֶׁל רַבּוֹ, וְאַחַר כָּךְ מֵנִיחַ אֶת שֶׁל אָבִיו. הָיָה אָבִיו וְרַבּוֹ בְּבֵית הַשֶּׁבִי, פּוֹדֶה אֶת רַבּוֹ, וְאַחַר כָּךְ פּוֹדֶה אֶת אָבִיו. וְאִם הָיָה אָבִיו חָכָם, פּוֹדֶה אֶת אָבִיו, וְאַחַר כָּךְ פּוֹדֶה אֶת רַבּוֹ.

---

him to the World to Come.[2] וְאִם אָבִיו חָכָם שֶׁל אָבִיו קוֹדֶמֶת — If, however, his father is also a Torah scholar, and he taught him some Torah wisdom as well, saving his father's item takes precedence over his teacher's.[3]

Similar rulings in regard to helping a father or a teacher in other ways: הָיָה אָבִיו וְרַבּוֹ נוֹשְׂאִין מַשָּׂאוּי — If his father and his teacher were both carrying packages, and both need help unloading them, מֵנִיחַ אֶת שֶׁל רַבּוֹ וְאַחַר כָּךְ מֵנִיחַ אֶת שֶׁל אָבִיו — he first unloads his teacher's package, and then unloads his father's. הָיָה אָבִיו וְרַבּוֹ בְּבֵית הַשֶּׁבִי — Likewise, if his father and his teacher were both in captivity, and both needed to be ransomed, פּוֹדֶה אֶת רַבּוֹ וְאַחַר כָּךְ פּוֹדֶה אֶת אָבִיו — he first ransoms his teacher and then ransoms his father, because his father brought him only into this world, but his teacher brings him into the World to Come. וְאִם הָיָה אָבִיו חָכָם פּוֹדֶה אֶת אָבִיו וְאַחַר כָּךְ פּוֹדֶה אֶת רַבּוֹ — Here, too, if his father is also a scholar, he first ransoms his father and then ransoms his teacher.[4]

NOTES

2. Whenever this Mishnah mentions "his teacher" it refers to the teacher who taught him most of his Torah wisdom [רַבּוֹ הַמּוּבְהָק] (Rav). The student owes such a teacher even more than he owes his father, and he therefore must save this teacher's lost item before he saves his father's lost item.

3. Since his father also taught him Torah, he too has a share in bringing him to the World to Come. Although this share is less than the teacher's share, the combination of bringing him into this world and also, in part, into the World to Come, gives the father precedence over the teacher (Tiferes Yisrael).

4. The same is true for unloading packages; if his father is a scholar he helps unload his father's package first and then his teacher's (Shitah Mikubetzes).

Chapter Three

This chapter discusses the laws of a שׁוֹמֵר, *shomer* (plural, שׁוֹמְרִים, *shomrim*), which means *watchman* or *custodian*. This is a person who is responsible to watch and take care of property that belongs to someone else. The property entrusted to his care is called a פִּקָּדוֹן, *pikadon* (deposited item).

⇨ The Four *Shomrim*

The Torah (*Exodus* 22:6-14) refers to several different *shomrim*. Based on those verses, Mishnah 7:8 lists four types of *shomrim*, each with his own responsibilities and liabilities:

(1) שׁוֹמֵר חִנָּם, an unpaid *shomer*, who watches the property of another for free. He must watch and take care of the item he was given, as must every *shomer*, and may not use it for his own purposes. However, if the item is stolen or lost, he does not have to pay the owner unless this was caused by his negligence (פְּשִׁיעָה).

(2) שׁוֹמֵר שָׂכָר, a paid *shomer*, who is paid to watch someone's property. Because he is paid, he must watch the item more carefully than an unpaid *shomer*. He is responsible even for loss that did not result from his negligence. Nevertheless, he is not required to pay if the loss resulted from an accident that he could not have prevented (אֹנֶס).

(3) שׂוֹכֵר, a renter, who pays to use another person's property. Tannaim disagree whether his liability is like that of an unpaid *shomer* or of a paid *shomer* (see Mishnah 7:8 and Gemara 93a).

(4) שׁוֹאֵל, a borrower, who may use another person's property without paying for it. A borrower has the highest degree of responsibility. He must pay even for loss caused by an unpreventable accident. However, he is not liable for damage that was caused by using the object for the purpose for which he borrowed it (Gemara 96b-97a).

⇨ The *Shomer's* Oath

When a *shomer* claims that he does not have to pay (for example, an unpaid *shomer* says that the item was stolen) but he cannot prove it, the Torah requires him to swear that his claim is true and that the item is not in his possession. In addition, he must swear that he was not negligent, and that he had not used the item for his own purposes without permission (see Gemara 6a).

If he *had* used the item without permission, he is considered a thief. Like any thief, he is liable even for loss caused by an unavoidable accident (Mishnah 3:9).

משניות בבא מציעא / פרק ג: המפקיד

[א] הַמַּפְקִיד אֵצֶל חֲבֵירוֹ בְּהֵמָה אוֹ כֵלִים, וְנִגְנְבוּ אוֹ שֶׁאָבְדוּ, שָׁלֵם וְלֹא רָצָה לִשָּׁבַע, שֶׁהֲרֵי אָמְרוּ, שׁוֹמֵר חִנָּם נִשְׁבָּע וְיוֹצֵא, נִמְצָא הַגַּנָּב, מְשַׁלֵּם תַּשְׁלוּמֵי כֶפֶל, טָבַח וּמָכַר, מְשַׁלֵּם תַּשְׁלוּמֵי אַרְבָּעָה וַחֲמִשָּׁה. לְמִי מְשַׁלֵּם, לְמִי שֶׁהַפִּקָּדוֹן אֶצְלוֹ.

— רע״ב —

פרק שלישי — המפקיד. (א) המפקיד. ולא רצה לישבע. שבועת השומרין. שהיה יכול ליפטר אם נשבע שלא פשע בה ושלא שלח בה יד: למי שהפקדון אצלו. דכיון דשלם קנה כל תשלומיה. ואפילו לא שלם, אלא כיון שאמר:

בבית דין הריני משלם, קנה כל תשלומיה, לא שנא תשלומי כפל, ולא שנא תשלומי ארבעה וחמשה:

---

[1] This Mishnah refers to an unpaid *shomer* (watchman). As stated in the introduction to this chapter, an unpaid *shomer* does not have to pay the owner if the item he was watching was stolen or lost without negligence on his part. However, he must prove that this is what happened. If he cannot prove it, he must either pay the owner or take "the oath of the *shomrim*" (that is, he swears that the item was indeed stolen or lost, that he was not negligent, and that he had not used it for his own purposes).

The Mishnah states the laws that apply when an unpaid *shomer* claims that the item was stolen, and later the thief is caught:

הַמַּפְקִיד אֵצֶל חֲבֵירוֹ בְּהֵמָה אוֹ כֵלִים — Someone gave his friend an animal or utensils to watch for him for free, וְנִגְנְבוּ אוֹ שֶׁאָבְדוּ — and the *shomer* later claimed that they were stolen or lost, שָׁלֵם וְלֹא רָצָה לִשָּׁבַע — but he paid the owner and did not want to swear, although he could have sworn to avoid paying; שֶׁהֲרֵי אָמְרוּ שׁוֹמֵר חִנָּם נִשְׁבָּע וְיוֹצֵא — as [the Sages] said: "An unpaid *shomer* may swear and leave the court without having to pay." נִמְצָא הַגַּנָּב מְשַׁלֵּם תַּשְׁלוּמֵי כֶפֶל — The law is that if the thief is caught, he must make the double payment,[1] טָבַח וּמָכַר מְשַׁלֵּם תַּשְׁלוּמֵי אַרְבָּעָה וַחֲמִשָּׁה — and if the item he stole was a sheep or ox and he slaughtered or sold it, he must make the fourfold or fivefold payment.[2] לְמִי מְשַׁלֵּם — Whom does [the thief] pay? לְמִי שֶׁהַפִּקָּדוֹן אֶצְלוֹ — He pays the one with whom the item was entrusted, namely, the *shomer*. The thief must pay the *shomer* (rather than the owner) because, through paying the owner for the theft, the *shomer* became its new owner.[3]

NOTES

[1]
1. The Torah commands a thief to pay the owner "double" — that is, the item he stole (or its value) plus an additional fine of the same amount (*Exodus* 22:3).

2. The Torah states that one who steals a sheep and then sells or slaughters it must pay the owner *four* times the value — that is, the sheep itself plus an additional fine of three times as much. If the animal was not a sheep but an ox, he must pay the owner *five* times the value — that is, the ox itself plus an additional fine of four times as much (there, 21:37).

3. Because the *shomer* chose to pay the owner for the object, and not swear, it is considered his property from the moment it was put in his care (see the next paragraph). Therefore, when the thief stole the item, it already belonged to the *shomer*, and thus it is the *shomer* whom he must pay.

Although the *shomer* paid for the item *after* the owner entrusted it to him,

[45] MISHNAH BAVA METZIA / Chapter 3: *Hamafkid*

— רע"ב —

(ב) הַשּׂוֹכֵר פָּרָה מֵחֲבֵירוֹ. וְעָמַד שׂוֹכֵר וְהִשְׁאִילָהּ לְאַחֵר בִּרְשׁוּת הַמַּשְׂכִּיר. שֶׁאִם לֹא נָתַן לוֹ הַמַּשְׂכִּיר רְשׁוּת, הֲלֹא קַיְּימָא לָן (וגמרא לו, א), שׁוֹמֵר שֶׁמָּסַר לְשׁוֹמֵר חַיָּיב: יִשָּׁבַע הַשּׂוֹכֵר. לַמַּשְׂכִּיר שֶׁמֵּתָה כְּדַרְכָּהּ, וּפָטוּר. שֶׁהַשּׂוֹכֵר פָּטוּר מִן הָאוֹנָסִין: וְהַשּׁוֹאֵל. שֶׁהוּא חַיָּיב בָּאוֹנָסִין, מְשַׁלֵּם לַשּׂוֹכֵר, בִּשְׁבוּעָה שֶׁהוּא נִשְׁבַּע לַמַּשְׂכִּיר:

נִשְׁבַּע וְלֹא רָצָה לְשַׁלֵּם, נִמְצָא הַגַּנָּב, מְשַׁלֵּם תַּשְׁלוּמֵי כֶפֶל, טָבַח וּמָכַר, מְשַׁלֵּם תַּשְׁלוּמֵי אַרְבָּעָה וַחֲמִשָּׁה. לְמִי מְשַׁלֵּם, לְבַעַל הַפִּקָּדוֹן.

[ב] הַשּׂוֹכֵר פָּרָה מֵחֲבֵירוֹ וְהִשְׁאִילָהּ לְאַחֵר, וּמֵתָה כְּדַרְכָּהּ, יִשָּׁבַע הַשּׂוֹכֵר שֶׁמֵּתָה כְדַרְכָּהּ, וְהַשּׁוֹאֵל יְשַׁלֵּם לַשּׂוֹכֵר.

The Mishnah turns to the related case, where the *shomer* swore instead of paying:

נִשְׁבַּע וְלֹא רָצָה לְשַׁלֵּם — **If he swore and did not want to pay,** נִמְצָא הַגַּנָּב מְשַׁלֵּם תַּשְׁלוּמֵי כֶפֶל — **here, too, the law is that if the thief is caught, he must make the double payment,** טָבַח וּמָכַר מְשַׁלֵּם תַּשְׁלוּמֵי אַרְבָּעָה וַחֲמִשָּׁה — **and if the item he stole was a sheep or ox and he slaughtered or sold it, he must make the fourfold or fivefold payment.** לְמִי מְשַׁלֵּם — **However, whom does he pay** in this case? לְבַעַל הַפִּקָּדוֹן — He pays the **original owner of the watched item,** since he owned it the whole time, and it never became the property of the *shomer*.

[2] As taught in the introduction to this chapter, a renter is not liable for loss or damage caused by an unavoidable accident (for example, an animal's natural death), but a borrower *is* liable for such an accident. The Mishnah discusses the case of a person who rents an animal and then lends it out to someone else.

הַשּׂוֹכֵר פָּרָה מֵחֲבֵירוֹ וְהִשְׁאִילָהּ לְאַחֵר — **If someone rented a cow from his friend and lent it to another** person (with the owner's permission),[1] וּמֵתָה כְּדַרְכָּהּ — **and it then died a natural death** for which the renter is not responsible but the borrower is, יִשָּׁבַע הַשּׂוֹכֵר שֶׁמֵּתָה כְּדַרְכָּהּ — **the renter swears** to the owner **that it died a natural death** without any negligence on his part, וְהַשּׁוֹאֵל יְשַׁלֵּם לַשּׂוֹכֵר — **and the borrower pays** the value of the cow to **the renter.** When the cow died a natural death, at which point the owner loses the cow and any right to be paid for it (because a renter does not pay for

---

NOTES

it became his retroactively, from the moment he received it. The reason is as follows: Whenever an item entrusted to a *shomer* is stolen, the owner would prefer that the *shomer* pay him for it rather than swear and not pay. To encourage the *shomer* to pay, the owner can tell him (when he gives him the item): "If it is stolen and you agree to pay, this giving of the item should retroactively be considered a *gift* to you. You will thus be its owner from the start and receive all the payments if the thief is caught." In fact, this is understood to be the owner's intent even if he does not say it aloud. Accordingly, as soon as the *shomer* agrees to pay, it emerges that the item was a gift to him from the start, and so it was the *shomer's* property that the thief stole (*Tos. Yom Tov*).

[2]

1. A renter is forbidden to lend the rented item to someone else without the owner's permission. If he does, he is responsible for anything that happens to it (*Rav*).

משניות בבא מציעא / פרק ג: המפקיד

אָמַר רַבִּי יוֹסֵי, כֵּיצַד הַלָּה עוֹשֶׂה סְחוֹרָה בְּפָרָתוֹ שֶׁל חֲבֵרוֹ, אֶלָּא תַּחֲזוֹר פָּרָה לַבְּעָלִים.

[ג] **אָמַר** לִשְׁנַיִם, גְּזַלְתִּי לְאֶחָד מִכֶּם מָנֶה, וְאֵינִי יוֹדֵעַ אֵיזֶה מִכֶּם, אוֹ אָבִיו שֶׁל אֶחָד מִכֶּם הִפְקִיד לִי מָנֶה, וְאֵינִי יוֹדֵעַ אֵיזֶה הוּא, נוֹתֵן לָזֶה מָנֶה וְלָזֶה מָנֶה, שֶׁהוֹדָה מִפִּי עַצְמוֹ.

— רע"ב —

אמר רבי יוסי כיצד הלה עושה סחורה וכו'. והלכה כרבי יוסי: (ג) אמר לשנים גזלתי אחד מכם. והם אינם תובעים לו כלום, אלא הוא בא לצאת ידי שמים. נותן לזה מנה ולזה מנה. אבל שנים שתבעוהו,

ויהודה שגזל לאחד מהם, ישבע כל אחד מהם שלו גזל, ונותן מנה לזה ומנה לזה. קנס קנסוהו חכמים מפני שעבר על לא תגזול. וכן שנים שתבעוהו לאחד, כל אחד אומר אבי הפקיד אצלך מנה, והוא אומר אביו של אחד מכם הניח לי מנה, ואיני יודע איזהו, הרי כל אחד מהם נשבע שאביו הניח אצלו מנה, ונותן מנה לזה ומנה לזה. דאיהו פשע בנפשיה, דהוה ליה למידק ולזכור מי הניח אצלו הממנה:

---

unavoidable accidents), it became the property of the renter.[2] The borrower therefore pays the renter and not the original owner.

The next Tanna disagrees:

אָמַר רַבִּי יוֹסֵי — R' Yose said: כֵּיצַד הַלָּה עוֹשֶׂה סְחוֹרָה בְּפָרָתוֹ שֶׁל חֲבֵרוֹ — How can that one (the renter) be allowed to do business with the cow of his friend? That is, the renter does *not* become the owner of the cow; thus, if he takes the borrower's payment, he is profiting from something that is not his! אֶלָּא תַּחֲזוֹר פָּרָה לַבְּעָלִים — Rather, the law is that the [borrower] returns the value of the cow to the owner. Since the cow always belonged to the original owner, it is the owner whom he must pay.

[3] This Mishnah deals with several cases where a person said to two people that he is obligated to pay one of them but he does not know which one:

אָמַר לִשְׁנַיִם — If one person said to two others (who had made no claim against him), גְּזַלְתִּי לְאֶחָד מִכֶּם מָנֶה, וְאֵינִי יוֹדֵעַ אֵיזֶה מִכֶּם — "I stole a *maneh* (100 *zuz*) from one of you but I do not know from which one," אוֹ אָבִיו שֶׁל אֶחָד מִכֶּם הִפְקִיד לִי מָנֶה, וְאֵינִי יוֹדֵעַ אֵיזֶה הוּא — or he said, "The father of one of you deposited a *maneh* with me before he died but I do not know which one," נוֹתֵן לָזֶה מָנֶה וְלָזֶה מָנֶה — the law in both cases is that that he must give a *maneh* to this one and a *maneh* to this one, שֶׁהוֹדָה מִפִּי עַצְמוֹ — because he admitted his obligation by himself. That is, since he came forward and admitted that he must pay, without any claim having been made against him, he shows that he wants to fulfill his moral duty (and not merely his legal obligation). This can be accomplished only by giving a *maneh* to each person, so that the rightful owner is certainly paid.[1]

NOTES

2. Since the owner cannot get his animal back nor will he be paid anything for it (because it died in a manner for which the renter is not responsible), he lost all his rights to it the moment it died. At that point, therefore, it became the property of the renter. As the new owner of the animal, the renter is entitled to the borrower's payment (*Tos. Yom Tov,* from Gemara 35b).

[3]

1. There are two types of monetary obligations: legal obligations (which a

[47] **MISHNAH BAVA METZIA** / Chapter 3: *Hamafkid*

— רע״ב —

(ד) שנים שהפקידו אצל אחד זה מנה וזה מאתים. כגון דאפקידו תרווייהו כי הדדי זה בפני זה: נותן לזה מנה ולזה מנה וכו׳. דאמר להו, אתון לא קפדיתו אהדדי, ולא חשדתם זה את זה שמא חבירו יתבע המאתים, אנא נמי לא רמאי אנפשאי למידק המאתים של מי הן. ונעשה כאילו הניחו כל השלש מאות בצרור אחד, דלא הוי ליה למידק מה יש לזה בתוכו ומה יש לחבירו:

[ד] **שְׁנַיִם** שֶׁהִפְקִידוּ אֵצֶל אֶחָד, זֶה מָנֶה, וְזֶה מָאתַיִם, זֶה אוֹמֵר, שֶׁלִּי מָאתַיִם, וְזֶה אוֹמֵר, שֶׁלִּי מָאתַיִם, נוֹתֵן לָזֶה מָנֶה וְלָזֶה מָנֶה, וְהַשְּׁאָר יְהֵא מֻנָּח עַד שֶׁיָּבֹא אֵלִיָּהוּ.

[4] This Mishnah speaks of a situation where someone received money from two people but he does not know how much he received from each one:

שְׁנַיִם שֶׁהִפְקִידוּ אֵצֶל אֶחָד — **Two** people **deposited** money **with one** *shomer*; זֶה מָנֶה, וְזֶה מָאתַיִם — **one** of them deposited **a** *maneh* (one hundred *zuz*) **and the other** deposited **two hundred** *zuz*.[1] זֶה אוֹמֵר שֶׁלִּי מָאתַיִם, וְזֶה אוֹמֵר שֶׁלִּי מָאתַיִם — When they came to collect their money, **one said, "The two hundred** *zuz* **are mine," and the other said, "The two hundred** *zuz* **are mine,"** and the *shomer* did not remember which of them deposited the two hundred *zuz*. נוֹתֵן לָזֶה מָנֶה וְלָזֶה מָנֶה — The law is that **he must give a** *maneh* **to one and a** *maneh* **to the other,** because each of them deposited at least that amount with him. וְהַשְּׁאָר יְהֵא מֻנָּח עַד שֶׁיָּבֹא אֵלִיָּהוּ — **And the remaining** *maneh*, which is the amount in dispute, **should be put away**[2] **until the Prophet Elijah comes** and tells us to whom the money belongs,[3] or until one of the claimants admits that he was lying.[4]

— NOTES —

human court can force a person to fulfill) and moral obligations (which cannot be enforced by a human court, but which a person must fulfill if he wishes to avoid punishment from the Court of Heaven). In our Mishnah's case, the moral obligation of the thief or *shomer* is greater than his legal obligation. He is legally obligated to pay only the amount that he *certainly* owes, namely, one *maneh*. [He fulfills this obligation by paying just one *maneh*, which is divided between the two "owners" (*Tiferes Yisrael*).] His moral duty, however, is to pay a full *maneh* to each one (*Rav*).

The preceding applies where the "owners" did not make claims against this person. If, however, they did make claims against him, and each swore that his claim is true, he would be *legally* obligated to pay an entire *maneh* to each one. Although a person cannot usually be obligated to pay more than what he *certainly* owes (even where claims have been made against him), the Sages

punished him because he is a thief, or in the case of a *shomer*, because he was negligent in that he forgot who the owner was (*Rav*). [This legally enforceable punishment does not apply where no claims were made and the person admitted to his obligation on his own (see *Rambam, Hilchos Gezeilah* 4:10).]

[4]

1. They deposited their money with the *shomer* at the same time and in the presence of each other (*Rav*). See note 4.

2. In the care of the *shomer* (*Tiferes Yisrael*, first explanation).

3. See Mishnah 1:8 note 16.

4. Although we learned earlier that a *shomer* who is responding to claims must pay each claimant the full amount he is seeking (see note 1 on the previous Mishnah), this *shomer* need not pay each claimant 200 *zuz*; it is enough for him to pay each one 100 *zuz*. In the case discussed earlier, the *shomer* was negligent in that he forgot who the owner was,

אָמַר רַבִּי יוֹסֵי, אִם כֵּן, מַה הִפְסִיד הָרַמַּאי, אֶלָּא הַכֹּל יְהֵא מֻנָּח עַד שֶׁיָּבֹא אֵלִיָּהוּ.

[ה] וְכֵן שְׁנֵי כֵלִים, אֶחָד יָפֶה מָנֶה וְאֶחָד יָפֶה אֶלֶף זוּז. זֶה אוֹמֵר, יָפֶה שֶׁלִּי, וְזֶה אוֹמֵר, יָפֶה שֶׁלִּי, נוֹתֵן אֶת הַקָּטָן לְאֶחָד מֵהֶן, וּמִתּוֹךְ הַגָּדוֹל נוֹתֵן דְּמֵי קָטָן לַשֵּׁנִי,

— רע"ב —

מַה הִפְסִיד הָרַמַּאי. וּלְעוֹלָם לֹא יוֹדֶה עַל הָאֱמֶת: (ה) וְכֵן שְׁנֵי כֵלִים. לְרַבָּנַן אִצְטְרִיכָא לֵיהּ. וְלֹא זוּ אַף זוּ קָתָנֵי, לֹא מִבַּעְיָא בִּמְנֶה מַחְמִיס דְּלֵיכָּא פְּסֵידָא דִשְׁבִירַת כְּלִי, אָמְרוּ רַבָּנַן נוֹתֵן לָזֶה מָנֶה וְלָזֶה מָנֶה, אֶלָּא אֲפִילּוּ בִּשְׁנֵי כֵלִים דְּאִיכָּא פְּסֵידָא,

שֶׁצָּרִיךְ לִשְׁבֹּר הַכְּלִי הַגָּדוֹל כְּדֵי לָתֵת מִמֶּנּוּ דְּמֵי הַקָּטָן, וְלִכְשֶׁיָּבֹא אֵלִיָּהוּ נִמְלָא שֶׁבִּטֵּל הַכְּלִי הַגָּדוֹל הַפְסִיד, שֶׁנִּשְׁבַּר הַכְּלִי שֶׁלּוֹ, וּסְלָקָא דַעְתָּךְ אֲמִינָא דְּבַהָא מוֹדוּ רַבָּנַן לְרַבִּי יוֹסֵי שֶׁהַכֹּל יְהֵא מֻנָּח עַד שֶׁיָּבֹא אֵלִיָּהוּ. קָמַשְׁמַע לָן. וַהֲלָכָה כַּחֲכָמִים:

The next Tanna disagrees:

אָמַר רַבִּי יוֹסֵי — **R' Yose said:** אִם כֵּן מַה הִפְסִיד הָרַמַּאי — **If so,** that each owner receives the one *maneh* that is surely his, **what does the liar lose?** Since the one who gave only one *maneh* gets back all his money and does not lose anything, he has no monetary incentive to admit that he was lying. אֶלָּא הַכֹּל יְהֵא מֻנָּח עַד שֶׁיָּבֹא אֵלִיָּהוּ — **Rather, all** the money (300 *zuz*) **should be put away until Elijah comes,** or until one of the owners admits that he gave only a *maneh*. In this way, the liar will be motivated to tell the truth, because otherwise he loses even the amount that is rightfully his.

[5] The case of this Mishnah is similar to the last Mishnah's, except that it involves utensils rather than money:

וְכֵן שְׁנֵי כֵלִים אֶחָד יָפֶה מָנֶה וְאֶחָד יָפֶה אֶלֶף זוּז — **And the same** law applies where two people gave **two utensils** (one utensil each) to a *shomer;* **one utensil was worth a** *maneh* (one hundred *zuz*) **and one was worth a thousand** *zuz*. זֶה אוֹמֵר, יָפֶה שֶׁלִּי, וְזֶה אוֹמֵר, יָפֶה שֶׁלִּי — When the owners came to collect their utensils, **one said, "The better** utensil **is mine,"** and the other said, "**The better** utensil **is mine,"** and the *shomer* does not remember which of them gave him the better one. נוֹתֵן אֶת הַקָּטָן לְאֶחָד מֵהֶן — **The law is that he must give the smaller** (cheaper) utensil **to one of them,** וּמִתּוֹךְ הַגָּדוֹל נוֹתֵן דְּמֵי קָטָן לַשֵּׁנִי — **and from the larger** (expensive) utensil he **gives the value of the smaller** utensil **to the second** owner (that is, a part of the larger utensil that is worth the same as the smaller utensil is removed and given to the second owner).[1]

NOTES

so the Sages punished him by requiring him to pay everything that was being claimed. Here, however, he was not negligent, because the two owners gave him their money in front of each other, which shows that they trust each other. (The one who deposited the larger amount was not worried that the other might claim the larger amount as his.) Since there is trust between the owners themselves, the *shomer* is not required to prevent a dispute between them by keeping track of who gave the larger amount (*Rav*).

[5]

1. The larger utensil is broken into pieces if the pieces have some value (for example, the utensil is made of silver or gold). If, however, the pieces would be worth nothing, the utensil is sold, and the value of the smaller utensil is taken

[49] MISHNAH BAVA METZIA / Chapter 3: *Hamafkid*

— רע״ב —

(ו) אבודים. על ידי עכברים או רקבון: לא יגע בהן. למוכרן. לפי שרוצה אדם בקב שלו, מתשעה קבין של חבירו. קב שלו חביב עליו על ידי שעמל בו, מתשעה קבין של אחרים שיקח בדמיהן אם ימכרם. ולא אמרו רבנן

וְהַשְּׁאָר יְהֵא מֻנָּח עַד שֶׁיָּבֹא אֵלִיָּהוּ. אָמַר רַבִּי יוֹסֵי, אִם כֵּן, מַה הִפְסִיד הָרַמַּאי, אֶלָּא הַכֹּל יְהֵא מֻנָּח עַד שֶׁיָּבֹא אֵלִיָּהוּ.

[ו] **הַמַּפְקִיד** פֵּרוֹת אֵצֶל חֲבֵרוֹ, אֲפִלּוּ הֵן אֲבוּדִין, לֹא יִגַּע בָּהֶן.

הרי זה לא יגע בהן, אלא שלא אבדו [אלא] עד כדי חסרונם המפורש במשנתינו, (דלקמן) לחטים ולאורז תשעת חלאי קביץ לכור וכו׳. אבל אם אבדו יותר מכדי חסרונם, מודים חכמים לרבן שמעון בן גמליאל דמוכרם בבית דין. והלכה כחכמים:

---

because each owner is certainly entitled to at least the value of the smaller utensil. וְהַשְּׁאָר יְהֵא מֻנָּח עַד שֶׁיָּבֹא אֵלִיָּהוּ — **And the rest** of the larger utensil **should be put away until Elijah** the Prophet **comes** and tells us to whom it belongs, or until one of the claimants admits that he was lying.

As in the previous Mishnah, R' Yose disagrees:

אָמַר רַבִּי יוֹסֵי — **R' Yose said:** אִם כֵּן מַה הִפְסִיד הָרַמַּאי — **If so,** that each owner receives what is surely his, **what does the liar lose?** Since the one who gave the smaller utensil gets it (or its value) back, he has no monetary incentive to admit that he was lying. אֶלָּא הַכֹּל יְהֵא מֻנָּח עַד שֶׁיָּבֹא אֵלִיָּהוּ — **Rather, everything** (i.e., both utensils) **should be put away until Elijah** the Prophet **comes,** or until one of the owners admits that he gave the smaller utensil.[2]

[6] The following three Mishnayos discuss situations where items of food were given to a *shomer* to safeguard. This Mishnah teaches what a *shomer* may do if he sees that the quantity of the food is decreasing (for example, it is being eaten by mice) and he wants to prevent further loss:

הַמַּפְקִיד פֵּרוֹת אֵצֶל חֲבֵרוֹ — **If someone deposits produce with his friend,** אֲפִלּוּ הֵן אֲבוּדִין — **the law is that even if it is becoming ruined,** לֹא יִגַּע בָּהֶן — **[the *shomer*] may not touch it** (that is, he may not sell it), even though that would save the owner from losing more. In general, a person prefers a small amount of his own produce to a large amount of produce that he receives from others. Thus, even if the volume of his produce is decreasing, he would rather keep it than sell it and buy other produce.[1]

NOTES

from the money and given to the second owner (*Meiri*).

Like the previous Mishnah, the case is where the owners deposited their utensils with the *shomer* in each other's presence. Thus, the *shomer* is not responsible to remember who gave what, and does not have to give the larger utensil (or its value) to each one (see note 4 there).

2. The Tanna Kamma, however, disagrees with R' Yose not only in the case of money

(as in the previous Mishnah) but even in the case of utensils, despite the fact that the larger utensil must be broken (*Rav*).

[6]

1. The Gemara (38a) says: "A person prefers a *kav* of his own produce to nine *kavs* of someone else's produce." His own produce is more valuable to him because he produced it with his own hard work (*Rav*).

The Mishnah refers to produce that is

משניות בבא מציעא / פרק ג: המפקיד

רַבָּן שִׁמְעוֹן בֶּן גַּמְלִיאֵל אוֹמֵר, מוֹכְרָן בִּפְנֵי בֵית דִּין, מִפְּנֵי שֶׁהוּא כְּמֵשִׁיב אֲבֵדָה לַבְּעָלִים.

[ז] הַמַּפְקִיד פֵּרוֹת אֵצֶל חֲבֵרוֹ, הֲרֵי זֶה יוֹצִיא לוֹ חֶסְרוֹנוֹת,

— רע״ב —

(ז) המפקיד פירות אצל חבירו. וערבן הנפקד עם פירותיו, והיה מסתפק מהן, ואינו יודע שיעור מה שאכל. כשבא להחזירן יוציא לו חסרונות, יפחות כמה הס רגילים לחסור:

The next Tanna disagrees:

רַבָּן שִׁמְעוֹן בֶּן גַּמְלִיאֵל אוֹמֵר — **Rabban Shimon ben Gamliel says:** מוֹכְרָן בִּפְנֵי בֵית דִּין — **[The *shomer*] may sell it in front of the court;** that is, he may sell it once the court gives him permission.[2] מִפְּנֵי שֶׁהוּא כְּמֵשִׁיב אֲבֵדָה לַבְּעָלִים — This is allowed **because he is like one who returns lost property to its owner.** According to this Tanna, the owner would presumably want to have his produce sold in order to avoid further loss (even though it will be replaced by the produce of others). Therefore, selling his produce is as beneficial to him as returning his property.[3]

[7] Produce tends to decrease in quantity over time due to natural causes (for example, it is being ruined by mice or decay). Therefore, if produce was entrusted to a *shomer* and it decreased while in his possession, he may simply give back what remains. He does not have to pay for the loss, since it is normal for produce to become ruined over time. The Mishnah teaches what happens when a *shomer* of produce cannot just return the owner's produce, because it became mixed with his own produce and he does not know how much of the owner's produce is left:

הַמַּפְקִיד פֵּרוֹת אֵצֶל חֲבֵרוֹ — **If someone deposited produce with his friend,** and the *shomer* mixed it with his own produce,[1] and then he ate some of the mixed produce but does not know how much he ate, הֲרֵי זֶה יוֹצִיא לוֹ חֶסְרוֹנוֹת — when he returns the produce to the owner **he may deduct for natural decreases;** that is, he deducts the proportion by which that type of produce usually decreases over the period of time it was in his safekeeping.[2]

NOTES

being depleted at the normal rate for that type of produce (see the following Mishnayos). If the rate of depletion is faster than usual, the *shomer* may sell it (*Rav*).

2. *Meiri*.

3. Even so, selling the produce is permitted only where the owner is not in town and cannot be asked what he wants done with it. If he *is* in town, the *shomer* should inform him of the situation and let him decide what to do (*Maggid Mishneh, Hilchos She'eilah U'Fikadon* 7:1).

[7]

1. A *shomer* is forbidden to mix the

owner's produce with his own, because if he does the owner will not get back his own produce, which he prefers (see note 1 on the previous Mishnah). The *shomer* discussed here either broke this law or he was given permission by the owner to do this (*Meiri*).

2. The *shomer* cannot calculate the amount by which the owner's produce decreased naturally, because he does not know how much was eaten by him and how much was eaten by mice. He may nevertheless deduct the *usual* proportion by which this type of produce decreases over the period of time he had it in his

[51] MISHNAH BAVA METZIA / Chapter 3: *Hamafkid*

לְחִטִּין וּלְאֹרֶז תִּשְׁעָה חֲצָאֵי קַבִּין לְכוֹר, לִשְׂעוֹרִין וּלְדֹחַן תִּשְׁעָה קַבִּין לְכוֹר, לְכֻסְּמִין וּלְזֶרַע פִּשְׁתָּן שָׁלֹשׁ סְאִין לְכוֹר. הַכֹּל לְפִי הַמִּדָּה, הַכֹּל לְפִי הַזְּמָן. אָמַר רַבִּי יוֹחָנָן בֶּן נוּרִי, וְכִי מָה אִכְפַּת לָהֶן לָעַכְבָּרִין, וַהֲלֹא אוֹכְלוֹת בֵּין מֵהַרְבֵּה וּבֵין מִקִּמְעָא,

— רע״ב —

תשעת חצאי קבין לכור. הכור שלשים סאין, והסאה ששה קבין: הכל לפי המדה. כן לכל כור וכור: הכל לפי הזמן. שהניחם בידו. לכל שנה ושנה יניח לו כך: מה איכפת להו לעכברים. כך אוכלים ממדה מועטת כמו ממדה מרובה. הלכך תשעה חצאי קבין לשנה, בין לכור בין לעשרה כורין:

The Mishnah defines the usual rates of decrease for some types of produce: לְחִטִּין וּלְאֹרֶז תִּשְׁעָה חֲצָאֵי קַבִּין לְכוֹר — **With regard to wheat and rice,** the usual decrease each year is **nine half-*kavs* for a** *kor* (which is 180 *kavs*), a proportion of one-fortieth; לִשְׂעוֹרִין וּלְדֹחַן תִּשְׁעָה קַבִּין לְכוֹר — **with regard to barley and millet,**[3] **nine *kavs* for a** *kor* (180 *kavs*), a proportion of one-twentieth; לְכֻסְּמִין וּלְזֶרַע פִּשְׁתָּן שָׁלֹשׁ סְאִין לְכוֹר — **with regard to spelt and flax seed, three** *se'ahs* (18 *kavs*) **for a** *kor* (180 *kavs*), a proportion of one-tenth.[4] הַכֹּל לְפִי הַמִּדָּה הַכֹּל לְפִי הַזְּמָן — **Everything depends on the quantity, and everything depends on the time.** The greater the quantity, the more the *shomer* may deduct (the amounts listed above are for each *kor*), and the longer the time it was in the *shomer's* care, the more he may deduct (the amounts listed above are for each year).[5]

The next Tanna disputes the rule that "everything depends on the quantity": אָמַר רַבִּי יוֹחָנָן בֶּן נוּרִי וְכִי מָה אִכְפַּת לָהֶן לָעַכְבָּרִין — **R' Yochanan ben Nuri said: — But why would the mice care** how much produce there is? וַהֲלֹא אוֹכְלוֹת בֵּין מֵהַרְבֵּה וּבֵין מִקִּמְעָא — **Would they not eat the same amount whether from a large quantity or from a small quantity?!** The *shomer,* therefore, may not deduct a larger amount just because the deposited amount was larger.

NOTES
---

possession. The Tanna will define the usual rate of decrease for various types of produce.

Had he left the owner's produce alone, he could have simply returned it as is. And had he just added his own produce to the owner's (without removing any), returning the produce would still be simple, because he could make the following calculation: He measures the proportion of the mixture that is missing (if any) and deducts the same proportion from the amount of produce that was given to him. For example, if the mixture is missing one-tenth, he returns the original volume minus one-tenth (*Rambam Commentary*). In the Mishnah's case, however, he cannot make this calculation because he ate some of the mixture and does not know how much he ate.

3. These translations of אֹרֶז (rice) and דֹחַן (millet) follow *Tosafos, Berachos* 37a ד״ה רש״י, and the generally accepted halachah (see *Mishnah Berurah* 208:25).

4. The Mishnah does not refer to pure seeds of flax, but to seeds that were still in their husks when they were given to the *shomer*. Husks of flax become dry, fall off, and are blown away by the wind, which results in a large decrease (see *Rashi* 40a ד״ה זרע).

5. For example, if he was given a *kor* of wheat for two years, he would deduct a fortieth (nine half-*kavs*) for the first year, plus a fortieth of what remains for the second year (*Tiferes Yisrael*).

אֶלָּא אֵינוֹ מוֹצִיא לוֹ חֶסְרוֹנוֹת אֶלָּא לְכוֹר אֶחָד בִּלְבַד. רַבִּי יְהוּדָה אוֹמֵר, אִם הָיְתָה מִדָּה מְרֻבָּה אֵינוֹ מוֹצִיא לוֹ חֶסְרוֹנוֹת, מִפְּנֵי שֶׁמּוֹתִירוֹת.

— רע"ב —

אם היתה מדה מרובה. שהפקיד אצלו הרבה, מעשרה כורים ולמעלה, לא יוציא לו חסרונות: מפני שהן מותירות. שבזמות הגורן כשמפקידים, החטים יבשים, ובזמות הגשמים כשמחזירן, נופחות. ובאכילת עכברים אינן מחסרין כל כך לכל כור וכור, דכולי האי לא אכלי עכברים מעשרה כורין, הלכך נפיחתו משלמת למה שעכברים אוכלים. ואין הלכה לא כרבי יהודה ולא כרבי יוחנן בן נורי. וכל השיעורים הללו בארץ ישראל ובימי התנאים. אבל בשאר ארצות ובזמנים הללו, הכל כפי מה שרגילים הזרעים לחסר באותה מדינה ובאותו זמן:

אֶלָּא אֵינוֹ מוֹצִיא לוֹ חֶסְרוֹנוֹת אֶלָּא לְכוֹר אֶחָד בִּלְבַד — **Rather, the law is that he deducts only the decreases** listed above, which are **for one** *kor,* even if the produce given to him was much larger (for example, he deducts nine half-*kavs* from wheat, even if its original measure was ten *kors*).[6]

A third opinion:

רַבִּי יְהוּדָה אוֹמֵר — **R' Yehudah says:** אִם הָיְתָה מִדָּה מְרֻבָּה אֵינוֹ מוֹצִיא לוֹ חֶסְרוֹנוֹת — **If the amount** of produce **was large,** and the *shomer* was given the produce in the summer and returns it in the winter, **he does not deduct** anything for **decreases** caused by mice, מִפְּנֵי שֶׁמּוֹתִירוֹת — **because** produce tends to **expand** in the winter.[7] The volume of the expansion is about the same as the volume eaten by mice. The overall volume should thus remain the same, and so the *shomer* may not deduct anything.[8]

[8] This Mishnah states the deductions that a *shomer* may make from wine and oil:[1]

NOTES
---

6. The amount that mice normally eat in a year is nine half-*kavs*. This, therefore, is always the amount the *shomer* may deduct whether he received one *kor* or a much larger amount (*Rav*). However, if he received less than a *kor,* he deducts a fortieth of what he was given (see *Tosafos* ד"ה אלא).

The Tanna Kamma disagrees with this opinion, because the greater the amount of produce, the more mice it will attract (*Tos. Yom Tov,* from *Tosafos* ד"ה וכי).

7. In the rainy season, produce absorbs moisture and swells.

8. According to R' Yehudah, the proportion that mice eat of a small amount of produce (less than ten *kors*) is greater than the proportion they eat of a large amount of produce (ten *kors* or more). Therefore, R' Yehudah said that his ruling applies when the original amount was "large" (ten *kors* or more), for only in that case does the wintertime expansion match the amount eaten by mice. If the original amount was smaller than ten *kors,* the mice will eat more than the volume by which it expands. The *shomer* may deduct the difference (*Tos. HaRosh*).

All the measurements mentioned in this Mishnah were relevant in Eretz Yisrael in the time of the Tannaim. In other times and places, the rates of decrease may be different (*Rav*).

[8]

1. As in the previous Mishnah, the *shomer* mixed the owner's wine or oil with some of his own, and then used some but does not know how much he used (*Tos. Yom Tov*). As a result, he cannot calculate how much of the owner's wine or oil is left (see note 2 there).

[ח] **יוֹצִיא** לוֹ שְׁתוּת לַיַּיִן. רַבִּי יְהוּדָה אוֹמֵר, חֹמֶשׁ. יוֹצִיא לוֹ שְׁלֹשֶׁת לֻגִּין שֶׁמֶן לְמֵאָה, לֹג וּמֶחֱצָה שְׁמָרִים, לֹג וּמֶחֱצָה בֶּלַע. אִם הָיָה שֶׁמֶן מְזֻקָּק אֵינוֹ מוֹצִיא לוֹ שְׁמָרִים. אִם הָיוּ קַנְקַנִּים יְשָׁנִים אֵינוֹ מוֹצִיא לוֹ בֶּלַע.

— רע״ב —

(ח) יוציא לו שתות ליין. אם הפקיד אצלו יין וערבו עם יינו. הקנקנים בולעים שתות: רבי יהודה אומר חומש. שהקרקע שלהן עושים ממנו הקנקנים באתריה דרבי יהודה בלע חומש. והכל לפי המקום:

יוֹצִיא לוֹ שְׁתוּת לַיַּיִן — **With regard to wine, [a** *shomer***] deducts a sixth** because this proportion is absorbed by the sides of the clay container. רַבִּי יְהוּדָה אוֹמֵר חֹמֶשׁ — But **R' Yehudah says** that **a fifth** is deducted.[2]

The Mishnah discusses oil:

יוֹצִיא לוֹ שְׁלֹשֶׁת לֻגִּין שֶׁמֶן לְמֵאָה — **[A** *shomer***] deducts three** *logs* **of oil for every one hundred** *logs* (3 percent). לֹג וּמֶחֱצָה שְׁמָרִים — **Of these three** *logs,* **one-and-a-half** *logs* **are deducted because of the** **sediment** that settled. The oil received by the *shomer* presumably contained one-and-a-half *logs* of sediment, which then settled at the bottom of the container. Therefore, when he returns the oil, which is now pure, he may deduct one-and-a-half *logs*.[3] לֹג וּמֶחֱצָה בֶּלַע — **And the other one-and-a-half** *logs* are deducted because of the **absorption** of oil into the sides of the container.[4] Thus, the total deduction is three *logs*.

These deductions may not be made in the following cases:

אִם הָיָה שֶׁמֶן מְזֻקָּק אֵינוֹ מוֹצִיא לוֹ שְׁמָרִים — **If the oil was pure** and free of sediment when it was given to the *shomer,* **he may not deduct** the one-and-a-half *logs* for sediment. אִם הָיוּ קַנְקַנִּים יְשָׁנִים אֵינוֹ מוֹצִיא לוֹ בֶּלַע — **If the containers** in which the oil was stored **were old, he may not deduct** the one-and-a-half *logs* for absorption, because they have already absorbed as much as they can.[5]

NOTES

2. R' Yehudah and the Tanna Kamma do not disagree, because they refer to different types of containers. The clay of which containers were made in the area where R' Yehudah lived was more absorbent than the clay used in the Tanna Kamma's area (*Rav,* from Gemara).

3. The Mishnah speaks of oil that was given to the *shomer* soon after it was squeezed, when it still contained sediment. It takes a while for the sediment to settle to the bottom of the container (*Meiri*).

[The Mishnah did not mention sediment in regard to wine, because the sediment of wine is considered part of the wine and is returned together with it. This is not true of the sediment of oil, which has no value and is thrown out (*Rashash*).]

4. Although a fifth or sixth of *wine* is absorbed, only 1.5 percent of *oil* is absorbed, because oil is thicker than wine (*Tiferes Yisrael*).

In contrast to the deductions mentioned in the previous Mishnah, which may be made each year anew, the deductions for sediment and absorption may be made only once, because after the liquid has been absorbed into the container and its sediment has settled, it does not decrease any further.

5. After a container has held oil for a long time, it has absorbed so much that it cannot absorb any more (Gemara). This is true only for oil, which is thick, and not for wine (*Ri MiLunel*).

[54] משניות בבא מציעא / פרק ג: המפקיד ג/ט

— רע"ב —

רַבִּי יְהוּדָה אוֹמֵר, אַף הַמּוֹכֵר שֶׁמֶן מְזֻקָּק לַחֲבֵרוֹ כָּל יְמוֹת הַשָּׁנָה, הֲרֵי זֶה מְקַבֵּל עָלָיו לֹג וּמֶחֱצָה שְׁמָרִים לְמֵאָה.

[ט] **הַמַּפְקִיד** חָבִית אֵצֶל חֲבֵרוֹ, וְלֹא יִחֲדוּ לָהּ הַבְּעָלִים מָקוֹם, וְטִלְטְלָהּ

אף המוכר וכו'. כשם שאמרו שמרים במפקיד, כך אמרו במוכר. שהמוכר שמן לחבירו, ונותן לו מתוך חביותיו שמן מזוקק תמיד, שהוא מסתפק ממנו, הרי הלוקח מקבל עליו לפחות לו לוג ומחצה, מחמת שמרים, לכל מאה לוג.

ואין הלכה כרבי יהודה: (ט) לא יחדו לה הבעלים מקום. בבית שומר, לומר לו זוית זו השאילני:

The following Tanna holds that the deduction for sediment may be made not only by a *shomer* of oil, but also by a seller of oil:

אַף הַמּוֹכֵר שֶׁמֶן מְזֻקָּק לַחֲבֵרוֹ כָּל יְמוֹת — **רַבִּי יְהוּדָה אוֹמֵר** — R' Yehudah says: הַשָּׁנָה — This deduction may be made **even where someone sold his fellow pure oil for the entire year,** and it was agreed that the seller would keep the oil with him and deliver it to the buyer in portions over the course of the year. The oil contained sediment at the time of the sale, but the sediment settled by the time the oil was delivered.[6] הֲרֵי זֶה מְקַבֵּל עָלָיו לֹג וּמֶחֱצָה שְׁמָרִים לְמֵאָה — It is understood that **this** buyer **accepts** a deduction of **one-and-a-half** *logs* **for every hundred** *logs* (1.5 percent) to account for the sediment. Since sediment was present in the oil at the time of the sale, the amount specified in the sale refers to an amount that contains sediment. The buyer knows that 100 *logs* of oil with sediment will become 98.5 *logs* once the sediment settles. He therefore agrees that if the oil is delivered pure, he will receive only 98.5 *logs*.[7]

[9] The rest of the chapter discusses the responsibilities of a *shomer*. A paid or unpaid *shomer* does not have to pay the owner if the deposited item was lost or ruined as a result of an unavoidable accident. However, if he used the item for his own benefit, he is considered a thief, who is responsible for *anything* that happens to it. The Mishnah deals with situations where the *shomer* used the item and then put it back into safekeeping:

הַמַּפְקִיד חָבִית אֵצֶל חֲבֵרוֹ וְלֹא יִחֲדוּ לָהּ הַבְּעָלִים מָקוֹם — **Someone deposited a barrel** of wine or oil **with his friend and the owner did not designate a place** in the *shomer*'s property in which the barrel must be kept,[1] וְטִלְטְלָהּ

— NOTES —

6. Although the Mishnah said that "pure oil" was sold, it does not mean that the buyer specified that he wanted pure oil; rather, no specification was made either way. The Mishnah means that although the oil contained sediment when it was sold, the oil received by the buyer will be pure, because the sediment will have settled by the time of delivery (*Meiri*, first explanation).

7. The Sages, however, disagree with R' Yehudah; in their opinion, the seller may

not deduct anything. Since it is expected that the oil will be pure at the time of delivery, the amount specified in the sale is understood as referring to pure oil. Therefore, when the seller delivers the pure oil, he must provide the full amount (see *Rashi* to 40b ד"ה אסור).

[9]

1. That is, the owner did not request that a certain area in the *shomer*'s house be lent to him for the exclusive use of storing his barrel. The *shomer* may therefore

[55] MISHNAH BAVA METZIA / Chapter 3: *Hamafkid*

וְנִשְׁבְּרָה, אִם מִתּוֹךְ יָדוֹ נִשְׁבְּרָה, לְצָרְכּוֹ חַיָּב, לְצָרְכָּהּ פָּטוּר. אִם מִשֶּׁהִנִּיחָהּ נִשְׁבְּרָה, בֵּין לְצָרְכּוֹ בֵּין לְצָרְכָּהּ פָּטוּר.

— רע״ב —

לצרכו. להשתמש בה: לצרכה. שהיתה במקום שקרובה להשתבר: אם משהניחה. שכלה תשמישו, הניחה במקום משתמר. בין שטלטלה מתחלה לצרכו, בין שטלטלה לצרכה, פטור. דאמרינן משהחזירה הרי היא ברשות הבעלים כבתחלה, ואינו עליה אלא כשומר חנם, ופטור על אונסיה, ואף על פי שלא הודיע לבעלים לומר נטלתיה והחזרתיה. ורישא דמתניתין רבי ישמעאל היא, דאמר בגונב טלה מן העדר והחזירו למקומו שהוא פטור, דלא בעינן דעת בעלים. והאי דקתני לא יחדו לה הבעלים מקום, לא מיבעיא קאמר, לא מיבעיא יחדו לה הבעלים מקום, והחזירה למקומה לאחר שנשתמש בה לצרכו, שהוא פטור, ואף על פי שלא הודיע לבעלים, שהרי החזירה למקום המיוחד לה, אלא אפילו לא יחדו לה הבעלים מקום, דלאו למקום מיוחד לה החזירה, הואיל והחזירה למקום משתמר, דלא בעינן דעת בעלים:

וְנִשְׁבְּרָה — **and [the *shomer*] moved it and it broke** as a result of an unavoidable accident. אִם מִתּוֹךְ יָדוֹ נִשְׁבְּרָה — **If it broke** when it was still **in his hands** (i.e., before he put it down in a safe place), the law depends on why he moved it: לְצָרְכּוֹ — If he moved the barrel **for his own needs** and he used it,[2] חַיָּב — **he is obligated** to pay for the breakage. Since he used it without permission, he is considered a thief,[3] who is liable even for unavoidable accidents. לְצָרְכָּהּ — But if he moved the barrel **for *its* needs** (for example, to take it from an unsafe place to a safe one), פָּטוּר — **he is exempt** from payment, because he never became a thief; rather, he always remained a *shomer*, who is not liable for unavoidable accidents.

The Mishnah now states the law where the barrel broke *after* the thief put it down in a safe place in his house:

אִם מִשֶּׁהִנִּיחָהּ נִשְׁבְּרָה — **If it broke after he put it down** in a safe place, בֵּין לְצָרְכּוֹ בֵּין לְצָרְכָּהּ — it makes no difference **whether** he had moved it **for his needs or for its needs**, פָּטוּר — either way **he is exempt** from payment. Even though he became a thief when he used the barrel for his own purposes, he was released from the responsibilities of a thief when he puts it in a safe place, because that is like returning it to its owner.[4] At that point, he went back to being a *shomer*, who is not responsible for unavoidable accidents.

NOTES

store it in any safe place in his property. [It is explained in note 8 why the Mishnah specifies this case.]

2. For example, he stood on it to reach a high place (*Tos. Yom Tov*).

3. He is deemed a thief even though he did not take any of the oil or wine for himself; rather, he used the barrel for just a short time and then returned it. This is an application of the rule: שׁוֹאֵל שֶׁלֹּא מִדַּעַת גַּזְלָן הֲוֵי, *One who borrows without permission is a thief* (*Tos. Yom Tov*, from Gemara).

4. Once a thief returns the article he stole, he is no longer responsible for it. If it is lost or damaged after it has been returned, he does not have to pay. Likewise, a *shomer* who stole the item (by using it for his own benefit) is responsible for it only until he returns it. Unlike a thief, however, a *shomer* does not need to return it to the owner himself or put it on the owner's property. Putting the object down in a safe place in the *shomer's* own house is as good as returning it to the owner, since that is where the owner wants it to be. [See, however, note 6 for a different opinion.]

— רע"ב —

יִחֲדוּ לָהּ הַבְּעָלִים מָקוֹם, וְטִלְטְלָהּ וְנִשְׁבְּרָה, בֵּין מִתּוֹךְ יָדוֹ וּבֵין מִשֶּׁהִנִּיחָהּ, לְצָרְכּוֹ חַיָּב, לְצָרְכָּהּ פָּטוּר.

וּבֵין משהניחה לצרכו חייב. סיפא זו אתאן לרבי עקיבא, דאמר בגונב טלה מן העדר והחזירו למקומו, ונאנס, לעולם הוא חייב, עד שיודיע לבעלים שגנב והחזיר. והכא נמי לאחר שנשתמש בה לצרכו ונעשה גזלן עליה, אף על פי שהניחה במקום המשתמר, חייב. והאי דקתני בסיפא יחדו לה הבעלים מקום, לא מיבעיא קאמר, לא מיבעיא לא יחדו שהוא חייב משהניחה לאחר שנשתמש לצרכו, דהא לא הניחה במקום המיוחד לה, אלא אפילו יחדו לה מקום, שחזר והניחה במקומה, חייב, דבעינן דעת בעלים. ורישא רבי ישמעאל וסיפא רבי עקיבא. והכי מוקמינן לה בגמרא:

The previous ruling follows the view of R' Yishmael, who holds that a *shomer* is released from the responsibilities of a thief as soon as he returns the item by putting it in a safe place in his house. It is not necessary for him to tell the owner that he has returned it.[5] R' Akiva, however, holds that he remains fully responsible until he tells the owner.[6] The Mishnah now teaches how R' Akiva would rule in cases similar to those discussed above: יִחֲדוּ לָהּ הַבְּעָלִים מָקוֹם — **If the owner designated a place for [the barrel]**,[7] וְטִלְטְלָהּ וְנִשְׁבְּרָה — **and [the *shomer*] moved it** out of that place **and it broke** due to an unavoidable accident, בֵּין מִתּוֹךְ יָדוֹ וּבֵין מִשֶּׁהִנִּיחָהּ — **whether** it broke **while it was still in his hands** (i.e., before he put it back in the designated place) **or** it broke **after he put it down** in the designated place, the law depends on why he moved it: לְצָרְכּוֹ חַיָּב — If he moved it **for his own needs** and he used it, **he is obligated** to pay. Once he used the barrel he is considered a thief, and this Tanna (R' Akiva) holds that once a *shomer* becomes a thief, he continues being responsible for the item until he tells the owner that he has returned it. Thus, even if it broke after he put it back in its designated place, he must pay. לְצָרְכָּהּ פָּטוּר — **But if he moved the barrel for its own needs, he is exempt** from payment regardless of when it broke, since he never became a thief.[8]

NOTES

5. An ordinary thief is not considered to have returned the stolen item until he tells the owner that he has returned it. The owner must be told that he has his item back, because otherwise he would not know that he has to take care of it (see *Sma, Choshen Mishpat* 355:1). R' Yishmael holds that a *shomer* is different. Since the *shomer* is the one taking care of the item, it is enough that *he* knows of its return. There is no need for the owner to be told (*Tos. Yom Tov*).

6. According to R' Akiva, once a *shomer* uses the owner's item without permission, the owner presumably does not want him to be a *shomer* anymore. Therefore, he cannot just put it in a safe place and go back to watching it. He must tell the owner, so that the owner can watch it himself (*Tos. Yom Tov*).

7. [It is explained in the next note why the Mishnah specifies this case.]

8. [Although he moved the barrel out of its designated place, that does not make him a thief, since he acted for the benefit of the barrel.]

R' Akiva's opinion is presented in a case where the owner designated a specific place in which the barrel should be stored and he borrowed that place from the *shomer*. The Tanna thus teaches that R' Akiva's ruling applies *even* in this case. Despite the fact that the *shomer* put the barrel back in the place borrowed by the owner, he is not considered to have returned it to the owner, since he did not

[10] הַמַּפְקִיד מָעוֹת אֵצֶל חֲבֵרוֹ, צְרָרָן וְהִפְשִׁילָן לַאֲחוֹרָיו, אוֹ שֶׁמְּסָרָן לִבְנוֹ וּלְבִתּוֹ הַקְּטַנִּים וְנָעַל בִּפְנֵיהֶם שֶׁלֹּא כָרָאוּי, חַיָּב, שֶׁלֹּא שָׁמַר כְּדֶרֶךְ הַשּׁוֹמְרִים. וְאִם שָׁמַר כְּדֶרֶךְ הַשּׁוֹמְרִים, פָּטוּר.

[11] הַמַּפְקִיד מָעוֹת אֵצֶל שֻׁלְחָנִי,

— רע״ב —

(י) צררן. בסודרן. והפשילן לאחוריו, אף על פי שמירה מעולה היא, חייב. שהמוליך מעות של פקדון ממקום למקום, אין להם שמירה אלא בידו, דכתיב (דברים יד, כה) וצרת הכסף בידך, אף על פי שגרורים הם, יהיו בידך. ואם בבית הוא, אין להם שמירה אלא בקרקע, ובכותל בטפח הסמוך לתקרה, או בטפח הסמוך לארץ. שאין דרך הגנבים לחפש שם. ואם שמר בענין אחר, פושע הוי וחייב. אלא אם כן התנה מתחלה עם המפקיד, שעל מנת כן הוא מקבל הפקדון, שלא יתחייב בכל השמירות הללו: לבנו ולבתו הקטנים. אבל לגדולים, נשבעים הם שמסרו כדרך השומרים, ופטור. ולא אמרינן בהא שומר שמסר לשומר חייב, שדרך האדם להפקיד מה שהופקד בידו, ביד אשתו ובניו. וכל המפקיד, על דעת שיתנם הנפקד ביד אשתו ובניו הוא מפקיד:

---

[10] The Mishnah speaks of an unpaid *shomer*:

הַמַּפְקִיד מָעוֹת אֵצֶל חֲבֵרוֹ — If someone deposited coins with his friend, צְרָרָן וְהִפְשִׁילָן לַאֲחוֹרָיו — and [the *shomer*] tied them in a kerchief and slung them behind him, on his back,[1] אוֹ שֶׁמְּסָרָן לִבְנוֹ וּלְבִתּוֹ הַקְּטַנִּים — or he handed them over to his underage son or daughter to watch for him, וְנָעַל בִּפְנֵיהֶם שֶׁלֹּא כָרָאוּי — or[2] he did not lock the door before [the coins] properly, חַיָּב — he is obligated to pay the owner if the coins were stolen or lost as a result of these circumstances, שֶׁלֹּא שָׁמַר כְּדֶרֶךְ הַשּׁוֹמְרִים — because he did not watch them in the way that *shomrim* normally do, and thus he is considered negligent. וְאִם שָׁמַר כְּדֶרֶךְ הַשּׁוֹמְרִים פָּטוּר — But if he *did* watch the coins in the normal way of *shomrim*, he is exempt from payment.[3]

[11] The Mishnah cites more laws about someone who has to safeguard money:

הַמַּפְקִיד מָעוֹת אֵצֶל שֻׁלְחָנִי — If someone deposited coins with a moneychanger[1]

NOTES

tell the owner that he had returned it. R' Akiva's ruling would certainly apply where the owner had *not* designated a specific place, and the *shomer* just put it down in a safe place in his house.

The Tanna states the opposite in the first part of the Mishnah. There, he presented R' Yishmael's opinion in a case where the owner had *not* designated a place. This teaches that R' Yishmael considers the *shomer* to have properly returned the barrel (although he did not tell the owner) even where the owner had not designated a place in which to put it. R' Yishmael's ruling would certainly apply where the owner *had* designated a place for the barrel and the *shomer* put it back there (*Rav*, from Gemara).

[10]
1. This clause refers to a *shomer* who is traveling. The required way to watch a bundle of money when traveling is by holding it in one's hand (*Rav*), or by tying it to his garments in front of him so that he can always see it (*Rosh* #20).
2. *Tos. Yom Tov.*
3. This rule applies only in the case of an unpaid *shomer*. For a paid *shomer*, it is not enough to guard the item in "the normal way of *shomrim*"; rather, he must guard it as best he can (see *Tosafos* 42a ד״ה אמר).

[11]
1. A moneychanger is paid to exchange people's coins for them.

משניות בבא מציעא / פרק ג: המפקיד

אִם צְרוּרִין, לֹא יִשְׁתַּמֵּשׁ בָּהֶן. לְפִיכָךְ אִם אָבְדוּ אֵינוֹ חַיָּב בְּאַחֲרָיוּתָן. מַתִּירִין, יִשְׁתַּמֵּשׁ בָּהֶן. לְפִיכָךְ אִם אָבְדוּ חַיָּב בְּאַחֲרָיוּתָן. אֵצֶל בַּעַל הַבַּיִת, בֵּין צְרוּרִין וּבֵין מַתִּירִין לֹא יִשְׁתַּמֵּשׁ בָּהֶן. לְפִיכָךְ אִם אָבְדוּ אֵינוֹ חַיָּב בְּאַחֲרָיוּתָן.

— רע״ב —

(יא) אם צרורין. וחתומין, או קשורים קשר משונה, לא ישתמש בהן. אבל אם אינם חתומים או קשורים קשר משונה, אף על פי שצרורין, הרי הן כמתירין, וכאילו אינם קשורים כלל, ומותר להשתמש בהם: **להשתמש בהן:** חייב באחריותן. ואפילו לא נשתמש בהן הוי עליהם שומר שכר, מפני שיכול להשתמש בהם, וחייב בגניבה ואבדה. ואם נשתמש, הוי מלוה גביה, וחייב אף באונסין:

---

to safeguard but did not pay him to do so, **אִם צְרוּרִין לֹא יִשְׁתַּמֵּשׁ בָּהֶן** — the law is that **if they were** given in a bundle that was **tied** and sealed, or that was tied with an unusual knot, **he may not use them**, because the owner tied the bundle in this way to show that he does not want him to use the coins.[2] **לְפִיכָךְ אִם אָבְדוּ אֵינוֹ חַיָּב בְּאַחֲרָיוּתָן** — **Therefore, if [the coins] were lost** without negligence on his part,[3] **he is not responsible for them.** In view of the fact that he was neither paid to watch the coins nor allowed to use them, he is an unpaid *shomer*, who is not liable for loss (unless he was negligent). **מַתִּירִין יִשְׁתַּמֵּשׁ בָּהֶן** — **However, if [the coins] were loose,**[4] **he** *may* **use them.** Since a moneychanger always needs coins for his business, and the owner did not tell him (or indicate in any way) that he may not use the coins, it may be assumed that the owner allows him to use them and give back other coins instead. **לְפִיכָךְ אִם אָבְדוּ חַיָּב בְּאַחֲרָיוּתָן** — **Therefore, if they were lost, he** *is* **responsible for them.** Although he was not directly paid for watching the coins, the right to use them is a benefit that makes him a "paid *shomer*." He is thus liable for their loss.[5]

The Mishnah now teaches the law where coins were given to a *shomer* who is not a moneychanger:

אֵצֶל בַּעַל הַבַּיִת — **If** coins were deposited **with an** ordinary **householder** for him to safeguard, **בֵּין צְרוּרִין וּבֵין מַתִּירִין** — it makes no difference **whether they were tied up or loose,** **לֹא יִשְׁתַּמֵּשׁ בָּהֶן** — **he may not use them.** Since an ordinary householder does not need extra cash,[6] we assume that the owner does not let him use the coins even if he gave them to him loose. **לְפִיכָךְ אִם אָבְדוּ אֵינוֹ חַיָּב בְּאַחֲרָיוּתָן** — **Therefore, if they were lost, he is not responsible**

NOTES

2. *Tos. Yom Tov.*

3. The *shomer* watched the money in the normal way and it was nevertheless lost. See previous Mishnah.

4. Or even if the coins were in a bundle tied with a regular knot (*Rav*). Securing coins in this way is normal and thus does not show that the owner forbids the moneychanger to use them (*Tos. Yom Tov*).

5. As soon as the coins were given to him, even before he started using them, the moneychanger had the status of a paid *shomer* because he was *allowed* to use them right away. Like any paid *shomer*, he is liable for loss even if he was not negligent, but he is not liable for a loss that could not have been prevented [אֹנֶס]. Once he uses the coins, he becomes a *borrower*, who is liable even for unpreventable loss (*Rav*).

6. [Although an ordinary householder needs money for his household expenses, he usually has enough available for that purpose.]

[59] **MISHNAH BAVA METZIA** / Chapter 3: *Hamafkid*

— רע״ב —

רבי יהודה אומר בשולחני. והלכה כרבי יהודה: (יב) ילקה בחסר וביתר. במה שחסר הפקדון, ובמה שהותיר. כגון שהפקיד אצלו רחל טעונה למר או מעוברת, ונגזזה או ילדה לאחר ששלח בה יד, משלם אותה ואת גיזותיה ואת ולדותיה,

חֶנְוָנִי כְּבַעַל הַבַּיִת, דִּבְרֵי רַבִּי מֵאִיר. רַבִּי יְהוּדָה אוֹמֵר, חֶנְוָנִי כְּשֻׁלְחָנִי.

[יב] **הַשּׁוֹלֵחַ** יָד בַּפִּקָּדוֹן, בֵּית שַׁמַּאי אוֹמְרִים, יִלְקֶה בְחָסֵר וּבְיָתֵר.

---

for them. In this case, where the *shomer* is forbidden to use the coins, he is just an unpaid *shomer*, who is not liable for loss.

The Mishnah cites a dispute as to whether a storekeeper who was given coins to watch is treated like an ordinary householder or a moneychanger: חֶנְוָנִי כְּבַעַל הַבַּיִת — **A storekeeper is like a householder.** Since a storekeeper does not need a large amount of cash all the time,[7] the owner presumably does not let him use the coins (even if he gave them to him loose) just as he would not let a householder use them. The storekeeper is thus an unpaid *shomer*, who is not liable for loss. דִּבְרֵי רַבִּי מֵאִיר — **These are the words of R' Meir.** רַבִּי יְהוּדָה אוֹמֵר — **But R' Yehudah says:** חֶנְוָנִי כְּשֻׁלְחָנִי — **A storekeeper is like a moneychanger,** because many times a storekeeper does need extra cash for his business. The owner, therefore, presumably lets the storekeeper use the coins (unless he tied them up in an unusual way), just as he lets a moneychanger use them. A storekeeper is thus a paid *shomer*, who *is* liable for loss.

[12] The following Mishnah deals with the law of שְׁלִיחוּת יָד, *shelichus yad* (literally, *sending the hand*). This is where a *shomer* takes the deposited item in order to keep all or some of it permanently for himself, or to use it in a way that would permanently ruin all or some of it. If any *shomer* (even an unpaid one) does this, he is considered a thief, who is responsible for all losses, even those that he could not have prevented.[1]

In the Mishnah's first case, after the *shomer* took the item for himself (*shelichus yad*), it went through a physical change that affected its value. He later lost the item in a way that he could not have prevented. The Mishnah cites a disagreement among Tannaim as to how much the *shomer* must pay: הַשּׁוֹלֵחַ יָד בַּפִּקָּדוֹן — **If [a *shomer*] took the deposited item** for himself, and then it physically changed, after which he lost it unavoidably, בֵּית שַׁמַּאי אוֹמְרִים — **Beis Shammai say:** יִלְקֶה בְחָסֵר וּבְיָתֵר — **He suffers** the value of

---

NOTES

7. He can frequently buy goods for his store on credit (*Rashi, Kiddushin* 53b ד״ה חנווני כבעה״ב).

[12]
1. If he did not intend to take it permanently, nor did he intend to spoil it, but just borrowed it without permission, he has not committed *shelichus yad*. He is nevertheless considered a thief, but for a different reason: "One who borrows without permission is a thief" (Mishnah 9 note 3). There are several differences between the two reasons, including that a *shomer* who commits *shelichus yad* is deemed a thief immediately, whereas one who borrows without permission does not have the responsibilities of a thief until he uses the item (see *Tiferes Yisrael*).

— רע״ב —

וּבֵית הִלֵּל אוֹמְרִים, בִּשְׁעַת הוֹצָאָה. וּמִמָּא שֶׁהוּא לוֹקֶה בַּמָּה שֶׁחִסְּרָהּ אֶצְלוֹ. וּבְיָתֵר, שֶׁאִם נִתְעַבְּרָה אוֹ טָעֲנָה גָמַר כְּשֶׁהִיא אֶצְלוֹ, מְשַׁלֵּם אוֹתָהּ טְעוּנָה וּמְעֻבֶּרֶת כְּמוֹת שֶׁהִיא עַכְשָׁיו, וַהֲרֵי לוֹקֶה בְּיָתֵר: וּבֵית הִלֵּל אוֹמְרִים בִּשְׁעַת הוֹצָאָה. מִבֵּית הַבְּעָלִים, אִם טְעוּנָה טְעוּנָה, וְאִם רֵקָנִית רֵקָנִית:

---

the change, whether the change is **a decrease or an increase.** For example, a case of "decrease" is where he stole a pregnant animal that then gave birth, which is a decrease in the mother. Later he lost both the animal and the newborn. It is not enough for him to pay what the animal was worth at the time of the theft; rather, he must pay the value of the animal (after it gave birth) *and* the value of the newborn.[2] An example of "increase" is where he stole an animal that was not pregnant and then it became pregnant[3] (and later he lost the animal). Here, too, it is not enough for him to pay what the animal was worth at the time of the theft, before it became pregnant; rather, he must pay the value of the animal in its pregnant state. It emerges that no matter whether the item decreased or increased after the theft, the *shomer* has to pay for the change.[4]

Beis Hillel disagree:

וּבֵית הִלֵּל אוֹמְרִים — But Beis Hillel say: בִּשְׁעַת הוֹצָאָה — **He pays according to** its value at **the time of** its **removal** from the owner's possession. He pays only what it was worth at the time of the theft, and no more.[5]

A third opinion:

NOTES

2. [A non-pregnant animal plus a newborn are worth more together than a pregnant animal.]
Another example of "decrease" is where a *shomer* stole a sheep that had wool and then its wool was shorn off. He must pay the value of the sheep (without wool) *and* the value of the removed wool, which amounts to more than what the sheep was worth when it was stolen (*Rav*).

3. Or he stole a sheep that did not have wool and then it grew wool (*Rav*).

4. Under Biblical law, the *shomer* is obligated to pay only what the item was worth when he took it. A *shomer* who takes the item for himself has the same law as a thief. If a thief steals something that then goes up in value, he pays only what it was worth at the time of the theft (see *Bava Kamma* 9:1). According to Beis Shammai, however, the Sages punished a thief by requiring him to pay for the change. If the item physically decreased, he pays for what it lost (for example, if a pregnant animal gave birth, he pays the value of the newborn), and if the item physically increased, he pays for what it gained (for example, if the animal became pregnant, he pays the value added by its pregnancy). Thus, it is only under Rabbinic law that a thief, or a *shomer* who took the item illegally, must pay the extra amount (see Gemara 43b and *Bava Kamma* 95a).

5. If he stole a pregnant animal that then gave birth, he pays only the value of the pregnant animal (and not the newborn as well). And if he stole a non-pregnant animal that then became pregnant, he pays only the value of a non-pregnant animal (*Rav*). According to Beis Hillel, the Sages did not punish a thief, or a *shomer* who took the item illegally, by requiring him to pay the value of the newborn or the value of the pregnancy. Thus, we follow the original, Biblical law, which states that a thief pays what the item was worth at the time of the theft.

[61] MISHNAH BAVA METZIA / Chapter 3: *Hamafkid*

— רע״ב —

רַבִּי עֲקִיבָא אוֹמֵר, בִּשְׁעַת הַתְּבִיעָה. הַחוֹשֵׁב לִשְׁלוֹחַ יָד בְּפִקְדּוֹן, בֵּית שַׁמַּאי אוֹמְרִים, חַיָּב. וּבֵית הִלֵּל אוֹמְרִים, אֵינוֹ חַיָּב עַד שֶׁיִּשְׁלַח בּוֹ יָד, שֶׁנֶּאֱמַר, אִם לֹא שָׁלַח יָדוֹ בִּמְלֶאכֶת רֵעֵהוּ. כֵּיצַד, הִטָּה אֶת הֶחָבִית וְנָטַל הֵימֶנָּה רְבִיעִית וְנִשְׁבְּרָה, אֵינוֹ מְשַׁלֵּם אֶלָּא רְבִיעִית,

רבי עקיבא אומר בשעת התביעה. כמו שהוא הפקדון בשעת העמדה בדין. דכתיב (ויקרא ה, כד) לאשר הוא לו יתננו ביום אשמתו, יתן כמו שהוא ביום אשמתו, ביום שמתחייב בו בדין. והלכה כבית הלל: החושב לשלוח יד בפקדון. אמר בפני עדים אטול פקדונו של פלוני לטלמי׳: בית שמאי מחייבים. דכתיב (שמות כב, ח) על כל דבר פשע, משעה שדבר לשלוח יד הוי פושע: עד שישלח יד. דכתיב (שם ז) אם לא שלח ידו במלאכת רעהו. והאי על כל דבר פשע דרשי ביה בית הלל, אמר לעבדו ולשלוחו לשלוח יד בפקדון, מנין שהוא חייב, תלמוד לומר על כל דבר פשע. השתא מפרש למלתייהו דבית הלל. ואית ספרים דלא גרסי כילד: ביצד הטה את החבית. ונשברה. משתא באונפה נפשה היא: לאחר זמן: אינו משלם אלא רביעית. דשליחות יד אינו מתחייב באונסים עד שימשוך או יגביה, דהוי קניה:

בִּשְׁעַת הַתְּבִיעָה — He pays according to its value at **the time of the claim** against him in court. He pays only for an increase in value that occurred before he is tried in court, and not for an increase in value that occurred later.[6]

The Mishnah presents a dispute as to whether *shelichus yad* includes speech:

הַחוֹשֵׁב לִשְׁלוֹחַ יָד בְּפִקְדּוֹן — **If** [a *shomer*] **intends to take** the **deposited item for himself,** that is, he says in front of witnesses that he intends to take the item, but he did not yet do so, **בֵּית שַׁמַּאי אוֹמְרִים חַיָּב** — **Beis Shammai say** that he immediately becomes **responsible** even for unavoidable loss, because even a statement of intent is considered *shelichus yad*.[7] **וּבֵית הִלֵּל אוֹמְרִים** — **But Beis Hillel say:** **אֵינוֹ חַיָּב עַד שֶׁיִּשְׁלַח בּוֹ יָד** — **He is not responsible** for unavoidable loss **until** he physically **takes it for himself,** **שֶׁנֶּאֱמַר** — **because it is stated** (*Exodus* 22:7): *If he [the shomer] did not lay his hand upon his fellow's property,* which implies a physical act, and not just speech.

The Mishnah elaborates upon Beis Hillel's opinion:

כֵּיצַד — **How** does a *shomer* perform *shelichus yad*? **הִטָּה אֶת הֶחָבִית וְנָטַל הֵימֶנָּה רְבִיעִית** — **If he tilted a barrel** of wine **and took a** *revi'is* **from it** for himself,[8] **וְנִשְׁבְּרָה** — **and later [the barrel] broke** because of an unavoidable accident and all the wine spilled out, **אֵינוֹ מְשַׁלֵּם אֶלָּא רְבִיעִית** — **he pays** the owner **only** for the *revi'is* of wine, and not for the rest. In order to be liable for *shelichus yad,* the *shomer* must perform an act of acquisition (*kinyan*) with the item, for example, pulling or lifting it. Merely tilting a barrel is not a *kinyan*.

NOTES

6. R' Akiva derives this law from *Leviticus* 5:24 (see *Rav*).

7. The source for this law is *Exodus* 22:8 (see *Rav*).

8. The *shomer* tilted the barrel so that the wine would flow to the top, and then he scooped out a *revi'is* of wine from it.

הִגְבִּיהָהּ וְנָטַל הֵימֶנָּה רְבִיעִית, וְנִשְׁבְּרָה, מְשַׁלֵּם דְּמֵי כֻלָּהּ.

— רע"ב —

הגביהה ונטל. לאו דוקא נטל, דמכי אגבהה על מנת ליטול חייב באונסיה, אפילו לא נטל ממנה כלום. ואם נטל רביעית מן החבית, והחמיץ היין הנשאר בחבית אחר כן, אף על פי שלא הגביה החבית, משלם כל היין, שהוא גרס יין שהחמיץ, וגירי דידיה הוא דאהנו ליה:

Thus, the *shomer* is not liable for the entire barrel, but only for the *revi'is* that he lifted out of it. **הִגְבִּיהָהּ וְנָטַל הֵימֶנָּה רְבִיעִית** — However, if **he lifted** [the barrel] with the intention to **take a** *revi'is* **of wine from it** for himself, **וְנִשְׁבְּרָה** — **and then [the barrel] broke** because of an unavoidable accident, **מְשַׁלֵּם דְּמֵי כֻלָּהּ** — **he must pay for its entire value.** By *lifting* the barrel, he performed a *kinyan* on the barrel as a whole, and he is therefore liable for the entire barrel.[9]

NOTES

9. As soon as he lifted the barrel, even before he took any wine, he is guilty of *shelichus yad* [since he *intended* to take some wine] (*Rav*).

Even though the *shomer* did not intend to take the whole barrel, but only a *revi'is*, he is liable for the entire barrel. According to the law of *shelichus yad*, intent to take part of the item makes the *shomer* liable for all of it (see *Rashi* 41a ד"ה ור' נתן). However, the act of *shelichus yad* (i.e., the *kinyan*) must be done with the entire item, and not just the part he wants to keep. Thus, if the *shomer* lifted only a *revi'is*, he would not be liable for the whole barrel, as the Mishnah stated above. But if he lifted the whole barrel with intent to take a *revi'is*, he becomes responsible for it all.

Chapter Four

משניות בבא מציעא / פרק ד: הזהב

— רע״ב —

פרק רביעי – הזהב.
(א) הזהב קונה את הכסף. כל דבר שהוא חשוב להיות מטבע,

[א] הַזָּהָב קוֹנֶה אֶת הַכֶּסֶף, וְהַכֶּסֶף אֵינוֹ קוֹנֶה אֶת הַזָּהָב. הַנְּחֹשֶׁת קוֹנָה

וְחָרִיף לִינָּתֵן בְּהוֹצָאָה, דִּין מָעוֹת יֵשׁ לוֹ, וְאֵינוֹ קוֹנֶה אֶת שֶׁכְּנֶגְדוֹ שֶׁאֵינוֹ חָשׁוּב מַטְבֵּעַ, וְאֵינוֹ חָרִיף בְּהוֹצָאָה כְּמוֹתוֹ. וּמִי שֶׁאֵין טִבְעוֹ חָשׁוּב וְחָרִיף, דִּין פֵּרוֹת יֵשׁ לוֹ, וּמְשִׁיכָתוֹ הוּא קִיּוּם דָּבָר. לְפִיכָךְ מִכִּי מָשַׁךְ הָאֶחָד דִּינְרֵי זָהָב, קָנָה הַשֵּׁנִי דִּינְרֵי כֶסֶף בְּכָל מָקוֹם שֶׁהֵם, וְאֵין אֶחָד מֵהֶם יָכוֹל לַחְזוֹר בּוֹ, דְּדִינְרֵי זָהָב הָווּ פֵּרוֹת לְגַבֵּי דִינְרֵי כֶסֶף: **וְהַכֶּסֶף אֵינוֹ קוֹנֶה אֶת הַזָּהָב.** דְּדִינְרֵי כֶסֶף שֶׁהֵם חֲרִיפִים בְּהוֹצָאָה, דִּין מָעוֹת יֵשׁ לָהֶם לְגַבֵּי דִּינְרֵי זָהָב. וְאִם מָשַׁךְ הָאֶחָד דִּינְרֵי כֶסֶף, לֹא קָנָה הָאַחֵר דִּינַר זָהָב עַד שֶׁיִּמְשׁוֹךְ, דְּמָעוֹת אֵינָן קוֹנוֹת. וְהַיְנוּ טַעְמָא נַמֵּי שֶׁנְּחֹשֶׁת קוֹנָה אֶת הַכֶּסֶף, דִּפְרוּטוֹת שֶׁל נְחֹשֶׁת שֶׁאֵין טִבְעָן חָשׁוּב כָּל כָּךְ, הָווּ פֵּרוֹת לְגַבֵּי דִּינְרֵי כֶסֶף, וְהַכֶּסֶף אֵינוֹ קוֹנֶה אֶת הַנְּחֹשֶׁת:

---

[1] Movable objects cannot be acquired simply by paying for them. The sale of a movable object is not final until the buyer does some other act of *kinyan*[1] to it, such as lifting it (*hagbahah*) or drawing it from where it is (*meshichah*).[2] Once he does one of these acts of *kinyan*, the buyer takes over ownership of the item even if he has not yet paid for it (and he now owes the seller the money). Before he makes such an act of *kinyan*, he does not own the item even if he already paid the seller for it.[3]

A question arises in a case where two people trade different types of coins: Which coins are the ones being "bought" and which are the ones paying for the purchase? The trade will be final only when the coin that is being "bought" is taken by the person buying it:

הַזָּהָב קוֹנֶה אֶת הַכֶּסֶף — If gold coins are traded for silver ones, taking **the gold** coins causes the other person to **acquire the silver** coins.[4] This is because the gold coins are considered the object being bought, so that a *kinyan* on them completes the sale. וְהַכֶּסֶף אֵינוֹ קוֹנֶה אֶת הַזָּהָב — But **taking the silver** coins **does not** cause the other person to **acquire the gold** coins, because the silver coins are considered the "money" in this exchange, and taking money for an item does *not* complete its sale.[5] הַנְּחֹשֶׁת קוֹנָה

NOTES

[1]
1. A *kinyan* is an act through which a person acquires ownership of property, either from someone else or from *hefker*.
2. See *Kiddushin* 1:4,5. This is in contrast to real estate (houses or land), which can be acquired simply by paying for it (*Kiddushin* 1:5).
3. By Biblical law, even movable property is acquired by paying for it. However, the Rabbis were concerned that a buyer might pay for his purchase and then leave it temporarily with the seller. If a fire were then to break out, the seller would not bother to save it since it was no longer his. The Rabbis therefore said that the sale is not final even after money has been paid until the buyer makes some other *kinyan*, in which he actually takes the item from the seller (*Tos. Yom Tov* to Mishnah 2, from Gemara 47b).

4. That is, the sale is final and the buyer must now pay the seller the number of silver coins they agreed on (*Tos. Yom Tov*, from Gemara). [However, the seller does not actually "acquire" any specific coins until the buyer pays him.]

5. As we explained in the introduction to this Mishnah.

The reason gold coins are considered the object being sold and silver the "money" is that whenever one kind of coin is used to acquire another kind of coin, the kind that can be more easily spent in the marketplace is considered to be the "money" (*Rav*). Since gold coins

[65] MISHNAH BAVA METZIA / Chapter 4: *Hazahav*

— רע"ב —

מעות הרעות. שנפסלו:
אסימון. שנעשה כמדת
המטבע היולא, אלא
שעדיין לא טבעו עליו
צורה:

אֶת הַכֶּסֶף, וְהַכֶּסֶף אֵינוֹ קוֹנֶה אֶת הַנְּחֹשֶׁת.
מְעוֹת הָרָעוֹת קוֹנוֹת אֶת הַיָּפוֹת, וְהַיָּפוֹת
אֵינָן קוֹנוֹת אֶת הָרָעוֹת. אֲסִימוֹן קוֹנֶה אֶת
הַמַּטְבֵּעַ, וְהַמַּטְבֵּעַ אֵינוֹ קוֹנֶה אֶת אֲסִימוֹן.
מִטַּלְטְלִין קוֹנִים אֶת הַמַּטְבֵּעַ, וְהַמַּטְבֵּעַ אֵינוֹ קוֹנֶה אֶת הַמִּטַּלְטְלִין.

אֶת הַכֶּסֶף — If silver and copper coins are being traded, then taking **the copper** coins causes the other person to **acquire the silver** coins.[6] This is because the copper coins are considered the object being bought, so that a *kinyan* on them completes the sale. וְהַכֶּסֶף אֵינוֹ קוֹנֶה אֶת הַנְּחֹשֶׁת — **But** taking **the silver** coins **does not** cause the other person to **acquire the copper** coins, because the silver coins are considered the "money" in this exchange.[7] מְעוֹת הָרָעוֹת קוֹנוֹת אֶת הַיָּפוֹת — If coins that are still in use in that country are traded for those that have been taken out of circulation, taking **the bad coins** (the ones no longer used) causes the other person to **acquire the good ones**, because the bad coins are considered the object being bought; וְהַיָּפוֹת אֵינָן קוֹנוֹת אֶת הָרָעוֹת — but taking **the good ones does not** cause the other person to **acquire the bad ones**, since the good coins are considered the "money" in this exchange. אֲסִימוֹן קוֹנֶה אֶת הַמַּטְבֵּעַ — If a minted coin is being traded for an unminted coin,[8] taking **the unminted coin** causes the other person to **acquire the minted coin**, because the unminted coin is considered the object being bought; וְהַמַּטְבֵּעַ אֵינוֹ קוֹנֶה אֶת אֲסִימוֹן — but taking **the minted coin does not** cause the other person to **acquire the unminted coin**, because the minted coin is the money.

The Mishnah teaches the basic rule with regard to buying movable objects: מִטַּלְטְלִין קוֹנִים אֶת הַמַּטְבֵּעַ — Taking **movable objects** causes the seller to **acquire the coin** that is given in payment, וְהַמַּטְבֵּעַ אֵינוֹ קוֹנֶה אֶת הַמִּטַּלְטְלִין — **but** taking **the coin does not** cause the buyer to **acquire the movable objects**.[9]

NOTES

are worth much more than silver ones, many merchants are reluctant to take them as payment because they would then have to make change for them. Silver coins, on the other hand, are readily accepted.

6. That is, the person who sold the copper coins is now owed the number of silver ones they agreed on (see note 4).

7. Although there are places where merchants would prefer to get the cheaper copper coins as payment rather than the more expensive silver ones, there are other places where the merchants do not accept copper coins at all, only silver ones. The copper coins are therefore viewed as the object being bought, and the silver coins are the payment for them (*Tos. Yom Tov,* from Gemara).

8. Unminted coins are pieces of gold or silver or copper made into the shape of coins that have not yet been stamped with an image ("minted") by the government. Since they cannot yet be used as money in the market, they are considered the object being bought (*Tos. Yom Tov*).

9. It does not matter whether the coin is gold, silver, or copper. A coin is always considered payment for a movable object.

משניות בבא מציעא / פרק ד: הזהב

זֶה הַכְּלָל, כָּל הַמִּטַּלְטְלִין קוֹנִין זֶה אֶת זֶה.

[ב] **בֵּיצַד**, מָשַׁךְ הֵימֶנּוּ פֵּרוֹת וְלֹא נָתַן לוֹ מָעוֹת, אֵינוֹ יָכוֹל לַחֲזֹר בּוֹ. נָתַן לוֹ מָעוֹת וְלֹא מָשַׁךְ הֵימֶנּוּ פֵּרוֹת, יָכוֹל לַחֲזֹר בּוֹ.

— רע"ב —

בל המטלטלים קונים זה את זה. אם החליף אלו באלו, כיון שמשך האחד קנה חבירו, והאי כל, לאתויי אפילו כיס מלא מעות בכיס מלא מעות: (ב) **נתן** לו מעות ולא משך ממנו פירות יכול לחזור בו. ודבר תורה מעות קונות, כדאמרינן גבי הקדש, דכתיב (ויקרא כז, יט) ונתן הכסף וקם לו. ומה טעם אמרו משיכה קונה ולא מעות, גזירה שמא יניח לוקח מקחו בבית מוכר זמן מרובה, ותפול דליקה בשכונת המוכר, ולא יחוש לערוח ולהציל, לפיכך העמידוס ברשותו לחזור בו אם ירצה, דכיון דאם יתייקרו, ברשותו יתייקרו, ויחזור בו מן המכר, ויהא השכר שלו, כדידיה חשיב להו, וטרח ומציל:

The Mishnah moves on to discuss trading movable objects for each other: זֶה הַכְּלָל — **This is the rule** with regard to trading one movable object for another: כָּל הַמִּטַּלְטְלִין קוֹנִין זֶה אֶת זֶה — **All movable objects acquire one another;** that is, as soon as one person takes one of the objects, the other person acquires the other object wherever it is, and the deal is final.[10]

[2] The Mishnah now gives the reason for the laws taught in the previous Mishnah. It also qualifies the extent of those laws:[1]

בֵּיצַד — **How so?** Why is it that taking the gold or copper coins acquires the silver coins, but taking the silver coins does not acquire the gold or copper coins? מָשַׁךְ הֵימֶנּוּ פֵּרוֹת וְלֹא נָתַן לוֹ מָעוֹת — Because the general rule is that when a person buys produce,[2] if **[the buyer] drew the produce from [the seller] but did not yet give him the money,** אֵינוֹ יָכוֹל לַחֲזֹר בּוֹ — **he cannot back out** of the sale, because taking the produce is the *kinyan* that makes the sale final. נָתַן לוֹ מָעוֹת וְלֹא מָשַׁךְ הֵימֶנּוּ פֵּרוֹת — In contrast, **if [the buyer] gave [the seller] money but did not yet draw the produce from him,** יָכוֹל לַחֲזֹר בּוֹ — **he can back out** of the sale.[3] Since gold and copper coins are considered "produce" in comparison to silver coins,[4] when gold or copper coins are traded for silver coins, taking the gold or copper (the "produce") acquires the silver (the "money"), but taking the silver does not acquire the gold or copper coins.

This would imply that simply paying money for an item accomplishes nothing. The Mishnah qualifies this rule:

─────────── NOTES ───────────

10. This kind of exchange is a new *kinyan*, known as *kinyan chalifin*. In this *kinyan* neither object is considered "money." The *kinyan* works simply on the basis of exchange. The exchange takes effect as soon as *one* of the objects is acquired by the other person. See Mishnah 8:4 for an example of this.

[2]

1. *Tos. Yom Tov.*

2. The word "produce," which usually refers to food items that grow from a tree or the ground, is used in this chapter as a general name for any movable object that is bought with money.

3. That is, either one of them can back out of the sale (*Tiferes Yisrael*).

4. For the reasons explained in Mishnah 1, notes 5 and 7.

— רע"ב —

אבל אמרו מי שפרע וכו'. אף על פי שיכול לחזור בו, מורידין אותו בבית דין, ואומרים עליו, מי שפרע מדור המבול ומדור הפלגה ומאנשי סדום ועמורה ומן המערבים שטפפו ביס, הוא עתיד ליפרע ממי שאינו עומד בדבורו, ואחר כך מחזיר לו את מעותיו: רבי שמעון אומר כל שהכסף בידו ידו על העליונה. רבי שמעון אמלתיה דתנא קמא קאי, דאומר, נתן לו מעות ולא משך ממנו פירות, יכול לחזור בו בין מוכר בין לוקח. ואתא רבי שמעון למימר, דזמנין דמי שהכסף בידו, דהיינו המוכר שקבל את הכסף, ידו על העליונה, ובידו לקיים את המקח אם ירצה, ואין הלוקח יכול לחזור בו. כגון שהיתה עליתו של לוקח שכורה אצל המוכר, והשתא אם המוכר רוצה שיהיה המקח קיים אין הלוקח יכול לחזור בו, אף על פי שלא משך, דטעמא מאי אמור רבנן משיכה קונה ולא מעות, גזירה שמא יאמר לו מוכר ללוקח נשרפו חטיך בעלייה, הכא דעליה דלוקח היא, אי נפלה דליקה איהו טרח ומייתי לה. ואין הלכה כרבי שמעון. אלא אף על פי שעלייתו של לוקח שכורה אצל המוכר, כל זמן שלא משך, יכול לחזור בו בין לוקח בין מוכר:

[67] MISHNAH BAVA METZIA / Chapter 4: *Hazahav* 4/2

אֲבָל אָמְרוּ, מִי שֶׁפָּרַע מֵאַנְשֵׁי דוֹר הַמַּבּוּל וּמִדּוֹר הַפַּלָגָה, הוּא עָתִיד לְהִפָּרַע מִמִּי שֶׁאֵינוֹ עוֹמֵד בְּדִבּוּרוֹ. רַבִּי שִׁמְעוֹן אוֹמֵר, כָּל שֶׁהַכֶּסֶף בְּיָדוֹ, יָדוֹ עַל הָעֶלְיוֹנָה.

אֲבָל אָמְרוּ — [The Sages], however, said that although a person can technically back out of a sale even after the money has been given, מִי שֶׁפָּרַע מֵאַנְשֵׁי דוֹר הַמַּבּוּל וּמִדּוֹר הַפַּלָגָה — the One Who punished the people of the Generation of the Flood and of the Generation of the Dispersion for their sins,[5] הוּא עָתִיד לְהִפָּרַע מִמִּי שֶׁאֵינוֹ עוֹמֵד בְּדִבּוּרוֹ — He will someday punish the person who does not stand by his word and backs out of a deal after the money has been paid.[6]

The first Tanna holds that since paying money is not enough to finalize a sale, *either* side can back out of it.[7] R' Shimon disagrees:

רַבִּי שִׁמְעוֹן אוֹמֵר — R' Shimon says: כָּל שֶׁהַכֶּסֶף בְּיָדוֹ יָדוֹ עַל הָעֶלְיוֹנָה — The one who has the money in his hand has the upper hand; that is, once the buyer has paid the seller, the seller (who has the money) can back out of the sale, but not the buyer.[8]

------- NOTES -------

5. The Generation of the Dispersion refers to the people who built the Tower of Babel, whom God punished by dispersing (scattering) them all over the world (see *Genesis* 11:1-9).

6. The courts pronounce a curse against the person who backed out of the deal, saying that God will punish him (see *Rav*).

7. See note 3.

8. *Tos. Yom Tov.*
As explained in the previous Mishnah (note 3), under Biblical law a sale is final as soon as the seller takes the money. The Rabbis enacted that the sale should not be final because of their concern that if later there was a fire in the seller's property, the seller would make no effort to save the item, since it no longer belonged to him. R' Shimon argues that this concern can be addressed by letting just the *seller* back out of the sale. Since the seller knows that if the price of the item goes up while he is still holding it, he will be able to back out and sell it at a higher price, he will make the effort to save the item from the fire. There is therefore no need to give the buyer this option as well (Gemara 47b, as explained by *Tos. Yom Tov*; see *Rav* for a different understanding of the Gemara).

‎‏— רע״ב —‏

‏(ג) האונאה ארבעה בסף. ארבעה מעות כסף שהם שש מעות בדינר, והסלע ארבעה דינרין: מעשרים‏

‏[ג] הָאוֹנָאָה אַרְבָּעָה כֶסֶף מֵעֶשְׂרִים וְאַרְבָּעָה כֶּסֶף לְסֶלַע, שְׁתוּת לַמִּקָּח. עַד מָתַי מֻתָּר לְהַחֲזִיר, עַד כְּדֵי שֶׁיַּרְאֶה לְתַגָּר:‏

וארבעה בסף לסלע. אם היה המקח בדמי הסלע שהוא עשרים וארבע מעות, והטעתא היא אונאה שתות למקח, חייב להשיב לו כל אונאתו ארבעה כסף: **עד מתי מותר להחזיר.** מי שנתאנה: **והא** דנקט לשון מותר, לאשמועינן דליכא אפילו מי שפרע להחזיר המקח, או שיתן לו אונאתו: **עד כדי שיראה.** המקח לתגר, או לאחד מקרוביו. ואם שהה יותר, מחל על אונאתו. והמוכר לעולם חוזר, שהרי אין המקח בידו שיוכל להראות לתגר או לקרובו אם נתאנה. ואם נודע שבא לידו דבר כיוצא, במי שמכרו, וידע שטעה ושתק ולא תבע, אינו יכול לחזור ולתבוע, שהרי מחל:

---

[3] The rest of this chapter deals with the prohibition of *ona'ah* (price fraud) in sales. This means that one may not take advantage of someone who does not know the true price of an item by selling it to him for more than the market value, or buying it from him for less than the market value.[1] If the difference between the market value and the price paid is significant enough, the person who was cheated can demand to be paid back the amount he was cheated. The Mishnah explains how big that difference must be:[2]

הָאוֹנָאָה אַרְבָּעָה כֶסֶף מֵעֶשְׂרִים וְאַרְבָּעָה כֶּסֶף לְסֶלַע — The amount considered **ona'ah** is **four silver *ma'ahs*** for an item that was sold for a ***sela*, when a *sela* is worth twenty-four silver *ma'ahs*;**[3] שְׁתוּת לַמִּקָּח — that is, **one-sixth** of the market value **of the item** that was **purchased.** In other words, if the market value of the item was twenty-four *ma'ahs* (a *sela*), and the price paid was either four *ma'ah* more or four *ma'ah* less than that, the sale stands but the person who was cheated is refunded the amount he was cheated (four *ma'ahs*).[4]

In addition to the amount of the *ona'ah,* the right to demand a refund also depends on how long after the sale the person who was cheated asks for a refund. The Mishnah now addresses this issue:

עַד מָתַי מֻתָּר לְהַחֲזִיר — **Until when is he permitted to return** the item he bought or demand to be paid back the difference in price?[5] עַד כְּדֵי שֶׁיַּרְאֶה לְתַגָּר

--- NOTES ---

[3]
1. See *Leviticus* 25:14. If, however, the two sides know the market value but agree upon a different price, there is no prohibition (see Gemara 51a-51b).
2. It should be noted that if the difference is *less* than the amount the Mishnah will state, there is no need to pay back anything, since people are generally willing to overlook such a small difference. And if the difference is *more* than the amount the Mishnah will state, the sale is simply canceled; the buyer returns the item and gets a *full* refund. It is only when the difference is *exactly* the amount the Mishnah will state that the sale remains in place and the one who was cheated gets back

the difference (see *Meiri*). See note 5.
3. There are six *ma'ah* in a *dinar*, and four *dinar* in a *sela* (*Rav*).

[The Mishnah could have said simply "four *ma'ah* for a *sela*." But the relative worth of the *ma'ah* and the *sela* sometimes changed, so the Mishnah identifies the type of *ma'ah* and *sela* it means (*Rashash*).]

4. If the object was sold for 28 *ma'ahs*, the buyer is entitled to get 4 *ma'ahs* back from the seller; and if it was sold for 20 *ma'ahs*, the seller is entitled to get 4 *ma'ahs* back from the buyer.

5. The Tanna of our Mishnah holds that the person who was cheated not only has the right to let the sale stand and get

[69] **MISHNAH BAVA METZIA** / Chapter 4: *Hazahav* 4/4

— רע״ב —

ושמחו תגרי לוד. שהיו בקיאין בסחורה, ומוכרין ביוקר. ואין הלכה כרבי טרפון:

אוֹ לִקְרוֹבוֹ. הוֹרָה רַבִּי טַרְפוֹן בְּלוּד, הָאוֹנָאָה שְׁמוֹנָה כֶסֶף לְסֶלַע, שְׁלִישׁ לַמִּקָּח, וְשָׂמְחוּ תַגָּרֵי לוּד. אָמַר לָהֶם, כָּל הַיּוֹם מֻתָּר לְהַחֲזִיר. אָמְרוּ לוֹ, יַנִּיחַ לָנוּ רַבִּי טַרְפוֹן בִּמְקוֹמֵנוּ. וְחָזְרוּ לְדִבְרֵי חֲכָמִים.

[ד] **אֶחָד** הַלּוֹקֵחַ וְאֶחָד הַמּוֹכֵר יֵשׁ לָהֶן אוֹנָאָה.

או לקרובו — **Until enough time has passed to show** it **to a merchant or to his relative,** to have them appraise it and say whether he was cheated. Once this time has passed, he can no longer return the item or force the other person to give him back the difference.[6]

Another Tanna disagrees with these rules:

הוֹרָה רַבִּי טַרְפוֹן בְּלוּד — **R' Tarfon ruled in Lod:** **הָאוֹנָאָה שְׁמוֹנָה כֶסֶף לְסֶלַע** — The amount of *ona'ah* that one must pay back is **eight silver** *ma'ahs* for an object worth **a sela,**[7] **שְׁלִישׁ לַמִּקָּח** — which is **a third of the purchase** price; **וְשָׂמְחוּ תַגָּרֵי לוּד** — **and the merchants of Lod were happy** with this ruling, because they could charge up to a third more than the market value without having to give back the difference. **אָמַר לָהֶם** — But then [R' Tarfon] told them **כָּל הַיּוֹם מֻתָּר לְהַחֲזִיר** — that [a buyer] who is overcharged **is allowed to return** the object **for the entire day** on which he bought it. **אָמְרוּ לוֹ** — **They said to [R' Tarfon]: יַנִּיחַ לָנוּ רַבִּי טַרְפוֹן בִּמְקוֹמֵנוּ** — "R' Tarfon should leave **us as we were** before his rulings," **וְחָזְרוּ לְדִבְרֵי חֲכָמִים** — **and they went back to** their previous practice, which followed **the words of the Sages** (the first Tanna).[8]

[4] The Mishnah teaches who is subject to the laws of *ona'ah*:

אֶחָד הַלּוֹקֵחַ וְאֶחָד הַמּוֹכֵר יֵשׁ לָהֶן אוֹנָאָה — **Both the buyer and the seller are subject to** the laws of **ona'ah.** If they cheat each other (by overcharging or

---

— NOTES —

back the amount he was cheated, but he also has the right to cancel the sale entirely and get all his money back (but see Mishnah 4 note 4). The Mishnah teaches that if he decides to cancel the sale, he is not even subject to the curse against someone who backs out of a sale after paying for it [see Mishnah 2], because this curse does not apply to someone who backs out because he was cheated. This is why the Mishnah asks, "Until when is he *permitted* to return [the item]" (*Rav*).

6. If he waits longer than that, we assume that he has forgiven the overcharge and he can no longer ask for a refund (*Rav*).

This time limit applies only to the buyer. It cannot apply to the seller because he does not have the item anymore and cannot show it to anyone to see if he was underpaid. The seller can discover that he was underpaid only when he comes across a similar item later and sees what is being charged for it. When this happens, he must immediately return to the buyer and ask for the amount he was underpaid. If he does not, we assume that he forgave the underpayment and he can no longer demand it (*Rav*).

7. This is double the amount of the previous Tanna.

8. The merchants of Lod preferred the arrangement of the Sages, which gave the buyer less time to make a claim, even though they could get away with overcharging only up to one-sixth above market value (see Gemara 50b).

כְּשֵׁם שֶׁאוֹנָאָה לַהֶדְיוֹט, כָּךְ אוֹנָאָה לַתַּגָּר. רַבִּי יְהוּדָה אוֹמֵר, אֵין אוֹנָאָה לַתַּגָּר. מִי שֶׁהֻטַּל עָלָיו, יָדוֹ עַל הָעֶלְיוֹנָה. רָצָה, אוֹמֵר לוֹ תֵּן לִי מָעוֹתַי, אוֹ תֵּן לִי מַה שֶּׁאוֹנִיתָנִי.

— רע״ב —

(ד) אֵין לַתַּגָּר אוֹנָאָה. מִפְּנֵי שֶׁהוּא בָּקִי, וּמִסְתַּמָּא אָחוּלֵי אָחִיל גַּבֵּיהּ. וְהַאי דְּזַבְנָא הָכִי, מִשּׁוּם דְּאִתְרְמִי לֵיהּ זְבִינְתָּא אַחֲרִיתִי, וְהַשְׁתָּא הוּא דְּקָבָעֵי לְמֶיהְדַּר בֵּיהּ. וְאֵין הֲלָכָה כְּרַבִּי יְהוּדָה:

מִי שֶׁהֻטַּל עָלָיו יָדוֹ עַל הָעֶלְיוֹנָה. מִי שֶׁנִּתְאַנָּה לוֹקֵחַ. אִם נִתְאַנָּה: תֵּן לִי מָעוֹתַי. וּמַתְנִיתִין רַבִּי יְהוּדָה [הַנָּשִׂיא] הִיא, וְלֵית הִלְכְתָא כְּוָתֵיהּ. אֶלָּא אִם הָאוֹנָאָה שְׁתוּת, קָנָה, וּמַחֲזִיר אוֹנָאָה. יוֹתֵר מִשְּׁתוּת, בָּטֵל מֶקַח:

underpaying) by an amount equal to a sixth of the item's value, the other side can demand a refund.[1]

כְּשֵׁם שֶׁאוֹנָאָה לַהֶדְיוֹט כָּךְ אוֹנָאָה לַתַּגָּר — **Just as** the laws of *ona'ah* apply to **an ordinary person, so too they apply to a merchant.** Although a merchant is usually aware of the market value of the item he bought or sold, we do not assume that he forgave the amount of the *ona'ah*.[2] רַבִּי יְהוּדָה אוֹמֵר — **R' Yehudah says:** אֵין אוֹנָאָה לַתַּגָּר — The laws of *ona'ah* **do not apply to a merchant,** because he knows the market value of the object and presumably forgave the amount of the *ona'ah*.[3]

The Mishnah now explains how much of a refund can be demanded:

מִי שֶׁהֻטַּל עָלָיו יָדוֹ עַל הָעֶלְיוֹנָה — **The person upon whom [the *ona'ah*] was imposed** (the wronged party) **has the upper hand** in terms of how to settle the matter. רָצָה אוֹמֵר לוֹ תֵּן לִי מָעוֹתַי —For example, if the buyer was overcharged, **if he wishes, he can say, "Give me** back all **my money** and I will give you back the item I bought"; אוֹ תֵּן לִי מַה שֶּׁאוֹנִיתָנִי — or he can say, "**Give me back [the amount] you cheated** (overcharged) **me,** and I will keep the item."[4]

— NOTES —

1. How much of a refund they can demand will be discussed at the end of this Mishnah.

2. *Tiferes Yisrael; Meiri.*

3. The Mishnah speaks of a merchant whose business is to buy from suppliers and immediately resell the merchandise to others. We assume that when such a merchant sells cheaply, he did not make a mistake about the price; rather, he sold at less than market value because he needed cash immediately to buy other merchandise. He now regrets that decision and is therefore claiming *ona'ah* (*Rav*).

[Accordingly, this applies only to a merchant who *sold* merchandise. Even R' Yehudah agrees, however, that if a merchant *bought* for more than market value, he has a claim of *ona'ah* (*Tosafos*).]

4. Similarly, if the seller was underpaid, he can demand to be paid the difference, or he can decide to cancel the sale.

The Mishnah is discussing a case in which the amount of the *ona'ah* was exactly one-sixth of the market value (see Mishnah 3 note 2). The Tanna of our Mishnah holds that, in such a case, the wronged party can choose either to receive back the difference and let the sale stand, or to cancel the sale entirely and get a full refund (see Mishnah 3 note 5). The one who committed the *ona'ah* has no choice and must do whatever the wronged party decides. The Gemara (50b), however, cites another Tanna (R' Nassan), who says that where the *ona'ah* was exactly one-sixth, the wronged party *cannot* cancel the sale and get a full refund. He may only demand back the amount of the *ona'ah*. The halachah follows this last view (*Shulchan Aruch, Choshen Mishpat* 227:2).

— רע"ב —

(ה) כמה תהא סלע חסרה. מטבע היוצא, ותמיד הוא שוחק וחסר, כמה תחסר ואם הוציאה לא תהא אונאה: ארבע איסרין. לסלע: איסר לדינר. והוא אחד מן עשרים וארבעה בו. דשש מעה כסף [והוא] דינר, מטה שני פונדיונים, פונדיון שני איסרין: ארבעה פונדיונות. אחד משנים עשר. שמונה פונדיונות. שתות. כשאר אונאה. וכן הלכה:

[ה] **בַּמָּה** תְּהֵא הַסֶּלַע חֲסֵרָה, וְלֹא יְהֵא בָּהּ אוֹנָאָה, רַבִּי מֵאִיר אוֹמֵר, אַרְבַּע אִסָּרִין, אִסָּר לְדִינָר. רַבִּי יְהוּדָה אוֹמֵר, אַרְבַּע פֻּנְדְּיוֹנוֹת, פֻּנְדְּיוֹן לְדִינָר. רַבִּי שִׁמְעוֹן אוֹמֵר,

[5] In the times of the Mishnah, coins were made of precious metals, and their value was based on their weight. Therefore, even though the coins had a certain value when they were minted, they were actually worth less when they got worn down from use. This Mishnah discusses how much a coin can be worn down and still be used in the market at its minted value without concern for *ona'ah*:[1]

בַּמָּה תְּהֵא הַסֶּלַע חֲסֵרָה וְלֹא יְהֵא בָּהּ אוֹנָאָה — **How much can a *sela* coin be missing** (i.e., be worn down) **and not be** a problem of *ona'ah* if it is used at its minted value? רַבִּי מֵאִיר אוֹמֵר — **R' Meir says:** אַרְבַּע אִסָּרִין — **It can be missing up to four *issars*,** אִסָּר לְדִינָר — **which is one *issar* for each *dinar* in the *sela*;** that is, it can be missing up to one twenty-fourth of the weight of the *sela*.[2] רַבִּי יְהוּדָה אוֹמֵר — **R' Yehudah says:** אַרְבַּע פֻּנְדְּיוֹנוֹת — **It can be missing up to four *pundyons*,** פֻּנְדְּיוֹן לְדִינָר — **which is one *pundyon* for each *dinar* in** the *sela*, or up to one-twelfth of the weight of the *sela*.[3] רַבִּי שִׁמְעוֹן אוֹמֵר —

———— NOTES ————

[5]

1. A person paying with a worn-down *sela* coin for something costing a *sela* is actually giving less than a *sela*. He is thus cheating the seller (see *Rav*).
   To understand the rulings of this Mishnah, it is necessary to know the coinage of Mishnaic times. The largest coin in general use was a *sela*. A *sela* is worth four *dinars*, and a *dinar* is six *ma'ahs*. A *ma'ah* is two *pundyons*, and a *pundyon* is two *issars* (*Rav*). Thus, there are 24 *ma'ahs* in a *sela*, or 48 *pundyons* or 96 *issars*.
2. One *issar* is one twenty-fourth of a *dinar* (see chart). Since there are four *dinars* in a *sela*, four *issars* are one twenty-fourth of a *sela*. Thus, if a *sela* has lost

up to one twenty-fourth of its weight, it may still be used at its minted value of a *sela*. If it has lost a full twenty-fourth of its weight, the owner may no longer spend it as a full *sela*, since he would then be cheating the person he was paying (*Tos. Yom Tov*, from Gemara 52a).
   Although the amount considered to be *ona'ah* in the case of merchandise is one-sixth, that is because people are willing to overlook price differences smaller than a sixth. With coins, however, people are more particular and are not willing to overlook even a difference of one twenty-fourth (Gemara 52a, the view of Abaye; *Rav*, as explained by *Tos. R' Akiva Eiger*).
3. A *pundyon* is one-twelfth of a *dinar* (see chart). Thus, four *pundyons* are

	Number of dinars	Number of ma'ahs	Number of pundyons	Number of issars
in a *sela*	4	24	48	96
in a *dinar*	1	6	12	24
in a *pundyon*	--	--	1	2
in a *issar*	--	--	--	1

שְׁמוֹנָה פְּנְדְיוֹנוֹת, שְׁנֵי פְּנְדְיוֹנוֹת לְדִינָר.

[ו] **עַד** מָתַי מֻתָּר לְהַחֲזִיר, בַּכְּרַכִּים עַד כְּדֵי שֶׁיַּרְאֶה לְשֻׁלְחָנִי, וּבַכְּפָרִים עַד עַרְבֵי שַׁבָּתוֹת. אִם הָיָה מַכִּירָהּ, אֲפִלּוּ לְאַחַר שְׁנֵים עָשָׂר חֹדֶשׁ מְקַבְּלָהּ הֵימֶנּוּ, וְאֵין לוֹ עָלָיו אֶלָּא תַּרְעֹמֶת.

— רע״ב —

(ו) בכרכים. שיש שם שלחני, עד כדי שיראה לשולחני בכפרים. שאין שם שלחני עד ערבי שבתות. שבא להוליא בערב שבת לסעודת שבת, אז ידע אם יוכל להוליאה ויקבלנה ממנו: ואם היה מכירה. הכי קאמר, ואם חסיד הוא ורולה לעשות לפנים משורת הדין, אם מכיר שהיא הסלע שנתן

לו, יקבלנה ממנו אפילו לאחר שנים עשר חודש: **ואין לו עליו אלא תרעומת**. הכי קאמר, ואחר שאינו חסיד ולא רלה לקבלה ממנו, אין לזה עליו אלא תרעומת. דאיהו הוא דאפסיד אנפשיה, שלא החזירו בזמנו:

R' Shimon says: שְׁמוֹנָה פְּנְדְיוֹנוֹת — **It can be missing up to eight** *pundyons*, שְׁנֵי פְּנְדְיוֹנוֹת לְדִינָר — which is **two** *pundyons* **for each** *dinar* in the *sela*, or up to one-sixth of the weight.[4]

[6] The previous Mishnah taught that when a coin is too worn down, it may no longer be used at face value. Doing so is considered *ona'ah*. Therefore, if a person receives such a coin in a transaction he can give it back and demand a different one. Our Mishnah discusses how much time he has to give it back: עַד מָתַי מֻתָּר לְהַחֲזִיר — **Until when may he give back** a worn coin and demand a new one in its place? בַּכְּרַכִּים — **In the big cities,** עַד כְּדֵי שֶׁיַּרְאֶה לְשֻׁלְחָנִי — **until enough time has passed to show** the coin **to a moneychanger,** who can evaluate how much it has worn down.[1] וּבַכְּפָרִים — **And in the villages,** where there are no moneychangers, עַד עַרְבֵי שַׁבָּתוֹת — he has **until Friday,** when he must buy food for Shabbos. He will then see whether the sellers accept the coin at face value.

The rule we have just learned is the law. The Mishnah now teaches that it is proper for a pious person to go beyond the letter of the law: אִם הָיָה מַכִּירָהּ — **If he** (the person who gave the worn coin) **recognizes** it as the one he gave, אֲפִלּוּ לְאַחַר שְׁנֵים עָשָׂר חֹדֶשׁ מְקַבְּלָהּ הֵימֶנּוּ — then **even after twelve months** have passed **he should accept it** back **from him,** and replace it with a newer coin. וְאֵין לוֹ עָלָיו אֶלָּא תַּרְעֹמֶת — **However,** if he refuses to do so, **he** (the person who received the coin) **has only a complaint against him,**[2]

NOTES

one-twelfth of a *sela*. If a *sela* has lost up to one-twelfth of its weight, it may still be used at its minted value of a *sela*. If it has lost a full twelfth of its weight, the owner may no longer spend it as a full *sela*.

4. According to R' Shimon, just as a sixth is considered the measure of *ona'ah* with regard to merchandise (see Mishnah 3), so too is it considered the measure of *ona'ah* with regard to worn-out coins (*Rav*).

The Mishnah has presented three opinions with regard to how much a *sela* can be missing and still be used at its minted value. The same ratios would apply to other coins as well (*Tiferes Yisrael*).

[6]

1. Most people cannot evaluate this. Therefore, we must give him enough time to show it to a professional moneychanger, and not just to a relative, as with ordinary merchandise [see Mishnah 3] (*Tos. Yom Tov*).

2. Although it is not proper to hold a

ונותנה למעשר שני.
מחסרה כדי אונאה קלי.
ונותנה למעשר שני בשוויה,
ואינו חושש משום דסימון
שאין מעשר שני מתחלל
אלא במטבע שיש בו צורה,

וְנוֹתְנָהּ לְמַעֲשֵׂר שֵׁנִי וְאֵינוֹ חוֹשֵׁשׁ,
שֶׁאֵינוֹ אֶלָּא נֶפֶשׁ רָעָה.

[ז] **הָאוֹנָאָה** אַרְבָּעָה כֶסֶף, וְהַטַּעֲנָה

דאם מטבע יש עליה, דמי שאינו לוקחה בשוויה בתורת מטבע, אלא כמו נסכא של כסף, אינו אלא
נפש רעה: (ז) האונאה ארבעה בסף. למקח סלע, שהוא עשרים וארבע מעות כסף. נמצאת האונאה
שתות, כדאמרן. וחזר ושנאה משום דבעי למתני הטענה שתי כסף:

---

but he has no legal claim, because it is his own fault that he did not give the coin back during the time allowed.

Maaser sheni (the second tithe)[3] must be eaten in Jerusalem. A person living outside of Jerusalem may redeem his *maaser sheni* with money and bring the money to Jerusalem, where he uses it to buy food that he eats there. However, the sanctity of *maaser sheni* can be transferred only to a *minted* coin.[4] The Mishnah addresses whether the worn-down coin under discussion is still considered a minted coin for this purpose:[5]

וְנוֹתְנָהּ לְמַעֲשֵׂר שֵׁנִי — **One can give it** (the worn-down coin) **to *maaser sheni*,** that is, one may transfer sanctity of *maaser sheni* onto it, וְאֵינוֹ חוֹשֵׁשׁ — **and he need not be concerned** that it is not considered minted anymore, שֶׁאֵינוֹ אֶלָּא נֶפֶשׁ רָעָה — **because** anyone refusing to treat **it as a coin is just being meanspirited.**[6]

[7] Having discussed the amount of money that is considered *ona'ah*, the Mishnah digresses to teach the amounts of money that are necessary for other Torah laws. It begins by restating the law regarding *ona'ah*:

הָאוֹנָאָה אַרְבָּעָה כֶסֶף — **The** amount considered ***ona'ah*** is **four silver** *ma'ahs* for an item worth a *sela*.[1]

The next law relates to the Biblical oath for a מוֹדֶה בְּמִקְצָת, *someone who admits to part of a claim*.[2] The Mishnah teaches the minimum amount that

--- NOTES ---

grievance against a fellow Jew (see *Leviticus* 19:18), in this case he may, since it is proper for the person who gave him the worn-down coin to replace it (see Mishnah 6:1 note 1).

3. Produce grown in Eretz Yisrael is subject to a number of obligations (see Mishnah 8). One of these is *maaser sheni* (the second tithe), which must be separated from the crop and be eaten in Jerusalem (*Deuteronomy* 14:22-27).

4. *Maaser Sheni* 1:2.

5. The Mishnah is talking about coins that are so worn down that a person who received them as payment would have the right to give them back (*Rav*).

6. Although people do not want to take the worn-down coin at its face value, it is still a coin worth its current weight. Anyone who refuses to accept it as a coin (at this lower value) is just being mean and stingy. It may therefore be used for redemption of *maaser sheni* according to its current value (*Rav*).

[7]

1. This is one-sixth the value of the object, as we learned in Mishnah 3.

2. When one person makes a monetary claim against another person and the second person denies it, the second person has no obligation to prove his denial; rather, it is the person making the claim

שְׁתֵּי כֶסֶף, וְהַהוֹדָאָה שָׁוֶה פְרוּטָה. חָמֵשׁ
פְּרוּטוֹת הֵן, הַהוֹדָאָה שָׁוֶה פְרוּטָה,
וְהָאִשָּׁה מִתְקַדֶּשֶׁת בְּשָׁוֶה פְרוּטָה;
וְהַנֶּהֱנֶה בְּשָׁוֶה פְרוּטָה מִן הַהֶקְדֵּשׁ מָעַל,
וְהַמּוֹצֵא שָׁוֶה פְרוּטָה, חַיָּב לְהַכְרִיז,

— רע״ב —

שאין
שבועות הדיינין על טענה
שהיא פחותה משתי כסף.
שטענו, שוה שתי מעות
כסף יש לי בידך, וזה יודה
לו מהם שוה פרוטה ויכפור
השאר, או יודה לו הכל
ויכפור פרוטה: **והַהוֹדָאָה
שָׁוֶה פְרוּטָה.** להיות הודאה במקצת, ויתחייב שבועה: **הַמּוֹצֵא שָׁוֶה פְרוּטָה.** אבל בליר מהכי
אינו חייב להכריז, דכתיב (דברים כב,ג) אֲשֶׁר תֹּאבַד מִמֶּנּוּ, פרט לאבדה שאין בה שוה פרוטה:

---

must be claimed and the minimum amount that must be admitted in order for this oath to apply:

וְהַטַּעֲנָה שְׁתֵּי כֶסֶף — A person who admits to part of a monetary claim is obligated to swear only if **the claim** is for at least **two silver** *ma'ahs*, וְהַהוֹדָאָה שָׁוֶה פְרוּטָה — and the admission is at least **the value of a** *perutah*.[3]

The Mishnah now lists all the Torah laws that require a minimum value of a *perutah*:

חָמֵשׁ פְּרוּטוֹת הֵן — **There are five** areas of law where *perutos* are relevant: הַהוֹדָאָה שָׁוֶה פְרוּטָה — (1) A person who admits to part of a claim has to swear only if **the admission** is at least **the value of a** *perutah*, as mentioned above; וְהָאִשָּׁה מִתְקַדֶּשֶׁת בְּשָׁוֶה פְרוּטָה — (2) **a woman can be betrothed** with money, or with something worth money, only if it has **the value of** at least **a** *perutah*;[4] וְהַנֶּהֱנֶה בְּשָׁוֶה פְרוּטָה מִן הַהֶקְדֵּשׁ מָעַל — (3) **someone who derives benefit** that is **worth a** *perutah* **from property of the Holy Temple has committed** *me'ilah*;[5] וְהַמּוֹצֵא שָׁוֶה פְרוּטָה חַיָּב לְהַכְרִיז — (4) **someone who finds** an object **worth** at least **a** *perutah* **is obligated to announce**

NOTES

who must prove that money is owed to him. However, in certain circumstances the Torah requires the denier to at least swear an oath that he does not owe anything. One of these circumstances is where the person admits to part of the claim, but denies the other part of it (see *Exodus* 22:8 with *Rashi* and *Bava Kamma* 106b; see also *Bava Metzia* 3a,3b).

3. The *perutah* is a copper coin, while the *ma'ah* is a silver coin. There are 32 *perutos* in a *ma'ah* (see *Kiddushin* 12a). A person is not subject to this oath unless he admits to owing at least a *perutah* of the claim.

4. *Kiddushin* (betrothal) is the first stage of marriage. One of the ways to perform *kiddushin* is for the man to give the woman money or something worth money for the purpose of betrothal. If he does so, he must give something worth at least a *perutah* (see *Kiddushin* 1:1).

5. It is forbidden for a person to have personal benefit from Temple property (*hekdesh*). Doing so is called מְעִילָה, *me'ilah*. Someone who gets such benefit must pay the Temple the value of that benefit. Additionally, if he violated this prohibition deliberately he receives *malkus* (lashes). If he benefited from it mistakenly, he must add a penalty payment of one-fifth (see Mishnah 8 note 1) to the payment he makes to the Temple, and he must bring an *asham* offering to atone for his sin (see *Leviticus* 5:15-16). These additional consequences apply only if the benefit he had was worth at least a *perutah* (see Gemara 55a,55b; *Rambam, Hilchos Me'ilah* 7:8).

[75] **MISHNAH BAVA METZIA** / Chapter 4: *Hazahav*　　4/8

— רע״ב —

וְהַגּוֹזֵל אֶת חֲבֵרוֹ שָׁוֶה פְרוּטָה וְנִשְׁבַּע לוֹ, יוֹלִיכֶנּוּ אַחֲרָיו אֲפִלּוּ לְמָדָי.

[ח] **חֲמִשָּׁה** חֻמָשִׁין הֵן, הָאוֹכֵל תְּרוּמָה, וּתְרוּמַת מַעֲשֵׂר, וּתְרוּמַת

יוליכנו אחריו. אם הודה שנשבע לשקר, דאז אין לו כפרה עד שיחזירנו לידו ממש, ולא ליד שלוחו, דכתיב (במדבר ה, ז) ונתן לאשר אשם לו: (ח) האוכל תרומה. גדולה. זר שאכל תרומה גדולה בשוגג: ותרומת מעשר. מעשר מן המעשר:

— וְהַגּוֹזֵל אֶת חֲבֵרוֹ שָׁוֶה פְרוּטָה וְנִשְׁבַּע לוֹ — the find so he can return it;[6] (5) **and someone who robs his fellow of something worth** at least **a *perutah* and swears to him** that he does not owe him anything, and then admits that he lied, יוֹלִיכֶנּוּ אַחֲרָיו אֲפִלּוּ לְמָדָי — **must bring [the stolen object] back to him even** if he moved **to** a place as far away as **Media** (Persia). He cannot simply give it to an agent of the person who was robbed,[7] because a robber who swears falsely about not owing cannot receive atonement for his sin until the object is actually received by the person who was robbed.[8]

[8] The previous Mishnah listed five areas of law in which a *perutah* is required. This Mishnah lists five situations in which a *fifth* must be added to the basic amount (the principal) that must be paid:

חֲמִשָּׁה חֻמָשִׁין הֵן — **There are five** situations in which **fifths** must be added to the principal:[1]

(1) הָאוֹכֵל תְּרוּמָה — **If [a non-Kohen] mistakenly eats *terumah*** (the portion of the crop given to a Kohen),[2] וּתְרוּמַת מַעֲשֵׂר — **or *terumas maaser*** (the portion of the *maaser rishon* tithe that a Levi must give to a Kohen),[3] וּתְרוּמַת

NOTES

6. See Introduction to Chapter 2. If it is worth less than a *perutah* there is no obligation to return it (*Ran*; Gemara 27a).
7. Even if the agent was appointed by the victim to accept it for him.
8. This is learned from a verse (*Rav*). Our Mishnah teaches that this requirement applies only to a stolen object worth at least a *perutah*. See *Bava Kamma* 9:5 for further details.

[8]
1. These added payments are actually a quarter of the principal. They are called "fifths" because the addition comes to one-fifth of the *total* amount paid (principal plus addition). For example, if the principal is 100 *zuz*, then one must add 25 *zuz* and pay a total of 125 *zuz*. The additional 25 *zuz* is thus one-fifth of the total payment of 125 *zuz*.

2. Produce that grows in Eretz Yisrael is subject to various obligations. The first is called *terumah*. A small portion of the crop (about 2 percent) is separated and given to a Kohen. It may not be eaten by a non-Kohen.

3. After separating *terumah*, the owner of the produce separates *maaser rishon* (first tithe), and gives it to a Levi. *Maaser rishon* is 10 percent of what remains of the crop after the *terumah* has been separated. Before the Levi may eat his *maaser*, he must separate 10 percent of it to give to a Kohen. That portion is called *terumas maaser* (the *terumah* from the *maaser*). It too is forbidden to a non-Kohen, and it has all the laws of *terumah*.

מַעֲשֵׂר שֶׁל דְּמַאי, וְהַחַלָּה, וְהַבִּכּוּרִים, מוֹסִיף חֹמֶשׁ, וְהַפּוֹדֶה נֶטַע רְבָעִי וּמַעֲשֵׂר שֵׁנִי שֶׁלּוֹ, מוֹסִיף חֹמֶשׁ. הַפּוֹדֶה אֶת הֶקְדֵּשׁוֹ, מוֹסִיף חֹמֶשׁ.

— רע״ב —

ותרומת מעשר של דמאי. הלוקח תבואה מעם הארץ, צריך להפריש תרומת מעשר, אבל לא תרומה גדולה, שהיו הכל זהירים בה: **וחלה ובכורים**. כל הני חמשה חד נינהו, דכולהו איקרו תרומה, ומשום חד הם באלין: נטע רבעי. גמר קדש קדש ממעשר שני דמוסיף חומש. ותרוויהו נמי חד חשיב להו, דמחד קרא נפקי, כיון דממעשר יליף: [ומעשר שני] שלו. דוקא, מוסיף חומש, דאים ממעטרו (ויקרא כז, לא): הקדשו. ולא של אחרים, המקדיש כתיב (שם טו):

מַעֲשֵׂר שֶׁל דְּמַאי — or *terumas maaser* of *demai* (produce received from an unlearned person),[4] **וְהַחַלָּה** — or *challah* (the portion of a dough that must be given to a Kohen),[5] **וְהַבִּכּוּרִים** — or *bikkurim* (the first fruits, which are brought to the Temple and then given to the Kohanim),[6] **מוֹסִיף חֹמֶשׁ** — in all these cases, the non-Kohen must give the Kohen produce that is worth as much as what he ate, and **add a fifth** to it.[7]

(2) **וְהַפּוֹדֶה נֶטַע רְבָעִי וּמַעֲשֵׂר שֵׁנִי שֶׁלּוֹ מוֹסִיף חֹמֶשׁ** — A person who redeems his own *neta reva'i* (fruit of a tree in its fourth year)[8] or *maaser sheni* (the second tithe) **adds a fifth.**[9]

(3) **הַפּוֹדֶה אֶת הֶקְדֵּשׁוֹ מוֹסִיף חֹמֶשׁ** — A person who redeems his own *hekdesh*

— NOTES —

4. *Demai* is produce that is bought or received as a gift from an *am haaretz* (an unlearned person). Most *amei haaretz* separated all the required obligations from their produce, but some separated only *terumah* and nothing else. Because of this concern, the Rabbis decreed that someone who gets produce from an *am haaretz* must separate *maaser* from it, and *terumas maaser* must then be separated from the *maaser*. This *terumas maaser* must be given to a Kohen and is forbidden to a non-Kohen.

5. The Torah (Numbers 15:18-20) commands us to separate "*terumah*" from our dough and give it to a Kohen. This portion is called *challah*. It may not be eaten by a non-Kohen.

6. There are seven species of produce for which Eretz Yisrael is famed (Deuteronomy 8:8): wheat, barley, grapes, figs, pomegranates, olives, and dates. Every year, the first growths of these grains or fruits are set aside and taken to the Temple. They are known as *bikkurim*. After the *bikkurim* ritual is performed, they are given to the Kohanim to eat. They may not be eaten by non-Kohanim and are subject to all the laws of *terumah*.

7. The Torah says that a non-Kohen who mistakenly eats *terumah* must pay back produce worth the value of what he ate plus a fifth (see Leviticus 22:14 with Rashi). All the things listed here are called *terumah* by the Torah and they are therefore all subject to this rule. All of these "*terumos*" are counted together as the first of the five things for which one must add a fifth (see *Rav*).

8. The fruit of a tree in the first three years after it is planted is called *orlah*. The Torah (Leviticus 19:23) forbids eating or having benefit from this fruit. In the fourth year, the fruit of this tree is called נֶטַע רְבָעִי, *neta reva'i*. It must be taken to Jerusalem and eaten there, or it can be redeemed with money, and the money is then spent in Jerusalem on food eaten there. Its fruit is essentially treated the same as *maaser sheni* (see Mishnah 6).

9. If a person wants to transfer the sanctity of his own *neta reva'i* or *maaser sheni* produce onto coins, he must add a fifth to the value of the fruit. He takes all the coins to Jerusalem, and spends them on food that he eats there. If someone redeems *reva'i* or *maaser sheni* produce that belongs to someone else, there is no need to add a fifth (see *Rav*).

[77] MISHNAH BAVA METZIA / Chapter 4: *Hazahav* 4/9

הַנֶּהֱנֶה בְּשָׁוֶה פְרוּטָה מִן הַהֶקְדֵּשׁ, מוֹסִיף חֹמֶשׁ. וְהַגּוֹזֵל אֶת חֲבֵרוֹ שָׁוֶה פְרוּטָה וְנִשְׁבַּע לוֹ, מוֹסִיף חֹמֶשׁ.

[ט] אֵלּוּ דְּבָרִים שֶׁאֵין לָהֶם אוֹנָאָה, הָעֲבָדִים, וְהַשְּׁטָרוֹת, וְהַקַּרְקָעוֹת, וְהַהֶקְדֵּשׁוֹת.

— רע״ב —

הנהנה. בשוגג, חייב קרבן מעילה וחומש:
(ט) אלו דברים שאין להם אונאה וכו׳. דאמר קרא (ויקרא כה, יד) וכי תמכרו ממכר לעמיתך או קנה מיד עמיתך, דבר הנקנה מיד ליד. יצאו קרקעות שאינן מטלטלין,
יצאו עבדים שהוקשו לקרקעות, שטרות, [דכתיב] (שם) וכי תמכרו ממכר, [דבר] שגופו מכור וגופו קנוי, יצאו שטרות שאינם עומדים אלא לראיה שבהן, הקדשות, אמר קרא (שם) אחיו, אחיו ולא הקדש:

(an item he donated to the Temple) pays its value to the Temple and **adds a fifth.**[10]

(4) הַנֶּהֱנֶה בְּשָׁוֶה פְרוּטָה מִן הַהֶקְדֵּשׁ מוֹסִיף חֹמֶשׁ — **A person who** mistakenly **derives benefit** that is **worth a** *perutah* **from** *hekdesh* pays the value of his benefit and **adds a fifth.**[11]

(5) וְהַגּוֹזֵל אֶת חֲבֵרוֹ שָׁוֶה פְרוּטָה וְנִשְׁבַּע לוֹ — **And a person who robs his friend** of something **worth a** *perutah* **and** falsely **swears to him** that he did not rob it, and then admits that he lied, מוֹסִיף חֹמֶשׁ — returns the object that he stole and **adds a fifth.**[12]

[9] The Mishnah now returns to the subject of *ona'ah*. Mishnah 3 taught that if an item is sold for one-sixth above or below its market value, the wronged party can demand a refund. Our Mishnah lists items to which this law does not apply:

אֵלּוּ דְּבָרִים שֶׁאֵין לָהֶם אוֹנָאָה — **These are the things that are not subject to** the law of *ona'ah* when they are sold: הָעֲבָדִים — **Canaanite slaves,** וְהַשְּׁטָרוֹת — **documents** that allow their owner to collect money from someone,[1] וְהַקַּרְקָעוֹת — **land,** וְהַהֶקְדֵּשׁוֹת — **and things that belong to** *hekdesh*.[2] Even if there is a difference of one-sixth between the market price and the amount charged for these items, the wronged party cannot demand a refund. These are all learned from the verse about *ona'ah*.[3]

--- NOTES ---

10. See *Leviticus* 27:15.

11. See Mishnah 7 note 5.

12. See *Leviticus* 5:24. [The same applies whenever a person is sued for payment and he swears falsely that he does not owe it, and he later admits that he lied (see verses 20-24 there; *Tos. Yom Tov*).]

[9]

1. A person who is owed money can sell the debt to someone else. The standard way of doing this is by giving the document in which the debt is recorded to the buyer (see *Bava Basra* 75b-76a). This sale is not subject to the law of *ona'ah*.

2. There are certain holy items that are either sold by the Temple treasury or may be redeemed by the person who consecrated them. If someone consecrates items of value to the Temple treasury, they are sold by the Temple to raise money for the Temple's expenses. If someone consecrates an animal as a sacrificial offering and it becomes blemished (which disqualifies it from being offered), he may sell it and use the money to buy a new offering (*Rashi* 56a).

3. The verse (*Leviticus* 25:14) that is the

משניות בבא מציעא / פרק ד: הזהב

אֵין לָהֶן תַּשְׁלוּמֵי כֶפֶל, וְלֹא תַשְׁלוּמֵי
אַרְבָּעָה וַחֲמִשָּׁה. שׁוֹמֵר חִנָּם אֵינוֹ נִשְׁבָּע,

— רע"ב —

לא תשלומי כפל.
דכתיב בטוען טענת גנב
(שמות כב, ח) על כל דבר
פשע, כלל, על שור על
חמור וכו', פרט, על כל אבדה, חזר וכלל, כלל ופרט וכלל, אי אתה דן אלא כעין הפרט, מה הפרט
מפורש דבר המטלטל וגופו ממון, אף כל דבר המטלטל וגופו ממון. יצאו קרקעות שאינן מטלטלין,
יצאו עבדים שהוקשו לקרקעות, יצאו שטרות שאף על פי שהם מטלטלין אין גופן ממון, הקדשות,
אמר קרא (שם) רעהו, רעהו ולא של הקדש: **ולא תשלומי ארבעה וחמשה.** אם גנב וטבח ומכר
שור או שה של הקדש. דתשלומי ארבעה וחמשה אמר רחמנא, ולא תשלומי שלשה לשה וארבעה
לשור. דכיון דאמעיט מכפל, בציר להו חדא, שהכפל בטובח ומוכר בכלל תשלומי ארבעה וחמשה הן:

The Mishnah lists other laws that do not apply to the four items listed above: **אֵין לָהֶן תַּשְׁלוּמֵי כֶפֶל** — **They are not subject to the double payment** if they are **stolen**,[4] **וְלֹא תַשְׁלוּמֵי אַרְבָּעָה וַחֲמִשָּׁה** — **nor to the payment of four or five** times their value if they are a sheep or an ox stolen from *hekdesh* and then slaughtered or sold.[5] **שׁוֹמֵר חִנָּם אֵינוֹ נִשְׁבָּע** — **An unpaid** *shomer* who was given one of these items to watch and claims that it was stolen or lost **does not** have to **swear** that he was not negligent in watching it,[6]

---------------- NOTES ----------------

source for the law of *ona'ah* says: *When you sell something to your fellow, or you buy from the hand of your fellow, do not commit ona'ah one man against his brother.* The word *something* [literally, *a sold thing*] excludes a loan document because it implies that the "thing" that is transferred to the buyer in the sale is identical with the thing that is being sold. This is not true in the case of a document, where the thing that is given to the buyer — the document — is not really what was sold; rather it is the debt recorded in it that was sold (see *Sifra* to this verse). The words *from the hand* imply that the thing being sold can be passed from hand to hand. This excludes land. Canaanite slaves are also excluded because the Torah elsewhere compares them to land (see *Kiddushin* 22b). And the words *his brother* exclude *hekdesh* (*Rav*).

[We learned above (Mishnah 3 note 2) that where the difference is *more* than a sixth, the sale is automatically canceled. There is a question whether these items are excluded from that law as well. See Gemara 57a and *Choshen Mishpat* 227:29.]

4. A person who steals someone's property must pay back double what he stole (see Mishnah 3:1 note 1). Our Mishnah teaches that this does not apply to the four types of property listed above. This is learned from the verse (*Exodus* 22:8) that describes the type of items to which the double payment applies: *For every item ... whether an ox, a donkey, a sheep, or a garment ... regarding any lost item* ... These examples all have in common that they are movable, valuable in their own right, and privately owned. This excludes land [which is not movable], slaves [which are compared to land], documents of debt [whose value is not in the paper of the document but in the debt that is being transferred through it], and *hekdesh* [which is not privately owned] (*Rav*).

5. If a person steals a sheep or an ox and slaughters or sells it, he must pay the owner four or five times its value (see 3:1 note 2). Our Mishnah teaches that this does not apply to animals that belong to *hekdesh*. This is because the payment of four or five times includes the double payment of a regular thief, plus another two or three times the value of the sheep or ox. Since someone who steals *hekdesh* animals is not subject to the double payment, he is also not subject to these higher payments (see *Rav*).

6. Ordinarily, if an unpaid *shomer* claims that the item he was given to watch was stolen or lost, he must swear that he was not negligent in guarding it, and he is then exempt from paying for it (see

[79] **MISHNAH BAVA METZIA** / Chapter 4: *Hazahav*

וְנוֹשֵׂא שָׂכָר אֵינוֹ מְשַׁלֵּם. רַבִּי שִׁמְעוֹן אוֹמֵר, קָדָשִׁים שֶׁהוּא חַיָּב בְּאַחֲרָיוּתָן יֵשׁ לָהֶן אוֹנָאָה, וְשֶׁאֵינוֹ חַיָּב בְּאַחֲרָיוּתָן אֵין לָהֶן אוֹנָאָה.

— רע״ב —

נושא שכר אינו משלם. דכתיב (שם פ) כי יתן איש אל רעהו, כלל, חמור או שור או שה, פרט, וכל בהמה לשמור, חזר וכלל, כלל ופרט וכלל, אי אתה דן אלא כעין הפרט, מה הפרט מפורש דבר המיטלטל וכו׳. הקדשות, אמר קרא רעהו, ולא הקדש: קדשים שחייב באחריותן. אמר הרי עלי עולה, והפרישה, והוממה, ומכרה: יש להם אונאה. דכיון דאם מתה או נגנבה חייב באחריותה, דיליה היא, ואל תונו איש את אחיו (ויקרא כה, יד) קרינא ביה:

וְנוֹשֵׂא שָׂכָר אֵינוֹ מְשַׁלֵּם — **and a paid [*shomer*] does not** have to **pay** for them if they were stolen or lost.[7] All of these are learned from the verses dealing with these laws.

The Mishnah cites a Tanna who maintains that the law of *ona'ah* does apply to certain types of *hekdesh*:

רַבִּי שִׁמְעוֹן אוֹמֵר — **R' Shimon says: קָדָשִׁים שֶׁהוּא חַיָּב בְּאַחֲרָיוּתָן** — *Kodashim* (animals designated as offerings) **for which [a person] is responsible,** that is, those which he must replace if they are lost, **יֵשׁ לָהֶן אוֹנָאָה** — **are subject to** the law of *ona'ah* because they are considered his property.[8] **וְשֶׁאֵינוֹ חַיָּב בְּאַחֲרָיוּתָן** — **And those for which [a person] is not responsible,** that is, which he does not have to replace if they are lost, **אֵין לָהֶן אוֹנָאָה** — **are not subject to** the law of *ona'ah*, since they are not considered his property.[9]

— NOTES —

Mishnah 3:1). Our Mishnah teaches that this requirement of swearing does not apply to the four types of property listed above. This is learned from the examples given by the verse for the things for which a *shomer* swears (*Exodus* 22:6): "silver coins and vessels." These items have in common all the characteristics mentioned in note 4, and they therefore exclude the same types of property (Gemara 57b with *Rashi*).

7. Ordinarily, a paid *shomer* must pay for items that are stolen from him or lost (see Introduction to Chapter 3). Our Mishnah teaches that this does not apply to the four types of property listed above. Here, too, the verse (*Exodus* 22:9) is phrased in a way that is similar to the verse regarding an unpaid *shomer* (see note 6), and thus excludes these four types of property (see *Rav*).

8. There are two ways to donate an offering. A person can say about a specific animal, "This is hereby an *olah* offering," or he can say, "I take upon myself to bring an *olah* offering," without designating any specific animal. Later, he sets aside an animal and says, "This is for my obligation," and the animal then becomes consecrated as an *olah*. [*Olah* is used here merely as an example.]

If he donates the offering the first way, his only obligation is to bring *that* animal to the Temple to be offered on the Altar. If that animal gets lost or dies, he has no obligation to bring another one in its place because he never obligated himself to do anything more than bring the animal he originally designated as an *olah*. However, if he donates it the second way and the animal dies or is lost, he does have an obligation to replace it, since his original commitment was "to bring an *olah*," not any specific animal.

R' Shimon argues that where the owner is responsible to replace the donated animal, it is considered [in some measure] his property, even though it is *hekdesh* (holy). Therefore, if it became blemished and he sells it (see note 2), the phrase *Do not commit ona'ah one man against his brother* applies to the sale (*Rav, Rashi*).

9. The first Tanna, however, holds that any animal that is *hekdesh* cannot be considered his property, even if he is responsible for it.

משניות בבא מציעא / פרק ד: הזהב

רַבִּי יְהוּדָה אוֹמֵר, אַף הַמּוֹכֵר סֵפֶר תּוֹרָה, בְּהֵמָה, וּמַרְגָּלִית אֵין לָהֶם אוֹנָאָה. אָמְרוּ לוֹ, לֹא אָמְרוּ אֶלָּא אֶת אֵלּוּ.

[י] כְּשֵׁם שֶׁאוֹנָאָה בְמִקָּח וּמִמְכָּר, כָּךְ אוֹנָאָה בִדְבָרִים.

— רע״ב —

ושאינו חייב באחריותן. כגון דאמר הרי זו: אף המוכר ספר תורה. לפי שאין קץ לדמיה: מרגלית ובהמה. מפני שאדם רוצה לזווגן. מי שיש לו שור יפה לחרישה, מחזר על אחר שכמותו [ולמדו עמו בעול],

שאם בא להלמידו תחת חלק שור הבריח, מקלקל את הבריח. וכן מרגליות נאה למלאות עם חברתה בזהב מן היחידית. ואין הלכה לא כרבי יהודה ולא כרבי שמעון: (י) כך אונאה בדברים. שנאמר (ויקרא כה, יז) ולא תונו איש את עמיתו ויראת מאלהיך, זה נאמר באונאת דברים, שאין טובתן ורעתן מסורה להכיר אלא ללבו של מדבר, שיודע אם לרעה מתכוין אם לטובה:

R' Yehudah expands the list of items to which *ona'ah* does not apply:

רַבִּי יְהוּדָה אוֹמֵר — R' Yehudah says: אַף הַמּוֹכֵר סֵפֶר תּוֹרָה — Even when someone sells a Torah Scroll, בְּהֵמָה — an animal, וּמַרְגָּלִית — or a pearl, אֵין לָהֶם אוֹנָאָה — they are not subject to the law of *ona'ah*, because a person is sometimes willing to pay a high price for them.[10] אָמְרוּ לוֹ — [The Sages] said to [R' Yehudah]: לֹא אָמְרוּ אֶלָּא אֶת אֵלּוּ — When the Rabbis listed the items excluded from *ona'ah*, **they stated only these** four items mentioned above. We cannot expand the list to include other items.[11]

[10] Until now, the Mishnah has discussed the prohibition of *ona'ah* as it relates to business transactions. Our Mishnah introduces another prohibition of *ona'ah*:

כְּשֵׁם שֶׁאוֹנָאָה בְמִקָּח וּמִמְכָּר — **Just as** *ona'ah* is forbidden **in buying and selling,** כָּךְ אוֹנָאָה בִדְבָרִים — **so too** is *ona'ah* forbidden **with words,** meaning that one may not say something to another person that will pain him.[1]

NOTES

10. A Torah Scroll is priceless, so no amount is considered too much to pay for it (*Rav; Tiferes Yisrael*). A person is also sometimes willing to pay a very high price for a particular animal or pearl because it pairs well with one that he already has. For example, if he has an animal of certain strength, he needs to buy another one of equal strength so that he can team them up to plow together. Or, if he has a matching pearl, he can set them both together in a piece of jewelry. In either case, he is willing to pay much more than the market price for the animal or pearl he needs, so there is no issue of *ona'ah* (*Rav*).

11. The Sages reason that a person might buy *any* item because it pairs well with something he already has. Since the Torah says that *ona'ah* is forbidden, we are forced to conclude that *ona'ah* applies even to things that a person may want to pair with something else. It is only the four types of property listed by the Mishnah that were excluded [because their exclusion is learned from a verse; see note 3] (Gemara 58b).

[10]

1. The word *ona'ah* actually means to cause pain or distress. The Torah uses this word in connection with buying and selling (*Leviticus* 25:14), to refer to causing pain to someone by cheating him (overcharging or underpaying him). However, three verses later the Torah repeats the warning about *ona'ah* without referring to commercial dealings: *You shall not cause pain one man to his*

[81] MISHNAH BAVA METZIA / Chapter 4: *Hazahav*

— רע״ב —

(יא) אֵין מְעָרְבִין פֵּרוֹת בְּפֵרוֹת. בַּעַל הַבַּיִת הָאוֹמֵר לְחָבֵירוֹ פֵּירוֹת שָׂדֶה פְלוֹנִי אֲנִי מוֹכֵר לָךְ, לֹא יְעָרֵב בְּפֵירוֹת שָׂדֶה אַחֵר: וְאֵין צָרִיךְ לוֹמַר חֲדָשִׁים בִּישָׁנִים. פָּסַק לִמְכּוֹר לוֹ יְשָׁנִים, לֹא יְעָרֵב עִמָּהֶם חֲדָשִׁים, שֶׁהַיְשָׁנִים יְבֵשִׁים, וְטוֹחֲנִים קֶמַח יוֹתֵר מִן הַחֲדָשִׁים:

לֹא יֹאמַר לוֹ, בְּכַמָּה חֵפֶץ זֶה וְהוּא אֵינוֹ רוֹצֶה לִקַּח. אִם הָיָה בַּעַל תְּשׁוּבָה, לֹא יֹאמַר לוֹ, זְכֹר מַעֲשֶׂיךָ הָרִאשׁוֹנִים. אִם הוּא בֶן גֵּרִים, לֹא יֹאמַר לוֹ, זְכֹר מַעֲשֵׂה אֲבוֹתֶיךָ, שֶׁנֶּאֱמַר, וְגֵר לֹא תוֹנֶה וְלֹא תִלְחָצֶנּוּ.

[יא] אֵין מְעָרְבִין פֵּרוֹת בְּפֵרוֹת, אֲפִלּוּ חֲדָשִׁים בַּחֲדָשִׁים, וְאֵין צָרִיךְ לוֹמַר חֲדָשִׁים בִּישָׁנִים.

The Mishnah gives some examples of *ona'ah* with words: בְּכַמָּה חֵפֶץ זֶה — **"How much is this object?"** לֹא יֹאמַר לוֹ — **One should not say to [a seller]:** וְהוּא אֵינוֹ רוֹצֶה לִקַּח — **when he does not want to buy it,** because this pains the seller.[2] אִם הָיָה בַּעַל תְּשׁוּבָה — **Or, if someone had** been a sinner and he then **repented,** לֹא יֹאמַר לוֹ זְכֹר מַעֲשֶׂיךָ הָרִאשׁוֹנִים — [a person] should not say to him, **"Remember your earlier** sinful **deeds,"** because that causes him shame and pain. אִם הוּא בֶן גֵּרִים — **Or, if someone is the son of converts,** לֹא יֹאמַר לוֹ זְכֹר מַעֲשֵׂה אֲבוֹתֶיךָ — **[a person] should not say to him, "Remember the deeds of your** non-Jewish **parents** or **ancestors,"** because this too causes him shame and pain. שֶׁנֶּאֱמַר — **As it says** (*Exodus* 22:20): "וְגֵר לֹא תוֹנֶה וְלֹא תִלְחָצֶנּוּ" — **"You shall not cause pain to a convert, and you shall not oppress him."**[3]

[11] The final two Mishnahs in our chapter discuss a third type of *ona'ah* — unethical business practices. This Mishnah addresses selling merchandise that is mixed with something else:

אֵין מְעָרְבִין פֵּרוֹת בְּפֵרוֹת — **[A seller] may not mix produce** (grain) **from one** of his fields **into produce** from another of his fields, if he specifically told the buyer that he is giving him grain from one of the fields, אֲפִלּוּ חֲדָשִׁים בַּחֲדָשִׁים — **even** if he wants to mix **new** grain from one field **into new** grain from the other field, in which case there is no difference in the quality of the grains. וְאֵין צָרִיךְ לוֹמַר חֲדָשִׁים בִּישָׁנִים — **And it goes without saying** that he may not

--- NOTES ---

fellow, and you shall fear your God, for I am Hashem, your God. The Sages understand this verse to refer to causing pain to another person simply with words (*Rav*).

2. It gives the seller the false hope that he will make a sale, and then disappoints him. Furthermore, it is possible that the seller will lower the price to get this person to buy it, when he really has no interest in buying it. When other buyers hear this, they will refuse to pay the price the seller usually charges; thus, this person is actually causing him a monetary loss (*Meiri*).

3. The phrase "*you shall not oppress him*" refers to *ona'ah* in money dealings (see *Mechilta* to this verse).

The Torah states the prohibition to pain or cheat a convert to Judaism as a separate prohibition. But someone who pains a convert verbally also violates the general prohibition to pain or cheat any Jew (see note 1). Thus, he violates *two* prohibitions. [The Gemara (59b) teaches that there is actually a third prohibition that forbids paining a convert; see *Leviticus* 19:33.]

בֶּאֱמֶת, בַּיַּיִן הִתִּירוּ לְעָרֵב קָשֶׁה בְרַךְ, מִפְּנֵי שֶׁהוּא מַשְׁבִּיחוֹ. אֵין מְעָרְבִין שִׁמְרֵי יַיִן בְּיַיִן, אֲבָל נוֹתֵן לוֹ אֶת שְׁמָרָיו. מִי שֶׁנִּתְעָרֵב מַיִם בְּיֵינוֹ לֹא יִמְכְּרֶנּוּ בַחֲנוּת אֶלָּא אִם כֵּן הוֹדִיעוֹ,

— רע״ב —

מִפְּנֵי שֶׁמַּשְׁבִּיחוֹ. קָשֶׁה מַשְׁבִּיחַ אֶת הרך. לפיכך, פסק עמו רך מערב בו קשה, אבל פסק עמו קשה לא יערב בו את הרך: אֵין מְעָרְבִין שְׁמָרֵי יַיִן. של חבית זו, בְּיַיִן של חבית

אחרת: אֲבָל נוֹתֵן לוֹ אֶת שְׁמָרָיו. של יין עצמו: לֹא יִמְכְּרֶנּוּ בַחֲנוּת. פרוטה פרוטה: אֶלָּא אִם כֵּן הוֹדִיעַ. לכל אחד ואחד מהן, מים מעורבין בו:

---

mix **new** grain **into old** grain if he promised the buyer old grain, because old grain has certain advantages over new grain.[1] בֶּאֱמֶת, בַּיַּיִן הִתִּירוּ לְעָרֵב קָשֶׁה בְרַךְ — **In truth,**[2] **with regard to wine [the Sages] did permit** a seller **to mix sharp** wine **into mellow** wine, מִפְּנֵי שֶׁהוּא מַשְׁבִּיחוֹ — **because [the sharp wine] improves it.**[3] Therefore, if he agreed to sell him mellow wine, he may mix some sharp wine into it.[4]

Wine usually contains sediment at the bottom of the container.[5] Thus, when an entire jug or barrel of wine is sold, the buyer realizes he will be getting a certain amount of sediment in it. The Mishnah teaches the law for a smaller amount of wine that is sold and is poured from the top of the container without any sediment:

אֵין מְעָרְבִין שִׁמְרֵי יַיִן בְּיַיִן — **[A seller] may not mix wine sediment** from one barrel **into** clear **wine** from another barrel, because that ruins the wine,[6] אֲבָל נוֹתֵן לוֹ אֶת שְׁמָרָיו — **but he may give [the buyer] sediment** from its own barrel.[7]

It is forbidden to dilute wine that is being sold.[8] The Mishnah discusses what should be done with wine that had become diluted with water:

מִי שֶׁנִּתְעָרֵב מַיִם בְּיֵינוֹ — **If water got mixed into someone's wine,** לֹא יִמְכְּרֶנּוּ בַחֲנוּת אֶלָּא אִם כֵּן הוֹדִיעוֹ — **he should not sell it in the store** in small amounts

---

NOTES

[11]

1. Old grain has dried out and it therefore produces more flour when it is ground (*Rav*).

2. This expression indicates that the halachah follows the ruling that will now be stated (Gemara 60a).

3. The sharp wine makes the mellow wine last longer before spoiling and turning into vinegar (*Rosh*).

   This applies only when the wines are mixed right after they are pressed. Afterward, though, each wine has already developed its own character, and mixing them will just ruin them both (Gemara 60a, with *Rashi*).

4. But they did not permit mixing mellow wine into sharp wine. Therefore, if he agreed to sell him sharp wine, he may not mix mellow wine into it (*Rav*).

5. This comes from the tiny particles of grape that remain in the wine, which eventually settle to the bottom of the container.

6. *Tos. Yom Tov*.

7. That is, when he takes wine from the barrel, he may add some sediment from that barrel to the wine he poured off and include it in the sale to the buyer (*Choshen Mishpat* 228:15). That sediment does not ruin the wine at all. [Nor is he cheating the buyer. Since, if one were to buy the entire container of wine it would include sediment, when the seller pours some off into the buyer's container, he may give him some of that sediment (see *Aruch HaShulchan, Choshen Mishpat* 228:9).]

8. This is clearly dishonest, since the buyer is paying for pure wine, not wine mixed with water (see *Isaiah* 1:22).

[83] MISHNAH BAVA METZIA / Chapter 4: *Hazahav*

וְלֹא לְתַגָּר אַף עַל פִּי שֶׁהוֹדִיעוֹ, שֶׁאֵינוֹ אֶלָּא לְרַמּוֹת בּוֹ. מְקוֹם שֶׁנָּהֲגוּ לְהָטִיל מַיִם בַּיַּיִן, יָטִילוּ.

[יב] **הַתַּגָּר** נוֹטֵל מֵחָמֵשׁ גְּרָנוֹת וְנוֹתֵן לְתוֹךְ מְגוּרָה אֶחָת, מֵחָמֵשׁ גִּתּוֹת וְנוֹתֵן לְתוֹךְ פִּטָּם אֶחָד, וּבִלְבַד שֶׁלֹּא יְהֵא מִתְכַּוֵּן לְעָרֵב.

— רע״ב —

ולא לתגר. [ולא] ימכרנו ביחד, ואף על פי שהודיעו. לפי שאינו לוקחו אלא לרמות ולמכרו בחנות: מקום שנהגו להטיל מים ביין. דוקא בין הגתות, יטיל. דכיון שנהגו אין כאן טעות, שכל הייניות בחזקת כן: (יב) התגר נוטל מחמש גרנות. שהכל יודעים בו שלא גדלו בשדותיו, ומבני אדם הרבה לוקח, ובחזקת כן לוקחים ממנו: מגורה. אוצר שאוגרין בו תבואה: גורן, הוא שדשין בו את התבואה. ודרך התגר לקנות בתים מבעלי בתים בשעת הגורן, ולהכניס למגורה שלו: פיטס. גיגית גדולה: ובלבד שלא יתבוין לערבן. להוליך קול לקנות הרוב ממקום משובח [ולערב] בו ממקום אחר, ושכיניו סבורים שכל הפירות מאותו מקום:

---

to individual customers **unless he tells [the customer]** that there is water mixed into the wine; וְלֹא לְתַגָּר אַף עַל פִּי שֶׁהוֹדִיעוֹ — **and** he should **not** sell it **to a** wine **merchant even if he** *does* **tell him** that there is water mixed into it, שֶׁאֵינוֹ אֶלָּא לְרַמּוֹת בּוֹ — **because** there is concern **that it is** being bought by the merchant **only to cheat** his customers.[9] מְקוֹם שֶׁנָּהֲגוּ לְהָטִיל מַיִם בַּיַּיִן — However, in **a place where it is customary to add water to the wine** and sell it that way, יָטִילוּ — **[sellers] may add** water, because the buyers understand that they are getting diluted wine.

[12] This Mishnah continues the discussion of a seller mixing items together: הַתַּגָּר נוֹטֵל מֵחָמֵשׁ גְּרָנוֹת וְנוֹתֵן לְתוֹךְ מְגוּרָה אֶחָת — **A merchant may take** (buy) grain **from five threshing-places** of five different people **and put** all the grain **into one granary,** מֵחָמֵשׁ גִּתּוֹת וְנוֹתֵן לְתוֹךְ פִּטָּם אֶחָד — **and he may take** wine **from five winepresses and put** it all **into one vat,** because buyers are aware that wholesale merchants typically do this;[1] וּבִלְבַד שֶׁלֹּא יְהֵא מִתְכַּוֵּן לְעָרֵב — **but** this is only **as long as [the merchant] does not intend to mix** a little bit of low-quality merchandise into mostly high-quality merchandise, while having buyers believe that it is all high quality.[2]

NOTES

9. The merchant might be planning to sell the diluted wine to his customers without informing them that it was diluted.

Although we do not ordinarily suspect a person of being dishonest, wine merchants are more likely to justify doing this because they were not the ones who diluted it and did not even see it happen (see *Sma, Choshen Mishpat* 228:21).

[12]
1. Wholesale merchants buy grain or wine from several farms or vineyards and mix it all together. Since buyers know this, the merchant is not cheating them by selling them mixed merchandise (*Rav*).

2. That is, he may not buy *most* of the merchandise from a high-quality supplier (and only a little from a lower-quality supplier) so that word gets out that he sells high-quality merchandise. The buyers then think that *all* his merchandise is high quality, so that when he mixes some lower-quality merchandise into it he is cheating them (*Rav*).

רַבִּי יְהוּדָה אוֹמֵר, לֹא יְחַלֵּק הַחֶנְוָנִי קְלָיוֹת וֶאֱגוֹזִין לַתִּינוֹקוֹת, מִפְּנֵי שֶׁהוּא מַרְגִּילָן לָבוֹא אֶצְלוֹ. וַחֲכָמִים מַתִּירִין. וְלֹא יִפְחֹת אֶת הַשַּׁעַר. וַחֲכָמִים אוֹמְרִים, זָכוּר לַטּוֹב. לֹא יָבֹר אֶת הַגְּרִיסִין, דִּבְרֵי אַבָּא שָׁאוּל. וַחֲכָמִים מַתִּירִין.

— רע"ב —

ולא יפחות את השער. למכור בזול. מפני שהוא מרגיל לבא אצלו, ומקפח מזונות חביריו: זכור לטוב. שמתוך כך מוזלי פירות מוכרין בזול. וכן הלכה: גריסין. פולין גרוסות בריחים אחת לשתים: לא יבור. את הפסולת. לפי שמתוך שנראות יפות, הוא מעלה את דמיהן הרבה מדמי הפסולת שנטל מהן: וחכמים מתירין. שיכול הלוקח לראות ולהבחין כמה דמי הפסולת שנגרר, מאלו ישנן באחרים. וטוב לו להתעלות בדמיהן של אלו שהן מבוררים, מפני הטורח. והלכה כחכמים:

The Mishnah now addresses a number of business practices that are designed to lure customers away from other dealers:

לֹא יְחַלֵּק הַחֶנְוָנִי קְלָיוֹת וֶאֱגוֹזִין לַתִּינוֹקוֹת — רַבִּי יְהוּדָה אוֹמֵר — R' Yehudah says: — **A storekeeper should not give out toasted wheat kernels and nuts to the children** who visit his store, מִפְּנֵי שֶׁהוּא מַרְגִּילָן לָבוֹא אֶצְלוֹ — **because he accustoms them to come to him.** He thereby undermines the businesses of other storekeepers in the area.[3] וַחֲכָמִים מַתִּירִין — **But the Sages permit** this because he can tell the other storekeepers that if they want the children to come, they should give out even better snacks![4] R' Yehudah continues: וְלֹא יִפְחֹת אֶת הַשַּׁעַר — **[A storekeeper] should also not lower the price** below that of the rest of the market, because this, too, causes other storekeepers to lose business. וַחֲכָמִים אוֹמְרִים — **But the Sages say:** זָכוּר לַטּוֹב — **He is remembered for good** for doing this because it pushes all the storekeepers to lower their prices, and thereby benefits the public.[5]

The Mishnah discusses things that a seller does to make his merchandise look better:

לֹא יָבֹר אֶת הַגְּרִיסִין — **[A seller] may not sift** the waste from **crushed beans,** because removing the waste does not justify the much higher price he will charge for these nicer-looking beans;[6] דִּבְרֵי אַבָּא שָׁאוּל — **these are the words of Abba Shaul.** וַחֲכָמִים מַתִּירִין — **But the Sages permit** this because the customer is not being fooled; rather, he is willing to pay the much higher

---

NOTES

3. When parents send their children to the store, they will choose to go to the storekeeper who gives out snacks (*Rashi, Bava Basra* 21b).

4. *Tos. Yom Tov,* from Gemara 60a.

5. Typically, some merchants would wait to sell their own produce until the market basically ran out, and they would then put it up for sale at a high price. The buyers would thus lose out. If, however, one merchant sells his produce early on for *lower* than the market price, then those merchants are afraid that people might buy everything they need from him, and there will be no one left to buy their produce! They therefore put everything on the market now at the lower price, and all the buyers benefit (*Rav*).

6. Although a pound of unsifted beans contains, let us say, 5 percent of waste, he will raise the price by 20 percent because the beans now look nicer (see *Rav*).

[85] MISHNAH BAVA METZIA / Chapter 4: *Hazahav*

וּמוֹדִים שֶׁלֹּא יָבֹר מֵעַל פִּי הַמְּגוּרָה, שֶׁאֵינוֹ אֶלָּא כְּגוֹנֵב אֶת הָעַיִן. אֵין מְפַרְכְּסִין לֹא אֶת הָאָדָם, וְלֹא אֶת הַבְּהֵמָה וְלֹא אֶת הַכֵּלִים.

— רע״ב —

שלא יבור על פי המגורה. למעלה להראות יפות, ואת הפסולת שבתוכו לא בירר. לפי שאינו אלא כגונב את העין בסברתו. מתקנין ומיפין: לא את האדם. עבד כנעני הטומד לימכר:

וּמוֹדִים שֶׁלֹּא יָבֹר מֵעַל פִּי מְגוּרָה — price for being saved the trouble of sifting.[7] However, [the Sages] agree that [the seller] may not sift only those beans on the top of the bin, while leaving the beans underneath unsifted, **שֶׁאֵינוֹ אֶלָּא כְּגוֹנֵב אֶת הָעַיִן** — because this is just deceiving the eye of the buyer.[8] **אֵין מְפַרְכְּסִין לֹא אֶת הָאָדָם** — One may not artificially **improve the look** of whatever one is selling: **not** that **of a person** (a Canaanite slave), **וְלֹא אֶת הַבְּהֵמָה** — **nor** that **of an animal**, **וְלֹא אֶת הַכֵּלִים** — **nor** that **of utensils**, because he deceives the buyer into thinking that he is getting something better than he really is.[9]

NOTES

7. The Sages assume that the customer is quite capable of comparing the sifted beans to unsifted ones and see how much waste was removed. His decision to pay much more for the sifted ones is for the *service* of sifting provided by the seller (*Rav*).

8. Even if the seller tells the buyer that there is waste underneath the top layer of beans, the buyer is still somewhat misled into thinking that there is not so much waste there (*Tiferes Yisrael*).

9. For example, he may not dye the white hairs of an older slave black to make him look younger, or give an animal bran water to drink before bringing it to market to make it look fatter, or put a new coat of paint on an old utensil to make it look new (*Tiferes Yisrael*). However, one may make new utensils look nice so that people will be attracted to buying them, as long as he does not make them look like something they are not (see Gemara 60b, with *Rashi* ד״ה בחדתי).

Chapter Five

The Torah forbids lending money to a fellow Jew and charging him interest on the loan. This means that the lender cannot require the borrower to pay back more than he borrowed. It is similarly forbidden for the borrower to pay (or agree to pay) interest. The Biblical prohibitions involved in lending on interest are listed in Mishnah 11.

Certain other activities that are not actually loans, and extra compensations that are not actually "interest," were forbidden by the Rabbis because they resemble lending on interest. Most of the chapter focuses on these Rabbinic forms of prohibited interest.

Many of the cases discussed in this chapter are quite complicated and involve the types of transactions that were common in the days of the Mishnah but which are less familiar today. For these reasons and others, *Eizehu Neshech* is known as one of the more difficult chapters in Mishnah. Understanding this chapter requires special attention.

פרק ה: איזהו נשך

— רע"ב —

פרק חמישי — איזהו נשך. (א) איזהו נשך. דשקל מיניה מאי דלא יהיב ליה: המרבה בפירות. המרבה שכר לעצמו בפירות. ובין בהלוואת

[א] אֵיזֶהוּ נֶשֶׁךְ וְאֵיזֶהוּ תַרְבִּית, אֵיזֶהוּ נֶשֶׁךְ, הַמַּלְוֶה סֶלַע בַּחֲמִשָּׁה דִינָרִין, סָאתַיִם חִטִּין בְּשָׁלֹש, מִפְּנֵי שֶׁהוּא נוֹשֵׁךְ. וְאֵיזֶהוּ תַרְבִּית, הַמַּרְבֶּה בְּפֵרוֹת. כֵּיצַד,

כסף ובין בהלוואת פירות הוי רבית, שהרי מרבה ממונו. אלא דבסיפא רבית דרבנן קמפרש, שהוא דרך מקח וממכר:

---

[1] The first Mishnah of this chapter defines what is Biblically forbidden interest and what is Rabbinically forbidden interest. The Mishnah calls the Biblically forbidden interest on a loan *neshech* (bite), and the Rabbinically forbidden "interest" *tarbis* (increase).[1] The Mishnah gives examples of each type of interest:

אֵיזֶהוּ נֶשֶׁךְ — **What** type of interest **is** *neshech*, which is forbidden by Biblical law, וְאֵיזֶהוּ תַרְבִּית — **and what** type of interest **is** *tarbis*, which is forbidden by Rabbinic law?

The Mishnah answers:

הַמַּלְוֶה סֶלַע בַּחֲמִשָּׁה דִינָרִין — **What is** a case of *neshech*? **Someone who lends a** *sela* (a coin worth four *dinars*) **for five** *dinars*, that is, on condition that the borrower will pay him five *dinars* in return, סָאתַיִם חִטִּין בְּשָׁלֹש — **or he lends two** *se'ah* **of wheat for three** *se'ah*. Both of these arrangements are Biblically forbidden and are called *neshech* (bite), מִפְּנֵי שֶׁהוּא נוֹשֵׁךְ — **because [the lender] "takes a bite"** out of the borrower's funds by taking from him more than he gave.[2] וְאֵיזֶהוּ תַרְבִּית — **And what is** a case of *tarbis*? הַמַּרְבֶּה בְּפֵרוֹת — **Someone who increases** his wealth **by way of** buying **produce** and receiving more value than he paid for. If this is done in a way that resembles a loan it is forbidden by Rabbinic law.[3] כֵּיצַד — **How so?**

The Mishnah's illustration involves a complicated transaction made up of two separate agreements. The first agreement:

NOTES

[1]
1. The Torah actually refers to Biblically forbidden interest as both *neshech* and *tarbis* (see *Leviticus* 25:36). The Mishnah, however, uses the term *tarbis* (increase) for Rabbinically forbidden interest. This is because the Rabbinically forbidden interest discussed here "increases" the lender's wealth *without* taking a "bite" out of the borrower's money (the way Biblically forbidden interest does). The lender's increase comes through a natural rise in prices, without taking anything extra from the borrower (*Tiferes Yisrael*).

2. Both of these are straightforward loans, one of money and the other of produce. Since they require the borrower to pay back more than he borrowed, they are Biblically forbidden.

3. The reason it is forbidden only Rabbinically is not because it involves produce, but because it happens through a sale and not through a loan (*Rav*). *Lending* produce on interest is *Biblically* forbidden, as we learned in the previous case (see note 2). *Selling* produce in a way that *resembles* a loan is Rabbinically forbidden.

[89] MISHNAH BAVA METZIA / Chapter 5: *Eizehu Neshech*

— רע"ב —

דינר זהב. עשרים וחמשה
דינרי כסף: ובן השער. כך
היו נמכרין בעיר. והותר לו
לתת מעות עכשיו, על מנת
ליתן לו זה חטין כל ימות השנה בדמים הללו כשיעור מעותיו, ואף על פי שעכשיו אין לו חטין. דתנן
בפרקין (משנה ז) יצא השער פוסקין, אף על פי שאין לזה יש לזה, ויכול המוכר הזה לקנותם עתה במעות
הללו: עמדו חטין בשלשים דינרין אמר לו תן לי חיטי. וזה מותר אם נתן לו חטין. אבל אם פסק

לָקַח הֵימֶנּוּ חִטִּין בְּדִינַר זָהָב הַכּוֹר, וְכֵן
הַשַּׁעַר. עָמְדוּ חִטִּין בִּשְׁלֹשִׁים דִּינָרִין,

לָקַח הֵימֶנּוּ חִטִּין בְּדִינַר זָהָב הַכּוֹר — For example, **someone bought wheat from another** person at a price of **a gold *dinar*** (equal to twenty-five silver *dinars*) for a *kor* (thirty *se'ah*) of wheat; **וְכֵן הַשַּׁעַר** — **and that was the established price** in the market.[4] The buyer paid for the wheat in advance, with the understanding that the seller would give him the wheat during the course of the year as needed. This was permissible because wheat at this price is readily available in the market.[5] **עָמְדוּ חִטִּין בִּשְׁלֹשִׁים דִּינָרִין** — **In the meantime, the** price of **wheat** increased and it **stands at thirty** silver *dinars* per *kor*. Even so, if the buyer were to take delivery of the wheat now, there would be no problem of interest, because he is viewed as having taken possession of the wheat from the time he paid for it.[6] Thus, it was *his* wheat that went up in value.

―――― NOTES ――――

4. The term "established price" implies two conditions: (a) Wheat was readily available in the market; and (b) this was the price everyone was charging.

5. The buyer did not want to take the wheat now and store it through the year. He therefore made an agreement with the dealer that he would hold the wheat and deliver it to the buyer as needed during the course of the year. The buyer paid for a certain amount of wheat at the rate of a gold *dinar* for thirty *se'ah* of wheat, and he paid all the money in advance (see *Rav*).

Ordinarily, it is forbidden to pay in advance for goods that will not be delivered until a later date. The Rabbis prohibited this because the price of the goods might rise before they are delivered, and the buyer would then receive more value than he paid for in exchange for letting the seller have the money in advance. This resembles interest being paid on a loan. [The money paid in advance is like a loan (since the buyer does not receive anything for it until some later date), and delivering the goods to him later on is repaying that loan. Since later the goods are worth more than the money that was given in advance, it resembles repaying the loan with interest.]

However, the Rabbis permitted paying in advance in a case where the seller has the goods in his possession when the buyer pays him. Since the buyer *could* take them now, the money he pays in advance is not viewed as a loan but as a pure sale (even though the goods do not actually become his until they are delivered; see below, Mishnah 7 note 3). The Rabbis extended this leniency even further: Even if the seller does not yet have the goods, but he could easily buy them for this price in the market with the money he now gets from the buyer, he is permitted to take the buyer's money in advance. Since the seller could easily buy the goods, we view him as already "having" them; and since he "has" them, we view his contract with the buyer as a sale rather than a loan (see note 6).

This is why the Mishnah says that a gold *dinar* for a *kor* was the market price. It means to teach that even if the seller did not yet have the wheat in his possession, the contract for the wheat was permitted, since this was the established market price for wheat at that time (*Rav*).

6. Since the seller could have bought the wheat in the market immediately, we consider it as if he had wheat in his possession at the time of the sale. Thus,

אָמַר לוֹ, תֶּן לִי חִטַּי, שֶׁאֲנִי רוֹצֶה לְמָכְרָן וְלִקַּח בָּהֶן יָיִן. אָמַר לוֹ, הֲרֵי חִטֶּיךָ עֲשׂוּיוֹת עָלַי בִּשְׁלֹשִׁים דִּינָרִין, וַהֲרֵי לְךָ אֶצְלִי בָּהֶן יָיִן, וְיַיִן אֵין לוֹ.

— רע״ב —

לִתֵּת לוֹ בָּהֶן יַיִן, אָסוּר. שֶׁמָּא יוֹקִיר הַיַּיִן, הוֹאִיל וְאֵין לוֹ יַיִן. וְאַף עַל פִּי שֶׁפּוֹסֵק עִמּוֹ כְּשַׁעַר הַיָּין שֶׁל עַכְשָׁיו וּכְבָר יָצָא הַשַּׁעַר, הוֹאִיל וְאֵינוֹ נוֹתֵן לוֹ דָּמִים שֶׁנּוּכַל לוֹמַר יָכוֹל הוּא לִקְנוֹת יַיִן

בְּדָמִים שֶׁקִּבֵּל, אֶלָּא בָּא לַעֲשׂוֹת עָלָיו דְּמֵי הַחִטִּין חוֹב וְלִפְסוֹק עַל הַחוֹב יַיִן, אָסוּר אִם יַיִן אֵין לוֹ. דְּאִי הֲוָה לֵיהּ יַיִן, הֲוָה קָנוּי לוֹ מֵעַכְשָׁיו לָזֶה שֶׁבָּא לִפְסוֹק עַל הַחוֹב יַיִן, וְכִי מְיַיקַּר בִּרְשׁוּתֵיהּ מְיַיקַּר:

However, now that the price of wheat has gone up, the buyer decides that he wants to sell the wheat and buy something else. This leads to a second agreement, which *is* problematic: אָמַר לוֹ — [The buyer] now says to [the seller]: תֶּן לִי חִטַּי — "Give me my wheat, שֶׁאֲנִי רוֹצֶה לְמָכְרָן וְלִקַּח בָּהֶן יָיִן — because I want to sell it and buy wine with the money I get for it." אָמַר לוֹ — [The seller] says to [the buyer]: הֲרֵי חִטֶּיךָ עֲשׂוּיוֹת עָלַי בִּשְׁלֹשִׁים דִּינָרִין — "Instead of taking the wheat and selling it to buy wine, let your wheat that I owe you be considered a debt of thirty *dinars* upon me, וַהֲרֵי לְךָ אֶצְלִי בָּהֶן יָיִן — and you will now have a right to receive from me wine worth the amount I now owe you for [the wheat]";[7] וְיַיִן אֵין לוֹ — however, [the seller] does not have any wine right now. He is also not receiving any new money from the buyer with which to buy wine.[8] Therefore, even if wine is available in the market at an established price, the seller cannot be considered to "have" wine in his possession. Since the seller does not have wine, the buyer cannot be viewed as acquiring wine

— NOTES —

when the buyer paid him in advance, we view *him* as having "acquired" the wheat at that time. See the previous note.

[The buyer, of course, did not really acquire anything at that time. Our "viewing" him as acquiring it is only in regard to the prohibition of taking interest on a loan. Since, on the Biblical level, the prohibition of taking interest is only on a real loan, not on a sale, and it is the Rabbis who prohibited doing so with sales that resemble loans, they were lenient in cases where the transaction appears less like a loan and more like a sale. Thus, wherever we can "view" the buyer as having acquired the merchandise before the price went up, the Rabbis allowed the transaction (see *Rashi* 72b פוסק עמו).]

7. In other words, the seller tells the buyer that since he no longer wants wheat but wine, he will "buy" the wheat back from him at its current market price of thirty *dinars*. [This is permissible. Since the buyer would be permitted to take

the wheat if he still wanted it (as we just explained), he is also permitted to take its value in money.] However, instead of giving him the money, the seller will owe him the money, and pay off that obligation at a later date by supplying the buyer with wine worth thirty *dinars* (see *Meiri*).

8. The money he received from the buyer when they made a deal for wheat has now become a debt owed by the seller to the buyer. The buyer is contracting for wine in exchange for forgiving a debt, not for cash (*Rav; Meiri*).

Even this would be permitted if the seller had wine in his possession when he made this second deal, since we could then view the buyer as acquiring the wine immediately, in return for forgiving the debt (*Rav*). The problem arises because the seller does *not* have any wine at this time, and the buyer is getting only an obligation of wine for what is owed him.

[91] **MISHNAH BAVA METZIA** / Chapter 5: *Eizehu Neshech* 5/2

— רע"ב —

[ב] הַמַּלְוֶה אֶת חֲבֵרוֹ לֹא יָדוּר בַּחֲצֵרוֹ חִנָּם, וְלֹא יִשְׂכֹּר מִמֶּנּוּ בְּפָחוֹת, מִפְּנֵי שֶׁהוּא רִבִּית.

(ב) מרבין על השכר. בשכר המתנת השכירות, ואין מרבין על מכר, בשכר המתנת המקח. וטעמא, משום דשכירות אינה משתלמת אלא לבסוף, הילכך כי שקיל מיניה סלע בחדש דהוו להו שנים עשר סלעים אין זה שכר המתנת מעות, שהרי לא נתחייב לשלם לו שכירות עד סוף החדש. והאי דאמר ליה אם מעכשיו תתן לי הרי היא שלך בעשר סלעים, אי הוה מקדים ליה, הוה מחיל ליה מדמי השכירות ומוזיל ליה בפחות משויה. אבל גבי מכר, משנמשך המקח דינו ליתן המעות, וכי אמר ליה אם מעכשיו תתן הרי היא לך באלף זוז, הן הן דמיה, וכי מטפי טפי עלייהו לגורן, שכר המתנת מעות הוא:

from him at this time.[9] Thus, if the price of wine goes up between the time they make the new agreement and the time the wine is delivered, the buyer will be receiving from the seller something that is worth more than what he was owed. The arrangement is therefore Rabbinically forbidden.[10]

[2] This Mishnah gives further examples of Rabbinically forbidden interest. The first example involves a loan:

הַמַּלְוֶה אֶת חֲבֵרוֹ — **Someone who gives a loan to his friend** לֹא יָדוּר בַּחֲצֵרוֹ חִנָּם — **should not live in [the borrower's] courtyard**[1] **for free** (without paying rent), וְלֹא יִשְׂכֹּר מִמֶּנּוּ בְּפָחוֹת — **nor may he rent** it **from him for less** than the usual rate, מִפְּנֵי שֶׁהוּא רִבִּית — **because it is** Rabbinically forbidden **interest**.[2]

The Mishnah now introduces a new type of Rabbinically forbidden interest — charging a higher price for a sale or lease in exchange for waiting for the full payment:[3]

---- NOTES ----

9. It was only earlier, with regard to the wheat, that the buyer was viewed as acquiring ownership of it as soon as he paid, because he gave *money* that the seller could have used to buy wheat at that time. Here, though, the buyer is not giving him the money for the wine; he is merely agreeing to accept it as payment for the money he is owed.

10. **In summary:** We have learned three rules in this Mishnah regarding Rabbinically prohibited interest that takes place through sales:

(a) It is forbidden for a person to pay in advance for goods he will not receive until some later time, because the money paid in advance is viewed as a loan. Thus, if the price of the goods rises before they are delivered, the buyer will be receiving something worth more than the "loan" he gave when he paid in advance.

(b) However, if the seller actually has the goods in his possession at the time the deal is made, it is permitted to pay him in advance even though the goods will not be delivered until a later time.

(c) Even if the seller does not yet have the goods when he makes the deal with the buyer, but they are available in the market at that time at an established price, it is permissible to pay in advance — if the buyer pays in cash. If he is merely forgiving a debt or loan in return, it is forbidden.

[2]

1. That is, in a house belonging to the borrower.

2. Allowing the lender to live in a house for free, or for less than the going rate, is a gift to the lender. Since the borrower gives him this in addition to repaying the loan, it is forbidden interest. However, since the loan was not made *on condition* that the borrower would give this benefit to the lender, it is forbidden only by Rabbinic law. Only interest that is made part of the original loan agreement is Biblically forbidden (*Meiri*).

3. In the cases that follow, the buyer or

מַרְבִּין עַל הַשָּׂכָר, וְאֵין מַרְבִּין עַל הַמֶּכֶר. כֵּיצַד, הִשְׂכִּיר לוֹ אֶת חֲצֵרוֹ וְאָמַר לוֹ, אִם מֵעַכְשָׁיו אַתָּה נוֹתֵן לִי הֲרֵי הוּא לְךָ בְּעֶשֶׂר סְלָעִים לַשָּׁנָה, וְאִם שֶׁל חֹדֶשׁ בְּחֹדֶשׁ בְּסֶלַע לַחֹדֶשׁ, מֻתָּר. מָכַר לוֹ אֶת שָׂדֵהוּ וְאָמַר לוֹ, אִם מֵעַכְשָׁיו אַתָּה נוֹתֵן לִי הֲרֵי הִיא שֶׁלְּךָ בְּאֶלֶף זוּז, אִם לַגֹּרֶן בִּשְׁנֵים עָשָׂר מָנֶה, אָסוּר.

— רע״ב —

מכר לו את השדה וכו'. והוא הדין מטלטלין וכל סחורה, אם מכר לו יותר משויה בשכר המתנת מעות, אסור, והוא אבק רבית מדבריהם. וכל אבק רבית אם נתן, אינה יוצאה בדיינים. דאילו רבית קצוצה דאורייתא, יוצאה בדיינים:

מַרְבִּין עַל הַשָּׂכָר — It is permissible to increase the amount of rent a person charges someone who does not pay in advance, וְאֵין מַרְבִּין עַל הַמֶּכֶר — but it is not permissible to increase the price a person charges for a sale to a buyer who does not pay up front (at the time of the purchase).

The Mishnah illustrates these rules:

כֵּיצַד — How so? הִשְׂכִּיר לוֹ אֶת חֲצֵרוֹ — If someone rents his courtyard to [another person], וְאָמַר לוֹ — and says to him, אִם מֵעַכְשָׁיו אַתָּה נוֹתֵן לִי הֲרֵי הוּא לְךָ בְּעֶשֶׂר סְלָעִים — "If you give me the rent for the entire year now, לַשָּׁנָה — it is yours for ten *sela* for the year; וְאִם שֶׁל חֹדֶשׁ בְּחֹדֶשׁ — but if you pay me for it month by the month, בְּסֶלַע לַחֹדֶשׁ — then I give it to you for a *sela* per month (twelve *sela* for the year)," מֻתָּר — it is permitted. Since rent is really due at the end of each month, the true price is twelve *sela*, and the landlord's offer of ten *sela* for the year is a *discount* for getting paid in advance rather than a *charge* for waiting to get paid. מָכַר לוֹ אֶת שָׂדֵהוּ — However, if someone sells his field to [another person], וְאָמַר לוֹ — and he says to him, אִם מֵעַכְשָׁיו אַתָּה נוֹתֵן לִי — "If you give me the money for the field now, הֲרֵי הִיא שֶׁלְּךָ בְּאֶלֶף זוּז — it is yours for a thousand *zuz*; אִם לַגֹּרֶן — but if you want to delay paying me until the threshing time, when the grain from the field can be sold so you can raise money to pay me, בִּשְׁנֵים עָשָׂר מָנֶה — then it is yours for twelve *maneh* (1,200 *zuz*)," אָסוּר — it is forbidden. Since money for a sale is due as soon as the sale takes effect, the true price for the field is 1,000 *zuz*, and the demand for 1,200 *zuz* is a *charge* for waiting to get paid.[4] This is Rabbinically forbidden interest.

NOTES

renter acquires the rights to the property as soon as the deal is concluded, even if he does not pay for everything at that time. His ownership of these rights does not depend on completing the payment; rather, the money he has not yet paid is simply a debt he owes to the seller or landlord of the property.

4. Since the buyer now owes the seller money for the item he bought, he in effect "borrowed" the purchase price (1,000 *zuz*) from him. Since he later pays him 1,200 *zuz*, he has paid interest on this loan.

In short, when two prices are presented, the true price is considered to be the one that applies when the money is legally due. If that is the lower price, then the higher price is considered an extra charge for waiting to be paid. This is considered to be like interest on a loan and is Rabbinically forbidden (see *Rav*).

MISHNAH BAVA METZIA / Chapter 5: Eizehu Neshech

— רע"ב —

(ג) הבא מעות וטול את שלך אסור. הבא מותר מעות שעליך וטול שדה שלך, אסור לעשות כן. וכגון שאמר לו מוכר ללוקח, לכי מייתית קנה מטכשיו. לפיכך אסור לעשות כן, שאם יאכל מוכר הפירות בתוך כך, לכשיציא זה המעות נמצא שדה זו קנויה לו מיום המכר, וזה אכל הפירות בשכר המתנת מעותיו. ואם יאכל לוקח פירות מעתכשיו, שמא לא יביא מותר המעות, ויחזיר לו זה מה שקבל, ונמצא שלא היתה שדה קנויה לו, דהא לכי מייתית קני מעתכשיו אמר ליה, והא לא אייתי, ומעות הראשונות כמלוה בעלמא היו אצל מוכר, וזה אכל פירות בשכרו:

משנה

[ג] **מָכַר** לוֹ אֶת הַשָּׂדֶה, וְנָתַן לוֹ מִקְצָת דָּמִים וְאָמַר לוֹ, אֵימָתַי שֶׁתִּרְצֶה הָבֵא מָעוֹת וְטֹל אֶת שֶׁלְּךָ, אָסוּר.

---

[3] The Mishnah discusses another real estate transaction that can lead to Rabbinically forbidden interest:

וְנָתַן לוֹ מָכַר לוֹ אֶת הַשָּׂדֶה — If someone sells a field to [another person], מִקְצָת דָּמִים — and [the buyer] gives [the seller] part of the money, וְאָמַר לוֹ — and [the seller] says to him, אֵימָתַי שֶׁתִּרְצֶה הָבֵא מָעוֹת וְטֹל אֶת שֶׁלְּךָ — "Whenever you want, bring the rest of the **money and take what is yours** (the field) and it will be considered yours from now, and if you do not bring the rest of the money, the sale will be nullified and I will return your money to you";[1] אָסוּר — **it is forbidden** for either the buyer or the seller to take the crops of this field until we see what happens. This is because it might result in a form of Rabbinically forbidden interest. If the field ends up belonging to the buyer, then any produce taken by the *seller* while he was waiting for the final payment is a benefit he is getting in return for waiting for his money.[2] And if the field ends up staying with the seller, then any produce taken by the *buyer* while the sale was still pending is a benefit he is getting for letting the seller use the money of the first payment while the sale was still pending.[3]

NOTES

[3]

1. That is, when you give me the rest of the money, the field will belong to you retroactively from when you made the first payment. But if you do not give me the rest of the money then the sale is canceled and I will give you back the first payment (*Rav*).

2. If the buyer ends up bringing the rest of the money, then the sale takes effect retroactively from the time of the first payment. If so, the seller really has no right to take produce from the field from that time on. Why then is he taking the crop? It is because he is taking an extra payment in return for waiting to receive the rest of his money from the buyer. [This is not Biblically forbidden because the debt did not come about through a loan but through a sale. Nevertheless, it is Rabbinically forbidden.]

3. If the buyer is unable to come up with the rest of the money (or simply changes his mind), and the sale is canceled, it turns out that the *buyer* had no right to take anything from the field because it never belonged to him. Why then is he taking crops? It is in return for allowing the seller to use the money of the first payment until the sale is decided. [This money is like a loan from the buyer to the seller until it is returned to him.]

Since neither the buyer nor the seller may take the produce until we see whether the sale is completed, the crops are given to a third person to hold. If the sale is eventually completed, they are given to the buyer, and if not, they are given to the seller (see Gemara 65b).

הִלְוָהוּ עַל שָׂדֵהוּ וְאָמַר לוֹ, אִם אִי אַתָּה נוֹתֵן לִי מִכָּאן וְעַד שָׁלֹשׁ שָׁנִים הֲרֵי הִיא שֶׁלִּי, הֲרֵי הִיא שֶׁלּוֹ. וְכָךְ הָיָה בַּיְתוֹס בֶּן זוֹנִין עוֹשֶׂה עַל פִּי חֲכָמִים.

— רע״ב —

הרי היא שלו. וכגון דאמר ליה, קני מעכשיו אם לא אביא לך מכאן עד שלש שנים. דלא אסמכתא היא, אלא קנין גמור, שעל מנת מכר גמור החזיק בה, יקבלם. והפירות יהיו מונחים ביד שליש, אם יחזיר הלוה מעותיו למלוה עד שלש שנים, יתן הפירות ללוה, ואם לאו יתן הפירות למלוה, שהיתה השדה קנויה לו משעת הלואה, ואותה הלואה דמי השדה היתה:

The next case involves a loan arrangement under which the lender might end up collecting a field that is worth more than the amount of the loan:

הִלְוָהוּ עַל שָׂדֵהוּ — If someone lends another person money on the security of his field, meaning that if the borrower does not repay the loan, the lender can take that field, וְאָמַר לוֹ — and [the lender] said to [the borrower], אִם אִי אַתָּה נוֹתֵן לִי מִכָּאן וְעַד שָׁלֹשׁ שָׁנִים — "If you do not give me back the money within the next three years,[4] הֲרֵי הִיא שֶׁלִּי — then [the field] is mine as of now," הֲרֵי הִיא שֶׁלּוֹ — then if the borrower does not pay back within three years, [the field] is [the lender's]. This is permitted even if the field is worth more than the loan, because the lender actually owned the field from the moment he gave the borrower the money. This means that the money he gave the "borrower" was never really a loan but a payment for the field. He simply *bought* the field at a cheap price.[5] וְכָךְ הָיָה בַּיְתוֹס בֶּן זוֹנִין עוֹשֶׂה עַל פִּי חֲכָמִים — And this is what Baisos the son of Zonin would do, with the approval of the Sages.[6]

NOTES

4. Literally, *from now until three years*.

5. [A loan is where the lender is repaid sometime *after* he gives the money. Where he receives property in return for the money *at the time* he gives the money, it is not a loan but a sale.] Since the agreement in this case was for the lender to take ownership of the field from the time he gave the money (if the borrower did not repay it within three years), this is not a "loan" but a sale — with a condition that if the money is repaid within three years, the sale will be nullified. Therefore, even if the field is worth more than the amount of the loan, there is no problem of interest (*Rav*). This is even Rabbinically permitted because it resembles a sale not a loan.

[However, here too the crops must be given to a third person to hold until we know whether the sale goes through or not. This is because the deal can be considered a "sale" only if the lender ends up with the field. If the borrower *does* repay him within three years and gets back his field, then the deal really was a loan (because the lender got back money, not a field), and anything the lender took from the field during those years was interest on that loan. And if the borrower does *not* pay back the loan, anything *he* took from the field would be considered stolen, since it turns out that the field really belonged to the lender during those three years (*Rav*; *Rashi*, as explained by *Pnei Yehoshua*).]

6. The Mishnah is proving that this is the accepted halachah by recalling the practice of Baisos (who lived shortly after the destruction of the Second Temple), who would make this kind of "loan" with the approval of the great Sages of that day.

MISHNAH BAVA METZIA / Chapter 5: Eizehu Neshech

— רע"ב —

(ד) אֵין מוֹשִׁיבִין חֶנְוָנִי [ד] **אֵין** מוֹשִׁיבִין חֶנְוָנִי לְמַחֲצִית שָׂכָר,
לְמַחֲצִית שָׂכָר. לֹא יֹאמַר
בַּעַל הַבַּיִת לְחֶנְוָנִי, הֲרֵי פֵּירוֹת נִמְכָּרִים בַּשּׁוּק אַרְבַּע סְאִין בְּסֶלַע, וְאַתָּה מוֹכֵר בַּחֲנוּת פְּרוּטָה פְּרוּטָה
וּמִשְׂתַּכֵּר סְאָה, הֵילָךְ פֵּירוֹת וְשֵׁב וּמְכוֹר בַּחֲנוּת, וְהָרְוָחִים נַחֲלוֹק. וּטְעָמָא דְמִלְּתָא, מִשּׁוּם דְּקַיְימָא לָן (גמרא
קד,ב) הָךְ עִסְקָא פַּלְגָּא מִלְוֶה וּפַלְגָּא פִּקָּדוֹן. סְתָם הַמְקַבֵּל פַּרְקְמַטְיָא לְמַחֲצִית שָׂכָר, מְקַבֵּל עָלָיו אַחֲרָיוּת
חֲצִי הַקֶּרֶן בְּאוֹנָסִין וְזוֹלָא, הִילְכָּךְ הַהִיא פַּלְגָא הֲוָה מִלְוֶה בְּאוֹנָסִין מִלְוֶה דְּמִחַיֵּיב כֵּיוָן בְּאוֹנָסִין מִלְוֶה הִיא אֶצְלוֹ, שֶׁהֲרֵי הִיא שׁוּמָא

[4] The following Mishnah deals with interest related to investments.

It was common in Mishnaic times for a person who had money to invest, or merchandise to sell, to make a deal with a broker to take the merchandise and find buyers for it, or to buy merchandise with the money and then sell it at a profit, and divide the profits with the investor. Since all investments involve risk, and since the investor wanted the broker to share in the risks as well the profits, these deals were typically arranged in the following manner: Half the investment (money or merchandise) would be considered a loan to the broker,[1] while the other half would be considered the investor's property. Since the broker puts the half he "borrowed" back into the investment, he and the investor are now equal partners in it. The broker then buys and sells with all of it and tries to earn a profit for the investment. If it makes money, they each take half the profits; and if it loses money they each suffer half the losses.[2]

Although this means that the investor may get back more than he gave the broker, this is not an interest payment, since that extra money is profit from the investor's half of the investment, not from the loan. Our Mishnah will now teach that there is one more requirement that must be met to prevent such a deal from being forbidden as interest:

The Mishnah begins with a case of investing with a storekeeper:

אֵין מוֹשִׁיבִין חֶנְוָנִי לְמַחֲצִית שָׂכָר — **One may not have a storekeeper sit** and sell

---
NOTES

[4]

1. Technically, the arrangement was for the broker to be responsible for the loss or drop in value of half the merchandise or money. However, whenever someone receives something and is responsible to pay it back in full no matter what happens to it, he has in effect received a loan. Since the broker is responsible to pay back half the losses, he has in effect borrowed half the investment (see *Rav*).

2. This is because the broker must repay the half that was a loan even if the investment loses money (the same as with any loan). For example, if the investor put up 200 *zuz*, half the money (100 *zuz*) is considered a loan to the broker, while the other half represents the investor's share. If the investment ends up losing half its value, the remaining 100 *zuz* is divided between them, and the broker must still pay the investor the 100 *zuz* he "borrowed" from him. The final result is that the investor ends up with 150 *zuz* (50 less than he started with), and the broker is out 50 *zuz*.

Similarly with the profits: if the investment earned a 100 *zuz* profit, the investor receives half (50 *zuz*) as the return on his half of the investment, while the broker receives the other half as the return on his half of the investment. The broker must also give the investor back the 200 *zuz* that was invested — half because it still belongs to the investor and the other half as repayment of the "loan" the broker took from him at the beginning of the investment. The final result is that the investor ends up with 250 *zuz* (50 more than he started with) and the broker receives 50 *zuz*.

משניות בבא מציעא / פרק ה: איזהו נשך

וְלֹא יִתֵּן מָעוֹת לִקַּח בָּהֶן פֵּרוֹת לְמַחֲצִית שָׂכָר, אֶלָּא אִם כֵּן נוֹתֵן לוֹ שְׂכָרוֹ כְּפוֹעֵל. אֵין מוֹשִׁיבִין תַּרְנְגוֹלִין לְמֶחֱצָה, וְאֵין שָׁמִין עֲגָלִין וּסְיָחִין לְמֶחֱצָה, אֶלָּא אִם כֵּן נוֹתֵן לוֹ שְׂכַר עֲמָלוֹ וּמְזוֹנוֹ.

— רע"ב —

אלו במעות בשער השוק, ודינו ליטול חצי שכר. נמצא מתעסק בחציו של בעל הבית שהוא פקדון אצלו, בשכר המתנת מעות המלוה, לפיכך אסור. אלא אם כן נותן לו שכר עמלו שהוא עמל באותו החצי, כפועל בטל של אותה מלאכה דבטל מינה. אם היה נגר או נפח, כמה אדם רוצה ליטול ליבטל ממלאכה כבדה כזו, ולעשות מלאכה קלה: אין מושיבין תרנגולים למחצה. לשום ביצים בדמים להושיבה עליהם לגדל אפרוחים, למחצית שכר מה שיהיו האפרוחים שוים יותר על דמי הביצים. דהואיל וזה מקבל עליו אחריות חצי דמי הביצים אם יתקלקלו או אם ימותו, הוה ליה פלגא מלוה, נמצא זה מגדל את חציו השני בשכר המתנת מעותיו: ומזונו. מזון שהוא מוליא באפרוחים: ואין שמין עגלים וסייחין למחצה. שכשיו הם שוים כך וכך, קבלם עליך לגדלם שנתים למחצית שכר, ולמחצית הפסד אם ימותו:

---

produce in exchange **for half of the earnings,** that is, one may not tell a storekeeper, "Here is produce at a certain price, sell it for a higher price and we will split the profits";[3] — **וְלֹא יִתֵּן מָעוֹת לִקַּח בָּהֶן פֵּרוֹת לְמַחֲצִית שָׂכָר** — **nor may one give** a storekeeper **money with which to buy produce** to sell in exchange **for half of the earnings,** **אֶלָּא אִם כֵּן נוֹתֵן לוֹ שְׂכָרוֹ כְּפוֹעֵל** — **unless one** also **gives [the storekeeper] his wages as a worker.** This is because half the produce (or money) is a loan from the investor to the storekeeper, and the other half is money that belongs to the investor. Since the storekeeper is an equal partner with the investor in this deal,[4] and yet he is doing *all* the work (buying and selling) on behalf of both of them, if he does not get paid for half his work, it is because he is performing a free service for the investor in exchange for the loan he received from him. This free service is forbidden interest. The investor must therefore pay the storekeeper for half his work.[5]

The same rule applies to someone investing in raising chickens or young animals:

אֵין מוֹשִׁיבִין תַּרְנְגוֹלִין לְמֶחֱצָה — **One may not** give eggs to a farmer to **have his hens sit on them** in order to hatch chicks, which he will then raise **for half** the profits and losses,[6] **וְאֵין שָׁמִין עֲגָלִין וּסְיָחִין לְמֶחֱצָה** — **nor may one assess** the value of **calves or colts** (young horses) and give them to a herdsman to raise **for half** the profits and losses,[7] **אֶלָּא אִם כֵּן נוֹתֵן לוֹ שְׂכַר עֲמָלוֹ וּמְזוֹנוֹ** — **unless**

--- NOTES ---

3. This deal is made according to the arrangement described in the introduction. The storekeeper is also responsible for half the losses, because he receives half the produce as a loan (*Rav*).

4. As explained in the introduction to the Mishnah.

5. Only half the work is being done for the investor. The other half is being done on behalf of the storekeeper's own share of the investment.

6. That is, he will get half the profits, but he will also be responsible for half of any losses (for example, if the chicks die). This is another example of the type of investment described in the introduction to this Mishnah. Half the eggs the farmer will receive will belong to the investor, while the other half will be a "loan" to the farmer.

7. Very young cows and horses need to be raised and fed until they grow large

[97] MISHNAH BAVA METZIA / Chapter 5: *Eizehu Neshech* — 5/4

אֲבָל מְקַבְּלִין עֲגָלִין וּסְיָחִין לְמֶחֱצָה, וּמְגַדְּלִין אוֹתָן עַד שֶׁיְּהוּ מְשֻׁלָּשִׁין, וַחֲמוֹר עַד שֶׁתְּהֵא טוֹעֶנֶת.

— רע״ב —

אבל מקבלים עגלים וסייחים קטנים. בלא שומא. שאם ימותו לא ישלם כלום, ואם יחיו יחלקו ביניהם: שיהיו משולשים. פירש כשיעמדו על שליש גדולן, ואז יחלקו: ובחמור עד שתהא טוענת. משאוי. כך היה מנהגם לגדלם קודם חלוקה:

[the investor] gives [the farmer or herdsman] payment for his work in raising the investor's half of the animals, **and** for half **his food** that he feeds the animals. Providing the work or food for free is Rabbinically forbidden as interest.

The Mishnah now teaches when it is *not* necessary to pay for the work:

אֲבָל מְקַבְּלִין עֲגָלִין וּסְיָחִין לְמֶחֱצָה — **However, [a herdsman] may accept calves or colts for half** the profits *without* first assessing their value, in which case he is *not* responsible for half the losses.[8] If so, he is not receiving any of the animals as a loan; he is simply caring for the owner's animals in exchange for half the profits. Therefore, there is no need to pay him for his work or the feed.[9]

As a side issue, the Mishnah teaches how long a herdsman is expected to raise the young animals in his care:

וּמְגַדְּלִין אוֹתָן עַד שֶׁיְּהוּ מְשֻׁלָּשִׁין — **He must raise [the calves and colts] until they are** grown **to a third** of their full size, before he may return them and split the profits with the investor. **וַחֲמוֹר עַד שֶׁתְּהֵא טוֹעֶנֶת** — If the agreement was to raise **a young donkey,** he must raise it **until it can carry** a load.[10]

— NOTES —

enough to take care of themselves. This involves a lot of work. People would therefore give their young animals to professional herders to do the work for them. One way of arranging to pay for this was to make the type of arrangement explained in this Mishnah, giving the herder half the profits and making him responsible for half the losses [for example, if the animals die]. Thus, half the animals are given to him as a "loan" and half simply as the owner's share of the investment (see *Rav*). In order that it should be clear how much the herdsman is responsible for, the value of the young animals is assessed before they are given to him (*Tos. Yom Tov* ד״ה אבל מקבלין).

[The "profit" in this case is the difference in value between the very young animals he receives and the animals he gives back to the investor.]

8. Wherever the receiver is expected to be responsible for half the losses, the value of the property is assessed and written down before it is given to him. If they are given to him without such an assessment, the agreement does not call for him to be responsible for half the losses (*Tos. Yom Tov, Tosafos*). And whenever the receiver is not responsible for the losses, the arrangement is not considered a loan; see note 1.

9. Since there is no loan, the work cannot be considered an interest payment. Rather, it is being done in exchange for half the profits.

10. These were the standard arrangements in the time of the Mishnah (*Rav; Rashi*). The Mishnah teaches that unless they specifically make a different arrangement, neither side is allowed to back out of it until the young animals reach the sizes mentioned here (see *Gemara* 69a).

[ה] **שָׁמִין** פָּרָה וַחֲמוֹר, וְכָל דָּבָר שֶׁהוּא עוֹשֶׂה וְאוֹכֵל, לְמֶחֱצָה. מָקוֹם שֶׁנָּהֲגוּ לַחֲלֹק אֶת הַוְּלָדוֹת מִיָּד חוֹלְקִין, מָקוֹם שֶׁנָּהֲגוּ לְגַדֵּל, יְגַדְּלוּ.

— רע"ב —

(ה) שמין פרה. גדולה וחמור גדול שראויין למלאכה, ומלאכתן כולה למקבל: למחצה. לחלוק שבח שישביחו, בדמים וולדות:

לחלוק את הולדות מיד. כשתבא שעת חלוקתן. בבהמה דקה שלשים יום, ובגסה חמשים יום:

[5] The previous Mishnah taught that if a herdsman takes young animals into his care and he shares in both the profits and the losses, the investor must pay him separately for half the work and half the food he gives the animals. Our Mishnah teaches that this is not the case with fully grown animals:

שָׁמִין פָּרָה וַחֲמוֹר וְכָל דָּבָר שֶׁהוּא עוֹשֶׂה וְאוֹכֵל לְמֶחֱצָה — One may assess the value of **a** grown **cow, a** grown **donkey, or any other** animal **that does** work **and** thereby covers the expense of what it **eats,** and place it in the care of a herdsman **for half** the profits and losses.[1] Since the herdsman can use these animals for work, that is considered his payment for taking care of and feeding the animals.[2]

All offspring produced by the grown animals are considered profit, so the herdsman and the investor each own half of them. The Mishnah discusses when the herdsman may take his share of the offspring:[3]

מָקוֹם שֶׁנָּהֲגוּ לַחֲלֹק אֶת הַוְּלָדוֹת מִיָּד — **In a place where the custom is to divide the offspring immediately,** that is, as soon as they no longer need the care of an expert herdsman, **חוֹלְקִין** — **they may divide them** immediately. **מָקוֹם שֶׁנָּהֲגוּ לְגַדֵּל** — **In a place where the custom is to** have the herdsman **raise** young animals until they are grown, **יְגַדְּלוּ** — **they may leave the animals with the herdsman to raise** until they are grown, and the herdsman cannot force the investor to divide the offspring before then.[4]

The previous Mishnah taught that if someone wants to give a herdsman calves or colts to raise in exchange for half the profits and losses, he must

---
NOTES

[5]
1. "Assessing the value" of an animal before giving it to someone to care for means that the caregiver will be responsible for half the losses (see note 7 of the previous Mishnah).
2. In the previous Mishnah, however, he received animals that are too young to do any work. The investor must therefore pay him for his work and the feed (*Meiri*).
3. The herdsman would prefer to divide the offspring as soon as they are born. This would free him from having to take care of the investor's half of the offspring.

Since he has no share in any increase in their value, he does not want to have to raise them. However, young animals must be cared for by an expert for the first part of their lives (thirty days for sheep and goats, and fifty days for cattle). It is therefore understood that the herdsman will care for *all* the offspring at least for that first period (*Rav, Rashi*).

4. Whenever people enter into a contract without specifying certain details of it, it is assumed that they mean to follow the local custom for such kinds of arrangements. They are therefore bound by the contract to keep those rules.

[99] MISHNAH BAVA METZIA / Chapter 5: *Eizehu Neshech*

שמין עגל עם אמו. ואין
צריך ליתן עמל ומזון לעגל,
אלא לחם. ואין הלכה
כרבן שמעון בן גמליאל:
ומפרין על שדהו. לשון
פרה ורבה. ואית דגרסת ומפרין בזיי"ן לשון פרזות תשב ירושלים (זכריה ב,ח). כלומר מרחיב על שדהו.
והוא שיאמר לו [חוכר למחכיר], אתה רגיל ליקח בחכירות שדך עשרת כורין לשנה, הלוני מחתים
זוז שאוכל להוציא לזבל שדה זו ולזרעה ולחרשה, ואני מעלה לך בחכירותה שנים עשר כורין לשנה,
ואחזיר לך מעותיך. זה מותר, דהוי כאילו מעדיף לו שני כורים הללו מפני שחוכר ממנו שדה טובה
ומשובחת, שחכירותה יפה מחכירות שדה רעה:

רַבָּן שִׁמְעוֹן בֶּן גַּמְלִיאֵל אוֹמֵר, שָׁמִין עֵגֶל
עִם אִמּוֹ, וְסֶיָּח עִם אִמּוֹ. וּמַפְרִיז עַל שָׂדֵהוּ,
וְאֵינוֹ חוֹשֵׁשׁ מִשּׁוּם רִבִּית.

---

pay the herdsman for half his work and half the food. The Mishnah now cites a Tanna who limits this requirement:

רַבָּן שִׁמְעוֹן בֶּן גַּמְלִיאֵל אוֹמֵר — **Rabban Shimon ben Gamliel says:** שָׁמִין עֵגֶל עִם אִמּוֹ וְסֶיָּח עִם אִמּוֹ — **One may assess** the value of **a calf** along **with its mother, or** of **a colt** along **with its mother,** and give them to a herdsman to raise for half the profits and losses, without having to pay him anything extra for his work and the food he provides. These expenses are covered by the value of the mother's work and the child's manure.[5]

Rabban Shimon ben Gamliel concludes with another leniency in the laws of interest:

וּמַפְרִיז עַל שָׂדֵהוּ — **A person may increase** the amount he charges for rent **on his field,** in exchange for lending the renter money to improve the quality of the field, וְאֵינוֹ חוֹשֵׁשׁ מִשּׁוּם רִבִּית — **and he need not be concerned about** the extra rent being considered **interest,** because the increased charge is on account of the improved quality of the field, which can now be expected to produce more.[6]

NOTES

5. The mother is a fully grown animal and her work covers the expense of her food and care. Since the young animal nurses from its mother and follows her everywhere, the herdsman does not have to feed it or work extra to care for it, except for the occasional times when he has to carry it on his shoulder to bring it somewhere. That small effort is covered by the manure produced by the calf or colt, which the herdsman can use to fertilize his fields (*Rav, Rashi, Tos. Yom Tov*). [Animal droppings were used as fertilizer.]

The Tanna of Mishnah 4, who disagrees with Rabban Shimon ben Gamliel, holds that the manure cannot be considered a payment by the investor. This is because people generally give up ownership of any manure left by their animals in someone else's property (see Mishnah 8:7 note 5). Here too, the investor is not *giving* the calf's manure to the herdsman, he is simply *giving up ownership* of it. Therefore, although the herdsman takes it for himself, it cannot be considered a *payment* for his work (*Tos. Yom Tov*).

6. For example, the person renting the field was paying ten *kors* of wheat a year as rent. He then borrowed 200 *zuz* from the owner to make improvements in the field (for example, to buy extra fertilizer). He agrees to pay back the 200 *zuz*, as well as twelve *kors* a year in rent (an additional two *kors*). Rabban Shimon ben Gamliel permits this because he views the 200 *zuz* the owner gave the renter to improve the field, not as a *loan* to the renter but as an *investment* by the owner in his field. [It is the same as if the owner asked someone else to make improvements for him in his field to get it ready for the renter.] Thus, the extra two *kors* the renter will now pay

— רע״ב —

(ו) אין מקבלין צאן ברזל. כל אחריות הנכסים על המקבל, וגם אומר עליו במעות, וכל זמן שאין נותן לו מעותיו חולקים השכר. ואף על גב דמשנה יתירה היא, דהא תנא ליה לעיל (משנה ד),

[ו] **אֵין מְקַבְּלִין צֹאן בַּרְזֶל מִיִּשְׂרָאֵל, מִפְּנֵי שֶׁהוּא רִבִּית. אֲבָל מְקַבְּלִין צֹאן בַּרְזֶל מִן הָעוֹבְדֵי כּוֹכָבִים, וְלֹוִין מֵהֶן וּמַלְוִין אוֹתָן בְּרִבִּית. וְכֵן בְּגֵר תּוֹשָׁב.**

אין מושיבים חנוני למחצית שכר משום דמקבל עליה פלגא בהפסד, וכל שכן הכא דקבל כל האחריות עליו. נקט ליה משום סיפא, אבל מקבלים צאן ברזל מן העכו״ם:

[6] The Mishnah discusses another type of investment that is forbidden because of interest:

אֵין מְקַבְּלִין צֹאן בַּרְזֶל מִיִּשְׂרָאֵל — **A person may not accept from a** fellow **Jew** an investment with a *tzon barzel* arrangement, under which he guarantees to return the amount of the original investment plus half of any profits,[1] מִפְּנֵי שֶׁהוּא רִבִּית — **because** the profit in **this** case is considered **interest.**[2]

The Mishnah discusses the laws of interest on a loan between a Jew and a non-Jew:

אֲבָל מְקַבְּלִין צֹאן בַּרְזֶל מִן הָעוֹבְדֵי כּוֹכָבִים — **One may, however, accept** an investment with a *tzon barzel* arrangement from non-Jews, וְלֹוִין מֵהֶן וּמַלְוִין אוֹתָן בְּרִבִּית — **and** in fact **one may** actually **borrow from them and lend to them with interest;**[3] וְכֵן בְּגֵר תּוֹשָׁב — **and the same** holds true **with a** *ger toshav*.[4]

— NOTES —

the owner is not interest on a *loan*, but part of an increased *rent* he is now paying for a much-improved field. Since the improved field can now be expected to produce a lot more than it did before, the renter is willing to pay the owner a much higher rent (*Rav, Rashi*).

[6]

1. *Tzon barzel* literally means "iron sheep." However, the Mishnah is not specifically discussing an investment in sheep. A *tzon barzel* investment refers to *any* kind of investment in which a dealer guarantees to give back to the investor all the money he invested (or the value of the items he invested), even if the investment fails and the money is lost. On the other hand, if the investment earns a profit, the investor will get a share of it. [This is called a *tzon barzel* arrangement because, like iron, the original amount is preserved for the investor, and it is called "sheep," because these arrangements were originally made with investments in sheep (*Rashi*).]

2. One of the basic differences between an investment and a loan is that an investment carries with it a risk of loss, whereas a loan must always be repaid in full. Since the investor in this case is guaranteed to get back the amount he invested even if the investment loses money, the investment is really a loan (see above, Mishnah 4 note 1). Any profit he gets is therefore considered interest on the loan, which is forbidden between Jews.

3. The Torah states clearly that we may *pay* interest to non-Jews (*Deuteronomy* 23:21). And since the Torah says (*Leviticus* 25:36) that the reason we may not *lend* with interest is because we must be concerned for the welfare of our *brother* (i.e., fellow Jew) and give him the loan for free, we understand that this does not apply to non-Jews [who must be treated with decency, but are not considered brothers] (*Tur, Yoreh Deah* 159).

4. A *ger toshav* is a non-Jew who is allowed to live in Eretz Yisrael because he has accepted not to worship idols. Although the Torah generally requires us to be more concerned for the welfare of a

[101] MISHNAH BAVA METZIA / Chapter 5: *Eizehu Neshech*

מַלְוֶה יִשְׂרָאֵל מְעוֹתָיו שֶׁל עוֹבֵד כּוֹכָבִים מִדַּעַת הָעוֹבֵד כּוֹכָבִים, אֲבָל לֹא מִדַּעַת יִשְׂרָאֵל.

— רע״ב —
מדעת העכו״ם. כגון ישראל שלוה מעות מעכו״ס ברבית, וביקש להחזירם לו, מלאו ישראל אחר ואמר תנם לי ואני אעלה לך כדרך שאתה מעלה לו. אם העמידו אצל עכו״ס, אף על פי שישראל נותנם לו במעות העכו״ס, מותר. ואם לא העמידו אצל עכו״ס, אסור. דהוא ניהו דקא מוזיף ליה בריבית:

מַלְוֶה יִשְׂרָאֵל מְעוֹתָיו שֶׁל עוֹבֵד כּוֹכָבִים — **A Jew may lend a non-Jew's money** (i.e., money he borrowed from a non-Jew[5]) to another Jew and charge him interest on it, provided that this is done **with the agreement of the non-Jew**, who is then considered to be the person lending with interest to the second Jew;[6] אֲבָל לֹא מִדַּעַת יִשְׂרָאֵל — **but not** if this is done only **with the agreement of the first Jew**, because the first Jew is then considered to be the one lending with interest to the second Jew.[7]

[7] We learned in Mishnah 1 that it is forbidden to pay in advance for merchandise that will not be delivered until a later date, because its price might go up before it is delivered and the buyer will end up getting more value than he paid for. This resembles interest on a loan because it looks like the seller is giving more in exchange for being allowed to use the money he was paid in advance.[1] The Rabbis therefore prohibited it. However, since the prohibition is only Rabbinic,[2] the Rabbis included several leniencies in it.

One of these leniencies is that it is permitted to pay in advance for merchandise the seller already has in his possession, even though the buyer will not receive it until sometime later.[3] Our Mishnah discusses the law where the seller does not yet have the merchandise:

--- NOTES ---

ger toshav (*Leviticus* 25:35), the prohibition of charging interest on a loan applies only to a fellow Jew [see previous note] (*Taz, Yoreh Deah* 159:1).

5. For which he is paying interest.

6. For example, Reuven borrowed money from a non-Jew who is charging him interest, and he is ready to repay the loan. Shimon says to Reuven, "Instead of repaying the loan now, lend me the money, and when I repay you I will also cover the extra interest the non-Jew will be charging you because of this delay." This is permitted if Reuven takes Shimon to the non-Jew and has him agree to this arrangement. In this case, we view Reuven as having repaid the loan to the non-Jew, who then took the money and lent it to Shimon (see *Rav*).

The Gemara (71b) adds that Reuven must actually hand the money to the non-Jew and have him pass it to Shimon in order for this to be permitted.

7. If Reuven does not take Shimon to the non-Jew and get his agreement [and have him hand the money to Shimon], then Reuven is considered to be the one lending money to Shimon and he is forbidden to charge him interest on it. Although Reuven is paying interest to have this money, he may still not charge interest on a loan *he* is making to a fellow Jew (*Rav*).

[7]

1. Since the seller has the use of the money before he gives anything in return, the money is considered a "loan" (see above, Mishnah 1 note 6).

2. Biblical law forbids interest on money that was *loaned*. The extra payment in our case, which comes about through a *sale*, is forbidden only by Rabbinic law (see *Rav* to Mishnah 1).

3. This is because we view the sale as having taken place as soon as the money was paid, so that the goods already

[ז] **אֵין** פּוֹסְקִין עַל הַפֵּרוֹת עַד שֶׁיֵּצֵא הַשַּׁעַר. יָצָא הַשַּׁעַר, פּוֹסְקִין, וְאַף עַל פִּי שֶׁאֵין לָזֶה, יֵשׁ לָזֶה. הָיָה הוּא תְחִלָּה לַקּוֹצְרִים, פּוֹסֵק עִמּוֹ עַל הַגָּדִישׁ, וְעַל הֶעָבִיט שֶׁל עֲנָבִים,

— רע״ב —

(ז) היה הוא תחלה לקוצרים. ויש לו גדיש ועדיין לא יצא השער, פוסק עמו באיזה שער שירצה. דכיון דיש לו אין כאן רבית, דמטכסיט אותו גדיש קנוי לו. ואף על גב דלא משך, כיון דכי אין לו נמי לא הוה אלא אבק רבית דרבנן, כי יש לו לא גזור: **על העביט**. כלי גדול שעוצרים בו את הענבים לפני דריכה, והם מתחממים, להוציא יינס יפה. ושל זיתים קרוי מעטן:

אֵין פּוֹסְקִין עַל הַפֵּרוֹת — **We may not set a price and pay in advance for produce** that the seller does not have now **עַד שֶׁיֵּצֵא הַשַּׁעַר** — **until a market price** for that type of produce **becomes established.**[4] Before that time, the seller may not be able to buy the produce for the money he receives from the buyer, and he therefore cannot be viewed as "having" the produce.[5] **יָצָא הַשַּׁעַר** — **Once the** market **price becomes established, פּוֹסְקִין** — **we can set a price and pay in advance, וְאַף עַל פִּי שֶׁאֵין לָזֶה, יֵשׁ לָזֶה** — **because even though this one** (the seller) **does not** yet **have** that produce, **that one** (a different person) **does have** it. Since the seller can easily buy the produce at the going rate with the money he receives from the buyer, we consider it as if he already has the produce when the buyer pays him in advance.[6]

The law we just learned applies where the seller does not actually have the produce at the time he is paid in advance. If he *does* have it, the buyer can surely be viewed as "acquiring" it immediately even if there is no established market price yet. The Mishnah now elaborates on the extent of this leniency:

הָיָה הוּא תְחִלָּה לַקּוֹצְרִים — **If [the seller] was the first of the harvesters** to bring in his grain, and he already has a stack of it waiting to be processed,[7] but there is not yet an established market price for it, **פּוֹסֵק עִמּוֹ עַל הַגָּדִישׁ** — **[a buyer] may set a price and pay in advance for** grain from **that stack**, even though that grain is not yet ready to be sold.[8] **וְעַל הֶעָבִיט שֶׁל עֲנָבִים** — **Similarly,**

--- NOTES ---

"belonged" to the buyer before the price went up. Thus, when the price went up, it is the *buyer's* goods that became more valuable, and he is not receiving anything extra from the seller (see Mishnah 1 note 5).

4. When a new crop is harvested, the market price for it fluctuates until it becomes clear how much produce will be available. Once the full crop reaches the market, the price stops fluctuating and a regular price becomes established.

5. Since he cannot be viewed as having produce, the buyer who is paying him now in advance cannot be viewed as "acquiring" the produce at this time. Thus, the money paid in advance is considered a loan, and if the price of this produce rises before the seller delivers it to the buyer, the seller will be giving the buyer more than was advanced, which would be like paying interest on the loan (see *Tos. Yom Tov*).

6. And since the seller "has" the produce, the buyer can be viewed as taking ownership of it at the time he gives the money (see Mishnah 1 note 6). This avoids the problem of interest on money paid in advance (see *Rav* and *Tos. Yom Tov*).

7. Before grain is sold, the cut stalks are threshed and winnowed to separate the stalks and the chaff from the grain.

8. The Rabbis were lenient where the grain is already harvested and in the

[103] MISHNAH BAVA METZIA / Chapter 5: *Eizehu Neshech* — 5/7

— רע״ב —

עַל הַבֵּיצִים שֶׁל יוֹצֵר. אִם הִכְנִיס עָפָר וַעֲשָׂאוֹ בַּלִּים לַעֲשׂוֹת מֵהֶן קְדֵרוֹת, פּוֹסֵק עִמּוֹ עַל הַקְּדֵירוֹת בְּאֵיזֶה שַׁעַר שֶׁיִּרְצֶה, וְאַף עַל פִּי שֶׁלֹּא יָצָא הַשַּׁעַר: **וְעַל הַסִּיד.** פּוֹסֵק עִמּוֹ בְּאֵיזֶה שַׁעַר שֶׁיִּרְצֶה, מִשֶּׁשִּׂקְּטַנּוּ בַּכִּבְשָׁן הָעֵצִים וְהָאֲבָנִים לִשְׂרֹף, וְלַעֲשׂוֹת מֵהֶן סִיד:

וְעַל הַמַּעֲטָן שֶׁל זֵיתִים, וְעַל הַבֵּיצִים שֶׁל יוֹצֵר,
וְעַל הַסִּיד מִשֶּׁשִּׂקְּעוֹ בַּכִּבְשָׁן. וּפוֹסֵק עִמּוֹ עַל
הַזֶּבֶל כָּל יְמוֹת הַשָּׁנָה. רַבִּי יוֹסֵי אוֹמֵר, אֵין פּוֹסְקִין
עַל הַזֶּבֶל אֶלָּא אִם כֵּן הָיְתָה לוֹ זֶבֶל בָּאַשְׁפָּה;

— he may agree on a price and pay in advance for wine that will be made from **a tub of grapes** that the seller is preparing to press; וְעַל הַמַּעֲטָן שֶׁל זֵיתִים — and for oil that will be made from **a vat of olives** that the seller is preparing to press;[9] וְעַל הַבֵּיצִים שֶׁל יוֹצֵר — and for earthenware vessels that will be made from the clay **balls** that **a potter has**;[10] וְעַל הַסִּיד מִשֶּׁשִּׂקְּעוֹ בַּכִּבְשָׁן — **and for plaster once** the materials from which **it** will be made **has been put in the furnace.**[11]

The Mishnah records three views with regard to paying in advance for fertilizer when there is not yet an established market price for it:[12]

וּפוֹסֵק עִמּוֹ עַל הַזֶּבֶל כָּל יְמוֹת הַשָּׁנָה — **One may set a price and pay in advance for fertilizer all year round,** that is, even during the winter. Although not everyone has it then, many people do. Thus, even if the seller does not have it, he can easily buy it from someone else at the price for which he is selling it to the buyer.

The second view:

רַבִּי יוֹסֵי אוֹמֵר — **R' Yose says:** אֵין פּוֹסְקִין עַל הַזֶּבֶל אֶלָּא אִם כֵּן הָיְתָה לוֹ זֶבֶל בָּאַשְׁפָּה — **One may not set a price and pay in advance for fertilizer unless [the seller] has fertilizer in his compost heap,** even during the summer.[13]

NOTES
---

seller's possession, and allowed us to view the buyer as taking immediate ownership of the stack [even though he is paying for finished grain, not raw grain] (*Rav*).

9. Grapes were piled into a tub, where they would become warm and ripe, so that the juice would flow more easily from them when they were pressed. Olives were similarly placed in a vat before they were pressed for oil (*Rav*). Once the seller has placed the grapes in the tub or the olives in the vat, the Rabbis permitted us to view it as if he already has the wine or oil that will be made from them.

10. Pottery is made by mixing clay and water and shaping the mixture into balls, and then shaping the balls into utensils.

11. Plaster is made from limestone and wood that are burned in a furnace (*Rav*).

12. In earlier times, people would put straw in the street during the winter so that people and animals would trample it while it decayed. A few months later it was gathered and used to fertilize the fields. Thus, during the summer months everyone had fertilizer, but during the winter months not everyone did (see *Rav*).

13. R' Yose holds that fertilizer is like any other merchandise: if there is no established market price for it, the seller must actually have it in his possession before he can take money for it in advance (*Rav*).

וַחֲכָמִים מַתִּירִין. וּפוֹסֵק עִמּוֹ כַּשַּׁעַר הַגָּבוֹהַּ.
רַבִּי יְהוּדָה אוֹמֵר, אַף עַל פִּי שֶׁלֹּא פָסַק עִמּוֹ
כַּשַּׁעַר הַגָּבוֹהַּ, יָכוֹל הוּא לוֹמַר, תֵּן לִי כָזֶה, אוֹ
תֵּן לִי מְעוֹתָי.

— רע"ב —

וחכמים מתירין. איכא בין חכמים לתנא קמא, דתנא קמא כל ימות השנה קאמר. ופליג עליה רבי יוסי ואמר לא שנא ימות החמה ולא שנא ימות הגשמים, עד שיהיה לו למוכר זבל באשפות. וחכמים מתירין דוקא בימות החמה, שאף על פי שאין לו, יש לאחרים. שהכל יש להן זבל, שכבר נרקב וגמור בימות הגשמים. אבל בימות הגשמים לא. והלכה כחכמים: בשער הגבוה. אם יפחות השער ממה שהוא עכשיו, תן לי כשער הזול. גבוה, היינו בזול, שנותנין פירות גבוהים ורבים בדמים מועטים: תן לי בזה או תן לי מעותי: שהרי לא משך, יכול לחזור בו. ואפילו מי שפרע ליכא, הואיל ולא נתן מעותיו על מנת לקבל עכשיו אלא לאחר זמן, ובתוך כך נשתנה השער, סתם דעתיה דאינש אתרעא זילא פסיק. ואין הלכה כרבי יהודה:

The third view:

וַחֲכָמִים מַתִּירִין — **The Sages permit** paying in advance even if the seller does not have fertilizer, but only during the summer, when everyone has it and it can be bought anywhere.

The Mishnah now returns to a case in which the seller does not have the produce, but it has an established market price. As we learned, a buyer can pay for the produce in advance and thus guarantee that he will not have to pay more for it later if the price goes *up*. The Mishnah discusses what happens if the buyer is concerned that the price will go *down*, and he will end up having paid too much for it:

וּפוֹסֵק עִמּוֹ כַּשַּׁעַר הַגָּבוֹהַּ — [The buyer] may agree to a price and pay in advance on condition that if the price for the produce goes down, the seller will give it to him **for the better price.**[14]

The previous ruling implies that if the buyer does *not* make this condition and the price goes down, the seller can give the buyer the produce at the original, higher price. R' Yehudah disagrees:

רַבִּי יְהוּדָה אוֹמֵר — **R' Yehudah says:** **אַף עַל פִּי שֶׁלֹּא פָסַק עִמּוֹ כַּשַּׁעַר הַגָּבוֹהַּ** — **Even if [the buyer] did not agree to a price and pay in advance for** produce at **the better price,** i.e., even if he did not make this condition explicitly when he agreed to the original contract, **יָכוֹל הוּא לוֹמַר תֵּן לִי כָזֶה** — if the price went down **[the buyer] can** still **say** to him, "**Give me** the produce **at this** better (lower) price, **אוֹ תֵּן לִי מְעוֹתָי** — **or give me** back **my money.**" According to R' Yehudah, every buyer intends this when he agrees to an advance contract, and it is therefore as if he made this condition explicitly.[15]

[8] The next two Mishnahs discuss the laws of lending "a *se'ah* for a *se'ah,*" that is, lending a certain amount of produce (a *se'ah*, for example) on condition that the borrower will pay back the same amount of produce. This

---
NOTES

14. Literally, *the higher price*, that is, the price for which the buyer gets a greater amount of produce (*Rav*).

15. Since the seller is taking money in advance and not giving him the produce right away, there is an unspoken agreement that if the price goes down the seller will have to give it to him at the better price (*Rav*).

MISHNAH BAVA METZIA / Chapter 5: *Eizehu Neshech*

[ח] מַלְוֶה אָדָם אֶת אֲרִיסָיו חִטִּים בְּחִטִּין לְזֶרַע, אֲבָל לֹא לֶאֱכֹל. שֶׁהָיָה רַבָּן גַּמְלִיאֵל מַלְוֶה אֶת אֲרִיסָיו חִטִּין בְּחִטִּין לְזֶרַע,

— רע"ב —

(ח) חטין בחטין לזרע. סאה בסאה מותר להלוות לאריסים, דוקא כשרגילה לזרעו.
וטעמו, דבאתרא דחמרים הוא שנותן הזרע, אם אין לו זרע לזרוע השדה, יסלקנו בעל הבית. וכשלוה האריס מבעל הבית וחוזר, וכשיוקירו חטין יתן חטין, אין זו הלואה, אלא הרי הוא כיורד לתוכה מטכסיו, על מנת שיטול בעל הבית מחלה הזרע לאריסים, והאריסים יטלו השאר, שכר טרחם. ועל מנת כן ירד, שיטול פחות משאר אריסין כשיעור הזרע, ואין כאן רבית: שהיה רבן גמליאל. כלומר, לכך הולרך לשנות משנה זו, לפי שהיה רבן גמליאל מחמיר שאם החולו נוטל כשער הזול. ואשמעינן מתניתין, לא שהלכה כן, אלא שרלה להחמיר על עלמו:

---

kind of loan is generally prohibited, as the next Mishnah will say.[1] However, our Mishnah begins the discussion of this subject by teaching about a case where it is permitted:

מַלְוֶה אָדָם אֶת אֲרִיסָיו חִטִּין לְזֶרַע — A person may lend his sharecroppers[2] **wheat for wheat**, that is, he may give them a certain amount of wheat kernels and they will later give back the same amount, provided that the kernels will be used **for planting**. In that case the kernels are not viewed as a loan, but as part of the sharecropping agreement.[3] אֲבָל לֹא לֶאֱכֹל — But he may **not** lend them wheat for wheat if it is to be used **for eating**, because that is a real loan, and if the price of wheat goes up, the sharecroppers will be giving back something worth more than they borrowed.[4]

The Tanna found it necessary to teach this law for the following reason: שֶׁהָיָה רַבָּן גַּמְלִיאֵל מַלְוֶה אֶת אֲרִיסָיו חִטִּין בְּחִטִּין לְזֶרַע — **Because Rabban Gamliel**

NOTES

[8]

1. The Rabbis prohibited this arrangement because the price might go up between the time of the loan and the time when it is repaid, and the borrower would then be giving the lender back something worth more than he borrowed (see Mishnah 9). The same prohibition applies to lending any item (that gets consumed) on condition that the borrower will pay back the same amount of that kind of item.
[If someone unlawfully made this sort of loan and the price of the item indeed went up, the borrower may not pay back the same *amount* of produce; he may pay back only the *value* of the produce as it was at the time of the loan (*Yoreh Deah* 162:1).]

2. A sharecropper is someone who farms someone else's field in exchange for giving the landowner a percentage of the crop (see Introduction to Chapter 9).

3. It is customary for the sharecropper to use his own seed for planting. In this case, however, he does not have seed, so he borrows seed (wheat kernels) from the landowner. In return, he agrees to give him back that amount of seed *in addition to* the percentage of the crop that goes to the landowner. The Mishnah teaches that we do not view the borrowed seed as a loan, but as part of the sharecropping agreement. Instead of the sharecropper providing the seed and the landowner getting the usual percentage (a quarter of the crop, for example), the landowner will provide the seed and the sharecropper will pay him the usual percentage (a quarter of the crop) plus the amount of seed he received from him (*Rav*).

4. If the wheat kernels are not used for planting, they cannot be considered part of the sharecropping agreement, since they have nothing to do with farming the field. Rather, they must be viewed as a loan. Thus, they are subject to the law forbidding the loan of a *"se'ah* for a *se'ah."*

בְּיוֹקֶר וְהוּזְלוּ, אוֹ בְזוֹל וְהוּקְרוּ, נוֹטֵל מֵהֶן כְּשַׁעַר הַזּוֹל, וְלֹא מִפְּנֵי שֶׁהֲלָכָה כֵן, אֶלָּא שֶׁרָצָה לְהַחְמִיר עַל עַצְמוֹ.

[ט] **לֹא** יֹאמַר אָדָם לַחֲבֵרוֹ, הַלְוֵנִי כּוֹר חִטִּים וַאֲנִי אֶתֵּן לְךָ לַגֹּרֶן.

---

would lend his sharecroppers wheat for wheat for the purpose of **planting**, בְּיוֹקֶר וְהוּזְלוּ — and if he gave it to them **at a high price and [the wheat] became cheaper**, אוֹ בְזוֹל וְהוּקְרוּ — or if he gave it to them **at a low price and [the wheat] became more expensive**, נוֹטֵל מֵהֶן כְּשַׁעַר הַזּוֹל — he would take the wheat back **from them** only **at the cheaper price**, because he did not want it to look like he was taking interest.[5] וְלֹא מִפְּנֵי שֶׁהֲלָכָה כֵן — Since this was known to be Rabban Gamliel's practice, the Tanna of our Mishnah teaches that this was **not because the law is so**, that is, not because Rabban Gamliel had to do so, אֶלָּא שֶׁרָצָה לְהַחְמִיר עַל עַצְמוֹ — **but because he wanted to be strict with himself.** The law, however, is that it is permissible to lend a sharecropper a *se'ah* for a *se'ah* if it will be used for planting, and take back a full *se'ah* whatever the price.[6]

[9] The Mishnah now teaches the basic prohibition of lending a *se'ah* for a *se'ah*:

לֹא יֹאמַר אָדָם לַחֲבֵרוֹ — **A person may not say to his friend**, הַלְוֵנִי כּוֹר חִטִּים — "**Lend me a *kor* of wheat** וַאֲנִי אֶתֵּן לְךָ לַגֹּרֶן — **and I will give you** back a *kor* of wheat **at threshing time**."[1] The Rabbis forbid this due to a concern that the price of wheat might be higher when he is ready to repay the loan, so that giving back a *se'ah* of wheat would mean that the borrower is giving back something worth more than he borrowed.[2]

NOTES
---

5. For example, if Rabban Gamliel lent them a *se'ah* of seed when it was worth two *selas*, and at the time of repayment the price of a *se'ah* had gone down to one *sela*, he would take back only a *se'ah* of wheat, even though its value now was only half of what is was when he lent them the *se'ah*. And if he lent them a *se'ah* when it was worth one *sela*, and at the time of repayment it had gone up to two *selas*, he would take back only half a *se'ah*, which was now equal to the value of the *se'ah* he originally lent them (*Tos. Yom Tov*).

[Rabban Gamliel agreed that it was not forbidden to lend seed in this way, which is why he agreed to lend it. However, to avoid even the appearance of interest, he was strict and would take back wheat only at the lower price.]

6. If the price of wheat goes up, it is permissible to take back a full *se'ah*. However, if the price of the wheat goes *down*, it is still only permissible to take back one *se'ah*, not two, even though they are now worth only as much as the one *se'ah* he lent. Taking two *se'ah* for one is always considered forbidden interest regardless of its worth (see *Yoreh Deah* 162:1 and *Pischei Teshuvah* 3 there).

[9]

1. That is, when the crop has been harvested and the stalks have been threshed to separate the kernels from them; in other words, when the new crop has been made into grain.

2. The Mishnah speaks about a loan of wheat that is supposed to be repaid at threshing time because it is unusual for wheat to be more expensive at threshing time [when a lot of new wheat comes to market] than at planting time. The Mishnah teaches that, even so, it is forbidden

[107] **MISHNAH BAVA METZIA** / Chapter 5: *Eizehu Neshech*

— רע"ב —

(ט) הלויני עד שיבא בני. דכיון שיש לו, שפיר דמי. דלא גזור רבנן אלא כשאין לו. ואפילו אין לו אלא סאה אחת, לוה עליה כמה כורין. דכל חדא וחדא אמרינן זו תהא תחתיה. שהרי אינה קנויה למלוה, וביד הלוה למכרה ולאכלה, וכשלוה, כל אחת ואחת לוה בהיתר: **ובן היה הלל אומר לא תלוה אשה**. ואין הלכה כהלל. אלא הלכה כחכמים שאומרים לוין סתם ופורעין סתם:

אֲבָל אוֹמֵר לוֹ, הַלְוֵינִי עַד שֶׁיָּבֹא בְנִי, אוֹ עַד שֶׁאֶמְצָא מַפְתֵּחַ. וְהִלֵּל אוֹסֵר. וְכֵן הָיָה הִלֵּל אוֹמֵר, לֹא תַלְוֶה אִשָּׁה כִּכָּר לַחֲבֶרְתָּהּ עַד שֶׁתַּעֲשֶׂנּוּ דָמִים, שֶׁמָּא יוֹקִירוּ חִטִּים, וְנִמְצְאוּ בָאוֹת לִידֵי רִבִּית.

The Mishnah teaches that there is a type of *se'ah*-for-*se'ah* loan that is subject to a dispute between Tannaim:

אֲבָל אוֹמֵר לוֹ — However, one may say to [his friend], הַלְוֵינִי עַד שֶׁיָּבֹא בְנִי "Lend me wheat **until my son**, who has my wheat, **comes**," אוֹ עַד שֶׁאֶמְצָא מַפְתֵּחַ — or, "Lend me wheat **until I find the key** to my granary so I can open it and repay you with wheat I have inside it." The Rabbis did not forbid lending a *se'ah* for a *se'ah* if the borrower has the same item in storage but he simply cannot get to it at that moment.[3] וְהִלֵּל אוֹסֵר — **Hillel, however, forbids** making the loan even when the borrower has the type of item he is borrowing. In his opinion, the Rabbis prohibited lending a *se'ah* for a *se'ah* in all circumstances.

The Mishnah discusses another case of a *se'ah*-for-*se'ah* loan, which is also subject to a dispute between Hillel and the Sages:

וְכֵן הָיָה הִלֵּל אוֹמֵר — **Hillel would also say:** לֹא תַלְוֶה אִשָּׁה כִּכָּר לַחֲבֶרְתָּהּ עַד שֶׁתַּעֲשֶׂנּוּ דָמִים — **A woman may not lend a loaf** of bread **to her friend until she makes [the loaf] into a loan of money**, that is, until she fixes a price for the loaf and tells the friend to pay her back the *value* of the loaf she borrowed. שֶׁמָּא יוֹקִירוּ חִטִּים — **This is because we are concerned that the price of wheat might go up**, וְנִמְצְאוּ בָאוֹת לִידֵי רִבִּית — **and** these women **will end up having done** a loan with **interest**, since the borrower will be repaying something worth more than she borrowed. The Sages, however, permit lending a loaf for a loaf, because it is something small and any change in price is likely to be so small as to be considered a gift rather than interest given for the loan.[4]

NOTES

to lend a *se'ah* for a *se'ah* (*Tos. Yom Tov*).

3. This is because we consider it as if the lender immediately acquired the *se'ah* that the borrower has in storage. Therefore, even if he does not actually take it until the price has gone up, it is not "interest"; he has simply gained money on produce that already "belonged" to him (see *Rav*; *Rashi* 44b).

4. Neighbors are not usually particular with each other about very small sums of money. A woman might well give such a small sum of money to her neighbor even if it had not been for the loan (see *Tos. Yom Tov*; *Tosafos* 75a ד"ה וכדברי). However, Hillel is concerned that people are sometimes particular even over such small sums (*Tosafos* there).

משניות בבא מציעא / פרק ה: איזהו נשך

[י] אוֹמֵר אָדָם לַחֲבֵרוֹ, נַכֵּשׁ עִמִּי וַאֲנַכֵּשׁ עִמָּךְ, עֲדֹר עִמִּי וְאֶעֱדֹר עִמָּךְ, וְלֹא יֹאמַר לוֹ, נַכֵּשׁ עִמִּי וְאֶעֱדֹר עִמָּךְ, עֲדֹר עִמִּי וַאֲנַכֵּשׁ עִמָּךְ. כָּל יְמֵי גָרִיד אֶחָד, כָּל יְמֵי רְבִיעָה אֶחָד. לֹא יֹאמַר לוֹ, חֲרֹשׁ עִמִּי בַגָּרִיד

- רע"ב -

(י) נכש עמי. היום, ואנכש עמך למחר. נכוש הוא עקירת העשבים הרעים הגדלים בתבואה: עדור. חפור: לא יאמר לו נכש עמי ואעדור עמך. פעמים שזו קשה מזו, ויש כאן אגר נטר: כל ימי גריד

אחד. ולא חיישינן אם יום אחד גדול מחבירו. וכן כל ימי רביעה אחד. ומותר לומר עדור עמי יום זה של גריד. ואני אעדור עמך יום אחר של גריד, וכן ברביעה: **גריד.** ימות החמה: **רביעה.** ימות הגשמים: **לא יאמר לו חרוש עמי בגריד ואני אחרוש עמך ברביעה.** שימי רביעה קשים למלאכה שבשדות:

---

[10] The previous two Mishnahs have dealt with the prohibition of lending an item for an item (for example, a *se'ah* for a *se'ah*). This Mishnah now discusses doing work in return for work, that is, agreeing to work for a person now on condition that he will later work for you:

אוֹמֵר אָדָם לַחֲבֵרוֹ — **A person may say to his friend,** נַכֵּשׁ עִמִּי וַאֲנַכֵּשׁ עִמָּךְ — "**Weed** my field **with me today and I will weed** your field **with you tomorrow,**" עֲדֹר עִמִּי וְאֶעֱדֹר עִמָּךְ — or, "**Hoe** my field **with me** today **and I will hoe** your field **with you** tomorrow." Although one person is "lending" the other a day of work, he is being paid back with the same type of work, so there is no problem of interest.[1] וְלֹא יֹאמַר לוֹ — **But he may not say to him,** נַכֵּשׁ עִמִּי וְאֶעֱדֹר עִמָּךְ — "**Weed with me** today **and I will hoe with you tomorrow,**" עֲדֹר עִמִּי וַאֲנַכֵּשׁ עִמָּךְ — or, "**Hoe with me** today **and I will weed with you** tomorrow." The person working on the second day may not repay the "loan" with a *different* type of work, because it might be harder (and thus more valuable) than the work done for him, and that is a Rabbinically forbidden form of interest.

The Mishnah teaches that it is sometimes forbidden for the two workers to arrange to do even the *same* type of work for each other:

כָּל יְמֵי גָרִיד אֶחָד — **All the days of the dry-earth** season (summer) **are** viewed as **one** period, and a person may work for another person on a summer day on condition that he will do the same type of work for him on a different day in the summer.[2] כָּל יְמֵי רְבִיעָה אֶחָד — Similarly, **all the days of the rainy** season (winter) **are** viewed as **one** period, and a person may work for another person on a winter day on condition that the second person will do the same type of work for him on a different day during the winter.[3] לֹא יֹאמַר לוֹ — But **a person may not say to another** person, חֲרֹשׁ עִמִּי בַגָּרִיד — "**Plow with me**

NOTES

[10]

1. We are not concerned that the work done by the second person might be harder than that done by the first person and thus be considered a form of interest (*Meiri*).

2. Work in the fields was done from sunrise to sunset (see Gemara 83b). Nevertheless, we are not concerned that the day he gives back may be longer or may be hotter than the day he worked. Workers were paid by the day, and small differences in time or temperature did not change the wages they were paid for a day in that season.

3. Even though that day might be longer or might have harsher weather conditions than the first person's day of work.

וַאֲנִי אֶחֱרשׁ עִמְּךָ בָּרְבִיעָה. רַבָּן גַּמְלִיאֵל אוֹמֵר, יֵשׁ רִבִּית מֻקְדֶּמֶת, וְיֵשׁ רִבִּית מְאֻחֶרֶת. כֵּיצַד, נָתַן עֵינָיו לִלְווֹת הֵימֶנּוּ, וְהָיָה מְשַׁלֵּחַ לוֹ וְאוֹמֵר, בִּשְׁבִיל שֶׁתַּלְוֵנִי, זוֹ הִיא רִבִּית מֻקְדֶּמֶת. לָוָה הֵימֶנּוּ, וְהֶחֱזִיר לוֹ אֶת מְעוֹתָיו, וְהָיָה מְשַׁלֵּחַ לוֹ וְאָמַר, בִּשְׁבִיל מְעוֹתֶיךָ שֶׁהָיוּ בְטֵלוֹת אֶצְלִי, זוֹ הִיא רִבִּית מְאֻחֶרֶת. רַבִּי שִׁמְעוֹן אוֹמֵר, יֵשׁ רִבִּית דְּבָרִים, לֹא יֹאמַר לוֹ, דַּע כִּי בָא אִישׁ פְּלוֹנִי מִמָּקוֹם פְּלוֹנִי.

וַאֲנִי אֶחֱרשׁ עִמְּךָ בָּרְבִיעָה — **and I will plow with you during the rainy** season," because working the field is clearly more difficult in the rainy season (when the soil is wet and muddy) than in the dry season.[4]

The various types of forbidden interest we have learned about in this chapter are all forms of interest that are "paid" between the time of the loan and the time it is repaid, or together with the repayment. The Mishnah will now teach that interest is forbidden even if it is paid before the loan is given or if it is given freely after the loan has been repaid:

רַבָּן גַּמְלִיאֵל אוֹמֵר — **Rabban Gamliel says:** יֵשׁ רִבִּית מֻקְדֶּמֶת — **There is a** prohibition on paying **"early interest,"** וְיֵשׁ רִבִּית מְאֻחֶרֶת — **and there is** also a prohibition on paying **"late interest."**[5] כֵּיצַד — **How so?** נָתַן עֵינָיו לִלְווֹת הֵימֶנּוּ — If someone **has set his mind on borrowing from [another person],** וְהָיָה מְשַׁלֵּחַ לוֹ וְאוֹמֵר בִּשְׁבִיל שֶׁתַּלְוֵנִי — **and he sends him** gifts and says, **"These are for you, so that you will lend me** money," זוֹ הִיא רִבִּית מֻקְדֶּמֶת — **that is "early interest"** and is forbidden. לָוָה הֵימֶנּוּ וְהֶחֱזִיר לוֹ אֶת מְעוֹתָיו — **If he borrowed from him and** already **gave him back his money,** וְהָיָה מְשַׁלֵּחַ לוֹ וְאָמַר בִּשְׁבִיל מְעוֹתֶיךָ שֶׁהָיוּ בְטֵלוֹת אֶצְלִי — **and he** later **sent him gifts and said, "This is to compensate you for your money that was not being used** by you while it was **by me,"** זוֹ הִיא רִבִּית מְאֻחֶרֶת — **this is "late interest,"** and it too is forbidden.

Another form of forbidden interest:

רַבִּי שִׁמְעוֹן אוֹמֵר — **R' Shimon says:** יֵשׁ רִבִּית דְּבָרִים — **There is** a prohibition of **interest** even **with words.** That is, the borrower may not even *say* something to the lender that will benefit him. How so? לֹא יֹאמַר לוֹ — **He should not say to him,** דַּע כִּי בָא אִישׁ פְּלוֹנִי מִמָּקוֹם פְּלוֹנִי — **"You should know that So-and-so is coming from such-and-such a place,"** if the lender needs this information.[6]

NOTES

4. In this case, the second worker would be repaying the first with something more valuable than he was "loaned." It is permitted, however, to arrange that the first person will work in the winter and the second will do the same work in the summer. Since it is easier to work the fields in the summer, the second worker will be repaying with something *less* valuable than he was "loaned."

5. Early interest and late interest are forbidden only by Rabbinic law (*Meiri*). Biblical law forbids only interest charged at the time of the loan.

6. This is forbidden only if the borrower would not have given the lender this

[110] **משניות בבא מציעא / פרק ה: איזהו נשך** ה/יא

— רע"ב —

(יא) עוברים משום לא תתן וכו׳. מלוה לוה עובר משום בל תשיך (דברים כג, כ), שהוא לשון מפעיל לאחרים, לא תגרום שאחיך ישוך, ועובר על ולאחיך לא

[יא] **וְאֵלּוּ** עוֹבְרִין בְּלֹא תַעֲשֶׂה, הַמַּלְוֶה, וְהַלֹּוֶה, וְהֶעָרֵב, וְהָעֵדִים. וַחֲכָמִים אוֹמְרִים, אַף הַסּוֹפֵר. עוֹבְרִים מִשּׁוּם לֹא תִתֵּן, וּמִשּׁוּם בַּל תִּקַּח מֵאִתּוֹ,

תשיך (שם פסוק כא), ולפני עור לא תתן מכשול (ויקרא יט, יד). ערב ועדים, עוברים על ולא תשימון עליו נשך (שמות כב, כד) בלבד:

---

[11] This Mishnah teaches which people involved in a loan with interest violate a Biblical prohibition, and how many prohibitions are involved in a loan with interest:

וְאֵלּוּ עוֹבְרִין בְּלֹא תַעֲשֶׂה — **These** are the people involved in a Biblically forbidden loan with interest who **transgress a negative commandment:**[1] הַמַּלְוֶה — **the lender,** וְהַלֹּוֶה — **the borrower,** וְהֶעָרֵב — **the guarantor,**[2] וְהָעֵדִים — **and the witnesses** to the loan;[3] וַחֲכָמִים אוֹמְרִים — **and the Sages say:** אַף הַסּוֹפֵר — **Even the scribe** who writes up the loan document transgresses a negative commandment.[4]

The Mishnah lists all the negative commandments involved in lending with interest:

עוֹבְרִים מִשּׁוּם "לֹא תִתֵּן" — **These** people **transgress [the prohibition]:** *Your money you shall not give him for interest (neshech), and for increase you shall not give your food (Leviticus 25:37);*[5] וּמִשּׁוּם "בַּל תִּקַּח מֵאִתּוֹ" — **and**

NOTES

information had it not been for the loan. But if he was friendly with the lender and in the habit of sharing such information with him, it is permitted (see *Yoreh Deah* 160:7).

There is a question whether this "interest" is Rabbinically forbidden (*Sefer HaTerumos* 46:3:13) or even Biblically forbidden [if it was made as a condition of the loan] (see *Tosafos, Kiddushin* 8b ד"ה צדקה).

It is also forbidden for a borrower to greet the lender when he meets him if he was not in the habit of doing this before the loan (Gemara 75b; *Yoreh Deah* 160:11).

[11]

1. They are guilty of transgressing at least one of the prohibitions listed by the Mishnah below.

A "negative commandment" is one that is stated by the Torah in the form of "You shall not ..."

2. A person who guarantees to repay

the loan if the borrower does not do so.

3. If they are aware that the loan is being made with interest (see *Tos. R' Akiva Eiger*).

4. Since the document enables the lender to prove that he is owed the money. The Tanna Kamma, however, does not consider him a party to the loan merely because he wrote up the document.

5. This counts as *two* prohibitions: *you shall not give … for interest* and *for increase you shall not give.* Although the verse refers to *interest (neshech)* and *increase* separately, they are really one and the same thing — one is not allowed to charge interest. The verse says the words *you shall not give* twice, once for interest and once for increase, because it wants to impose *two* separate prohibitions against the same act of lending with interest (*Rambam, Hil. Malveh VeLoveh* 4:1). [Although the verse says these words first with regard to lending money and then with regard to food, both prohibitions of

[111] **MISHNAH BAVA METZIA** / Chapter 5: *Eizehu Neshech*   5/11

וּמִשּׁוּם לֹא תִהְיֶה לּוֹ כְּנֹשֶׁה, וּמִשּׁוּם לֹא תְשִׂימוּן עָלָיו נֶשֶׁךְ, וּמִשּׁוּם וְלִפְנֵי עִוֵּר לֹא תִתֵּן מִכְשֹׁל וְיָרֵאתָ מֵאֱלֹהֶיךָ אֲנִי ה'.

[the prohibition]: *You shall not take from him* interest and increase (verse 36 there);[6] "וּמִשּׁוּם "לֹא תִהְיֶה לוֹ כְּנֹשֶׁה — and [the prohibition]: *You shall not act toward him as a harsh creditor* (Exodus 22:24);[7] וּמִשּׁוּם "לֹא תְשִׂימוּן עָלָיו נֶשֶׁךְ" — and [the prohibition] (there): *You shall not place interest on him*;[8] וּמִשּׁוּם "וְלִפְנֵי עִוֵּר לֹא תִתֵּן מִכְשֹׁל וְיָרֵאתָ מֵאֱלֹהֶיךָ אֲנִי ה'" — and [the prohibition]: *And before a blind person you shall not place a stumbling block*,[9] *and you shall fear your God, I am Hashem* (Leviticus 19:14).[10]

NOTES

lending with interest apply to both types of loans; see *Tos. Yom Tov* to Mishnah 1.]

The two prohibitions of *giving* a loan on interest apply only to the lender and not to the others listed above (*Rav; Rambam, Hil. Malveh VeLoveh* 4:1-2). The lender violates them as soon as he makes the loan (see *Tos. Yom Tov*).

6. The prohibition of *taking* interest and increase also applies only to the lender (*Rav*), who violates it when he takes the interest payment (*Tos. Yom Tov*).

7. This prohibition, too, applies only to the lender (*Rav*). Some say that *any* loan with interest is considered acting like a harsh creditor and is thus a violation of this prohibition, but others say that the lender transgresses this prohibition only if he *pressures* the borrower to pay the interest (see *Rashi* to Exodus 22:24; *Tos. Yom Tov*).

8. This prohibition applies to all the people listed in the first half of the Mishnah, except for the borrower. They are all viewed as participants in "placing" the debt of interest on the borrower (*Rav; Rambam*).

9. This is a prohibition against causing someone to commit a sin. The "blind person" in the verse means someone who is blind to the fact that he is sinning,

either because he is not aware that what he is doing is wrong, or because he is too caught up in his desires to see the truth (see *Rambam, Hilchos Rotze'ach* 12:14). The borrower causes the lender to commit all the sins listed above when he takes the loan with interest.

10. The last part of this verse, *and you shall fear your God, I am Hashem,* is not relevant to the discussion in our Mishnah. The Mishnah adds it in order to end the chapter on a positive note (*Tiferes Yisrael*).

In sum, then, the lender violates all the prohibitions mentioned in the Mishnah; the borrower violates *before a blind person you shall not place a stumbling block,* and the guarantor and the witnesses (and, according to the Sages, the scribe) violate *you shall not place interest upon him.*

In addition to the prohibitions mentioned in our Mishnah, the borrower also violates two more prohibitions: לֹא תַשִּׁיךְ לְאָחִיךָ, *You shall not cause your brother to take interest* (Deuteronomy 23:20); and וּלְאָחִיךָ לֹא תַשִּׁיךְ, *To your brother, you shall not cause him to take interest* (verse 21 there) (see *Rav*). [The Mishnah does not mention these prohibitions because it wants to discuss only those that apply to the lender (*Tiferes Yisrael*).]

Chapter Six

משניות בבא מציעא / פרק ו: השוכר את האמנין

פרק ששי — השוכר
יין האומנין. (א) השוכר.
והטעו זה את זה. אחד
מן האומנין שלחו בעל
הבית לשכור את חביריו,
והטעה אותם. כגון
שאמר לו בעל הבית
לשכור כל אחד בארבעה

— רע"ב —

[א] הַשּׂוֹכֵר אֶת הָאֻמָּנִין וְהִטְעוּ זֶה אֶת
זֶה, אֵין לָהֶם זֶה עַל זֶה אֶלָּא
תַּרְעֹמֶת. שָׂכַר אֶת הַחַמָּר וְאֶת הַקַּדָּר לְהָבִיא
פְּרְיָפָרִין וַחֲלִילִים לְכַלָּה אוֹ לְמֵת, וּפוֹעֲלִין
לְהַעֲלוֹת פִּשְׁתָּנוֹ מִן הַמִּשְׁרָה, וְכָל דָּבָר שֶׁאָבֵד,

דינרים ליום, והלך הוא ושכרם בשלשה. אין להם עליו אלא תרעומת, דהא סבור וקביל בשלשה, אלא
שיכולים לומר לו, לית לך אל תמנע טוב מבעליו (משלי ג,כז). פירש אחר, הטעו זה את זה, שחזרו
בהם, ולא רצו ללכת לעשות מלאכתו של בעל הבית כמו שסכרו עמו. או בעל הבית חזר בו, כגון שאמר
להם אי חפשי בכם, בבקר קודם שילכו אצל המלאכה: **ואת הקדר.** בריי"ש גרסינן, כלומר בעל הקרון:
פריפרין. עלים משופין לעשות אפריון: **חלילים.** למת או לחתן: **המשרה.** מים שטורין בהן פשתן:

─────────── NOTES ───────────

[1] This chapter deals with laws about hiring workers and animals. The Mishnah begins by discussing a conflict that can arise between workers: הַשּׂוֹכֵר אֶת הָאֻמָּנִין וְהִטְעוּ זֶה אֶת זֶה — **If someone hired craftsmen** to work for him, **and one** of them **deceived the others** about conditions of the job, for example, an employer appointed a craftsman as an agent to hire others for a rate of four *dinars* a day, and the agent went and hired others for three *dinars* a day, אֵין לָהֶם זֶה עַל זֶה אֶלָּא תַּרְעֹמֶת — [the other craftsmen] can **have nothing but complaints against** [the agent]. Since they agreed to do the job for the lower wage, they have no legal claim to the extra *dinar,* although they may have complaints against the agent for not telling them that the employer was willing to pay a higher wage.[1]

The Mishnah discusses cases where workers agreed to perform a job and then backed out of their commitment:

שָׂכַר אֶת הַחַמָּר וְאֶת הַקַּדָּר לְהָבִיא פְּרְיָפָרִין — **Someone hired a donkey driver or a wagon driver**[2] **to deliver smooth pieces of wood** to make a bridal chair,[3] וַחֲלִילִים לְכַלָּה אוֹ לְמֵת — **or to deliver flutes** to play music **for a bride** and groom at their wedding **or to play mournful music for the dead** at a funeral,[4] וּפוֹעֲלִין לְהַעֲלוֹת פִּשְׁתָּנוֹ מִן הַמִּשְׁרָה — **or** he hired **workers to lift his flax out of the** water in which it was soaking,[5] וְכָל דָּבָר שֶׁאָבֵד — **or to do anything that**

─────────── NOTES ───────────

[1]

1. Although a person may not hold resentment against someone else without a valid reason (see *Leviticus* 19:18), this agent has truly wronged the other workers and they may bear a grudge against him until he asks for forgiveness (*Nesivos Ohr,* p. 58 ד"ה הנה בש"ס).

2. Literally, *a potter.* The Mishnah uses this term to refer to a wagon driver because people who made pots usually had wagons [which they used to transport their goods, and they were often hired to carry things in these wagons] (*Tos. Yom Tov*; see *Rav*).

3. It was common to carry a bride to her wedding on a special chair covered with a decorative canopy (see *Meiri, Sotah* 49a).

4. Mournful music was played at funerals in order to inspire weeping (*Rambam Commentary, Shabbos* 23:4).

If these items are not brought in time for the wedding or funeral, the employer will lose the opportunity of using them (see *Tos. Yom Tov*).

5. The flax plant is used to make linen thread. After harvesting the stalks of flax, one would soak them in water to soften

[115] MISHNAH BAVA METZIA / Chapter 6: *Hasocheir es Haumanin* 6/2

וְחָזְרוּ בָהֶן, מָקוֹם שֶׁאֵין שָׁם אָדָם, שׂוֹכֵר עֲלֵיהֶן, אוֹ מַטְעָן.

[ב] **הַשּׂוֹכֵר** אֶת הָאֻמָּנִין וְחָזְרוּ בָהֶן,

— רע״ב —

מקום שאין שם אדם. [שהוא] אינו מוצא פועלים לשכור, והפשתן אבד: שוכר עליהם. בני אדם כשיעור שכרן, אבל לא ביותר משיעור שכרן: או מטען. אומר שיתן להם זוז יתר, ואינו נותן אלא מה שהתנה מתחלה: (ב) השוכר את האומנין. בקבלנות, כך מלאכה בכך וכך מעות: וחזרו בהם. לאחר שעשו מקצתה:

will cause him **a loss** if it is not done by a certain time, וְחָזְרוּ בָהֶן — **and [the drivers or workers] changed their minds** and refused to do the job; in all these cases, מָקוֹם שֶׁאֵין שָׁם אָדָם — in **a place where** the employer can find **no one else to do the job for the same price,**[6] שׂוֹכֵר עֲלֵיהֶן — **he may hire** others **on the [original workers'] account,** that is, he may hire other workers for higher wages, and charge the difference to the original workers.[7] אוֹ מַטְעָן — **Or, he may trick [the original workers]** into doing the job; that is, he may offer to pay them more, and once they do the job, he need pay them only the original amount that was agreed upon.[8]

[2] The previous Mishnah taught that if workers back out of a job and thereby cause the employer a loss, they may be penalized. Where backing out will not cause the employer a loss, though, they may back out without penalty, as long as they have not yet begun working. However, if they quit in the *middle* of a job, they are penalized, as the Mishnah now teaches:

הַשּׂוֹכֵר אֶת הָאֻמָּנִין וְחָזְרוּ בָהֶן — **If someone hired craftsmen** to do a job, **and they** started the job but then **changed their minds** and refused to complete it,

———————— NOTES ————————

them, dry them in an oven, and beat them to remove the fibers, which would then be spun into thread. If the stalks were not removed from the water at the right time, they would begin to rot and the employer would lose the flax (*Tiferes Yisrael*).

6. And since these jobs must be done right away, the employer will have to hire other workers at a higher price and thus suffer a loss.

7. For example, if the original workers had agreed to do the job for 4 *dinars* and now the employer cannot find anyone to do it for less than 6 *dinars,* the original workers are required to pay him the extra 2 *dinars* that the job will now cost.

[The employer may charge the original workers up to the amount they were promised for the job, but not more than that (*Rav,* from Gemara 78a). For example, if the original workers had been hired for 4 *dinars,* the employer may hire other workers for up to eight *dinars* and charge the difference (4 *dinars*) to the original workers. But if the new workers charge more than 8 *dinars,* the original workers are responsible for only 4 *dinars* (*Tos. Yom Tov*).]

8. However, if the workers' backing out does not cause the employer a loss — either because other workers are available for the same wage, or because the job does not have to be done immediately and the employer can thus wait until he finds other workers for the same wage — the original workers may not be penalized in any way, although the employer may have a legitimate complaint against them for causing him the inconvenience of finding new workers [see note 1] (see *Rav*).

משניות בבא מציעא / פרק ו: השוכר את האמנין [116]

יָדָן עַל הַתַּחְתּוֹנָה. אִם בַּעַל הַבַּיִת חוֹזֵר בּוֹ, יָדוֹ עַל הַתַּחְתּוֹנָה. כָּל הַמְשַׁנֶּה, יָדוֹ עַל הַתַּחְתּוֹנָה,

— רע"ב —

ידם על התחתונה
אם הוקרו פועלים,
ואינו מוצא מי שיגמרנה
בשכר שהיה מגיע לאלו

על העתיד לעשות, מעכב משכרם ממה שפסו, כל מה שיצטרך להוציא עד שתגמר מלאכתו בשכר שפסק עם אלו. ואם החלו פועלים וימצא מי שיגמרנה בפחות, ישומו להם מה שעשו, ויתן להם מה שפסק. עשו חציה, יתן להם חצי שכרן. ואין יכולים לומר, לו הרי פועלים אחרים תחתינו לגמור מלאכתך, ותן לנו כל שכרנו חוץ ממה שיטלו אלו: ואם בעל הבית חוזר בו ידו על התחתונה. יתן להם לפי מה שעשו. ואם הוזלה מלאכת הפועלים, על כרחן יתן להם כמו שפסק, חוץ ממה שצריך להוציא בהשלמתה: כל המשנה ידו על התחתונה. כגון נתן צמר לצבע לצבעו אדום, וצבעו שחור. אם השבח יותר על היליאה, אין נותן לו שכרו שלם, אלא דמי יליאה טלים וסממנים. ואם היליאה יתירה על השבח, נותן לו את השבח:

יָדָן עַל הַתַּחְתּוֹנָה — [the craftsmen] **have the lower hand** with regard to their wages; that is, we calculate the wages for the work they completed in a way that favors the employer and not the workers.[1] אִם בַּעַל הַבַּיִת חוֹזֵר בּוֹ — **If, however, the employer changed his mind** and fired the workers in the middle of the job, יָדוֹ עַל הַתַּחְתּוֹנָה — **[the employer] has the lower hand;** that is, the wages are calculated in a way that favors the workers and not the employer.[2]

The Mishnah gives another case where a worker has the lower hand:

כָּל הַמְשַׁנֶּה — **Any** craftsman **who deviates** from the instructions given to him, for example, he was given wool and told to dye it red but instead he dyed it black, יָדוֹ עַל הַתַּחְתּוֹנָה — **he has the lower hand** when he collects payment

---
NOTES

1. When workers do only part of a job, their wages can be calculated in one of two ways: (1) They can be paid according to the percentage of the work that they did; for example, if they did half the job, they will receive half the amount they were promised; (2) they can be paid the full amount they were promised minus whatever it will cost the employer to have the job completed. If workers back out in the middle of a job, their wages are calculated by whichever method gives them less.

To illustrate: Workers were hired to do a job for 6 *dinars* and they quit after doing half the job. The price of workers has gone up, and such a job now costs 8 *dinars*; since half the job remains undone, the employer will have to pay 4 *dinars* for workers to complete it. If the wages for the original workers are calculated by the first method, they will receive 3 *dinars* (half of the 6 *dinars* that they were promised). If their wages are calculated by the second method, they will receive only 2 *dinars* (the full amount of 6 minus the 4 that the employer will have to pay to hire new workers). Since they backed out in the middle of the job, their wages are calculated by the second method and they receive only 2 *dinars*.

However, if the price of workers has gone down and the employer can now hire workers to complete the job for only 2 *dinars,* the reverse applies. If their wages are calculated the first way, they will receive 3 *dinars*. If their wages are calculated the second way, they will receive 4 *dinars* (the full amount of 6 minus the 2 that it will cost the employer to hire new workers). In this case, their wages are calculated the first way and they receive 3 *dinars* (*Rav*).

[If the price of workers has not changed and workers can be found to do the rest of the job for 3 *dinars,* both methods of calculation will produce the same result, and the original workers receive 3 *dinars*.]

[2] 2. That is, they are paid whichever is *more*: the wage for the percentage of the work that they did, or the amount promised for the whole job minus whatever it will cost to hire new workers (see the previous note).

וְכָל הַחוֹזֵר בּוֹ, יָדוֹ עַל הַתַּחְתּוֹנָה.

[ג] הַשּׂוֹכֵר אֶת הַחֲמוֹר לְהוֹלִיכָהּ בָּהָר, וְהוֹלִיכָהּ בַּבִּקְעָה, בַּבִּקְעָה, וְהוֹלִיכָהּ בָּהָר, אֲפִלּוּ זוֹ עֶשֶׂר מִילִין

— רע"ב —

וכל החוזר בו ידו על התחתונה. לאתויי המוכר שדה לחבירו באלף זוז ונתן לו מהם מאתים זוז, וחזר בו המוכר, יד לוקח על העליונה, רצה אומר לו תן לי מעותי, רצה אומר לו תן לי קרקע כנגד מעותי. ואם לוקח חוזר בו, יד מוכר על העליונה, רצה אומר לו הילך מעותיך, רצה אומר לו הילך קרקע כנגד מעותיך: (ג) בהר והוליכה בבקעה בבקעה והוליכה בהר. ברא"ש ההר. ואף על פי שהדרך חלק וישר, חייב כשמתה מחמת אוירא שלא החליקה ולא הוחמה. דהואיל ושינה בה, יכול לומר לו, לא מתה זו אלא מתה מחמת שלא היתה למודה באויר הר, וקשה לה, או לא היתה למודה באויר בקעה, וקשה לה. ומשום הכי לא מפליג הכא בין הוחלקה להוחמה כמו דמפליג בסיפא:

for his work; that is, his pay is calculated in a way that favors the employer.[3]

Another case where a person has the lower hand:

וְכָל הַחוֹזֵר בּוֹ יָדוֹ עַל הַתַּחְתּוֹנָה — **And anyone who goes back on his word** during a sale **has the lower hand.** That it, if two people are involved in the sale of a piece of land and one of them backs out after part of the money is paid, the one who backed out has the lower hand with regard to working out the details.[4]

[3] The next three Mishnahs discuss laws of renting animals. As a rule, a renter (שׂוֹכֵר) is obligated to pay for damage that happens to the rented object because of his negligence, and for damage that he could have prevented; he does not have to pay for damage that was unavoidable (see Introduction to Chapter 3; Mishnah 7:8). This Mishnah discusses whether a renter who does not keep to the terms of the rental is obligated to pay for damage that occurs:

הַשּׂוֹכֵר אֶת הַחֲמוֹר לְהוֹלִיכָהּ בָּהָר וְהוֹלִיכָהּ בַּבִּקְעָה — **If someone rents a donkey** and agrees that he will lead it only **on a mountain** but instead **he leads it in a valley,** בַּבִּקְעָה וְהוֹלִיכָהּ בָּהָר — or he agrees to lead it **in a valley but leads it on a mountain**[1] — אֲפִלּוּ זוֹ עֶשֶׂר מִילִין — **even if this** path on the mountain **is**

NOTES

3. Since the craftsman has improved the wool, the employer must pay him for his work. However, he is not paid what he was promised, because he did not do the job he was hired to do. Instead, he can be paid in one of two ways: (1) He can be reimbursed for his expenses (for example, the equipment and dyes that he used); or (2) he can be paid for the value of the improvement to the wool (that is, the difference between the value of undyed wool and that of black wool). He has the lower hand and therefore receives whichever amount is less (*Rav*).

[If the dyer ruined the wool instead of improving it, he must pay the employer its value (*Bava Kamma* 9:3-4).]

4. For example, someone offered to sell a field to his friend for 1,000 *zuz*. After the buyer paid 200 *zuz,* one of them decided not to go through with the sale. If it was the seller who backed out, the buyer has the upper hand and can choose whether he wants to receive back his money or receive the portion of the field that he paid for (in this case, ⅕th of the field). If it was the buyer who backed out, the seller has the upper hand and can choose whether to give back the money or give the buyer a portion of the field (*Rav*).

[3]

1. He rented the donkey to carry goods to a place that can be reached by two paths — one that goes over a mountain

משניות בבא מציעא / פרק ו: השוכר את האמנין

— רע"ב —

וְזוֹ עֶשֶׂר מִילִין, וָמֵתָה חַיָּב. הַשּׂוֹכֵר אֶת הַחֲמוֹר וְהִבְרִיקָה אוֹ שֶׁנַּעֲשֵׂית אַנְגַּרְיָא, אוֹמֵר לוֹ, הֲרֵי שֶׁלְּךָ לְפָנֶיךָ. מֵתָה אוֹ נִשְׁבְּרָה,

אם החליקה פטור. שהבר היא רצויה להחליק יותר, שראש ההר חד ומשופע ולצדדין: ואם הוחמה חייב. שהבקעה מעלה הבל, לפי

שההרים סביבה ואין אויר שולט בה. ואם הוחמה מחמת העלותה בהר, חייב. שהמעלה גרמה לה, והוא שינה להוליכה בהר: והבדיקה. כסמית בדוק שבעין. פירש אחר, התליטו רגליה: או שנעשית אנגריא. שנלקחה לעבודת המלך. ודוקא כשאמר לו חמור זה, ושכרו למשאוי. אבל אם שכרו לרכוב עליו, אפילו אמר לו חמור זה, אינו יכול לומר לו הרי שלך לפניך. שמא תפול תחתיו בגשר, או תשליכנו באחת הפחתים. וכן אם השכיר לו חמור סתם אפילו למשאוי, אינו יכול לומר לו הרי שלך לפניך, אלא חייב להעמיד לו בהמה אחרת. ואם אינו מעמיד לו בהמה אחרת, אינו חייב ליתן לו כלום מכל שכר הדרך שהלך עמו: מתה או נשברה חייב. המשכיר למכור [הטור והגבלה] לכלבים, ולהוסיף מעות, ולהעמיד לו חמור. או ישכור לו אחר בדמי נבילה, שהרי חמור זה שיעבד לו. או יחזור לו שכרו:

עֶשֶׂר מִילִין — **וְזוֹ** — and that path in the valley is also **ten mils** long,[2] and thus the renter did not take the donkey any farther than he agreed to take it — **וָמֵתָה חַיָּב** — if [the donkey] dies on the way for no known reason, [the renter] is obligated to pay for it. This is because air on a mountain is different from air in a valley, and the owner can claim that the renter caused the donkey's death by bringing it to an environment that it was not used to.[3]

The Mishnah discusses whether an owner is responsible to provide a renter with a replacement animal if the rented animal becomes unusable:

הַשּׂוֹכֵר אֶת הַחֲמוֹר וְהִבְרִיקָה — Someone rents a donkey, and it becomes blind[4] **אוֹ שֶׁנַּעֲשֵׂית אַנְגַּרְיָא** — or is temporarily seized for the king's service.[5] If the renter demands a replacement,[6] **אוֹמֵר לוֹ הֲרֵי שֶׁלְּךָ לְפָנֶיךָ** — [the owner] can say to him: "Your animal is here before you," i.e., "The donkey that I gave you can still be used to some extent; therefore, I do not have to replace it."[7] **מֵתָה אוֹ נִשְׁבְּרָה** — However, if [the donkey] died or broke a limb

---

— NOTES —

and another that goes through a valley (*Maharam*). The owner stipulated that the renter should take the donkey on a specific path, but the renter took the other path.

2. A *mil* is a unit of distance.

3. Air on a mountain is usually cool, while air in a valley is warm, since the mountains surrounding it prevent cool air from entering. [Although the donkey seems to have died from natural causes, for which the renter should not be liable], the owner can claim that its death was in fact the renter's fault, because it was used to only one kind of air — either mountain or valley — and it died because the renter took it to an unfamiliar environment (*Rav*).

4. Literally, *it was lit up*. The Mishnah uses this term as a euphemism for blindness (*Tos. Yom Tov*).

5. It was common for officers of a king to seize an animal for their needs; they would use it until they found a different one, when they would return the first one and seize the second (*Rashi* 78b).

6. [Since these events are definitely beyond the renter's control, he does not have to pay the owner for the injury or loss.]

7. A blind donkey can still carry things as long as a person leads it, and a donkey that was confiscated by the king's men will be returned eventually. Thus, the renter will still be able to use the donkey for the job he rented it for (Gemara 78b [first opinion]).

However, if the donkey can no longer do the job it was rented for, the owner must provide a replacement. For example, if the renter hired the donkey to

חַיָּב לְהַעֲמִיד לוֹ חֲמוֹר. הַשּׂוֹכֵר אֶת הַחֲמוֹר לְהוֹלִיכָהּ בָּהָר, וְהוֹלִיכָהּ בַּבִּקְעָה, אִם הֶחֱלִיקָה, פָּטוּר. וְאִם הוּחַמָּה, חַיָּב. לְהוֹלִיכָהּ בַּבִּקְעָה וְהוֹלִיכָהּ בָּהָר, אִם הֶחֱלִיקָה, חַיָּב. וְאִם הוּחַמָּה, פָּטוּר. אִם מֵחֲמַת הַמַּעֲלָה, חַיָּב.

and cannot perform work at all, חַיָּב לְהַעֲמִיד לוֹ חֲמוֹר — [the owner] must provide [the renter] with another donkey for the rest of the term of the rental, or return the rental money.

The Mishnah returns to the case where someone rented a donkey and took it on a path other than the one stipulated by the owner. Having earlier stated the law when the animal died from an unknown cause, the Mishnah now states the law when the animal died because of a specific reason:

הַשּׂוֹכֵר אֶת הַחֲמוֹר לְהוֹלִיכָהּ בָּהָר וְהוֹלִיכָהּ בַּבִּקְעָה — If someone rents a donkey and agrees to lead it on a mountain but instead leads it in a valley, the law is as follows: אִם הֶחֱלִיקָה פָּטוּר — If [the donkey] slipped and died, [the renter] is exempt from paying for it. Although he did not obey the owner's instructions, its death cannot be considered the renter's fault, since if he had taken it on a mountain as agreed, it would have been even more likely to slip, due to the mountain's steepness.[8] וְאִם הוּחַמָּה חַיָּב — However, if [the animal] was affected by the heat of the valley and died, [the renter] is obligated to pay for it. In this case, he is responsible for the animal's death, for if he had kept to the agreement and taken it on a mountain, where the air is cooler, it would not have died from the heat.

In the next case, the reverse is true:

לְהוֹלִיכָהּ בַּבִּקְעָה וְהוֹלִיכָהּ בָּהָר — If a person rents a donkey and agrees to lead it in a valley but instead leads it on a mountain, the law is as follows: אִם הֶחֱלִיקָה חַיָּב — If it slipped on the mountain and died, [the renter] is obligated to pay for it, for if he had kept to the agreement and taken it in a valley, it would not have slipped; וְאִם הוּחַמָּה פָּטוּר — but if it died because it was affected by the heat on the mountain, [the renter] is exempt. In this case, he is not responsible for its death, because if he had taken it to a valley as agreed, it would have been even more likely to die from heat. אִם מֵחֲמַת הַמַּעֲלָה חַיָּב — However, if the donkey became overheated and died because of the strain of climbing the mountain,[9] [the renter] is obligated to pay, because he caused its death by leading it up the mountain.

NOTES

ride on it, the owner must offer a replacement if it becomes blind, because a blind donkey is not safe to ride (Rav).

The Mishnah's law applies only if the renter had specified that he wanted to rent *this particular donkey*. As long as this donkey can be used to some extent, the owner does not have to supply a replacement. However, if the renter had not asked for a specific donkey, the owner must provide an animal that is fully usable. If anything happens to the rented donkey, he must offer another one (Rav).

8. Thus, its death is considered an unavoidable accident and the renter is exempt (see Tos. Yom Tov).

9. That is, the animal was clearly straining and sweating during the climb, which

[ד] **הַשּׂוֹכֵר** אֶת הַפָּרָה לַחֲרשׁ וְחָרַשׁ בָּהָר וְחָרַשׁ בַּבִּקְעָה, אִם נִשְׁבַּר הַקַּנְקָן, פָּטוּר. בַּבִּקְעָה וְחָרַשׁ בָּהָר, אִם נִשְׁבַּר הַקַּנְקָן, חַיָּב.
לָדוּשׁ בְּקִטְנִית, וְדָשׁ בִּתְבוּאָה, פָּטוּר. לָדוּשׁ בִּתְבוּאָה וְדָשׁ בְּקִטְנִית, חַיָּב, מִפְּנֵי שֶׁהַקִּטְנִית מַחֲלֶקֶת.

— רע״ב —

(ד) השוכר את הפרה לחרוש וכו׳. וכל כלי המחרישה לבעל הפרה, ונעריו הולכים עם בהמתו וחורשים בה: **נשבר הקנקן.** יתד המחרישה שבו הברזל: **חייב.** שהריס קשים לחרוש מן הבקעה מפני הסלעים שיש שם: **ודש בתבואה.** פטור אם החליקה:

[4] הַשּׂוֹכֵר אֶת הַפָּרָה לַחֲרשׁ וְחָרַשׁ בָּהָר בַּבִּקְעָה — If someone rents a cow and a plow and agrees with the owner that he will use it **to plow on a mountain,** but instead **he plows in a valley,** אִם נִשְׁבַּר הַקַּנְקָן פָּטוּר — **if the plow beam**[1] **breaks** while he is plowing, **he is exempt** from paying for it. Although he did not obey the owner's instructions, the damage cannot be considered his fault, since if he had kept to the agreement and plowed on a mountain, where the ground is hard and rocky, the plow would have been even more likely to break.[2] בַּבִּקְעָה וְחָרַשׁ בָּהָר — However, if the renter agrees to plow **in a valley** but instead **plows on a mountain,** אִם נִשְׁבַּר הַקַּנְקָן חַיָּב — **if the plow beam breaks** while he is plowing, **he is obligated** to pay for it, because his negligence caused the damage, since if he had kept to the agreement and plowed in a valley, where the ground is soft, the plow would probably not have broken.

A similar case:

לָדוּשׁ בְּקִטְנִית וְדָשׁ בִּתְבוּאָה פָּטוּר — If a person rents a cow and agrees that he will use it **to thresh beans**[3] but instead **he threshes grain,** if the cow slips while threshing and is hurt, **he is exempt** from paying for the damages. Had he kept to the agreement and threshed beans, which are more slippery than grain, the cow would have been even more likely to slip. Thus, the injury cannot be considered the renter's fault. לָדוּשׁ בִּתְבוּאָה וְדָשׁ בְּקִטְנִית חַיָּב — However, if he agrees **to thresh grain but** instead **threshes beans,** if the cow slips and is hurt, **he is obligated** to pay for its injury, מִפְּנֵי שֶׁהַקִּטְנִית מַחֲלֶקֶת — **because beans are** more **slippery** than grain, and thus the animal would probably not have been injured if the renter had kept to the agreement and threshed grain.

— NOTES —

[4]
1. The [wooden] beam to which the plow's blade is attached (*Rav*).

2. Rather, the damage to the plow is considered an unavoidable accident, for which a renter is exempt (see *Meiri*).

3. Threshing is the removal of the hard shells of grain or beans from their edible kernels. This was done by spreading out the beans or grain and having an animal pull a heavy instrument over them (see *Rashi, Menachos* 22a ד״ה דיישי דישא).

shows that it died from the strain of the climb (*Ritva*). In the previous case, the animal climbed the mountain with no visible effort and became overheated only later. In that case, it is clear that it died from the heat on the mountain and not from the strain of the climb (*Tos. Yom Tov*).

[ה] הַשּׂוֹכֵר אֶת הַחֲמוֹר לְהָבִיא עָלֶיהָ חִטִּים, וְהֵבִיא עָלֶיהָ שְׂעוֹרִים, חַיָּב. תְּבוּאָה וְהֵבִיא עָלֶיהָ תֶבֶן, חַיָּב, מִפְּנֵי שֶׁהַנֶּפַח קָשֶׁה לַמַּשּׂאוֹי. לְהָבִיא לֶתֶךְ חִטִּים, וְהֵבִיא לֶתֶךְ שְׂעוֹרִים, פָּטוּר, וְאִם הוֹסִיף עַל מַשָּׂאוֹ, חַיָּב.

— רע"ב —

(ה) והביא עליה שעורים. שהן קלים מחטין: חייב. בקלקולה אם הוסיף שלשה קבין. ולא אמרינן, הואיל והשעורים קלין יש לו להוסיף עד כדי כובד לתך חטין שהוא משא החמור: מפני שהנפח קשה. לבהמה כמשאוי. אף על פי שאין משאו כבד כמשא החטין, הרי נפחן כנפח החטין, והנפח כמשאוי: לתך. חצי כור. והכור שלשים סאין:

---

[5] This Mishnah discusses one who overloads a rented animal:

הַשּׂוֹכֵר אֶת הַחֲמוֹר לְהָבִיא עָלֶיהָ חִטִּים — If someone rents a donkey and agrees that he will carry a certain amount of wheat on it, וְהֵבִיא עָלֶיהָ שְׂעוֹרִים — but instead he carries barley on it, and because barley is lighter than wheat, he adds more to the load; even though the larger load of barley weighs the same as the smaller load of wheat would have weighed, if the donkey becomes injured, חַיָּב — [the renter] is obligated to pay for the damage.[1] תְּבוּאָה — Similarly, if he agreed to carry a certain amount of grain on the donkey וְהֵבִיא עָלֶיהָ תֶבֶן — but instead he carries straw on it, and because straw is lighter than grain, he adds to the load; even though the larger load of straw weighs the same as the grain would have weighed, if the donkey becomes injured, חַיָּב — [the renter] is obligated to pay for the damage. מִפְּנֵי שֶׁהַנֶּפַח קָשֶׁה לַמַּשּׂאוֹי — In both these cases, the renter must pay because even though he did not add to the *weight* of the load, the extra volume is hard for a donkey to bear, and likely caused its injury.

In the next case, the renter did not add to either the weight or the volume of the agreed-upon load:

לְהָבִיא לֶתֶךְ חִטִּים — If a person rents a donkey and agrees to carry a *lesech* (a unit of volume) of wheat on it, וְהֵבִיא לֶתֶךְ שְׂעוֹרִים — but instead he carries a *lesech* of barley on it, if the donkey is injured, פָּטוּר — [the renter] is exempt from paying for the damage. Although he did not obey the owner's instructions, he did not increase the volume of the load and in fact made the load lighter by carrying barley instead of wheat; therefore, he is not at fault for the animal's injury. וְאִם הוֹסִיף עַל מַשָּׂאוֹ — However, if [the renter] adds to the volume of the load, and loads enough barley to equal the weight of a *lesech* of wheat, חַיָּב — he is obligated to pay if the donkey is hurt, because it was likely harmed because of the extra volume, as mentioned above.

The Mishnah now states the law when a renter loads the animal with the material he had agreed to load it with, but adds to the agreed-upon load:[2]

--- NOTES ---

[5]
1. He is liable only if he adds enough barley so that the load weighs as much as the agreed-upon load of wheat would have weighed. If he adds less than that amount, he does not have to pay if the animal is injured (*Rambam Commentary*; see *Rav*).

2. *Rambam Commentary.*

משניות בבא מציעא / פרק ו: השוכר את האמנין

וְכַמָּה יוֹסִיף עַל מַשָּׂאוֹ וִיהֵא חַיָּב, סוֹמְכוֹס אוֹמֵר מִשּׁוּם רַבִּי מֵאִיר, סְאָה לְגָמָל, שְׁלֹשָׁה קַבִּין לַחֲמוֹר.

[ו] כָּל הָאֻמָּנִין שׁוֹמְרֵי שָׂכָר הֵן, וְכֻלָּן שֶׁאָמְרוּ, טֹל אֶת שֶׁלְּךָ וְהָבֵא מָעוֹת,

— רע״ב —

סומכוס אומר וכו׳. והלכה כסומכוס. ואם הוסיף פחות משיעור זה, פטור אם הוזק החמור, ונותן שכר התוספות בלבד: (ו) כל האומנין. קבלנים שמקבלים עליהם לעשות מלאכה בבתיהם:

שומרי שכר. להתחייב בגניבה ואבידה. דבהכי הנאה דתפס ליה אאגרא: וכולן שאמרו טול את שלך. שכבר גמרתיו, ואיני מעכבו לתפסו על שכרי, ומאחר שהולכנו תביא מעות, הרי הוא משם ואילך שומר חנם:

וְכַמָּה יוֹסִיף עַל מַשָּׂאוֹ וִיהֵא חַיָּב — **And, if the renter loads the animal with the agreed-upon material, how much must he add to the load to be liable if the animal is injured?** סוֹמְכוֹס אוֹמֵר מִשּׁוּם רַבִּי מֵאִיר — **Sumchos says in the name of R' Meir:** If he agreed to carry a *lesech,* he is liable if he adds סְאָה לְגָמָל — **a** *se'ah* **on a camel,**[3] שְׁלֹשָׁה קַבִּין לַחֲמוֹר — **or three** *kav* **on a donkey.**[4] If he adds less than this amount, he is not obligated to pay if the animal is injured.

[6] The next three Mishnahs discuss laws of a *shomer,* one who watches someone else's object. As we have learned (see Introduction to Chapter 3), different types of *shomrim* have different levels of liability. An unpaid *shomer* (שׁוֹמֵר חִנָּם; one who watches an object without pay) is liable to pay only if the object he is guarding is damaged due to his negligence. A paid *shomer* (שׁוֹמֵר שָׂכָר; one who is paid to watch an object) is liable even for damage that was not the result of his negligence, such as if the object was stolen or lost; he is exempt only for damage that is unavoidable. The Mishnah begins by discussing whether a craftsman working on other people's items is considered a paid *shomer* or an unpaid *shomer* for the items he is working on: כָּל הָאֻמָּנִין שׁוֹמְרֵי שָׂכָר הֵן — **All craftsmen** who work in their own homes or shops on other people's items **are** considered **paid** *shomrim* for the items they are working on. For example, a tailor who is given a garment to mend is considered a paid *shomer* for the garment.[1] Although the craftsman is not paid to watch the object, he receives benefit from it, since he is entitled to hold the object as security and not return it until he is paid for his work.[2] Since he benefits from having the object in his possession, he is considered a paid *shomer.* וְכֻלָּן שֶׁאָמְרוּ טֹל אֶת שֶׁלְּךָ וְהָבֵא מָעוֹת — **However,** once any

---

NOTES

3. 1/15th of its load [a *lesech* is 90 *kav* and a *se'ah* is 6 *kav;* 90 ÷ 6 = 15] (*Tiferes Yisrael*).

4. 1/30th of its load (90 ÷ 3 =30). A donkey is weaker than a camel and cannot bear an addition of even 1/30th of its load (*Tiferes Yisrael*).

[6]

1. As such, he is obligated to pay for the garment if it is damaged due to his negligence, and even if it is stolen or lost.

2. Thus, he receives the benefit of not having to pursue the owner for his payment (Gemara 80b).

[The fee he receives for his work does not make him a paid *shomer,* because that is simply payment for his labor and is not benefit from having the item in his possession (see *Rashi* 80b ד״ה ר׳ מאיר אומר).]

[123] MISHNAH BAVA METZIA / Chapter 6: *Hasocheir es Haumanin*

שׁוֹמֵר חִנָּם. שְׁמֹר לִי וְאֶשְׁמֹר לָךְ, שׁוֹמֵר שָׂכָר. שְׁמֹר לִי, וְאָמַר לוֹ, הַנַּח לְפָנַי, שׁוֹמֵר חִנָּם.

— רע״ב —

שמור לי ואשמור לך. שמור לי היום ואשמור לך למחר. אבל שמור לי אתה זה, ואני שומר לך זה האחר במקומו, והכל בזמן אחד. זו שמירה בבעלים היא, ופטור: הנח לפני שומר חנם. אבל הנח לפניך, או הנח סתם, אפילו שומר חנם לא הוי. דלא קביל עליה נטירותא כלל:

[craftsman] finishes his work and **says** to the owner of the item, **"Take your [item] and bring money** to pay my fee," that is to say, "I will not hold your item as security; take it and then pay me," שׁוֹמֵר חִנָּם — his status changes to that of **an unpaid** *shomer,* since he has given up his right to hold the item as security and thus receives no benefit from it.[3]

Another case of a paid *shomer:*

שְׁמֹר לִי וְאֶשְׁמֹר לָךְ — If someone says to his friend, **"Watch** my item **for me** today, **and I will watch** your item **for you** tomorrow," שׁוֹמֵר שָׂכָר — each is considered a **paid** *shomer* for the other's item, because the fact that his friend watches his item is considered payment for watching his friend's item.[4]

In order for a person to become a *shomer* for an object, he must accept the responsibility of guarding it. The Mishnah gives an example of how one can do this:

שְׁמֹר לִי וְאָמַר לוֹ הַנַּח לְפָנַי שׁוֹמֵר חִנָּם — If one person says to another, **"Watch** my item **for me,"** and [the other] replies, **"Put it down before me,"** he is considered **an unpaid** *shomer;*[5] that is, this statement indicates that he agrees to watch the item, and he is now responsible for it.[6]

[7] A person who gives a loan may take an object from the borrower as security for the loan (i.e., if the borrower does not repay the loan, the lender can use that object to collect what he is owed). This Mishnah discusses some laws that apply while the lender holds the object of security:

NOTES

3. Accordingly, he is not liable if the object is stolen or lost, but only if it is damaged due to his negligence.

4. *Meiri.*
[This law applies only if each person watches the other's item at a different time (for example, one person watches the other's item today and the other watches his item tomorrow). However, if they watch each other's items at the same time, neither is obligated to pay for any damage that happens to the other's item. This is based on the principle that if a *shomer* accepts an item to watch while the object's owner is working for him, the *shomer* is not obligated to pay for damage to the object (see Mishnah 8:1). If two people watch each other's objects, they are each working for each other, and thus each is exempt from any liability for the object he is watching (*Rav*).]

5. Since he is not paid to watch it, he is an unpaid *shomer.* If he was being paid to watch the item, he would be considered a paid *shomer* as soon as he said, "Put it down before me" (*Tosafos* 99a ד״ה כך תקנו).

6. However, if he used a different phrase, such as, "Place it before *yourself,*" or, simply, "Place it down," he does not become a *shomer,* since these statements do not indicate that he agrees to watch it (*Rav*).

[124] משניות בבא מציעא / פרק ו: השוכר את האמנין ו/ז

— רע"ב —

(ז) הלוהו מעות על המשכון שומר שכר. בין הלוהו מעות בין משכנו כך ואחר כך הלוהו, ומאי שכר שכר מצוה: הלוהו מעות

[ז] **הַלְוָהוּ** עַל הַמַּשְׁכּוֹן, שׁוֹמֵר שָׂכָר. רַבִּי יְהוּדָה אוֹמֵר, הַלְוָהוּ מָעוֹת, שׁוֹמֵר חִנָּם. הַלְוָהוּ פֵרוֹת, שׁוֹמֵר שָׂכָר. אַבָּא שָׁאוּל אוֹמֵר, מֻתָּר אָדָם לְהַשְׂכִּיר מַשְׁכּוֹנוֹ שֶׁל עָנִי

שומר חנם. דלית ליה לרבי יהודה שכר מצוה לענין דינא: הלוהו פירות שומר שכר. דדרך פירות להרקיב. ואין הלכה כרבי יהודה: מותר אדם להשכיר. לאחרים: משכונו של עני. שבידו

הַלְוָהוּ עַל הַמַּשְׁכּוֹן שׁוֹמֵר שָׂכָר — **If one lends someone against a security**, that is, the lender took an item from the borrower to guarantee the loan, the lender **is considered a paid** *shomer* for the item of security.[1] Although the lender is not paid to watch the item, he benefits from having given the loan, because at the time he gives the loan he is exempt from giving charity and thus saves money.[2] Because of this benefit, he is considered a paid *shomer* for the item of security.

R' Yehudah differentiates between different types of loans:

רַבִּי יְהוּדָה אוֹמֵר — **R' Yehudah says:** **הַלְוָהוּ מָעוֹת שׁוֹמֵר חִנָּם** — **If he lent someone money** against a security, the lender **is** considered **an unpaid** *shomer* for the security item, because the benefit of being exempt from charity is not enough to make a lender a paid *shomer*.[3] **הַלְוָהוּ פֵרוֹת שׁוֹמֵר שָׂכָר** — However, if **he lent someone produce** against a security, he is considered **a paid** *shomer* for the security. In this case, the lender benefits by the loan, for his produce would eventually have rotted, and he will now be repaid with fresh produce.[4]

The Mishnah mentions another law about a lender who holds an item of security:

אַבָּא שָׁאוּל אוֹמֵר — **Abba Shaul says:** **מֻתָּר אָדָם לְהַשְׂכִּיר מַשְׁכּוֹנוֹ שֶׁל עָנִי** — **A person** who lent money to a poor man against a security **is allowed to rent the poor man's security** to others on the poor man's behalf without his knowledge;

───── NOTES ─────

[7]
1. Therefore, the lender is liable to pay for the item even if it is stolen or lost.
2. While a person does a mitzvah, he is exempt from other mitzvos. Accordingly, if a person is giving a loan (which is a mitzvah [*Exodus* 22:24]) and a poor person asks him for charity, he does not have to give the charity (*Bava Kamma* 56b). Thus, one who gives a loan can save money that he would otherwise have been obligated to give to charity; this is considered enough of a benefit to make him a paid *shomer* for the item of security (*Rav, Tos. Yom Tov*).
3. R' Yehudah argues that the lender is

exempt from charity only at the moment when he is giving the loan (since that is when he is doing the mitzvah), and it is not that likely that he will be asked for charity at that exact moment and thereby save money. The possibility that he *might* save money in this manner is not enough of a benefit to make him a paid *shomer* (*Ritva* 82a).

4. [Although it is generally forbidden to lend produce and be repaid with produce, due to a Rabbinic prohibition against collecting interest (as we have learned in Mishnah 5:9), our Mishnah refers to those cases where it is permitted (see there notes 3-4).]

[125] **MISHNAH BAVA METZIA** / Chapter 6: *Hasocheir es Haumanin*

לִהְיוֹת פּוֹסֵק עָלָיו וְהוֹלֵךְ, מִפְּנֵי שֶׁהוּא כְּמֵשִׁיב אֲבֵדָה.

[ח] הַמַּעֲבִיר חָבִית מִמָּקוֹם לְמָקוֹם וּשְׁבָרָהּ, בֵּין שׁוֹמֵר חִנָּם בֵּין שׁוֹמֵר שָׂכָר, יִשָּׁבַע. רַבִּי אֱלִיעֶזֶר אוֹמֵר, זֶה וָזֶה יִשָּׁבַע,

— רע״ב —

להיות פוסק עליו וכו׳. שכר: והולך. תמיד ופוחת מן החוב. ודוקא במשכון דנפיש אגריה וזוטר פחתיה, כגון מרא וקרדום וכיולא בהן. וכן הלכה:
(ח) בין שומר חנם ובין שומר שכר ישבע. קא סלקא [דעתיה] ישבע שלא פשע ויפטר: רבי אליעזר אומר זה וזה ישבע וכו׳. כלומר, אף אני שמעתי מרבותי כרבי מאיר דזה וזה ישבע, אבל תמה אני על זה ועל זה היאך נפטרין בשבועה. דשומר שכר היאך פטור בשבועה, הא בלא פשיעה נמי חייב, שאין זה אונס, אלא דומיא דגניבה ואבידה שהן קרובים לפשיעה ולאונס. ועוד, אי שלא במקום מדרון נשברה, אפילו שומר חנם היכי מלי משתבע שלא פשע, הא ודאי פשיעה היא. ורבי מאיר סבר, שבועה זו לא מן הדין היא אלא תקנת חכמים היא. שאם אי אתה פוטר המעביר

לִהְיוֹת פּוֹסֵק עָלָיו וְהוֹלֵךְ — that is, the lender can set a rental fee for [the security item] and rent it out, using the rental income to steadily deduct from the poor man's debt. Although a lender is forbidden to use an item he is holding for security, he is permitted to rent it out in this manner מִפְּנֵי שֶׁהוּא כְּמֵשִׁיב אֲבֵדָה — because it is as though he is returning lost property to its owner; that is, by renting out the security item, the lender is giving the borrower money that would otherwise have been lost to him.[5]

[8] Another law related to *shomrim*:

הַמַּעֲבִיר חָבִית מִמָּקוֹם לְמָקוֹם וּשְׁבָרָהּ — If someone was moving his friend's barrel from place to place, and he tripped and broke it, בֵּין שׁוֹמֵר חִנָּם בֵּין שׁוֹמֵר שָׂכָר — whether he was an unpaid *shomer* (i.e., he was not paid to move the barrel) or a paid *shomer* (i.e., he was paid to move the barrel), יִשָּׁבַע — he swears that he did not cause the barrel to break and he is then exempt from paying for it.

Assuming that the Tanna Kamma means that the *shomer* swears that he was not negligent in guarding the barrel and is then exempt,[1] R' Eliezer responds:

רַבִּי אֱלִיעֶזֶר אוֹמֵר — R' Eliezer says: I too heard from my teachers that זֶה וָזֶה יִשָּׁבַע — both this one [an unpaid *shomer*] and that one [a paid *shomer*]

— NOTES —

5. Therefore, if the borrower is poor, it can be assumed that he allows the rental, even if he does not know about it (*Shach, Choshen Mishpat* 72:2).

This law applies only to an object that can be rented out for a fair amount of money without undergoing a lot of wear and tear, such as a shovel or axe. Otherwise, it cannot be assumed that the borrower allows it to be rented out (*Rav*).

[8]

1. The usual case where a *shomer* swears an oath and is then exempt from paying is the case of an unpaid *shomer*, who is exempt from paying for damage that is not the result of his negligence — as long as he swears that he was indeed not negligent in guarding the object (see Mishnah 3:1). R' Eliezer assumed that when the Tanna Kamma said that the *shomer* swears and is thereby exempt, he referred to the usual oath, that is, an oath that he was not negligent (see *Rav*).

וְתָמֵהַּ אֲנִי אִם יְכוֹלִין זֶה וָזֶה לִשָּׁבַע.

— רע"ב —

חבית ממקום למקום מן התשלומין על ידי שבועה

זו, אין לך אדם שיעביר חבית לחבירו ממקום למקום, לפיכך תקנו שישבע שלא בכוונה שברתיה ויפטר:

וְתָמֵהַּ אֲנִי אִם יְכוֹלִין זֶה וָזֶה לִשָּׁבַע — swear and are then exempt from paying for the barrel. **However, I wonder how both these** *shomrim* **can be** exempt simply by **swearing** that they were not negligent. After all, a paid *shomer* is obligated to pay for damage even if it is not the result of his negligence (unless it is unavoidable — and tripping is not unavoidable). Moreover, if he had been walking on a flat path, the *shomer* was indeed negligent, since he should have been more careful not to trip; in that case, even an unpaid *shomer* should be obligated to pay![2]

NOTES

2. In fact, the Tanna Kamma never meant that the *shomer* should swear that he was not negligent in guarding the barrel — since, as R' Eliezer argued, based on the regular rules of *shomrim*, a *shomer* who trips and breaks a barrel should not be exempt simply by swearing that he was not negligent. What the Tanna Kamma meant was that the *shomer* swears that he did not break the barrel *deliberately*, and he is then exempt based on a special Rabbinic exemption that applies to carrying barrels. Since it is very common for barrels to break while being moved, the Sages were concerned that if the regular rules of *shomrim* applied, no one would ever agree to move a barrel, for fear that he would have to pay for it in case of an accident. They therefore ruled that if any *shomer* breaks a barrel while moving it, he is exempt from paying as long as he swears that he did not break it deliberately (*Rav*).

Chapter Seven

פרק ז: השוכר

[א] הַשּׂוֹכֵר אֶת הַפּוֹעֲלִים וְאָמַר לָהֶם לְהַשְׁכִּים וּלְהַעֲרִיב, מְקוֹם שֶׁנָּהֲגוּ שֶׁלֹּא לְהַשְׁכִּים וְשֶׁלֹּא לְהַעֲרִיב, אֵינוֹ רַשַּׁאי לְכוֹפָן. מְקוֹם שֶׁנָּהֲגוּ לָזוּן, יָזוּן, לְסַפֵּק בִּמְתִיקָה, יְסַפֵּק. הַכֹּל כְּמִנְהַג הַמְּדִינָה.

— רע"ב —

פרק שביעי – השוכר את הפועלים. (א) השוכר את הפועלים. אינו יכול לכופן. ואף על גב דטפחא להו אאגרייהו משאר פועלים, לא מני אמר להו, האי דטפאי לכו אאגרייכו,

אדעתא דמקדמיתו ומחשכיתו בהדדאי. דאמרי ליה, האי דטפאת לן, אדעתא דעבדינן לך עובדתא שפירתא: במתיקה. לפתן: הכל במנהג המדינה. הכל, לאתויי דנהיגי פועלים למיכל ולמשתי בצפרא בביתו של בעל הבית, קודם שילאו למלאכתם. דאי אמר לו בעל הבית, קדימו לעבידתייכו בשדה ואביא לכם מאכלכם שם, אמרי ליה, לא, אלא עתה נאכל בבית קודם שנלך השדה, כמנהג המדינה:

---

[1] A person who hires a worker for a day's labor can set the terms of employment (for example, working hours, wages, etc.) as he wishes, as long as the worker agrees to those terms before he begins working.[1] This Mishnah discusses how the terms are decided if nothing is specified when the worker is hired:

הַשּׂוֹכֵר אֶת הַפּוֹעֲלִים — **If someone hires workers** without specifying what their work hours will be, וְאָמַר לָהֶם לְהַשְׁכִּים וּלְהַעֲרִיב — **and he** later **tells them to come** to work **early** in the morning **or to continue** working **late** at night,[2] מְקוֹם שֶׁנָּהֲגוּ שֶׁלֹּא לְהַשְׁכִּים וְשֶׁלֹּא לְהַעֲרִיב — if they are in **a place where [workers] are not accustomed to come early or stay late,** אֵינוֹ רַשַּׁאי לְכוֹפָן — **[the employer] cannot force them** to do so. Since he did not specify the work hours when he hired them, he must follow the local custom and cannot demand that they work longer than what is usual in that place.

Other matters that depend on local custom:

מְקוֹם שֶׁנָּהֲגוּ לָזוּן — In **a place where [employers] are accustomed to give** their **workers food,** יָזוּן — **[the employer] must give them food.** לְסַפֵּק בִּמְתִיקָה — **If** it is customary **to** also **supply** workers with **relish** to dip their food in, יְסַפֵּק — **he must supply** relish as well. הַכֹּל כְּמִנְהַג הַמְּדִינָה — In general, **everything** that was not specified when the workers were hired **must be done according to local custom.**

The Gemara (86a-86b) states that the following clause is missing from the Mishnah and must be inserted: Where it is customary to give workers food, if the employer tells them explicitly that he will give them food, it is assumed that he means to promise them *more* food than is usually given to workers — otherwise, there would be no reason for him to promise food, since local custom requires him to give it regardless. The following story illustrates this law:

NOTES

[1] 1. *Tos. Yom Tov, Lechem Shamayim;* see note 4.

2. A standard workday is from sunrise to sunset (Gemara 83b). This employer tells his workers to start work before sunrise and continue after sunset (*Meiri*).

[129] MISHNAH BAVA METZIA / Chapter 7: *Hasocheir*

מַעֲשֶׂה בְּרַבִּי יוֹחָנָן בֶּן מַתְיָא שֶׁאָמַר לִבְנוֹ, צֵא שְׂכֹר לָנוּ פּוֹעֲלִים. הָלַךְ וּפָסַק לָהֶם מְזוֹנוֹת. וּכְשֶׁבָּא אֵצֶל אָבִיו, אָמַר לוֹ, בְּנִי אֲפִלּוּ אַתָּה עוֹשֶׂה לָהֶם כִּסְעוּדַת שְׁלֹמֹה בִּשְׁעָתוֹ, לֹא יָצָאתָ יְדֵי חוֹבָתְךָ עִמָּהֶן, שֶׁהֵן בְּנֵי אַבְרָהָם, יִצְחָק, וְיַעֲקֹב. אֶלָּא עַד שֶׁלֹּא יַתְחִילוּ בִּמְלָאכָה צֵא וֶאֱמֹר לָהֶם, עַל מְנָת שֶׁאֵין לָכֶם עָלַי אֶלָּא פַּת וְקִטְנִית בִּלְבַד.

— **מַעֲשֶׂה בְּרַבִּי יוֹחָנָן בֶּן מַתְיָא שֶׁאָמַר לִבְנוֹ** — It once happened that R' Yochanan ben Masya said to his son: **צֵא שְׂכֹר לָנוּ פּוֹעֲלִים** — "Go out and hire workers for us." **הָלַךְ וּפָסַק לָהֶם מְזוֹנוֹת** — [The son] went and hired workers, **and** although it was the local custom to provide workers with food, **he** nevertheless **promised** explicitly **to give them food.** **וּכְשֶׁבָּא אֵצֶל אָבִיו אָמַר לוֹ** — When he came back to his father, [his father] said to him: **בְּנִי אֲפִלּוּ אַתָּה עוֹשֶׂה לָהֶם כִּסְעוּדַת שְׁלֹמֹה בִּשְׁעָתוֹ** — "My son, even if you will prepare for [the workers] a meal like the feast of King Solomon in his time, **לֹא יָצָאתָ יְדֵי חוֹבָתְךָ עִמָּהֶן** — you will not have fulfilled your obligation to them. By promising food, you obligated yourself to give them *more* than what is usually given to workers. Even if you give them a kingly feast, they can claim that they deserve better, **שֶׁהֵן בְּנֵי אַבְרָהָם יִצְחָק וְיַעֲקֹב** — since they are the children of Abraham, Isaac, and Jacob, and they can claim they deserve a banquet as lavish as the one served by their forefather Abraham."[3]

R' Yochanan instructed his son what to tell the workers:

אֶלָּא עַד שֶׁלֹּא יַתְחִילוּ בִּמְלָאכָה צֵא וֶאֱמֹר לָהֶם — "Rather," R' Yochanan told his son, "before they start work, go out and tell them: **עַל מְנָת שֶׁאֵין לָכֶם עָלַי אֶלָּא פַּת וְקִטְנִית בִּלְבַד** — 'You are being hired on the condition that you have no claim against me for anything other than bread and beans.' " This way, they will not be able to demand more than this simple meal.[4]

NOTES

3. The Gemara (86b) explains that the feast served by Abraham to the three angels (described in *Genesis* 18:6-8) was even more lavish than the royal feasts served by King Solomon (described in *I Kings* 5:2-3).

4. [Even though this simple meal is presumably less than was usually given to workers by local custom, if an employer stipulates to give the workers such a meal, he need not give them any more.]

This condition must be made before the workers start their work, because at that point they have only a verbal agreement with their employer, and the details of such an agreement can be changed. Once they begin work, though, the terms can no longer be changed (*Rav*).

רַבָּן שִׁמְעוֹן בֶּן גַּמְלִיאֵל אוֹמֵר, לֹא הָיָה צָרִיךְ לוֹמַר, הַכֹּל כְּמִנְהַג הַמְּדִינָה.

[ב] **וְאֵלּוּ** אוֹכְלִין מִן הַתּוֹרָה, הָעוֹשֶׂה בִמְחֻבָּר לַקַּרְקַע בִּשְׁעַת גְּמַר מְלָאכָה, וּבְתָלוּשׁ מִן הַקַּרְקַע עַד שֶׁלֹּא נִגְמְרָה מְלַאכְתּוֹ.

A different opinion:

רַבָּן שִׁמְעוֹן בֶּן גַּמְלִיאֵל אוֹמֵר — **Rabban Shimon ben Gamliel says:** לֹא הָיָה צָרִיךְ לוֹמַר — **[R' Yochanan's son] did not have to say** anything to clarify the terms of employment, הַכֹּל כְּמִנְהַג הַמְּדִינָה — because **everything is done according to the local custom.** Even though he promised the workers food, he does not have to give them more than what workers are customarily given in that place.[5]

[2] Having discussed when workers are entitled to receive food from their employers based on local custom or through agreement with their employer, the Mishnah discusses a Torah law that allows a worker to eat from his employer's food, regardless of local custom. The Torah states (*Deuteronomy* 23:25-26) that when a laborer is hired to work with produce, he is entitled to eat from that produce as he works, without the employer's permission, under certain conditions. The next seven Mishnahs discuss details of this law:

וְאֵלּוּ אוֹכְלִין מִן הַתּוֹרָה — **These** workers are entitled **by Torah** law **to eat** from the food they are working with: הָעוֹשֶׂה בִמְחֻבָּר לַקַּרְקַע — **One who works on produce that is attached to the ground** may eat from it בִּשְׁעַת גְּמַר מְלָאכָה — **when its work is complete,** that is, if it is fully ripe and he is harvesting it. וּבְתָלוּשׁ מִן הַקַּרְקַע — In contrast, someone who works **with produce that has** already **been detached from the ground** may eat from it only עַד שֶׁלֹּא נִגְמְרָה מְלַאכְתּוֹ — **when its work is not yet complete,** that is, if it is not yet processed to the point when *terumah* and *maaser* must be separated.[1]

NOTES

5. According to Rabban Shimon ben Gamliel, when an employer is required to feed his workers by local custom and nevertheless promises them food, he does not mean to promise them *extra* food; he is simply pledging to keep to the local custom.

[2]

1. Produce that grows in Eretz Yisrael may not be eaten until several portions, known as *terumah* and *maaser,* are removed from it (see Mishnah 4:8 for a list of these portions). *Terumah* and *maaser* do not have to be separated until the

בְּדָבָר שֶׁגִּדּוּלוֹ מִן הָאָרֶץ. וְאֵלּוּ שֶׁאֵינָן אוֹכְלִין, הָעוֹשֶׂה בִּמְחֻבָּר לַקַּרְקַע בְּשָׁעָה שֶׁאֵין גְּמַר מְלָאכָה, וּבִתְלוּשׁ מִן הַקַּרְקַע מֵאַחַר שֶׁנִּגְמְרָה מְלַאכְתּוֹ, וּבְדָבָר שֶׁאֵין גִּדּוּלוֹ מִן הָאָרֶץ.

[ג] **הָיָה** עוֹשֶׂה בְּיָדָיו, אֲבָל לֹא בְּרַגְלָיו,

— רע״ב —

אף כל דבר שהוא גדולי קרקע ולא נגמרה מלאכתו למעשר, כשהוא בשעת גמר מלאכה פועל אוכל בו. יצא החולב והמחבץ והמגבן, שאינן גדולי קרקע. ויצא המבדיל בתמרים והגרוגרות המחוברים יחד, שנגמרה מלאכתם למעשר. ויצא המנכש בשומים ובבצלים, שמסיר הקטנים שאינן גדלים לטולם, מבין האחרים, להרחיב מקום לגדולים, שאין זו שעת גמר מלאכה. שכל אלו וכיוצא בהן, אין פועל אוכל בהן:

בְּדָבָר שֶׁגִּדּוּלוֹ מִן הָאָרֶץ — And this privilege applies only to a person who works **with things that grow from the ground.**[2]

The Mishnah states which workers do not have this privilege:

וְאֵלּוּ שֶׁאֵינָן אוֹכְלִין — **And these** workers **may not eat** from the food they are working with: הָעוֹשֶׂה בִּמְחֻבָּר לַקַּרְקַע בְּשָׁעָה שֶׁאֵין גְּמַר מְלָאכָה — **Someone who works with produce that is attached to the ground** may not eat from it **when its work is not** yet **complete,** that is, if he is doing any job before the harvest. וּבִתְלוּשׁ מִן הַקַּרְקַע מֵאַחַר שֶׁנִּגְמְרָה מְלַאכְתּוֹ — **And** someone who works **with produce that was detached from the ground** may not eat from it **after its work is complete,** that is, if it is already processed to the point when *terumah* and *maaser* must be separated.[3] וּבְדָבָר שֶׁאֵין גִּדּוּלוֹ מִן הָאָרֶץ — In addition, anyone who works with food **that does not grow from the ground** may not eat from that food, no matter what kind of work he is doing.[4]

[3] This Mishnah states what type of work entitles a worker to eat from the produce he is working with:

הָיָה עוֹשֶׂה בְּיָדָיו אֲבָל לֹא בְּרַגְלָיו — **If [a worker] was working with his hands but not with his feet** (for example, he was harvesting produce by hand),[1]

NOTES

produce is considered fully processed. Different types of produce reach this point at different times. For example, vegetables that are sold in bundles are not considered fully processed until they are bundled (see *Maasros* 1:5-8). Only one who works with such vegetables *before* they are bundled is entitled to eat from them.

When a person prepares dough from certain species of grain, after separating *terumah* and *maaser,* he must separate another portion known as *challah.* When a laborer works with grain that will be made into dough, it is not considered fully processed until it becomes obligated for *challah* to be taken (which is at a later point than when it becomes obligated in *terumah* and *maaser*), and he may eat from it until that point (*Rav*).

2. These laws are derived from verses in the Torah (*Rav*).

3. Or, if it is produce that will be subject to the removal of *challah,* when it is processed to the point that *challah* must be separated (see note 1).

4. For example, a worker hired to milk cows or make cheese may not drink from the milk or eat from the cheese (*Rav*).

[3]

1. Meiri.

[132] **משניות בבא מציעא / פרק ז: השוכר**

בְּרַגְלָיו, אֲבָל לֹא בְּיָדָיו, אֲפִלּוּ בִּכְתֵפוֹ, הֲרֵי זֶה אוֹכֵל. רַבִּי יוֹסֵי בְּרַבִּי יְהוּדָה אוֹמֵר, עַד שֶׁיַּעֲשֶׂה בְּיָדָיו וּבְרַגְלָיו.

[ד] **הָיָה** עוֹשֶׂה בִּתְאֵנִים לֹא יֹאכַל בַּעֲנָבִים, בַּעֲנָבִים לֹא יֹאכַל בִּתְאֵנִים. אֲבָל מוֹנֵעַ אֶת עַצְמוֹ עַד שֶׁמַּגִּיעַ לִמְקוֹם הַיָּפוֹת וְאוֹכֵל.

— רע״ב —

(ג) עד שיעשה בידיו ורגליו. מה שור בידיו וברגליו אף פועל בידיו וברגליו, דהא אתקש חוסם לנחסם. ואין הלכה כרבי יוסי ברבי יהודה:

בְּרַגְלָיו אֲבָל לֹא בְּיָדָיו — or if he was working **with his feet but not with his hands** (for example, he was pressing grapes with his feet),[2] **אֲפִלּוּ בִּכְתֵפוֹ** — or **even** if he was working only **with his shoulder** (for example, he was hired to support a load with his shoulder),[3] **הֲרֵי זֶה אוֹכֵל** — this worker **may eat** from the produce he is working with. The Torah gave a worker this privilege no matter what type of work he is doing.[4]

Another Tanna disagrees:

רַבִּי יוֹסֵי בְּרַבִּי יְהוּדָה אוֹמֵר — R' Yose the son of R' Yehudah says: **עַד שֶׁיַּעֲשֶׂה בְּיָדָיו וּבְרַגְלָיו** — A worker may eat from the produce he works with **only if he is working** with both **his hands and his feet**. Otherwise, he does not have this privilege.[5]

הָיָה עוֹשֶׂה בִּתְאֵנִים לֹא יֹאכַל בַּעֲנָבִים — If [a worker] was working with figs, he may not eat from his employer's grapes; **בַּעֲנָבִים לֹא יֹאכַל בִּתְאֵנִים** — if he was working with grapes, he may not eat from his employer's figs. He may eat only from the type of produce he is working with.[1] **אֲבָל מוֹנֵעַ אֶת עַצְמוֹ עַד שֶׁמַּגִּיעַ לִמְקוֹם הַיָּפוֹת וְאוֹכֵל** — However, [a worker] may restrain himself from eating until he reaches an area of better quality produce, and eat his fill from there.[2]

The Mishnah discusses when a worker may eat from the produce:

--- NOTES ---

2. *Meiri.* [In earlier times, grapes were pressed for juice by stomping on them.]
3. *Kol HaRamaz.*
4. Subject to the guidelines discussed in Mishnah 2.
   Since the Torah did not state what type of work entitles a worker to eat from the produce he is working with, he has this privilege no matter how he is working (see *Tos. Yom Tov*).
5. Just as the Torah gave a worker the privilege of eating from produce with which he is working, the Torah teaches that a person must allow his ox (or other animal) to eat from produce with which it is working (*Deuteronomy* 25:4; see Mishnah 4). The Gemara teaches (89a) that, with regard to certain matters, a worker's privilege to eat produce is compared to that of an ox. R' Yose derives from this comparison that a worker may eat as he works only when he works as an ox works, i.e., with both his hands and his feet, just as an ox works with both its hands (i.e., its forelegs) and feet (i.e., its hind legs) (*Rav*).

[4]

1. Even if he was hired to work with both figs and grapes, he may eat from each type of fruit only while he is currently working with it (*Tos. Yom Tov*).
2. Even though he will thus eat more of the better fruits than he would have if he had also eaten from the inferior fruits (see *Rabbeinu Yehonasan*).

MISHNAH BAVA METZIA / Chapter 7: *Hasocheir*

— רע״ב —

(ד) מפני השב אבדה לבעלים. שלא יבטל ממלאכתו ויאכל: אמרו פועלים אוכלים בהליכתן מאומן לאומן. כשגמרו שורה זו והולכים להתחיל בחברתה. ואף על גב דהשתא שעתא לאו שעת מלאכה היא, ניחא ליה לבעל הבית בהא: בהליכתה אוכלת ממשאוי שעל גבה עד שתהא פורקת: (ה) אפילו בדינר. אפילו היא שוה דינר:

וְכֻלָּן לֹא אָמְרוּ אֶלָּא בִּשְׁעַת מְלָאכָה. אֲבָל מִשּׁוּם הָשֵׁב אֲבֵדָה לַבְּעָלִים אָמְרוּ, פּוֹעֲלִין אוֹכְלִין בַּהֲלִיכָתָן מֵאֻמָּן לְאֻמָּן, וּבַחֲזִירָתָן מִן הַגַּת. וּבַחֲמוֹר כְּשֶׁהִיא פוֹרֶקֶת.

[ה] **אוֹכֵל** פּוֹעֵל קִשּׁוּת אֲפִלּוּ בְּדִינָר,

וְכֻלָּן לֹא אָמְרוּ אֶלָּא בִּשְׁעַת מְלָאכָה — **Regarding all** workers, [the Sages] said that by Torah law, they may eat from their employers' produce **only while they are actually working.** אֲבָל מִשּׁוּם הָשֵׁב אֲבֵדָה לַבְּעָלִים — **However, in order to prevent owners** (i.e., employers) **from suffering a loss**[3] due to their workers eating while they work,[4] אָמְרוּ — **[the Sages] decreed**[5] פּוֹעֲלִין אוֹכְלִין בַּהֲלִיכָתָן מֵאֻמָּן לְאֻמָּן — **that workers may eat while they walk from one row to** the next **row,** that is, when they finish harvesting one row of plants or grapes and are walking to the next row to continue their work, וּבַחֲזִירָתָן מִן הַגַּת — **and when they are coming back from the winepress** to harvest the next load of grapes.[6] Although at those times, the laborers are not actually working with produce attached to the ground, the Sages realized that an employer would prefer that his workers eat while they are walking back and forth rather than while they are actually working.

Just as the Torah gave workers the privilege of eating produce they are working with, it teaches that if an animal is threshing produce, one is forbidden to muzzle it and prevent it from eating from the produce (*Deuteronomy* 25:4). The Mishnah discusses the extent of this prohibition:

וּבַחֲמוֹר כְּשֶׁהִיא פוֹרֶקֶת — **As for a donkey,** if it is carrying a load of food, one must allow it to eat from that food **until it is unloaded,** because the prohibition to muzzle an animal while it works applies not only when an animal threshes but even when it carries food on its back.[7]

[5] The Mishnah discusses how much produce a worker may eat while he works:

אוֹכֵל פּוֹעֵל קִשּׁוּת אֲפִלּוּ בְּדִינָר — **A worker may eat a cucumber, even** if it is

---

— NOTES —

3. Literally, *to return a loss to the owner.*
4. Which will cause them to do a less efficient job (*Meiri*).
5. *Tos. Yom Tov.*
6. After workers harvested a load of grapes, they would bring the grapes to the winepress and then return to the vines to harvest more grapes. They may bring some grapes with them from the winepress to eat on their way back to the vines (see *Meiri*).

7. Although the Torah states that it is forbidden to muzzle an animal while it *threshes,* in which case the produce is at the animal's feet where the animal can see it (see Mishnah 6:4 note 3), the same applies even when an animal is carrying a load on its back; even though it cannot see the food, one may not prevent it from eating from it (*Tos. Yom Tov*).

משניות בבא מציעא / פרק ז׳ / השוכר

וְכוֹתֶבֶת אֲפִלּוּ בְדִינָר. רַבִּי אֶלְעָזָר (בֶּן) חִסְמָא אוֹמֵר, לֹא יֹאכַל פּוֹעֵל יָתֵר עַל שְׂכָרוֹ. וַחֲכָמִים מַתִּירִין, אֲבָל מְלַמְּדִין אֶת הָאָדָם שֶׁלֹּא יְהֵא רַעַבְתָן, וִיהֵא סוֹתֵם אֶת הַפֶּתַח בְּפָנָיו.

[ו] **קוֹצֵץ** אָדָם עַל יְדֵי עַצְמוֹ, עַל יְדֵי בְּנוֹ וּבִתּוֹ הַגְּדוֹלִים, עַל יְדֵי עַבְדּוֹ וְשִׁפְחָתוֹ

— רע״ב —

לא יאכל פועל יותר על שכרו. דאמר קרא (דברים כג,כה) כנפשך, כשכירותו שעליו הוא מוסר את נפשו לעלות בכבש ולתלות באילן: מלמדין. אומרים לו דרך ארץ הוגנת. ותנא קמא פליג ואמר אין מלמדין. והלכה כחכמים: ויהא סותם את הפתח. שימנעו מלשכרו: (ו) קוצץ. ליטול מעות ולא יאכל: על ידי עצמו. בשביל עצמו:

worth a **dinar**,[1] וְכוֹתֶבֶת אֲפִלּוּ בְדִינָר — and he may eat **a date, even if it is worth a dinar.**[2] A worker who is allowed to eat from his employer's produce may eat as much as he wants[3] — no matter how much the produce is worth.

The Mishnah cites two other opinions:

לֹא יֹאכַל פּוֹעֵל — **R' Elazar** ben **Chisma says:** רַבִּי אֶלְעָזָר (בֶּן) חִסְמָא אוֹמֵר יָתֵר עַל שְׂכָרוֹ — **A worker may not eat** an amount of produce worth **more than his wages** for the day.[4] וַחֲכָמִים מַתִּירִין — **But the Sages** say that a worker is **permitted** by law to eat as much as he wants; אֲבָל מְלַמְּדִין אֶת הָאָדָם שֶׁלֹּא יְהֵא רַעַבְתָן — however, **we teach a person not to be a glutton,** because if a worker will eat too much, וִיהֵא סוֹתֵם אֶת הַפֶּתַח בְּפָנָיו — **he will close the doors** of employment **before himself,** that is, people will refuse to hire him.[5]

[6] The Mishnah discusses whether a worker can arrange to give up his right or the right of other workers to eat produce while working:

קוֹצֵץ אָדָם עַל יְדֵי עַצְמוֹ — **A person can make an agreement for himself** with his employer that he will not eat produce as he works, and in return, the employer will pay him extra. Although the Torah grants a worker the right to eat as he works, he can give up this right if he wishes.[1] עַל יְדֵי בְּנוֹ וּבִתּוֹ הַגְּדוֹלִים — A person can also make such an agreement **on behalf of his adult son or daughter,**[2] עַל יְדֵי עַבְדּוֹ וְשִׁפְחָתוֹ — **on behalf of his adult**

NOTES

[5]
1. A *dinar* was a considerable amount of money.
2. [Certain types of dates and cucumbers were expensive foods in the time of the Mishnah.]
3. Subject to the rules taught in the previous Mishnahs.
4. R' Elazar derives this law from a verse in the Torah (*Rav*).

5. The Tanna Kamma, on the other hand, holds that a worker should be allowed to eat as much as he wants (up to the amount of his wages). One should not tell a worker to cut back on his eating, because if he is hungry he might not work as well (*Rav, Hon Ashir*).

[6]
1. See *Meiri*.
2. That is, a boy over the age of 13 or a girl over the age of 12 (*Tos. Yom Tov*).

הַגְּדוֹלִים, עַל יְדֵי אִשְׁתּוֹ, מִפְּנֵי שֶׁיֵּשׁ בָּהֶן דָּעַת. אֲבָל אֵינוֹ קוֹצֵץ עַל יְדֵי בְנוֹ וּבִתּוֹ הַקְּטַנִּים, וְלֹא עַל יְדֵי עַבְדּוֹ וְשִׁפְחָתוֹ הַקְּטַנִּים, וְלֹא עַל יְדֵי בְהֶמְתּוֹ, מִפְּנֵי שֶׁאֵין בָּהֶן דָּעַת.

Canaanite **slave or maidservant,**[3] עַל יְדֵי אִשְׁתּוֹ — or **on behalf of his wife**[4]; that is, if a person's adult child, slave, or wife is hired to work with produce, he can make an agreement with their employer that they will not eat while they work, in return for a higher wage. The agreement is binding, and the child, slave, and wife are forbidden to eat while they work — provided that they know about the agreement and consent to it. מִפְּנֵי שֶׁיֵּשׁ בָּהֶן דָּעַת — **Since** they are adults, **they have** enough **understanding** to legally give up their rights; thus, if they consent to the agreement, it is binding.

In the following cases, though, one cannot make such an agreement: אֲבָל אֵינוֹ קוֹצֵץ עַל יְדֵי בְנוֹ וּבִתּוֹ הַקְּטַנִּים — **But [a person] cannot make** such **an agreement on behalf of his minor son or daughter,**[5] וְלֹא עַל יְדֵי עַבְדּוֹ וְשִׁפְחָתוֹ הַקְּטַנִּים — **nor on behalf of his minor** Canaanite **slave or maidservant,** וְלֹא עַל יְדֵי בְהֶמְתּוֹ — **nor on behalf of his animal** (i.e., if he hires out his animal to work with produce, he cannot agree to muzzle it as it works, in return for extra money).[6] מִפְּנֵי שֶׁאֵין בָּהֶן דָּעַת — He cannot make an agreement that his minor children or slaves will not eat while they work, even though they consent to the agreement, **because [minors] do not have** enough **understanding** to legally give up their rights; thus, an agreement that they make is not binding.[7] And a person cannot make an agreement to muzzle his animal, because it is Biblically prohibited to muzzle an animal while it works, and this prohibition cannot be waived through an agreement.[8]

[7] The Mishnah discusses laborers who are hired to work with fruit that is *neta reva'i,* which may not be eaten outside Jerusalem unless it is redeemed for money:[1]

NOTES

3. [See Mishnah 1:5 for a definition of Canaanite slave and maidservant.] The Mishnah refers to a master who hired out his Canaanite slave to work for someone else. If the slave is working with produce, he has the right to eat from it as he works just as a Jewish worker does.
4. The Mishnah refers to a wife who is an adult (*Rashash*).
5. That is, a boy younger than 13 or a girl younger than 12 (*Tos. Yom Tov*).
6. As we have learned in Mishnah 4, it is forbidden to prevent an animal from eating from produce with which it is working.
7. An agreement made by a minor is not legally binding, because he is considered to lack sufficient understanding of what he is agreeing to. Accordingly, since the Torah granted these minors the right to eat while they work, they do not lose that right even if they agree to give it up.
8. *Ritva* 92b.

[7]
1. [It is forbidden to eat or benefit from any fruit that grows on a tree during the first three years after it is planted. This fruit is known as *orlah.*] Fruit that grows on a tree during its fourth year is known as *neta reva'i* and may be eaten only in Jerusalem. If a person is unable to take the fruit to Jerusalem, he may redeem it for money that he takes to Jerusalem and uses to buy food to eat there (see Mishnah 4:8).

פרק ז: השוכר

[ז] הַשּׂוֹכֵר אֶת הַפּוֹעֲלִים לַעֲשׂוֹת בְּנֶטַע רְבָעִי שֶׁלּוֹ, הֲרֵי אֵלּוּ לֹא יֹאכֵלוּ. אִם לֹא הוֹדִיעָן, פּוֹדֶה וּמַאֲכִילָן. נִתְפָּרְסוּ עִגּוּלָיו, נִתְפַּתְּחוּ חָבִיּוֹתָיו, הֲרֵי אֵלּוּ לֹא יֹאכֵלוּ.

רע"ב

מפני שיש בהן דעת. **(ז)** וידעי, וקא מחלי: נטע רבעי. פירות של אילן בשנה הרביעית שאינן נאכלין אלא בירושלים, או פודה אותן, ומעלה הדמים לירושלים:

נתפרסו עגוליו. עגולי דבלה שנתפרדו, ושכר פועלים לחברן. **או חביות שנפתחו, ושכר פועלים לסתמן: הרי אלו לא יאכלו.** שכבר נגמרו מלאכתם, והוקבעו למעשר, והרי הן טבל:

הַשּׂוֹכֵר אֶת הַפּוֹעֲלִים לַעֲשׂוֹת בְּנֶטַע רְבָעִי שֶׁלּוֹ — If someone hires workers to harvest[2] his *neta reva'i* fruit, **הֲרֵי אֵלּוּ לֹא יֹאכֵלוּ** — these workers **may not eat** from the fruit while they harvest it, because *neta reva'i* may not be eaten outside Jerusalem. Moreover, the employer does not have to redeem the fruit to make it permissible for them to eat — as long as the workers accepted the job knowing that they would be working with *neta reva'i*.[3] **אִם לֹא הוֹדִיעָן** — However, if [the employer] did not let [the workers] know when he hired them that they would be harvesting fruit from which they cannot eat,[4] **פּוֹדֶה וּמַאֲכִילָן** — he must redeem the *neta reva'i* to make it permissible to eat, and allow [the workers] to eat from it. Since the workers accepted the job expecting to be allowed to eat as they work, the employer must arrange for them to be able to do so.[5]

A similar case:

נִתְפָּרְסוּ עִגּוּלָיו — If someone's **cakes of figs**[6] **became separated,** and he hires workers to re-press them into cakes, **נִתְפַּתְּחוּ חָבִיּוֹתָיו** — or **his barrels** of wine **opened,** and he hires workers to reseal them, **הֲרֵי אֵלּוּ לֹא יֹאכֵלוּ** — **these** workers **may not eat** from the figs or drink from the wine while they work, because the figs and the wine have already been fully processed and a worker does not have the right to eat from food that is fully processed.[7]

NOTES

2. *Tiferes Yisrael.*

3. Since they knew they would be working with *neta reva'i,* if they expected the employer to redeem the fruit, they should have stipulated this when they were hired (*Tos. Yom Tov*).

   For the same reason, they cannot demand that the employer pay them extra to make up for the fact that they cannot eat the produce (*Rabbeinu Yehonasan*).

4. For example, he hired workers to harvest fruit but did not tell them that the fruit was *neta reva'i* (*Tos. Yom Tov*).

5. If they had known that they would not be allowed to eat as they worked, they likely would not have accepted the job. Therefore, if they are not allowed to eat, they will have been hired under false pretenses [מֶקַּח טָעוּת] (*Tos. Yom Tov*).

6. It was common to dry figs and press them together to form large cakes (see Mishnah 2:1 note 2).

7. *Rashi.*

   As we learned in Mishnah 2, a worker does not have the right to eat from produce that has been detached from the ground once it is fully processed to the point when *maaser* must be separated from it. Figs are considered fully processed in this regard when they are pressed into cakes, and wine is fully processed when it is filtered and poured into barrels (*Maasros* 1:7-8). Even though these figs separated from their cakes and the wine barrels became unsealed, the figs and wine are nevertheless considered fully processed and the workers may not eat from them.

— רע"ב —

(ח) שׁוֹמְרֵי פֵּרוֹת. שׁוֹמְרֵי גִתּוֹת וַעֲרֵימוֹת וּפֵירוֹת תְּלוּשִׁים. אֲבָל שׁוֹמְרֵי גִנּוֹת וּפַרְדֵּסִים, אֵין אוֹכְלִים לֹא מֵהִלְכוֹת מְדִינָה וְלֹא מִן הַתּוֹרָה. דְשׁוֹמֵר לָאו כְּעוֹשֶׂה מַעֲשֶׂה דָמֵי: **מֵהִלְכוֹת מְדִינָה.** שֶׁכְּבָר נָהֲגוּ כֵן:

אִם לֹא הוֹדִיעָן, מְעַשֵּׂר וּמַאֲכִילָן.

[ח] **שׁוֹמְרֵי** פֵּרוֹת אוֹכְלִין מֵהִלְכוֹת מְדִינָה, אֲבָל לֹא מִן הַתּוֹרָה. אַרְבָּעָה שׁוֹמְרִין הֵן, שׁוֹמֵר חִנָּם, וְהַשּׁוֹאֵל, נוֹשֵׂא שָׂכָר, וְהַשּׂוֹכֵר.

אִם לֹא הוֹדִיעָן — However, if [the employer] did not let [the workers] know when he hired them that they would be working with food that was fully processed,[8] מְעַשֵּׂר וּמַאֲכִילָן — he must separate *maaser* from the figs and the wine,[9] and allow [the workers] to eat from them. Although workers are usually not entitled to eat from processed food, in this case, they must be allowed to eat, because they accepted the job with that expectation.[10]

[8] The Mishnah discusses the law of a *shomer* who watches and safeguards produce but does not work with it:

שׁוֹמְרֵי פֵּרוֹת — *Shomrim* who watch produce that has been detached from the ground אוֹכְלִין מֵהִלְכוֹת מְדִינָה — are allowed to eat from the produce **according to the local custom**,[1] אֲבָל לֹא מִן הַתּוֹרָה — **but not according to the Torah**, because the Torah gave the right to eat produce only to one who *works* with it, and watching produce is not like working with it.[2]

Once the Tanna mentions *shomrim*, he goes on to list the categories of *shomrim*, and the laws that apply to each one:

אַרְבָּעָה שׁוֹמְרִין הֵן — **There are four** categories of *shomrim* mentioned in the Torah:[3] שׁוֹמֵר חִנָּם — **an unpaid** *shomer*, וְהַשּׁוֹאֵל — **a borrower**, נוֹשֵׂא שָׂכָר — **a paid** *shomer*, וְהַשּׂוֹכֵר — **and a renter**.

NOTES
---

8. For example, he hired workers to press figs into cakes. The workers assumed that they would be working with figs that were not yet pressed into cakes and are thus not fully processed, and thus, they would be entitled to eat from the figs. However, the employer assigned them to work with figs that had already been pressed into cakes once before, and thus were fully processed (*Tos. Yom Tov*).

9. Since this food is fully processed to the point when *maaser* must be separated, it cannot be eaten until *maaser* (as well as the other necessary portions; see Mishnah 4:8) is separated from it.

10. See note 5.
Similarly, if workers were hired to work with any type of forbidden food, if they did not know when they were hired that the food was forbidden, the employer must pay them extra to make up for the fact that they cannot eat as they work (see *Talmid HaRashba*).

[8]

1. If the owner and the worker do not specify their own conditions, they must follow the local custom, as taught in Mishnah 1.

2. The Mishnah's ruling applies only to a *shomer* who watches produce that has been detached from the ground (but is not yet fully processed). Since someone who *works* with this type of produce may eat it according to the Torah (see Mishnah 2), the general custom permits even a *shomer* to do so. The law is different where the *shomer* is guarding a field or orchard, where the produce is still attached to the ground. Since even one who actually works with attached produce (before the harvesting) is not permitted by the Torah to eat it, a *shomer* does not have that right even according to the general custom (see *Rav*).

3. *Exodus* 22:6-14.

משניות בבא מציעא / פרק ז: השוכר

שׁוֹמֵר חִנָּם נִשְׁבָּע עַל הַכֹּל, וְהַשּׁוֹאֵל מְשַׁלֵּם אֶת הַכֹּל. וְנוֹשֵׂא שָׂכָר וְהַשּׂוֹכֵר נִשְׁבָּעִים עַל הַשְּׁבוּרָה, וְעַל הַשְּׁבוּיָה, וְעַל הַמֵּתָה,

— רע"ב —

נשבע על הכל. על כל המאורעות הכתובות בשאר שומרים לחיוב, נשבע שכך עלתה לו ופטור: משלם את הכל.

גנבה ואבדה ואונסים: נושא שכר וכו'. וכולהו נפקא לן מקראי פרשת ואלה המשפטים. פרשה ראשונה כי יתן איש אל רעהו וגו' (שמות כב,ו) נאמרה בשומר חנם, שכן פטר בו גנבה ואבדה. שניה, כי יתן איש אל רעהו חמור או שור או שה (שם פסוק ט') נאמרה בשומר שכר, שכן חייב בו גנבה ואבדה, דכתיב בה (שם פסוק י"א) אם גנב יגנב מעמו ישלם לבעליו, אין לי אלא גנבה, אבדה מנין, תלמוד לומר אם גנב יגנב, מכל מקום. ועוד, קל וחומר, ומה גנבה שקרובה לאונס חייב, אבדה שקרובה לפשיעה לא כל שכן. ושוכר, כיון שאין כל הנאה שלו דינו כשומר שכר. והשואל, מפורש בפרשה שלישית, וכי ישאל איש מעם רעהו ונשבר או מת בעליו אין עמו שלם ישלם (שם פסוק יג):

All *shomrim* must pay the owner if the item in their care suffers loss or damage as a result of their negligence. The Torah mentions two other instances of loss or damage, where some *shomrim* pay and some do not: (a) loss that was not caused by negligence but which the *shomer* could have prevented had he taken extra care; and (b) a complete accident, which the *shomer* could not have prevented. The Mishnah states the cases in which each type of *shomer* must pay. It begins with the unpaid *shomer*:

שׁוֹמֵר חִנָּם נִשְׁבָּע עַל הַכֹּל — An **unpaid *shomer* may swear** that the item he was watching was lost **in all** of the cases stated in the Torah (avoidable and unavoidable accidents) and he thereby exempts himself from payment.[4] He is liable only for negligence.[5]

The law of the borrower:

וְהַשּׁוֹאֵל מְשַׁלֵּם אֶת הַכֹּל — **The borrower must pay for all** types of loss, even those that resulted from unavoidable accidents.[6]

The law of the paid *shomer* and the renter:

וְנוֹשֵׂא שָׂכָר וְהַשּׂוֹכֵר — The **paid *shomer* and the renter**[7] נִשְׁבָּעִים עַל הַשְּׁבוּרָה וְעַל הַשְּׁבוּיָה וְעַל הַמֵּתָה — **may swear that** an animal in their care suffered **breakage** of a limb, **capture, or** a natural **death** (which the Torah gives as examples of unavoidable accidents) and thus exempt themselves from

---

NOTES

4. If any type of *shomer* claims that the item was lost or damaged in a way for which he is not liable, but he cannot prove his claim, the Torah requires him to swear that it is true. If he does not want to swear, he must pay (see Mishnah 3:1).

5. The Sages derive the laws of the unpaid *shomer* from verses 6-8 there (see *Rav*).

6. As stated in verse 13 there (*Rav*). Since a borrower benefits from having the item in his care (he may use it) and he does not pay for that benefit, his responsibility is greater than that of all the other *shomrim*. Even a borrower, however, is not liable for damage that resulted from using the object for the purpose for which he borrowed it (Gemara 96b-97a), because the owner of the item clearly allowed him to use it in that way.

7. Referring to a renter, the Torah states only that he is not treated like a borrower (verse 14). Tannaim disagree whether he is regarded as a paid *shomer* (because the right to use the item is like payment) or an unpaid *shomer*. The Tanna of our Mishnah holds that a renter is like a paid *shomer* (Gemara 93a).

— רע״ב —

(ט) זאב אחד אינו אונס. ונושא שכר ושוכר חייבין עליו. דכתיב (שמות כב,יב) הטרפה לא ישלם, יש טרפה שהוא משלם, ויש טרפה שאינו משלם: בשעת משלחת זאבים. כשחיה רעה משולחת, קופצת היא על אדם אחד. ואין הלכה כרבי יהודה ולא כידוע הבבלי:

וּמְשַׁלְּמִין אֶת הָאֲבֵדָה וְאֶת הַגְּנֵבָה.

[ט] **זְאֵב** אֶחָד אֵינוֹ אֹנֶס, שְׁנֵי זְאֵבִים אֹנֶס. רַבִּי יְהוּדָה אוֹמֵר, בִּשְׁעַת מִשְׁלַחַת זְאֵבִים אַף זְאֵב אֶחָד אֹנֶס. שְׁנֵי כְלָבִים אֵינוֹ אֹנֶס. יַדּוּעַ הַבַּבְלִי אוֹמֵר מִשּׁוּם רַבִּי מֵאִיר, מֵרוּחַ אַחַת אֵינוֹ אֹנֶס, מִשְׁתֵּי רוּחוֹת אֹנֶס.

---

payment, וּמְשַׁלְּמִין אֶת הָאֲבֵדָה וְאֶת הַגְּנֵבָה — **but they must pay in a case of loss or theft** (which are given as examples of mishaps that can be avoided).[8]

[9] We learned in the previous Mishnah that a paid *shomer* (or renter) must pay the owner if the item in his care is lost or stolen, but he does not have to pay in the event of an unavoidable accident. This Mishnah cites cases in which a shepherd — a paid *shomer* — loses sheep from his flock, and it teaches whether these are unavoidable losses or not:

זְאֵב אֶחָד אֵינוֹ אֹנֶס — A loss of sheep caused by the attack of **a single wolf** is **not unavoidable,** because a shepherd can drive away one wolf. He must therefore pay for the loss, since he is a paid *shomer*.[1] שְׁנֵי זְאֵבִים אֹנֶס — **But** a loss caused by **two wolves** is **unavoidable,** because a shepherd cannot drive away two wolves together. He is thus exempt from payment. רַבִּי יְהוּדָה אוֹמֵר — R' Yehudah says: בִּשְׁעַת מִשְׁלַחַת זְאֵבִים — **During a time when wolves are sent out** to attack, אַף זְאֵב אֶחָד אֹנֶס — **even** a loss caused by **a single wolf is unavoidable,** because at such times beasts are especially bold and dangerous.[2]

The Mishnah cites a dispute about an attack by dogs:

שְׁנֵי כְלָבִים אֵינוֹ אֹנֶס — A loss caused by an attack of **two dogs** is **not unavoidable,** because a shepherd can drive dogs away even if two come at once. יַדּוּעַ הַבַּבְלִי אוֹמֵר מִשּׁוּם רַבִּי מֵאִיר — **However, Yaddua the Babylonian says in the name of R' Meir:** מֵרוּחַ אַחַת אֵינוֹ אֹנֶס — **If** both dogs approached **from one direction,** the loss is **not unavoidable,** because the shepherd could have driven each one away on its own; מִשְׁתֵּי רוּחוֹת אֹנֶס — **but if** they approached **from two directions, the loss is unavoidable.**

The Mishnah cites more cases:

--- NOTES ---

8. The laws of the paid *shomer* are derived from verses 9-11 (see *Rav*). The examples of breakage, capture, death, and theft appear in that passage.

[9]

1. However, if he tried to chase the wolf away and failed, the loss of the sheep is an unavoidable accident, for which he is not liable (*Shulchan Aruch, Choshen Mishpat* 303:5).

2. When wild beasts are provoked by Heaven into attacking [as can be seen from an increase in the intensity or number of attacks in the area], even a single beast will jump on a person (*Rashi*).

משניות בבא מציעא / פרק ז: השוכר

הַלִּסְטִים הֲרֵי זֶה אֹנֶס. הָאֲרִי, וְהַדֹּב, וְהַנָּמֵר, וְהַבַּרְדְּלָס, וְהַנָּחָשׁ הֲרֵי זֶה אֹנֶס. אֵימָתַי, בִּזְמַן שֶׁבָּאוּ מֵאֲלֵיהֶן. אֲבָל אִם הוֹלִיכָן לִמְקוֹם גְּדוּדֵי חַיָּה וְלִסְטִים אֵינוֹ אֹנֶס.

[י] **מֵתָה** כְּדַרְכָּהּ הֲרֵי זֶה אֹנֶס, סִגְּפָהּ וָמֵתָה אֵינוֹ אֹנֶס. עָלְתָה לְרָאשֵׁי צוּקִין וְנָפְלָה הֲרֵי זֶה אֹנֶס; הֶעֱלָהּ לְרָאשֵׁי צוּקִין, וְנָפְלָה וָמֵתָה אֵינוֹ אֹנֶס.

— רע״ב —

הלסטים. חד לסטים הרי זה אונס: (י) **סגפה.** עינה אותה ברעב, או שהושיבה בקיץ בחמה ובחורף בצנה: **עלתה לראשי צוקין.** שתקפתה, ועלתה לראשי הרים גבוהים:

הַלִּסְטִים הֲרֵי זֶה אֹנֶס — A loss caused by even a single **armed robber is unavoidable**,[3] הָאֲרִי וְהַדֹּב וְהַנָּמֵר וְהַבַּרְדְּלָס וְהַנָּחָשׁ הֲרֵי זֶה אֹנֶס — and **a loss caused by a lion, a bear, a leopard, a hyena, or a snake is unavoidable**. אֵימָתַי — **When are these losses unavoidable?** בִּזְמַן שֶׁבָּאוּ מֵאֲלֵיהֶן — **When** [armed robbers or such beasts] **come to the shepherd's flock on their own.** אֲבָל אִם הוֹלִיכָן לִמְקוֹם גְּדוּדֵי חַיָּה וְלִסְטִים — **But if** [the shepherd] **leads** [the flock] **to a place where there are groups of beasts or armed robbers** and his sheep are attacked, אֵינוֹ אֹנֶס — **this is not an unavoidable loss.**[4]

[10] The Mishnah continues defining when the loss of an animal is unavoidable and when the loss is not unavoidable:

מֵתָה כְּדַרְכָּהּ הֲרֵי זֶה אֹנֶס — **If it dies of natural causes, this is an unavoidable accident;** סִגְּפָהּ וָמֵתָה אֵינוֹ אֹנֶס — **but if he afflicted it** (for example, he starved it or exposed it to severe heat or cold) **and later it died, this is not an unavoidable accident.**[1] עָלְתָה לְרָאשֵׁי צוּקִין וְנָפְלָה — **If it went up to the tops of steep mountains** on its own, against the will of the *shomer*,[2] **and fell** to its death, הֲרֵי זֶה אֹנֶס — **this is an unavoidable accident;** הֶעֱלָהּ לְרָאשֵׁי צוּקִין וְנָפְלָה וָמֵתָה — **but if he brought it up to the tops of steep mountains and it fell and died,** אֵינוֹ אֹנֶס — **this is not an unavoidable accident.**[3]

The Mishnah teaches a method through which *shomrim* can exclude themselves from their normal obligations:

— NOTES —

3. Even if the shepherd himself is armed, he is not required to risk his life in order to fight off an armed robber (*Tos. Yom Tov*).

4. This would be considered negligence on the part of the shepherd [for which even an unpaid *shomer* must pay] (*Meiri*).

[10]
1. Not only is such behavior avoidable, but it is negligent. Thus, even an unpaid *shomer* would have to pay in this circumstance (*Tos. Yom Tov*).

The shepherd is held responsible even if the animal did not die right away, because its abuse might have caused an internal injury that eventually led to its death (*Tos. Yom Tov*).

2. The shepherd tried to stop the animal but it overpowered him (*Rav*).

3. In fact, it is negligence (see note 1).

Even if the shepherd did not *take* the animal up the mountain, but he could have prevented it from doing so, he is liable (*Tos. Yom Tov*). This, however, is not negligence, so only a paid *shomer* would have to pay, while an unpaid *shomer* would be exempt.

[141] **MISHNAH BAVA METZIA** / Chapter 7: *Hasocheir*   7/11

— רע״ב —

מַתְּנָה שׁוֹמֵר חִנָּם לִהְיוֹת פָּטוּר מִשְּׁבוּעָה, וְהַשּׁוֹאֵל לִהְיוֹת פָּטוּר מִלְּשַׁלֵּם, נוֹשֵׂא שָׂכָר וְהַשּׂוֹכֵר לִהְיוֹת פְּטוּרִין מִשְּׁבוּעָה וּמִלְּשַׁלֵּם. [יא] **כָּל** הַמַּתְנֶה עַל מַה שֶּׁכָּתוּב בַּתּוֹרָה

מתנה שומר חנם להיות פטור משבועה: והאי לאו מתנה על מה שכתוב בתורה הוא, אלא שאומר לו, אי אפשי להיות שומר לך אלא בכך. ושומר לא נחית לשמירה

עד דמשיך לבהמה, והאי כי משיך, כבר פירש על מנת שאין לו עליו שבועה, ולא שעבד נפשיה לירד בתורת שומרין אלא למקצת, ולמה שירד ירד: (יא) כל המתנה על מה שכתוב בתורה תנאו בטל. כולה מתניתין רבי מאיר היא, דסבר המתנה על מה שכתוב בתורה אפילו בדבר שבממון תנאו בטל. ואינה הלכה. אלא בדבר שבממון אפילו שהתנה על מה שכתוב בתורה, תנאו קיים:

מַתְּנָה שׁוֹמֵר חִנָּם לִהְיוֹת פָּטוּר מִשְּׁבוּעָה — **An unpaid *shomer* can make a condition that he will be exempt from swearing** in a case where he would normally have to swear. When the *shomer* accepts the item, he can say to the owner that he agrees to watch it only on condition that if it is lost or stolen, he does not have to swear in order to exempt himself from payment.[4] וְהַשּׁוֹאֵל לִהְיוֹת פָּטוּר מִלְּשַׁלֵּם — **And a borrower,** who must pay for all types of loss, can make a condition **that he will be exempt from paying.** נוֹשֵׂא שָׂכָר וְהַשּׂוֹכֵר לִהְיוֹת פְּטוּרִין מִשְּׁבוּעָה וּמִלְּשַׁלֵּם — And **a paid *shomer* and a renter** can make a condition **that they will be exempt from swearing** in cases of unavoidable loss (where they would normally be required to swear) **and from paying** in cases of theft and loss (where they would normally be obligated to pay).

[11] Having taught that a *shomer* may make a condition to exempt himself from his normal responsibilities, the Mishnah teaches some laws about conditions in general. Most legal acts can be made to depend on the fulfillment of a condition — the legal act takes effect only if the condition is fulfilled. However, a condition is valid only if it meets certain guidelines. If an act is made to depend on an invalid condition, it is as if the act was performed without any condition, and thus the act takes effect regardless of whether the condition is fulfilled.[1] The Mishnah gives some guidelines about which conditions are valid and which are not valid:

כָּל הַמַּתְנֶה עַל מַה שֶּׁכָּתוּב בַּתּוֹרָה — **If anyone makes a condition that goes**

NOTES

4. Generally, an unpaid *shomer* who claims that the item was lost or stolen (without negligence on his part) does not have to pay, provided that he swears his claim is true (see Mishnah 8). This Mishnah teaches that he can exempt himself from having to swear.

He can even stipulate that he is exempt from payment if he was negligent. The Mishnah does not mention this case, because it is unusual for an owner to entrust his property to a *shomer* who will not pay for negligence (*Rabbeinu Yehonasan*).

[Our Mishnah seems to contradict the general rule stated in the next Mishnah, that one cannot make a condition that goes against the Torah. See note 2 there.]

[11]

1. For example, a man betroths a woman on condition that she give him a sum of money. If the condition is valid, she is betrothed only if she gives him the money. If the condition is not valid (i.e., it does not meet the guidelines for a proper condition, as the Mishnah will explain) she is betrothed regardless of whether she gives him the money or not.

רע״ב

כל תנאי שיש בו מעשה מתחלה. שהקדים מעשה שיש עליו לעשות, לתנאי שהוא מבקש ממנו. כגון

תְּנָאוֹ בָטֵל. וְכָל תְּנַאי שֶׁיֵּשׁ מַעֲשֶׂה בִתְחִלָּתוֹ תְּנָאוֹ בָּטֵל.

הרי מעשה זה שלך אם תעשה דבר פלוני. דלא דמי לתנאי בני גד ובני ראובן אם יעברו ונתתם, היינו תנאי קודם למעשה. והוי מעשה קיים: **תנאו בטל.** ואף על פי שלא קיים בעל התנאי את התנאי:

against something written in the Torah, תְּנָאוֹ בָטֵל — **his condition is not valid.**[2] For example, a man betroths a woman on the condition that he does not have to engage in marital relations. Since the Torah obligates a husband to provide his wife with marital relations,[3] this condition is not valid.[4]

In addition, a condition must be worded in a specific manner:

וְכָל תְּנַאי שֶׁיֵּשׁ מַעֲשֶׂה בִתְחִלָּתוֹ — **Any condition in which** the person states **the action** being done **before** stating the condition it depends on, תְּנָאוֹ בָטֵל — **is not a valid condition.** For example, if a person gives someone a gift and says, "I give you this gift on condition that you walk a mile," the condition is invalid because he mentioned the action he is doing ("I give you this gift") before the condition ("on condition that you walk a mile").[5] For the condition to be valid, he would have to say, "If you walk a mile, I will give you this gift."[6]

── NOTES ──

2. [This is not a contradiction to the law taught in the previous Mishnah — that a *shomer* may make a condition that he be exempt from the obligations that the Torah sets for a *shomer*. In that case, the condition does not go against the Torah's laws, because the Torah does not require a person to accept the responsibilities and obligations of a *shomer*. The Torah simply says that when a person agrees to become one of the four *shomrim*, he is subject to a specific set of laws. This person is saying that he is not willing to become one of the *shomrim* described in the Torah. Instead, he agrees to guard the object under a different set of terms, which he now arranges with the owner of the object (*Rav* to Mishnah 10, *Ramban*).]

3. *Exodus* 21:10; *Kesubos* 47b.

4. Since the condition is not valid, the legal act that depended on the condition takes effect, but the condition does not have to be fulfilled. Accordingly, the betrothal is valid and the husband is required to engage in marital relations.

[There is a dispute among Tannaim whether this law applies even to conditions that involve only money. For example, if a man betroths a woman on the condition that he will not provide her with food, the condition *is* valid according to R' Yehudah, even though it goes against the Torah — which obligates a husband to provide his wife with food (*Exodus* 21:10). Since the obligation to feed one's wife is purely a monetary matter, she can give up her right to receive food, because a person can waive any monetary right. Thus, if she agrees to the condition, it is valid. R' Meir, however, disagrees. He maintains that any condition against the Torah's laws is invalid — even if it involves only money (Gemara 94a).]

5. Since the condition is not valid, the gift belongs to the recipient even if he does not fulfill the condition.

6. This law is learned from the condition made by Moses with the tribes of Gad and Reuven. Before the Jews entered Eretz Yisrael, they conquered the land of Gilead, which is east of the Jordan River. The tribes of Gad and Reuven wanted to settle in that land rather than in Eretz Yisrael. Moses agreed to this on condition that the men of those tribes join the rest of the Jews in their battles to conquer Eretz Yisrael (*Numbers* Chapter 32). The law is that no condition is valid unless it is similar to the condition made by Moses. Since Moses stated the condition before he stated the action (there 32:29), all conditions must be worded the same way

[143] MISHNAH BAVA METZIA / Chapter 7: *Hasocheir*

וְכָל שֶׁאֶפְשָׁר לוֹ לְקַיְּמוֹ בְּסוֹפוֹ, וְהִתְנָה עָלָיו מִתְּחִלָּתוֹ תְּנָאוֹ קַיָּם.

— רע"ב —

וכל שאפשר לו לקיימו בסופו. והיה תנאי קודם למעשה תנאו קיים. אבל אי אפשר לו לקיימו, התנאי בטל והמעשה קיים. שאינו אלא כמפליג בדברים. שאין בלבו לשום תנאי, אלא להקניט בעלמא מרחיק ודוחה את חבירו בדברים:

The Mishnah states what kind of condition *is* valid:

וְכָל שֶׁאֶפְשָׁר לוֹ לְקַיְּמוֹ בְּסוֹפוֹ — **Any** condition **that is possible to eventually fulfill,** וְהִתְנָה עָלָיו מִתְּחִלָּתוֹ — **and [the one making the condition] stated the condition at the beginning,** before stating the action (as taught earlier), תְּנָאוֹ קַיָּם — **it is a valid condition.** However, if a condition is impossible to fulfill,[7] or if the action was stated first, it is not valid.

NOTES

in order to be valid (*Rav*). [Other guidelines for conditions are also inferred from Moses' condition; see *Kiddushin* 3:4.]

7. For example, if a man gave his wife a *get* (bill of divorce) and said, "If you fly up to the sky, you will be divorced," the divorce takes effect even though she obviously cannot fly (Gemara 94a).

Such a condition is not valid because we assume that it was not meant seriously but was simply said to annoy the other person (*Rav*).

Chapter Eight

משניות בבא מציעא / פרק ח: השואל את הפרה

פרק שמיני

— רע"ב —

השואל את הפרה. (א) השואל את הפרה ושאלה בעלה עמה. אם היו בעליה של פרה אצל השואל לעשות מלאכתו, בין שהיו שאולים אצלו או שכורים, בין באותה מלאכה של פרה, בין לעשות מלאכה אחרת, אם מתה פטור: שנאמר

[א] הַשּׁוֹאֵל אֶת הַפָּרָה וְשָׁאַל בְּעָלֶיהָ עִמָּהּ, אוֹ שָׂכַר בְּעָלֶיהָ עִמָּהּ, שָׁאַל אֶת הַבְּעָלִים אוֹ שְׂכָרָן וּלְאַחַר כָּךְ שָׁאַל אֶת הַפָּרָה וָמֵתָה, פָּטוּר, שֶׁנֶּאֱמַר, אִם בְּעָלָיו עִמּוֹ לֹא יְשַׁלֵּם. אֲבָל שָׁאַל אֶת הַפָּרָה וְאַחַר כָּךְ שָׁאַל אֶת הַבְּעָלִים אוֹ שְׂכָרָן וָמֵתָה, חַיָּב,

אם בעליו עמו לא ישלם. והכי משמע, אם בעל השור עמו, עם השואל. שהוא שאול או שכור לו פרתו, לא ישלם: אבל שאל את הפרה בו'. אם היה עמו בשעת אונסים ולא היה עמו בשעת שאלה, חייב. דלא הוי שאלה בבעלים לאפטורי, אלא אם כן היה עמו בשעת שאלה:

---

[1] We learned in the previous chapter (Mishnah 7:8) that someone who borrows an item must pay for any damage or loss that happens to it, even if it was the result of a complete accident and there was nothing he could have done to prevent it. The Mishnah now teaches an exception to this rule:

הַשּׁוֹאֵל אֶת הַפָּרָה וְשָׁאַל בְּעָלֶיהָ עִמָּהּ — If someone borrowed a cow and borrowed its owner along with it, that is, at the time he borrowed the cow, he asked its owner to do some work for him without pay, and the owner agreed;[1] אוֹ שָׂכַר בְּעָלֶיהָ עִמָּהּ — or if at the time he borrowed the cow he hired its owner along with it; שָׁאַל אֶת הַבְּעָלִים אוֹ שְׂכָרָן — or if he first borrowed or hired the owner, וּלְאַחַר כָּךְ שָׁאַל אֶת הַפָּרָה — and afterward, while the owner was still working for him, he borrowed the cow as well; וָמֵתָה — in each of these cases, if [the cow] died, even if the owner is no longer working for him at that time, פָּטוּר — he is exempt from paying for it, because the owner was working for him when he borrowed the cow. שֶׁנֶּאֱמַר "אִם בְּעָלָיו עִמּוֹ לֹא יְשַׁלֵּם" — As it states (Exodus 22:14): *if its owner is working with him, [the borrower] shall not pay.* This teaches that as long as the animal's owner is working for the borrower when he borrows it, he does not have to pay for its damage or loss.[2]

אֲבָל שָׁאַל אֶת הַפָּרָה — However, if he first borrowed the cow, וְאַחַר כָּךְ שָׁאַל אֶת הַבְּעָלִים אוֹ שְׂכָרָן — and only afterward borrowed or hired the cow's owner, וָמֵתָה — and [the cow] then died, חַיָּב — [the borrower] is obligated to pay

---

— NOTES —

[1]
1. Even if the work the owner does for the borrower has nothing to do with the work that will be done by the cow (*Rav*); for example, the borrower asked the owner to bring him a drink of water and he agreed to do it (*Tiferes Yisrael,* from Gemara 97a).

2. The words *if its owner is with him* mean that he is with him as his employee. The Gemara shows that these words refer to the time when the cow is borrowed (and not when it dies). Thus, the verse teaches that if the owner was working for the borrower at the time he borrowed the cow, the borrower is free from paying for the cow when it dies (*Rav*). This will be explained further in note 4.

The borrower is free from paying in this case even if the owner is no longer working for him when the cow dies (Gemara 96a).

MISHNAH BAVA METZIA / Chapter 8: Hashoeil es Haparah

— רע״ב —

שנאמר בעליו אין
עמו שלם ישלם. והכי
קא ממעטינן קרא, בעליו
אין עמו בשעת שאלה, אף
על פי שהיה עמו בשעת
שבירה ומיתה, שלם ישלם:

[ב] **הַשּׁוֹאֵל** אֶת הַפָּרָה, שֶׁאֲלָה חֲצִי הַיּוֹם וּשְׂכָרָהּ חֲצִי הַיּוֹם, שֶׁאֲלָה הַיּוֹם וּשְׂכָרָהּ לְמָחָר, שָׂכַר אַחַת וְשָׁאַל אַחַת וָמֵתָה, שֶׁנֶּאֱמַר, בְּעָלָיו אֵין עִמּוֹ שַׁלֵּם יְשַׁלֵּם.

---

for it, because the owner of the cow was not working for the borrower when the cow was borrowed.[3] "בְּעָלָיו אֵין עִמּוֹ שַׁלֵּם יְשַׁלֵּם" — שֶׁנֶּאֱמַר — As it states (22:13 there): *if the owner is not working with him, [the borrower] shall surely pay.*[4]

[2] We learned in Mishnah 7:8 that a renter does *not* have to pay for accidental losses that he could not have prevented. Our Mishnah deals with someone who was both a renter and a borrower and the animal he was using died accidentally. The question is whether it was a rented animal that died or a borrowed one. The Mishnah begins by presenting three cases of how he became both a renter and a borrower, and then gives the law for all three cases: הַשּׁוֹאֵל אֶת הַפָּרָה — **Someone borrows a cow,** שֶׁאֲלָה חֲצִי הַיּוֹם וּשְׂכָרָהּ חֲצִי הַיּוֹם — and either (1) **he borrowed it for half the day and rented it for the other half of the day,** שֶׁאֲלָה הַיּוֹם וּשְׂכָרָהּ לְמָחָר — or (2) **he borrowed it for a full day and rented it for the next day,** שָׂכַר אַחַת וְשָׁאַל אַחַת — or (3) **he rented one cow from the owner and borrowed another one from him;** וָמֵתָה — **and [the cow] died,** but we do not know whether it died during the time it was borrowed or during the time it was rented, or whether it was the borrowed cow that died or the rented one.[1]

NOTES

3. Even if the owner was working for the borrower when the cow died, since he was not working for him when he borrowed the cow, he is obligated to pay. The key moment is when the cow is borrowed, not when it dies (*Rav*).

4. There is seemingly no need for the Torah to say this. Since the verse quoted above said that the borrower does not have to pay if the owner is working for him, it is obvious that if he is not working for him he does have to pay. Why then does the Torah say it? We must therefore say that when the verse says *the owner is not [working] with him,* it does not mean that he is not working for him at all; rather, it means that he was not working with him when he *borrowed the cow.* Even though he is working with him when the animal dies, if he was not working for him when he borrowed the cow, the borrower must pay (*Rav, Tiferes Yisrael,* from Gemara 96a). [The time of borrowing is considered the key because that is when the borrower becomes responsible not only for returning the animal but also for feeding it (*Gemara*).]

Although the Mishnah discusses a case in which the cow died on its own (which is the case discussed by the verse), the same law applies if the cow was stolen, lost, or died because the borrower was negligent. Moreover, this law applies not only to a borrower but to all *shomrim.* Thus, if an unpaid *shomer* took the job of caring for an object while its owner was working for him, he does not have to pay for anything that happens to it even if he was negligent (*Rambam Commentary; Tos. R' Akiva Eiger*).

[2]

1. If it was the borrowed cow that died, or if the cow died during the time in which it was borrowed, then the borrower must

[148] **משניות בבא מציעא / פרק ח: השואל את הפרה**

הַמַּשְׁאִיל אוֹמֵר שְׁאוּלָה מֵתָה, בַּיּוֹם (ב) הַמַּשְׁאִיל אוֹמֵר
שְׁאוּלָה מֵתָה. ואתא חייב
שֶׁהָיְתָה שְׁאוּלָה מֵתָה, בְּשָׁעָה שֶׁהָיְתָה בחווסיה: איני יודע. שמא
שְׁאוּלָה מֵתָה, וְהַלָּה אוֹמֵר אֵינִי יוֹדֵעַ, חַיָּב. מן האווסיס: חייב. הא

— רע״ב —

מתניתין לא אפשר לאוקמה כמשמטה, דהא קיימא לן (צ״ו,ב תוס׳ ד״ה רב נחמן בשם רש״י) מנה לי
בידך והלה אומר איני יודע, ישבע שבועת היסת שאינו יודע, ופטור. להכי מוקמינן לה בגמרא (צ״ח,א),
כגון שיש עסק שבועה דאורייתא ביניהם. כגון דאמר ליה, שתי פרות מסרתי לך, חד יומא בשאלה,
וחד יומא בשכירות, ומתו תרוייהו בעידן שאלה. ואמר ליה שואל, חדא אין, בעידן שאלה מתה, וחדא
לא ידענא. והוי ליה מודה במקצת וחייב שבועה, ומתוך שאינו יכול לישבע, משלם. ודמיא להך, מנה
לי בידך, ואמר ליה היאך, חמשין ידענא וחמשין לא ידענא. הוי ליה מחוייב שבועה ואינו יכול לישבע,
ומתוך שאינו יכול לישבע, משלם:

Whatever the case, there were no witnesses to say what really happened. The Mishnah now teaches that the law in these cases depends on the claims made by the borrower and lender. There are four possible sets of claims and the law is different for each of them. The first set of claims:

הַמַּשְׁאִיל אוֹמֵר שְׁאוּלָה מֵתָה — **If the lender says, "The borrowed [cow] is definitely the one that died";** בַּיּוֹם שֶׁהָיְתָה שְׁאוּלָה מֵתָה — or, in the case where he borrowed it for one day and rented it for another, the lender says, **"It definitely died on the day it was borrowed";** בְּשָׁעָה שֶׁהָיְתָה שְׁאוּלָה מֵתָה — or in the case where he borrowed it for half a day and rented it for the other half of the day, the lender says, **"It definitely died during the time it was borrowed";** וְהַלָּה אוֹמֵר אֵינִי יוֹדֵעַ — **and** in all of these cases, **the other one** [the borrower] **says, "I do not know** what happened": חַיָּב — [the borrower] **is obligated** to pay for the cow.[2] Since the borrower would have to swear an oath in this case to free himself from paying, and he cannot swear that he is exempt because he admits that he does not know what really happened, he is required to pay.[3]

--- NOTES ---

pay for it. If the rented cow died, or the cow died during the time it was rented, then he does not have to pay for it.

2. The simple meaning of the Mishnah is that the borrower must pay because the lender is certain of his claim and the borrower is not. Although the Gemara cites a dispute about this, the accepted view is that a person who does not know whether he is obligated to pay cannot be forced to pay based simply on someone else's definite claim [בָּרִי וְשֶׁמָּא לָאו בָּרִי עָדִיף]. For this reason, Rav (based on Gemara 97b) explains that the Mishnah is speaking about a special case where, in addition to their claims, the borrower is also obligated to make an oath about his claim. This will be explained in the next note.

3. The rule is that whenever a person must swear a Biblical oath to free himself

from paying — and he cannot do so — he is obligated to pay [מִתּוֹךְ שֶׁאֵינוֹ יָכוֹל לִשָּׁבַע מְשַׁלֵּם] (Gemara 98a). Since the borrower must swear an oath and he cannot do so, he must pay for the cow in question even though the lender cannot prove his claim.

The borrower is required to swear an oath because the Mishnah speaks of a case where he actually borrowed another cow, besides the one they are disputing. Both cows were partially borrowed and partially rented, and both died. The lender is now demanding to be paid for both, claiming that both died during the time they were borrowed. The borrower admits that one of them died while it was borrowed and he must pay for it, but he is unsure whether the other one died while it was borrowed or while it was rented. Since he admits to part of the lender's

[149] **MISHNAH BAVA METZIA** / Chapter 8: *Hashoeil es Haparah*

הַשּׂוֹכֵר אוֹמֵר שְׁכוּרָה מֵתָה, בְּיוֹם שֶׁהָיְתָה שְׁכוּרָה מֵתָה, בְּשָׁעָה שֶׁהָיְתָה שְׁכוּרָה מֵתָה, וְהַלָּה אוֹמֵר אֵינִי יוֹדֵעַ, פָּטוּר. זֶה אוֹמֵר שְׁאוּלָה וְזֶה אוֹמֵר שְׂכוּרָה, יִשָּׁבַע הַשּׂוֹכֵר שֶׁשְּׂכוּרָה מֵתָה.

— רע״ב —

ישבע השוכר ששכורה מתה. הא נמי לא אפשר לאוקמה כמשמטה, דהא קיימא לן (בבא קמא לה,ב) טענו חטים והודה לו בשעורים, פטור אף

The second set of claims:

הַשּׂוֹכֵר אוֹמֵר שְׁכוּרָה מֵתָה — **If the renter**[4] says, "The rented [cow] is definitely the one that **died**," בְּיוֹם שֶׁהָיְתָה שְׁכוּרָה מֵתָה — or, in the case where he borrowed the cow for one day and rented it for another day, the renter says, "It definitely **died on the day it was rented**"; בְּשָׁעָה שֶׁהָיְתָה שְׁכוּרָה מֵתָה — or, in the case where he borrowed it for half a day and rented it for half a day, he says, "It definitely **died during the time it was rented**"; וְהַלָּה אוֹמֵר אֵינִי יוֹדֵעַ — and in all of these cases **the other one** [the cow's owner] says, "**I do not know** what happened," פָּטוּר — [the renter] is **exempt** from paying for the cow that died because the renter is not obligated to swear an oath in this case.[5]

The third set of claims:

זֶה אוֹמֵר שְׁאוּלָה — **If this one** [the cow's owner] says, "It was definitely **the borrowed [cow]** that died," or he says, "The cow definitely died while it was borrowed," וְזֶה אוֹמֵר שְׂכוּרָה — **and this one** [the renter] says, "It was definitely **the rented [cow]** that died," or he says, "The cow definitely died while it was rented," יִשָּׁבַע הַשּׂוֹכֵר שֶׁשְּׂכוּרָה מֵתָה — **the renter should swear that**

— NOTES —

claim, he must swear the Biblical oath of a מוֹדֶה בְּמִקְצָת, *someone who admits to part of a claim* (see Mishnah 4:7; *Shevuos* 6:1). Since he cannot swear that the second cow died while it was rented, he must pay for it.

In the last case, where one cow was borrowed and one was rented and it is not clear whether the borrowed cow died or the rented one died, the Mishnah speaks of a case where there was yet a third cow involved and that too was borrowed. Two of the three cows died. The borrower admits that he has to pay for one of them (since one of the two was surely borrowed), but he is unsure whether he has to pay for the other, since it might have been the rented cow. Here too, since he admits that he must pay for at least one of the cows, he must swear the oath of someone who admits to part of a claim in order to free himself from paying for the other one. And since he cannot swear, he must pay.

4. This is the same person the Mishnah previously called "the borrower"; that is, the one who rented and borrowed the cows. The Mishnah now calls him "the renter" because he claims that the cow definitely died while he was renting it (*Tos. Yom Tov*).

5. Although we explained in note 3 that there were actually two cows involved (or three), and the renter (borrower) admits that he must pay for one of them, he still does not have to swear about the other one. The oath for *someone who admits to part of a claim* applies only when the one making the claim says that he is *definitely* owed the money. If he only claims that he is *possibly* owed the money, no oath is required. Since the cow's owner admits that he does not know whether the renter must pay for the cow in question, the renter is not obligated to swear. Therefore, he does not have to pay for the cow in question (*Tosafos* 97b ד״ה ה״נ).

זֶה אוֹמֵר אֵינִי יוֹדֵעַ וְזֶה אוֹמֵר אֵינִי יוֹדֵעַ, יַחֲלֹקוּ.

[ג] **הַשּׁוֹאֵל** אֶת הַפָּרָה וְשִׁלְחָהּ לוֹ בְּיַד בְּנוֹ,

— רע״ב —

מדמי שטורים. והכי נמי, מה שהודה לו לא טענט, ומה שטעט לא הודה לו, ומה מקום יש לשבועה זו].

להכי מוקמינן בגמרא (שח,ב), דשבועה זו על ידי גלגול. דאמר ליה, אשתבע לי שבועת השומרים שאתה חייב לישבע לי דכדרכה מתה, ומגו דמשתבע דכדרכה מתה, משתבע נמי על ידי גלגול דשכורה מתה: **יחלוקו**. מתניתין סומכוס היא, דאמר ממון המוטל בספק חולקים. ואינה הלכה. אלא הלכה המוציא מחבירו עליו הראיה, וישבע הנשבע שאינו יודע, ופטור: **(ג) ביד בנו**. המשאיל שלחה לשואל, ביד בנו ועבדו ושלוחו של משאיל או ביד בנו ועבדו ושלוחו של שואל, פטור אם מתה בדרך. והאי שלוחו

---

the rented cow died, or that the cow died while it was being rented, and then he does not have to pay.[6] Since he is sure that he is right about which animal died or when it died, there is nothing to prevent him from swearing that his claim is true. Thus, if he swears he does not have to pay.[7]

The fourth set of claims:

זֶה אוֹמֵר אֵינִי יוֹדֵעַ — If **this one** [the cow's owner] **says, "I do not know** what happened," וְזֶה אוֹמֵר אֵינִי יוֹדֵעַ — **and this one** [the renter] **says, "I do not know** what happened," יַחֲלֹקוּ — **they divide** the loss of the cow: the borrower pays for half its value and the owner loses the other half.[8]

[3] A borrower becomes responsible for the item he borrows as soon as he takes it from the lender. This Mishnah explains when he becomes responsible in cases where he does not take the item directly from the lender but has it sent to him. The Mishnah begins by listing six cases in which the lender chooses the person to bring a cow to the borrower and then teaches the law for these six cases:

הַשּׁוֹאֵל אֶת הַפָּרָה — **If someone** arranged **to borrow a cow,** וְשִׁלְחָהּ לוֹ בְּיַד בְּנוֹ

--- NOTES ---

6. Since in this case the owner of the cow claims that it was definitely the borrowed cow that died, and the renter admits that one of the two cows died while it was borrowed, he is required to swear the Biblical oath of a מוֹדֶה בְּמִקְצָת, *someone who admits to part of a claim*. However, since the renter says he is sure that it was a rented cow that died, he can swear this oath and free himself from paying (see *Tiferes Yisrael*).

7. *Tiferes Yisrael;* see *Rashi* 98b ד״ה ואמאי. [*Rav* explains this clause of the Mishnah differently; see *Tos. Yom Tov* for a discussion of why *Rav* did not follow his own explanation of the earlier part of the Mishnah in this case as well.]

8. The renter is not obligated to swear (that it died while it was rented) because the owner of the cow does not claim definitely that it did (see note 5). On the other hand, the renter is not completely free from paying because he admits that he might be obligated. They therefore split the value of the cow in question, with the renter paying half and the owner losing half.

This follows the opinion of Sumchos, who holds that when two people have a claim about something and we do not know who is right, they divide the money in question (see *Bava Kamma* 5:1 note 2). However, the Sages hold that when one person already has the money in his possession, the other person cannot take any of it unless he proves that it is his (see there and Mishnah 1:1 here, note 6). In this case, the borrower has the money in his possession, and the owner must prove that he deserves to be paid. If he cannot prove it, the borrower swears that he does not know what happened and he does not have to pay anything (*Rav*).

[151] MISHNAH BAVA METZIA / Chapter 8: Hashoeil es Haparah   8/3

בְּיַד עַבְדּוֹ, בְּיַד שְׁלוּחוֹ, אוֹ בְּיַד בְּנוֹ, בְּיַד עַבְדּוֹ, בְּיַד שְׁלוּחוֹ שֶׁל שׁוֹאֵל וָמֵתָה, פָּטוּר. אָמַר לוֹ הַשּׁוֹאֵל, שַׁלְחָהּ לִי בְּיַד בְּנִי, בְּיַד עַבְדִּי, בְּיַד שְׁלוּחִי, אוֹ בְּיַד בִּנְךָ, בְּיַד עַבְדְּךָ, בְּיַד שְׁלוּחֶךָ,

— רע"ב —

של שואל, איכא דמוקי לה (בבא קמא קד,ח,ה) בשכירו ולקיטו שדר בביתו, אבל לא עשאו שליח בעדים. דאי איכא עדים דשליח שויה, חייב השואל באונסיה משמסרה לו. ואיכא דאמרי, אפילו עשאו שליח בעדים, אינו מתחייב על ידו באונסיה. דהכי קאמר ליה, אינש מהימנא הוא, אי בעית לשדורי בידיה, שדר: אמר לו השואל שלחה לי וכו׳. ביד עבדך, חייב. האי עבדך, בעבד עברי קאמר. דאילו עבד כנעני, יד עבד כיד רבו, והוי כאילו לא יצאת מרשות משאיל, וכאילו משאיל עצמו הוליכה לו, ופטור השואל אם נאנסה בדרך:

בְּיַד עַבְדּוֹ בְּיַד שְׁלוּחוֹ — and [the lender] sent it to him in the hands of [the lender's] son, or in the hands of his servant, or in the hands of his messenger; אוֹ בְּיַד בְּנוֹ בְּיַד עַבְדּוֹ בְּיַד שְׁלוּחוֹ שֶׁל שׁוֹאֵל — or he sent it to him in the hands of [the borrower's] son, or in the hands of his servant, or in the hands of his messenger;[1] וָמֵתָה — and [the cow] died on the way before reaching the borrower, פָּטוּר — [the borrower] is exempt. Since in these cases the lender chose the person to bring the cow, that person is considered to be acting on behalf of the lender, and the cow is therefore still in his possession. The borrower is not responsible for the cow until it actually reaches him.[2]

The Mishnah now lists six cases in which the borrower chooses the person to bring the cow, and another six cases in which, although the lender chose the person, the borrower agreed to have it sent through him:

שַׁלְחָהּ לִי בְּיַד אָמַר לוֹ הַשּׁוֹאֵל — However, if the borrower said to [the lender], בְּנִי בְּיַד עַבְדִּי בְּיַד שְׁלוּחִי — "Send [the cow] to me in the hands of my son," or "in the hands of my servant," or "in the hands of my messenger"; אוֹ בְּיַד בִּנְךָ בְּיַד עַבְדְּךָ בְּיַד שְׁלוּחֶךָ — or he said, "Send it to me in the hands of your son," or "in the hands of your servant,"[3] or "in the hands of your messenger," in other words, the borrower chose the person to bring the cow to him;

NOTES

[3]

1. The Mishnah does not mean that the borrower told the lender to send the cow with this messenger. He merely sent this messenger to the lender to arrange to get the cow. He thereby indicated to the lender that he considered this person trustworthy, but he did not actually instruct the lender to give it to him. Thus, if the lender sent the cow with him, he is considered the lender's agent, not the borrower's (Rav; Tos. Yom Tov, from Rosh).

2. Rashi, Bava Kamma 104a [א] ד"ה פטור.

3. He told the lender to send it with the lender's Hebrew servant [עֶבֶד עִבְרִי]. Since a Hebrew servant is not actually the property of his master, merely someone who is required to work for him for a certain amount of time (see 1:5 note 6), he can become the agent of the borrower. However, if the lender sends it with his Canaanite slave (even if the borrower told him to do so), the cow is still considered to be in the lender's possession because a Canaanite slave is the property of his master. Thus, as long as the cow is in the slave's hands, it has not left the lender's possession, and the borrower is not responsible for it until it reaches him (Rav; see Eruvin 7:6).

משניות בבא מציעא / פרק ח: השואל את הפרה [152]

— רע״ב —

וכן בשעה שמחזירה. אם שלח השואל ביד בנו ועבדו או שלוחו, או ביד [בנו ועבדו] ושלוחו של משאיל, לא יצאת מרשותו של שואל עד שתבא ליד המשאיל, ואם

אוֹ שֶׁאָמַר לוֹ הַמַּשְׁאִיל, הֲרֵינִי מְשַׁלְּחָהּ לְךָ בְּיַד בְּנִי, בְּיַד עַבְדִּי, בְּיַד שְׁלוּחִי, אוֹ בְּיַד בִּנְךָ, בְּיַד עַבְדְּךָ, בְּיַד שְׁלוּחֶךָ, וְאָמַר לוֹ הַשּׁוֹאֵל, שַׁלַּח, וְשִׁלְּחָהּ וָמֵתָה, חַיָּב. וְכֵן בְּשָׁעָה שֶׁמַּחֲזִירָהּ.

נאנסה בדרך, חייב. אמר לו המשאיל שלחה לי, או שאמר השואל הריני משלחה וכו׳, המשאיל שלח, ושלחה ונאנסה בדרך, פטור. ומתניתין דוקא כשמחזירה בתוך ימי שאלתו שהוא חייב באונסיה. אבל אם החזירה לאחר ימי שאלתו, דין שומר שכר יש לו [הוחיל ונהנה ממנה] ולא דין שואל, ואם שלחה ביד בנו ועבדו או שלוחו, בין שלו בין של משאיל, ונאנסה בדרך, פטור:

הֲרֵינִי — אוֹ שֶׁאָמַר לוֹ הַמַּשְׁאִיל — or, even if the lender said to [the borrower], מְשַׁלְּחָהּ לְךָ בְּיַד בְּנִי בְּיַד עַבְדִּי בְּיַד שְׁלוּחִי — "I am sending it to you in the hands of my son," or "in the hands of my servant," or "in the hands of my messenger," אוֹ בְּיַד בִּנְךָ בְּיַד עַבְדְּךָ בְּיַד שְׁלוּחֶךָ — or he said, "I am sending it in the hands of your son," or "in the hands of your servant," or "in the hands of your messenger," וְאָמַר לוֹ הַשּׁוֹאֵל שַׁלַּח — and the borrower said, "Send it";[4] וְשִׁלְּחָהּ וָמֵתָה — and he then sent it and [the cow] died on the way, before it reached the borrower, חַיָּב — [the borrower] is obligated to pay for the cow. In all of these cases, the one bringing the cow is acting on behalf of the borrower; the cow is thus already considered to be in the borrower's hands and he is therefore responsible for it.

Having taught when a borrower's obligation starts, the Mishnah teaches when it ends:

וְכֵן בְּשָׁעָה שֶׁמַּחֲזִירָהּ — And so too, when [the borrower] returns [the cow]: if the borrower sends back the cow with someone he chooses, he is still responsible for it until it reaches the lender; therefore, if it dies on the way, he must pay for it.[5] If the lender tells him to send it back with a certain person, that person is acting on behalf of the lender. Therefore, if it dies on the way, the borrower does not have to pay, since it has already been returned to the lender.

[4] In Mishnah 2 we learned about a dispute between a borrower and a lender, which centered on the question of a cow's status at the time it died. The Mishnah now teaches about a dispute between a buyer and seller, which arises from a question about the item's status at the time of the transaction:[1]

── NOTES ──

4. By telling the lender to send it with this person, it is as if he told the lender, "Appoint this person to bring the cow on my behalf" (Raavad, cited by Shitah Mekubetzes).
5. However, if the cow was borrowed for only a certain number of days, the borrower pays for it only if it dies during those days. Once they are over and he cannot use the cow anymore, he is no longer a

borrower and his status is merely that of an ordinary shomer (since he must still take care of the cow until it is returned). Even a paid shomer is not responsible for damage beyond his control. Thus, if the animal dies before it is returned, he does not pay for it (Rav).

[4]

1. Meiri.

[ד] **הַמַּחֲלִיף** פָּרָה בַּחֲמוֹר וְיָלְדָה, וְכֵן הַמּוֹכֵר שִׁפְחָתוֹ וְיָלְדָה, זֶה אוֹמֵר, עַד שֶׁלֹּא מָכַרְתִּי, וְזֶה אוֹמֵר, מִשֶּׁלְּקַחְתִּי, **יַחֲלֹקוּ.**

— רע״ב —

(ד) **המוכר שפחתו וילדה.** דעבד כנעני נקנה בכסף, וכשנתן המטות נקנית לו השפחה בכל מקום שהיא, ואין ידוע אם עד שלא ילדה נתן הכסף והטובר שלו, או לאחר שילדה, והולד של בעלים. אבל פרה אינה נקנית בכסף, אלא במשיכה, וכיון דמשך, מידע ידע אי ילדה כבר אי לא ילדה. להכי איצטריך למתני המחליף, דעל ידי חליפין כיון שמשך האחד נקנה האחר בכל מקום שהוא, לפיכך אין ידוע אם ילדה אם לא ילדה: **יחלוקו.** ומתניתין סומכוס היא, ולית הילכתא כוותיה:

הַמַּחֲלִיף פָּרָה בַּחֲמוֹר וְיָלְדָה — **If someone trades a cow for a donkey, and** after making the trade it is discovered that **[the cow] had given birth,**[2] and we do not know whether it gave birth before the trade took place, in which case the calf belongs to the first owner of the cow, or whether it gave birth after the trade took place, in which case it belongs to the new owner of the cow;[3] וְכֵן הַמּוֹכֵר שִׁפְחָתוֹ וְיָלְדָה — **and so too,** if **someone sells his** Canaanite **slavewoman, and** after selling her it was discovered that **she had given birth,**[4] and we do not know whether she gave birth before the sale, in which case the child belongs to her first owner, or whether she gave birth after the sale, in which case the child belongs to the new owner; זֶה אוֹמֵר עַד שֶׁלֹּא מָכַרְתִּי — in both of these cases, if **this one** [the seller] **says,** "She gave birth **before I sold** her, so the offspring belongs to me," וְזֶה אוֹמֵר מִשֶּׁלְּקַחְתִּי — **and this one** [the buyer] **says,** "She gave birth **after I bought** her, so the offspring belongs to me," יַחֲלֹקוּ — **they divide** the value of the calf or child.[5]

NOTES

2. When two people agree to trade their belongings, as soon as one of them makes a *kinyan* on the item he is getting, the other one acquires the other item in the trade — even if it is in a different place. This type of transaction is known as חֲלִיפִין, *chalifin*. In our case, the owners of the cow and the donkey agreed to trade animals. The owner of the cow pulled the donkey into his possession, thereby making a *kinyan* on it (*meshichah* — see intoduction to Mishnah 4:1). As a result, the cow automatically became the property of the other person (the one who originally owned the donkey). The cow itself was not present (*Rav*). When the new owner came to take the cow, it was discovered that it had given birth.

3. If the cow was still pregnant when it was traded, the unborn calf was included in the trade.

[The reason the Mishnah does not discuss this in regard to a cow that was sold in an ordinary manner is that a cow must usually be present when it is sold in order for the *kinyan* to be effective (see *Kiddushin* 1:4). It would then be obvious whether it gave birth before the transaction or afterward. The Mishnah therefore speaks of a case where the cow was traded and thus did not need to be present at the place of the transaction (*Rav*).]

4. A Canaanite slave can be acquired simply by paying money to his or her owner (*Kiddushin* 1:3). Therefore, she herself did not have to be present at the sale (*Rav*). Later, they find that she had given birth.

5. This Mishnah also follows the opinion of Sumchos (see Mishnah 2 note 8). The Sages, however, hold that if one of them has the calf in his possession, he keeps it unless the other one can prove when the calf was born. If neither one has it in his possession (such as if the cow gave birth on public land and the calf is still there), the calf belongs to the original owner (Gemara 100a).

משניות בבא מציעא / פרק ח: השואל את הפרה

הָיוּ לוֹ שְׁנֵי עֲבָדִים, אֶחָד גָּדוֹל וְאֶחָד קָטָן, וְכֵן שְׁתֵּי שָׂדוֹת, אַחַת גְּדוֹלָה וְאַחַת קְטַנָּה, הַלּוֹקֵחַ אוֹמֵר גָּדוֹל לָקַחְתִּי, וְהַלָּה אוֹמֵר אֵינִי יוֹדֵעַ, זָכָה בַגָּדוֹל. הַמּוֹכֵר אוֹמֵר קָטָן מָכַרְתִּי, וְהַלָּה אוֹמֵר אֵינִי יוֹדֵעַ, אֵין לוֹ אֶלָּא קָטָן. זֶה אוֹמֵר גָּדוֹל, וְזֶה אוֹמֵר קָטָן,

— רע״ב —

זה אומר גדול וזה אומר קטן. זה אומר דמי עבד גדול, וזה אומר דמי עבד קטן. דאילו עבד ממש, הא קיימא לן (גמרא ק,א) דאין נשבעין על העבדים. וטור, מה שטענו לא הודה לו, ומה שהודה לו לא טענו, ולא היה כאן מקום לשבועה:

The Mishnah now teaches about another disagreement between a buyer and seller. In this case the law depends on the claims of the two people. The Mishnah first presents the cases of the dispute and then discusses the law for them: הָיוּ לוֹ שְׁנֵי עֲבָדִים אֶחָד גָּדוֹל וְאֶחָד קָטָן — **Someone had two slaves, one large and one small,** and he sold one of them, but he and the buyer disagree about which slave was sold; וְכֵן שְׁתֵּי שָׂדוֹת אַחַת גְּדוֹלָה וְאַחַת קְטַנָּה — **and so too,** if someone had **two fields, one large and one small,** and he sold one of them, but he and the buyer disagree about which field he sold.

The law in these cases depends on their claims. The Mishnah lists four sets of claims and the law in each case.[6] The first set of claims:

הַלּוֹקֵחַ אוֹמֵר גָּדוֹל לָקַחְתִּי — If **the buyer says, "I** definitely **bought the large slave or field,"** וְהַלָּה אוֹמֵר אֵינִי יוֹדֵעַ — **and the other one** [the seller] **says, "I do not know** which one I sold you," זָכָה בַגָּדוֹל — **[the buyer] has the right to the large one.** Since the seller would have to swear an oath in this case to free himself from giving the buyer what he claims, and he cannot swear since he admits he does not know, he must pay the claim.[7]

The second set of claims:

הַמּוֹכֵר אוֹמֵר קָטָן מָכַרְתִּי — If **the seller says, "I** definitely **sold you the small slave or field,"** וְהַלָּה אוֹמֵר אֵינִי יוֹדֵעַ — **and the other one** [the buyer] **says, "I do not know** which one you sold me," אֵין לוֹ אֶלָּא קָטָן — **[the buyer] has the right only to the small one.** The seller is not obligated to swear in this case because the buyer is not making a definite claim.[8]

The third set of claims:

זֶה אוֹמֵר גָּדוֹל — If **this one** [the buyer] **says, "I definitely bought the large** slave or field," וְזֶה אוֹמֵר קָטָן — **and this one** [the seller] **says, "I definitely sold**

--- NOTES ---

6. This part of the Mishnah parallels the discussion in Mishnah 2.

7. As explained in Mishnah 2 note 2, one cannot force someone to pay based only on a claim. Thus, the fact that the buyer is sure and the seller is unsure is not enough reason to force the seller to give in to the larger claim. However, since the seller agrees that he did sell a slave or field, he is admitting to part of the buyer's claim. Therefore, to be free from paying the full claim, he must swear the oath of a מוֹדֶה בְּמִקְצָת, *one who admits to part of a claim,* that he does not owe everything the buyer claims. Since he cannot do so (because he admits he does not know), he must pay the full claim (*Tos. Yom Tov*; see Mishnah 2 note 3).

See below, note 10.

8. Although the seller agrees that he owes something, he does not have to swear in this case that he does not owe

יִשָּׁבַע הַמּוֹכֵר שֶׁהַקָּטָן מָכַר. זֶה אוֹמֵר אֵינִי יוֹדֵעַ וְזֶה אוֹמֵר אֵינִי יוֹדֵעַ, יַחֲלקוּ.

[ה] הַמּוֹכֵר זֵיתָיו לְעֵצִים, וְעָשׂוּ פָּחוֹת

— רע״ב —

(ה) המוכר זיתיו לעצים. שיקוץ אותן לשרפס. והשהה אותן בקרקעו. ועשו. זיתים רעים שאין בסאה שלהם רביעית שמן:

יִשָּׁבַע הַמּוֹכֵר שֶׁהַקָּטָן מָכַר — **the seller must swear that he sold** him **the small one,** and then the buyer receives only the small one.[9]

The fourth set of claims:

זֶה אוֹמֵר אֵינִי יוֹדֵעַ — If **this one** [the buyer] **says, "I do not know** which one I bought," וְזֶה אוֹמֵר אֵינִי יוֹדֵעַ — **and this one** [the seller] **says, "I do not know** which one I sold you," יַחֲלקוּ — **they divide** the difference in value between the large one and small one; the seller gives the buyer half the extra value and the buyer loses the other half.[10]

[5] Another dispute between a buyer and seller:

הַמּוֹכֵר זֵיתָיו לְעֵצִים — If **[a person] sells his olive trees** to someone to cut down and use **for firewood,**[1] but the buyer did not cut them down right away and left them growing in the seller's land; וְעָשׂוּ פָּחוֹת

NOTES
---

the larger amount, because the buyer is not certain that the seller owes the larger amount (see Mishnah 2 note 5).

9. Since the seller agrees that he did sell a slave or field, he admits that he owes something. Therefore, he must swear that he does not owe everything the buyer claims, as explained in note 7. Since in this case the seller is sure of his claim, he can swear the oath and be free from paying the larger amount (*Rav*).

10. This again follows the view of Sumchos (see note 5). The Sages, however, say that the buyer gets only the small field or slave. Since the fields or slaves are in the seller's possession, the buyer must prove his claim is correct (*Meiri*).

The Gemara notes that the Mishnah cannot be speaking of cases where the buyer is actually demanding the larger slave or field, because a person cannot be forced to swear about land or slaves (*Shevuos* 6:5). Moreover, admitting to having sold the smaller one would not technically be considered admitting to part of the claim, because the small slave or field is not part of the large one being claimed by the buyer (*Rav*). Instead, we must explain this set of cases of the Mishnah as follows:

A person ("the buyer") gave money to someone else ("the seller") and asked him to use the money to buy a slave or field for him. [Thus, the "seller" in this case is not actually the person selling the slave or field, but a broker arranging the sale, to the buyer.] In the end, however, the "seller" was not able to arrange the sale and the buyer now wants his money back. The buyer says, "I gave you enough money to buy a large field (or slave), which you should now return," but the seller says, "I do not remember if you gave me that much money; you might have given me only enough for a small field (or slave)." Since they are arguing about money, not about a slave or field, and the seller admits he owes part of the amount being claimed, he must swear that he was not given enough money to buy a large field (or slave). Since he cannot do so, he must pay (*Rav*, based on Gemara 100a and *Rashi* there ד״ה דמי; see *Tos. Yom Tov*). [The other three sets of claims also can be explained as referring to a dispute over money.]

[5]

1. This is permitted in the case of olive trees that produce little fruit (*Meiri*). [Normally, it is forbidden to cut down a fruit tree (*Deuteronomy* 20:19). However, if a tree produces so little fruit that it is

משניות בבא מציעא / פרק ח: השואל את הפרה

מַרְבִּיעִית לִסְאָה, הֲרֵי אֵלּוּ שֶׁל בַּעַל הַזֵּיתִים. עָשׂוּ רְבִיעִית לִסְאָה, זֶה אוֹמֵר, זֵיתַי גִּדְּלוּ, וְזֶה אוֹמֵר, אַרְצִי גִדְּלָה, יַחֲלֹקוּ. שָׁטַף נָהָר זֵיתָיו וּנְתָנָם לְתוֹךְ שְׂדֵה חֲבֵרוֹ, זֶה אוֹמֵר, זֵיתַי גִּדְּלוּ, וְזֶה אוֹמֵר, אַרְצִי גִדְּלָה, יַחֲלֹקוּ.

— רע״ב —

הרי אלו של בעל הזיתים. דפחות מרביעית לא קפדי אנשי. ורביעית שאמרו, חוץ מן הסולאה שהוא מוציא במסיקתן ובעלירתן. ומתנייתין כשמכר זיתיו על מנת לקוץ סתם. אבל אם אמר לו לקוץ מיד, אפילו פחות מרביעית לבעל הקרקע. ואם אמר לקוץ לכשתרצה, אפילו יותר מרביעית לבעל הזיתים: וזה אומר ארצי גדלה יחלוקו. בגמרא (קא,א) מוקי לה, כגון ששטף נהר הזיתים עם גושיהן, דהיינו עם הקרקע שבסביבותיהן שהן יכולים לחיות על ידו, ומפני כן הם פטורים מערלה.

מַרְבִּיעִית לִסְאָה — in the meantime, [the trees] produced olives of such low quality that when they are pressed, they will yield **less than a quarter** *log* of oil for every *se'ah* of olives;[2] הֲרֵי אֵלּוּ שֶׁל בַּעַל הַזֵּיתִים — the law is that **these olives belong to the** new **owner of the olive trees.**[3] עָשׂוּ רְבִיעִית לִסְאָה — However, if [the trees] produced olives that yield **a quarter** *log* or more of oil for every *se'ah* of olives, and both people claim the olives: זֶה אוֹמֵר זֵיתַי גִּדְּלוּ — **This one** [the owner of the trees] **says, "My olive trees grew these olives, so they belong to me,"** וְזֶה אוֹמֵר אַרְצִי גִדְּלָה — **and that one** [the owner of the land] **says, "My land grew these olives, so they belong to me,"** יַחֲלֹקוּ — **they divide** the olives between them, since they are both right: the olives need both the trees and the land in order to grow.[4]

In the previous case, the trees grew in the owner's land and were then sold. In the Mishnah's next case, the trees grew in one place and then ended up in someone else's land:

שָׁטַף נָהָר זֵיתָיו — **If a** flooding **river swept away someone's olive trees** וּנְתָנָם לְתוֹךְ שְׂדֵה חֲבֵרוֹ — **and deposited them in his neighbor's field,** where they took root and grew olives,[5] זֶה אוֹמֵר זֵיתַי גִּדְּלוּ — **and this one** [the owner of the trees] **says, "My olive trees grew these olives, so they belong to me,"** וְזֶה אוֹמֵר אַרְצִי גִדְּלָה — **and that one** [the owner of the land] **says, "My land grew these olives, so they belong to me,"** יַחֲלֹקוּ — **they divide** the olives between

— NOTES —

not worth doing the work needed to keep it alive, one may cut it down (see *Bava Kamma* 91b; *Sheviis* 4:10).]

2. *Log* and *se'ah* are volume measurements; a *se'ah* contains 24 *log*. These olives produce so little oil that after earning back the money he spends to harvest and press 24 *log* of them, he is left with not even a quarter-*log* of oil as profit (*Tiferes Yisrael*, from Gemara 101a). [A quarter *log* is also known as a רְבִיעִית, *revi'is*.]

3. The owner of the land could also have a claim on them, since they grew from his land. However, since they produce so little oil, we assume that he waives whatever claim he might have to them (*Rav*).

4. Unlike the previous Mishnah, they do not divide them out of doubt. Each one has a right to half the olives because the olives grew both from the tree and from the land (*Rambam Commentary*).

[The Mishnah speaks of a case where the owner of the land did not say when the trees should be cut down. However, if he said that they should be cut down immediately, then any olives that grow afterward belong to the owner of the land (*Rav*, from Gemara 100b).]

5. Although the owner of the trees has no right to leave them in this field, the

— רע"ב —

וכל שלש שנים הראשונות הוא דיחלוקו, דאף על גב דקרקע של זה מגדלן, מכל מקום, אי לאו גושייהו, לא הוי מני אכיל מנייהו משום ערלה. אבל לאחר שלש [שנים] הכל לבעל הקרקע, דאמר ליה, אי אנא נטעי, לאחר שלש מי לא הוה אכילנא: (ו) **הַמַּשְׂכִּיר** בַּיִת לַחֲבֵרוֹ. סתם. ובימות החמה שלשים יום. כלומר, אם בא להוציאו קודם הפסח, צריך שיודיענו שלשים יום מימות החמה, דהיינו חמשה עשר באלול, שמהם, שלשים יום עד החג שהוא התחלת ימות הגשמים. ואם לא הודיעו חמשה עשר באלול, אינו יכול להוציאו עד הפסח. וממילא שמעתין, שהמשכיר בית סתם בימות החמה, צריך להודיעו שלשים יום קודם שיוליאנו:

[ו] **הַמַּשְׂכִּיר** בַּיִת לַחֲבֵרוֹ, בִּימוֹת הַגְּשָׁמִים אֵינוֹ יָכוֹל לְהוֹצִיאוֹ, מִן הֶחָג וְעַד הַפֶּסַח; בִּימוֹת הַחַמָּה, שְׁלֹשִׁים יוֹם.

them for the first three years. After that, all the fruit belongs to the owner of the land.[6]

[6] The rest of this chapter deals with the laws of renting a house:

הַמַּשְׂכִּיר בַּיִת לַחֲבֵרוֹ — **If someone rents a house to [another person]** without specifying how long the lease will last,[1] בִּימוֹת הַגְּשָׁמִים אֵינוֹ יָכוֹל לְהוֹצִיאוֹ מִן הֶחָג וְעַד הַפֶּסַח — **[the owner] cannot force him to leave in the winter**,[2] from the Succos **holiday until Pesach**, because almost all available houses are rented during that period and it is difficult to find a new place to live; בִּימוֹת הַחַמָּה שְׁלֹשִׁים יוֹם — and if he wishes to have him leave during the winter, he must tell him **during the summer**,[3] at least **thirty days** before the start of the winter season (i.e., before the rains come), when houses are still available for rent.[4]

─── NOTES ───

owner of the field allowed them to stay (*Tos. Yom Tov; Ritva*).

6. *Rav.* The owner of the trees really should have no right to any of the fruit, because the owner of the land can say to him that if the trees had not come into his field, he would have planted his own trees in their place and had all the fruit for himself. [Therefore, he is not benefiting from the trees that were swept into his field.] However, the Mishnah teaches that the owner of the trees does have a right to share the fruit of the first three years during which the trees are in his neighbor's land. The reason for this is as follows:

The Torah states that for the first three years after a tree is planted, its fruit is forbidden as *orlah* (*Leviticus* 19:23). Had the owner of the land planted his own trees, their fruit would have been forbidden to be eaten for three years. The reason he gets to eat the fruit now is only because these grown trees were brought by the flood into his land and started growing in it. Thus, during the first three years, the owner of the field must divide the olives with the owner of the trees. After that, the

owner of the land keeps all future olives for himself (*Rav*, from *Gemara* 101a). However, he must pay the owner of the trees the value of the trees (*Tosafos*).

[Actually, when a tree is uprooted and replanted, it too is subject to the law of *orlah* and its fruit cannot be eaten for three years. In the Mishnah's case, however, the trees were uprooted together with a large clod of soil surrounding them. Since this soil was enough to keep them alive, when they take root again in another field they are not subject to *orlah* (*Rav*; see *Orlah* 1:3).]

[6]
1. For example, they agreed how much money he will pay each month, but they did not say how long he can stay (*Rav; Tos. Yom Tov*).
2. Literally, *the days of rain*. [In Eretz Yisrael it rains only during the winter months, from shortly after Succos until Pesach (see *Taanis* 1:2,3).]
3. Literally, *the days of sun*.
4. *Rav*, from *Gemara* 101b. That is, he must tell him by the 15th of Elul, thirty days before Succos.

וּבַכְּרַכִּים, אֶחָד יְמוֹת הַחַמָּה וְאֶחָד יְמוֹת הַגְּשָׁמִים, שְׁנֵים עָשָׂר חֹדֶשׁ. וּבַחֲנוּיוֹת, אֶחָד עֲיָרוֹת וְאֶחָד כְּרַכִּים, שְׁנֵים עָשָׂר חֹדֶשׁ. רַבָּן שִׁמְעוֹן בֶּן גַּמְלִיאֵל אוֹמֵר,

— רע״ב —

וּבכרכים. שהכל נמשכים שם לגור, והבתים אין מצויין לשכור, צריך להודיעו שנים עשר חודש קודם יציאתו, בין בימות החמה בין בימות הגשמים. וכשם שמשכיר צריך להודיע, כך שוכר צריך להודיע, בעיירות שלשים יום ובכרכים שנים עשר חדש. ואם לא הודיעו אינו יכול לצאת, אלא נותן לו שכרו:

By the same token, if he wants the tenant to leave during the summer, he must tell him thirty days in advance.[5] This is the law for towns. וּבַכְּרַכִּים — **However, in the big cities,** where many people want to live and it is always difficult to find houses to rent, אֶחָד יְמוֹת הַחַמָּה וְאֶחָד יְמוֹת הַגְּשָׁמִים — whether he wants his tenant to leave in **the summer** or in **the winter,** שְׁנֵים עָשָׂר חֹדֶשׁ — he must tell him **twelve months** in advance.

The rule for stores is somewhat different:

וּבַחֲנוּיוֹת — **In** the case of **stores** that are being rented, אֶחָד עֲיָרוֹת וְאֶחָד כְּרַכִּים — **whether** they are in **towns** or in **big cities,** שְׁנֵים עָשָׂר חֹדֶשׁ — the owner must tell the renter **twelve months** in advance that he wishes for him to leave. This is because storekeepers often sell on credit and if they are forced to leave on short notice, the customers who owe them money will not know where to find them and will not pay the storekeepers what they owe. The owners must therefore give the storekeepers twelve months' notice, to give them time to collect their debts.[6] רַבָּן שִׁמְעוֹן בֶּן גַּמְלִיאֵל אוֹמֵר — **Rabban Shimon**

NOTES

5. By right, when a lease agreement does not specify for how long the rental is, the owner should be allowed to force the tenant to leave at any time. The Rabbis, however, decreed that he cannot do so unless he gives the tenant enough time to find another place to live. Thus, in the summer (when houses are available for rent), he must give him thirty days' notice, and in the winter (when it is difficult to find a house to rent) he cannot force the tenant out at all unless he notified him thirty days before winter began (*Meleches Shlomo*; Gemara 101b).

However, if the lease specified when the rental would end, the tenant can be forced to leave even in the winter, since he knew in advance that the rental would end at that time (*Rif*).

Just as the owner must give the tenant time to find another place to live, so too the tenant must give the owner enough time to find another person to rent his house. Thus, if the tenant wants to leave during the summer, he must tell the owner thirty days ahead of time, and if he wants to leave during the winter, he must inform the owner thirty days before winter starts [since very few people are looking for a house in the winter] (*Rav; Nimukei Yosef*).

6. *Tos. Yom Tov.* If he sells on credit during those twelve months, he can tell the buyers where he will be moving so that they can find him later (*Sma, Choshen Mishpat* 312:10).

Similarly, if the storekeeper wants to leave, he must tell the owner twelve months in advance. This is because any storekeeper who takes over this store will also want to wait twelve months at his old location before moving into this store. The owner therefore needs time to have another renter in place (*Tos. Yom Tov*).

חֲנוּת שֶׁל נַחְתּוֹמִים וְשֶׁל צַבָּעִים, שָׁלֹשׁ שָׁנִים.

[ז] הַמַּשְׂכִּיר בַּיִת לַחֲבֵרוֹ, הַמַּשְׂכִּיר חַיָּב בַּדֶּלֶת, בַּנֶּגֶר, וּבַמַּנְעוּל, וּבְכָל דָּבָר שֶׁמַּעֲשֵׂה אֻמָּן. אֲבָל דָּבָר שֶׁאֵינוֹ מַעֲשֵׂה אֻמָּן, הַשּׂוֹכֵר עוֹשֵׂהוּ. הַזֶּבֶל שֶׁל בַּעַל הַבַּיִת,

— רע"ב —
של נחתומים ושל צבעים שלש שנים. מפני שהקיפן מרובה לזמן ארוך. והלכה כרבן שמעון בן גמליאל: (ז) ובנגר. שנועלין בו את הדלת, ותוחבים אותו בקורת האסקופה: הזבל של בעל הבית. וכגון שנעשה זבל מתורי דשוכר, דאי מתורי דעלמא, הזבל של השוכר:

ben Gamliel says: חֲנוּת שֶׁל נַחְתּוֹמִים וְשֶׁל צַבָּעִים — If it is **a store used by bread sellers** or **fabric dyers**,[7] שָׁלֹשׁ שָׁנִים — he must let the renters know **three years** in advance, because such businesses sometimes allow buyers to wait a very long time before paying their bills. Therefore, they need to stay in place for three years to be able to collect what is owed them.

[7] More laws about renting a house:

הַמַּשְׂכִּיר בַּיִת לַחֲבֵרוֹ — When someone **rents a house to [another person]**, הַמַּשְׂכִּיר חַיָּב בַּדֶּלֶת בַּנֶּגֶר וּבַמַּנְעוּל — **[the owner] must provide a door** for the house, **a bolt** to secure the door from the inside, **a lock** to secure the door from the outside, וּבְכָל דָּבָר שֶׁמַּעֲשֵׂה אֻמָּן — **and anything** else **that requires a professional** to make or fix it.[1] אֲבָל דָּבָר שֶׁאֵינוֹ מַעֲשֵׂה אֻמָּן — **But something that does not require a professional,** הַשּׂוֹכֵר עוֹשֵׂהוּ — **the renter must make** or fix it himself.[2]

In the times of the Mishnah, houses were built with a courtyard in front, which in turn led to the public street. The Mishnah teaches who may keep things left behind by outsiders who used the courtyard for some reason:

הַזֶּבֶל שֶׁל בַּעַל הַבַּיִת — **Manure**[3] left behind by someone else's animal **belongs to the owner of the house,** not to the renter. Since the courtyard was not included in the rental of the house,[4] it still belongs to the owner and it therefore

---
NOTES
---

7. [People would make their own wool, linen, or cotton fabrics, and then take them to a dyer to have them dyed a certain color.]

[7]

1. Anything that is needed to make the house livable (i.e., it is a basic part of a normal dwelling), and that only a professional would build or fix, is the owner's responsibility (*Tos. Yom Tov*, from *Rambam, Hilchos Sechirus* 6:3). For example, he is responsible for the windows (Gemara 101b).

2. For example, he is responsible for plastering the roof, since this does not require a professional (Gemara 101b). [In the times of the Mishnah, the roofs of the houses were flat and had to be plastered regularly to keep them waterproof. This was something all people did for themselves.]

3. Animal droppings were collected and used as fertilizer.

4. The Mishnah speaks of a case where the rental was only for the house and not the courtyard. Thus, the person renting the house receives only the right to walk through the courtyard, but not the right to use it (*Tos. Yom Tov*, according to *Rashi*).

משניות בבא מציעא / פרק ח: השואל את הפרה [160]

— רע"ב —

היוצא מן התנור. אפר ונעשה זבל: **(ח) נתעברה** לשוכר. לא ירבה לו שכר חדש, שהעבור בכלל שנה:

וְאֵין לַשּׂוֹכֵר אֶלָּא הַיּוֹצֵא מִן הַתַּנּוּר וּמִן הַכִּירַיִם בִּלְבָד.

[ח] **הַמַּשְׂכִּיר** בַּיִת לַחֲבֵרוֹ לְשָׁנָה, נִתְעַבְּרָה הַשָּׁנָה, נִתְעַבְּרָה לַשּׂוֹכֵר. הִשְׂכִּיר לוֹ לֶחֳדָשִׁים,

---

acquires the manure for him.[5] וְאֵין לַשּׂוֹכֵר אֶלָּא הַיּוֹצֵא מִן הַתַּנּוּר וּמִן הַכִּירַיִם בִּלְבָד — The renter has the right to keep **only what is left over in the oven and the stove** in the courtyard; that is, the ash left behind by people using the oven or stove.[6] The right to use these ovens and stoves are usually included in the rental of the house. They therefore acquire for the renter any ashes left in them.[7]

[8] Every few years, an extra month is added to the Jewish calendar, creating a leap year.[1] Our Mishnah teaches how this affects the payment of rent: הַמַּשְׂכִּיר בַּיִת לַחֲבֵרוֹ לְשָׁנָה — **If someone rents a house to [another person] for a year,** and they agreed that he would pay a certain amount for the year: נִתְעַבְּרָה הַשָּׁנָה — **if a month is** then **added to the year** (because a leap year was declared), so that the year is now thirteen months long instead of twelve,[2] נִתְעַבְּרָה לַשּׂוֹכֵר — **it is added for the renter,** and he does not have to pay extra for that month, because the added month is included in the "year."[3] הִשְׂכִּיר לוֹ לֶחֳדָשִׁים — However, if **he rented it to him by the month,** and they agreed

---

NOTES

5. When the owner of an animal leaves its manure in a courtyard, we assume that he gives up his right to it. Since a person's property can acquire things for him [this is known as קִנְיָן חָצֵר, *acquisition by a courtyard* — see *Gittin* 8:1], and the owner of the courtyard still has the rights to it, the courtyard acquires the manure for him (Gemara 102a; *Rashi* ד"ה בחצר דמשכיר and ד"ה ותורי דאתו מעלמא; *Tos. Yom Tov*).

However, if the renter's own animal leaves manure in the courtyard, it belongs to the renter (*Rav*). Since he lives right next to the courtyard, we assume he does not give up his rights to the manure left there by his animals (*Ritva*).

6. Ashes were also used as fertilizer (*Rav*).

7. Just as the property someone owns acquires for him, so too the property that a person rents acquires for him (*Tos. Yom Tov*, according to *Rashi*).

[8]

1. This is done to make sure that the Jewish calendar, in which the months follow the cycle of the moon, remains in line with the seasons, which follow the yearly cycle of the sun. Since twelve lunar months add up to only 354 days, while a solar year comes to 365¼ days, an extra month (a second Adar) is added approximately once every three years to make up the difference (see our General Introduction to *Rosh Hashanah* for a fuller explanation).

2. In the times of the Mishnah, the Sanhedrin would decide each year whether to declare a leap year, based on certain calculations and observations (see *Sanhedrin* 11b-13b). In our Mishnah's case, the Sanhedrin declared a leap year after the person had already rented the house. [Nowadays, leap years follow a fixed cycle of seven leap years in nineteen years; see General Introduction to *Rosh Hashanah*.]

3. When someone says he will rent for "a year," he means that he will rent from this date until the same date the following year. It does not matter if the year lasts twelve months or thirteen (*Rav*; *Shitah Mekubetzes*).

[161] **MISHNAH BAVA METZIA** / Chapter 8: *Hashoeil es Haparah*   8/8

— רע"ב —

מעשה בצפורי. בגמרא (קב,ב) פריך, מעשה לסתור, דהא רישא תנא או כולה דשוכר או כולה דמשכיר, וייתי מעשה דיחלוקו. ומשני, חסורי מחסרא והכי קתני, ואם אמר לו בשנים עשר זהובים לשנה, יחלוקו, דלא ידעינן

נִתְעַבְּרָה הַשָּׁנָה, נִתְעַבְּרָה לַמַּשְׂכִּיר. מַעֲשֶׂה בְּצִפּוֹרִי בְּאֶחָד שֶׁשָּׂכַר מֶרְחָץ מֵחֲבֵרוֹ בִּשְׁנֵים עָשָׂר זָהָב לְשָׁנָה, מִדִּינַר זָהָב לַחֹדֶשׁ. וּבָא מַעֲשֶׂה לִפְנֵי רַבָּן שִׁמְעוֹן בֶּן גַּמְלִיאֵל וְלִפְנֵי רַבִּי יוֹסֵי, וְאָמְרוּ, יַחְלְקוּ אֶת חֹדֶשׁ הָעִבּוּר.

אי תפוס לשון ראשון או לשון אחרון, ומעשה נמי וכו'. ואין הלכה כרבן שמעון בן גמליאל ורבי יוסי. אלא הלך אחר פחות שבלשונות. דקרקע בחזקת מרה קיימא. לפיכך כולו למשכיר, בין שהיה לשון ראשון פחות, בין שהיה לשון אחרון פחות:

נִתְעַבְּרָה הַשָּׁנָה — **if a month is** then **added to the year, נִתְעַבְּרָה לַמַּשְׂכִּיר** — **it is added for the owner**; that is, the renter must pay for the extra month, since the agreement was that he would pay per month. that he would pay a certain amount for each month,

The Mishnah now teaches what the law is in a case where both expressions were used. It does so by telling about an incident in which this actually happened:

מַעֲשֶׂה בְּצִפּוֹרִי בְּאֶחָד שֶׁשָּׂכַר מֶרְחָץ מֵחֲבֵרוֹ — **It once happened in** the city of **Tzippori that someone rented a bathhouse from [another person], בִּשְׁנֵים עָשָׂר זָהָב לְשָׁנָה מִדִּינַר זָהָב לַחֹדֶשׁ** — **and their agreement was that he would rent it "for twelve gold *dinars* for a year, at one gold *dinar* per month."** The year was then declared a leap year. The renter argued that he should not have to pay for the extra month, since the first part of their agreement gave a price for the year, while the owner argued that the renter should pay for the extra month, since the second part of their agreement stated that the price was per month. **וּבָא מַעֲשֶׂה לִפְנֵי רַבָּן שִׁמְעוֹן בֶּן גַּמְלִיאֵל וְלִפְנֵי רַבִּי יוֹסֵי וְאָמְרוּ** — **The case came before Rabban Shimon ben Gamliel and R' Yose** to decide, **and they said: יַחְלְקוּ אֶת חֹדֶשׁ הָעִבּוּר** — **They should divide** the rent for **the added month** because of the doubt as to who is correct. Since the monthly rent was one gold *dinar*, the renter pays half a gold *dinar* and the owner loses the other half a *dinar*.[4]

NOTES

4. Whenever two parts of a statement contradict each other, there is a dispute whether the first part of the statement should be considered binding or the second (see *Bava Basra* 7:3; *Temurah* 5:4; *Tos. Yom Tov*). Rabban Shimon ben Gamliel and R' Yose were unsure of the law. They therefore ruled that the renter and owner should split the money (see *Rav; Tos. Yom Tov*).

In ruling that they should split the money, Rabban Shimon ben Gamliel and R' Yose followed the opinion of Sumchos [as explained in Mishnah 2 note 8] (*Ramban; Ritva*). According to the Sages, however, whoever has the money in his possession keeps it unless the other person can prove it should be his. In this case, the question is whether the renter has the right to use the bathhouse for an extra month without paying for it. Since the house belongs to the owner, he is considered to be in possession of it, and if the renter wants to use it for the extra month, he must pay for it (*Rav*).

[ט] **הַמַּשְׂכִּיר** בַּיִת לַחֲבֵרוֹ וְנָפַל, חַיָּב לְהַעֲמִיד לוֹ בַּיִת. הָיָה קָטָן לֹא יַעֲשֶׂנּוּ גָּדוֹל, גָּדוֹל לֹא יַעֲשֶׂנּוּ קָטָן; אֶחָד לֹא יַעֲשֶׂנּוּ שְׁנַיִם, שְׁנַיִם לֹא יַעֲשֶׂנּוּ אֶחָד; לֹא יִפְחֹת מֵהַחַלּוֹנוֹת, וְלֹא יוֹסִיף עֲלֵיהֶן, אֶלָּא מִדַּעַת שְׁנֵיהֶם.

— רע"ב —

(ט) חייב להעמיד לו בית. [לימי שכירתו]: היה גדול לא יעשנו קטן וכו׳. והוא דהראהו לו בית ואמר לו בית כזה אני משכיר לך. אבל העמידו על הבית ואמר לו בית זה אני משכיר לך, ונפל, אינו חייב לבנותו. ואם אמר לו בית סתם, יעמיד לו מקום שיקרא בית, בין גדול בין קטן:

[9] A final law about renting a house:

הַמַּשְׂכִּיר בַּיִת לַחֲבֵרוֹ וְנָפַל — If someone rents a house to [another person] and it collapses, חַיָּב לְהַעֲמִיד לוֹ בַּיִת — [the owner] must provide a different **house for the [renter]** for as long as he was supposed to rent the original house.[1] הָיָה קָטָן לֹא יַעֲשֶׂנּוּ גָדוֹל — If [the original house] was small, he cannot provide him with **a large [house] instead**,[2] if the renter prefers a small one; גָּדוֹל לֹא יַעֲשֶׂנּוּ קָטָן — and if [the original house] was large, he cannot provide him with **a small** house instead, if the renter wants a large one.[3] אֶחָד לֹא יַעֲשֶׂנּוּ שְׁנַיִם — If it had **one** room, [the owner] cannot provide a house that has **two** rooms; שְׁנַיִם לֹא יַעֲשֶׂנּוּ אֶחָד — if it had **two** rooms, he cannot provide a house that has only **one** room; in both of these cases, the renter can say he prefers the other type of house. לֹא יִפְחֹת מֵהַחַלּוֹנוֹת וְלֹא יוֹסִיף עֲלֵיהֶן — [The owner] can also **not give** a house with **fewer windows nor** a house with **more windows,** if the renter insists on a house with the original number of windows. אֶלָּא מִדַּעַת שְׁנֵיהֶם — In all of these cases, a change may not be made **unless they both agree** to the change.[4]

NOTES

[9]

1. Since the owner agreed to rent him "a house" (not a specific house), if the first house he provided fell down, he must provide another one. However, if they agreed that he would rent him "this house" and it collapsed, the owner does not have to provide another one, since they agreed only about this specific house (Rav; Tiferes Yisrael). Nor does he have to rebuild the house that fell down (Tos. Yom Tov).

However, if the renter paid for the entire lease in advance, the owner must give him back the money for the time remaining on the lease (Shulchan Aruch, Choshen Mishpat 312:17).

2. Literally, he cannot make it large.

3. This is true only if he showed him a house and told him, "I will rent you a house like this." However, if he did not specify what kind of house he was renting, he can give him any place that can be called a "house," no matter its size (Rav).

4. However, if the house is the same in all these ways but it is painted or decorated differently, it is considered an acceptable replacement (Rama, Choshen Mishpat 312:17).

Chapter Nine

Most of this chapter discusses laws that apply when a person rents a field to farm it. This can be done in three ways:

(1) Sharecropping (אֲרִיסוּת): The renter pays the owner a percentage of the crops — for example, a half or a third — and keeps the rest. As a result, the owner does not receive a set amount for rent; the amount he receives depends on how much the field produces.

(2) Tenant-farming (חֲכִירוּת): The renter pays the owner a set amount of produce from the field's crops — for example, ten *kors* of wheat[1] — and keeps the rest. He must pay this amount regardless of how much the field produces; if the field does not produce ten *kors* of wheat, the renter will have to buy wheat from the market to pay the owner.

(3) Leasing (שְׂכִירוּת): The renter pays the owner a fixed amount of money, regardless of how much the field produces.[2]

While some laws discussed in this chapter apply to all rentals, others apply to only one or two types.

NOTES

1. A *kor* is a large unit of volume.
2. As a rule, tenant-farming and leasing have the same laws (*Tos. Yom Tov;* see, though, Mishnah 6).

ט/א

— רע"ב —

פרק תשיעי – המקבל שדה מחבירו. (א) המקבל שדה. באריסות, למחצה לשליש ולרביע.
או בחכירות, כך וכך כורין לשנה: **לחרוש** אחריה. אחר הקצירה או העקירה, כדי להפוך שרשים של עשבים

[א] הַמְקַבֵּל שָׂדֶה מֵחֲבֵרוֹ, מָקוֹם שֶׁנָּהֲגוּ לִקְצֹר, יִקְצֹר. לַעֲקֹר, יַעֲקֹר. לַחֲרֹשׁ אַחֲרָיו, יַחֲרֹשׁ. הַכֹּל כְּמִנְהַג הַמְּדִינָה. כְּשֵׁם שֶׁחוֹלְקִין בַּתְּבוּאָה, כָּךְ חוֹלְקִין בַּתֶּבֶן וּבַקַּשׁ. כְּשֵׁם שֶׁחוֹלְקִין בַּיַּיִן, כָּךְ חוֹלְקִין בַּזְּמוֹרוֹת וּבַקָּנִים, וּשְׁנֵיהֶם מְסַפְּקִין אֶת הַקָּנִים.

רעים שבו וימותו. **ובקנים**. המעמידים את הגפנים: **ושניהם מספקים את הקנים**. מה טעם אמר, מה טעם חולקים בקנים, לפי שעניהם מספקים את הקנים החדשים בכל שנה:

---

[1] A field can be rented either for a percentage of its crops or for a fixed payment (see Introduction to this chapter). Whatever the type of rental, before the rental begins, the owner and renter can set any terms they wish. The Mishnah discusses how certain terms are decided if nothing is specified when the rental is arranged:

הַמְקַבֵּל שָׂדֶה מֵחֲבֵרוֹ — If **someone rents a field from his friend** and they do not specify how the crops are to be harvested, מָקוֹם שֶׁנָּהֲגוּ לִקְצֹר יִקְצֹר — **if** they are in **a place where [farmers] are accustomed** to harvest the crops **by cutting** them, **he must cut** them; לַעֲקֹר יַעֲקֹר — **where they are accustomed to harvest the crops by uprooting** them, **he must uproot** them.[1] לַחֲרֹשׁ אַחֲרָיו יַחֲרֹשׁ — Similarly, in a place where it is customary **to plow** the field **after [the harvest]** in order to destroy the weeds, **[the renter] must plow** the field. הַכֹּל כְּמִנְהַג הַמְּדִינָה — In general, **everything** that was not specified between the renter and owner must be done **according to local custom.**

The Mishnah turns to a sharecropper. It teaches that he shares more than just the crop with the field's owner:[2]

כְּשֵׁם שֶׁחוֹלְקִין בַּתְּבוּאָה כָּךְ חוֹלְקִין בַּתֶּבֶן וּבַקַּשׁ — **Just as they** [a sharecropper and owner] **share the grain, so they share the straw and the stubble** (the inedible parts of a stalk of grain).[3] כְּשֵׁם שֶׁחוֹלְקִין בַּיַּיִן כָּךְ חוֹלְקִין בַּזְּמוֹרוֹת וּבַקָּנִים — Similarly, if a sharecropper rents a vineyard, **just as [he and the owner] share the wine** produced by the vineyard's grapes, **so they share the branches** that are trimmed from the grapevines **and,** at the end of the season, they share **the poles** that supported the vines as they grew. וּשְׁנֵיהֶם מְסַפְּקִין אֶת הַקָּנִים — They

---

NOTES

[1]

1. Grain can be harvested in either of two ways: It can be cut (with a sickle or similar tool) or the whole plant can be uprooted from the ground. Each method has advantages and disadvantages. [For example, cutting the grain is easier, while uprooting it leaves the ground cleaner (see *Tos. Yom Tov*).] If the renter and owner disagree about which method to use, the renter must follow the local custom.

2. *Tos. Yom Tov.*

3. A stalk of grain consists of three parts: the kernel, which is eaten; the straw, which is cut with the grain and used for animal feed; and the stubble, which is usually left in the ground when the grain is cut, and was used as fuel for fire (see *Tos. Yom Tov; Shabbos* 3:1). A sharecropper must give the owner a percentage of the straw and stubble just as he gives him a percentage of the edible kernels.

[165] MISHNAH BAVA METZIA / Chapter 9: Ham'kabeil

— רע"ב —

(ב) בית השלחין. קרקע יבשה שאין די לה מי גשמים: או בית האילן. ובשביל האילן היה מקבלה על האריס, שנוטל חלק בפירות בלא טורח: יבש המעיין שבה, שממנו משקין

[ב] הַמְקַבֵּל שָׂדֶה מֵחֲבֵרוֹ, וְהִיא בֵית הַשְּׁלָחִין אוֹ בֵית הָאִילָן, יָבֵשׁ הַמַּעְיָן וְנִקְצַץ הָאִילָן, אֵינוֹ מְנַכֶּה לוֹ מִן חֲכוֹרוֹ. אִם אָמַר לוֹ, חֲכֹר לִי שְׂדֵה בֵית הַשְּׁלָחִין זֶה, אוֹ שְׂדֵה בֵית הָאִילָן זֶה,

מתוכה: **מן חבירו.** אם קבלה בחכירות כך וכך כורין לשנה. דמטיקרא לא גלי דעתיה דמשום מעין או אילן טפי לה בחכירותה: **חכור לי בית השלחין זו.** גלי דעתיה דבשביל שהיא בית השלחין טפי לה וחכרה ממנו:

---

share these poles because **they both provide the poles.** That is, they both share the cost of setting up the poles at the beginning of the season; therefore, they share the poles after the grapes are harvested.[4]

[2] The Mishnah discusses whether a renter can deduct from the rent if the field loses certain advantages:

וְהִיא בֵית, הַמְקַבֵּל שָׂדֶה מֵחֲבֵרוֹ — **Someone rents a field from his friend,** הַשְּׁלָחִין — **and it is a field that requires irrigation,**[1] i.e., its crops cannot grow on rainwater alone but must be watered by other means; however, the field contains a spring from which it can be easily watered. אוֹ בֵית הָאִילָן — **Or,** he rents **a field that contains** a **fruit tree,** which provides him with fruit, in addition to the field's crops.[2] יָבֵשׁ הַמַּעְיָן — **If the spring dries up**[3] וְנִקְצַץ הָאִילָן — **or the** fruit **tree is cut down,** אֵינוֹ מְנַכֶּה לוֹ מִן חֲכוֹרוֹ — **[the renter] may not deduct** anything **from the rent,** even though he lost the advantage of the spring or tree.[4] אִם אָמַר לוֹ חֲכֹר לִי שְׂדֵה בֵית הַשְּׁלָחִין זֶה — However, **if [the renter] had originally said to [the owner], "Rent me this field that requires irrigation"** (i.e., a field with a spring),[5] אוֹ שְׂדֵה בֵית הָאִילָן זֶה — or, **"Rent me this field that contains**

--- NOTES ---

4. [A sharecropper is responsible for working the field and protecting it; all other tasks (such as setting up poles to support the grapevines) are shared by the sharecropper and the owner. In contrast, a farmer who pays a fixed rent must do all the work in the field on his own (*Rashi; Beur HaGra, Choshen Mishpat* 320:14).]

The Mishnah refers to a place that has no specific custom about how these things are shared. Otherwise, they follow the local custom, as the Mishnah taught earlier (*Ritva*).

[2]

1. Literally, *a thirsty field.*
2. Such a field is desirable, because the renter is entitled to fruit from the tree even though the tree requires no work on his part (*Rav*).

3. Since the crops need irrigation, the farmer now has to carry water from other sources [which will take more effort] (*Gemara* 103b-104a).

4. [Even if the renter claims that he had agreed to the original price only because the field contained a spring or tree], since he did not mention this specifically at the time of rental, he cannot change the terms even if the field loses that advantage (*Rav*).

5. Since most fields that need to be irrigated contain their own water sources, when a person says, "This field that requires irrigation," he implies a field that contains a spring (see *Tiferes Yisrael*).

יָבֵשׁ הַמַּעְיָן וְנִקְצַץ הָאִילָן, מְנַכֶּה לוֹ מִן חַכּוֹרוֹ.

[ג] הַמְקַבֵּל שָׂדֶה מֵחֲבֵרוֹ וְהוֹבִירָהּ, שָׁמִין אוֹתָהּ כַּמָּה רְאוּיָה לַעֲשׂוֹת וְנוֹתֵן לוֹ. שֶׁכָּךְ כּוֹתֵב לוֹ, אִם אוֹבִיר וְלֹא אַעֲבִיד, אֲשַׁלֵּם בְּמֵיטָבָא.

— רע״ב —

(ג) המקבל שדה. למחצה לשליש ולרביע: הובירה. שלא חרש בה ולא זרעה: אם אוביר. אטשנה בורה ולא אעביד. ולא אטשה בה פטולה הראויה לה: אשלם במיטבא. כפי מה שהיתה ראויה לעשות אם היתה חרושה וזרועה כראוי:

יָבֵשׁ הַמַּעְיָן וְנִקְצַץ הָאִילָן — if the spring dried up or the tree was cut down, **מְנַכֶּה לוֹ מִן חַכּוֹרוֹ** — he can deduct from the rent. By specifying the field's qualities when he rented it, he made it clear that he agreed to the price only because the field had an extra advantage. Accordingly, if it loses that advantage, he can deduct from the rent.[6]

[3] A sharecropper pays the field's owner a percentage of the crops that grow in the field. This Mishnah discusses the law if the sharecropper does not plant any crops:

הַמְקַבֵּל שָׂדֶה מֵחֲבֵרוֹ וְהוֹבִירָהּ — If someone rents a field from his friend as a sharecropper but leaves it fallow (i.e., he does not plow it or plant any crops), **שָׁמִין אוֹתָהּ כַּמָּה רְאוּיָה לַעֲשׂוֹת** — we evaluate [the field] to see how much it could produce if it is planted, **וְנוֹתֵן לוֹ** — and [the sharecropper] must give [the owner] what he would have received as his share if crops had been planted.[1] **שֶׁכָּךְ כּוֹתֵב לוֹ** — This is because [a sharecropper] writes the following to [the owner] in the rental document: **אִם אוֹבִיר וְלֹא אַעֲבִיד** — "If I leave the field fallow and do not work it, **אֲשַׁלֵּם בְּמֵיטָבָא** — I will pay you based on what the field would produce if it were planted properly."[2]

NOTES

6. He pays the owner the price that someone would pay for the field as it is now, i.e., without a spring or tree (see *Meiri*).

These laws apply to any type of field rental (*Tos. Yom Tov,* from Gemara 104a). A sharecropper deducts from the amount of produce that he gives the owner, and a renter who pays a fixed price deducts from that price.

[3]

1. For example, if he had agreed to pay the owner one-third of the crop, and it is estimated that the field could have produced 60 *kors* of wheat, he must give the owner 20 *kors* of wheat.

[The same applies if the sharecropper plants only part of the field: he must pay the owner what he would have received had the whole field been planted (*Tiferes Yisrael*).]

2. The Mishnah's law applies even if the sharecropper did not actually write this, because this clause is usually included in the agreement, and it can be assumed that he agreed to work the field under the usual terms [unless he specifically said otherwise] (*Tos. Yom Tov*).

[A renter who pays a fixed price (either in produce or money) must pay that amount regardless of whether he plants the field or not (*Tos. Yom Tov*).]

[ד] הַמְקַבֵּל שָׂדֶה מֵחֲבֵרוֹ וְלֹא רָצָה לְנַכֵּשׁ, וְאָמַר לוֹ, מָה אִכְפַּת לָךְ, הוֹאִיל וַאֲנִי נוֹתֵן לְךָ חֲכוֹרָהּ, אֵין שׁוֹמְעִין לוֹ, מִפְּנֵי שֶׁיָּכוֹל לוֹמַר לוֹ, לְמָחָר אַתָּה יוֹצֵא מִמֶּנָּה, וּמַעֲלָה לְפָנַי עֲשָׂבִים.

[ה] הַמְקַבֵּל שָׂדֶה מֵחֲבֵרוֹ וְלֹא עָשְׂתָה, אִם יֵשׁ בָּהּ כְּדֵי לְהַעֲמִיד כְּרִי,

— רע״ב —

(ד) ולא רצה לנכש. לנקות התבואה מעשבים רעים, שמתישים כח הקרקע ומעכבין התבואה מלעלות: מה איכפת לך. אם יחסר חלקי, שהעשבים מכחישין הצבלים. אתן לך חכירוך כך וכך כורין שפסקתי עמך: (ה) המקבל שדה מחבירו. למחצה לשליש ולרביע כחכרים: ולא עשתה. תבואה אלא מעט. ובא לו האריס למנוע מלהתעסק בה עוד, שאין בה כדי טרחו: אם יש בה כדי לעשות מתבואתה כרי. שיש בו כדי לכסות הרחת שזורים בה התבואה, והוא קרוב לסאתים. חייב לעפל בה בעל כרחו:

---

[4] הַמְקַבֵּל שָׂדֶה מֵחֲבֵרוֹ — **Someone rented a field from his friend** for a fixed payment, וְלֹא רָצָה לְנַכֵּשׁ — **but he did not want to weed the field, and** as a result, the field will produce fewer crops,[1] וְאָמַר לוֹ — **and he said to [the owner],** מָה אִכְפַּת לָךְ הוֹאִיל וַאֲנִי נוֹתֵן לְךָ חֲכוֹרָהּ — **"Why does it matter to you** whether I weed the field? **Since I give you a set payment for [the field]** no matter how much it produces, the weeds will not affect the amount you receive."[2] אֵין שׁוֹמְעִין לוֹ — **We do not listen to him** and he must weed the field, מִפְּנֵי שֶׁיָּכוֹל לוֹמַר לוֹ — **because [the owner] can say to him,** לְמָחָר אַתָּה יוֹצֵא מִמֶּנָּה וּמַעֲלָה לְפָנַי עֲשָׂבִים — "Although the weeds may not affect me now, **tomorrow** (i.e., when your rental is over), **you will leave [the field], and** if you do not weed it now, **it will grow weeds for me** then and affect my crops."[3]

[5] A law that applies to a sharecropper:

הַמְקַבֵּל שָׂדֶה מֵחֲבֵרוֹ — **Someone rents a field from his friend** as a sharecropper, וְלֹא עָשְׂתָה — **but it did not produce** a significant amount, and he does not think it worth his time to tend the few crops that are growing. The owner, however, wants the sharecropper to tend to whatever crops there are.[1] אִם יֵשׁ בָּהּ כְּדֵי לְהַעֲמִיד כְּרִי — **The law is that if there is** enough produce growing

--- NOTES ---

[4]

1. If the weeds are left in the soil, they weaken it and reduce its ability to produce crops (*Rav*).

[The Mishnah refers to a case where the field is in a place that has no custom as to whether or not farmers weed their fields. If there is a local custom, they must follow the custom, as we learned in Mishnah 1 (*Tos. Yom Tov*).]

2. [A sharecropper, who pays the owner a percentage of the field's crops, obviously cannot make such a claim, because if the field produces less, the owner will receive less (*Tos. Yom Tov*).]

3. If the renter does not clear the field, the owner will be left with a field full of weeds (*Meiri*). Even if they are later destroyed, those weeds will have left seeds that will sprout more weeds in the future (see *Tos. Yom Tov*).

[5]

1. Since the rent is paid with a percentage of the crops, the owner will not receive anything if the sharecropper abandons the field.

A renter who pays a fixed price (either in produce or money) may stop working

חַיָּב לְטַפֵּל בָּהּ. אָמַר רַבִּי יְהוּדָה, מַה קִּצְבָה בַּכְּרִי, אֶלָּא אִם יֵשׁ בָּהּ כְּדֵי נְפִילָה.

[ו] הַמְקַבֵּל שָׂדֶה מֵחֲבֵרוֹ, וַאֲכָלָהּ חָגָב אוֹ נִשְׁדְּפָה, אִם מַכַּת מְדִינָה הִיא,

— רע"ב —

מה קצבה בכרי. אין קצבה זו רצויה, שתהיה שדה גדולה בשיעור כרי ושדה קטנה בשיעור כרי. ואינה דומה טפולה של שדה גדולה, לטפולה של שדה קטנה: אלא אם יש

בו כדי נפילה. כלומר כשיעור מה שזרע בה, חייב לטפל בה. ואין הלכה כרבי יהודה: (ו) המקבל שדה. בתחכירות כך וכך כורין: מכת מדינה. שאכל חגב או נשדפו, רוב שדות של אותה מדינה או אותה בקעה:

---

in [the field] that, when harvested, it will **form a pile** of grain,[2] בָּהּ — [the sharecropper] must continue to take care of [the field].[3] If the field cannot produce that amount, he may abandon the crops.[4]

Another opinion:

אָמַר רַבִּי יְהוּדָה — R' Yehudah said: מַה קִּצְבָה בַּכְּרִי — Why should there be a fixed limit of a pile of grain for every field? It should depend on the size of the field: a large field requires more work than a small field, and thus should need to produce more grain to be worth the effort. אֶלָּא אִם יֵשׁ בָּהּ כְּדֵי נְפִילָה — Rather, the sharecropper must continue to tend the crops only if there is enough produce growing in [the field] to yield as much grain as was originally used to plant the field.[5]

[6] A law that applies to a renter who pays a fixed price:

הַמְקַבֵּל שָׂדֶה מֵחֲבֵרוֹ — If someone rents a field from his friend for a fixed payment, וַאֲכָלָהּ חָגָב אוֹ נִשְׁדְּפָה — and [its crops] were eaten by locusts or ruined by strong winds,[1] the law is as follows: אִם מַכַּת מְדִינָה הִיא — If it is

--- NOTES ---

the field at any time and the owner can have no complaints — because the renter must pay the agreed-upon price regardless [although he must prevent damage to the field, as we learned in the previous Mishnah] (*Tos. Yom Tov*).

2. [That is, if he continues to tend to the crops, they will produce enough grain to make a pile.] "A pile" here refers to a heap of grain large enough that if a winnowing shovel (the shovel used to scoop up the grain and toss it in the air to winnow it [see *Shabbos* 17:2]) is thrust into the pile, the grain will cover the bottom part of the shovel (*Rav,* Gemara 105a).

3. When a sharecropper rents a field, he usually signs a document that says: "I will plow, plant ... and present you with a pile of grain." As long as the field can produce enough grain for the sharecropper to fulfill this agreement, he must continue to tend the crops.

This law applies even if the sharecropper did not actually sign such a document; since these are the usual terms, they apply to everyone [unless he specified otherwise] (*Tos. Yom Tov*).

4. [In Mishnah 3, we learned that a sharecropper who does not plant the field properly must nevertheless pay the owner the full amount that he should have received. In our Mishnah, though, the sharecropper is allowed to abandon the field without paying for it, because *he* is not neglecting his responsibility; rather, the *field* is defective and did not produce a proper crop.]

5. For example, if he planted ten *kors* of seeds, he need work the field only if it will produce at least ten *kors* of grain.

[6]

1. Strong winds tore the kernels of grain off the stalks and blew them away (*Tiferes Yisrael*).

מְנַכֶּה לוֹ מִן חֲכוֹרוֹ, אִם אֵינָהּ מַכַּת מְדִינָה, אֵין מְנַכֶּה לוֹ מִן חֲכוֹרוֹ. רַבִּי יְהוּדָה אוֹמֵר, אִם קִבְּלָהּ הֵימֶנּוּ בְּמָעוֹת, בֵּין כָּךְ וּבֵין כָּךְ אֵינוֹ מְנַכֶּה לוֹ מֵחֲכוֹרוֹ.

[ז] **הַמְקַבֵּל** שָׂדֶה מֵחֲבֵרוֹ בַּעֲשֶׂרֶת כּוֹר חִטִּים לְשָׁנָה, לָקְתָה, נוֹתֵן לוֹ מִתּוֹכָהּ.

— רע"ב —

אינו מנכה. דאמר לו מזלך גרם: בין כך ובין כך. אפילו היא מכת מדינה אינו מנכה. שעל המעות לא נגזרה גזירה: (ז) ולקתה. שהיו החטים שדופות: נותן לו. עשרת כורים שפסק עמו, מחטים שדופות הללו. ולא מצי למימר ליה, חטים יפות קא בעינא מינך:

---

a regional disaster, that is, the locusts or strong winds ruined most of the fields in that area,[2] מְנַכֶּה לוֹ מִן חֲכוֹרוֹ — **he can deduct from his rent.** The fact that most local fields were affected indicates that this calamity was the result of a Heavenly decree on the whole area; therefore, both the owner and renter must share in the loss.[3] אִם אֵינָהּ מַכַּת מְדִינָה — **But if it is not a regional disaster,** that is, most of the fields in the area were not affected, אֵין מְנַכֶּה לוֹ מִן חֲכוֹרוֹ — **[the renter] cannot deduct from his rent.** In this case, the owner can argue that since only the renter's crops were damaged, it must be due to the renter's bad fortune, and he must absorb the loss himself.[4]

According to R' Yehudah, there is an exception to this law:

רַבִּי יְהוּדָה אוֹמֵר — **R' Yehudah says:** אִם קִבְּלָהּ הֵימֶנּוּ בְּמָעוֹת — **If he rented [the field] from [the owner] for money** (and not for a payment of produce), בֵּין כָּךְ וּבֵין כָּךְ אֵינוֹ מְנַכֶּה לוֹ מֵחֲכוֹרוֹ — **in either case** (i.e., whether it was a regional disaster or not), **he cannot deduct from his rent.** Even if the disaster was the result of a Heavenly decree on the whole area, the fact that only produce was destroyed indicates that the decree was against produce and not against money. Since the owner is not paid in produce, he was not included in the decree and should not lose out because of the disaster.[5]

[7] A law about a renter who pays a fixed payment of produce:

הַמְקַבֵּל שָׂדֶה מֵחֲבֵרוֹ בַּעֲשֶׂרֶת כּוֹר חִטִּים לְשָׁנָה — **If someone rents a wheat field from his friend** for a fixed payment of **ten** *kors* **of wheat a year,** לָקְתָה — **even if [the field] was damaged** (e.g., by a storm) and as a result, its crop was of poor quality, נוֹתֵן לוֹ מִתּוֹכָהּ — **he pays [the owner] with ten** *kors* of

---
NOTES

2. It is considered a regional disaster if this calamity affected either most of the fields in that town or most of the fields in that immediate area (*Rav*).

3. *Levush, Choshen Mishpat* 322:1.
   He can deduct an amount in proportion to the amount of crops that were ruined (*Tos. Yom Tov*). For example, if half the crops were ruined, he pays the owner half of the agreed-upon payment.

4. The Mishnah discusses a renter who pays a fixed fee. A sharecropper, who pays a percentage of the crops, obviously ends up paying less if some crops are damaged [regardless of whether other fields also suffered damage] (*Rav, Tos. Yom Tov*).

5. R' Yehudah agrees, though, that if the renter was to pay a fixed amount of produce, he can deduct from the rent in the event of a regional disaster (*Tiferes Yisrael*).

משניות בבא מציעא / פרק ט: המקבל [170]

הָיוּ חִטֶּיהָ יָפוֹת, לֹא יֹאמַר לוֹ, הֲרֵינִי לוֹקֵחַ מִן הַשּׁוּק, אֶלָּא נוֹתֵן לוֹ מִתּוֹכָהּ.

[ח] **הַמְקַבֵּל** שָׂדֶה מֵחֲבֵרוֹ לְזָרְעָהּ שְׂעוֹרִים, לֹא יִזְרָעֶנָּה חִטִּים. חִטִּים, יִזְרָעֶנָּה שְׂעוֹרִים. רַבָּן שִׁמְעוֹן בֶּן גַּמְלִיאֵל אוֹסֵר.

— רע״ב —

(ח) **המקבל** שדה מחבירו לזרעה שעורים. בתכירות, כך וכך שעורים או חטים או מעות, לא יזרענה חטים. שהחטים מכחישות הקרקע [יותר] מן השעורים: **רבן שמעון בן גמליאל אוסר.** שקשה לקרקע כשזורעים אותה שנה ממין זה ושנה ממין אחר. ולעניין פסק הלכה, הכל לפי הקרקע ולפי המקום. אם התנה עמו בדבר שמכחיש הקרקע מעט, אינו יכול לשנות ולזרוע דבר שמכחיש הרבה. ואיפכא שרי:

---

wheat from [that field]; he does not have to buy wheat of better quality in order to pay the rent. **הָיוּ חִטֶּיהָ יָפוֹת** — Likewise, if [the field's] wheat was of especially **good quality,** **לֹא יֹאמַר לוֹ הֲרֵינִי לוֹקֵחַ מִן הַשּׁוּק** — he cannot say to [the owner], "I will buy ordinary wheat from the market to give you, and I will keep all the high-quality wheat for myself"; **אֶלָּא נוֹתֵן לוֹ מִתּוֹכָהּ** — rather, he must give [the owner] ten *kors* of the wheat that grew in [that field].[1]

[8] Another law that applies to a renter who pays a fixed price (of either money or produce):

הַמְקַבֵּל שָׂדֶה מֵחֲבֵרוֹ לְזָרְעָהּ שְׂעוֹרִים — If someone rents a field from his friend for a fixed payment and agrees **to plant it** with barley, **לֹא יִזְרָעֶנָּה חִטִּים** — he **may not plant it** with wheat, because wheat weakens the land more than barley does.[1] **חִטִּים יִזְרָעֶנָּה שְׂעוֹרִים** — However, if he agreed to plant **wheat, he may plant it** with **barley,** since that will place less strain on the land.[2] **רַבָּן שִׁמְעוֹן בֶּן גַּמְלִיאֵל אוֹסֵר** — But **Rabban Shimon ben Gamliel forbids** making any change. This is because switching crops from year to year weakens the soil, and therefore any change can weaken the land.[3]

NOTES

[7]

1. Although the owner is paid a set amount of wheat no matter how much the field produces, it is understood as part of the rental agreement that if possible, he will be paid from the wheat that grows in the field (*Rabbeinu Yehonasan*).

[The Mishnah gives the law for a renter who pays a fixed price. It is obvious that a sharecropper pays with the produce that grows in the field, no matter its quality (*Tos. Yom Tov*).]

[8]

1. A sharecropper, though, may plant wheat even if he agreed to plant barley. Since wheat is more valuable than barley, it can be assumed that in the case of a sharecropper, where the owner receives a portion of the crop, he allows the farmer to plant wheat even though it weakens the soil, because it will provide him with a greater profit (*Tos. Yom Tov*).

2. [If he had agreed to pay a specific amount of wheat for the rent, he will have to buy wheat from the market to pay the owner (see *Tos. Yom Tov*).]

3. A land is weakened if different crops are planted in it each year (*Rav*). Thus, although barley is generally easier on the land than wheat is, barley will harm the field if it had been planted with wheat the year before. Because of this concern, Rabban Shimon ben Gamliel rules that the farmer may never change from the agreed-upon crop (*Tos. Yom Tov*).

The Tanna Kamma, however, holds

[171] MISHNAH BAVA METZIA / Chapter 9: *Ham'kabeil*

תְּבוּאָה, לֹא יִזְרָעֶנָּה קִטְנִית. קִטְנִית, יִזְרָעֶנָּה תְּבוּאָה. רַבָּן שִׁמְעוֹן בֶּן גַּמְלִיאֵל אוֹסֵר.

[ט] **הַמְקַבֵּל** שָׂדֶה מֵחֲבֵרוֹ לְשָׁנִים מֻעָטוֹת, לֹא יִזְרָעֶנָּה פִשְׁתָּן, וְאֵין לוֹ בְקוֹרַת שִׁקְמָה. קִבְּלָהּ הֵימֶנּוּ לְשֶׁבַע שָׁנִים,

— רע"ב —

(ט) **לשנים מועטות.** פחות משבע שנים: **לא יזרענה פשתן.** שזרע פשתן מכחיש בארץ הרבה, ושרשיו נשארים בקרקע עד שבע שנים: **ואין לו בקורת שקמה.** עץ תאנה של יער הוא, וקולסים ענפיו לקורות הבנין, והם חוזרים וגדלים. ופחות משבע שנים אין נעשות קורות. הלכך קבלה לפחות משבע שנים לא יקוץ קורות שבה, דלאו אדעתא דקורות נחית, דבשנים מועטות אינם חוזרים לקורות. אבל קבלה לשבע שנים, שנה ראשונה זורעה פשתן, וקוצץ שקמה שבה:

A similar law:

תְּבוּאָה לֹא יִזְרָעֶנָּה קִטְנִית — **If a renter agreed to plant grain** in the rented field, **he may not plant it** with **beans**, because beans weaken the land more than grain does. קִטְנִית יִזְרָעֶנָּה תְּבוּאָה — However, **if he agreed to plant beans, he may plant it** with **grain**, since that will place less strain on the land.[4] רַבָּן שִׁמְעוֹן בֶּן גַּמְלִיאֵל אוֹסֵר — But **Rabban Shimon ben Gamliel forbids** making any change, because any change can weaken the land.[5]

[9] הַמְקַבֵּל שָׂדֶה מֵחֲבֵרוֹ לְשָׁנִים מֻעָטוֹת — **If someone rents a field from his friend for a few years**, i.e., less than seven years, לֹא יִזְרָעֶנָּה פִשְׁתָּן — **he may not plant it** with **flax**, because flax weakens the land and it does not return to full strength for seven years.[1] Since he rented the field for less than seven years, he will return it in a weaker state than he received it.[2] וְאֵין לוֹ בְקוֹרַת שִׁקְמָה — Likewise, **he does not have** the right to cut **beams** of wood **from a sycamore tree** in the field,[3] because a sycamore tree takes seven years to grow back fully, and if he cuts its branches, he will not return it in the same state as he received it.[4]

קִבְּלָהּ הֵימֶנּוּ לְשֶׁבַע שָׁנִים — However, **if he rented [the field] from him for seven**

NOTES

that if the owner was concerned about this, he would have specified that the sharecropper may plant *only* wheat (*Kos HaYeshuos* 107a).

4. The Mishnah's examples apply to the soil of Eretz Yisrael (Gemara 107a). As far as other places, it depends on the condition of the local soil: the renter may not switch to a crop that will place a greater strain on the soil than the agreed-upon crop would have, but he may switch to a crop that will place less of a strain on the soil (*Rav*).

5. See note 3.

[9]

1. *Rav, Rashi.*
2. This law applies only to a renter who pays a fixed price. A sharecropper, though, may plant flax, because flax is valuable, and it can be assumed that in the case of a sharecropper, where the owner receives a portion of the crop, he allows the farmer to plant flax even though it weakens the soil, because it will provide him with a greater profit (*Tos. Yom Tov*).

3. The Mishnah refers to a case where it was customary for a renter to enjoy the right to take fruit and wood from the trees in the field (*Meiri*). If the field contains a sycamore (a type of wild fig tree whose branches were used to make beams), a short-term renter may not cut its branches (*Rav*).

4. This law applies to all types of rentals.

שָׁנָה רִאשׁוֹנָה יִזְרָעֶנָּה פִּשְׁתָּן, וְיֵשׁ לוֹ בְקוֹרַת שִׁקְמָה.

[י] הַמְקַבֵּל שָׂדֶה מֵחֲבֵרוֹ לְשָׁבוּעַ אֶחָד בְּשֶׁבַע מֵאוֹת זוּז, הַשְּׁבִיעִית מִן הַמִּנְיָן. קִבְּלָהּ הֵימֶנּוּ שֶׁבַע שָׁנִים בְּשֶׁבַע מֵאוֹת זוּז, אֵין הַשְּׁבִיעִית מִן הַמִּנְיָן.

שָׁנָה רִאשׁוֹנָה יִזְרָעֶנָּה פִּשְׁתָּן — during **the first year** of the rental **he may plant it with flax** וְיֵשׁ לוֹ בְקוֹרַת שִׁקְמָה — **and he has** the right to cut **beams from a sycamore tree,** because by the time the rental period is over, the field or tree will have returned to its original state.[5]

[10] Every seventh year, the *shemittah* (Sabbatical year) is observed, during which it is forbidden to work the land of Eretz Yisrael or plant crops there. This Mishnah discusses whether a person who rents a field must count *shemittah*, when he cannot work the field, as part of the rental:

הַמְקַבֵּל שָׂדֶה מֵחֲבֵרוֹ לְשָׁבוּעַ אֶחָד בְּשֶׁבַע מֵאוֹת זוּז — **If someone rents a field from his friend** saying, "I am renting the field **'for one seven-year period'** for the price of **seven hundred** *zuz*,"[1] הַשְּׁבִיעִית מִן הַמִּנְיָן — the *shemittah* **is counted** as part of the seven years. Since he specified "one seven-year period," he keeps the field for seven years in a row, even though he will not be able to work the land during one of those years.[2] קִבְּלָהּ הֵימֶנּוּ שֶׁבַע שָׁנִים בְּשֶׁבַע מֵאוֹת זוּז — However, if **he rented it from him** saying, "I am renting the field **'for seven years'** for seven hundred *zuz*," אֵין הַשְּׁבִיעִית מִן הַמִּנְיָן — the *shemittah* year **is not counted** as part of the seven years. In this case, the renter implied that he was renting the field for seven years during which it can be used.[3] Therefore, he keeps the field for seven years aside from the *shemittah* year (eight years in total).

[11] The Mishnah turns to a new subject. The Torah states that a worker must be paid right after he finishes his work; an employer who pays his worker

---

NOTES

5. The Mishnah refers to a case where the branches were fully grown when the rental period began. If, for example, the branches had been cut two years before the rental period began, the renter can cut beams in the fifth year of the rental, because he will be returning the tree as he got it — with two years' of growth on the branches (*Tos. Yom Tov*).

[10]

1. Although the Mishnah gives a case where the field was rented for money, the law is the same if the field was rented for a fixed amount of crops or for a percentage of the crops (*Rambam, Hilchos Sechirus* 8:3, with *Maggid Mishneh*).

2. Since he rented the field for a period of seven years, he knew that one of those years would be *shemittah*, when he would not be able to work the field, and he nevertheless agreed to the rental (see *Rabbeinu Yehonasan*). Therefore, he cannot keep the field for an extra year to make up for the year of *shemittah,* and he cannot demand a discount for that year (see *Tos. Yom Tov*).

3. The expression "for seven years" implies that he is paying for each year separately, and he surely does not intend to pay for a year when he cannot use the field (see *Rabbeinu Yehonasan*).

— רע"ב —

[יא] שָׂכִיר יוֹם גּוֹבֶה כָּל הַלַּיְלָה. שָׂכִיר לַיְלָה גּוֹבֶה כָּל הַיּוֹם. שְׂכִיר שָׁעוֹת גּוֹבֶה כָּל הַלַּיְלָה וְכָל הַיּוֹם. שְׂכִיר שַׁבָּת, שְׂכִיר חֹדֶשׁ, שְׂכִיר שָׁנָה, שְׂכִיר שָׁבוּעַ, יָצָא בַיּוֹם, גּוֹבֶה כָּל הַיּוֹם;

(יא) שכיר יום גובה כל הלילה. שלאחריו. שנאמר (ויקרא יט,יג) לא תלין פעולת שכיר אתך עד בקר. ואי אפשר לומר שבשכיר לילה מדבר, שהרי אין שכירות משתלמת אלא בסופה, דכתיב (שם כה,גג) כשכיר

שנה בשנה, ודרשינן מיניה [בבא מציעא סה, א] שכירות של שנה זו משתלמת בתחלת שנה אחרת, אלמא לא משתעבד ליה לשכיר יום עד שקיעת החמה. וכי כתיב (דברים כד,טו) לא תבא על כרכך בשכיר לילה תוקמיה, שנשתעבד לו לבקר משכלתה שכירותו. וכן לא תלין נמי לא תוקמיה בשכיר לילה, דהא לא משתעבד ליה עד הבקר: שכיר שעות גובה כל היום וכל הלילה. הכי קאמר, שכיר שעות דיום גובה כל היום, שכיר שעות דלילה גובה כל הלילה. שמטה: יצא ביום. שכלתה שכירותו לבקר או ביום, גובה כל היום. וכיון ששקעה חמה מה טובר עליו:

---

late transgresses a prohibition. This Mishnah discusses what is considered "late" for various types of workers with regard to this law:

שְׂכִיר יוֹם גּוֹבֶה כָּל הַלַּיְלָה — **Someone who is hired** to work **for an** entire **day** and finishes at sunset **collects** his wages during **the entire night** that follows, i.e., that night is the proper time for him to be paid. If the employer does not pay him before dawn, the employer transgresses the Torah's command to pay a worker on time. שְׂכִיר לַיְלָה גּוֹבֶה כָּל הַיּוֹם — **Someone who is hired** to work **for an** entire **night** and finishes at dawn **collects** his wages during **the entire day** that follows, i.e., that day is the proper time for him to be paid. If the employer does not pay him before sunset, the employer transgresses the Torah's command.[1] שְׂכִיר שָׁעוֹת — **Someone who is hired for** only **a few hours** must be paid based on when he finishes working: גּוֹבֶה כָּל הַלַּיְלָה — If he finishes during the night, **he collects** his wages **that entire night**, i.e., he must be paid before dawn; וְכָל הַיּוֹם — **and** if he finishes work during the day, he collects his wages **that entire day**, i.e., he must be paid before sunset.

The Mishnah discusses when to pay workers who work for longer periods of time:

שְׂכִיר שַׁבָּת שְׂכִיר חֹדֶשׁ שְׂכִיר שָׁנָה שְׂכִיר שָׁבוּעַ — **In the case of someone hired** to work **for a week, someone hired for a month, someone hired for a year,** or **someone hired for a seven-year period,** the law is as follows: יָצָא בַיּוֹם גּוֹבֶה כָּל הַיּוֹם — **if he finished** his work **during the day,**[2] **he collects** his wages

---

NOTES

[11]

1. In two places, the Torah forbids paying a worker late. One verse states (*Leviticus* 19:13): *You may not keep the wages of a worker with you overnight until morning.* This refers to a day worker; he must be paid during the night following his work, before morning. Another verse states (*Deuteronomy* 24:15): *You shall give him his wages on that day; the sun shall not set upon him.* This verse, which contains both a positive mitzvah to pay a worker on time and a prohibition not to pay him late, refers to a night worker; he must be paid during the day following his work, before sunset (*Rav; Talmid HaRashba*).

2. Literally, *he left during the day.*

יָצָא בַלַּיְלָה, גּוֹבֶה כָּל הַלַּיְלָה וְכָל הַיּוֹם.

[יב] אֶחָד שְׂכַר אָדָם, וְאֶחָד שְׂכַר בְּהֵמָה, וְאֶחָד שְׂכַר כֵּלִים, יֵשׁ בּוֹ מִשּׁוּם בְּיוֹמוֹ תִתֵּן שְׂכָרוֹ, וְיֵשׁ בּוֹ מִשּׁוּם לֹא תָלִין פְּעֻלַּת שָׂכִיר אִתְּךָ עַד בֹּקֶר.

— רע״ב —

יצא בלילה. שכלתה שכירותו בלילה: **גובה כל הלילה וכל היום.** דכיון דמשכה פעולתו משתחשך הוה ליה שכיר לילה ואינו עובר עליו בבקר, עד למחרת בשקיעת החמה: **(יב) ואחד שכר בהמה. ואחד שכר כלים.** דכתיב (ויקרא יט,יג) לא תלין פעולת שכיר אתך, כל שפעולתו אתך, ואפילו בהמה וכלים:

יָצָא — **בַּלַּיְלָה גּוֹבֶה כָּל הַלַּיְלָה וְכָל הַיּוֹם** — If he finished his work at night, he collects his wages anytime during that entire night and the entire next day, i.e., he must be paid before the next sunset.[3]

[12] The Mishnah states what type of wages are required to be paid on time:

אֶחָד שְׂכַר אָדָם — Whether someone owes a person's wages (i.e., wages for hiring a worker), וְאֶחָד שְׂכַר בְּהֵמָה — or payment for renting an animal, וְאֶחָד שְׂכַר כֵּלִים — or payment for renting utensils, יֵשׁ בּוֹ מִשּׁוּם "בְּיוֹמוֹ תִתֵּן שְׂכָרוֹ" — he is subject to the requirement to pay on time, based on the verse (Deuteronomy 24:15): You shall give him his wages on that day, וְיֵשׁ בּוֹ מִשּׁוּם "לֹא תָלִין פְּעֻלַּת שָׂכִיר אִתְּךָ עַד בֹּקֶר" — and based on the verse (Leviticus 19:13): You may not keep the wages of a worker with you overnight until morning.[1]

NOTES
---

3. The Gemara (111a) explains that this last law is the opinion of a different Tanna than the previous laws in the Mishnah. While the first Tanna taught that a worker who works for a few hours by day must be paid before sunset and someone who works for a few hours at night must be paid before morning, this Tanna (whom the Gemara identifies as R' Shimon) holds as follows: The Torah states (Deuteronomy 24:15) that a worker must be paid on the day he finishes his work. By Jewish law, a "day" begins at sunset and ends at the next sunset. Accordingly, no matter when a worker finishes working, he must be paid before the next sunset, which is the end of that "day." (Thus, if he finishes work during the day, his employer has less time to pay him than if he finishes at night — when there is a longer time until sunset.)

Although the Mishnah cites R' Shimon only with regard to a worker who works for a long period of time, R' Shimon holds that the same applies whether one works for a few hours or a few years; no matter when he finishes working, he must be paid before the next sunset (Tos. Yom Tov).

[Both the Tanna Kamma and R' Shimon agree to the Mishnah's first law, that when a worker works for an entire day and finishes at sunset, he must be paid before morning, based on the Torah's command: You may not keep the wages of a worker with you overnight until morning (see note 1).]

[12]

1. As we have learned (see Mishnah 11 note 1), one of these verses forbids paying day workers later than dawn, and the other forbids paying night workers later than sunset. Both prohibitions apply to all forms of rental: if it is a day rental, it must be paid before dawn, and if it a night rental, it must be paid before sunset (Meleches Shlomo).

[175] **MISHNAH BAVA METZIA** / Chapter 9: *Ham'kabeil*

אֵימָתַי, בִּזְמַן שֶׁתְּבָעוֹ. לֹא תְבָעוֹ, אֵינוֹ עוֹבֵר עָלָיו. הִמְחָהוּ אֵצֶל חֶנְוָנִי אוֹ אֵצֶל שֻׁלְחָנִי, אֵינוֹ עוֹבֵר עָלָיו. שָׂכִיר, בִּזְמַנּוֹ נִשְׁבָּע וְנוֹטֵל. עָבַר זְמַנּוֹ

— רע״ב —

לא תבעו אינו עובר עליו. דכתיב אתך, לדעתך שלא מדעתו: [המחהו.] נתקן מחללו, והעמידו אצל חנוני ואמר לו, תן לפועל זה בדינר פירות ואני אשלם. או אמר לשלחני, תן לו בדינר מעות עליו. דכתיב אתך, ולא שהמחהו אצל חנוני: שכיר בזמנו נשבע ונוטל. משום דבעל הבית טרוד בפועליו, ולפעמים סבור שנתן, והוא לא נתן, שקלוה לשבועה מבעל הבית ושדיוה אשכיר: שלא בזמנו. אף על גב דבעל הבית טרוד בפועליו, כי מטא זמן חיוביה רמי אנפשיה ומדכר, ולא תשיד בעל הבית

The Mishnah discusses when this prohibition applies and when it does not apply:

אֵימָתַי — **When** does a person violate the prohibition against paying a worker late? בִּזְמַן שֶׁתְּבָעוֹ[2] — **When [the worker]** asked him for his wages and the employer did not pay within the proper time. לֹא תְבָעוֹ אֵינוֹ עוֹבֵר עָלָיו — But if **[the worker] did not ask him** for his wages, **[the employer] does not transgress** the prohibition if he does not pay on time, because we can assume that the worker agrees not to be paid right away.[3] הִמְחָהוּ אֵצֶל חֶנְוָנִי — Similarly, if **[the employer] directed [the worker] to a storekeeper**, that is, he arranged for a storekeeper to give the worker food equal to the value of his wages, אוֹ אֵצֶל שֻׁלְחָנִי — **or** he directed the worker **to a moneychanger**, that is, he arranged for a moneychanger to pay the worker,[4] אֵינוֹ עוֹבֵר עָלָיו — **[the employer] does not transgress** the prohibition if the storekeeper or moneychanger does not pay the worker before the end of that day or night.[5]

Having discussed the proper time for various workers to be paid, the Mishnah teaches a law that applies during that time period:

שָׂכִיר בִּזְמַנּוֹ — If **a worker** asks for his payment **during the time** when he is supposed to be paid (as defined in the previous Mishnah), and the employer claims that he already paid him, נִשְׁבָּע וְנוֹטֵל — **[the worker] can swear** that he had not been paid **and collect** the money from the employer. The worker is believed and not the employer, because we suspect that the employer is preoccupied with his business and simply thinks that he paid the worker but he did not actually do so.[6] עָבַר זְמַנּוֹ — However, once **the proper time**

NOTES

2. Or the owner of the rented animal or object.
3. The Gemara (112a) derives from a verse in the Torah that the prohibition against paying a worker late does not apply in such a case (*Rav*).
4. The employer asked a storekeeper or moneychanger to give the worker food or money, and promised to pay him back (*Rav*).
5. The Gemara (112a) derives from a verse in the Torah that the prohibition against paying a worker late does not apply in such cases (*Rav*).

6. Usually, when a person claims that someone owes him money and the other person denies it, the defendant is believed — as long as he swears that he is telling the truth. (Sometimes the defendant is Biblically obligated to swear, and sometimes Rabbinic law obligates him to swear [see Mishnah 4:7].) Thus, when a worker claims that his employer owes him money and the employer denies the claim, the defendant (i.e., the employer) should be allowed to swear that he is telling the truth and be exempt from paying. However, the Sages made an exception

אֵינוֹ נִשְׁבָּע וְנוֹטֵל. אִם יֵשׁ עֵדִים שֶׁתְּבָעוֹ, הֲרֵי זֶה נִשְׁבָּע וְנוֹטֵל. גֵּר תּוֹשָׁב יֵשׁ בּוֹ מִשּׁוּם בְּיוֹמוֹ תִתֵּן שְׂכָרוֹ, וְאֵין בּוֹ מִשּׁוּם לֹא תָלִין פְּעֻלַּת שָׂכִיר אִתְּךָ עַד בֹּקֶר.

— רע״ב —

שֶׁהוּא טוֹרֵחַ עַל כָּל תָּלִין: גֵּר תּוֹשָׁב. שֶׁקִּבֵּל עָלָיו שֶׁלֹּא לַעֲבוֹד עֲבוֹדָה זָרָה וְאוֹכֵל נְבֵלוֹת, אֵין בּוֹ מִשּׁוּם לֹא תָלִין, דִּכְתִיב בְּרֵישָׁא דִקְרָא רֵעֶךָ, רֵעֲךָ וְלֹא גֵּר תּוֹשָׁב:

---

for the worker to be paid **has passed**, if the worker claims that he was not paid and the employer claims that he paid him, אֵינוֹ נִשְׁבָּע וְנוֹטֵל — **[the worker] cannot swear and collect** his wages; rather, the employer can swear that he paid the worker and he is then exempt from paying. This is because we assume that even a busy employer makes sure to pay his workers before the deadline so as not to transgress the Torah's command against paying late; therefore, once the deadline has passed, the employer is believed and not the worker.[7] אִם יֵשׁ עֵדִים שֶׁתְּבָעוֹ — But **if there are witnesses** who testify that **[the worker] asked [the owner]** for payment right before the deadline and the employer pushed him off until later, הֲרֵי זֶה נִשְׁבָּע וְנוֹטֵל — **then** even after the deadline **[the worker] can swear** that he was not paid **and collect** his wages.[8] In this case, the worker is believed even after the deadline, because the employer was clearly not concerned about missing the deadline.

The Mishnah concludes with a unique case:

גֵּר תּוֹשָׁב יֵשׁ בּוֹ מִשּׁוּם "בְּיוֹמוֹ תִתֵּן שְׂכָרוֹ" — If someone hires **a *ger toshav*** (a non-Jew who agrees not to worship idols)[9] as a night worker, **he is subject to the verse** (*Deuteronomy* 24:15): **You shall give him his wages on that day,** and he must therefore be paid before sunset.[10] וְאֵין בּוֹ מִשּׁוּם "לֹא תָלִין פְּעֻלַּת שָׂכִיר אִתְּךָ עַד בֹּקֶר" — **However, if he is hired as a day worker, he is not subject**

--- NOTES ---

in this case. Since an employer is often preoccupied with his business, we suspect that he mistakenly thinks that he paid his worker even though he did not. Because of this concern, the Sages ruled that the employer is not believed; instead, the worker is believed, as long as he swears to his claim (*Rav*).

7. Since an employer usually makes sure to pay his workers before the deadline, after that time we do not suspect that the employer is making a mistake. Therefore, the usual law of claims applies, which means that the defendant (in this case, the employer) is believed (see the previous note).

[The Mishnah refers to cases where neither the worker nor the employer has any proof to his claim. If either of them produces witnesses that he is telling the truth, he is believed.]

8. For example, a laborer worked the whole day Sunday, and was thus required to be paid before Monday morning. Witnesses testified that the worker asked the employer for payment right before dawn on Monday morning, and the employer promised to pay later. The worker claims that he was not paid, while the employer claims to have eventually paid him. Since the testimony of the witnesses proves that the employer was not concerned about paying after the deadline, the worker is believed just as he is believed before the deadline (see *Tiferes Yisrael*).

9. A *ger toshav* (literally, *resident foreigner*) is a non-Jew who agrees not to worship idols, and lives among the Jews in Eretz Yisrael (see *Rav*).

10. *Rashi* 111b ד״ה ואין בו משום.

As we have learned (see Mishnah 11 note 1), this verse refers to night workers. The Gemara explains that the wording of this verse implies that it refers

— רע"ב —

(יג) המלוה את חבירו: והגיע זמן ולא פרעו: לא ימשכננו. ליקח ממנו משכון בעל כרחו, ואפילו בשוק. אלא על ידי שליח בית דין, שיקח ממנו ברשות בית דין: ולא יכנס לביתו. אפילו שליח בית דין לא יכנס לביתו. וכל שכן בעל חובו עצמו: היה לו שני כלים. וחובו כנגד שניהם, וממשכנו בשניהם: נוטל אחד ומחזיר אחד. בשעה שהוא צריך לזה יחזירנו, ויעכב השני אצלו, כדמפרש ואזיל, מחזיר את הכר בלילה ואת המחרישה ביום:

[יג] **הַמַּלְוֶה** אֶת חֲבֵרוֹ לֹא יְמַשְׁכְּנֶנּוּ אֶלָּא בְּבֵית דִּין, וְלֹא יִכָּנֵס לְבֵיתוֹ לִטֹּל מַשְׁכּוֹנוֹ, שֶׁנֶּאֱמַר, בַּחוּץ תַּעֲמֹד. הָיוּ לוֹ שְׁנֵי כֵלִים, נוֹטֵל אֶחָד וּמֵנִיחַ אֶחָד,

---

to the verse (*Leviticus* 19:13): **You may not keep the wages of a worker with you overnight until morning,** and thus, he does not have to be paid before the next morning.[11]

[13] The chapter ends with a new topic. If a borrower does not repay a loan when it is due, the lender may take an object from him as security for the loan; when the borrower repays the loan, the lender returns the security. The Mishnah discusses a number of laws that apply when taking an object as security:[1]

הַמַּלְוֶה אֶת חֲבֵרוֹ — **If someone lends money to his friend** and the loan comes due but the borrower does not repay it, לֹא יְמַשְׁכְּנֶנּוּ אֶלָּא בְּבֵית דִּין — [the lender] **may not take** an object **from [the borrower]** as **security except through a court,** that is, the lender may not simply take an object from the borrower, but must have the court send an agent to collect it. וְלֹא יִכָּנֵס לְבֵיתוֹ לִטֹּל מַשְׁכּוֹנוֹ — In addition, the agent of the court **may not go into [the borrower's] house to take his** property as **security;** rather, he must wait for the borrower to bring out the object,[2] שֶׁנֶּאֱמַר "בַּחוּץ תַּעֲמֹד" — **for it is stated** (*Deuteronomy* 24:10-11): *You may not come into his house to take his security; you must stand outside.*

The Torah commands (*Exodus* 22:25-26; *Deuteronomy* 24:12-13) that if the security is an object that the borrower needs to use, the lender must return it whenever the borrower needs it. The Mishnah gives an example of this law: הָיוּ לוֹ שְׁנֵי כֵלִים — **If [the borrower] had two utensils** that the lender takes as security,[3] and the borrower needs one during the day and the other at night, נוֹטֵל אֶחָד וּמֵנִיחַ אֶחָד — **[the lender] takes one and leaves** the other **one** with the borrower, depending on which one the borrower needs at the time. For

---

NOTES

not only to Jews but also to anyone living among them, such as a *ger toshav* (Gemara 111b).

11. *Rashi* there.

As we have learned, this verse refers to day workers. The wording of this verse implies that it refers only to Jews (*Rav*).

[13]

1. [A lender can also take a security at the time he gives the loan, but such a security is not subject to this Mishnah's laws (*Shulchan Aruch, Choshen Mishpat* 97:6,14,16).]

2. However, the court's agent may take an item that he finds outside the borrower's house (*Tiferes Yisrael*).

3. He takes both objects because together they equal the value of the loan (*Rav*).

משניות בבא מציעא / פרק ט: המקבל

וּמַחֲזִיר אֶת הַכַּר בַּלַּיְלָה וְאֶת הַמַּחֲרֵשָׁה בַּיּוֹם. וְאִם מֵת אֵינוֹ מַחֲזִיר לְיוֹרְשָׁיו. רַבָּן שִׁמְעוֹן בֶּן גַּמְלִיאֵל אוֹמֵר, אַף לְעַצְמוֹ אֵינוֹ מַחֲזִיר אֶלָּא עַד שְׁלֹשִׁים יוֹם, וּמִשְּׁלֹשִׁים יוֹם וּלְהַלָּן מוֹכְרָן בְּבֵית דִּין. אַלְמָנָה, בֵּין שֶׁהִיא עֲנִיָּה בֵּין שֶׁהִיא עֲשִׁירָה, אֵין מְמַשְׁכְּנִין אוֹתָהּ,

— רע״ב —

מת. הלוה. אין משיב הטבוט ליורשים, שאין כאן מצות השבת העבוט דהשב תשיב לו את העבוט כתיב (דברים כד, יג), לו ולא ליורש: עד שלשים יום. זמן בית דין. ואין הלכה כרבן שמעון בן גמליאל: בין שהיא עניה בין שהיא עשירה

וכו׳. משום דאיכא למאן דאמר, עניה הוא דאין ממשכנין. שמתוך שאתה צריך להחזיר לה והיא נכנסת ויוצאת אצלך, אתה משיאה שם רע בשכנותיה. אבל עשירה דליכא למימר הכי, אימא ממשכנין, קמשמע

וּמַחֲזִיר אֶת הַכַּר — example, if the lender takes the borrower's plow and pillow, **בַּלַּיְלָה וְאֶת הַמַּחֲרֵשָׁה בַּיּוֹם** — he returns the pillow every night and takes it back in the morning, and he returns the plow every day and takes it back at night.[4] **וְאִם מֵת אֵינוֹ מַחֲזִיר לְיוֹרְשָׁיו** — However, if [the borrower] died, and his heirs inherit his possessions, [the lender] does not have to return the security to [the borrower's] heirs when they need it, because the obligation to return a security when the borrower needs it applies only to the borrower himself and not to his heirs.[5]

According to the previous Tanna, as long as the borrower is alive, the lender must continue to return the security item every day as long as the borrower needs it. The next Tanna disagrees:

רַבָּן שִׁמְעוֹן בֶּן גַּמְלִיאֵל אוֹמֵר — Rabban Shimon ben Gamliel says: **אַף לְעַצְמוֹ אֵינוֹ מַחֲזִיר אֶלָּא עַד שְׁלֹשִׁים יוֹם** — Even when the lender must return the security to the borrower himself (i.e., while the borrower is alive), he need return it only until thirty days have passed; **וּמִשְּׁלֹשִׁים יוֹם וּלְהַלָּן מוֹכְרָן בְּבֵית דִּין** — from thirty days and on, he can sell [the security] in court and keep the money as payment for the loan.[6]

Another prohibition that relates to taking a security:

אַלְמָנָה בֵּין שֶׁהִיא עֲנִיָּה בֵּין שֶׁהִיא עֲשִׁירָה אֵין מְמַשְׁכְּנִין אוֹתָהּ — When a widow

---

NOTES

4. This applies only if the borrower has no other pillow or plow and cannot work or sleep without these items (*Rambam Commentary*).

[The lender will think it worthwhile to take a security even though he must return it every day, because taking these items every day will encourage the borrower to repay the debt (*Tos. Yom Tov;* see there for several additional reasons).]

5. This law is derived from a verse in the Torah (*Rav*).

Since the lender does not have to return the security to the heirs, once the borrower dies the lender can sell the security to collect the debt (*Rashi*).

[Usually, when a borrower dies before repaying a loan, the lender may claim the loan only from real estate left by the borrower but not from movable objects he owned. However, if the lender was holding an object of the borrower's as security, he may collect the loan from that object after the borrower died (see Gemara 115a).]

6. Thirty days is the standard amount of time given by a court for their orders to be carried out (*Rav;* see Mishnah 10:4 note 7). Thus, once a security is taken from the borrower, he has thirty days to come up with money to pay back the loan; after that, the lender can sell the security.

MISHNAH BAVA METZIA / Chapter 9: Ham'kabeil

שֶׁנֶּאֱמַר, וְלֹא תַחֲבֹל בֶּגֶד אַלְמָנָה. הַחוֹבֵל אֶת הָרֵחַיִם עוֹבֵר בְּלֹא תַעֲשֶׂה, וְחַיָּב מִשּׁוּם שְׁנֵי כֵלִים, שֶׁנֶּאֱמַר, לֹא יַחֲבֹל רֵחַיִם וָרֶכֶב. וְלֹא רֵחַיִם וָרֶכֶב בִּלְבַד אָמְרוּ, אֶלָּא כָּל דָּבָר שֶׁעוֹשִׂין בּוֹ אֹכֶל נֶפֶשׁ, שֶׁנֶּאֱמַר, כִּי נֶפֶשׁ הוּא חֹבֵל:

— רע"ב —

לָן הַאי תָּנָא דְלָא. דִכְתִיב (שם פסוק יז) לֹא תַחֲבוֹל בֶּגֶד אַלְמָנָה, אֶחָד עֲנִיָּה וְאֶחָד עֲשִׁירָה במַשְׁמַע: מִשּׁוּם שְׁנֵי כֵלִים. הָעֶלְיוֹנָה רֶכֶב, וְהַתַּחְתּוֹנָה רֵחַיִם:

---

borrows, **whether she is poor or rich, we may not take security from her,** שֶׁנֶּאֱמַר "וְלֹא תַחֲבֹל בֶּגֶד אַלְמָנָה" — **as it is stated** (*Deuteronomy* 24:17): *You may not take the clothing of a widow as security.*[7]

The Torah forbids taking as security an object that is used to prepare food. As an example, it forbids taking millstones. The Mishnah elaborates: הַחוֹבֵל אֶת הָרֵחַיִם עוֹבֵר בְּלֹא תַעֲשֶׂה — **Someone who takes a mill as security transgresses a prohibition;** וְחַיָּב מִשּׁוּם שְׁנֵי כֵלִים — **moreover, he is liable for two transgressions, because a mill consists of two utensils,** a bottom stone and a top stone,[8] שֶׁנֶּאֱמַר "לֹא יַחֲבֹל רֵחַיִם וָרֶכֶב" — **and it is stated** (24:6 there): *He may not take the lower millstone or the upper millstone as security.* Since the Torah mentions both stones explicitly, taking each one is considered a separate transgression even though they are part of the same tool.[9]

Although the Torah states only that a lender may not take millstones as security, the same applies to similar items:

וְלֹא רֵחַיִם וָרֶכֶב בִּלְבַד אָמְרוּ — **They did not say** that it is forbidden to take **only a lower millstone or upper millstone;** אֶלָּא כָּל דָּבָר שֶׁעוֹשִׂין בּוֹ אֹכֶל נֶפֶשׁ — **rather, anything that is used to prepare food** (such as a pot) may similarly not be taken as security.[10] שֶׁנֶּאֱמַר "כִּי נֶפֶשׁ הוּא חֹבֵל" — **This is because it is stated** (there): *He may not take the lower millstone or the upper millstone as security,* **because he is taking a life as security.** With this statement, the Torah teaches that the reason one may not take a millstone as security is because it is something that the borrower uses to sustain his life (by preparing food). Accordingly, it is equally forbidden to take anything that is used to prepare food.[11]

NOTES

7. Clothing is just an example. It is forbidden to take any object from a widow as security (*Tos. R' Akiva Eiger*).

8. A mill consists of two round stones, one on top of the other. [Grain is placed between them and the top stone is turned, crushing the grain.]

The Mishnah refers to a hand mill, which was small enough to be carried [and was used for grinding grain at home] (*Tos. Yom Tov*).

9. The Torah did not simply say "He may not take a mill," but mentioned both millstones. This teaches that taking each stone is a separate transgression (*Meiri*).

10. *Rabbeinu Yehonasan.*

11. *Sma, Choshen Mishpat* 97:11.

Chapter Ten

משניות בבא מציעא / פרק י: הבית והעליה

רע"ב

פרק עשירי – הבית והעליה. (א) הבית והעליה של שנים. הבית של אחד, ועליה של אחר: שניהם חולקים.

[א] הַבַּיִת וְהָעֲלִיָּה שֶׁל שְׁנַיִם שֶׁנָּפְלוּ, שְׁנֵיהֶם חוֹלְקִים בָּעֵצִים וּבָאֲבָנִים וּבֶעָפָר, וְרוֹאִים אֵלּוּ אֲבָנִים הָרְאוּיוֹת לְהִשְׁתַּבֵּר.

לפי שאין ניכר אלו אבנים של עליון, ואלו אבנים של תחתון: ורואים אלו אבנים הראויות להשתבר. שאם נתבם הבית מיסודו ונפל תחתיו, יש לדעת שהתחתונות נשברו. ואם עליונו של כותל נפל להלן ממנו הרבה, הטליונות נשברו, שנפלו ממקום גבוה, והתחתונות שלמות שנפלו ממקום נמוך. וריש דתנא שניהם חולקים, מיירי שנפל הכותל בלילה, ופנו את האבנים מיד, וליכא למימר, אי בחבסה נפל ותתאה אתבור, אי בבטשה נפל וטליתא אתבור:

---

[1] This chapter deals with laws that apply to properties situated one on top of the other. The first three Mishnahs discuss neighbors who live in a two-story house that has two separate apartments — one on the ground floor and one on the upper floor.

This Mishnah discusses a case where each apartment was owned by a different person, and the house collapsed. It teaches how the owners divide the usable materials found in the rubble:

הַבַּיִת וְהָעֲלִיָּה שֶׁל שְׁנַיִם שֶׁנָּפְלוּ — If a two-story house[1] belonging to two people **collapsed,** **שְׁנֵיהֶם חוֹלְקִים בָּעֵצִים וּבָאֲבָנִים וּבֶעָפָר** — the two of them divide the usable **wood, stones, and earth** that they find in the rubble,[2] based on the size of the two apartments.[3] For example, if both apartments were the same size, each owner takes half of the material.[4]

The Mishnah discusses how the stones are divided if some are whole and some are broken. If it can be determined how the house collapsed, the following method is used to divide the stones:

וְרוֹאִים אֵלּוּ אֲבָנִים הָרְאוּיוֹת לְהִשְׁתַּבֵּר — We determine which stones were more likely to have broken; that is, we examine the way the house fell and determine which story's stones were more likely to have broken in the collapse. The owner of that story receives the broken stones.[5]

NOTES

[1]

1. Literally, *a ground floor and an upper floor.*
2. A house usually had [stones (or bricks) in its structure, wood in the ceilings, and] earth that was used to cement the stones together (*Tos. Yom Tov*).
3. *Tos. Yom Tov.*
4. [By law, each owner owns the building materials that came from his apartment.] However, since we cannot tell which parts of the rubble came from which apartment, the owners simply divide the materials according to the size of the apartments (*Rav*).
5. For example, if the house caved in, presumably the stones from the lower floor broke and caused the rest of the structure to collapse; the stones from the upper floor, though, likely remained whole. Therefore, the owner of the upper story gets the whole stones, and the owner of the ground floor gets the broken ones. If, however, the house fell to its side (e.g., it was blown over by a strong wind), the stones of the upper story were more likely to have broken, since they fell from a greater height than the lower stones did. In that case, the owner of the upper story receives the broken stones, and the owner of the ground floor takes the whole ones (*Rav, Rashi*).

If it cannot be determined how the house fell (for example, it fell at night when no one saw it fall, and passersby

[183] MISHNAH BAVA METZIA / Chapter 10: *Habayis Veha'aliyah* 10/2

אִם הָיָה אֶחָד מֵהֶן מַכִּיר מִקְצָת אֲבָנָיו, נוֹטְלָן, וְעוֹלוֹת לוֹ מִן הַחֶשְׁבּוֹן.

[ב] הַבַּיִת וְהָעֲלִיָּה שֶׁל שְׁנַיִם, נִפְחֲתָה הָעֲלִיָּה, וְאֵין בַּעַל הַבַּיִת רוֹצֶה לְתַקֵּן, הֲרֵי בַּעַל הָעֲלִיָּה יוֹרֵד וְדָר לְמַטָּה, עַד שֶׁיְּתַקֵּן לוֹ אֶת הָעֲלִיָּה.

— רע״ב —

מִקְצָת אֲבָנָיו. וְהֵן שְׁלֵמוֹת: נוֹטְלָן. וּכְגוֹן שֶׁהַלָּה מוֹדֶה בְּמִקְצָת מֵהֶן שֶׁהוּא אֱמֶת, וּבְמִקְצָת חוֹמֶר שֶׁאֵינוֹ יוֹדֵעַ, שֶׁכֵּיוָן שֶׁהוּא מוֹדֶה בְּמִקְצָת הָוֵה לֵיהּ מְחוּיָּב שְׁבוּעָה דְּאוֹרַיְיתָא וְאֵינוֹ יָכוֹל לִישָּׁבַע, וְכָל הַמְחוּיָּב שְׁבוּעָה וְאֵינוֹ יָכוֹל לִישָּׁבַע מְשַׁלֵּם. אֲבָל אִם אָמַר עַל כּוּלָן אֵינִי יוֹדֵעַ, יִשָּׁבַע שֶׁאֵינוֹ יוֹדֵעַ, וְחוֹלֵק עִם חֲבֵרוֹ בְּשָׁוֶה: (ב) הַבַּיִת וְהָעֲלִיָּה. הַמַּשְׂכִּיר לַחֲבֵרוֹ עֲלִיָּה שֶׁעַל גַּבֵּי בֵיתוֹ, וְאָמַר לוֹ עֲלִיָּה זוֹ שֶׁעַל גַּבֵּי בַיִת זֶה אֲנִי מַשְׂכִּיר לְךָ, וְנִפְחֲתָה הָעֲלִיָּה אַרְבָּעָה טְפָחִים עַל אַרְבָּעָה טְפָחִים, דְּהַשְׁתָּא אִם בָּא זֶה לְהִשְׁתַּמֵּשׁ בַּעֲלִיָּה צָרִיךְ שֶׁיִּשְׁתַּמֵּשׁ חֶצְיוֹ לְמַעְלָה וְחֶצְיוֹ לְמַטָּה: וְאֵין בַּעַל הַבַּיִת רוֹצֶה לְתַקֵּן. הָעֲלִיָּה: הֲרֵי בַּעַל הָעֲלִיָּה יוֹרֵד וְדָר לְמַטָּה. לְגַמְרֵי. דְּהָא שַׁעְבֵּד בֵּיתֵיהּ לַעֲלִיָּה. וְלֹא כָפִינַן לֵיהּ לְדוּר חֶצְיוֹ לְמַעְלָה וְחֶצְיוֹ לְמַטָּה:

אִם הָיָה אֶחָד מֵהֶן מַכִּיר מִקְצָת אֲבָנָיו — If one of [the owners] recognized some of his stones among the unbroken stones, **נוֹטְלָן** — he may take them, even if they are more valuable than the other stones,[6] **וְעוֹלוֹת לוֹ מִן הַחֶשְׁבּוֹן** — and they are counted toward the total amount of unbroken stones he is entitled to. For example, if he is supposed to get 50 unbroken stones, he can take the stones he recognizes as part of his 50 stones.[7]

[2] This Mishnah discusses a two-story house that is owned by one person, who lives on the ground floor and rents out the second story to someone else:

הַבַּיִת וְהָעֲלִיָּה שֶׁל שְׁנַיִם — A two-story house is occupied by two people:[1] the owner of the house lives on the ground floor and a tenant lives in the upper story. **נִפְחֲתָה הָעֲלִיָּה** — If the floor of the upper story fell in[2] **וְאֵין בַּעַל הַבַּיִת רוֹצֶה לְתַקֵּן** — and the owner of the house does not want to fix it, **הֲרֵי בַּעַל הָעֲלִיָּה יוֹרֵד וְדָר לְמַטָּה** — [the occupant] of the upper story may go down and live below, in the ground-floor apartment, **עַד שֶׁיְּתַקֵּן לוֹ אֶת הָעֲלִיָּה** — until [the owner] fixes the floor of the upper story for him.[3]

NOTES

moved the rubble from its original position), the two owners divide both the whole and broken stones based on the size of their apartments, as taught in the Mishnah's first ruling (*Rav, Tos. Yom Tov*).

6. For example, the stones he identifies are larger or of better quality than the other stones (*Tos. Yom Tov*, from Gemara 116b).

He may take these stones only if there is a reason for his claim to be believed, for example, if the other owner admits that those stones are indeed his (see *Rav*, Gemara 116b).

7. The unbroken stones are divided in the manner described earlier in the Mishnah: if it can be determined how the house fell, they are divided based on that calculation; otherwise, they are divided according to the size of the apartments. If one owner recognizes some stones, he does not gain *more* stones; he can simply choose the ones he recognized — even if they are more valuable — in place of other stones (Gemara 116b).

[2]

1. *Tos. Yom Tov*.

2. A large enough section of the floor collapsed so that the tenant no longer has full use of his apartment (see *Rav*).

3. This law does not apply in every case.

משניות בבא מציעא / פרק י: הבית והעליה

רַבִּי יוֹסֵי אוֹמֵר, הַתַּחְתּוֹן נוֹתֵן אֶת הַתִּקְרָה, וְהָעֶלְיוֹן אֶת הַמַּעֲזִיבָה.

[ג] הַבַּיִת וְהָעֲלִיָּה שֶׁל שְׁנַיִם שֶׁנָּפְלוּ, אָמַר בַּעַל הָעֲלִיָּה לְבַעַל הַבַּיִת לִבְנוֹת

— רע"ב —

מעזיבה. [טיח של] טיט שנותנים על התקרה. רבי יוסי סבר מעזיבה אשווי גומות היא, ולאשווי גומות על העליון לאשווי. ורבנן סברי מעזיבה אחזוקי תקרה היא, ואחזוקי

תקרה תתחון בעי לאחזוקי. והלכה כחכמים: (ג) הבית והעליה של שנים. בית של זה ועליו של זה: אמר בעל עליה לבעל הבית לבנות. החומה והתקרה התחתונה המוטלים עליו לבנות:

According to the next Tanna, the landlord is responsible for only part of the repair:

רַבִּי יוֹסֵי אוֹמֵר — R' Yose says: הַתַּחְתּוֹן נוֹתֵן אֶת הַתִּקְרָה — The occupant of the lower apartment [the landlord] is required to provide only the wood of the ceiling (i.e., the ceiling of the lower apartment, which is the floor of the upper apartment), וְהָעֶלְיוֹן אֶת הַמַּעֲזִיבָה — and the occupant of the upper apartment provides the plaster that covers the wood. This plaster is not needed to strengthen the floor but simply ensures that it is smooth and flat. Since the upper apartment is livable without the plaster, the landlord is not obligated to provide it.[4]

[3] The Mishnah returns to the case of a two-story house owned by two people that collapsed. If the owner of the upper story wants to rebuild his apartment, the owner of the ground floor is obligated to rebuild the ground floor to enable the upper floor to be rebuilt on top of it.[1] The Mishnah discusses the law when the owner of the upper apartment wants to rebuild but the owner of the ground floor does not:

הַבַּיִת וְהָעֲלִיָּה שֶׁל שְׁנַיִם שֶׁנָּפְלוּ — A two-story house belonging to two people collapsed. אָמַר בַּעַל הָעֲלִיָּה לְבַעַל הַבַּיִת לִבְנוֹת — If the owner of the upper

--- NOTES ---

The Mishnah refers to a unique case, where the landlord had said at the time of rental, "I am renting you this upper story, which is on top of this ground floor." By adding the words, "which is on top of this ground floor," he is indicating that if the upper apartment becomes unusable, he will provide the lower apartment as a replacement (Rav, from Gemara 116b). [If he did not mean to promise this, there would have been no need for him to add that extra phrase, since it is obvious that the upper story is on top of the ground floor (Rashi).] Accordingly, if the floor of the upper apartment collapses, the tenant may live in the lower apartment until it is fixed.

If the landlord did not use such an expression at the time of rental, the tenant does not have the right to live on the ground floor. Whether or not the landlord is obligated to repair the floor at all depends on the phrases used and the terms set at the time of rental (as discussed in Mishnah 8:9).

4. The Tanna Kamma, on the other hand, holds that the plaster also serves to reinforce the ceiling, and makes the upper apartment livable; therefore, the landlord must provide plaster (Rav), and the tenant can live downstairs until the landlord does so (Rabbeinu Yehonasan).

[3]

1. When the two neighbors move in, it is understood that the owner of the ground-floor apartment will do his part to ensure that the upper apartment can continue to exist (Rashba, cited by Tzeror HaKesef). Thus, he is required to rebuild the ground floor so that the upper floor can be rebuilt.

[185] **MISHNAH BAVA METZIA** / Chapter 10: *Habayis Veha'aliyah*   10/3

וְהוּא אֵינוֹ רוֹצֶה לִבְנוֹת, הֲרֵי בַעַל הָעֲלִיָּה בּוֹנֶה אֶת הַבַּיִת וְדָר בְּתוֹכוֹ עַד שֶׁיִּתֶּן לוֹ אֶת יְצִיאוֹתָיו. רַבִּי יְהוּדָה אוֹמֵר, אַף זֶה דָר בְּתוֹךְ שֶׁל חֲבֵרוֹ צָרִיךְ לְהַעֲלוֹת לוֹ שָׂכָר.

— רע״ב —

בּוֹנֶה בַיִת. וְתִקְרָה הַתַּחְתּוֹנָה שֶׁעָלָיו, וְיוֹשֵׁב בַּבַּיִת עַד שֶׁיִּתֵּן לוֹ יְצִיאוֹתָיו, וְאַחַר כָּךְ יוֹצֵא מִמֶּנּוּ וּבוֹנֶה עֲלִיָּתוֹ: אַמַר רַבִּי יְהוּדָה אַף זֶה דָר בְּתוֹךְ שֶׁל חֲבֵרוֹ. אִם כֵּן הוּא, בַּעַל הָעֲלִיָּה זוּ כְּשֶׁזֶּה מַחֲזִיר לוֹ יְצִיאוֹתָיו, נִמְצָא שֶׁדָּר כָּל הַיָּמִים הַלָּלוּ בְּתוֹךְ שֶׁל חֲבֵירוֹ. וְאַף עַל פִּי שֶׁזֶּה אֵינוֹ חָסֵר, דְּהָא בִּלְאוֹ הָכִי לָא הֲוֵי בָנֵי לָהּ, מִכָּל מָקוֹם זֶה נֶהֱנָה, שֶׁאִלּוּלֵי בַּיִת זֶה לֹא הָיָה לוֹ מָקוֹם לָדוּר שָׁם. וּקְסָבַר זֶה נֶהֱנֶה וְזֶה אֵינוֹ חָסֵר, חַיָּב. אֶלָּא בּוֹנֶה אֶת הַכֹּל, וּמַקְרֶה אֶת הָעֲלִיָּה לְמַעְלָה וְכָל הַצָּרִיךְ לָהּ, וְיוֹשֵׁב בַּבַּיִת הַתַּחְתּוֹן: דְּהַוִי לֵיהּ זֶה לֹא נֶהֱנָה, שֶׁהֲרֵי עֲלִיָּתוֹ מוּכֶנֶת לוֹ לָדוּר בָּהּ, וְזֶה לֹא חָסֵר, דְּהָא לֹא הֲוָה בָּנֵי לָהּ וְלֹא חֲזִי לֵיהּ:

story told the owner of the ground floor to rebuild his apartment so that the upper story can be rebuilt on top of it, וְהוּא אֵינוֹ רוֹצֶה לִבְנוֹת — **but [the ground-floor's owner] does not want to rebuild,** הֲרֵי בַעַל הָעֲלִיָּה בּוֹנֶה אֶת הַבַּיִת — **the owner of the upper story may rebuild the ground floor** himself, וְדָר בְּתוֹכוֹ עַד שֶׁיִּתֶּן לוֹ אֶת יְצִיאוֹתָיו — **and live in it until [the owner of the ground floor] pays him for his building expenses.**[2] Since the owner of the ground floor is obligated to ensure that the upper story can be rebuilt, the owner of the upper apartment has the right to use the ground floor until its owner pays for his share of the construction.[3]

Another opinion:

רַבִּי יְהוּדָה אוֹמֵר — **R' Yehudah says:** אַף זֶה דָר בְּתוֹךְ שֶׁל חֲבֵרוֹ — **Even** in such a case, **this one** [the owner of the upper story] is nevertheless **living in his friend's** property;[4] since he thereby receives monetary benefit from his friend, צָרִיךְ לְהַעֲלוֹת לוֹ שָׂכָר — **he will have to pay [the owner of the ground floor] rent** for the time he lives there, because anyone who receives monetary benefit from someone else's property must pay for that benefit.[5]

— NOTES —

2. Once the owner of the ground floor pays for his apartment, the owner of the upper story leaves and rebuilds his own apartment (*Rav*).

3. *Bava Kamma* 20b, with *Rashi* ד״ה הבית לעלייה.

4. Although the owner of the upper story has the right to live on the ground floor, as soon as the ground-floor owner pays for it, it is considered his retroactively from the time it was rebuilt [since he owns the right to whatever apartment is on the rebuilt ground floor]. Thus, the owner of the upper story will have been living in someone else's property without paying rent (*Rav*).

5. R' Yehudah maintains that whenever someone derives monetary benefit from another person's property, he must pay for that benefit — even if the other person lost nothing because of it [זֶה נֶהֱנֶה וְזֶה לֹא חָסֵר]. Since the owner of the upper story benefits by living on the ground floor — because he does not have to rent another place to live — he must pay rent for living there, even though he did not cause its owner any loss (because its owner did not even want to rebuild it) (*Rav*).

The *Tanna Kamma*, on the other hand, holds that a person who benefits from someone else's property is obligated to pay for that benefit only if the other person suffered a loss as a result. If the second person suffered no loss, the first person does not have to pay for the benefit. Since the owner of the ground floor suffered no loss as a result of the other owner living in his apartment, the owner of the upper story does not have to pay rent for living there (*Rabbeinu Yehonasan*).

[186] **משניות בבא מציעא / פרק י: הבית והעליה** י/ד

— רע"ב —

(ד) בית הבד. בית לעצור זיתים: וגנה אחת על גביו. ובית הבד של אחד וגנה של אחר: ונפחת. בארבעה טפחים על ארבעה טפחים, ואינו ראוי לזרוע כבתחלה: ביפין. תקרה עשויה בעגול כמין קשת ועליה יתן בעל הגנה עפר ויזרע:

אֶלָּא בַּעַל הָעֲלִיָּה בּוֹנֶה אֶת הַבַּיִת וְאֶת הָעֲלִיָּה וּמְקָרֶה אֶת הָעֲלִיָּה, וְיוֹשֵׁב בַּבַּיִת עַד שֶׁיִּתֵּן לוֹ אֶת יְצִיאוֹתָיו.

[ד] **וְכֵן** בֵּית הַבַּד שֶׁהוּא בָנוּי בַּסֶּלַע, וְגִנָּה אַחַת עַל גַּבָּיו, וְנִפְחַת, הֲרֵי בַעַל הַגִּנָּה יוֹרֵד וְזוֹרֵעַ לְמַטָּה, עַד שֶׁיַּעֲשֶׂה לְבֵית בַּדּוֹ כִּפִּין.

אֶלָּא בַּעַל הָעֲלִיָּה בּוֹנֶה אֶת הַבַּיִת וְאֶת הָעֲלִיָּה — **Rather,** in order to avoid having to pay rent, **the owner of the upper story should rebuild both the ground floor and the upper story,** וּמְקָרֶה אֶת הָעֲלִיָּה — **and build a roof over the upper story;** וְיוֹשֵׁב בַּבַּיִת עַד שֶׁיִּתֵּן לוֹ אֶת יְצִיאוֹתָיו — **he should** then **live in the lower apartment until [the owner of the ground floor] pays his expenses.** Since he now has another apartment available to live in (namely, the upper apartment), he does not gain any monetary benefit by living on the ground floor and thus does not have to pay rent for living there.[6]

[4] The Mishnah discusses a different case where two properties, each owned by a different person, are situated one above the other:

וְכֵן בֵּית הַבַּד שֶׁהוּא בָנוּי בַּסֶּלַע — **Similarly, a chamber for an olive press was built in the rock** of a mountain (like a cave),[1] וְגִנָּה אַחַת עַל גַּבָּיו — **and a garden** belonging to someone else **was** planted in the earth that covered the **top of [the chamber].** וְנִפְחַת — If part of the chamber's roof **fell in,** causing part of the garden to collapse,[2] the owner of the press is required to repair the roof.[3] If he does not want to do so, הֲרֵי בַעַל הַגִּנָּה יוֹרֵד וְזוֹרֵעַ לְמַטָּה — **the owner of the garden may go down and plant** his seeds **below** in the dirt floor of **the chamber,** עַד שֶׁיַּעֲשֶׂה לְבֵית בַּדּוֹ כִּפִּין — **until [the owner of the olive press] makes a** new **dome** (i.e., a roof)[4] **for his olive-press chamber,** on which the garden can be replanted.

— NOTES —

6. Even though the upper apartment is rebuilt, he should live on the ground floor because that will encourage the other owner to pay his share of the building expenses.

[4]
1. A person hollowed out a chamber in the side of a mountain, and installed in it a press for squeezing oil from olives (*Rashi*).
2. Enough of the roof fell in that the garden can no longer be used as before (*Rav*).

3. Although these two people share the roof, it is expected that the owner of the olive press will be the one to repair the roof if it breaks, because without the roof, his olive press will be ruined by the rain (*Tos. Yom Tov*). [Since this is the standard expectation, if they wanted to arrange otherwise, they would have had to say so explicitly when they acquired their properties (*Perishah, Choshen Mishpat* 165:1).]

4. [Such chambers usually had dome-shaped ceilings.]

[187] **MISHNAH BAVA METZIA** / Chapter 10: *Habayis Veha'aliyah* 10/5

— רע״ב —

פטור מלשלם. דמאי
הוה ליה למיעבד, אנוס
הוא: נתנו לו זמן. בית
דין, שלשים יום לסתור
ולקוץ: (ה) ונפל. לתוך
גנת חבירו:

הַכֹּתֶל וְהָאִילָן שֶׁנָּפְלוּ לִרְשׁוּת הָרַבִּים
וְהִזִּיקוּ, פָּטוּר מִלְּשַׁלֵּם. נָתְנוּ לוֹ זְמַן לָקֹץ אֶת
הָאִילָן וְלִסְתֹּר אֶת הַכֹּתֶל, וְנָפְלוּ בְּתוֹךְ הַזְּמַן,
פָּטוּר; לְאַחַר הַזְּמַן, חַיָּב.

[ה] **מִי** שֶׁהָיָה כָּתְלוֹ סָמוּךְ לְגִנַּת חֲבֵרוֹ וְנָפַל, וְאָמַר לוֹ, פַּנֵּה

The Mishnah turns to other laws concerning property that fell down. If a person's property causes damage in the public domain, he must pay for that damage if it is the result of his negligence, but not if it was unavoidable.[5] The Mishnah discusses whether a person must pay for damage caused by a falling wall or tree that he owned:

הַכֹּתֶל וְהָאִילָן שֶׁנָּפְלוּ לִרְשׁוּת הָרַבִּים וְהִזִּיקוּ — If someone's **wall or tree fell into a public domain** (e.g., a street) **and caused damage,** פָּטוּר מִלְּשַׁלֵּם — under ordinary circumstances **he is not obligated to pay** for the damages, because it is an unavoidable accident.[6]

In the next case, the court saw that the wall or tree was in danger of falling, and they warned the owner to take it down within a set amount of time:

נָתְנוּ לוֹ זְמַן לָקֹץ אֶת הָאִילָן וְלִסְתֹּר אֶת הַכֹּתֶל — **If [the court] gave him a set time** (for example, thirty days)[7] **to cut down the tree or demolish the wall** but before he could take it down, it fell and caused damage, the law is as follows: וְנָפְלוּ בְּתוֹךְ הַזְּמַן — **If it fell within the time** set by the court, פָּטוּר — **[the owner] is not obligated** to pay for damages. Since it was not expected that the tree or wall would fall so soon, its collapse is considered an accident.[8] לְאַחַר הַזְּמַן — However, if it fell **after the time** set by the court had passed, חַיָּב — **he is obligated** to pay for any damages it caused, because he was negligent by not taking it down when he was supposed to do so.

[5] Continuing the discussion of a wall that falls and causes damage, the Mishnah discusses a wall that falls into private property:

מִי שֶׁהָיָה כָּתְלוֹ סָמוּךְ לְגִנַּת חֲבֵרוֹ — **Someone had a wall next to his friend's garden,** וְנָפַל — **and [the wall] fell** into the garden. וְאָמַר לוֹ פַּנֵּה

NOTES

5. These laws are discussed more fully in *Bava Kamma* Chapter 3.

6. The Mishnah refers to a sturdy wall or tree that fell because of an earthquake or powerful storm. Since there was no reason to suspect that it would fall, its owner is not responsible for the damage it causes. If, however, the wall or tree was not sturdy, the owner is responsible if it falls (*Tos. Yom Tov*).

The owner is exempt from damage that occurred as the wall or tree fell (e.g., if it hit somebody), as well as damage that occurred right after the fall (e.g., if someone tripped over the rubble). However, if he does not clear away the rubble in a timely manner, he *is* responsible if someone is later hurt by it (see *Tos. Yom Tov*).

7. A court would usually give thirty days for their orders to be carried out (*Rav* to Mishnah 9:13). If they estimated that the wall or tree was in danger of falling sooner, they would give the owner less time (*Rabbeinu Yehonasan*).

8. *Rabbeinu Yehonasan*.

משניות בבא מציעא / פרק י: הבית והעליה

אֲבָנֶיךָ, וְאָמַר לוֹ, הִגִּיעוּךָ, אֵין שׁוֹמְעִין לוֹ. מִשֶּׁקִּבֵּל עָלָיו, אָמַר לוֹ, הֵילָךְ אֶת יְצִיאוֹתֶיךָ וַאֲנִי אֶטֹּל אֶת שֶׁלִּי, אֵין שׁוֹמְעִין לוֹ. הַשּׂוֹכֵר אֶת הַפּוֹעֵל לַעֲשׂוֹת עִמּוֹ בְּתֶבֶן וּבְקַשׁ, וְאָמַר לוֹ, תֶּן לִי שְׂכָרִי, וְאָמַר לוֹ, טֹל מַה שֶּׁעָשִׂיתָ בִּשְׂכָרְךָ, אֵין שׁוֹמְעִין לוֹ.

— רע״ב —

הִגִּיעוּךְ. זָכָה בָהֶן, וּפַנֵּה אוֹתָן לְעַצְמְךָ: אֵין שׁוֹמְעִין לוֹ. אִם אֵין זֶה רוֹצֶה אֵין קוֹנֶה אוֹתָן, וְחַיָּב הַלָּה לְפַנּוֹתָן: בְּתֶבֶן וּבְקַשׁ. לְלַקֵּט לוֹ מִשֶּׁלּוֹ אוֹ מִשֶּׁל הֶפְקֵר: אֵין שׁוֹמְעִין לוֹ. אַף עַל גַּב דְּבְכָל דּוּכְתָא אִית לָן שָׁוֶה כֶסֶף כְּכֶסֶף, גַּבֵּי שָׂכִיר אֵינוּ כֵן, דְּלֹא תְלִין פְּעֻלַּת שָׂכִיר כְּתִיב (ויקרא יט,יג), [וּמַאי] דְּאַתְנִי בַּהֲדֵיהּ מַשְׁמַע:

אֲבָנֶיךָ — [The owner of the garden] said to [the owner of the wall], "Clear away your stones," וְאָמַר לוֹ הִגִּיעוּךְ — and [the owner of the wall] replied, "They are yours"; that is, "You may keep the stones; clear them away yourself." אֵין שׁוֹמְעִין לוֹ — If the owner of the garden does not want the stones, **we do not listen to [the owner of the wall]**; that is, the stones remain his,[1] and since they are causing damage,[2] he is obligated to remove them.[3]

In the next case, the owner of the garden agreed to accept the stones and cleared them away. The owner of the wall then changed his mind:

מִשֶּׁקִּבֵּל עָלָיו — If, after [the owner of the garden] accepted the stones and cleared them away, אָמַר לוֹ — [the owner of the wall] said to him, הֵילָךְ אֶת יְצִיאוֹתֶיךָ וַאֲנִי אֶטֹּל אֶת שֶׁלִּי — "Here are your expenses for clearing away the stones, **and I will take back my stones**,"[4] אֵין שׁוֹמְעִין לוֹ — **we do not listen to him**; that is, the owner of the garden may keep the stones. Since the owner of the garden already acquired the stones as his own, the owner of the wall no longer has any right to them.

The Mishnah discusses an unrelated case with a similar ruling:

הַשּׂוֹכֵר אֶת הַפּוֹעֵל לַעֲשׂוֹת עִמּוֹ בְּתֶבֶן וּבְקַשׁ — **Someone hired a worker to work for him gathering straw and stubble**.[5] וְאָמַר לוֹ תֶּן לִי שְׂכָרִי — **After completing the job, [the worker] said to [the employer], "Give me my wages,"** וְאָמַר לוֹ טֹל מַה שֶּׁעָשִׂיתָ בִּשְׂכָרְךָ — and [the employer] said to him, **"Take what you did** (i.e., the straw that you gathered) **as your wages."** אֵין שׁוֹמְעִין לוֹ — If the worker does not want to be paid with straw, **we do not listen to [the employer]**,

---

NOTES

[5]

1. [Although a person automatically acquires objects that are in his property, that is only if he wants to do so; if the owner of the garden does not want the stones, they do not become his even though they are in his garden (see Rashi).]

2. The stones and rubble cover the garden and prevent it from being used (Rabbeinu Yehonasan).

3. Even if the wall fell because of an accident, he must clear away the stones as soon as possible to prevent any further damage (see Tos. Yom Tov).

4. The owner of the wall changes his mind, and decides to keep the stones and to assume the responsibility for taking them away. Since the owner of the garden has already taken them away, the owner of the wall offers to reimburse him for his work.

5. The inedible parts of a stalk of grain; see Mishnah 9:1 note 3.

[189] MISHNAH BAVA METZIA / Chapter 10: *Habayis Veha'aliyah* — 10/5

מְשַׁקְבֵּל עָלָיו, וְאָמַר לוֹ, הֵילָךְ שְׂכָרְךָ וַאֲנִי אֶטֹּל אֶת שֶׁלִּי, אֵין שׁוֹמְעִין לוֹ. הַמּוֹצִיא זֶבֶל לִרְשׁוּת הָרַבִּים, הַמּוֹצִיא מוֹצִיא, וְהַמְזַבֵּל מְזַבֵּל. אֵין שׁוֹרִין טִיט בִּרְשׁוּת הָרַבִּים, וְאֵין לוֹבְנִים לְבֵנִים.

— רע"ב —

המוציא מוציא והמזבל מזבל. כשזה מוציאו מן הרפת לרשות הרבים יהא מוכן הנושאו לזבל, ואינו רשאי להשהותו שם:

---

and he must give the worker cash, since a worker has the right to be paid with money and not with goods.[6] **מְשַׁקְבֵּל עָלָיו** — However, if **[the worker] accepted** the straw as payment, **וְאָמַר לוֹ הֵילָךְ שְׂכָרְךָ וַאֲנִי אֶטֹּל אֶת שֶׁלִּי** — and the employer then changed his mind and said to him, "Here are your wages in cash, and I will take back my straw," **אֵין שׁוֹמְעִין לוֹ** — we do not listen to [the employer] and the worker may keep the straw. Since the worker has acquired the straw as his own, the employer no longer has any right to it.[7]

Having discussed (in the previous Mishnah) a wall that fell and caused damage in a public domain, the Mishnah focuses on other items that can cause damage in a public domain. It first discusses manure — which was often taken out to a street to be given to farmers for use as fertilizer:

הַמּוֹצִיא זֶבֶל לִרְשׁוּת הָרַבִּים — When **one takes out** his **manure into the public domain** to give to a farmer,[8] **הַמּוֹצִיא מוֹצִיא** — as soon as **the one taking out** the manure **takes it out** to the street, **וְהַמְזַבֵּל מְזַבֵּל** — **the one who is fertilizing** his field must remove the manure from the street and **fertilize** his soil with it. Since manure can cause damage if it is left in a public place,[9] a person may bring it there only if someone is ready to take it away immediately.

In earlier times, cement and bricks were made by soaking clay and then kneading it. If bricks were being made, the clay was then formed into bricks and laid out to dry. The Mishnah discusses whether these procedures may be done in a public domain:

אֵין שׁוֹרִין טִיט בִּרְשׁוּת הָרַבִּים — **One may not soak clay in a public domain** in order to make cement or bricks, **וְאֵין לוֹבְנִים לְבֵנִים** — **and one may not make bricks** in a public domain, because these procedures take a long time, and if they are done in a public area, they will likely cause damage to passersby,[10]

NOTES

6. Although most debts can be paid with anything of value, we learn from a verse in the Torah that a worker is entitled to be paid in cash (see *Rav*).

7. The Mishnah refers to a case where the worker brought the straw to his property or did some other act of acquisition [קִנְיָן] (such as lifting it). Thus, the straw belongs to him, and the employer no longer has any right to it (*Tiferes Yisrael*).

8. People who owned animals would give their manure to farmers to use as fertilizer. In order to make it easier for the farmers, the owners of the animals would remove the manure from the animal's stalls and put it in the street.

9. For example, someone might slip on the manure and injure himself or ruin his clothes.

10. Clay was usually left to soak for a long time before it was kneaded into cement or bricks. Likewise, once bricks are formed, they are left to dry for a long time (*Tiferes Yisrael*). If the clay is left to soak or the bricks left to dry in a public place, it is likely that passersby will trip over them or dirty their clothes (*Rabbeinu Yehonasan*).

י/ה

רע״ב

גובלין טיט. לתת מיד
בבנין: והבונה [בונה.
מקבלן מיד] המביא,
ובונה: מתקן. מזמן ברשות
הרבים כל שלשים יום, ואינו
חייב בנזקין. ואין הלכה
כרבן שמעון בן גמליאל:

אֲבָל גּוֹבְלִין טִיט בִּרְשׁוּת הָרַבִּים, אֲבָל לֹא לְבֵנִים. הַבּוֹנֶה בִּרְשׁוּת הָרַבִּים, הַמֵּבִיא אֲבָנִים מֵבִיא, וְהַבּוֹנֶה בּוֹנֶה. וְאִם הִזִּיק, מְשַׁלֵּם מַה שֶּׁהִזִּיק. רַבָּן שִׁמְעוֹן בֶּן גַּמְלִיאֵל אוֹמֵר, אַף מְתַקֵּן הוּא אֶת מְלַאכְתּוֹ לִפְנֵי שְׁלֹשִׁים יוֹם.

אֲבָל גּוֹבְלִין טִיט בִּרְשׁוּת הָרַבִּים — **However,** a person **may knead clay in a public domain** to make it into cement if he will remove the cement right away to use, אֲבָל לֹא לְבֵנִים — **but** he may **not** knead clay in a public domain in order to make **bricks,** because for this the clay must be kneaded for a long time, and may cause damage to passersby.[11]

The Mishnah now discusses a person who is building a structure at the edge of his property, right next to a public domain. It teaches whether he may bring building materials through the public domain:

הַבּוֹנֶה בִּרְשׁוּת הָרַבִּים — **When someone is building** right next to **the public domain,** and he must bring stones for the building through the public domain,[12] הַמֵּבִיא אֲבָנִים מֵבִיא — as soon as **the person bringing the stones takes** them into the public domain, וְהַבּוֹנֶה בּוֹנֶה — **the builder** must take them from there and **build** with them. The one bringing the stones may not leave them in a public place for the builder to pick up later, since passersby might trip over them.

The Mishnah adds:

וְאִם הִזִּיק — **And if [the stones] caused damage** during the short time they were in the public domain, מְשַׁלֵּם מַה שֶּׁהִזִּיק — **[the owner] must pay for the damage.** Although he is permitted to bring the stones into the public domain in this manner, he must still make sure that they do not cause damage and he is responsible if they do.[13]

The next Tanna holds that when doing construction, a person may keep materials in the public domain:

רַבָּן שִׁמְעוֹן בֶּן גַּמְלִיאֵל אוֹמֵר — **Rabban Shimon ben Gamliel says:** אַף מְתַקֵּן הוּא אֶת מְלַאכְתּוֹ לִפְנֵי שְׁלֹשִׁים יוֹם — **One may even prepare** in the public domain for **his** construction **work** for **thirty days before** he begins the work. The Sages allowed a person to store his building materials in the public domain for up to thirty days before he begins to build. Moreover, even if the materials cause damage during that time, he does not have to pay for it.[14]

NOTES

11. *Tiferes Yisrael*.

12. Since the structure is right next to the public domain, the builder must stand in the public domain to build it, and must therefore bring stones through there (see *Meiri*).

13. The same applies if one puts manure or kneads clay in a public domain in the permitted manner — i.e., where they are quickly removed — as the Mishnah described earlier. Even though these activities are permitted, he is responsible if any damage occurs (*Meiri*). [Needless to say, if one brings items into a public domain in a *forbidden* manner (e.g., he soaks clay there), he is certainly responsible for any damage that occurs.]

14. Rabban Shimon ben Gamliel

[191] MISHNAH BAVA METZIA / Chapter 10: *Habayis Veha'aliyah*

— רע״ב —

(ו) שתי גנות. של שני בני אדם סמוכות זו לזו, האחת קרקעיתה גבוה, ושאצלה קרקעיתה נמוך: והירק בנתים. בזקיפת הגובה, שזו גבוה מזו: של עליון. שהרי עפרו הוא וממנו הוא יונק: של תחתון. שעל אוירו היא מונחת:

[ו] **שְׁתֵּי** גִּנּוֹת זוֹ עַל גַּב זוֹ וְהַיָּרָק בֵּינְתַיִם, רַבִּי מֵאִיר אוֹמֵר, שֶׁל עֶלְיוֹן. רַבִּי יְהוּדָה אוֹמֵר, שֶׁל תַּחְתּוֹן. אָמַר רַבִּי מֵאִיר, אִם יִרְצֶה הָעֶלְיוֹן לִקַּח אֶת עֲפָרוֹ,

---

[6] Returning to the chapter's original subject, the Mishnah discusses another case of two properties, each owned by a different person, that are situated one above the other:

שְׁתֵּי גִנּוֹת זוֹ עַל גַּב זוֹ — **Two gardens** are next to each other, and the surface of **one** is **higher than** the surface of **the other**, so that there is a vertical wall of earth between them, **וְהַיָּרָק בֵּינְתַיִם** — **and vegetables** are growing out of the vertical area **between [the two gardens].**[1] Thus, the roots of these vegetables are in the ground of the upper garden, while the plants themselves are hanging over the lower garden. It is a matter of dispute who owns the vegetables: **רַבִּי מֵאִיר אוֹמֵר** — **R' Meir says:** **שֶׁל עֶלְיוֹן** — **The vegetables belong to** the owner of **the upper** garden because they are nourished from his earth.[2] **רַבִּי יְהוּדָה אוֹמֵר** — But **R' Yehudah says:** **שֶׁל תַּחְתּוֹן** — **They belong to** the owner of **the lower** garden because they are in his airspace.[3]

R' Meir and R' Yehudah offer arguments to support their opinions:

אָמַר רַבִּי מֵאִיר — **R' Meir said:** **אִם יִרְצֶה הָעֶלְיוֹן לִקַּח אֶת עֲפָרוֹ** — **If the**

NOTES

disagrees with the Tanna Kamma on two points: (1) He holds that a person may store construction materials in a public domain for 30 days; and (2) he maintains that whenever a person is allowed to do an activity in the public domain, he is not responsible for any damage it causes. Thus, he holds that also in the cases permitted by the Mishnah earlier (e.g., bringing in manure to take it out right away), the owner is not responsible if any damage occurs (Gemara 118b).

[6]
1. For example, wild vegetables, such as garlic or onion plants, sprouted by themselves from the earth, and are hanging over the lower garden (see *Rashi*). See diagram.

2. [All the earth below the upper garden belongs to the owner of that garden (*Rav*).]

3. [The air above the lower garden belongs to the owner of that garden.]

Both Tannaim agree that the *roots* of the vegetables belong to the owner of the upper garden, because they are nourished from the ground and are completely in the ground, which is part of the upper garden (see Gemara 118b, with *Rashi*). Their disagreement is only about the greenery that grows above the ground. R' Meir holds that since it is nourished from the ground, it belongs to the owner of the ground (i.e., the owner of the upper garden). R' Yehudah holds that since it is situated in the airspace of the lower garden, it belongs to the owner of that garden (see *Rav*).

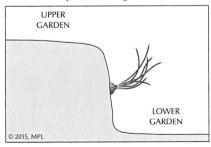

[192] משניות בבא מציעא / פרק י: הבית והעליה

אֵין כָּאן יָרָק. אָמַר רַבִּי יְהוּדָה, אִם יִרְצֶה הַתַּחְתּוֹן לְמַלֹּאות אֶת גִּנָּתוֹ, אֵין כָּאן יָרָק. אָמַר רַבִּי מֵאִיר, מֵאַחַר שֶׁשְּׁנֵיהֶן יְכוֹלִין לִמְחוֹת זֶה עַל זֶה, רוֹאִין מֵהֵיכָן יָרָק זֶה חָי. אָמַר רַבִּי שִׁמְעוֹן, כֹּל שֶׁהָעֶלְיוֹן יָכוֹל לִפְשֹׁט אֶת יָדוֹ וְלִטֹּל, הֲרֵי הוּא שֶׁלּוֹ, וְהַשְּׁאָר שֶׁל תַּחְתּוֹן.

— רע״ב —

מאחר ששניהם יכולים למחות. שלא יהא ירק זה כאן. עליון ליטול עפרו, ותחתון למלאות גינתו: רואין מהיכן ירק זה חי. ממקום שהוא יונק וגדל, ולו ינתן: כל שעליון יכול לפשוט ידו וליטול הרי אלו שלו. כדקאמר רבי מאיר, הואיל ומעפרו הוא חי: והשאר של תחתון.

דטליוין גופיה אפקורי מפקיר ליה לגבי דתחתון. שגנאי הוא לו ליטול רשות ליכנס לתוך חבירו וללוקחו. והלכה כרבי שמעון:

---

owner of **upper** garden **decides to take away his earth,** i.e., if he decides to remove the dirt under his garden until his garden is level with the lower one, אֵין כָּאן יָרָק — **there would be no vegetables here!** Since there would be no plants if he removes his earth, anything that grows in that earth should be his.

אָמַר רַבִּי יְהוּדָה — **R' Yehudah said:** אִם יִרְצֶה הַתַּחְתּוֹן לְמַלֹּאות אֶת גִּנָּתוֹ — **If** the owner of the **lower** garden **decides to fill his garden** with earth until it is level with the upper garden, אֵין כָּאן יָרָק — **there would be no vegetables here!** Since there would be no plants if he removes his airspace, anything that grows in that airspace should be his.[4]

R' Meir responds to the above arguments:

אָמַר רַבִּי מֵאִיר — **R' Meir said:** מֵאַחַר שֶׁשְּׁנֵיהֶן יְכוֹלִין לִמְחוֹת זֶה עַל זֶה — **Since both of them can block each other,** i.e., they can each prevent the growth of the vegetables, they are both equal in this respect, and these arguments do not give either person an advantage. רוֹאִין מֵהֵיכָן יָרָק זֶה חָי — **Rather, we check where these vegetables draw their nourishment** in order to determine who owns them. Since they are nourished from the ground, they belong to the owner of the upper garden, who owns that ground.[5]

The Mishnah cites a third opinion as to who owns the vegetables:

אָמַר רַבִּי שִׁמְעוֹן — **R' Shimon said:** כֹּל שֶׁהָעֶלְיוֹן יָכוֹל לִפְשֹׁט אֶת יָדוֹ וְלִטֹּל — **Any** vegetable **that the** owner of the **upper** garden **can stretch out his hand and take** while he is in his garden הֲרֵי הוּא שֶׁלּוֹ — **belongs to him.** וְהַשְּׁאָר שֶׁל תַּחְתּוֹן — **But the other** vegetables (i.e., those he cannot reach) **belong to**

--- NOTES ---

4. Meiri.

5. Since both people can equally prevent the vegetables from growing, that ability cannot determine who owns them. Therefore, R' Meir returns to his original argument: that the owner of the upper garden gets the vegetables because they are nourished by his soil, as we explained earlier in the Mishnah.

R' Yehudah, too, will respond with his original claim: that it is the location of the vegetables, and not their source of nourishment, that decides whose they are — and they are located in the lower garden's airspace (see Ramban).

the owner of the **lower** garden. According to R' Shimon, by law the vegetables all belong to the owner of the upper garden; however, it can be assumed that he gives up his right to the vegetables that he cannot reach.[6]

NOTES

6. In principle, R' Shimon holds like R' Meir, that the vegetables should all belong to the owner of the upper garden because they are nourished by his soil. R' Shimon maintains, however, that the owner of the upper garden is embarrassed to ask permission to walk through the lower garden to take the vegetables he cannot reach from his garden. Since he cannot get these vegetables, he gives up his right to them and allows the owner of the lower garden to take them (*Rav*).

Appendix
Glossary

Appendix: Laws of Tumah

The laws of *tumah* come up throughout the Mishnah. Indeed, the last of the Six Orders of Mishnah — *Seder Tohoros* — is devoted entirely to this topic. Since these laws unfortunately do not play a significant role in daily Jewish life nowadays (as the Temple is not standing) and most people are unfamiliar with them, we present here a short introduction to this very intricate topic.

Tumah is a type of halachic impurity that attaches itself to people, utensils, and foods under certain circumstances or as a result of special conditions. The laws of *tumah* and its counterpart *taharah* (purity) are Scriptural decrees, whose roots cannot be understood through ordinary human logic and experience (*Rambam, Hil. Mikvaos* 11:12). For this reason, their terminology cannot be simply translated. Therefore, we will use a number of Hebrew terms to explain the Mishnah's discussions of these laws, with which the reader must be familiar to follow the explanations of many Mishnahs.

◆§ Sources of *Tumah*

The Torah classifies certain people and items as "sources of *tumah*." These include a human corpse, a *neveilah* (any animal carcass except for that of a kosher animal killed through *shechitah*), a *sheretz* (the carcass of one of eight species of creeping things listed in *Leviticus* 11:29-30), a *zav* (a man who experienced emissions that resemble, but are not identical to, seminal emissions), a *niddah* (menstruant woman), and others that are listed in the first chapter of *Keilim*. Each of these main sources of *tumah* is known as an *av hatumah* (literally, *father of tumah*) except for a human corpse, whose more stringent *tumah* is known as *avi avos hatumah* (*father of fathers of tumah*). An *av hatumah* [and certainly an *avi avos hatumah*] transmits *tumah* to people, utensils, and foods and beverages that touch it or come in contact with it in various other ways.

◆§ Objects That Can Become *Tamei*

As mentioned above, there are three categories of things that can become *tamei* through contact with a source of *tumah*: (a) people; (b) utensils (objects that have been fashioned to be used in some way, such as chairs, dishes, lamps, or clothing, in contrast to blocks of wood, gold, clay, or random strands of wool, etc.); and (c) beverages, or foods that have become wet through contact with one of seven liquids (dew, water, wine, olive oil, blood, milk, or honey). These different categories are subject to different levels of *tumah* (as will be explained below).

[3] **APPENDIX** / Laws of Tumah

⇝ The Transfer of *Tumah* and Degrees of *Tumah*

Tumah is passed from an *av hatumah* to a person, utensil, food, or beverage that comes in contact with it, and these in turn can have the ability to pass the *tumah* further. The *tumah* weakens, however, each time it is passed on. Thus, when an *av hatumah* transmits *tumah* to a person or object, the person or object becomes a רִאשׁוֹן לְטוּמְאָה, *rishon of tumah* (first degree of received *tumah*). This level of *tumah* is too weak to transmit *tumah* to people or utensils, and it can transmit further *tumah* only to foods and beverages. These in turn can become *tamei* as a שֵׁנִי לְטוּמְאָה, *sheni of tumah* (second degree of received *tumah*). [These terms are generally abbreviated simply as *av, rishon,* and *sheni.*]

A *sheni* is too weak to transmit *tumah* to *chullin* (non-holy) food that it touches — which makes it impossible for ordinary food to possess a third degree of acquired *tumah*. Due to the greater degree of stringency associated with *terumah,* however, it can become *tamei* as a *shelishi,* or third degree of received *tumah,* if it is touched by a *sheni*. But even the *tumah* of *terumah* can go no further than this third degree. [Food that is *kodesh* (such as the parts of offerings) can receive an additional degree of *tumah*. If *kodesh* food is touched by a *shelishi,* it becomes a *revi'i* (fourth degree of received *tumah*).]

Although usually *chullin* foods touched by a *rishon* become *tamei* as a *sheni,* the Rabbis made a special decree that *beverages* touched by *tamei food* (whether the food is *tamei* as a *rishon* or as a *sheni*) always become a *rishon*. They can then render other foods a *sheni* by touching them.

⇝ How *Tumah* Is Transmitted

All main sources of *tumah* (*avos hatumah*) can transmit their *tumah* to other objects if one touches them (מַגָּע). Most *avos* also transmit *tumah* to one who carries them even without touching them (מַשָּׂא), or even causes them to be moved without touching or carrying them (הֶיסֵּט).

Avos hatumah that are living persons (such as a *zav* or a *niddah*) also render *tamei* any bed, chair, etc. that they sit or lie upon (מִשְׁכָּב וּמוֹשָׁב), even if it is covered and they do not touch it directly or move it. Also, the bed or chair (called a מִדְרָס) is an exception to the rule discussed above, because it itself becomes an *av hatumah,* rather than a *rishon,* and has the capacity to render people and utensils *tamei* (not only foods and beverages as a *rishon* does).

A human corpse (as well as certain parts of a corpse) can also transmit *tumah* through *tumas ohel* (tent-*tumah* or roof-*tumah*). A corpse renders people or objects *tamei* through *tumas ohel* (a) if the corpse is in the same tent (under the same roof) as they are; or (b) if the corpse forms a roof over them; or (c) if they form a roof over the corpse. The details of these complex laws are discussed in Tractate *Oholos*.

⇝ Items That Do Not Become *Tamei*

Live animals do not become *tamei*; animal food not fit for human consumption also cannot become *tamei*; nor can anything attached to the ground (such as a tree or plant) become *tamei*.

Utensils made of stone or unbaked earth do not become *tamei*. Flat wooden utensils that have no receptacle or hollow in which something can be contained (e.g., a wooden cutting board) also cannot be rendered *tamei*.

Foods that have not been "prepared" (מֻכְשָׁר) for *tumah* by being wetted by one of the seven liquids mentioned above do not become *tamei*. [These laws are the subject of Tractate *Machshirin*.] Once they have been "prepared" they can become *tamei* even after they are dry.

Earthenware utensils (כְּלֵי חֶרֶס) are unique in that they become *tamei* only if their *inside* (or even their interior airspace) is touched; even if a corpse (the most severe source of *tumah*) touches only the outside of an earthenware utensil, it remains *tahor*. Also, an earthenware utensil that is *tamei* transmits *tumah* only to objects that touch its interior.

◆§ Removing *Tumah*

Tumah is removed from people and most utensils that become *tamei* as a *rishon* through immersion in a *mikveh*. Earthenware utensils, however, cannot be purified of *tumah*; foods and beverages (other than water) also cannot be purified of *tumah*.

After immersing in a *mikveh*, the person (or utensil) is known as a טְבוּל יוֹם, *tevul yom* (one who immersed that day), and will no longer render *tamei* any food or beverage he touches. He may also eat *maaser sheni* immediately after immersion. However, he still renders *terumah* or *kodesh* that he touches *tamei* until nightfall (הַעֲרֵב שֶׁמֶשׁ) of the day of his immersion.

A person who is an *av hatumah* (such as a *zav*, or a person who touched a human corpse) requires additional procedures to remove his or her *tumah*. The procedures vary with each type of *tumah*, and sometimes include the bringing of offerings, or the passage of certain time periods.

The *tumah* of a non-living *av hatumah* (such as *neveilah*, or corpses) cannot be removed.

◆§ Consequences of *Tumah*

Tamei persons and objects may not enter the Temple (*Beis HaMikdash*). *Terumah, maaser sheni*, and *kodesh* foods that become *tamei* may not be eaten and must be burned. By contrast, *chullin* foods that become *tamei* may be eaten (although some people were careful to eat only *tahor* foods), and *tamei* utensils may be used for ordinary, non-sacred purposes.

Glossary

Adar — the twelfth month of the Jewish calendar.

Altar — the structure in the **Temple** Courtyard upon which the blood of offerings was poured and on which part or all of their meat or flour were burned. See also **Inner Altar**.

am haaretz [plural, **amei haaretz**] — an unlearned person. This refers to someone who is not careful in his observance of the laws of **tumah** and **taharah**. *Amei haaretz* were also suspected of not separating **maaser**.

amah [plural, **amos**] — cubit; a measure of distance equaling six **tefachim**. Opinions regarding its modern equivalent range between 18.9 and 22.7 inches (48-57.7 cm.).

Antechamber — the **Ulam**; the Hall in the **Sanctuary** Building that led into the Sanctuary.

aravah [plural, **aravos**] — twigs of a willow tree. See **Four Species**.

Ark — the sacred chest that stood in the **Holy of Holies** in the **Mishkan** and the First **Temple**. It contained the Tablets of the Ten Commandments and the Torah Scroll written by Moses.

asham [plural, **ashamos**] — guilt offering; an offering brought to atone for one of several specific sins or as part of certain purification procedures. It is one of the **kodshei kodashim**.

asheirah — a tree that was designated for worship or under which an idol is placed.

asmachta — a Scriptural source that hints at a Rabbinic law.

av [plural, **avos**] **hatumah** — literally, father of **tumah**. See *tumah*.

avi avos hatumah — literally, father of fathers of **tumah**; a corpse. See *tumah*.

avodah [plural, **avodos**] — (a) a part of the sacrificial service in the **Temple**; (b) the Temple service as a whole.

Azazel — (a) the he-goat chosen by lottery to be thrown off a cliff on Yom Kippur; (b) the cliff from which it was thrown.

bagrus — the state of being a **bogeress**.

bamah — (a) major *bamah;* the **Altar** that stood next to the **Mishkan** when the Mishkan was located in Gilgal, Nov, and Givon; (b) minor *bamah;* altar built by an individual on which he offered his personal, voluntary offerings.

bechor — (a) firstborn male child; (b) a firstborn male kosher animal. Such an animal is born with sacrificial sanctity, and must be given to a **Kohen** who then offers it (if unblemished) as a *bechor* offering in the **Temple** and eats its meat.

bein hashemashos — the twilight period preceding night. The legal status of *bein hashemashos* as day or night is uncertain.

beis av — a family group within a **mishmar**.

beis din — Rabbinic court.

Beis HaMikdash — **Temple** in Jerusalem.

beis kor — 75,000 square **amos**.

beis se'ah — an area 50 **amos** by 50 *amos*.

Bircas HaMazon — the blessings recited after a meal.

bogeress — see **naarah**.

chadash — literally, new; the new crop of any of the five grains (wheat, barley, rye, spelt, oats). *Chadash* may not be eaten until the **omer** offering is brought on the second day of **Pesach**.

chalitzah — see **yibum**.

challah — the portion separated from a dough made of the five grains; it must be given to a **Kohen**.

chalal — the male child of a **Kohen** and

a woman who is forbidden specifically to Kohanim (for example, a divorcee). Although his father is a Kohen, a *chalal* is not a Kohen. The son of a *chalal* is also a *chalal,* and his daughter is a **chalalah**.

chalalah — (a) the female child of a **Kohen** and a woman who is forbidden specifically to Kohanim; (b) the daughter of a **chalal;** (c) a woman forbidden specifically to Kohanim who cohabited with a Kohen; (d) a woman who cohabited with a *chalal*. A *chalalah* is prohibited to marry a Kohen or eat **terumah**.

chametz — grain that was mixed with water and allowed to leaven before being baked. Only five grains — wheat, barley, spelt, rye, and oats — can become *chametz*.

Chanukah — Festival of Lights; the eight-day holiday that commemorates the Maccabean victory over the Greeks.

chatas [pl. **chataos**] — sin offering; an offering usually brought in atonement for the inadvertent transgression of a prohibition punishable by **kares** when transgressed deliberately.

chatzitzah — literally, an interposition; foreign matter attached or adhering to the person or object that needs to be immersed in a **mikveh**, which prevents the water from coming in contact with the whole of its surface. This invalidates the immersion.

chaver [plural, **chaveirim**] — (a) one who observes the laws of **tumah** and **taharah** even with respect to non-consecrated foods; (b) a Torah scholar, scrupulous in his observance of mitzvos.

chavitin — a **minchah** offering that consists of flour and oil; half of it was offered with the morning **tamid** and half with the afternoon *tamid*. The **Kohen Gadol** brings a *chavitin* every day; an ordinary **Kohen** brings it on his first day of service in the **Temple**.

cherem — (a) a vow in which one uses the expression "*cherem*" to consecrate property, placing it under the ownership of the **Temple** or the **Kohanim;** (b) land or property upon which a ban has been declared, forbidding its use to anyone.

chilazon — an aquatic creature from whose blood the blue *techeiles* dye was produced.

Chol HaMoed — the intermediate days of the festivals of **Pesach** and **Succos**. These festivals begin and end with a holy day (**Yom Tov**), during which most forms of work (**melachah**) are forbidden, and they are separated by intermediate days — known as "Chol HaMoed," literally, the ordinary part of the festival — during which certain forms of *melachah* are permitted.

chullin — literally, ordinary things; any substance that is not sanctified or consecrated. See **kodesh**.

Curtain — the **Paroches;** the curtain that divided between the **Holy** and the **Holy of Holies** in the **Sanctuary**.

Cutheans — a non-Jewish tribe brought by the Assyrians to settle the part of **Eretz Yisrael** left vacant by the exile of the Ten Tribes. The Cutheans' subsequent conversion to Judaism was considered questionable and their observance of many laws was lax.

demai — produce of **Eretz Yisrael** obtained from an **am haaretz**. The Rabbis required that **maasros** be separated from *demai* because the *am haaretz* might not have done so.

eglah arufah — literally, decapitated calf; when a murder victim is found and the murderer is not known, the **beis din** measures to determine the city closest to where the corpse lies. The elders of that city decapitate a calf, in accordance with the procedures outlined in *Deuteronomy* 21:1-9.

emurin — the fats and internal organs of an animal offering that are burned on the **Altar**.

Eretz Yisrael — the Land of Israel.

Erev Pesach — the fourteenth of **Nissan**, the day before **Pesach**.

erusin — betrothal; the first act of marriage [also known as **kiddushin**]. This is effected by the man giving the

GLOSSARY

woman an object of value to betroth her. At this point, the couple is not yet permitted to have marital relations, but is legally married in most respects and the woman requires a **get** before she can marry again. The period between *erusin* (*kiddushin*) and **nisuin** is also called *erusin*.

eruv — popular contraction of **eruvei tavshilin** or **eruvei techumin**.

eruv tavshilin — food cooked before a **Yom Tov** that falls on Friday and is intended to be eaten on **Shabbos**. If one prepares such food before the Yom Tov, one is permitted on that Yom Tov to prepare food for Shabbos.

eruvei techumin — literally, merging of boundaries; a legal device that allows a person to shift his **Shabbos** residence from the place where he is to any place up to 2,000 **amos** away. One accomplishes this by placing a specific amount of food at the desired location before the start of Shabbos or by being there himself when Shabbos begins. That place is then viewed as the person's Shabbos residence, and his 2,000-*amah* **techum** limit is measured from there.

esrog — citron; one of the **Four Species**.

Four Species — it is a Biblical obligation to take the following four species on Succos: the **lulav** (branch of a palm tree), **esrog** (citron), **hadassim** (twigs of a myrtle tree), and **aravos** (twigs of a willow tree).

fourfold and fivefold payments — the fine that must be paid by a **ganav** who stole a sheep or ox and slaughtered or sold it. In addition to the value of the sheep or ox, he must pay a fine of three times as much (in the case of the sheep) or four times as much (in the case of the ox).

fund for the upkeep of the Temple — fund comprised of voluntary contributions that was used to pay for repairs to the **Temple**.

ganav — a thief who steals secretly.

gazlan — a thief who robs openly, by force or by threatening force.

get [plural, **gittin**] — bill of divorce; the document that, when placed in the wife's possession, effects the end of the marriage.

gezeirah shavah — one of the thirteen principles of Biblical derivation. If a similar word or phrase occurs in two passages in the Torah, the principle of *gezeirah shavah* teaches that these passages are linked to each other, and the laws of one passage are applied to the other. Only those words that are designated by the Oral Sinaitic Law for this purpose may serve as a basis for a *gezeirah shavah*.

Golden Altar — see **Inner Altar**.

hadassim — twigs of a myrtle tree; one of the **Four Species**.

hagbanah — see **kinyan**.

half-pras — measure of volume that is equivalent to two eggs.

Hallel — prayer of praise to God that is recited on **Pesach, Succos, Shavuos, Chanukah,** and **Rosh Chodesh**. It consists of *Psalms* 113-118.

hekdesh — (a) items consecrated to the **Temple** treasury or as offerings. *Hekdesh* can have two levels of sanctity: **monetary sanctity** and **physical sanctity**. Property owned by the Temple treasury is said to have monetary sanctity. Such property can be redeemed or sold by the Temple treasurers, with the proceeds of the redemption or sale becoming *hekdesh* in its place. Consecrated items that are fit for the Temple service (e.g., unblemished animals or sacred vessels) are deemed to have physical sanctity; (b) the state of consecration; (c) the Temple treasury.

Holy — the chamber in the Temple that contained the **Shulchan, Menorah,** and the **Inner (Golden) Altar**.

Holy of Holies — the most sacred part of the **Temple**. During most of the First Temple era, it contained the Holy Ark; later it was empty of any utensils. Even the **Kohen Gadol** is prohibited from entering it except on **Yom Kippur**.

Inner Altar — structure inside the main chamber of the **Temple** building on which the **ketores** offerings were burned. See also **Altar**.

Iyar — the second month of the Jewish calendar.

kares — cutting off of the soul or premature death; Divinely imposed punishment decreed by the Torah for certain classes of transgression.

kav — measure of volume equivalent to 24 eggs.

kebeitzah — an egg's volume.

keifel — the fine that a **ganav** must pay. In addition to returning the stolen item (or its value), he must pay a fine of the same value.

keilim [singular, **kli**] — utensil or vessel.

keren — literally, horn; damage that an animal does through unusual behavior, such as a tame animal goring another animal with its horns.

kesubah — (a) the marriage contract that a groom hands over to his bride when they get married, in which his commitments toward her are recorded; (b) the payment that a husband (or his estate) must make to his wife if their marriage ends in divorce or his death. If she was a virgin when she got married, the payment is at least 200 *zuz*; if she was not a virgin, the payment is at least 100 *zuz*.

Kesuvim — see **Writings**.

ketanah — an underaged girl. See **naarah**.

ketores — a mixture of aromatic spices and other substances that was burned twice every day in the **Temple**, and a third time on **Yom Kippur**.

kezayis — the volume of an olive; minimum amount of food whose consumption is considered "eating."

Kiddush — the blessing recited over wine before the evening and morning meals on the **Sabbath** and **Yom Tov**.

kiddushin — see **erusin**.

kilayim — "mixtures"; various forbidden mixtures, including: **shaatnez** (cloth made from a blend of wool and linen); cross-breeding of animals; cross-breeding (or side-by-side planting) of certain food crops; and working with different species of animals yoked together.

kinyan — an act through which a person acquires ownership of property; examples of a *kinyan* are **hagbahah** (lifting the object) and **meshichah** (drawing it away from where it is).

kiyor — large basin of water that stood in the **Temple** Courtyard to which faucets were attached. The **Kohanim** washed their hands and feet with water from the *kiyor*.

kodashim — sacrificial food.

kodashim kalim — offerings of lesser holiness (one of the two classifications of sacrificial offerings). They may be eaten anywhere in Jerusalem by any **tahor** person. They include the **todah**, regular **shelamim**, **bechor**, **nazir's** ram, **maaser**, and **pesach** offerings. This category of offerings is not subject to the stringencies applied to **kodshei kodashim**.

kodesh — (a) portions of sacrificial offerings; (b) any consecrated item.

kodshei kodashim — most-holy offerings (one of the two classifications of sacrificial offerings). They may be eaten only in the **Temple** Courtyard and only by male **Kohanim**. They include the **olah** (which may not be eaten at all), **chatas**, **asham**, and communal **shelamim**. These are subject to greater stringencies than **kodashim kalim**.

Kohen [plural, **Kohanim**] — member of the priestly family descended in the male line from Aaron. The Kohen performs the service in the **Temple**.

Kohen Gadol — High Priest.

konam — a word that can substitute for **korban**. It is used in **nedarim**; for example, "This object is *konam* to me."

korban — a sacred offering.

lavud — rule stating that a gap of less than three **tefachim** is legally viewed as closed.

lechem hapanim — *panim* breads. The twelve loaves of bread baked in a special way that were placed on the **Shulchan** in the **Temple** each **Shabbos**. They remained until the next Shabbos, when they were eaten by the **Kohanim**.

Levi [plural, **Leviim**] — male descendant of the tribe of Levi in the male line, who performs secondary services in the **Beis HaMikdash**.

lishkah — the **lishkah** (or **terumas halishkah**) is the name of a fund in which the annual half-**shekel** contributions were collected. This fund was used to pay for the communal offerings and general expenses related to the Temple service.

log [plural, **lugin**] — liquid measure equal to the volume of six eggs.

lulav — branch of a palm tree; one of the **Four Species**.

maamar — The Sages decreed that before performing **yibum**, the **yavam** first "betroth" the **yevamah** by performing one of the acts that normally effect **erusin**. This act of pre-*yibum* betrothal is called **maamar**.

Maariv — the evening prayer service.

maasar ani — the tithe for the poor, given in the third and sixth years of the **shemittah** cycle.

maasar beheimah — the animal tithe. The newborn kosher animals born to one's herds and flocks each year are gathered into a pen and made to pass through an opening one at a time. Every tenth animal is designated as **maaser**. It is brought as an offering in the **Temple** and is eaten by the owner.

maaser [plural, **maasros**] — tithe. It is a Biblical obligation to give two tithes, each known as *maaser*, from the produce of the Land of Israel. The first tithe (**maaser rishon**) is given to a **Levi**. The second tithe (**maaser sheni**) is taken to Jerusalem and eaten there, or redeemed with coins that are then taken to Jerusalem for the purchase of food to be eaten there. In the third and sixth years of the seven-year **shemittah** cycle, the *maaser sheni* obligation is replaced with **maasar ani**, the tithe for the poor.

maaser rishon — see **maaser**.

maaser sheni — see **maaser**.

mamzer (fem. **mamzeress**) — a child born from a forbidden union that is punishable by **kares**, or from a parent who is a *mamzer* or *mamzeress*. The Torah forbids marriage or cohabitation between a *mamzer* or *mamzeress* and a regular Jew.

maror — the bitter herb that one is obligated to eat on the first night of **Pesach**.

matzah — unleavened bread; dough that was baked before it was allowed to ferment or rise. It is a Biblical obligation to eat matzah on the first night of **Pesach**.

mazik — a person who damages the body or property of someone else, or whose property does such damage.

mechussar kapparah [plural, **mechussarei kapparah**] — literally, lacking atonement; the status accorded to a **tevul yom** in the interval between sunset of the day of his immersion and the time he brings his offerings. During that period, he retains a vestige of his earlier **tumah** and is thus forbidden to enter the **Temple** Courtyard or partake of the offerings.

mei chatas — see **parah adumah**.

me'ilah — unlawfully benefiting from **Temple** property or removing such property from the Temple ownership. One who does so inadvertently must pay the value of the item plus a quarter. He must also bring an **asham** offering.

melachah [plural, **melachos**] — labor; specifically, one of the thirty-nine labor categories whose performance is forbidden by the Torah on **Shabbos** and **Yom Tov**. These prohibited categories are known as *avos melachah*. Activities whose prohibition is derived from one of these thirty-nine categories are known as **tolados** (singular, *toladah*) — subcategories.

melikah — the unique manner in which bird offerings were slaughtered. *Melikah* differs from **shechitah** in two respects: (a) The cut is made with the **Kohen's** thumbnail rather than with a knife. (b) The neck is cut from the back rather than from the throat. Only birds for sacrificial purposes may be slaughtered by *melikah;* all others require *shechitah.*

melog — property that a bride brings into the marriage that is not recorded in the **kesubah** document. It belongs to her but the husband has the right to use it, and any profit generated from it is his.

Menorah — the seven-branched gold candelabra that stood in the main chamber of the **Temple.**

meshichah — see **kinyan.**

metzora — a person who has contracted **tzaraas** (mistakenly described as leprosy), an affliction of the skin described in *Leviticus* Chs. 13 and 14.

mezuzah [plural, **mezuzos**] — a parchment scroll that contains the passages of *Deuteronomy* 6:4-9 and 11:13-21; it is affixed to the doorpost.

midras — literally, treading; an object that acquired **tumah** when a **zav, zavah, niddah,** or woman after childbirth rests his or her weight on it. It is an **av hatumah.**

mikveh — a body of standing water containing at least forty *se'ah.* It is used to purify (by immersion) people and utensils of their **tumah**-contamination. A *mikveh* consists of waters naturally collected, without direct human intervention. Water drawn in a vessel is not valid for a *mikveh.*

mil — distance of 2,000 **amos.**

minchah — (a) [upper case] the afternoon prayer service; (b) [plural, **menachos**] a flour offering, generally consisting of fine wheat flour, oil, and frankincense, part of which is burned on the **Altar.**

minyan — quorum of ten adult Jewish males necessary for the communal prayer service and other rituals.

Mishkan — the portable Temple used during the forty years of national wandering in the Wilderness. After the Jews entered **Eretz Yisrael,** it was situated in different places (Gilgal, Shiloh, Nov, and Givon) until the **Beis HaMikdash** was built in Jerusalem.

mishmar [plural, **mishmaros**] — literally, watch; one of the twenty-four watches of **Kohanim** and **Leviim** who served in the **Temple** for a week at a time on a rotating basis. These watches were subdivided into family groups, each of which served on one day of the week. A family group is called a **beis av** (literally, father's house).

mi'un — By Rabbinic enactment, an underaged orphan girl may be given in marriage by her mother or brothers. She can annul the marriage anytime before reaching adulthood by declaring her unwillingness to continue in the marriage. This declaration and process are called *mi'un.*

monetary sanctity — the level of sanctity of items consecrated to the **Temple,** not to be offered on the **Altar** but to be sold for their value, with the proceeds being used for Temple purposes. See **hekdesh.**

muad — an animal that habitually does damage in a certain way.

muktzeh — literally, set aside; (a) a class of objects that the Sages prohibited moving on **Shabbos** or **Yom Tov;** (b) an animal set aside to be sacrificed for idolatry.

mussaf — (a) additional offerings brought on **Shabbos, Rosh Chodesh,** or **Yom Tov;** (b) [upper case] the prayer service recited on the days that these offerings are brought.

naarah — There are three stages in the life of a maturing girl. She is a **ketanah** (minor) from the day of her birth until she reaches the age of twelve and grows two pubic hairs, at which point she becomes a *naarah* (partial adult). She remains a *naarah* for six months, after which she becomes a **bogeress** (full adult).

nasin (fem. **nesinah**) — a descendant of the Gibeonites, a group of Canaanites who tricked Joshua into making a peace treaty with them. An ordinary Jew is forbidden to marry a *nasin* or a *nesinah.*

nazir [plural, **nezirim**] — one who took a special vow that prohibits him, for a minimum period of thirty days, from cutting his hair, drinking wine (or eating any part of a grape), and becoming **tamei** from a corpse.

neder — a vow that renders objects, in contrast to actions, prohibited. There are two basic categories of vows: (a) prohibitive vows; (b) vows to donate to **hekdesh**. See **hekdesh**.

nesachim [singular, **nesech**] — libations; a liquid (usually wine) that is poured upon the **Altar**. It accompanies certain offerings or may be donated separately.

nesinah — see **nasin**.

neveilah — carcass of an animal that was not killed through **shechitah**.

Neviim — see **Prophets**.

nezirus — the state of being a **nazir**.

niddah — a woman who has menstruated but has not yet completed her purification process, which concludes with immersion in a **mikveh**.

Nissan — the first month of the Jewish calendar.

nisuch hamayim — the mitzvah of pouring water on the **Altar** on each day of **Succos**.

nisuin — the second act of marriage, after which the couple is allowed to live together. It is effected by a procedure called *chuppah*. The period between *nisuin* and the end of the marriage is also known as *nisuin*. See **erusin**.

nizak — a person who suffers damage to his body or his property.

nolad — literally, newborn. Objects that are **muktzeh** because they did not exist (or were not usable) before **Shabbos** or **Yom Tov** began.

nossar — part of an offering left over after the time permitted for eating it has passed.

olah [plural, **olos**] — burnt offering; an offering that is burned in its entirety on the **Altar**.

omer — a communal **minchah** offering brought on the 16th of **Nissan**. Once it was brought, the new grain crop (**chadash**) became permitted to be eaten.

ona'ah — price fraud; taking advantage of someone who does not know the true price of an item, by selling it to him for more than the market value, or buying it from him for less than the market value.

orlah — literally, sealed; fruit that grows on a tree during the first three years of the tree's existence. The Torah prohibits any benefit from such fruit.

parah adumah — literally, red cow. A completely red cow is slaughtered and burned; its ashes are mixed with spring water and then used in the purification process of people or objects who have contracted **tumah** from a human corpse.

Paroches — see **Curtain**.

Pesach — Passover; the **Yom Tov** that celebrates the Exodus of the Jewish nation from Egypt.

pesach offering — offering brought on the afternoon of the 14th day of **Nissan** and eaten after nightfall.

physical sanctity — the level of sanctity possessed by items consecrated to be used as offerings. See **hekdesh**.

Prophets (Neviim) — the second of the three sections of the Written Torah. It consists of the following books: *Joshua, Judges, Samuel, Kings, Isaiah, Jeremiah, Ezekiel, Twelve Prophets*.

prozbul — The Torah states that all loans are canceled at the end of the **shemittah** year. The Rabbis enacted a law allowing for loans to be collected after the *shemittah* year through a process whereby the lender authorizes the court in advance of *shemittah* to collect all his debts. The document that authorizes the court to assume responsibility for the collection of those debts is called a *prozbul*.

regel [plural, **regalim**] — (a) any of the three pilgrimage festivals: **Pesach**, **Shavuos**, and **Succos**; (b) damage that an animal does in the course of walking or other normal movement.

reshus harabim — literally, public domain; any unroofed, commonly used street, public area, or highway at least sixteen **amos** wide and open at both ends. According to some, it must be used by at least 600,000 people.

reshus hayachid — literally, private domain; any area measuring at least four **tefachim** by four *tefachim* and enclosed by partitions at least ten *tefachim* high. According to most opinions, it needs to be enclosed only on three sides to qualify as a *reshus hayachid*. Private ownership is not necessary.

revi'i of tumah — see **tumah**.

revi'is — a quarter of a **log**.

rishon of tumah — first degree of acquired **tumah**. See *tumah*.

Rosh Chodesh — (a) festival celebrating the new month; (b) the first of the month.

Rosh Hashanah — the **Yom Tov** that celebrates the new year. It falls on the first and second days of **Tishrei**.

Sadducees — heretical sect active during the Second **Temple** era, named after Tzaddok, a disciple of Antigenos of Socho. They denied the Divine origin of the Oral Law and refused to accept the Sages' interpretation of the Torah.

Sanctuary — (a) the **Holy**; (b) the main **Temple** building that included the Holy and the **Holy of Holies.**

Sanhedrin — (a) the High Court of Israel; the Supreme Court consisting of seventy-one judges whose decisions on questions of Torah law are definitive and binding on all courts; (b) [lower case] a court of twenty-three judges authorized to adjudicate capital and corporal cases.

sela — see **shekel.**

shaatnez — see **kilayim.**

Shabbos — the seventh day of the week (Saturday); a holy day when **melachah** and certain other activities are forbidden.

Shacharis — the morning prayer service.

Shavuos — the festival that celebrates the giving of the Torah to the Jewish nation at Mount Sinai.

shechitah — (a) ritual slaughter; the method prescribed by the Torah for slaughtering a kosher animal to make it fit for consumption. It consists of cutting through most of the esophagus and windpipe, from the front of the neck, with a specially sharpened knife that is free of nicks; (b) one of the four essential blood **avodos.**

shein — literally, tooth; damage that an animal does through eating or any other activity from which it benefits.

shekel (plural, **shekalim**) — Scriptural coin equivalent to the Aramaic **sela** or four *dinars*. In Mishnaic terminology, the Scriptural half-*shekel* (two *dinars*) is called a *shekel,* and the Scriptural shekel is called by its Aramaic name, *sela.*

shelamim — peace offering; generally brought by an individual on a voluntary basis; part is burned on the **Altar**, part is eaten by a **Kohen** (and the members of his household), and part is eaten by the owner.

shelishi of tumah — see **tumah.**

Shemini Atzeres — the eighth and concluding day of the **Succos** celebration. In many respects, it is a **Yom Tov** in its own right.

shemittah — the Sabbatical year, occurring every seventh year, during which the land of **Eretz Yisrael** may not be cultivated.

Shemoneh Esrei — literally, eighteen; the silent standing prayer that is the main feature of the daily prayer services. It is also called *Amidah.*

sheni of tumah — see **tumah.**

sheretz — carcass of one of eight species of creeping animals (rodents and reptiles) listed in *Leviticus* 11:29-30.

shevuah — (a) a vow to perform or not to perform an action; (b) an oath stating that something is true.

shogeg — inadvertent action.

shomer — literally, guardian, watchman; a person who is responsible to watch and take care of property that belongs to someone else.

Shulchan — the sacred Table in the **Sanctuary.**

Simchas Beis HaSho'eivah — celebration

GLOSSARY

held in the **Temple** on each night of **Chol HaMoed** on **Succos**.

sotah — a woman suspected of adultery. If a woman was warned by her husband not to be alone with a certain man and she disobeyed his warning, she and her husband are not allowed to live together unless she drinks the "bitter waters," which prove her guilt or innocence. These consist of water from the **Temple** mixed with dust from the Temple floor, into which the writing of certain verses that include the Name of God has been dissolved.

succah — (a) the temporary dwelling in which one must dwell during the festival of **Succos**; (b) [upper case] the Talmudic tractate that deals with the laws pertaining to the festival of Succos.

Succos — festival during which we dwell in a **succah** to commemorate the protection provided by God to the Jewish people in the Wilderness.

taharah — the absence of **tumah**.

tahor — not **tamei**.

tam — an animal that is not expected to do damage in a particular way; see **keren**.

tamei — possessing **tumah**.

tamid — a communal offering that was offered in the **Temple** twice daily — once in the morning and once after the conclusion of the Temple services (always before nightfall). It consisted of lambs in their first year.

techum [plural, **techumim**] — **Shabbos** boundary; the distance of 2,000 **amos** from a person's Sabbath residence that he is permitted to travel on Shabbos or **Yom Tov**. See **eruv techumin**.

tefach [plural, **tefachim**] — a handbreadth; the length of an average fist. Opinions regarding its modern equivalent range between 3.15 and 3.8 inches (8-9.6 cm.).

tefillin — phylacteries; they are worn on the head and the left arm.

Temple — (a) the Holy Temple in Jerusalem (**Beis HaMikdash**); (b) the **Mishkan**.

terumah [plural, **terumos**] — the first portion of the crop separated and given to a **Kohen**, usually between $\frac{1}{40}$ and $\frac{1}{60}$ of the total crop. It has a level of sanctity that prohibits it from being eaten by a non-Kohen, or by a Kohen in a state of **tumah**.

terumas hadeshen — the daily service of removing a portion of ash from the **Outer Altar** in the **Temple**.

terumas halishkah — (a) money withdrawn from the **lishkah** fund; (b) an alternative name of the fund itself.

tevel — produce of **Eretz Yisrael** that has become subject to the obligation of **terumah** and **maaser**. *Tevel* is forbidden for consumption until *terumah* and all the other tithes have been designated.

tevilah — immersion in a **mikveh** for the purpose of purification from **tumah**-contamination.

tevul yom — literally, one who immersed that day — a person who had been rendered ritually impure with a Biblical **tumah** from which he purified himself with immersion in a **mikveh**. A residue of the *tumah* lingers until nightfall of the day of his immersion, leaving him *tamei* in regard to offerings, **terumah**, and entering the **Temple** Courtyard. A person in this reduced state of *tumah* is known as a *tevul yom*, and he renders *terumah* and **kodashim** invalid through contact.

Tishah B'Av — literally, the ninth of Av; annual fast day that commemorates the fall of the First and Second **Temples**.

Tishrei — the seventh month of the Jewish calendar.

todah — a thanksgiving offering brought when a person wants to show gratitude to God, particularly after surviving a life-threatening situation.

toladah [plural, **tolados**] — see **melachah**.

tumah [plural, **tumos**] — a type of impurity that attaches itself to people, utensils, and foods. There are different levels of *tumah*. The highest level, **avi avos hatumah** [literally, *father of fathers of tumah*], is limited to a human corpse.

The next level is known as **av hatumah**, primary [literally, *father of*] *tumah*. This category includes a **neveilah**, a **sheretz**, a **niddah**, a **zavah**, a **metzora**, a woman after childbirth, and a person who received *tumah* directly from a corpse. An *av hatumah* transmits *tumah* to people, utensils, foods, and beverages that come in contact with it, for example, by touching it. These in turn have the ability to pass the *tumah* further. The *tumah* weakens, however, each time it is passed on. Thus, when an *av hatumah* transmits *tumah* to a person or object, he or it become **rishon of tumah** (first degree of acquired *tumah*). This level of *tumah* is too weak to transmit *tumah* to people or utensils; it can transmit *tumah* only to foods and beverages, which become **sheni of tumah** (second degree of acquired *tumah*). A *sheni* is too weak to transmit *tumah* to **chullin** (non-holy) food that touches it, which makes it impossible for ordinary food to possess a third degree of acquired *tumah*. However, a *sheni* can transmit *tumah* to **terumah** and **kodesh**, making either one a **shelishi of tumah** (third degree of acquired *tumah*), and a *shelishi* can transmit *tumah* to **kodesh**, making it a **revi'i of tumah** (fourth degree of acquired *tumah*).

tzaraas — see **metzora**.

tzitzis — the fringes that by Torah law must be placed on a four-cornered garment.

tzon barzel — property that a bride brings into the marriage and is recorded in the **kesubah**. The husband owns it and may use it as he wishes, but if the marriage ends in his death or divorce, he must pay her the amount the property was worth at the time of marriage.

Ulam — see **Antechamber**.

Writings — the third of the three sections of the Written Torah. It consists of the following Books: *Psalms, Proverbs, Job, Song of Songs, Ruth, Lamentations, Ecclesiastes, Esther, Daniel, Ezra-Nehemiah, Chronicles*.

yavam — see **yibum**.

yevamah — see **yibum**.

yibum — levirate marriage. When a man dies childless, the Torah provides for one of his brothers to marry the widow. This marriage is called *yibum*. Before this, the widow is forbidden to marry anyone else. The surviving brother, upon whom the obligation to perform the mitzvah of *yibum* falls, is called the *yavam*. The widow is called the *yevamah*. *Yibum* is effected only through cohabitation. If the brother should refuse to perform *yibum*, he must release her from her *yibum*-bond by performing the rite of *chalitzah*, in which she removes his shoe before the court and spits before him and declares: *So should be done to the man who will not build his brother's house* (Deuteronomy 25:5-9).

Yisrael [plural, **Yisraelim**] — a Jew who is not a **Kohen** or a **Levi**.

Yom Kippur — Day of Atonement; a day of prayer, penitence, fasting, and abstention from **melachah**.

Yom Tov [plural, **Yamim Tovim**] — holiday; specifically, the first and last days of **Pesach, Shavuos**, the first day of **Succos, Shemini Atzeres, Yom Kippur**, and the two days of **Rosh Hashanah**. Outside of **Eretz Yisrael**, an additional day of Yom Tov is added to each of these festivals, except **Yom Kippur** and **Rosh Hashanah**. Most forms of **melachah** are forbidden on Yom Tov.

yovel — fiftieth year [Jubilee]; the year following the conclusion of a set of seven **shemittah** cycles. On **Yom Kippur** of that year, the shofar is sounded to proclaim freedom for the Jewish servants, and to signal the return to the original owner of fields that had been sold in **Eretz Yisrael** during the previous forty-nine years.

zav [plural, **zavim**] — a man who has become **tamei** because of a specific type of bodily emission. If three emissions were experienced during a three-day period, the man must bring offerings upon his purification.

zavah [plural, **zavos**] — By Biblical law,

GLOSSARY

after a women concludes her seven days of **niddah,** there is an eleven-day period during which any menses-like bleeding renders her a *minor zavah,* who is **tamei** until she experiences seven consecutive days without bleeding and immerses in a **mikveh.** If the bleeding lasts for three days, she is a *major zavah* and must bring offerings upon her purification.

zonah — a woman who cohabited with a non-Jew, a Canaanite slave, or one of the forbidden close relatives; a married woman who cohabited with any man who is not her husband. The Torah forbids marriage between a *zonah* and a **Kohen.** A *zonah* is forbidden to eat **terumah.**

תפילה על הנפטר אחר לימוד משניות
Prayer after the Study of Mishnah for the Deceased

[18] תפילה על הנפטר אחר לימוד משניות

It is customary to recite this prayer whenever Mishnayos are studied in memory of a deceased.

אָנָּא יהוה מָלֵא רַחֲמִים, אֲשֶׁר בְּיָדְךָ נֶפֶשׁ כָּל חַי, וְרוּחַ כָּל בְּשַׂר אִישׁ. יְהִי נָא לְרָצוֹן לְפָנֶיךָ תּוֹרָתֵנוּ וּתְפִלָּתֵנוּ בַּעֲבוּר נִשְׁמַת (deceased's Hebrew name) בֶּן/בַּת (father's Hebrew name) וּגְמוֹל נָא עִמָּהּ בְּחַסְדְּךָ הַגָּדוֹל, לִפְתּוֹחַ לָהּ שַׁעֲרֵי רַחֲמִים וָחֶסֶד, וְשַׁעֲרֵי גַּן עֵדֶן. וּתְקַבֵּל אוֹתָהּ בְּאַהֲבָה וּבְחִבָּה, וּשְׁלַח לָהּ מַלְאָכֶיךָ הַקְּדוֹשִׁים וְהַטְּהוֹרִים, לְהוֹלִיכָהּ וּלְהוֹשִׁיבָהּ תַּחַת עֵץ הַחַיִּים, אֵצֶל נִשְׁמוֹת הַצַּדִּיקִים וְהַצִּדְקָנִיּוֹת, חֲסִידִים וַחֲסִידוֹת, לֵהָנוֹת מִזִּיו שְׁכִינָתֶךָ, לְהַשְׂבִּיעָהּ מִטּוּבְךָ הַצָּפוּן לַצַּדִּיקִים. וְהַגּוּף יָנוּחַ בַּקֶּבֶר בִּמְנוּחָה נְכוֹנָה, בְּחֶדְוָה וּבְשִׂמְחָה וְשָׁלוֹם, כְּדִכְתִיב: יָבוֹא שָׁלוֹם, יָנוּחוּ עַל מִשְׁכְּבוֹתָם, הֹלֵךְ נְכֹחוֹ. וּכְתִיב: יַעְלְזוּ חֲסִידִים בְּכָבוֹד, יְרַנְּנוּ עַל מִשְׁכְּבוֹתָם. וּכְתִיב: אִם תִּשְׁכַּב לֹא תִפְחָד, וְשָׁכַבְתָּ וְעָרְבָה שְׁנָתֶךָ.

for a male:

וְתִשְׁמוֹר אוֹתוֹ מֵחִבּוּט הַקֶּבֶר, וּמֵרִמָּה וְתוֹלֵעָה. וְתִסְלַח וְתִמְחוֹל לוֹ עַל כָּל פְּשָׁעָיו, כִּי אָדָם אֵין צַדִּיק בָּאָרֶץ, אֲשֶׁר יַעֲשֶׂה טּוֹב וְלֹא יֶחֱטָא. וּזְכוֹר לוֹ זְכִיּוֹתָיו וְצִדְקוֹתָיו אֲשֶׁר עָשָׂה. וְתַשְׁפִּיעַ לוֹ מִנִּשְׁמָתוֹ לְדַשֵּׁן עַצְמוֹתָיו בַּקֶּבֶר מֵרֹב טוּב הַצָּפוּן לַצַּדִּיקִים, דִּכְתִיב: מָה רַב טוּבְךָ אֲשֶׁר צָפַנְתָּ לִּירֵאֶיךָ. וּכְתִיב: שֹׁמֵר כָּל עַצְמוֹתָיו, אַחַת מֵהֵנָּה לֹא נִשְׁבָּרָה. וְיִשְׁכּוֹן בֶּטַח בָּדָד וְשַׁאֲנָן מִפַּחַד רָעָה, וְאַל יִרְאֶה פְּנֵי גֵּיהִנֹּם. וְנִשְׁמָתוֹ תְּהֵא צְרוּרָה בִּצְרוֹר הַחַיִּים, וּלְהַחֲיוֹתוֹ בִּתְחִיַּת הַמֵּתִים עִם כָּל מֵתֵי עַמְּךָ יִשְׂרָאֵל בְּרַחֲמִים. אָמֵן.

for a female:

וְתִשְׁמוֹר אוֹתָהּ מֵחִבּוּט הַקֶּבֶר, וּמֵרִמָּה וְתוֹלֵעָה. וְתִסְלַח וְתִמְחוֹל לָהּ עַל כָּל פְּשָׁעֶיהָ, כִּי אָדָם אֵין צַדִּיק בָּאָרֶץ, אֲשֶׁר יַעֲשֶׂה טּוֹב וְלֹא יֶחֱטָא. וּזְכוֹר לָהּ זְכִיּוֹתֶיהָ וְצִדְקוֹתֶיהָ אֲשֶׁר עָשָׂתָה. וְתַשְׁפִּיעַ לָהּ מִנִּשְׁמָתָהּ לְדַשֵּׁן עַצְמוֹתֶיהָ בַּקֶּבֶר מֵרֹב טוּב הַצָּפוּן לַצַּדִּיקִים, דִּכְתִיב: מָה רַב טוּבְךָ אֲשֶׁר צָפַנְתָּ לִּירֵאֶיךָ, וּכְתִיב: שֹׁמֵר כָּל עַצְמוֹתָיו, אַחַת מֵהֵנָּה לֹא נִשְׁבָּרָה. וְתִשְׁכּוֹן בֶּטַח בָּדָד וְשַׁאֲנָן מִפַּחַד רָעָה, וְאַל תִּרְאֶה פְּנֵי גֵּיהִנֹּם. וְנִשְׁמָתָהּ תְּהֵא צְרוּרָה בִּצְרוֹר הַחַיִּים, וּלְהַחֲיוֹתָהּ בִּתְחִיַּת הַמֵּתִים עִם כָּל מֵתֵי עַמְּךָ יִשְׂרָאֵל בְּרַחֲמִים. אָמֵן.

[19] PRAYER AFTER THE STUDY OF MISHNAH FOR THE DECEASED

It is customary to recite this prayer whenever Mishnayos are studied in memory of a deceased.

אָנָּא Please, O Hashem, full of mercy, for in Your hand is the soul of all the living and the spirit of every human being, may You find favor in our Torah study and prayer for the soul of (deceased's Hebrew name) son/daughter of (father's Hebrew name) and do with it according to Your great kindness, to open for it the gates of mercy and kindness and the gates of the Garden of Eden. Accept it with love and affection and send it Your holy and pure angels to lead it and to settle it under the Tree of Life near the souls of the righteous and devout men and women, to enjoy the radiance of Your Presence, to satiate it from Your good that is concealed for the righteous. May the body repose in the grave with proper contentment, pleasure, gladness, and peace as it is written: "Let him enter in peace, let them rest on their beds — everyone who has lived in his proper way." And it is written: "Let the devout exult in glory, let them sing joyously upon their beds." And it is written: "If you lie down, you will not fear; when you lie down, your sleep will be sweet." And protect him/her from the tribulations of the grave and from worms and maggots. Forgive and pardon him/her for all his/her sins, for there is no person so wholly righteous on earth that does good and never sins. Remember for him/her the merits and righteous deeds that he/she performed, and cause a spiritual flow from his/her soul to keep his/her bones fresh in the grave from the abundant good that is concealed for the righteous, as it is written: "How abundant is Your goodness that You have concealed for Your reverent ones," and it is written: "He guards all his bones, even one of them was not broken." May it rest secure, alone, and serene, from fear of evil and may it not see the threshold of Gehinnom. May his/her soul be bound in the Bond of Life. And may it be brought back to life with the Revivification of the Dead with all the dead of Your people Israel, with mercy. Amen.

This volume is part of
THE ArtScroll® SERIES
an ongoing project of
translations, commentaries and expositions on
Scripture, Mishnah, Talmud, Midrash, Halachah,
liturgy, history, the classic Rabbinic writings,
biographies and thought.

For a brochure of current publications visit your local
Hebrew bookseller or contact the publisher:

Mesorah Publications, ltd

313 Regina Avenue / Rahway, New Jersey 07065
(718) 921-9000 / www.artscroll.com

Many of these works are possible
only thanks to the support of the
MESORAH HERITAGE FOUNDATION,
which has earned the generous support of concerned people,
who want such works to be produced
and made available to generations world-wide.
Such books represent faith in the eternity of Judaism.
If you share that vision as well,
and you wish to participate in this historic effort
and learn more about support and dedication opportunities –
please contact us.

Mesorah Heritage Foundation

313 Regina Avenue / Rahway, New Jersey 07065
(718) 921-9000 ext. 5 / www.mesorahheritage.org

Mesorah Heritage Foundation is a 501(c)3 not-for-profit organization.